D1542973

Deleted by RCPL

PARA!

This book is dedicated to
the officers and men of The Parachute Regiment
past, present and future

UTRINQUE PARATUS

PETER HARCLERODE

PARA!
Fifty Years of
The Parachute Regiment

'Where is the prince who can afford so to cover his country with troops for its defence, as that ten thousand men descending from the clouds might not, in many places, do an infinite deal of mischief before a force could be brought together to repel them?'

Benjamin Franklin, 1784

Raleigh County Public Library
P. O. Box 1876
221 N. Kanawha St.
Beckley, WV 25802-1876

ARMS AND
ARMOUR

Arms and Armour Press
A Cassell Imprint
Villiers House, 41–47 Strand, London WC2N 5JE.

Distributed in the USA by Sterling Publishing Co. Inc.,
387 Park Avenue South, New York, NY 10016-8810.

Distributed in Australia by Capricorn Link (Australia) Pty. Ltd,
P.O. Box 665, Lane Cove, New South Wales 2066.

© Peter Harclerode, 1992
Reprinted in 1993

All rights reserved. No part of this book may be reproduced or
transmitted in any form or by any means electronic or
mechanical, including photocopying, recording or any
information storage and retrieval system, without permission in
writing from the Publisher.

British Library Cataloguing in Publication Data: a catalogue
record for this book is available from the British Library

ISBN 1-85409-097-6

Jacket illustration: Lieutenant Colonel 'H' Jones winning the
Victoria Cross at Goose Green during the Falklands campaign
of 1982; painted by Terence Cuneo. (Reproduced by courtesy
of the artist and 2 PARA)

Cartography by Peter Burton.

Designed and edited by DAG Publications Ltd. Designed by
David Gibbons; edited by Philip Jarrett; typeset by Ronset
Typesetters, Darwen, Lancashire; camerawork by M&E
Reproductions, North Fambridge, Essex; printed and bound in
Great Britain by Hartnolls Ltd, Bodmin, Cornwall.

CONTENTS

Foreword by Lieutenant General
Sir Michael Gray   9

Acknowledgments   11

Prologue   13

1. Early Days   19
Baptism of Fire – Operation
'Colossus'   20
Formation of 1st Parachute
Brigade   23
Formation of 1st Airborne
Division   24
Formation of 2nd Parachute
Brigade   25
The Red Beret   25
Formation of the Parachute
Regiment   25
Airborne Forces Depot and Battle
School   26
Parachute Training   27
Battle Training   28

**2. Operations in North Africa,
Sicily and Italy, 1942–1943**   30
North Africa 1942–43 – 1st
Parachute Brigade Operations   30
1st Parachute Brigade – Ground
Operations, December 1942–
April 1943   42
Sicily & Italy 1943 – 1st Airborne
Division Operations   51

**3. Formation of 6th Airborne
Division**   58

**4. 6th Airborne Division
Operations in Normandy, June
to September 1944**   61
The Advance to the Seine   84

**5. 1st Airborne Division
Operations at Arnhem,
September 1944**   92

**6. North-West Europe,
December 1944 to May 1945**   125
The Ardennes   125
Operation 'Varsity'   128
The Advance to the Baltic   135

**7. 2nd Independent Brigade
Group in Italy, Southern France
and Greece, November 1943
to October 1945**   146
Operation 'Hasty'   148
Operation 'Dragoon'   149

**8. 5th Parachute Brigade in the
Far East, 1945–1946**   156

**9. Parachute Battalions in India,
1941–1945**   165

**10. 6th Airborne Division
Operations in Palestine,
1945–1948**   193

**11. Post-War Reorganisation
and Operations in the Middle
East, Cyprus and Malaya,
1948–1958**   210
The Middle East, 1951–54   213
Malaya, 1955–57   214
Cyprus 1956   216
Suez and Operation
'Musketeer'   221
Jordan, 1958   233

**12. Operations in the Middle
East, Cyprus, the Far East,**

British Guiana and Anguilla, 1961–1969 **235**
The Persian Gulf 1961–64 235
1 PARA Operations in Cyprus, 1964 236
3 PARA Operations in the Radfan, 1964 237
Borneo Confrontation, 1963–66: No. 1 (Guards) Independent Company Operations, 1964–65 244
Gurkha Independent Parachute Company Operations in Borneo, 1964–65 254
2 PARA Operations in Borneo, 1965 261
C (Independent) Company 2 PARA Operations in Borneo, 1965 267
D (Patrol) Company 3 PARA Operations in Borneo, 1966 269
C (Patrol) Company 2 PARA Operations in the Radfan, 1966 271
3 PARA in British Guiana, 1965–66 272
2 PARA Operations in Aden 1966 273
1 PARA Internal Security Operations in Aden, 1967 274
Anguilla, 1969 279

13. Northern Ireland **281**
1 PARA 283
Bloody Sunday – 30 January 1972 288
2 PARA 293
Operation 'Demetrius' – 9 August 1971 294
Operation 'Motorman' – 31 July 1972 295
Warren Point – 27 August 1979 296
3 PARA: South Armagh, 1976 297

14. Operation 'Corporate': The Falklands Campaign, 1982 **302**
Landings at San Carlos – 21 May 307
2 PARA Advance to Camilla Creek 314
The Battle for Darwin and Goose Green 318
3 PARA – The Advance

Eastwards 340
2 PARA – The Move to Fitzroy 345
3 PARA – The Battle of Mount Longdon 350
2 PARA – The Battle of Wireless Ridge 359
The Return Home 367

15. The Parachute Regiment and Airborne Forces Today **368**
Reorganisation of Airborne Forces, 1977 368
5 Airborne Brigade 369
The Regular Army Parachute Battalions 369
The Territorial Army Parachute Battalions 371
The Parachute Regiment Group 372
The Depot The Parachute Regiment & Airborne Forces 372
'P' Company and the Pre-Parachute Selection Course 374
The Parachute Course Administrative Unit 376
The Parachute Regiment Battle School 376
The Red Devils 377
No. 1 Parachute Training School RAF and the Basic Parachute Course 378
The Future for the Parachute Regiment and Airborne Forces 380

Bibliography **383**

Appendix 1. Colonels Commandant The Parachute Regiment, 1942–1992 **385**

Appendix 2. Regimental Colonels and Regimental Adjutants of The Parachute Regiment 386

Appendix 3. Honorary Colonels of Territorial Army Battalions and Independent Companies of The Parachute Regiment, 1947–1992 387

Appendix 4. Commanding
Officers of the Regular and
Territorial Army Battalions and
Independent Companies of The
Parachute Regiment, The Depot
The Parachute Regiment &
Airborne Forces, and The

Parachute Regiment Battle
School, 1940–1992   389

Appendix 5. Battle Honours of
The Parachute Regiment   398

Index   **399**

LIST OF MAPS

The Bruneval Raid   17
1st Parachute Brigade in North
Africa, 1942–3   31
6th Airborne Division, D-Day, 6
June 1944 and Advance to the
Seine   62
The Air Route for Operation
'Market Garden'   94
Arnhem, 17–25 September 1944   96
Operation 'Varsity': 6th
Airborne DZ, 24 March 1945   128
Advance to the Baltic, 26 March
to 2 May 1945   136

Burma   157
Cyprus   217
Operation 'Musketeer': Suez,
1956   222
3 PARA in the Radfan, 1964   238
Borneo   245
Aden   274
Northern Ireland   282
Belfast   284
The Battle for Goose Green and
Darwin, 28–29 May 1982   319
Mount Longdon and Wireless
Ridge, 11–14 June 1982   351

FOREWORD
by Lieutenant General Sir Michael Gray, KCB, OBE
Colonel Commandant The Parachute Regiment

When you read this contemporary history of The Parachute Regiment and the family that is Airborne Forces, bear in mind two important factors. Firstly that, at the time of writing, the men who created this most remarkable narrative are mostly still alive and the author has been able to talk with them about their experiences. The foundations of this story were laid during those grim, early years of the Second World War. They have been built upon with honour and still continue to develop to this day. Secondly, the British parachutist emerged from a national crisis in 1940. Under Winston Churchill's leadership, determined young men from nearly all the regiments and corps of the British and Indian Armies, and from Canada, volunteered and were given a unique opportunity to create a force which would take the fight directly into the enemy's camp. This they did with the close co-operation of their comrades in the Royal Air Force. It is a remarkable story of ingenuity and courage; and of soldiers who were determined to succeed, no matter what the odds.

Supreme fitness was required to build up the body and mind in order to create total self-confidence and to overcome the initial fear of leaping into the unknown. Stamina was needed to carry the tortuously heavy loads of equipment and ammunition into battle. Above all, parachutists needed the spirit of the warrior and to be imbued with the will to overcome the opposition even when faced with vastly superior odds, and the endurance to carry on and continue to fight to the bitter end when that was necessary.

It is the mixture of these qualities and skills, together with parachuting, which create a thinking soldier who, in the process, forms a close bond with his comrades. He knows the capabilities of the men around him; they know and respect him. He is physically and mentally robust, and is thus able to handle stress in all of its forms. He believes that nothing can stop him; his morale is high, he is self-disciplined and totally motivated to win. Such is the Airborne Soldier.

Read these chapters and you will marvel at the commitment and dedication of the men whom they portray over the period of the last fifty years. The men of The Parachute Regiment and Airborne Forces are the best, the very best which our nation has to offer, and it was prophetic in 1947 when the then Colonel Commandant, Field Marshal The Viscount Montgomery, wrote of them in his foreword to the book *The Red Beret*: "What manner of men are these? They are, in fact, men apart — every man an emperor".

ACKNOWLEDGMENTS

The production of this book has been very much a team effort, and I owe a great debt of gratitude to a number of people who put a considerable amount of time and effort into helping me assemble material. Without such assistance, it would never have been published.

Some of the information herein has not been published previously, and this is based on interviews with former members of The Parachute Regiment or on documents provided by them. In addition, I was granted access to the archives of the Airborne Forces Museum, and I am most grateful to Colonel David Parker, the Regimental Colonel of The Parachute Regiment, and to his predecessor, Colonel Hamish MacGregor, for their kindness in granting me that facility.

Lieutenant General Sir Michael Gray, Colonel Commandant of The Parachute Regiment, was kind enough to write the Foreword and in addition checked all chapters before submission to the publishers. He also provided me with a great deal of material from his own extensive collection of papers. I would like to express my sincere thanks to him for his great support and assistance.

General Sir Kenneth Darling also provided me with considerable help and information concerning 6th Airborne Division and the post-war period of The Parachute Regiment, fielding my unending series of questions with unfailing kindness and good humour. Colonel John Waddy, Brigadier Vic Coxen and Brigadier 'Dicky' Richards, devoted considerable effort to checking my chapters covering the operations of 1st Airborne Division, the thorny subject of Arnhem, 2nd Independent Parachute Brigade and the wartime Indian Airborne Forces respectively. I am most grateful to them.

Previous books about The Parachute Regiment have tended to neglect the sterling work carried out by 2 PARA and the independent patrol companies that saw service in the SAS role during the Borneo Confrontation and subsequently in the Radfan. I have attempted to rectify that situation and would like to thank Colonel John Head, Lieutenant Colonel Tom Brooke, Major The Lord Patrick Beresford and Major Charles Fugelsang for providing me with photographs and information about the tours of operations carried out by No. 1 (Guards) Independent Company. Similarly, Brigadier David Morgan, Lieutenant Colonel John Cross and Major 'Phil' Phillips supplied me with much material relating to the operations of the Gurkha Independent Parachute Company during the same period, while Major General Peter Chiswell, Colonel John Winter and Major Alex Young provided me with accounts concerning D (Patrol)

11

Company, 3 PARA, and C (Independent) Company, 2 PARA, respectively. To all of them I extend my thanks.

I was rendered great assistance by Brigadier Joe Starling and Colonel Peter Walter, who helped with my coverage of operations in Aden and the Radfan. Others who also provided me with much help include: Lieutenant Colonel Bill Corbould, Major Jack Watson, Major Denis Reid, Major Nick Nicholas, Captain John Carruthers, Mr Roger Field, Mr Gavin Coxen, Mr Bert Goodall, Mr Ken Siret, Mr Reg Curtis and Mr Ted Farr. I am most grateful to them all.

Three fellow writers allowed me to use material concerning operations in Northern Ireland that has been published previously in books of their own: David Barzilay, author of *The British Army in Ulster* Vols. 1, 2 and 3, Brigadier Peter Morton, who wrote *Emergency Tour – 3 PARA in South Armagh*, and Max Arthur who is author of *Men of The Red Beret*. My thanks to all of them for their kindness.

Major David Benest, the Regimental Adjutant, also spent long hours checking all my chapters and offering constructive advice. Moreover, he provided an extremely valuable contribution in the form of his account of 2 PARA's operations during the Falklands War, and part of my chapter on that campaign is based on his story. I am most grateful to him and to Major Pat Butler, who provided me with help on 3 PARA's operations.

I would like to extend special thanks to Major Jeremy Hickman and Mrs Pat Blake of The Parachute Regimental Association, both of whom were instrumental in enabling me to contact many of those who subsequently gave me so much help, and to Mrs Diana Andrews and Stan Ward of the Airborne Forces Museum, who spent many hours helping me trace material in the archives. My thanks also go to Jane Carmichael, Keeper of Photographs at the Imperial War Museum, and her staff for supplying many of the photographs used in this book. In addition, I must also express my gratitude to Express Newspapers for their kindness in granting permission for reproduction of photographs taken in Northern Ireland and during the Falklands War.

Finally, I would like to express my appreciation to Lieutenant Colonel Donald Campbell, formerly SO1 Director Public Relations (Army), and Mr John Harding of the Army Historical Branch of the Ministry of Defence for their help in submitting the book for clearance by the Ministry of Defence.

Peter Harclerode, June 1992

PROLOGUE

I t was a bright, moonlit night as 12 Armstrong Whitworth Whitley bombers of No. 51 Squadron RAF, commanded by Wing Commander Charles Pickard, took off from Thruxton soon after 2230 hours on the night of 27 February 1942. Instead of a bomb load, each aircraft carried ten parachutists. This airborne force, under the command of Major Johnny Frost of The Cameronians, consisted of C Company 2nd Parachute Battalion accompanied by nine sappers of 1st Parachute Squadron, Royal Engineers, four signallers and a flight sergeant of the RAF. Inside each aircraft, the troops sat jammed together on the floor in some discomfort. The noise and vibration were such that conversation was difficult, but spirits were high and songs were sung with great gusto as the bombers headed through the night for their destination on the coast of France. Little did they know it, but the men of C Company and those attached to them were about to make history.

Towards the end of 1941, the RAF had suffered increasing losses of bombers carrying out missions over Europe. This was due to the efficiency of the German radar, which enabled the enemy to track incoming aircraft and to direct and guide their own night fighters to intercept them. A chain of radar posts had been established along the French coast for this purpose, and one of these was detected by RAF aerial reconnaissance aircraft north of the village of Bruneval, some 12 miles north of Le Havre.

British radar specialists at the Telecommunications Research Establishment already possessed a considerable amount of information about the German acquisition radar, codenamed 'Freya'. However, they were anxious to obtain data on the narrow-beam radar, codenamed 'Wurzburg', which was used to vector the Luftwaffe's night fighters for interception. As luck would have it, the radar at Bruneval was one of this type. It was decided that an operation should be mounted to obtain key components of this radar for subsequent examination. Initially, the use of commandos was considered, but the radar site was well defended against seaborne assault. It was therefore decided, as surprise and speed would be the keys to success in this particular instance, that the operation should be carried out by an airborne force which would subsequently be evacuated by sea.

2nd Parachute Battalion was allocated the task, and the Commanding Officer, Lieutenant Colonel Edward Flavell, selected Major Johnny Frost's C Company to carry it out. The company itself had only recently been formed, and some of its members had not completed their parachute training. When briefed by a liaison officer from Headquarters, 1st Airborne

Division, Frost was informed that his company was to provide a demonstration for the War Cabinet. He was told that training would be carried out in an area near Alton Priors, in Wiltshire, where the terrain was very similar to that on which the demonstration would take place in due course. He was also advised that his company would have to be split into four groups, each to be specially trained and equipped for specific tasks. Frost was not at all happy about the reorganization of his company, and made his feelings clear during a visit to divisional headquarters, where he had intended to state his objections to the divisional commander, Major General F. A. M. 'Boy' Browning. Unfortunately for Frost, Browning was away, and he therefore saw the GSO 1 and the liaison officer who had briefed him previously. His objections fell on stony ground, and he came away puzzled by the attitude shown towards his own plan, which retained the company's normal organization of three platoons. On the following day, however, the liaison officer from 1st Airborne Division arrived at 2nd Parachute Battalion's base where, after swearing Frost to secrecy, he informed the latter that he and his company would in fact be carrying out an operation in enemy-occupied France. On hearing this, Frost dropped his objections and turned his attention fully to preparing his company for the task ahead.

After a period spent training on Salisbury Plain, C Company and its attached section of sappers travelled to Inverary in Scotland. There, on the banks of Loch Fyne, the company underwent training in night embarkations on the landing craft that would evacuate them on completion of their operation. During this period, the company was visited by the Chief of Combined Operations, Admiral Mountbatten, who addressed both the company and the crews of the landing craft. His speech gave them the first hints as to the operation for which they were training — Frost had until then kept all details of it to himself.

After returning to its base at Tilshead, C Company carried out its first practice drop with No. 51 Squadron. Despite the fact that the aircrews had never dropped parachutists before, this exercise was successful and passed without incident. Further training in embarking on landing craft in conjunction with the Royal Navy was also carried out on the Dorset coast. Unlike the airborne training, this proved to be fraught with problems and failures.

A full moon was required for the operation, and a rising tide was required for the landing craft to be able to carry out the evacuation from the beach at Bruneval. The four days on which the operation could be carried out were during the period 24 to 27 February. On 23 February a final rehearsal was conducted, but this proved disastrous: despite perfect weather conditions, the landing craft became grounded 60 yards offshore and the best efforts of C Company failed to push them off.

The groups into which Frost's force was organized were named 'Nelson', 'Jellicoe', 'Hardy', 'Drake' and 'Rodney'. 'Nelson', 40-strong and under the command of Captain John Ross and Lieutenant Euen Charteris, would clear and secure the enemy positions defending the beach from which the force would be evacuated. 'Jellicoe', 'Hardy' and 'Drake', under

Frost himself, would have the task of capturing the radar site and a nearby villa occupied by German technicians and guards. Captain Dennis Vernon and his sappers, together with Flight Sergeant Cox, would accompany Frost's group. Cox was a radar expert and would supervise the dismantling of the equipment by the sappers. 'Rodney', the reserve element commanded by Lieutenant John Timothy, would take up positions between the radar site and the main likely enemy approach, to block any counterattack.

The enemy forces at Bruneval were divided into three groups. The radar site was manned by technicians who were protected by a detachment of guards, the total number of men at that location numbering approximately 30. Three hundred yards to the north lay a group of buildings surrounded by woods. Called Le Presbytère, this was occupied by more technicians and troops, estimated at over 100 in strength. Finally, there was a garrison of 40 men based in Bruneval itself. The beach, linked to the village by a narrow road, was defended by pillboxes and positions on the clifftops and down below.

Before take-off on the night of 27 February, the men of C Company were in great spirits. As the sticks marched out to their respective aircraft, Piper Ewing played the regimental marches of the Scottish regiments represented among the ranks of the company. Shortly afterwards, the bombers lumbered down the runway at Thruxton and soon after 2230 hours took off into the night sky.

As the 12 Whitleys neared the French coast, the RAF despatchers busied themselves with removing the cover from the aperture in the floor of each aircraft's fuselage. Those in each stick sitting nearest the hole could see the waters of the Channel six hundred feet below. As the aircraft crossed the coastline they came under fire from enemy flak defences, and swung violently as their pilots took evasive action. None of the bombers was hit, however, and they continued to head for the dropping zones.

"Action Stations!" At the despatchers' cry, the troops swiftly cast aside the sleeping bags and blankets in which they had rested during the flight, and the No. 1 in each stick swung his legs into the aperture beside him, watching intently the red light which glowed above him. The green light in each aircraft suddenly came on, and above the noise of the engines came the shouted command "Go!". Tumbling into the bright, moonlit sky went the men of C Company and those accompanying them. As Frost floated earthwards beneath his canopy, he recognized the layout of the snow-covered ground below him from the maps, air photographs and models which he and his men had studied at length during their preparations for the operation. There was no wind and the only sound was the noise of the departing aircraft. The snow provided a soft landing, and within ten minutes Frost and his men had rallied without incident at their rendezvous point and were ready to move off. As they headed for their objective they saw the men of 'Nelson' group landing.

As they moved towards the radar site, 'Jellicoe', 'Hardy' and 'Drake' encountered no opposition nor any indication of any enemy alertness. Once the villa was surrounded and all his men were in position, Frost blew his whistle to start the assault. As he did so, the noise of exploding grenades and automatic weapons came from the direction of the radar site. Inside the villa, Frost and his men encountered only one enemy soldier, who had opened fire from an upstairs window. He was summarily dealt with. Meanwhile, the enemy at the radar site had been overwhelmed and two prisoners captured. It was learned from them that there were only a small number of troops based at the site, but that others were based further inland. At that point, Frost and his men came under fire from enemy in the area of Le Presbytère and Private McIntyre was killed as he left the villa. Shortly afterwards, Captain Dennis Vernon, accompanied by his section of sappers and Flight Sergeant Cox, arrived at the radar site and work was immediately begun to dismantle the radar equipment.

The fire from Le Presbytère grew heavier, and soon afterwards enemy vehicles were spotted moving up behind the woods. Frost grew anxious, particularly as the new No. 38 radio sets with which his force had been equipped for the operation had failed to work and he thus had no communication with his other groups. Shortly afterwards the sappers and Flight Sergeant Cox completed dismantling the radar and loaded the pieces on to trolleys. Without further ado, Frost and his men headed for the beach. As they reached the area of the clifftop, however, a machine gun in a pillbox opened fire on them and Company Sergeant Major Strachan was severely wounded in the stomach. It rapidly became apparent that the beach defences had not been taken by the men of 'Nelson', and this was soon confirmed by Captain John Ross, who shouted up from the beach. Frost started to make his way across to Lieutenant John Timothy, who was commanding the 'Rodney' group, to order him to attack the enemy defences. At that point, however, he was told that the enemy had reoccupied the villa and were advancing toward the clifftop. He altered his plan and led his own group back to deal with this threat, which proved not to be serious and was quickly dispersed.

On returning to the clifftop, Frost found Lieutenant Euen Charteris waiting for him by the main pillbox. It was then that he learned that Charteris and two sections of 'Nelson', who had flown in Wing Commander Pickard's aircraft and the one following it, had been dropped two miles short of the dropping zone and had subsequently had to make their way across country to Bruneval. The going had been difficult, and whilst skirting round the village towards the clifftop Charteris and his men had encountered an enemy patrol, with which they had fought a sharp engagement. Attacking from a flank, they had cleared the pillbox and killed the machine gun crew. All the other defenders, except for one very frightened telephone orderly, had also perished.

By now it was 0215 hours and the force was ready to be evacuated. However, there was no sign of the landing craft and radio contact could not be established with them. Frost's signallers tried to call them in with a lamp and ultimately with red Very flares, which was the agreed emergency signal. However, this proved to be of no avail, and Frost decided to redeploy his force in positions at the entrance to the village and in the clifftop area. He

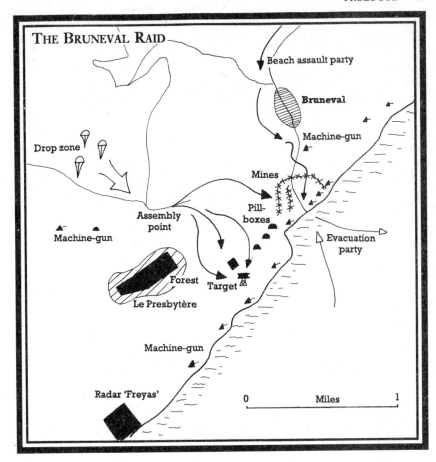

THE BRUNEVAL RAID

Beach assault party

Bruneval

Machine-gun

Drop zone

Mines

Pill-
boxes

Assembly
point

Machine-gun

Evacuation
party

Forest   Target

Le Presbytère

Machine-gun

Radar 'Freyas'

0   Miles   1

and his officers had just completed establishing the new positions when a shout from one of his signallers informed him that the landing craft had arrived. The plan had called for two craft to approach the beach at a time, the withdrawal being carried out in three phases. However, all six craft moved in at the same time as C Company began to assemble on the beach. As they did so, their crews opened fire with Bren guns on the clifftop where some of Frost's men were still in positions guarding against any attack from inland. They ceased fire only after a chorus of shouts from the beach.

The wounded and the sappers with the dismantled radar equipment were successfully loaded aboard one landing craft, but thereafter the withdrawal became somewhat chaotic. Matters were made no easier by the enemy who, on realising that a withdrawal was taking place, started mortaring the beach and throwing grenades down from the clifftop. After wading through the waves and scrambling aboard, the men of C Company were eventually embarked on the landing craft, which then withdrew out to sea. At 0330 hours the entire force was transferred to motor gunboats which took the landing craft in tow. It was only at that point, when a radio message was received, that it was realised that two signallers had been left behind. Having lost their way, they had reached the beach too late. Frost also learned why the landing craft had been late in reaching the beach. Whilst they were waiting offshore for the signal to pick up C Company, a German destroyer and two E-boats had passed by less than a mile away, and the six craft had been forced to remain motionless in the moonlight until the enemy had sailed out of range. At dawn on 28 February the small flotilla was met by a squadron of Spitfires and a number of destroyers which took up station on either side and escorted the gunboats to Portsmouth.

C Company was rightly accorded a heroes' welcome on its return. Not only had Major Johnny Frost and his men successfully accomplished their mission in capturing the radar equipment, but they had also provided a great boost for British morale in what were very dark times. Moreover, they had also won the newly formed airborne forces their spurs and, unbeknown to themselves, had earned a battle honour for what, two months later, on 1 August 1942, would become the British Army's youngest regiment.

"Well done, everyone. Let's remember Arnhem!" These words were spoken on 28 May 1982 by Captain David Wood, the Adjutant of the 2nd Battalion The Parachute Regiment, as he moved up with the Commanding Officer, Lieutenant Colonel 'H' Jones, to join A Company during the action at Goose Green in the Falkland Islands. Shortly afterwards, Captain Wood and Lieutenant Colonel Jones were both killed in a battle in which the battalion added another honour to those already emblazoned on its colours.

Three months earlier, on 28 February, the fortieth anniversary of the operation at Bruneval had taken place. During the years since 1942, the battalions of The Parachute Regiment had seen service in war-torn Europe, the deserts of North Africa and the Middle East, the troubled island of Cyprus, the jungles of South East Asia, the snowbound hills of Norway and the streets of Northern Ireland, truly living up to their motto *Utrinque Paratus* — "Ready For Anything".

The story of The Parachute Regiment begins, however, before the raid on Bruneval: in those dark days of 1940 when Britain stood alone against the might of Nazi Germany's war machine.

CHAPTER 1
Early Days

'We ought to have a corps of at least 5,000 parachute troops, including a proportion of Australians, New Zealanders and Canadians, together with some trustworthy people from Norway and France . . . advantage of the summer must be taken to train these troops, who can nonetheless play their part meanwhile as shock troops in home defence. Pray let me have a note from the War Office on the subject.' — So wrote Prime Minister Winston Churchill on 22 June 1940 to General Sir Hastings Ismay, the head of the Military Wing of the War Cabinet Secretariat.

In fact, the foundation stone for the training of airborne forces had already been laid by the Royal Air Force, which earlier that month had taken the decision to set up a parachute training centre at Ringway, near Manchester. This was the Central Landing School, commanded by Squadron Leader Louis Strange DSO MC DFC. He was assisted by Major John Rock of the Royal Engineers, who was tasked with "the military organisation of British airborne forces". The parachute jumping instructors (PJIs) comprised nine from the Army Physical Training Corps under Regimental Sergeant Major Mansie and fourteen from the Royal Air Force under Flight Sergeant (later Wing Commander) Bill Brereton.

The initial equipment for the school consisted of six ageing Whitley bombers and a thousand parachutes, but little else. Such was the obstructive attitude of the Air Ministry, despite the Prime Minister's directive and enthusiastic support, that the staff at Ringway rapidly had to become experts in the art of improvisation. Apparatus for 'synthetic' training had to be designed and built, whilst the Whitleys had to be adapted by having apertures cut in the floors of their fuselages and their rear gun turrets removed. Whilst the school was being set up, the search was on for volunteers to be trained as parachutists. It was eventually decided that one of the newly formed Commando units would be converted to the parachute role, and as a result No. 2 Commando was selected. The unit was subsequently moved to its new station at Knutsford, not far from the Central Landing School. On 3 July Lieutenant Colonel C.I.A. Jackson of the Royal Tank Regiment arrived to assume command of No. 2 Commando.

On 9 July B and C Troops of No. 2 Commando arrived at Ringway. Four days later, on 13 July, the Royal Air Force PJIs gave a demonstration of jumping from a Whitley, and on 22 July the trainees themselves carried out their first descents. Unfortunately, three days later, Driver Evans of the Royal Army Service Corps was killed when his parachute failed to deploy properly. By August, developments had been carried out on a barrage balloon with a 'cage' slung underneath. This enabled trainees to carry out their initial two jumps from a static platform before progressing to jumping from an aircraft. By September a total of 961 descents had been made by 290 trainees. Casualties were very low: two deaths, thirteen injured, thirty refusals and thirteen returned to their units (RTU) as unsuitable.

On 19 September the school was expanded to become the Central Landing Establishment, which now encompassed a parachute training school and a glider training school, the latter under command of Squadron Leader H. E. Hervey. Group Captain L. G. Harvey became station commander, while Wing Commander Sir Nigel Norman took over as commandant of the establishment. Squadron Leader Strange remained in command of the parachute training school, while Major John Rock was promoted to lieutenant colonel. In July the following year Wing Commander Maurice Newnham DFC took over command of the parachute training school, a post he continued to hold until the end of the war.

During those early days that first generation of parachute jumping instructors brought parachuting to the state where it became "safer than crossing the road", a phrase repeated many times by PJIs during the last 50 years. The original nucleus of RAF instructors came from RAF Henlow, where, before the war, pilots underwent parachute training in order to survive in the event of being forced to bale out. Instructors came from the Army and the RAF until October 1941, after which they were drawn solely from the Physical Training Branch of the RAF. They were commanded by Flight Lieutenant (later Wing Commander) J. C. Kilkenny OBE, and during the war their ranks were filled by individuals with a variety of backgrounds, including professional footballers, acrobats, boxers and male ballet dancers. The first six months of the parachute training school's existence saw between four and five hundred men undergoing basic training as parachutists.

During its period of conversion to the airborne role, No. 2 Commando consisted of a headquarters and a number of troops, each comprising 50 men. In total, the unit numbered some 500 of all ranks. In November 1940 it was redesignated 11th Special Air Service Battalion and was reorganised into a headquarters, a parachute wing and a glider wing. By the end of the year, the unit consisted of 22 sub-sections each consisting of ten men.

BAPTISM OF FIRE – OPERATION 'COLOSSUS'

Although it was only newly formed, and its members had no previous experience of airborne operations, the British Army's first parachute unit soon found itself committed to action, albeit on a small scale. In the dark days of early 1941, it was decided that an operation was to be carried out in Southern Italy with the purpose of disrupting water supplies to the ports of Taranto, Bari and Brindisi, which were all embarkation points for Italian forces campaigning in North Africa and Albania. It was also thought that such an operation would show the rest of the world that Britain was still very much a force to be reckoned with. Whilst these were the official reasons given for the operation, the real justification for it was that the War Office was anxious to test the ability of the fledgling airborne force, and thus the standards of training and equipment, as well as the ability of the RAF to deliver troops at predetermined locations at the right time.

The target was an aqueduct crossing a small watercourse called the Tragino at a point about 30 miles north-east of a small town called Salverno, in the province of Campania. The aqueduct provided the main water supply route for the province of Apulia and its population of two million inhabitants.

A total of 38 men, consisting of seven officers and 31 other ranks, were selected from 11th SAS Battalion to form the raiding force. Designated 'X' Troop, it was commanded by Major T. A. G. Pritchard of the Royal Welch Fusiliers. Attached to it for the operation were three Italian-speaking interpreters: Squadron Leader Lucky MC of the RAF, Rifleman Nastri of the Rifle Brigade and a civilian named Fortunato Picchi. Preparations began in January 1941 under the supervision of Lieutenant Colonel John Rock, the RAF element being under the watchful eye of Wing Commander Sir Nigel Norman. Eight Whitley aircraft of No. 91 Squadron, under the command of Wing Commander J. B. Tate, were allocated to carry 'X' Troop to its target area, a further two Whitleys being tasked to carry out a diversionary bombing raid against some railway yards at Foggia, some 60 miles to the north. The training for the operation was intensive, and lasted until the end of the first week of February. It included attacks on a full-scale mockup of part of the aqueduct, which was erected in Tatton Park.

The plan was for 'X' Troop, which included a party of seven sappers under Captain G. F. K. Daly of the Royal Engineers, to travel in their Whitleys on 7 February from England to Malta, whence the operation would be launched. This stage of the operation would involve a night flight of some 1,600 miles, some of it over enemy-occupied France. Three days later, on the night of 10 February, the entire force would be dropped by the Whitleys in the area of their objective at 2130 hours. Once the attack was completed, the raiding force would withdraw and make its way over 50 miles of mountainous terrain to the coast and the mouth of the River Sele where a submarine, HMS *Triumph*, would be waiting to take them off on the night of 15/16 February.

The initial stage of the operation, the flight to Malta, went as planned, with 'X' Troop emplaning at Mildenhall on the evening of 7 February and flying through the night without mishap. They had been preceded on 24 January by Lieutenant Anthony Deane-Drummond, of the Royal Signals, who had gone ahead to ensure that preparations were in hand for their arrival.

At 1830 hours on 10 February the six Whitleys took off from Malta, each carrying one officer and five other ranks with their weapons and equipment. The weather was perfect and visibility was excellent, and the flight proved uneventful. The dropping zone itself was approximately half a mile north of the aqueduct, and the first Whitley, flying at a height of 400 feet, reached it at 2142 hours and dropped its troops and their equipment within 250 yards. The next four aircraft then arrived and dropped their sticks, including two of the sappers, within 400 yards of the dropping zone, but two of the Whitleys failed to drop the weapons and explosives which they were also carrying, owing to icing-up of the container release mechanisms. The sixth Whitley, which was carrying Captain Daly and the other five sappers, was unfortunately unable to find the dropping zone, and eventually dropped its stick and equipment two hours later in a valley two miles to the north east of the objective.

Meanwhile, the rest of the force were attempting to retrieve the containers containing the arms and explosives, but were hampered by the fact that the lights on the containers themselves had proved inoperable. However, they succeeded in finding one weapon container and managed to collect 800lb of explosive, sufficient to carry out at least part of their mission. In the absence of Captain Daly a junior sapper officer, 2nd Lieutenant A. Paterson RE, took charge of the demolition task on the main viaduct with the assistance of another sapper, Sergeant Drury. It was discovered, however, that the centre pier was constructed of reinforced concrete which the limited amount of explosive was not sufficient to destroy. Paterson and Drury thus switched their attention to another pier and a small bridge crossing the River Ginestra nearby. At 0030 hours on 11 February the charges were blown and the pier was destroyed, taking half the aqueduct with it as it crumbled. As the raiding party watched, water poured through the breach and down the Tragino Valley. Almost immediately afterwards, the charges on the small wooden bridge exploded and destroyed it totally. 'X' Troop had successfully completed its mission.

At 0100 hours the raiders withdrew and moved off towards the coast in three groups commanded, respectively, by Major Pritchard, Captain C. G. Lea of the Lancashire Fusiliers and 2nd Lieutenant G. Jowett of the Highland Light Infantry. They were to move by night and lie up during the day to avoid any contact with local inhabitants or enemy forces. Unfortunately, all three groups were captured on 12 February. Pritchard's group was spotted by a farmer as it was resting in a cave. The alarm was raised and the inhabitants of a nearby village, followed by Italian troops and Carabinieri, appeared shortly afterwards. Pritchard realised that his small, poorly armed group could hold out only for a limited length of time, and that there was a risk of women and children being killed or wounded in any engagement. He therefore felt that he had no choice but to surrender. Luck had also deserted Lea's party, which had already been captured, as had Jowett and his men, who were ambushed.

The missing group of sappers, under Captain Daly, travelled for three nights and covered over 30 miles in their journey towards the coast. Exhausted and suffering from lack of food, they still had some 18 miles ahead of them when they encountered a group of Italian troops and police. Using Fortunato Picchi, the interpreter attached to their group, they tried to bluff their way out of this precarious situation by claiming that they were German troops on a special operation and demanding transport to take them to Naples. This ploy was nearly successful, but failed when the Italians demanded identification papers. Daly and his men were taken away as prisoners — all except for Fortunato Picchi, who was handed over to the Fascist militia. Despite being tortured under interrogation, he remained silent and was eventually court-martialled and executed by firing squad.

Had Daly and his men reached the coast, they would not have found HMS *Triumph* waiting for them. Whilst the operation was under way, one of the two Whitleys carrying out the diversionary bombing raid on the railway yards at Foggia had suffered engine trouble. The pilot had radioed the operational base in Malta, saying that he was heading for the mouth of the River Sele where he planned to ditch his aircraft, completely unaware that this was the rendezvous location for the evacuation of the raiding force. In view of the risk of his message having been monitored, thus exposing the submarine to possible detection by enemy naval forces, it was decided not to send HMS *Triumph*.

While Operation Colossus was of little value in terms of any effect on disruption of water supplies to the three Italian ports, and thus on the Italian operations in Albania and North Africa, it gave a valuable boost to morale in Britain as well as providing experience which was subsequently put to good use in later airborne operations.

FORMATION OF 1ST PARACHUTE BRIGADE

A joint memorandum issued by the Chiefs of Staff at the end of May 1941 directed that a parachute brigade was to be formed at the earliest opportunity, based upon an expansion of 11th SAS Battalion. In July authorisation was granted for the formation of a brigade headquarters, four parachute battalions and an airborne troop of sappers of the Royal Engineers. The call for volunteers was sent throughout the entire British Army. A maximum number of ten was placed on any one unit so as not to cause undue depletion. Recruitment teams visited units and, despite the unenthusiastic reception from commanding officers unwilling to release their best men, received a good response.

In early September 1941, Headquarters 1st Parachute Brigade was formed at Hardwick Hall, near Chesterfield in Derbyshire, under the command of Brigadier Richard Gale. It consisted of a small staff with Major P. E. Bromley-Martin of the Grenadier Guards as Brigade Major and Captain J. G. Squirrel as Staff Captain. Attached to it was a signals section and No. 1 Air Troop Royal Engineers. Initially, it had been decided that 11th SAS Battalion should be disbanded and its numbers divided among the four parachute battalions. However, after meeting the battalion's new commanding officer, Lieutenant Colonel Eric Down, Brigadier Gale decided that the unit should be kept together and redesignated 1st Parachute Battalion. The decision was also taken to form only two further parachute battalions initially, with the fourth to be formed at a later date. As a result, 2nd and 3rd Parachute Battalions were formed in September under the command of Lieutenant Colonels Edward Flavell and Gerald Lathbury respectively. Four months later, in January 1942, 4th Parachute Battalion was formed under the command of Lieutenant Colonel M. R. Hope Thomson. Each battalion consisted of a headquarters and three rifle companies.

The task of raising the new brigade and its battalions from scratch was enormous, and much credit must be given to Brigadier Gale and those of his officers on whose shoulders it fell. The job was not made any easier by commanding officers of some units attempting to rid themselves of unwanted individuals who were either physically below the standards required or whose disciplinary records left much to be desired. During the initial period of formation, the lack of good warrant officers and non-commissioned officers also caused problems, and officers had to make their presence felt on occasions when discipline had to be enforced. However, the enthusiasm among the volunteers for airborne forces was such that it was not long before such problems were overcome and the fledgling units began to take shape.

FORMATION OF 1ST AIRBORNE DIVISION

In late 1941 the War Office decided that an airlanding brigade of gliderborne troops would be formed in addition to 1st Parachute Brigade. In October, 31st Independent Infantry Brigade was selected for conversion to this role, subsequently being redesignated 1st Airlanding Brigade. Brigadier G. F. Hopkinson took over command of this formation on 31 October. At this point it was decided that 1st Parachute Brigade, 1st Airlanding Brigade and the glider units should be grouped together as a divisional formation. Consequently, Headquarters 1st Airborne Division was formed at the end of October and Brigadier Frederick 'Boy' Browning was appointed Commander Paratroops and Airborne Troops in the rank of major general. Initially the headquarters was based in King Charles Street, London, but on 22 December 1941 it moved to Syrencote House at Figheldean in Wiltshire.

Thus, airborne forces were well and truly established by the end of 1941, but they did not as yet possess any corporate identity in the form of a parent regiment. To remedy this, the War Office decided that all parachute battalions would form part of a new formation to be designated the Army Air Corps, which would also contain another new, yet to be formed, body — the Glider Pilot Regiment. On 24 February 1942 both were formed and became part of the British Army's wartime order of battle. Shortly afterwards, a number of changes in command appointments took place. Brigadier Richard Gale was appointed Director of Air at the War Office, and he was replaced by Brigadier Edward Flavell on promotion from commanding 2nd Parachute Battalion. Flavell had been replaced by Major Goften Salmond, who was subsequently found to be medically unfit and his place was taken by Major Johnny Frost. Lieutenant Colonel Gerald Lathbury handed over command of 3rd Parachute Battalion to Lieutenant

Colonel R Webb on being posted to the War Office. Subsequently, Webb was replaced by Lieutenant Colonel Geoffrey Pine Coffin.

FORMATION OF 2ND PARACHUTE BRIGADE

In early 1942 it was decided that a second parachute brigade was required to bring 1st Airborne Division up to a full establishment of three brigades. Consequently, on 17 July, Headquarters 2nd Parachute Brigade was formed and Lieutenant Colonel Eric Down, then commanding 1st Parachute Battalion, was promoted to the rank of brigadier and given command of the new formation.

To provide a nucleus for the brigade, 4th Parachute Battalion was transferred from 1st Parachute Brigade. At that time, in view of the insufficient number of volunteers successfully qualifying as parachutists, the War Office decided that in future parachute units would be formed by converting infantry battalions to the role. As a result, the 7th Battalion The Queen's Own Cameron Highlanders and the 10th Battalion The Royal Welch Fusiliers were transferred to 2nd Parachute Brigade. These were redesignated as 5th (Scottish) and 6th (Royal Welch) Parachute Battalions, and were commanded respectively by Lieutenant Colonel A. Dunlop of the Argyll and Sutherland Highlanders and Lieutenant Colonel C. H. V. Pritchard of the Royal Welch Fusiliers. Those officers and men not wishing to qualify as parachutists were permitted to transfer to other units, their places being taken by men who had successfully passed through the Airborne Forces Depot and Ringway.

THE RED BERET

In the middle of 1942 Major General Browning decided that airborne troops should have some form of distinctive headwear, and that 1st Airborne Division should possess its own emblem. He commissioned Major Edward Seago, the well known artist, to produce the latter. The result was the now famous design of the mythical warrior Bellerophon riding Pegasus, his winged steed. The beret was selected as a suitable item of headwear, and several colours were considered. Legend has it that Daphne du Maurier, the well-known novelist and wife of Major General Browning, was responsible for selecting the adopted colour of maroon, but she denied this. In fact, the choice of colours was placed before the Chief of Imperial General Staff, General Sir Alan Brooke, who was apparently unable to make up his mind and asked the opinion of a soldier on whose head the berets of different hues were being displayed. The man expressed his preference for maroon, and thus the choice was made.

FORMATION OF THE PARACHUTE REGIMENT

By the middle of 1942 the fledgling airborne forces had grown rapidly, and it was felt that the parachute battalions should have their own parent regiment. Accordingly, The Parachute Regiment was formed on 1 August and became part of the Army Air Corps along with the Glider Pilot Regiment.

AIRBORNE FORCES DEPOT & BATTLE SCHOOL

In addition to being the initial location of 1st Parachute Brigade during its period of formation, Hardwick Hall was also the home of the Airborne Forces Depot, which was formed in April 1942. Regardless of rank, all volunteers for parachute units had to undergo a selection course at the depot. This course, which lasted two weeks, was designed to weed out those who were not able to attain the rigorous standards of physical fitness demanded, and consisted of an unrelenting programme of intensive physical training and tests. Organised in small squads, each supervised by an Army Physical Training Corps instructor who kept them under continual close scrutiny, recruits carried out everything 'at the double'. The failure rate among volunteers was high, and the fate which they all dreaded was to be "RTU'd" — "Returned to Unit". The course also included jumping from mockup fuselages, swinging from trapezes and an airsickness test which consisted of recruits being swung for 20 minutes in a swingboat of a type similar to that found in fairgrounds.

Hardwick Hall was a somewhat unprepossessing place, consisting of red brick huts surrounded by barbed wire fences, and those who underwent the selection course in those early days remember it all too well. The majority of those in airborne forces passed through it only once or twice, being happy not to return because life there could be somewhat bleak.

Whilst it was co-located with the depot, the Battle School operated independently of it and was administratively self-contained. Training was carried out around the Derwent Valley and on the moors belonging to the Duke of Devonshire. This was conducted during the day and at night, with or without live ammunition and over varying types of terrain. One exercise was an initiative test which involved groups of trainees being dropped off individually by trucks in the areas of Mansfield and Nottingham. From there they had to make their way to a location near Chesterfield by a certain time at dawn the following day. Many trainees made use of the railways, but on several occasions found themselves being shunted around and subsequently heading off in the wrong direction. Generally speaking, only a small number reached the final rendezvous, the remainder having been captured by other troops and police searching for them and locked up in the cells of Chesterfield police station.

Major Ian Fenwick, a well known pre-war artist and cartoonist who was not a trainee at the time but wanted to try his luck, 'acquired' from a church vestry a set of clerical garments and proceeded to board a passenger train which stopped at Chesterfield. He had more or less convinced the ticket collector at Chesterfield of his reasons for the lack of a ticket when it was noticed that his trousers were far too short — the parson was obviously a very short man, whereas Fenwick was over six foot. He therefore soon found himself in the cells, where he proceeded to render one of his celebrated cartoons on the cell wall. How he got the materials to do so nobody knew, but early in the morning Major Derick Reid, the Chief Instructor of the Battle School, received an urgent telephone call from the station sergeant at Chesterfield police station, asking for someone with a pot of whitewash to be sent down to clean up the wall before his senior officer arrived on duty.

Another of the Battle School's exercises involved the ambushing of tanks with necklaces of mines. One of the instructors, who had formerly been a Royal Tank Regiment officer, considered this exercise to be most unreal because 15 cwt trucks acted as the tanks. He had discovered that a factory in Nottingham was just completing an order for tanks which were not suitable for operations in Europe. He and Major Reid approached the general commanding the area to see if they could 'borrow' three of these tanks, which were in full working order except for their armament. After a short conversation, and Major Reid's signature on the relevant paperwork, the Battle School acquired three brand new tanks which thereafter operated within the boundaries of Hardwick.

PARACHUTE TRAINING

Once the aspiring parachutists had succeeded in passing the selection course, they were sent on for parachute training at Ringway. By the middle of 1942 much progress had been made in improving parachuting techniques since the early days of two years earlier. The parachute course lasted two weeks. The first week was devoted to 'synthetic' ground training, during which the trainees learned how to exit correctly from an aircraft, how to control their parachutes in the air and how to land correctly. The fuselages of Whitleys, and subsequently Stirlings, Halifaxes, Albemarles and, eventually, Dakotas were positioned in the hangars at Ringway. Trainees jumped from these, learning the correct position for an exit. Other training aids included trapezes, on which trainees swung whilst learning flight drills, and wooden chutes down which they slid before falling and rolling. Later there was also the 'Fan', which consisted of a drum around which was wound a steel cable, the end of which was attached to a parachute harness. When a trainee jumped from a platform some 20 feet from the ground, his weight caused the drum to revolve; however, its speed was controlled by two vanes which acted as an air brake and thus allowed the trainee to land with the same impact as he would when using a parachute.

The end of the first week's training culminated in trainees carrying out their first two parachute descents from a tethered balloon. These were universally unpopular, the slow swaying ascent to the jump height of 700 feet often adding nausea to the tribulations of the trainees, who were inevitably suffering from nervousness. A 'stick' of four trainees sat in the cage suspended below the balloon. On a command from the RAF parachute jumping instructor, the first man to jump swung his legs into the circular aperture in the centre of the cage floor and adopted a position of sitting to attention whilst gripping the rim of the aperture behind and either side of him. On the command "Go!", he thrust himself forward, bringing his hands to his sides and keeping his feet together in the position of attention. This was followed by a stomach-churning 120-foot drop before the parachute opened. Needless to say, the sensation of the parachute opening was a thrilling one, but any feeling of bliss was soon interrupted by an instructor on the ground shouting instructions through a megaphone regarding the correct flight drills and position for landing. Those who were short and stocky had little difficulty in mastering the parachute roll, whilst those who were tall tended to find it more difficult

The second week of the course saw trainees making their five descents from aircraft. These were initially carried out in 'slow pairs', and then in 'quick pairs'. Subsequently, trainees jumped in sticks of five and finally in sticks of ten. Whilst it was not such a nauseating process as jumping from a balloon, parachuting from a Whitley could be somewhat disconcerting. If the correct position was not maintained when making an exit through the aperture in the fuselage floor, the result was one or two rather dramatic somersaults which normally resulted in the 'twists' — the front and rear sets of rigging lines becoming twisted together, restricting the proper development of the parachute canopy and thus increasing the rate of descent as well as preventing control of the parachute. The same problems were faced when jumping from other types of converted bombers, namely Halifaxes, Stirlings and Albemarles, which were subsequently pressed into service as paratroop transports but which had not been designed for such use. It was not until the arrival of the Dakota that exits could be made through a door in the side of the fuselage rather than an aperture in the floor, thus making life somewhat easier and relatively more enjoyable for the parachutist.

Other problems which faced parachutists included the 'blown periphery', which occurred when part of the periphery of the canopy was blown inwards and subsequently outwards through the rigging lines, this producing a second inverted canopy. Another type of blown periphery occurred when part of the canopy blew between two rigging lines, after which the canopy tended to roll up at the skirt. Other types of malfunctions included the 'streamer', in which a canopy failed to open at all.

By the end of the second week, unless they had fallen prey to any mishap such as injury, trainees had completed their total of seven descents at Ringway and were presented with the coveted parachute wings. Subsequently they returned to their units. However, there was little opportunity for them to rest on their laurels as they faced up to battle training.

BATTLE TRAINING

Battle training in airborne forces was tough and intensive. From the very start it was appreciated that airborne troops would have to be capable of fighting and surviving against larger and more heavily armed formations until link-ups with infantry or armoured formations could be effected. What they lacked in armour and firepower had to be made up in extremely high standards of physical fitness and individual skills such as weapon training and fieldcraft. The aim of such training was to produce troops of such a high calibre that they would be capable of taking on superior odds and holding their own against them. Each man was to possess a high degree of courage, self-discipline and self-reliance.

Training began with the individual soldier and the required skills, progressing to section, platoon, company and ultimately battalion level training. Exercises were carried out by day and night and frequently ended in long marches back to unit barracks. The ability to cover long distances at high speed in full battle order became a matter of pride to the newly formed parachute units — ten miles in two hours, twenty in four and, ultimately, fifty miles in twenty-four hours.

CHAPTER 2
Operations in North Africa, Sicily and Italy, 1942–1943

NORTH AFRICA 1942–43 — 1ST PARACHUTE BRIGADE OPERATIONS

In September 1942 it was decided that an airborne unit would be included amongst the Allied forces which would take part in the forthcoming campaign in North Africa. The unit detailed was the 2nd Battalion 503rd US Parachute Infantry, which had arrived in Britain in mid-June and had been placed under command of 1st Airborne Division. Major General Browning successfully argued that one battalion would be insufficient for the role and, as a result, 1st Parachute Brigade was allotted in addition to the American unit, being placed under command of the Supreme Allied Commander, General Dwight Eisenhower, who in turn allocated it to 1st British Army commanded by Lieutenant General Sir Kenneth Anderson. The Allies' initial objective was the capture of northern Tunisia and 1st British Army was tasked with landing east of Algiers and capturing the two ports of Bizerta and Tunis. To carry out this task Anderson had three brigades of infantry, including 1st Parachute Brigade, and a brigade of tanks.

However, 1st Parachute Brigade was not up to strength nor fully equipped to war scales. As a result, men and equipment had to be taken from 2nd Parachute Brigade and other units of 1st Airborne Division, depleting them somewhat. Before their departure for North Africa, the men of 1st Parachute Brigade had to learn a new skill — jumping from Dakotas of the US Army Air Force (USAAF). The RAF was unable to spare any aircraft for airborne operations in North Africa and thus the USAAF assumed the role of transporting and dropping the paratroops. However, because of the differences between American and British parachuting equipment and techniques, 1st Parachute Brigade, whose troops were used to making their exits through apertures in the fuselage floors of converted bombers, had to undergo a period of retraining after the arrival of the USAAF's No. 60 Group in England at the end of September. The first drop from Dakotas took place on 9 October, a total of 250 men being involved. Unfortunately four of them, including Lieutenant Street of 2nd Parachute Battalion, were killed. It was discovered that the static line on the British 'X' Type parachute was too short for use with the Dakota and had caused two of the canopies to become entangled with the aircraft's tailwheel. Subsequently, it was found that raising the tail of the aircraft during a drop helped to eliminate the risk of this happening.

Towards the end of October B and C Companies, the Mortar Platoon and Battalion Headquarters of 3rd Parachute Battalion departed their base at Bulford in Wiltshire and moved to nearby Netheravon airfield. The rest of the battalion, along with 1st and 2nd Parachute Battalions, soon afterwards travelled to Greenock, in Scotland, where on 29 October they were embarked on ships sailing in convoy for an undisclosed destination. Meanwhile, 3rd Parachute Battalion was preparing to fly to Gibraltar in readiness for an airborne operation in North Africa. The limitations on the number of Dakotas allotted to the operation were the reason that the battalion's A Company, commanded by Major Stephen Terrell, had to travel by sea with the rest of the brigade. Additional problems were encountered when it was discovered that the aircrafts' payload had been decreased by some 2,000lb because extra fuel tanks had been fitted, and the loading manifests for each aircraft having to be revised.

On 5 November the battalion moved to Hurn airfield, near Bournemouth. The aircraft arrived on the following day, and at this point Lieutenant Colonel Geoffrey Pine Coffin briefed his men on the task that lay ahead. Meanwhile, everyone awaited news of the Allied seaborne landings in North Africa, which would take place on Sunday 8 November. Two days later news of the success of the landings arrived, but the battalion was unable to take off from Hurn because of thick fog. On the following day the weather forecast indicated that the entire southern part of England, except for the west of Cornwall, would remain fog-bound. It was decided to move the battalion by train to Newquay and then by road to RAF St Eval. This was carried out by 2300 hours that night, by which time the Dakotas and their USAAF crews were awaiting the arrival of Lieutenant Colonel Pine Coffin and his men. At 2330 hours that night, the leading elements of the battalion took off and headed for Gibraltar, where they arrived at dawn on the next day, 10 November. Here Lieutenant Colonel Pine Coffin was informed that his battalion was to carry out an operation on the following day, its task being to capture an airfield at Bone, a port on

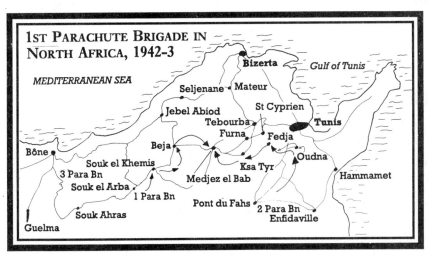

1ST PARACHUTE BRIGADE IN
NORTH AFRICA, 1942–3

MEDITERRANEAN SEA

Bizerta — Gulf of Tunis

Seljenane — Mateur
Jebel Abiod   St Cyprien
    Tebourba
    Furna   Fedja   Tunis
    Beja
Bône
    Souk el Khemis   Ksa Tyr   Oudna
3 Para Bn   Hammamet
    Souk el Arba   Medjez el Bab
        1 Para Bn
        Pont du Fahs   2 Para Bn
    Souk Ahras   Enfidaville
Guelma

the border between Tunisia and Algeria some 250 miles east of Algiers. The battalion was to fly early on the following morning to an airfield at Maison Blanche, near Algiers, from which the operation would be mounted.

At 0430 hours on 11 November the battalion took off from Gibraltar and flew to Maison Blanche, arriving at 0900 hours. Lieutenant Colonel Pine Coffin was briefed by Lieutenant General Sir Kenneth Anderson, Commander 1st British Army, on board the latter's headquarters ship in Algiers harbour. The battalion was to seize the airfield outside Bone, and would subsequently be relieved by No. 6 Commando which would carry out a seaborne landing at Bone itself. Owing to the inexperience of the American pilots in dropping paratroops at night, the operation would start with take-off at 0430 hours and P-Hour (the time at which the drop would take place) at 0830 hours.

On the morning of 12 November the battalion took off as planned and arrived over the target at exactly 0830 hours. The operation was successful, the American aircrews having delivered their sticks of paratroops accurately. Both of 3rd Parachute Battalion's companies, plus the Mortar Platoon and Battalion Headquarters, landed on and around the airfield. Casualties were light, numbering 14 in all, some breaking legs on the very hard, stony ground. Only one man was killed during the drop, having accidentally shot himself with his own Sten gun during the descent. Unbeknown to Lieutenant Colonel Pine Coffin and his men, their operation had been observed by a battalion of *fallschirmjaeger*, their German counterparts, who were en route for Bone in a formation of Junkers Ju 52 transports. Seeing that the airfield had already been taken by Allied troops, the Germans turned and headed back for their base at Tunis.

3rd Parachute Battalion swiftly occupied the airfield, but soon came under attack by the Luftwaffe in the form of Stuka dive bombers. However, they held firm and were eventually by joined by No. 6 Commando as planned. Shortly afterwards, a squadron of Spitfires arrived to provide air cover. Three days later, on 15 November, the battalion withdrew from Bone and moved west to the village of St Charles, where it met A Company and the rest of the unit which had travelled by sea. Together with the rest of 1st Parachute Brigade, they had disembarked on 13 November at Algiers, where they had remained whilst being subjected to enemy bombing.

Originally, Lieutenant General Anderson had decided to seize a key road junction at Beja and the El Aouina airfield at Tunis by an airborne operation, and 1st Parachute Battalion, commanded by Lieutenant Colonel James Hill, had been allocated the task. However, by the time that the battalion had arrived at Algiers there were reports that a large number of German troops, numbering some ten thousand, had been flown into Tunis. General Anderson therefore decided that 1st Parachute Battalion, supported by detachments of 16th Parachute Field Ambulance RAMC and 1st Parachute Squadron RE, would be dropped at Souk el Arba with the tasks of securing the crossroads there, contacting the French forces stationed at Beja, some 40 miles to the north east, and carrying out harrassing operations to the east.

Not least of 1st Parachute Battalion's problems in preparing for the operation was insufficient time. Added to this was the lack of transport, because 1st Parachute Brigade had not been permitted to bring any of its own vehicles owing to limitations on shipping space, and this hampered the movement of equipment to the mounting airfield after it had been unloaded from the ships in Algiers harbour. Much of the stores required for the operation did not arrive at the airfield at Maison Blanche until 1630 hours on the afternoon of 14 November. These had to broken down and packed into containers, while parachutes had to be unpacked from the crates in which they had travelled during the sea voyage and inspected by the parachute packing section from the RAF's No. 38 Wing which was attached to 1st Parachute Brigade. The battalion was to be flown in and dropped by Dakotas of No. 64 Group of the USAAF's 51st Wing. These were limited to 32 in number, and thus one of 1st Parachute Battalion's companies could not be carried in the first lift. Furthermore, the American aircrews had no previous experience of dropping paratroops, and there was no radio communication between aircraft nor intercom facilities between pilots and despatchers in each Dakota. There were no maps available other than French quarter-inch-to-the-mile maps designed for motorists, and thus there was little chance of the aircrews finding any predetermined dropping zones. Consequently, Lieutenant Colonel Hill decided to travel in the cockpit of the commander of 51st Wing and with him select the most suitable dropping zone in the area of the objective. At that point, Hill would retire to the rear of the aircraft and jump with his men.

The battalion took off for Souk el 'Arba, but encountered heavy cloud over the target area and was forced to turn back, arriving at Maison Blanche airfield at 1100 hours. The operation was postponed for two days. At 1100 hours on 16 November 1st Parachute Battalion once again took off from Maison Blanche. Its mission had been changed, and it was now to seize the town of Beja, persuade the French forces there to join the Allied cause, and carry out probing and harrassing operations. It was also to secure the area of the Souk el Khemis-Souk el Arba plain for use as landing strips by the RAF.

The drop took place without mishap, the only fatality being a man who was strangled by a rigging line which became entangled round his neck. Major Sir Richard des Voeux, who was a liaison officer accompanying the battalion, broke his leg on landing, and four men were slightly wounded by a Sten gun which was accidentally discharged. The main problem was caused by local Arabs, who attempted to spirit away the equipment containers. Shortly afterwards, the battalion rallied and formed up before moving off towards Beja as quickly as possible. On arrival at the area of the road junction, Hill and his men were confronted by a force of two battalions of French troops, numbering 3,000, who were dug in and supported by machine guns. However, they gave the paratroops a friendly reception, as did the mayor and people of Beja, who plied them with copious quantities of champagne and wine.

On opening negotiations with the French commander, Lieutenant Colonel Hill learned that the former had been threatened with reprisals if he permitted British forces to take Beja. Hill bluffed the Frenchman into believing that his force was somewhat larger than was the case, and informed him that British armoured divisions were already advancing to link up with him and his men. Fortunately, the French commander believed him and agreed that his units would hand over to 1st Parachute Battalion during the evening. During the rest of the day, as part of the charade designed to reinforce the impression of a larger force, 1st Parachute Battalion marched through Beja twice — first wearing helmets and then berets. The ruse worked, and reports reached the Germans in Tunis that a large British force had occupied the town. They responded by bombing the town.

Shortly afterwards, Lieutenant Colonel Hill discovered from the French that the Germans were in the habit of sending a patrol of eight armoured cars to the railway station at Sidi N'Sir, which was about 20 miles from Beja and was occupied by a company of French native infantry. The Germans, who arrived each day at 1000 hours, apparently exchanged pleasantries with the French and swapped cigarettes before returning to their base at Bizerta, on the coast. Hill decided that this would be an ideal opportunity to demonstrate that the enemy were not invincible and thus win over the French. He decided to ambush the German patrol and managed to persuade the French to allow him to send a company through their lines to Sidi N'Sir.

On the following day S Company, commanded by Major Peter Cleasby-Thompson, together with a small detachment of sappers, was despatched to make contact with the French commander at Sidi N'Sir and to ambush the German patrol. Having arrived at the village and received a friendly welcome from the French company commander, S Company lay up for the night before setting up the ambush on the following morning. Once the enemy patrol, which consisted of four large armoured cars and four small armoured reconnaissance vehicles, had driven through the ambush area and on towards Sidi N'Sir, S Company and its sapper detachment laid necklaces of No. 75 Hawkins anti-tank grenades across the road and settled down to wait for the Germans' return. The ground on one side of the road consisted of a steeply rising slope, and on the other side there was a large bog. Cleasby-Thompson positioned a 3-inch mortar on a hill nearby and two Bren gun groups in the bog to one side of the road, while the main ambush group was positioned on the hillside some 80 yards from the road. Lieutenants Philip Mellor and Arthur Kellas, equipped with a number of Gammon bombs, were hidden in a ditch at the side of the road. They did not have to wait long. The column of enemy vehicles appeared, and the company held its fire until the first Hawkins grenade was detonated. However, the leading armoured car passed over the necklace without exploding any of the grenades, and disappeared from sight round the corner. The second vehicle was not so fortunate and detonated a grenade, swerving over to one side and blocking the road. As the last vehicle entered the trap, another necklace of Hawkins grenades was pulled on to the road to block off any attempt at escape by reversing out of the ambush. S Company opened fire immediately the first grenade exploded, two of the armoured reconnaissance vehicles being destroyed and their crews killed by Gammon bombs thrown by the two officers hiding in the ditch. The leading armoured car, returning to investigate the absence of the rest of the column, reappeared but ran over one of the Hawkins grenades and was disabled. Meanwhile, the crew of the 3-inch mortar on the hill were bringing down fire on the tail of the column, forcing the remaining vehicles to move forward into the main killing ground. All four of the armoured cars had been destroyed and their crews killed by the time the rest of the enemy surrendered.

Casualties among S Company were light. They included Lieutenant Arthur Kellas, who had been wounded in the eye, and Company Sergeant Major Steadman. Loading the wounded on to the two armoured vehicles which were still in working order, the company withdrew to Sidi N'Sir and then returned to Beja. Lieutenant Colonel Hill ordered the two scout cars and prisoners to be driven around the town to demonstrate that the Germans could be defeated. S Company's action did much to convince the French to rally to the Allied cause, not least because it gave rise to a belief that 1st Parachute Battalion possessed a highly secret anti-tank weapon capable of destroying German armour.

On 20 November the enemy attacked the French forces at Medjez el Bab. On the previous day, at a meeting with the French divisional commander, the Germans had insisted that they be permitted to man the bridge there. The French, who had already been warned by Lieutenant Colonel Hill that any German attempt to cross the bridge would be resisted by 1st Parachute Battalion, rejected the German demands and announced that any advance would be blocked. R Company, commanded by Major Conron, had been deployed in support of the French at Medjez el Bab. When the Germans attacked at 1100 hours, they met stiff resistance from the French and British troops, the former suffering heavy casualties. Nevertheless, the enemy were beaten off, and subsequent aggressive patrolling by 1st Parachute Battalion helped to prevent any further attempts by the enemy to advance westwards.

Two days later, on 22 November, Lieutenant Colonel Hill learned that an Italian force numbering some 300, together with some tanks, was located in a harbour position nine miles to the north east of Sidi N'Sir, at the base of a small hill called Gue. He decided to attack it. On the following night 1st Parachute Battalion moved to Sidi N'Sir, where it rendezvoused with the French company of Senegalese infantry who were to be attached to it to help carry ammunition for the battalion's 3-inch mortars. Hill's plan called for the mortars, which would be controlled by the battalion's second in command, Major Alastair Pearson, to bring down heavy fire while the battalion advanced towards the enemy position. Meanwhile, a detachment of 27 sappers from 1st Parachute Squadron RE, under Captain Geary, would move round the hill and mine the road to the east with Hawkins grenades and thus hinder any withdrawal or attempt at reinforcement by the enemy.

R and S Companies, the Mortar Platoon, the French company and Battalion Headquarters moved across country, following a railway line. The Mortar Platoon started setting up its mortars, while the sapper detachment departed on its flanking move to the rear of the hill. Just before H Hour, as the two rifle companies were preparing for the assault, the night was suddenly rent by three loud explosions. Unfortunately, one of the No. 75 Hawkins grenades, being carried in sandbags by the sappers, had accidentally exploded and had detonated the others. All but two of the sappers were killed. All element of surprise was lost as the enemy immediately stood to and opened fire from the top of the hill. R and S Companies put in an immediate assault, with two platoons assaulting the enemy position on the hill itself, on which they encountered a mixed force of Germans and Italians. Lieutenant Colonel Hill observed that there were only three Italian light tanks on the position and proceeded to approach them himself, accompanied by a small group of his men. Inserting the barrel of his revolver through an observation port in the nearest tank, he fired a round into the vehicle. This resulted in the rapid surrender of the Italian crew. He approached the second tank and knocked on its turret with his walking stick, achieving the same results. However, when he tried the same with the third tank a German crew emerged, firing their weapons and throwing grenades from the turret. Lieutenant Colonel Hill was shot three times in the chest and Captain Miles Whitelock, his adjutant, was wounded by shrapnel from grenades. Needless to say, the tank crew were rapidly despatched. Major Alastair Pearson took over command of the battalion as Lieutenant Colonel Hill and Captain Whitelock were evacuated by means of a captured enemy motorcycle combination driven slowly down the nearby railway line to Beja. There they were operated on by the forward surgical team from 16th Parachute Field Ambulance.

Two days later, on 26 November, the battalion moved to a new location ten miles south of Mateur. From there it carried out a vigorous programme of patrolling during the next ten days or so, after which it withdrew into reserve in Algiers.

For a few days after its arrival in Algiers on 12 November, 2nd Parachute Battalion was kept in reserve at Maison Blanche, where it suffered the loss of some of its equipment from enemy bombing. On 18 November Headquarters 1st Parachute Brigade received orders for a battalion to be dropped at Sousse, which was on the coast some 60 miles by road south east of Tunis, and 2nd Parachute Battalion was given the task. Because of the limited number of aircraft available, only two companies would be flown in on the first lift on the morning of 19 November, the rest of the battalion following on the following day. Lieutenant Colonel Johnny Frost carried out a reconnaissance of the area from the air in order to select a suitable dropping zone for his battalion. On his return, however, he was informed that the operation was cancelled and that his battalion was to drop on Enfidaville, some 30 miles north west of Sousse. Having carried out another aerial reconnaissance, Frost returned to be told that the Enfidaville operation had also been cancelled.

On 27 November Headquarters 1st Parachute Brigade received orders from Headquarters 1st British Army for one of its battalions to be put on standby for an operation. Once again 2nd Parachute Battalion was given the task, and that afternoon it was revealed that the target area was Pont du Fahs, 40 miles south of Tunis, where the battalion was to attack and destroy enemy aircraft on the landing ground there. The battalion was then to move to Depienne, 12 miles from its initial objective, and then Oudna, a further 20 miles away, where it was to carry out similar tasks at both locations.

On 29 November 2nd Parachute Battalion, together with a troop of 1st Parachute Squadron RE and a section of 16th Parachute Field Ambulance, emplaned at Maison Blanche in 44 Dakotas of the USAAF's Nos. 62 and 64 Groups. Just before take-off Lieutenant Colonel Frost was informed that the enemy aircraft at Pont de Fahs and Depienne had departed. As a result, the battalion was to drop at Depienne and move to Oudna, where it was to carry out its task, after which it was to link up with units of 1st British Army at St Cyprien. There was no time for a further aerial reconnaissance, so Frost had to rely on being able to select a suitable dropping zone from the lead Dakota, in which he was travelling. The flight itself was unpleasant for the paratroops, bad weather causing considerable turbulence which resulted in many members of the battalion suffering from airsickness. As the aircraft approached Depienne, Frost fortunately saw a large open expanse of terrain suitable for use as a dropping zone.

The drop itself was unopposed but scattered, and there were seven casualties, one of which was fatal. Blowing the hunting horn which he always carried, Lieutenant Colonel Frost rallied his men, who then set about collecting their parachutes and containers. In this they were hindered by the local Arabs, who were intent on stealing as much as possible. As the battalion had been instructed to retrieve its parachutes and containers, a platoon of C Company, under Lieutenant Buchanan, had to be left behind to guard them and to look after those injured in the drop, thus reducing C Company to two platoons in strength. At 1600 hours that afternoon a patrol of three armoured cars from 56th Reconnaissance Regiment appeared on the road, heading north towards Cheylus. An hour later they returned and reported that there was a German roadblock four miles along the road. Just before midnight the battalion set off under cover of darkness for Oudna. The going was difficult, over stony and hilly terrain with rutted tracks, and the troops were weighed down with equipment and ammunition. Fortunately, they were able to commandeer some mules and carts on to which they loaded their 3-inch mortars and other heavy equipment. By 0430 hours on 30 November the battalion had covered 12 miles and a halt was called to give the troops some chance of rest, although the bitter cold made this virtually impossible. Three hours later the march was continued, and by 1100 hours the battalion had reached a location from which the landing ground could be observed.

At 1430 hours that afternoon A Company, commanded by Major Dick Ashford, moved down into the valley towards the landing ground while C Company and Battalion Headquarters moved to the left along some high ground. Suddenly, the battalion came under machine gun and mortar fire from the direction of the landing ground, a small number of men being hit. A Company, however, succeeded in reaching the landing ground and the cover of some buildings nearby. At that point, however, six German heavy tanks appeared and attacked the battalion, as did a number of Messerschmitt fighters which strafed the paratroops. These were followed by six Stuka dive bombers. However, the tanks were repulsed and the air attacks proved largely ineffective owing to the paratroops' good camouflage and concealment in the scrub on the hillside.

At dusk, Lieutenant Colonel Frost withdrew his battalion to the west to Prise de l'Eau, which offered a good location for a defensive position and where there was a good supply of water from a well. There they would wait to link up with the advancing units of 1st British Army on the following morning as they headed for Tunis. However, his men were by then exhausted and severely depleted in numbers, as well as being very low on ammunition. Frost was sure that the enemy would follow up on the following day, so he positioned an ambush on the track at the foot of the battalion's position. On the following morning, 1 December, a column of enemy armoured vehicles was observed approaching from the direction of Oudna. After a while the column halted at a range of about 2,000 yards and a small number of vehicles detached themselves and headed rapidly along the track towards the battalion's ambush position. Unfortunately, they surprised a party filling waterbottles at the well, and thus the ambush group was not able to engage them effectively, merely managing to kill the commander of the leading armoured vehicle, which succeeded in escaping. The other enemy vehicles also withdrew and rejoined their column, which then proceeded to deploy and open fire on the battalion, which replied with its 3-inch mortars. Within a very short space of time a direct hit was scored and the enemy withdrew out of range.

At that point C Company reported that three armoured vehicles, two tanks and an armoured car, were approaching from a different direction and that they were displaying the 1st British Army recognition signal, which was a yellow triangle. Frost naturally assumed that this was the leading element of the forces with which the battalion was to link up during the advance on Tunis. This illusion was shattered a few minutes later when C Company's commander, Major John Ross, reported that the vehicles were German and had taken prisoner three members of his company who had gone forward to meet them in the belief that they were British. The Germans then sent one of the captured men back to the battalion, informing Frost that he and his men were surrounded and demanding that they surrender. The situation was made even worse by a radio message from Headquarters 1st British Army, informing Frost that the advance on Tunis had been postponed. Rejecting the German demands for a surrender, Lieutenant Colonel Frost decided that the battalion must vacate its positions immediately and move to higher ground from which it would exfiltrate after dark and continue its march westwards towards Allied lines, which were about 50 miles away. After destroying the 3-inch mortars, for which there was no more ammunition, and the radio sets, whose batteries were exhausted, 2nd Parachute Battalion moved off. As it did so, the enemy armour opened fire and caused casualties among the paratroops, the splinters from the hard rocks around them taking their toll.

The battalion ascended the high ground to the north of Prise de l'Eau. The physical effort of climbing the hills whilst heavily laden in the heat of the day was taking its toll on Frost's men, who were suffering badly from thirst, and he decided that the battalion would halt and take up positions on the northern face of a hill called Djebel Sidi Bou Hadjeba. As luck would have it, a well was located there. The hill had two summits and B Company, commanded by Major Frank Cleaver, was positioned on the right with the remnants of C Company on the left, the remaining elements of A Company in reserve and Battalion Headquarters to the right and in the rear. Enemy troop movements could clearly be seen on the plain below the battalion.

During the afternoon, at about 1500 hours, the enemy mounted their initial assault with light tanks and infantry mounted in armoured half-tracks. Heavy artillery and mortar fire was brought down on the battalion and a fierce battle for the summit of Djebel Sidi Bou Hadjeba developed. Casualties mounted amongst 2nd Parachute Battalion, who had not had sufficient time to dig in. Those killed included Major Frank Cleaver, the commander of B Company, and one of C Company's platoon commanders, Lieutenant the Honourable Henry Cecil. The battalion's chaplain, Padre Macdonald, was among those wounded. At the height of the battle enemy aircraft appeared and provided a breathing space for Frost and his men by mistakenly attacking their own troops and halting their attack. It was all too evident to Frost that his battalion, which by then had suffered some 150 killed and wounded, could not hold on much longer and would have to make its escape after nightfall. He decided that the battalion would move by companies, each independently heading for the village of Massicault. Sadly, the wounded would have to be left behind in the care of Lieutenant Jock McGavin and his section of 16th Parachute Field Ambulance, protected by a platoon of B Company under Lieutenant Pat Playford.

At 1830 hours, after darkness had fallen, 2nd Parachute Battalion moved out of the defensive position and down the steep slopes of Djebel Sidi Bou Hadjeba. Making their individual ways over the rough terrain, which consisted in part of rough ploughland which made the going very difficult for the exhausted troops, as well as being interspersed with wadis, the companies marched on compass bearings. Resting for ten minutes in every hour, they moved through the moonless night until they came to the River Medjerda, where the troops were able to relieve their raging thirsts before once again continuing their march westwards. Elements of the battalion were lost during the march. Some of B Company became separated from the rest and were captured by enemy troops after being surrounded. Others evaded capture, including Captain Ronnie Stark, who succeeded in reaching the British lines while leading Lieutenant Douglas Crawley, a platoon commander in B Company, who had been temporarily blinded by a wound. Major John Ross, C Company's commander, along with six of his men, also reached British lines. Major Philip Teichman, the battalion's second in command, and Captain Jock Short, the Adjutant, together with a number of men from B Company, were ambushed. Teichman was killed and Short was wounded and captured.

Shortly before dawn on 2 December, Lieutenant Colonel Frost and his group, which consisted of Battalion Headquarters, Support Company and the sapper troop, halted in a wadi and a reconnaissance patrol was sent forward. It returned soon afterwards, having discovered an Arab farm a few minutes' march away. The battalion moved forward to the farm, which offered plenty of cover in which to lie up and a good supply of water. The farmer proved amenable and made the weary troops welcome, selling them food and generally helping them in any way that he could. Not long afterwards, news arrived of another body of troops resting in another farm a short distance away. Lieutenant Euen Charteris, the battalion's Intelligence Officer, was dispatched to discover who they were, and discovered that it was A Company, which immediately joined Frost and his small force. Frost learned from the Arabs that the nearest elements of 1st British Army were at Furna, further West than had been thought. The battalion was in dire need of ammunition and equipment, and Frost decided that an attempt had to be made to make contact with Headquarters 1st British Army to request support. As a result, Lieutenant Charteris and two men were dispatched to make their way to Furna to seek help. Unfortunately, they were ambushed and killed en route.

By now, Frost's force consisted of some 200 men, comprising Battalion Headquarters, A Company, Support Company and the sapper troop from 1st Parachute Squadron RE. There was no sign of B and C Companies. Suddenly the Arabs, who until then had been friendly and co-operative, departed in haste, and it soon became apparent to Frost and his men that enemy troops had arrived — indeed, they could be seen on a ridgeline a few hundred yards away. Shortly afterwards, more could be seen moving into the area on all sides. Fortunately the paratroops were well concealed in their positions and held their fire, thus making it more difficult for the enemy to gauge their strength. At approximately 1500 hours the enemy opened fire with mortars and subsequently with machine guns. However, the battalion was well dug in and effective cover was provided by the farm buildings and the thick hedges of cactus. At 1700 hours a small group of enemy troops approached A Company's positions and were wiped out. This resulted in the Germans laying down even heavier fire which forced a small picket, posted by Frost on the high ground above the farm, to withdraw to the main position.

Frost decided that the battalion would make a mass break-out after dark. On the sound of his hunting horn, his force would concentrate at Battalion Headquarters' location before charging the enemy's positions blocking the route to the hills and eventually re-forming on the Djebel el

Mengoub, which was on the line of march to Furna. However, at this point the enemy put in a heavy attack. This was repulsed by A Company, which waited until their adversaries were at close range before opening fire. Shortly after dusk the Germans launched another attack from the high ground above the farm, and this was also repulsed. Almost immediately afterwards, Frost gave the signal for the break-out on his hunting horn and the battalion, carrying its wounded, moved out with all speed. It met no opposition but became scattered in the dark. After a while, Frost and the men with him halted and he blew his hunting horn to guide the stragglers in to the rendezvous point. Eventually 110 men, out of the 200 who had broken out of the farm, made their way in to the sound of the horn. By now, none of them had more than five rounds of ammunition. After waiting for a short while to see if any more of his men appeared, Frost led his remaining force towards the ridgeline of Djebel el Mengoub. At about 0300 hours a large group of troops could be seen ahead on the same track and heading in the same direction. These turned out to be the men missing after the break-out, being led by Captain Dennis Vernon, the sapper troop commander.

An hour later the battalion reached a farm owned by a French family who provided the exhausted troops with food. Soon afterwards, however, news came of the approach of enemy armoured vehicles, and Frost and his men were forced to make their escape into the hills nearby. By now they could see the town of Medjez el Bab which, a local Arab informed them, was in the hands of the Allies. Heading towards the town, they encountered a troop of enemy armoured cars near a road junction, but these moved off in the direction of Tunis and the battalion was able to resume its march towards the Allied lines. Shortly afterwards, armoured vehicles were seen in the distance, and as they approached they were identified as American. The battalion's trials and tribulations were over. That afternoon, on 3 December, the remnants of 2nd Parachute Battalion marched smartly past the French positions outside Medjez el Bab.

It was a much depleted battalion which was eventually withdrawn to Souk el Khemis on 13 December to rest and reorganise. The Oudna operation had cost it dear. Sixteen officers and 250 other ranks had been lost. C Company had been decimated during the action on the Djebel Sidi Bou Hadjeba, while much of B Company, which had been with the Second in Command and the Adjutant, had been surrounded and killed or captured during the withdrawal from that location. Both companies had thus virtually ceased to exist. Eventually, reinforcements arrived in the form of 200 men, many of whom had previously been anti-aircraft gunners and thus had no previous infantry experience. Nevertheless, the battalion issued them with red berets and proceeded to take them in hand and make good their deficiencies as far as infantry skills were concerned.

Some members of the battalion who had been captured subsequently managed to escape and return to it. Corporal McConney was captured along with those injured in the drop and the platoon from C Company left to look after them and the parachutes and containers. Having concealed his fighting knife in the sling supporting a dislocated shoulder, he killed a guard and escaped, eventually making his way back to Allied lines. Members of B and C Companies who had been taken prisoner were being escorted to a PoW cage in a convoy escorted by Italian armoured cars. They overpowered their escort and escaped, eventually reaching the safety of Allied lines and ultimately returning to the battalion. The battalion's redoubtable chaplain, Padre Macdonald, and Lieutenant Jock McGavin, the commander of the 16th Parachute Field Ambulance section attached to 2nd Parachute Battalion, managed to distinguish themselves en route to captivity. Having been taken prisoner after staying with the wounded at Dejebel Sidi Bou Hadjeba, they were flown to Rome from Tunis. On landing in Rome their escort left them alone in the transport aircraft while enquiries were made as to their disposal. Lieutenant McGavin espied some cans of petrol and a pile of blankets, and within a very short space of time had set the aircraft ablaze, at which point he and Padre Macdonald made a rapid exit. Their mirth at the sight of the burning aircraft only served to infuriate the Italians, who were on the point of shooting both of them when a Luftwaffe officer intervened and saved their lives.

The Oudna operation was a disastrous episode which had been badly planned and based upon faulty intelligence. The blame must be laid squarely upon the shoulders of those at Headquarters 1st British Army who planned it, including Lieutenant General Sir Kenneth Anderson himself. 2nd Parachute Battalion was needlessly committed against a target which did not exist by the time it had been dropped, all enemy aircraft having left the landing ground at Oudna beforehand. Moreover, once the battalion had been dropped, little or no interest was shown in it by Headquarters 1st British Army and, for that matter, by its own parent formation, Headquarters 1st Parachute Brigade. No effort was made to provide support or maintain communications, or to assist in extracting the battalion once it was evident that its task had been carried out. The fact that any elements at all of 2nd Parachute Battalion survived the operation and the subsequent fighting withdrawal is testimony to the magnificent courage of its officers and men, and in particular to the determination and leadership of its Commanding Officer.

1ST PARACHUTE BRIGADE – GROUND OPERATIONS, DECEMBER 1942 – APRIL 1943

On 2 December, whilst 2nd Parachute Battalion was carrying out its fighting withdrawal from Oudna, 1st Parachute Brigade was informed by Headquarters 1st British Army that it was to be deployed in the infantry role. By 11 December, with 1st and 2nd Parachute Battalions having returned to the fold, the brigade was relocated at Souk el Khemis, with No. 1 Commando and 2nd Battalion 9th Regiment Tirailleurs Algeriennes under command, and had taken up defensive positions covering Beja under command of 5th Corps. During this period the weather had deteriorated, making any major operations impossible. An attack on Tunis from Medjez, which was held by 5th Corps, was cancelled because of the torrential rain. However, 1st Parachute Brigade was much encouraged by a visit from Lieutenant General Browning, who was well aware of the problems facing them.

On 3 January 1943, A Company 3rd Parachute Battalion took part in a night attack on an objective named 'Green Hill' while under command of a battalion of 36th Infantry Brigade. This hill was one of two, the other being named Commando Hill, which dominated the road which linked the town of Sedjenane with that of Mateur. The attack itself was unsuccessful, although A Company, commanded by Major Stephen Terrell, did gain the top of the hill. On 4 January 3rd Parachute Battalion was tasked with supporting two battalions of 36th Infantry Brigade, two of its rifle companies being attached to them: A Company to the 4th Battalion The Buffs, and B Company to a battalion of The Royal West Kent Regiment. C Company would be in the rear to prevent any attempt at infiltration by the enemy.

The attack on Green Hill took place just after dawn, and by 1000 hours the first crest had been gained. However the second crest, which was a further hundred yards on, was heavily fortified with gun emplacements, barbed wire and minefields. A Company, which was in an exposed position on the first crest and was under heavy enemy fire, called for artillery support. Unfortunately some of the shells fell on it owing to the proximity of its own position to that of its objective. In the evening however, B Company succeeded in temporarily seizing the second crest. The Germans then launched two counterattacks, the first being wiped out by heavy fire. This resulted in B Company nearly exhausting its ammunition and being driven off the hill by the second counterattack. On the same day, 3rd Parachute Battalion was withdrawn to Souk el Khemis and then to St Charles for rest.

On 7–8 January 1st Parachute Brigade, less 2nd Parachute Battalion, which remained under command of 78th Infantry Division, returned to Algiers to prepare for an airborne operation in support of 2nd US Corps. The brigade was to drop in the areas of Sfax and Gabes to cut enemy lines of communication between Tunis and Tripolitania. In the event the operation was cancelled, and on 4 January 1st Parachute Brigade was placed under command of 5th Corps, returning to its area by sea. Four days later the brigade was placed under command of 6th Armoured Division, Brigade Headquarters being located at Bou Arada with its two battalions deployed in the area of El Aroussa. On 30 January the brigade was transferred, along with 17th Regiment Royal Artillery, to the command of 19th French Corps, commanded by General Mathinet, for the purpose of relieving French units who were being withdrawn to re-equip. It was allocated the 4th Spahis, 4th Regiment Tirailleurs Tunisien, 43rd Regiment Infanterie Coloniale, 4th Chasseurs d'Afrique and six batteries of French artillery under command.

Almost immediately, 1st Parachute Brigade was ordered to attack an important feature, the massifs of Jebel Mansour and Jebel Alliliga. This task was given to Lieutenant Colonel Alastair Pearson's 1st Parachute Battalion, which was allocated a company of the French Foreign Legion under command and a battery of 17th Field Regiment RA in support. The attack was to take place on the night of 2–3 February. On the night of 31 January a large fighting patrol was sent out to probe the German positions on Djebel Mansour. Commanded by Captain 'Vic' Coxen, it was accompanied by the Commanding Officer. After successfully working its way to within a close distance of the top of the feature, the patrol was challenged. Putting in an immediate assault, Captain Coxen and his men overran some of the enemy positions and succeeded in capturing 14 prisoners and a number of machine guns which they purloined. After coming under fire from other enemy positions on the feature, and from Djebel Alliliga, which was about 500 yards away, the patrol withdrew under covering fire from French artillery.

On 2 February 1st Parachute Battalion, which had been relieved in its positions by the 3rd Battalion Grenadier Guards, carried out a night approach to Djebel Mansour. Captain 'Vic' Coxen and a small group went ahead and laid mine marking tape to guide the battalion to the start line. R and T Companies arrived without mishap and deployed along the start line, but S Company lost its way in the dark and headed too far to the left, encountering heavy machine gun fire and a minefield which caused several casualties. The rest of the battalion crossed the start line at 0500 hours, making its way up the scrub-covered hillside towards the enemy positions 500 yards away. As it did so, it came under heavy mortar and machine gun fire from the German mountain battalion holding the feature, but had reached its objective just before first light. By this stage the enemy had withdrawn, but a heavy barrage of mortar fire was brought down on the battalion, followed by a counterattack which was beaten off. The battle continued throughout the day, with S and T Companies eventually taking part of Djebel Alliliga for a while. At this point the Grenadiers and the Foreign Legion company under command of 1st Parachute Battalion were to have moved up to help occupy both the features, but heavy enemy artillery fire prevented them from doing so. The battalion had suffered heavy casualties, numbering approximately 105 in all, S Company in particular having lost a large number of men after coming under fire from one particular machine gun position. After trying unsuccessfully to tackle its second objective, Djebel Alliliga, 1st Parachute Battalion went firm on Djebel Mansour and requested that the 3rd Battalion Grenadier Guards should take on the task.

On the following day, 4 February, at 1500 hours, a company of the Grenadiers attacked Djebel Alliliga. It succeeded in reaching the top of the feature, by which time all of its officers had been killed or wounded and the company sergeant major had assumed command. Shortly afterwards, the enemy counterattacked and drove the Grenadiers off the hill, following this up with a series of counterattacks on 1st Parachute Battalion.

At 0700 hours on 5 February, 1st Parachute Battalion was attacked in force and was coming under heavy fire again from Djebel Alliliga. By then the battalion was very low on ammunition and was weak in numbers. It was decided that the position on Djebel Mansour was no longer tenable, and the Grenadiers and 1st Parachute Battalion withdrew at 1100 hours under cover of smoke laid down by tanks of 26th Armoured Brigade. During the withdrawal 3rd Parachute Battalion took up a covering position and 1st Parachute Battalion withdrew into reserve. It had lost nearly half of its strength: 35 killed, 132 wounded and 16 missing.

On 4 February 2nd Parachute Battalion found itself placed under command of 139th Infantry Brigade, commanded by Brigadier 'Swifty' Howlett, its first task being to take and hold a crossroads in the Ousseltia valley. When informed that the enemy threat was composed of ten battalions of infantry, supported by 100 tanks, Lieutenant Colonel Johnny Frost asked what support was available to him. He was told that no anti-tank guns could be spared, but that six tanks would be sent, although these would be of little use against the more powerful enemy armour. On the following day Lieutenant Colonel Frost, together with his company commanders and the rest of his 'R' Group, travelled in three Bren gun carriers to carry out a reconnaissance of the crossroads and the battalion's new positions. As they approached, Frost suddenly noticed that the surface of the road had been disturbed, and realised that the road had been mined. His shouted warning came too late, and one of the other carriers hit a mine and was blown up, killing two officers travelling in the vehicle: Major Dick Ashford, the commander of A Company, and Major 'Dinty' Moore, who commanded Headquarter Company.

In the event the enemy threat in the area did not materialise, and 2nd Parachute Battalion was relieved at the crossroads on 7 February and returned to the fold of 1st Parachute Brigade on the following day. Deployed in an area nicknamed 'Happy Valley', where it had relieved a French unit, the battalion was spread over a very wide front of three miles, and was somewhat stretched. It was, however, supported by a number of French units including some anti-tank guns, some artillery, two squadrons of Spahis and two dismounted squadrons of Chasseurs d'Afrique. The next two weeks or so were relatively quiet, but on 26 February the battalion, which was well dug in and well stocked with ammunition, was attacked by enemy infantry and by 0900 hours was under artillery fire. C Company was attacked first but beat off the enemy without any problem. The enemy, which comprised a mixed force of Austrians, Italian *Alpini* and German *Gebirgsjaeger* mountain troops, then attempted to carry out a flanking attack, but soon found themselves pinned down in a gully by the artillery supporting 2nd Parachute Battalion. Frost dismounted his Spahis and moved them forward to the Djebel Salah, a feature from which the French cavalrymen were able to cover the battalion's left flank. The enemy then attacked B Company, which was in the centre of the battalion's sector. After failing to make any progress, they turned their attention to infiltrating themselves into the large areas between the companies. However, here they met the fire of the battalion's medium machine guns and mortars which covered the areas of ground which the overstretched companies were unable to protect. By nightfall the battalion had broken up every enemy assault pitted against it, for little or no loss to itself. That night Captain

Ronnie Stark led a force of two platoons which swept across the battalion's front, flushing out and dealing with any enemy that they encountered. Just after dawn on the following morning, he and his men reappeared with 80 prisoners. During this action the enemy suffered 150 casualties, whilst 2nd Parachute Battalion lost one man killed and two wounded. Later that morning, Lieutenant Colonel Frost learned that some German armour had managed to penetrate the brigade on the left of the battalion and had reached 1st Parachute Brigade's B Echelon, 12 miles behind, where it had met stiff resistance, organised by the quartermasters of all three battalions, before being routed by British tanks of 6th Armoured Division which appeared in support.

Lieutenant Colonel Geoffrey Pine Coffin's 3rd Parachute Battalion, supported by 1st Parachute Squadron RE, suffered the brunt of the main assault on the morning of 26 February, enemy troops having infiltrated their positions during the previous night. Some very savage close-quarter fighting took place amongst A and B Companies and Battalion Headquarters, but eventually the enemy were forced to withdraw to a wadi where they took cover. Unfortunately for them, however, 3rd Parachute Battalion had registered the wadi amongst its mortar DFs and had set up its machine guns to cover the ground on the far side of it. Within an hour and a half, a total of 3,000 3-inch mortar bombs were dropped into the wadi with unerring accuracy, while the battalion's machine guns brought down a murderous fire on the slopes on the far side. Caught in a lethal trap, the enemy suffered very heavy casualties, totalling some 400 killed. Another 200 surrendered. 3rd Parachute Battalion, on the other hand, sustained very light losses, with only two officers and 12 other ranks killed, and between 30 and 40 wounded. 1st Parachute Battalion had also inflicted heavy casualties on the enemy, who had found themselves being 'channelled' by cleverly laid barbed wire entanglements into killing grounds selected by Lieutenant Colonel Alastair Pearson. Subjected to heavy fire at very close range, the enemy were routed and the attack failed.

On the night of 4 March 1st Parachute Brigade left the Bou Arada after being relieved by American troops, and moved to the Beja sector. The brigade took up positions with 1st Parachute Battalion on the right, south of the road between Tamera and Sedjenane, with 3rd Parachute Battalion on its left. Meanwhile, 2nd Parachute Battalion had been tasked by Headquarters 46th Infantry Division with clearing any enemy from the high ground above the town of Beja. On completing the task, during which it encountered no enemy troops, it was ordered to carry out an operation to capture a hill called Spion Kop. The battalion was to be supported by divisional artillery and a small composite force consisting of a company of infantry and a troop of tanks. In the event no artillery support was forthcoming, despite repeated calls for it once the battalion came under enemy fire, and the infantry company and troop of tanks withdrew after making contact with the enemy. As darkness fell, 2nd Parachute Battalion withdrew, and on the following day, 7 March, it rejoined 1st Parachute Brigade.

At 0800 hours on the following morning the enemy attacked 1st and 2nd Parachute Battalions under cover of artillery and mortar fire. The enemy forces consisted of four regiments: Witzig's parachute engineers, 10th Panzer Grenadiers, the Barenthin Regiment and the Tunisian Regiment. 1st Parachute Battalion was attacked by two companies which approached along the line of the road. S Company, commanded by Major Taffy Lloyd Jones, waited until the German troops were some 300 yards away before opening fire and enfilading them. At the same time, artillery and mortar fire was brought down on the enemy, who suffered some 40 casualties. At this point Brigadier Eric Down arrived at Lieutenant Colonel Alastair Pearson's battalion headquarters to observe the action. He subsequently distinguished himself in the battalion's eyes by personally taking a written message from the Commanding Officer to R Company.

In the meantime, 2nd Parachute Battalion had suffered a number of casualties and its companies were running low on ammunition. At 1000 hours Major Johnny Lane, commanding A Company, reported over the radio that he and his men were surrounded but were holding out. During the day enemy troops managed to work their way to within close range of the battalion's positions and eventually infiltrated into positions between the battalion and 1st Parachute Battalion. The Adjutant, Captain Willoughby Radcliffe, was killed whilst leading a small mule train loaded with ammunition for A Company. The enemy also attempted to outflank 1st Parachute Brigade by moving round to its right along a ridgeline to the south. However, this tactic was thwarted by the Vickers medium machine guns of 2nd Parachute Battalion, which were sited in a feature called Cork Wood. During this engagement Major Geoff Rotheray, commanding Headquarter Company, was killed.

By the afternoon the enemy attack had slackened, and Brigadier Flavell decided to mount a counterattack to drive out those enemy who had infiltrated between 1st and 2nd Parachute Battalions. This was successfully carried out by A Company 3rd Parachute Battalion, commanded by Major Stephen Terrell, which linked up with C Company 2nd Parachute Battalion once it had crossed over the road. A number of prisoners were taken, including several of Witzig's paratroops. By 1600 hours the enemy had been driven off. However, a flight of Stuka dive bombers attacked A Company 2nd Parachute Battalion just before dusk, causing some casualties.

During the next four days 1st Parachute Brigade, which from 10 March had a number of additional units, including 139th Infantry Brigade, under command, was engaged in defensive operations against powerful German forces of approximately divisional strength. Additional reinforcements, in the shape of the 5th Battalion The Sherwood Foresters, arrived and were soon committed on the 12 March to an attack on Djebel Bel, the feature of high ground adjacent to 1st Parachute Battalion's positions. Supported by a company of 1st Parachute Battalion, The Sherwood Foresters were initially successful but were eventually beaten off by a powerful enemy counterattack, suffering heavy casualties. That evening, 1st Parachute Battalion withdrew into reserve for a rest.

On the following day, 14 March, 2nd Parachute Battalion was subjected to heavy artillery bombardment of its positions in Cork Wood, followed by an enemy flanking attack which was almost successful. That evening, troops of the 10th Panzer Grenadier Regiment mounted another attack on Cork Wood and had achieved a degree of success until they were accidentally bombed by a squadron of Stukas. The following two days passed relatively quietly, although 1st Parachute Brigade and the units under its command were subjected to bombing and some accurate shellfire. On 17 March, however, the Germans once again attacked in force, penetrating the positions of 139th Infantry Brigade and some French units also under command. 1st and 3rd Parachute Battalions, who were by that time in reserve, moved forward to link up with 2nd Parachute Battalion and hold a line to cover the withdrawal of 139th Infantry Brigade, No. 1 Commando and the French units. On the following day, 8 March, the divisional commander ordered a withdrawal to new positions on a line running east to west at Djebel Abiad.

1st Parachute Battalion made its way back over the hills while 2nd Parachute Battalion carried out a difficult withdrawal along the bed of the Oued el Medene river. The going was difficult, the river being deep and fast-running. Periodically, salvoes of shells landed among the battalion and caused casualties, while enemy troops attempted to harry the rearguard. In all, casualties during the withdrawal totalled two killed, eleven wounded and five missing. Eventually, the battalion was able to climb out of the river and follow a railway line to the area where it was take up its new positions on three hills, known as 'The Pimples'. There it met the Second in Command, Major John Marshall, who had led the battalion's transport in its move by road during the withdrawal. On the evening of 20 March the battalion withdrew for a rest after handing over to the 2nd/5th Battalion The Leicestershire Regiment.

There was little respite for 1st Parachute Brigade, however, as on the following night the 10th Panzer Grenadier Regiment attacked the largest of 'The Pimples', called 'Bowler Hat', which was on the enemy-held side of the river and was overlooked by the enemy from two flanks. The Leicesters were pushed off the feature and Lieutenant Colonel Geoffrey Pine Coffin's 3rd Parachute Battalion was ordered to recapture the feature on the next night. However, it failed to do so, owing to inadequate time for reconnaissance and thorough planning, and thus 1st Parachute Battalion was given the task. However, Lieutenant Colonel Alastair Pearson remonstrated with the commander of 5th Corps, Lieutenant General Charles Allfrey, who was visiting the battalion, pointing out that his battalion was exhausted. A compromise was reached, Allfrey agreeing that 1st Parachute Battalion would capture the feature, thereafter handing it over to 3rd Parachute Battalion which would hold it. 1st Parachute Battalion carried out the attack at 2230 hours on the night of 23 March, taking the enemy by surprise and catching them asleep in their trenches with no sentries posted. By 0300 hours on 24 March 'Bowler Hat' had been retaken and a considerable number of prisoners captured, these being from an infantry unit which had taken over from the 10th Panzer Grenadier Regiment during the night.

On the same day, 1st Parachute Brigade received orders for an operation which was to be undertaken in conjunction with 36th and 138th Infantry Brigades. The task was the capture of the enemy positions at Tamera. 1st Parachute Brigade would be on the left of the two other brigades, with a unit of French Goums under command and 70th Field Regiment Royal Artillery in support. At 2300 hours on 27 March the three parachute battalions and the Goums crossed their start lines under cover of a heavy barrage laid down by the guns of 46th Infantry Division's artillery. 3rd Parachute Battalion, meanwhile, remained in its positions on 'Bowler Hat'. As was later discovered by Lieutenant Colonel Johnny Frost when he subsequently inspected them, the enemy defensive positions on the high ground consisted initially of a screen of observation and machine gun posts on the forward slopes, being concentrated on the most likely approaches. These and alternative positions, prepared to meet threats from different directions, were well stocked with stores and ammunition. On top of the feature were more positions in which there were signs marking routes to positions to the front and rear as well as to the flanks. On the reverse slope of the feature were well constructed dug-outs equipped with radios and electric light, trenches, barbed wire entanglements and minefields. In all, the enemy position at Tamera was formidable.

2nd Parachute Battalion's leading companies, A and B, moved forward as quickly as possible to be on schedule with the fire plan, the fire from the divisional artillery moving gradually ahead as the battalion advanced. Lieutenant Colonel Frost moved behind them with a small group which laid a white tape marking the axis advance as they moved through the darkness. The going was difficult, however, and the artillery barrage had passed the crest of the feature and had moved on to the reverse slopes before the battalion was ready to launch its assault. The enemy on the forward slope positions recovered as A and B Companies reached them. A Company met stiff resistance on the right, and B Company, which had made better progress, encountered a minefield and came under heavy fire while trying to work its way round it. Major Mickey Wardle, the company commander, was wounded, together with Captain Victor Dover. Lieutenant Douglas Crawley took over command but was also wounded shortly afterwards, while B Company was making its way to rejoin the rest of the battalion, which had regrouped on a false crest which had been mistaken in the dark for the top of the feature.

As dawn broke, Lieutenant Colonel Frost realised the situation and the battalion made haste to continue its assault. C Company, under Major John Ross, had been in reserve and now attacked uphill without delay. B Company, now commanded by Captain Simpson, a sapper officer attached to the battalion, carried out a left flanking movement while A Company and the rest of the battalion remained to set up a firm base. C Company met stiff opposition from elements of Witzig's parachute engineers, who counterattacked vigorously. Captain Dicky Spender was

RALEIGH COUNTY PUBLIC LIBRARY
BECKLEY, WEST VIRGINIA

killed thwarting an attempt by the enemy to outflank the company, killing four Germans in the process. Eventually the company's advance was halted and Major Ross, by then the only surviving officer, and his men were forced to withdraw after suffering heavy casualties. At this point Brigadier Flavell, aware of the position, despatched B Company 3rd Parachute Battalion, commanded by Major David Dobie, to help the sorely pressed 2nd Parachute Battalion. As Dobie and his men arrived, the German parachute sappers launched another fierce counterattack under cover of a heavy barrage of mortar and artillery fire which proved largely ineffective. The British artillery responded and, together with the battalion's own mortars, succeeded in breaking up the counterattack as it reached A Company. Meanwhile, B Company had successfully carried out its left flanking movement and proceeded to attack Witzig's regiment from the right and rear. Artillery support was called down and this proved effective, although some shells unfortunately fell among the company itself, causing casualties. By then, 2nd Parachute Battalion numbered only some 160 of all ranks. Consequently, Brigadier Flavell sent Major Stephen Terrell's A Company 3rd Parachute Battalion to reinforce the battalion further. Lieutenant Colonel Frost reorganised his force, forming a rifle company from the remaining elements of A, B and C Companies, under the command of Major John Ross, and designating it No. 1 Company. His other two companies, designated No. 2 and No. 3 Companies respectively, were those from 3rd Parachute Battalion.

At 0300 hours on the following morning, 29 March, the battalion recommenced its advance with No. 1 Company in the lead. Little opposition was encountered, however, and by the time the battalion reached its old positions in Cork Wood it had captured 50 members of the Tunisian Regiment, together with a large amount of equipment. On securing its objective the battalion sent out patrols which succeeded in taking further prisoners.

1st Parachute Battalion, meanwhile, had carried out a very successful attack which went almost as planned. After a long approach march, the battalion crossed the River Oued el Medene just as the artillery barrage started, subsequently taking its objective after a fierce fight. On the following morning it made a dawn attack and almost immediately encountered some Germans who surrendered after a very brief fight. Advancing into the woods on the higher part of the feature, the battalion was involved in an engagement with Italian troops of the *Bersaglieri* and took 400 of them prisoner. Moving up on to the left of 2nd Parachute Battalion, Lieutenant Colonel Pearson and his men continued their advance, encountering German troops who were well dug in on the high, rocky and heavily wooded terrain. By the time the fighting died down at the end of the day, 1st Parachute Brigade had achieved all of its objectives and had captured 770 prisoners, including 220 German paratroops.

During 1–14 April 1st Parachute Brigade encountered little sign of the enemy despite an active programme of patrolling. On the night of 14/15 April the brigade was relieved by the 39th Regimental Combat Team of the

9th US Division, and was withdrawn into 5th Corps reserve. Subsequently it was moved to Boufarik, near Algiers. On 27 April Brigadier Edward Flavell bade farewell to his brigade and returned to England to take up his next appointment. On the following day, Brigadier Gerald Lathbury assumed command of 1st Parachute Brigade.

During its five months of operations in North Africa, 1st Parachute Brigade suffered 1,700 casualties but captured more than 3,500 prisoners and inflicted over 5,000 casualties on enemy forces. Such was the standing of the British paratroops in the eyes of the enemy that their German adversaries had christened them *Rote Teufel* — "Red Devils". This esteem manifested itself during their journey by rail to Boufarik. As the train carrying the brigade slowly passed a prisoner-of-war camp situated near the railway line, the German inmates caught sight of the red berets and ran from their tents to cheer the paratroops whose fighting ability had aroused their admiration during the previous five months of fighting. As the Commander 1st Airborne Division, Major General 'Boy' Browning, stated in his message of congratulations to the brigade: "Such distinctions are seldom given in war, and then only to the finest fighting troops".

SICILY & ITALY 1943 — 1ST AIRBORNE DIVISION OPERATIONS

While 1st Parachute Brigade was engaged on operations, elsewhere in North Africa another parachute formation was being created in November 1942. This was 4th Parachute Brigade, commanded by Brigadier John Hackett and consisting of 156th Parachute Battalion, which had been formed in India in 1941 as 151st Parachute Battalion, 10th Parachute Battalion, and 11th Parachute Battalion. The two latter units had been formed from volunteers from British units serving in the Middle East, 10th Parachute Battalion initially consisting of a nucleus from the 2nd Battalion The Royal Sussex Regiment. During the following month the brigade headquarters was formed, and in January 1943 4th Parachute Squadron RE and 133rd Parachute Field Ambulance RAMC also started formation. At the end of February 1943 the brigade left its station at Kabrit for Palestine.

Meanwhile, in England, 1st Airborne Division's strength, somewhat depleted after 1st Parachute Brigade's departure for North Africa, had been bolstered by the formation of 3rd Parachute Brigade. This newly raised formation consisted of 7th (Light Infantry) Parachute Battalion, which had been formed from the 10th Battalion The Somerset Light Infantry; 8th (Midland) Parachute Battalion, formed from the 13th Battalion The Royal Warwickshire Regiment; and 9th (Eastern & Home Counties) Parachute Battalion, formed from the 10th Battalion The Essex Regiment. At the same time, 3rd Parachute Squadron RE and 224th Parachute Field Ambulance RAMC were raised as supporting-arm elements. The new brigade's commander was Brigadier Gerald Lathbury, who had previously commanded 3rd Parachute Battalion before taking up a staff appointment in the Air Directorate of the War Office.

On 9 March 1943 1st Airborne Division, with the exception of 3rd Parachute Brigade, two battalions of 1st Airlanding Brigade and the Airborne Light Tank Squadron, was ordered to mobilise by 1 May for operations in North Africa. The division sailed from England in two convoys, 2nd Parachute Brigade arriving at Oran on 26 April and 1st Airlanding Brigade a month later on 26 May. On 10 May 1st Parachute Brigade rejoined the division at Mascara, where it was undergoing training. During the rest of May and throughout June, all units of 1st Airborne Division trained hard and ceaselessly. The parachute units carried out a total of 8,913 descents and exercises were carried out up to brigade level.

From 19 June to 5 July the division moved from Mascara to Kairouan, near Sousse, which was to be its operational base. Here it was joined by 4th Parachute Brigade, less 11th Parachute Battalion which had remained in Palestine to carry out a number of minor airborne operations. In March, planning had begun for the invasion of Sicily. 1st Airborne Division was tasked with carrying out three brigade airborne operations, landing in advance of a seaborne landing by troops of 13th Corps. The division was allotted three objectives: the Ponte Grande, a road bridge south of Syracuse, which was to be taken by 1st Airlanding Brigade; the port of Augusta, which was allotted to 2nd Parachute Brigade; and the Primosole Bridge, which spanned the River Simeto and was the objective of 1st Parachute Brigade. In the middle of June, however, it was decided that the assault on the road bridge south of Syracuse would be carried out by 1st Airlanding Brigade, and 4th Parachute Brigade was allocated the role of divisional reserve. For this operation, 1st Airborne Division was placed under command of 8th Army, commanded by General Bernard Montgomery.

On the night of 9 July 1st Airlanding Brigade, commanded by Brigadier 'Pip' Hicks, took off for Syracuse. To avoid enemy flak, the USAAF tug aircraft pilots had been briefed to release their gliders 3,000 yards off the coastline. In the event, a combination of inexperienced tug pilots, adverse weather conditions and anti-aircraft fire resulted in the brigade suffering heavy losses even before it had landed, 78 of its gliders landing in the sea and others being scattered over a distance of some 25 miles. Only one Horsa glider succeeded in reaching its allotted landing zone. However, a platoon of the 2nd Battalion The South Staffordshire Regiment succeeded in capturing the Ponte Grande intact.

2nd Parachute Brigade had been due to emplane at 1845 hours on the 10 July, but at 2145 hours received the news that its assault on Augusta had been postponed for 24 hours. On the following day the operation was cancelled, as 13th Corps had been able to take the port and a bridge to the south and the airborne troops were not needed. 1st Parachute Brigade, having loaded its aircraft, was stood by on the afternoon of 12 July to carry out its allotted tasks. However, at 1745 hours the operation was postponed for 24 hours. On the following day the first aircraft took off at 1901 hours. By 2200 hours a total of 113 paratroop aircraft and 16 tug-glider combinations were airborne and heading for Sicily. All went well until the aircraft neared the Sicilian coastline, when anti-aircraft fire from Allied naval vessels was encountered. Some aircraft were hit, while others took evasive action or returned to base. Those aircraft which reached the dropping zones met heavy enemy anti-aircraft fire and searchlights. In the event, only 39 aircraft dropped their 'sticks' of paratroops on or near the dropping zones (DZs), 48 others dropping them up to half a mile away. Seventeen returned to base without dropping their troops, and 12 others were unable to find the DZs. Eleven aircraft were shot down, eight of which had succeeded in dropping their 'sticks', and several suffered severe damage. Of the 16 gliders carrying the brigade's heavy equipment, six crashed into the sea and six crashed on landing. Four succeeded in reaching their landing zones, while seven others landed safely some distance away. By the time it had rallied and mustered on its DZs, 1st Parachute Brigade numbered only 12 officers and 283 other ranks, out of a total of 1,856 all ranks.

The plan for the brigade's operation called for two platoons of 1st Parachute Battalion, together with 1st Parachute Squadron RE, to capture the Primasole Bridge. Meanwhile, two platoons of 3rd Parachute Battalion would attack and neutralise an enemy anti-aircraft battery nearby while the rest of the battalion deployed to cover the approaches from the north. 2nd Parachute Battalion was to take the high ground to the south of the bridge which consisted of three features codenamed 'Johnny I', 'II' and 'III'.

Lieutenant Colonel Alastair Pearson's 1st Parachute Battalion dropped at 2230 hours. By 0215 hours a small group of 50 men, commanded by Captain Rann, had taken the Primosole Bridge and captured some 50 Italian prisoners. By 0400 hours three 6-pounder anti-tank guns of 1st Airlanding Anti-Tank Battery RA, which had been landed by glider, had arrived and the size of the force had grown to approximately 120. The only other support weapons available were one Vickers medium machine gun, two 3-inch mortars and three PIATs. Even more worrying was the fact that none of the battalion's radio sets had appeared. By dawn there were some 200 men, including the sappers of 1st Parachute Squadron RE and two platoons of 3rd Parachute Battalion, holding the bridge. Brigadier Lathbury and Lieutenant Colonel Pearson had arrived shortly after the bridge had been captured, and the latter deployed his small force to cover the approaches to it.

Meanwhile, 2nd Parachute Battalion had been scattered in the drop, and by the time it rallied near the dropping zone it numbered only 170 of all ranks. Only A Company, commanded by Major Dickie Lonsdale, was able to muster most of its strength, and the Adjutant, Captain Victor Dover, and the Second in Command, Major Johnnie Lane, were both missing. At 0215 hours, with no sign of his missing men, Lieutenant Colonel Johnny Frost, who had been injured on landing, led his much-depleted battalion towards its objective of the high ground to the south of the bridge. Just over an hour later, at 0330 hours, the battalion's first objective had been taken, and by 0500 hours 2nd Parachute Battalion had occupied all three features on the high ground and had taken 100 Italian prisoners.

In the meantime, 3rd Parachute Battalion had experienced major problems during the drop. Only one officer and three men succeeded in joining up with 1st Parachute Battalion at the Primosole Bridge at 0130 hours. Two and a half hours later their numbers had increased to two platoons. Brigadier Lathbury and some of the members of his headquarters had jumped at 2330 hours, and found themselves on the ground after a surprisingly short time in the air. It transpired that the pilot of their Dakota had turned the aircraft just as they were about to jump, and they had been dropped on some high ground about three miles from the dropping zone. Although the Dakota's altimeter had read 500ft, Lathbury and the rest of his stick had jumped from a height of just over 200ft. Fortunately for the brigadier, he landed on soft ploughed ground.

Together with his batman, Private Lake, Lathbury headed for the Primosole Bridge. The two men paused en route on the dropping zone to collect some weapons and ammunition from a container. There they met Major David Hunter, the Brigade Major, and some of the other members of brigade headquarters. Setting off once more towards the bridge, Lathbury and his party shortly afterwards met Lieutenant Colonel Johnny Frost and 50 men of 2nd Parachute Battalion making their way to their objective. Lathbury divided his force into four sections, and as he neared the bridge he met a paratrooper who told him that 1st Parachute Battalion had taken it. However, as he and his men pressed on and started to cross the bridge, a number of grenades were thrown by an Italian soldier. Lathbury was wounded, but after being given first aid he was able to continue to make his way towards the northern side. By 0630 hours on 14 July the brigade headquarters was established on the southern bank of the river. Due to the non-arrival of radio sets, communications were virtually non-existent. Although the sole No. 22 Set which had arrived was in working order, contact could not be established with 4th Armoured Brigade, which was due to link up with the paratroops.

The enemy, in the form of German paratroops of the 4th *Fallschirmjaeger* Regiment, counterattacked from the west at 0630 hours. 2nd Parachute Battalion, which had not had time to dig in, came under machine gun and mortar fire which caused a number of casualties. A fighting patrol was sent out at 0730 hours to try and neutralise enemy machine guns sited on 'Johnny II', but was driven back by fire from armoured vehicles. At the same time, the long grass around the southernmost of the battalion's positions caught fire, and this caused further problems by providing a smokescreen behind which the enemy troops were able to advance to better positions. At the same time, the intense heat forced Frost's men to withdraw from their forward positions. At this point help arrived in the form of a forward observation officer and naval gunfire support. Captain Vere Hodge of 1st Airlanding Light Regiment RA arrived at 0700 hours, and by 0900 hours had established radio communications with a Royal Navy cruiser lying offshore. Shortly afterwards, the first salvoes of 6-inch shells burst among the enemy, and by 1000 hours the enemy advance had been halted and 2nd Parachute Battalion was able to push its perimeter forward again.

Shortly after doing so, it discovered a battery of Italian light howitzers in a valley beside 'Johnny I'. These were swiftly appropriated by the battalion's Mortar Platoon, which brought them into action against enemy positions north of the bridge, their effective fire attracting a counter-battery response from enemy artillery.

At 0930 hours radio contact with 4th Armoured Brigade was briefly established by the Brigade Major, who was able to pass on the information that the Primosole Bridge had been taken intact. However, he was told that relief was not possible at that stage, and radio contact was lost shortly afterwards. The enemy counterattacked again at 1310 hours, supported by artillery and aircraft. Infantry advanced under cover of smoke along the axis of the road, with close support from fighters. 3rd Parachute Battalion, which by then numbered only five officers and 35 other ranks, bore the brunt of this attack but held firm, and by 1500 hours had driven off two company attacks. Shortly afterwards, however, the enemy increased the pressure and by the middle of the afternoon 1st and 3rd Parachute Battalions had been forced to withdraw to the southern side of the river. Nevertheless, the enemy were prevented from reaching the bridge.

By the time darkness fell, 1st Parachute Brigade's position was somewhat precarious. The enemy had managed to cross the river further to the east, under cover of heavy mortar and artillery fire from some self-propelled guns which had been brought up once the paratroops had withdrawn to the southern bank. Lathbury and his men were under fire from the north, south and east, and it soon became plain that the situation was fast becoming untenable. Consequently, at 1935 hours, the order was given for a withdrawal in small groups to 2nd Parachute Battalion's positions. Shortly afterwards, however, the leading elements of 4th Armoured Brigade, including the 9th Battalion The Durham Light Infantry, arrived, and were followed by the rest of the brigade at midnight. On the following morning, 15 July, the Durham Light Infantry attacked the bridge, which by then was defended by German troops. The attack, which was carried out with support from tanks and artillery, was unsuccessful and the Durhams suffered heavy casualties. They subsequently withdrew and took over 2nd Parachute Battalion's positions.

The commander of 4th Armoured Brigade announced his intention to carry out another frontal assault, but was prevailed upon by Brigadier Lathbury and Lieutenant Colonel Alastair Pearson to carry out a night attack instead. Accordingly, before dawn on 16 July, Pearson himself, accompanied by his batman and his battalion provost sergeant, led the Durham Light Infantry across the river. The Durhams put in a successful attack and took the bridge with few casualties. At 0700 hours 1st Parachute Brigade withdrew and moved by transport to Syracuse. Of the 12 officers and 280 other ranks who had taken part in the Primosole Bridge operation, 27 had been killed, 78 wounded, and several were missing.

By 30 July 1st Airborne Division was once again concentrated at its base at Sousse in North Africa. During the following month many of the missing members of 1st Parachute Brigade made their appearance, all of them recounting how they had been dropped up to 30 miles from the dropping zone. The Adjutant of 2nd Parachute Battalion, Captain Victor Dover, and his stick had been dropped on Mount Etna and most of them had been captured. Dover and another man managed to avoid being caught, and for nearly a month had made their way back to British lines, at the same time trying to cause as much damage to the enemy as possible.

During August and September all three parachute brigades in 1st Airborne Division trained hard. 1st Parachute Brigade received reinforcements and all three battalions were brought up to full strength. During this period Brigadier Gerald Lathbury was absent while recovering from his wounds, and the brigade was commanded by Lieutenant Colonel Johnny Frost. At the beginning of September the division received orders for its part in the invasion of Italy. On 8 September it sailed in warships of the Royal Navy's 1st Cruiser Squadron for Italy, with 2nd and 4th Parachute Brigades in the lead and 1st Parachute Brigade in reserve. Their objective was the Italian port of Taranto, which they reached at 1700 hours on 9 September, in time to see the Italian fleet sailing for Malta to surrender to the Allies. Shortly afterwards, disaster occurred when HMS *Abdiel*, a fast minelayer carrying troops of 6th Parachute Battalion, struck a mine. On board were members of Battalion Headquarters, B and C Companies, the Machine Gun Platoon and the Mortar Platoon. The explosion set off the vessel's own mines in her magazines and the ship was torn in half. 6th Parachute Battalion suffered heavy casualties, including the Commanding Officer, Lieutenant Colonel Goodwin, six officers, Regimental Sergeant Major Langford and 51 other ranks. Four officers and 150 other ranks were injured and were taken to hospital after being landed. The other two battalions in 2nd Parachute Brigade landed without mishap. After moving through Taranto, 4th Parachute Battalion took up positions to the north west of it, while the 5th deployed in a village east of the town.

1st Parachute Brigade took up defensive positions around Taranto. Meanwhile, 2nd and 4th Parachute Brigades advanced northwards, the latter taking the town of Massafra before moving on to the village of Mottala. During the early stages of this advance Major General Hopkinson, the Commander 1st Airborne Division, was killed by an enemy machine gun while observing 10th Parachute Battalion in action against German troops of the 1st *Fallschirmjaeger* Division at Castellaneta. Brigadier Eric Down, the commander of 2nd Parachute Brigade, immediately assumed command of the division. Brigadier C. H. V. Pritchard, better known as 'Charlie Orange' to the members of 6th Parachute Battalion which he had previously commanded, took over command of 2nd Parachute Brigade.

By 13 September 1st Airborne Division had advanced about 20 miles from Taranto. 10th and 156th Parachute Battalions attacked the town of Goia del Colle, which was an important objective because of the airfield there. Some very aggressive patrolling on the part of both battalions and a night attack carried out by 10th Parachute Battalion persuaded the enemy to evacuate the area on the night of 16 September. Two days later the airfield had been pressed into service by the RAF, which flew in six squadrons of Hurricanes to provide close air support. On 19 September 4th Parachute Brigade, which had been relieved by 1st Airlanding Brigade, withdrew to Taranto after nine days of what was described as "interesting though not heavy fighting". During this period, 1st Parachute Brigade had remained in divisional reserve, eventually moving up to Castellaneta and then Altamura, from where it withdrew at the end of September.

In the early part of October a small group of eight men from 2nd Parachute Battalion, under the command of Captain 'Tim' Timothy, parachuted into an area north of Pescara. Their mission was to make contact with escaped Allied prisoners of war, large numbers of whom were known to be roaming the Italian countryside. They were then to guide them to rendezvous points on the coast, manned by patrols of the Special Air Service, from which they would be evacuated by the Royal Navy. Timothy became separated from his stick on landing, but moved to his allotted area and carried out his task alone. Eventually he encountered a sergeant from 2nd Parachute Battalion who had been captured in North Africa, and between them the two men assembled a group of some 400 prisoners, made their way to a rendezvous point and made contact with the SAS patrol manning it. Shortly afterwards, however, as the boats were approaching the shore, firing broke out nearby. In the ensuing confusion only 40 prisoners managed to escape, Timothy amongst them.

In late October 1st Airborne Division learned that it was to be withdrawn to Britain, with the exception of 2nd Parachute Brigade, which was to remain in Italy as an independent brigade group. In November the division sailed from Taranto for England, its personnel and equipment from its base at Sousse embarking at the same time.

At this juncture mention must be made of 11th Parachute Battalion, which had remained in Palestine when the rest of 4th Parachute Brigade moved to North Africa to join 1st Airborne Division. Commanded by Lieutenant Colonel R. M. C. Thomas, this battalion was formed at Shallufa, on the Suez Canal, and had moved with 4th Parachute Brigade to Ramat David in Palestine, where it completed its formation and its parachute training.

On 15 September 1943 A Company, together with a section of the Machine Gun Platoon and a section of mortars, took off from Cyprus and dropped on the island of Cos. At the time, plans were already under way for the invasion of Greece, and it was recognised by the Allies that the capture of the island of Rhodes would be a vital factor. It was also appreciated that the seizure of Cos, with its airfield, would make Rhodes indefensible. The dropping zone had been marked by men of the Special Boat Squadron, and the men of A Company received a warm welcome from the Italian garrison, which numbered some 4,000. The company remained on Cos until 25 September, during which it came under attack from the Luftwaffe, which operated with virtual impunity because of the inability of the RAF to provide air cover. After ten days the company was withdrawn by air and during the following month, December, 11th Parachute Battalion sailed from England to rejoin 4th Parachute Brigade.

CHAPTER 3
Formation of 6th Airborne Division

While 1st Airborne Division was undergoing its baptism of fire in Sicily and Italy, further developments were taking place with regard to airborne forces in the United Kingdom. The Airborne Forces Depot, which hitherto had existed unofficially, was formally established on 11 May as the Airborne Forces Depot and Development Centre. On 5 July Brigadier Edward Flavell, who was in the initial process of forming the newly established 5th Parachute Brigade, assumed command of the depot and development centre under the title of Commander Airborne Establishments. The depot remained at Hardwick Hall, where it was ideally located near to No. 1 Parachute Training School at Ringway, whilst the development centre, which was tasked with developing new equipment for airborne forces, was established at Amesbury Abbey, in Wiltshire, under the command of Lieutenant Colonel J. G. Squirrell.

On 23 April 1943 the War Office issued orders for the formation of a second airborne division. This was to consist of 3rd Parachute Brigade and two other formations which were to be formed: 5th Parachute Brigade and 6th Airlanding Brigade. The new formation was designated 6th Airborne Division, and its commander was to be Major General Richard Gale OBE MC, who had previously formed and commanded 1st Parachute Brigade before becoming Deputy Director of Air at the War Office. On 7 May Major General Gale travelled to the village of Figheldean in Wiltshire, where he set up his headquarters at Syrencote House. Such was the speed of events that his headquarters was not fully formed, added to which the War Office had laid down a phased programme of formation. This permitted 30 per cent of the headquarters to be formed immediately, a further 30 per cent to be formed on 1 June, and the remaining requirements to be subject to review in September.

The nucleus of the new division was formed by 3rd Parachute Brigade, by then commanded by Brigadier James Hill DSO MC, but it was weak in numbers, having supplied reinforcements for 1st Parachute Brigade. In late May Hill was informed by Major General Gale that he was to transfer one of his battalions to 5th Parachute Brigade, which was being formed. To replace it, he would receive a Canadian parachute battalion. Accordingly, 7th Parachute Battalion was transferred to 5th Parachute Brigade. This left Hill with his two other units: 8th Parachute Battalion, commanded by Lieutenant Colonel Alastair Pearson, who had distinguished himself with 1st Parachute Battalion in North Africa, and 9th Parachute Battalion, commanded by Lieutenant Colonel Terence Otway.

During May, 6th Airlanding Brigade was also formed, under the command of Brigadier The Honourable Hugh Kindersley. It comprised the 2nd Battalion The Oxfordshire & Buckinghamshire Light Infantry, the 1st Battalion The Royal Ulster Rifles and the 12th Battalion The Devonshire Regiment.

On 1 July 5th Parachute Brigade was formed, under the command of Brigadier Nigel Poett. In addition to 7th Parachute Battalion, which was commanded by Lieutenant Colonel Geoffrey Pine Coffin, it comprised 12th (Yorkshire) Parachute Battalion, which had been formed from the 10th Battalion The Green Howards, and 13th (Lancashire) Parachute Battalion formed from the 2nd/4th Battalion The South Lancashire Regiment. These two units were commanded by Lieutenant Colonels Reggie Parker and Peter Luard respectively.

On 11 August 1st Canadian Parachute Battalion joined 3rd Parachute Brigade. Commanded by Lieutenant Colonel George Bradbrooke, it had arrived in England a month earlier and had proceeded to No. 1 Parachute Training School to undergo training in British parachuting techniques before joining 6th Airborne Division. Brigadier Hill, although sorry to have lost 7th Parachute Battalion, was delighted at being able to add some of Canada's toughest fighting men to his command.

The formation of divisional units also took place from May until September. These included the division's pathfinder unit, 22nd Independent Parachute Company, under the command of Major Francis Lennox-Boyd. Like its sister unit, 21st Independent Parachute Company, which performed the same role in 1st Airborne Division, 22nd Independent Parachute Company consisted of a company headquarters and three platoons, each of which comprised one officer and 32 other ranks. Each platoon was made up of three 'sticks' commanded by a sergeant or corporal. For pathfinding tasks 'sticks' were equipped with 'Eureka' ground-to-air radio beacons which transmitted homing signals to 'Rebecca' receivers fitted in transport aircraft. In addition, coloured cloth panels laid out in the form of a 'T' were used to mark drop zones. At night, 6V battery-powered Holophane lamps were used to mark DZs: an orange lamp was placed at the end of each arm of the 'T', and a green one was put at the base. Operated by a member of the 'stick', this was used to signal the drop zone code letter to the approaching transport aircraft.

No time was wasted in raising and training the new division. Although it was not yet fully formed, work began almost immediately. In particular, those members of the parachute units who were not already qualified as parachutists had to undergo parachute selection and training. This applied particularly to the newly formed 12th and 13th Parachute Battalions, whose members had previously been ordinary infantrymen. Throughout the second half of 1943, all units within the division concentrated on individual military skills and tactical training at all levels, from the individual soldier through section, platoon, company, battalion, brigade and, eventually, divisional levels. Training took place during the day and night, exercises frequently beginning with parachute drops and glider landings and nearly always ending with a 20-mile march back to barracks. Much emphasis was placed on physical fitness, even for those employed in the administrative echelons and units. Every man in the division, including the divisional commander and those on the staff, marched, jumped and exercised. One consequence of the ceaseless and intensive training programme was the manifestation of a tremendous *esprit de corps*. Nor was staff training ignored. Major General Gale initiated a programme of exercises and study days for his officers, all of which included problems concerning administration and air movement. These were tailored to the types of operations in which the division was likely to be involved in the future. Gale had studied closely the airborne operations carried out by the Germans in 1940 at Eben Emael and in 1941 when they captured the Corinth Canal bridge. These staff exercises were designed to train his officers and men to operate under adverse conditions.

The division's administrative elements also trained hard during this period. All divisional exercises included full-scale resupply by RAF and USAAF aircraft, the division's Royal Army Service Corps units playing their part in despatching containers from aircraft as well as collecting stores from dropping zones and setting up resupply dumps in the field. Meanwhile, the parachute and airlanding field ambulances were fully exercised, 'wounded' personnel undergoing evacuation, being rendered 'first aid' or undergoing simulated field surgery. By the end of 1943 much had been accomplished. However, the required results were only just achieved in time. With little warning, 6th Airborne Division was ordered to mobilise on 23 December, less than eight months after its formation, and to prepare for operations by 1 February 1944.

CHAPTER 4
6th Airborne Division Operations in Normandy, June to September 1944

On the morning of 17 February 1944 Major General 'Boy' Browning, the Commander Airborne Troops, arrived at Headquarters 6th Airborne Division to brief Major General Gale on 6th Airborne Division's task during Operation 'Overlord', the invasion of Normandy. Gale had been eagerly anticipating this moment, but he was disappointed and dismayed when Browning outlined the operational plan, which called for one parachute brigade and one anti-tank battery to be placed under command of 3rd Infantry Division, which would be one of the Allied formations carrying out a seaborne assault on the Normandy coastline. The parachute brigade's task would be to seize the bridges over the Caen Canal and the River Orne at Benouville and Ranville.

Gale detailed 3rd Parachute Brigade for the task. However, Brigadier James Hill realised that the bridges would have to be seized in a *coup de main* operation for which parachute troops were not ideal. Accordingly, he requested that a company of gliderborne troops be placed under his command. Gale agreed, and accordingly D Company 2nd Battalion The Oxfordshire & Buckinghamshire Light Infantry, reinforced by two platoons from B Company, were allocated to 3rd Parachute Brigade. As well as being disappointed that 6th Airborne Division was not to be committed to the operation in its entirety, Gale was also worried that a single parachute brigade would not prove sufficient for the task. He made his feelings plain on the matter, and succeeded in convincing his superiors because, a few days later, on 23 February, the decision was taken to allocate increased numbers of aircraft to the operation and thus commit the whole of the division under command of 1st British Corps.

Gale and his staff immediately started planning for the operation. 6th Airborne Division would have under command 1st Special Service Brigade, commanded by Brigadier The Lord Lovat, and would be transported by aircraft of Nos. 38 and 46 Groups RAF. In essence, the overall Allied plan called for a massive seaborne assault on the coast of Normandy in the area between the Cherbourg Peninsula and the mouth of the River Orne, with the Americans on the right and the British 2nd Army on the left. The British assault would be carried out by two formations: 1st Corps on the left and 30th Corps on the right. 6th Airborne Division, which would be under command of 1st Corps, commanded by Lieutenant General Sir John Crocker, was to cover the left flank of the British assault, which was bounded by the Caen Canal and the River Orne, and to dominate the area east of Caen, whose features of high ground dominated the British left flank.

The division was allocated three primary tasks which were to be carried out before the seaborne landings: first, the capture of the bridges at

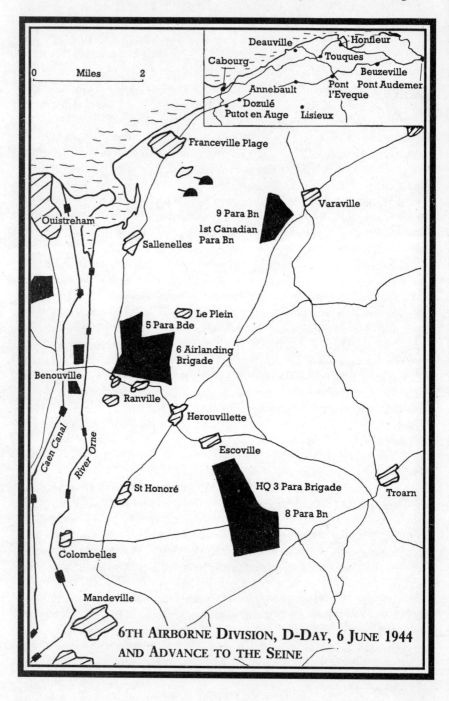

Deauville
Honfleur
Cabourg
Touques
Beuzeville
Annebault
Pont   Pont Audemer
l'Eveque
Dozulé
Putot en Auge   Lisieux

0   Miles   2

Franceville Plage

Ouistreham

Varaville

9 Para Bn
1st Canadian
Para Bn

Sallenelles

Le Plein
5 Para Bde

6 Airlanding
Brigade

Benouville

Ranville

Herouvillette

Escoville

St Honoré

HQ 3 Para Brigade

Troarn

8 Para Bn

Colombelles

Mandeville

**6TH AIRBORNE DIVISION, D-DAY, 6 JUNE 1944
AND ADVANCE TO THE SEINE**

Benouville and the establishment of a bridgehead to hold them; second, the destruction of the Merville coastal gun battery at Franceville Plage; and, third, the destruction of the bridges over the River Dives at Varaville, Robehomme, Bures and Troarn to delay any movement by enemy forces from the east. The division was also allocated two secondary tasks: first, the clearing and securing of the River Orne and Dives, including the capture of the towns of Sallanelles and Franceville Plage as well as the clearing of the coastal area between these towns and Cabourg at the mouth of the River Dives; and, second, after establishing a firm base east of the River Orne, to block any move by enemy reserve forces attempting to move towards the covering position from the east and south east.

Initially, Gale decided to commit 6th Airlanding Brigade to the operation to capture the two bridges at Benouville and Ranville, and tasked 3rd Parachute Brigade with neutralising the Merville Battery. Owing to the limited number of aircraft available from Nos. 38 and 46 Groups, 5th Parachute Brigade would have to be flown in, together with the 6th Airborne Armoured Reconnaissance Regiment and other divisional troops, on a second airlift. Divisional headquarters, together with elements of the divisional artillery regiment and anti-tank batteries, would land after 6th Airlanding Brigade. Detailed intelligence of enemy forces in the area had revealed that these consisted of two infantry low-category divisions plus two squadrons of armour and a number of *ad hoc* infantry units formed from training establishments. A more potent threat, however, was posed by the 12th SS (*Hitler Jugend*) Panzer Division, which was based 30 miles south-cast of Lisieux, and from the 21st Panzer Division based in the Rennes area. In addition, it was known that the 352nd Infantry Division was within striking distance.

In April, however, intelligence reports indicated that the Germans had erected anti-glider defences on the landing and dropping zones chosen by Gale and his staff. Initially, it was feared that the division's plans had been compromised, but further reports indicated that all areas of open ground along the coasts of France and Belgium had been similarly obstructed. As a mass glider landing was no longer feasible, Gale altered his plans. The task of capturing the bridges at Benouville and Ranville was now given to 5th Parachute Brigade, although the *coup de main* operation would still be carried out by D Company 2nd Battalion The Oxfordshire & Buckinghamshire Light Infantry, which had been undergoing intensive training for the task. The brigade would land soon after the bridges had been captured and, after clearing and securing the area of Benouville, Ranville and Le Bas de Ranville, would clear the landing zones for 6th Airlanding Brigade. 3rd Parachute Brigade's task of destroying the Merville Battery and the bridges over the River Dives remained unaltered, and the commandos of 1st Special Service Brigade would move inland to join up with the rest of the division as soon as possible after the seaborne landings.

During the rest of April and throughout May, 6th Airborne Division prepared assiduously for its coming baptism of fire. The tempo of training increased for all units, including divisional troops. Lieutenant Colonel

Terence Otway's 9th Parachute Battalion, tasked with silencing the Merville Battery, rehearsed on a dummy battery, complete with gun emplacements, minefield, anti-tank ditch and barbed wire fences. 8th Parachute Battalion, which was to destroy the bridges over the River Dives at Bures and Troarn, practised on similar bridges in the south of England, whilst 1st Canadian Parachute Battalion, whose objectives would be the bridges at Varaville and Robehomme, did likewise. In 5th Parachute Brigade, 7th Parachute Battalion, which would relieve the *coup de main* force at the bridges after landing, accompanied the gliderborne company to Devon, where it rehearsed on two similar bridges spanning the River Exe and a canal nearby. Meanwhile, 13th Parachute Battalion and sappers of 591st Parachute Squadron RE practised clearing anti-glider defences with explosives.

The preparations for Operation 'Overlord' culminated in a four-day test exercise which took place during 21 to 25 May, the 'enemy' being provided by elements of 1st Airborne Division and 1st Polish Independent Parachute Brigade. Unknown to nearly all members of 6th Airborne Division, this was the final rehearsal, because immediately afterwards, on 25 May, the entire division was moved into heavily guarded airfield transit camps. It was only at that point, and in briefings during the next few days, that all was revealed concerning the division's tasks for the invasion.

Take-off for Normandy had been scheduled for the evening of 4 June. On the morning of 3 June the battalions of both parachute brigades and the men of 22nd Independent Parachute Company paraded in full battle order and moved in transport to the launching airfields. While parachutes were fitted, containers were loaded aboard aircraft. At approximately midday, however, all units received a signal postponing the operation for 24 hours. On the following morning another signal was received, confirming that take-off would be later that day. That evening, 3rd and 5th Parachute Brigades departed from the transit camps for the airfields. First to take off were the pathfinders of 22nd Independent Parachute Company, who would mark the dropping zones. Meanwhile, the gliderborne *coup de main* force for the assault on the bridges over the Caen Canal and River Orne was already airborne and heading for its objectives. Soon after the two parachute brigades had taken off, they were followed by the gliders carrying Headquarters 6th Airborne Division and elements of divisional troops.

By the time the leading elements of 5th Parachute Brigade had landed, D Company 2nd Battalion The Oxfordshire & Buckinghamshire Light Infantry, commanded by Major John Howard, had seized both its objectives. First to link up with it was Brigadier Nigel Poett, who had jumped with the pathfinders. Shortly afterwards, the aircraft carrying his brigade arrived and it was not long before Lieutenant Colonel Geoffrey Pine Coffin and some of 7th Parachute Battalion appeared and relieved the *coup de main* force. Although the drop had gone smoothly, 7th Parachute Battalion was scattered. This was largely because each man was very heavily burdened with equipment, resulting in slow exits from the aircraft and subsequent dispersing of sticks. By 0230 hours only 40 per cent of the battalion had arrived at the battalion's RV point, and few of the containers with the mortars, machine guns and radios had been found. Hearing the whistle blasts signalling the successful capture of the two bridges, Lieutenant Colonel Pine Coffin had decided not to wait for any more of his battalion, but to move to the bridges without further delay. Having relieved Major Howard and his men, 7th Parachute Battalion established itself in defensive positions in Benouville, B Company engaging a small number of enemy while moving into a wood and hamlet at the northern end of the town.

12th Parachute Battalion had also been scattered during the drop. The first men to arrive at the RV point at a quarry half a mile north of the bridge were the Commanding Officer, Lieutenant Colonel Johnny Johnson, Major Gerald Ritchie, who commanded A Company, Captain John Turnbull, second in command of B Company, and the Regimental Sergeant Major. Most of the battalion had landed on the eastern side of the dropping zone, and it was some 45 minutes before more men arrived at the RV. By the time it moved off towards its objective, which was the village of Le Bas de Ranville, the battalion numbered no more than 60 per cent of its full strength. However, by 0400 hours it had secured the village and was digging in.

13th Parachute Battalion was also at only 60 per cent of its strength when it moved off from its RV. Like the other battalions, it had been scattered during the drop. It objective was the area of Ranville, which it was to secure and from which, in conjunction with 12th Parachute Battalion, it was to cover both bridges from the approaches to the south east. In addition, the battalion was also tasked with clearing the landing zone on which Major General Gale and his headquarters, together with some divisional troops, would be landing at 0330 hours. A Company, commanded by Major John Cramphorn, had been detailed to carry this out with the assistance of some sappers from 591st Parachute Squadron RE. It completed the task at 0300 hours, the first gliders landing at 0335 hours.

By dawn on the following day 5th Parachute Brigade was in firm possession of its objectives. 7th Parachute Battalion, which still only numbered some 200 plus the 70 men of D Company 2nd Battalion The Oxfordshire & Buckinghamshire Light Infantry, who were holding the eastern end of the Caen Canal bridge, was deployed in and around Benouville. A Company occupied the southern part of the town, while B Company was deployed in positions at the northern end and in the small hamlet called Le Port. 13th Parachute Batttalion had cleared Ranville by dawn, having encountered small groups of enemy troops on the northern edge of the village which was normally garrisoned by a company of 21st Panzer Division. Enemy retaliation came shortly after dawn. At 0700 hours 7th Parachute Battalion was confronted by some enemy light tanks which appeared and halted in full view of one of C Company's platoons which was positioned as an outpost at the Chateau de Benouville. To the platoon's surprise, the tank crews dismounted and held a discussion. The platoon opened fire, hitting some of the crewmen and scattering the others. The tanks sped away from the village, heading towards the coast. During the morning the enemy probed A Company's positions in the southern part of Benouville. Self-propelled guns moved to within close range and shelled the company, forcing one of the platoons to withdraw into the centre of the village. Later in the morning enemy infantry, supported by armour, reached the southern edge of the village, but A Company blocked their advance. At one point, a Mark IV tank reached the centre of the village but was knocked out with Gammon bombs.

Throughout the rest of the morning 7th Parachute Battalion, hampered by its lack of support weapons and radios, whose containers had not been found, was subjected to probing attacks by companies of enemy supported by tanks. The enemy also attempted to infiltrate the battalion's positions but was thwarted by active patrolling. At midday, the sound of pipes heralded the arrival of the leading elements of 1st Special Service Brigade and much-needed relief for the battalion. Bypassing the enemy, the commandos pushed through and linked up with the paratroops at 1330 hours. However, their arrival brought little respite to 7th Parachute Battalion, which continued to be subjected to enemy action. 12th Parachute Battalion, meanwhile, was subjected to heavy mortar and artillery fire. The enemy, in the form of the 125th Panzer Grenadier Regiment, attacked Ranville but was beaten off after losing a number of men, who were taken prisoner, and a tank which was destroyed. A further attack followed but was also repulsed. The battalion bore the brunt of both assaults but succeeded in beating them off with the help of 4th Airlanding Anti-Tank Battery RA, which destroyed three self-propelled guns and a tank.

The battalions of 3rd Parachute Brigade had also suffered mishaps during the drop, things beginning to go wrong from the start. Nearly all the pathfinders' Eureka beacons and lamps for marking Drop Zone 'V', on which 1st Canadian and 9th Parachute Battalions were due to land, had been lost. To make matters worse, the pathfinders for Drop Zone 'K', on which Headquarters 3rd Parachute Brigade and 8th Parachute Battalion would drop, had been dropped on to one of 5th Parachute Brigade's zones, DZ 'N'. Unaware of this, they had set up their Eureka beacon and lamps, and as a result the brigade headquarters and 8th Parachute Battalion were despatched over DZ 'N' instead of DZ 'K'. 3rd Parachute Brigade's advance party consisted of elements of brigade headquarters and of each battalion, together with a company of 1st Canadian Parachute Battalion, which was tasked with clearing obstructions from DZ 'V'. Their delivery also proved somewhat chaotic. Of the 14 converted Albemarle bombers carrying them, two dropped three and nine men respectively, six men made their exit from a third aircraft as it crossed the coast, and only four jumped over the dropping zone. A fourth Albemarle, under fire, was forced to make a second run and thus dropped its troops late. Two more aircraft reported technical problems. One losing time while flying along the coast to find the correct approach point, and the other was forced to return to base after being hit by anti-aircraft fire on its seventh approach to the dropping zone, which it was unable to locate. Major Bill Collingwood, the Brigade Major, was travelling in this aircraft and was waiting to jump when it was hit. He was knocked through the aperture and remained suspended beneath the fuselage, hanging by his static line, which had become wound round his leg. Although there was a 60lb kitbag attached to his leg, he was pulled back into the aircraft as it returned to England. He eventually arrived in Normandy during the evening, having flown in by glider with 6th Airlanding Brigade.

Twenty-six aircraft carried the main body of 3rd Parachute Brigade as well as forward observation parties from 53rd Airlanding Light Regiment RA, 224th Parachute Field Ambulance and elements of divisional troops. Of these, nine dropped their sticks in the marshy areas on either side of the River Dives, some two or three miles from the dropping zone, and the remainder were scattered over a wide area. Brigadier James Hill landed about half a mile south of Cabourg in four feet of water alongside the submerged bank of the river. It took him four hours to reach dry land next to the dropping zone, crossing numerous deep irrigation ditches in which many of his men were drowned. Along the way he met several soldiers whom he collected and took with him.

Meanwhile, the advance party of 9th Parachute Battalion had dropped on DZ 'V' without experiencing any problems and reached the battalion RV without mishap. Major Allen Parry, who was in command of the group, and his men set out the lights marking the company locations while Major George Smith and Company Sergeant Majors Harold and Miller made their way towards their objective, the Merville Battery, about a mile away. Shortly afterwards, RAF Lancaster bombers carried out a raid on the battery but missed it. Most of their bombs fell to the south, nearly hitting Smith's party.

Meanwhile, the aircraft bringing the main body of the battalion were approaching the French coast. Unfortunately, because most of the path-finding equipment for marking DZ 'V' had been damaged, there were only a few lights marking the dropping zone when they arrived. Moreover, visibility had deteriorated because of smoke from the bombing raid blowing across the DZ. As a result, few of the pilots saw the lights and consequently only a few sticks landed on the dropping zone, others dropping into the Dives marshes and some on the high ground between Cabourg and Dozule. By 0250 hours, Lieutenant Colonel Terence Otway had assembled some 150 of the 550 in his battalion. None of the gliders bringing in the jeeps, anti-tank guns or trailers had appeared. Moreover, the battalion's 3-inch mortars, all but one of its Vickers medium machine-guns, a party of sappers, a section of the field ambulance and a naval bombardment forward observation party were all missing. However, bearing in mind that the battery had to be destroyed by 0530 hours, Otway decided to press on.

Skirting the northern edge of the village of Gonneville, Otway and his men made their way to a crossroads where they met Major George Smith. He and his two warrant officers had cut their way through a barbed wire fence and, making their way through a minefield to an inner wire fence, had managed to locate some enemy positions. A taping party, led by Captain

The Honourable Paul Greenway, had successfully cleared and marked four lanes through the minefields, locating and disarming several tripwires. Otway divided his force into four groups. It was by then 0430 hours. At this point two of the three gliders carrying the 58-strong assault group commanded by Captain Robert Gordon-Brown suddenly appeared, flying in low over the battery. Both aircraft came under fire and were seen to be hit. One glider flew on into the darkness, eventually landing in a field two miles to the east, while the other headed for a large hedge at the edge of the minefield. The pilot suddenly spotted a minefield warning sign and managed to haul his glider up over the hedge and a lane beyond it, streaming his arrester parachute and crashing into an orchard beyond. The platoon inside, commanded by Lieutenant Hugh Pond, made a somewhat dazed exit, only to hear the sound of men approaching. Rapidly deploying into positions on either side of the lane, Pond and his men opened fire on some enemy troops as they approached.

It was then that Lieutenant Colonel Otway launched his attack. Bangalore torpedoes were detonated and the four assault groups went in, using two of the cleared lanes. Having penetrated the battery's defences, they had to fight their way to the gun casemates, coming under fire from two machine guns as they did so. One of these was silenced by Sergeant Knight.

On reaching the casemates, Otway's men eventually succeeded in gaining entry. During the action, 22 enemy were killed and the same number captured. The rest of the German gunners sought shelter in underground bunkers and remained undetected. The guns, which were 10cm calibre light howitzers, and thus much smaller than had been reported previously, were not destroyed because the sappers accompanying 9th Parachute Battalion, together with their explosive charges, had been dropped or landed some distance from the dropping zone and had not appeared. (On the following day, 7 June, the battery was attacked again by two troops of No. 3 Commando. Assaulting in daylight without the use of smoke as cover, the commandos suffered heavy losses. As they withdrew, they were engaged by the enemy gunners who brought one of the howitzers out of its casemate and engaged them over open sights, causing further casualties. The guns and their crews remained in their position until 17 August when they were withdrawn with other German forces in Normandy.)

At 0500 hours 9th Parachute Battalion withdrew, having paid a very heavy price. Out of the force which had attacked the battery, only about 80 were uninjured; about 65 had been killed, wounded or were missing. Subsequently, Lieutenant Colonel Otway proceeded to attack and seize the village of Le Plein on the Bavent ridge. At 0600 hours he and his men moved off. After being mistakenly bombed by high flying RAF bombers, they reached a crossroads between Le Plein and the neighbouring village of Hauger where B Company, which was in the lead, came under fire. Major George Smith led a company attack on the village, forcing a platoon of German troops back into Le Plein and killing about 15 of them in the process. As the battalion was in the process of clearing and securing a number of houses at the northern end of the village, an enemy platoon counterattacked but met the battalion's single Vickers machine gun, which proceeded to wreak havoc at close range, killing 12 enemy and forcing the remainder to withdraw. A platoon of B Company, commanded by Lieutenant Halliburton, attacked a large house near the church from the rear. Surrounded by a six-foot wall, it appeared to be the main enemy defensive position. As the leading section of the platoon crossed the wall it came under fire and Halliburton, who was in the lead, was killed. The platoon was forced to withdraw.

9th Parachute Battalion was now very weak in numbers, its strength being less than 100 men. Lieutenant Colonel Otway decided to establish defensive positions in the Chateau d'Amfreville and await the arrival of 1st Special Service Brigade. On moving into its new positions the battalion found a hoard of German rations, which were duly shared out, as well as a car and some horses, which were duly commandeered. The early afternoon saw the arrival of No. 6 Commando, which took up positions within the village.

Meanwhile, 8th Parachute Battalion had also been scattered during its drop. The battalion's initial task was to destroy the bridges at Bures and Troarn, the plan calling for the battalion to secure and hold Troarn while one company provided cover for sappers of 3rd Parachute Squadron RE, who would blow the bridge at Bures. However, when Lieutenant Colonel Alastair Pearson arrived at the battalion RV at a track junction near Touffreville at 0120 hours, he found only 30 men plus a jeep and trailer belonging to the engineer squadron. By 0330 hours this number had increased to 11 officers and 130 other ranks, but there was no sign of the other sappers who had dropped with the battalion. Pearson decided to send a small force to destroy the bridge at Bures while he waited at a crossroads a mile north of Troarn until he had enough men with which to attack the town. At 0400 hours his group moved off to the crossroads, which was in heavily wooded terrain east of the main road between Troarn and Le Mesnil. On the way, Pearson set up an ambush which comprised two PIAT detachments under the command of a junior NCO, Lance Corporal Stevenson, to cover the battalion's rear.

On arriving at the crossroads Pearson sent a patrol to reconnoitre the two bridges at Bures, one of which was a steel girder railway bridge and the other a similar but shorter one carrying a trackway. By 0915 hours both had been destroyed by sappers of No. 2 Troop 3rd Parachute Squadron RE, who had reached them at 0630 hours. After carrying out this task, No. 2 Troop joined up with 8th Parachute Battalion. Meanwhile, more men of the battalion arrived at the crossroads, including Lieutenant Thompson, some 50 men of A Company and the majority of the Mortar Platoon and Machine Gun Platoon. Thompson and his men had earlier met Major Tim Roseveare, the commander of 3rd Parachute Squadron RE, and some of his sappers who were on their way to blow the bridge at Troarn. Roseveare had ordered Thompson to set up a firm base at a road junction while he went forward to deal with the bridge. Thompson had done so, but had shortly afterwards made contact with the PIAT ambush party and had thus learned of the battalion's whereabouts. Not long afterwards six enemy vehicles drove into the ambush and were destroyed. The enemy, subsequently identified as being from 21st Panzer Division, withdrew on foot towards Troarn.

Lieutenant Colonel Pearson despatched patrols to reconnoitre the areas to the north and west of Troarn. He had received no confirmation of the Troarn bridge having been blown, so he despatched a group of sappers, together with No. 9 Platoon under Lieutenant Brown, to check whether the bridge had been destroyed and, if so, to increase any damage if necessary. Brown's platoon and the sappers made their way to the outskirts of Troarn, heading for the bridge, where they came under fire from a house near the church. After a brief skirmish they captured a small number of Germans who, they learned, were members of a 21st Panzer Division reconnaissance unit. Shortly afterwards they came under fire again from enemy troops located in houses near the church. After Brown's platoon had cleared these, the sappers went forward and inspected the bridge, in which they found a gap had been blown. Placing some charges, they increased the width of the gap to 70 feet. Having completed this task, and having been plied with food and wine by local townspeople, Brown and his force returned to the battalion.

1st Canadian Parachute Battalion found itself with most of its strength dropped some distance away from DZ 'V'. C Company had flown in as an advance group, along with brigade headquarters and elements of the pathfinder company. One stick, under the command of the company second in command, Captain John Hanson, landed some ten miles from the drop zone, whilst another found itself on the opposite side of the River Orne and only 1,200 yards from the invasion beaches. Eventually, those members of C Company who had reached the drop zone area made their way to Varaville, where their task was to neutralise the garrison. Meanwhile, the pathfinders set up the two remaining serviceable Eureka beacons to guide in the main forces. When the rest of 1st Canadian Parachute Battalion arrived, A Company was scattered over a large area and some of its members linked up with C Company, who were preparing for their attack on Varaville. Meanwhile, the remainder of A Company were covering the withdrawal of 9th Parachute Battalion. B Company had also been dropped over a wide area, two platoons landing in flooded marshes two miles from the dropping zone. One stick was dropped several miles to the north-east near Villers-sur-Mer, while five others landed in flooded areas near Robehomme which were criss-crossed with large drainage ditches, many of which were up to seven feet deep. Several men were forced to jettison their equipment to avoid being dragged underwater and drowned, while others, unable to free themselves from their heavy loads, perished.

Lieutenant Norman Toseland, the commander of No. 5 Platoon in B Company, was fortunate enough to land on firm ground. After meeting another member of his platoon he collected a group of men from the company and led them towards the Robehomme bridge, which was one of the battalion's objectives. As he did so, Toseland met another ten men from his platoon, together with men from 8th and 9th Parachute Battalions and some sappers from 3rd Parachute Squadron RE. On reaching the bridge, Toseland and his men met Major Clayton Fuller, who had landed in the River Dives nearby. By 0300 hours, however, the sappers tasked with blowing the bridge had not arrived. Sergeant Bill Poole, one of the sappers who had joined up with Toseland, collected all the plastic explosive carried by the infantrymen for making Gammon bombs. This amounted to 30lb in all. Sergeant Poole tried to blow the bridge but, with only a limited amount of explosive, merely managed to weaken it. At 0600 hours, however, another small group of sappers arrived with 200lb of explosive and the bridge was duly destroyed.

The Commanding Officer of 1st Canadian Parachute Battalion, Lieutenant Colonel George Bradbrooke, landed in marshes west of the River Dives. However, he quickly headed for the battalion RV, which was beside the drop zone, where he met his second in command, Major Jeff Nicklin, together with his Signals Officer, Lieutenant John Simpson, and his Intelligence Officer, Lieutenant R. Weathersbee. Also at the RV were men from 8th and 9th Parachute Battalions and a detachment of the Anti-Tank Platoon of the 2nd Battalion The Oxfordshire & Buckinghamshire Light Infantry, whose glider had landed in the wrong location. Not long afterwards, some members of Headquarter Company and a section of 224th Parachute Field Ambulance also appeared. Lacking information as to C Company's progress with its attack on Varaville, Lieutenant Colonel Bradbrooke despatched Lieutenant Weathersbee and two men to investigate and report back. Meanwhile, he led the rest of his force towards the crossroads at Le Mesnil. As he did so, he and his men came under fire and had to clear enemy troops out of houses along the road before they could continue. The enemy withdrew after an attack put in by men of Headquarter Company and the crossroads was reached at 1100 hours. Bradbrooke proceeded to set up his battalion headquarters there.

Meanwhile, C Company had been undertaking the four tasks allocated to it with a fraction of its normal strength of over 100 men. The company had been given the task of clearing the enemy garrison from Varaville, knocking out a 75mm gun emplacement at a road junction near the Chateau de Varaville, just east of the town, the demolition of the bridge over the River Divette, and the destruction of a radio transmitter station which was also near Varaville. Even for a full strength company this was a formidable task. As it was, when company commander Major Murray McLeod arrived at his company RV at 0030 hours, he found only a small number of his men waiting there. He himself, together with some of his men, had been on the dropping zone when the RAF Lancasters bombing the Merville Battery had flown over and some had emptied their bomb loads on the DZ. McLeod, along with everyone else, had been left badly shocked. His group was only 15 strong and could muster only one PIAT, three Sten guns, eight rifles and his own pistol. Regardless of this, he led his small force off to attack the enemy garrison at Varaville. As he did so, he met a small group from No. 9 Platoon who had survived the RAF's bombing of the dropping zone. Although they were still badly shocked, they were unhurt and in possession of all their weapons and equipment.

With only 25 minutes left before the arrival of the main body of 3rd Parachute Brigade, McLeod and his men made their way through the dark to Varaville. Passing through the village undetected, they reached the chateau gatehouse, which was some distance from the chateau itself and overlooked the enemy positions. These consisted of a long trench fortified with concrete and earthworks, with machine gun positions located at intervals and a bunker at each end. McLeod's men searched the deserted gatehouse and discovered that it was used as a barracks, housing 96 men. After positioning his force, McLeod went up to the second floor of the gatehouse where, shortly afterwards, he and some others came under fire from the 75mm gun in an emplacement to the rear of the enemy trench. An attempt to knock out the gun with a PIAT was unsuccessful. Before the operator could fire a second bomb, the gun once again fired at the gatehouse and set off some PIAT bombs beside him. Lieutenant 'Chug' Walker was killed and Major Murray McLeod was mortally wounded.

At that point Captain John Hanson, the company second in command, arrived with two other men, one carrying a machine gun. They were followed by Corporal Dan Hartigan and another man with a 2-inch mortar. Shortly afterwards a massive explosion was heard away to the south-east, and Hanson and his men realised that other members of C Company, under Sergeant Davies, had succeeded in destroying the Varaville bridge and thus had achieved one of their objectives.

At 1000 hours, after an effective bombardment of 2-inch mortar bombs had been put down by Corporal Hartigan on their positions, the enemy troops at the chateau surrendered and the battle for Varaville was over. During the afternoon, having waited for an enemy counterattack which never materialised, the Canadians were relieved by 1st Special Service Brigade. Hanson and his men, together with their prisoners, set off for Le Mesnil, where they would rejoin their battalion. On the way they came under fire on several occasions but dealt effectively with the enemy each time, arriving at Le Mesnil at 1800 hours.

As Brigadier James Hill had been making his way towards Sallenelles to discover how 9th Parachute Battalion had fared at the Merville Battery, he had heard the sound of low-flying aircraft carrying out a bombing raid. Shouting to his men to take cover, he had thrown himself to the ground on top of the Mortar Officer of 9th Parachute Battalion, Lieutenant Peters. On regaining his feet, he found that Peters had been killed, as had the majority of the group whom he had been leading. Only Hill, who had suffered a painful wound in his backside, and his headquarters defence platoon commander had survived, the rest being either badly wounded or dying. After rendering first aid and administering morphia to the wounded, the two men pressed on and eventually reached the Regimental Aid Post of 9th Parachute Battalion. After receiving treatment for his wound, Brigadier Hill headed for Headquarters 6th Airborne Division, which by then had been established in Ranville. On reporting to Major General Gale, he was told that 3rd Parachute Brigade had achieved all of its objectives. Immediately afterwards Hill underwent surgery, but by 1600 hours had reached his brigade headquarters at Le Mesnil. There he found Lieutenant Colonel Alastair Pearson in temporary command of the brigade and discovered that some of his staff were missing, including the Brigade Major, Major Bill Collingwood, and the DAA & QMG, Major Alec Pope. The latter had been dropped 15 miles east of the River Dives and, together with his stick and a group of others, had been surrounded by enemy troops. Refusing to surrender, they had all died fighting.

As dawn broke on the morning of 6 June, Major General Gale met Brigadier Nigel Poett, who informed him that the bridges had been captured and briefed him on 5th Parachute Brigade's dispositions. Meanwhile, the divisional headquarters was being set up in the Chateau de Heaume in Le Bas de Ranville. At 0700 hours the Allied sea and air bombardment of the assault beaches began, and this was the signal for radio silence in the division to be broken. Later in the morning, news arrived of 3rd Parachute Brigade and of 9th Parachute Battalion's attack on the Merville Battery.

That evening, at 2100 hours, the noise of hundreds of aircraft could suddenly be heard and the sky was filled with 250 aircraft towing the Horsa and Hamilcar gliders carrying 6th Airlanding Brigade and divisional troops. By all accounts it was an awe-inspiring sight as the gliders cast off and swooped on to the landing zones. The enemy reaction to the landings was swift. Mortar fire came down on Ranville and on the divisional headquarters. The Commander Royal Artillery was badly wounded, as was Major Gerry Lacoste the GSO 2 (Intelligence). Small-arms and mortar fire was directed at the landing zones, but casualties there were light. An hour and a half later units were moving off the landing zones towards their respective RV locations.

By midnight on D-day 6th Airborne Division had received its baptism of fire and was fully deployed, except for the 12th Battalion The Devonshire Regiment (less one company which had already landed by glider) and those divisional troops which had not already landed with 6th Airlanding Brigade. They would arrive by sea on the following day. 3rd Parachute Brigade was deployed over a four-mile front, with 9th Parachute Battalion at Le Plein in the north, 1st Canadian Parachute Battalion and Brigadier James Hill's brigade headquarters at Le Mesnil in the centre, and 8th Parachute Battalion in the southern part of the Bois de Bavent. 5th Parachute Brigade was holding La Bas de Ranville and Ranville with 12th and 13th Parachute Battalions respectively, with 7th Parachute Battalion as its reserve on the western edge of DZ 'N'. 6th Airlanding Brigade had two of its battalions deployed and ready to start operations to extend the bridgehead on the following morning, while 1st Special Service Brigade was holding the villages of Hauger, Le Plein and Amfreville, to the north and north-east of DZ 'N'.

On the following day 9th Parachute Battalion left the Chateau d'Amfreville in Hauger and made its way across country to the south of Breville to rejoin the brigade. By 1330 hours it had arrived at its new location in the area of the Chateau St Come and was digging in. The battalion's area of responsibility extended across the road from the grounds of the chateau to include a house called the Bois de Mont, located in a clearing surrounded by trees. After discussion with his brigade commander, Lieutenant Colonel Otway altered the disposition of his battalion so that the Bois de Mont became the area of the main defensive position, the chateau being denied to the enemy by patrolling. A Company was positioned along either side of the chateau drive, while B Company was located along a sunken lane which ran along the northern edge of the Bois de Mont wood, overlooking open ground stretching away towards Breville. C Company was deployed on the southern and western sides of the position and was the battalion's counterattack force. The Vickers guns of the Machine Gun Platoon were positioned in the ditch beside the road, near the gates to the chateau, and covered both ways along the Breville-Le Mesnil road. Battalion Headquarters and the Regimental Aid Post were located in the Bois de Mont itself.

On 8 June a patrol led by Lieutenant Dennis Slade reconnoitred the Chateau St Come and found it unoccupied, although signs of occupation by German troops were found. At midday an enemy patrol attacked A Company but was beaten off without difficulty. During the afternoon, attacks were mounted against A and C Companies by the 857th Grenadier Regiment, but were repulsed. Regimental Sergeant Major Cunningham led a small counterattack force consisting of a Vickers machine gun, a Bren group and some members of the Anti-Tank Platoon, moving swiftly to any area in the battalion's perimeter which was under threat. That night the battalion was resupplied with two 3-inch mortars and three Vickers machine guns. None of its mortars had been retrieved during the drop and these had been sorely missed, as had the members of the Mortar Platoon, of whom the majority were still missing. Shortly after the arrival of the new mortars, however, Sergeant Hennessy of the Mortar Platoon had trained some replacements to a very creditable standard. Meanwhile, Sergeant McGeever had formed a new Machine Gun Platoon and had mounted one of the Vickers on a jeep for use as a mobile support vehicle.

At dawn on 9 June the enemy laid down a heavy concentration of mortar fire on 9th Parachute Battalion and followed this up with a strong attack with infantry against A Company and part of B Company. Both waited until the enemy were only 50 yards away before opening fire and wreaking havoc, with support from the Mortar Platoon, amongst the German infantrymen, who broke and fled into the woods surrounding the chateau. An hour later the enemy mounted another assault, but this met the same fate.

During the morning, a report was received that Brigade Headquarters was under threat of attack. Lieutenant Colonel Terence Otway quickly gathered together a small force of some 30 men from Battalion Headquarters and C Company, together with a fire support group, under Major George Smith, which was equipped with two captured MG-42s. Moving rapidly through the wood to the south-east, Lieutenant Colonel Otway and his men trapped the enemy between themselves and the Brigade Headquarters Defence Platoon, killing 19 and taking one prisoner.

In the afternoon, two platoons of enemy infantry started to infiltrate through the wood to the east and south of A Company's positions. A platoon of C Company, led by Major Eddie Charlton, the battalion's Second in Command, and Lieutenant John Parfitt, carried out a counter-attack. Unfortunately, they encountered two machine guns and both Charlton and Parfitt, together with five others, were killed. Their bodies were recovered that night by a patrol.

Very early on the morning of 10 June, a section was sent into the area of the chateau to check for enemy activity. After searching the chateau itself and finding it empty, the section came under fire from a machine gun in buildings which it had already checked. One man was wounded in the leg but was rescued. That morning also saw the very welcome arrival of Captain Robert Gordon-Brown and 30 other members of the battalion, which increased the battalion's strength to 270 all ranks, although this was still a very low figure. Despite the fact that everyone was extremely tired, morale was very high. At 1100 hours the enemy put in a weak attack on A Company, but this was easily driven off. Shortly afterwards, after a platoon of A Company had been redeployed further forward about 50 yards into a ditch north-east of the gates to the chateau, some 50 enemy troops began digging in along the ditch beside the Breville road in full view of two of the battalion's Vickers guns. At a range of 500 yards they were in perfect enfilade. Supported by two Bren gun groups from B Company, the Vickers gunners virtually wiped out the entire enemy force. Not long afterwards, A Company's recently deployed forward platoon ambushed a German patrol at a range of ten yards, virtually annihilating it.

However, the enemy had reoccupied the chateau and by early afternoon were there in force. An infantry company advanced down the drive with support from two self-propelled guns which turned their attentions on A and B Companies. The battalion's supply of 3-inch mortar ammunition was by then running very low, so PIATs were brought into play as makeshift mortars. Combined with the firepower of some of A Company's Bren light machine guns, this measure proved effective in breaking up the enemy attack. Meanwhile, Sergeant McGeever's jeep-mounted Vickers gun engaged one of the self-propelled guns which had suddenly appeared to the north of the chateau. To the amazement of those watching, the self-propelled gun suddenly exploded and ground to a halt.

Shortly afterwards, two companies of enemy infantry attacked B Company in strength from the north, supported by heavy mortar fire. The battalion's own mortars, which by then had been resupplied with ammunition, replied and drove off the enemy with the assistance of B Company's Bren guns. At this point supporting fire was called down from HMS *Arethusa* via a Forward Observer Bombardment (FOB) at Brigade

Headquarters. Fifteen minutes later, salvoes of 6-inch shells crashed down 500 yards in front of the battalion's positions. Captain Paul Greenway stood up in full view of the enemy and shouted corrections to Lieutenant Colonel Terence Otway who relayed them by radio to the FOB. Although they suffered heavy casualties, the enemy's leading elements still managed to reach B Company's positions, where they received a further mauling which few survived. Among those taken prisoner was the commanding officer of the 2nd Battalion 857th Grenadier Regiment, who told his captors that his battalion had been destroyed and that the rest of his regiment had met a similar fate during fighting in Ranville and Amfreville.

At 2300 hours that night Major Ian Dyer led C Company forward to occupy the chateau which, after some skirmishing with small groups of enemy, he succeeded in doing. Throughout the rest of the night enemy patrols probed the company's positions and kept it busy, but the rest of the battalion saw little activity.

That same day, the commander of 1st Corps, Lieutenant General Sir John Crocker, had decided to extend the bridgehead to east of the River Orne. Consequently, 51st Highland Division crossed the bridges to take over the southern half of the sector from 6th Airborne Division. That night the 5th Battalion The Black Watch arrived at an assembly area a short distance south-west of 9th Parachute Battalion. Detached from 153rd Infantry Brigade and now under Brigadier James Hill's command, it had been given the task of attacking and capturing Breville from the south-west on the following day, 11 June, to dislodge the enemy from their vantage point on the high ground overlooking Ranville. The Chateau St Come was a vital factor in any successful attack on Breville from the south, as any assault from that direction would be vulnerable to counterattack through the area north of the chateau. Breville itself was held by a strong enemy force consisting of infantry supported by self-propelled guns.

The commanding officer of The Black Watch battalion planned his attack so that his main assault would approach Breville from the south-west under heavy artillery and mortar support from the guns of 51st Highland Division and the mortars of the two battalions. Before dawn, a company of The Black Watch took over the chateau from C Company while a reconnaissance patrol, commanded by Captain Hugh Smyth, moved along the road towards Breville to check the ground over which The Black Watch attack would approach. Before reaching Breville itself, the assaulting companies of The Black Watch had to move across 250 yards of open ground. As they were doing so, the supporting artillery and mortar fire lifted and the Highlanders were subjected to a heavy concentration of enemy mortar and machine gun fire which caused several casualties. Simultaneously, the enemy also brought down a heavy mortar bombardment on the area to the south-west through which The Black Watch reserve companies were advancing. Heavy casualties were caused there as well, and the attack ground to a halt, the Highlanders withdrawing to 9th Parachute Battalion's positions and eventually taking up positions around the Chateau St Come.

Meanwhile, 8th Parachute Battalion was busy operating from its base in the Bois de Bavent, near the road junction south-east of Escoville, dominating its area with vigour. Although it numbered only 50 per cent of its full strength, it had been patrolling ceaselessly and aggressively at night and lying up by day. The battalion's base was located in thick forest, through which it was impossible to move except by use of the network of tracks which were woven through it. The road runs through the forest, and this was dominated by the battalion from a point south of Le Mesnil through to Troarn. The thickness of the trees was such that visibility and fields of fire were limited to just a few yards. The enemy, conscious of the fact that the tracks and road provided the only means of access to different parts of the forest, kept them under almost constant mortar fire, track junctions proving to be death traps. Casualties were caused by mortar bombs bursting in the branches of trees, and the battalion soon learned to take cover rapidly at the sound of them arriving. Overhead cover was constructed in all trenches, and this helped to reduce the risk of head wounds caused by flying steel fragments and wooden splinters. However, conditions in the forest were grim. Everything was permanently wet through with rain, the dripping foliage being so thick that the sun could not penetrate it. Trenches became waterlogged, and the mud was slimy and slippery. To make matters worse, large mosquitoes infested the forest and plagued the battalion, their bites causing skin sores when scratched. Lieutenant Colonel Alastair Pearson himself was a sick man, suffering from a wound and covered in boils and sores. Despite these hardships, 8th Parachute Battalion's morale was as high as ever and its confidence undiminished. At night, patrols were sent out to gather information or to harry the enemy, frequently entering Troarn and Bures, which was held in strength by German troops.

1st Canadian Parachute Battalion, meanwhile, had also been seeing plenty of action. Having been resupplied on 7 June with much-needed mortars and large quantities of ammunition, its positions at the Le Mesnil crossroads were subjected to a strong attack by enemy infantry of the 857th and 858th Grenadier Regiments, supported by tanks and self-propelled guns. These had appeared in a long column along the road leading to Le Mesnil, apparently in the belief that the battalion did not possess mortars. Before they could deploy for an assault, however, the Canadian mortars opened fire to good effect. Despite heavy casualties the enemy infantry attacked B and C Companies. They were supported by a Mark IV tank, but this was driven off by PIATs. B Company then counterattacked with a bayonet charge, forcing the enemy to withdraw to a fortified farmhouse some 200 yards down the road. This was heavily defended with machine guns, and from it the Germans could threaten the Canadian positions with harassing fire and sniping.

At 0900 hours, after the attack on the crossroads had been repulsed, B Company was ordered to attack and clear the building. Two platoons, reinforced by men from Headquarter Company and commanded by Captain Peter Griffin, carried out the task. While two sections moved into a position to protect their flank, Captain Griffin and the rest of his force put in a frontal assault through an orchard and caught the enemy by surprise. Lieutenant Norman Toseland led his men in a bayonet charge, coming under fire as they made for a hedgerow at the end. Four of Toseland's men were killed and two were wounded. The flank protection party also took casualties, three men being killed and three wounded by a machine gun which was subsequently knocked out by Captain Griffin and his men as they cleared the farmhouse and some outbuildings. Griffin halted the attack after spotting a large number of enemy troops and armoured vehicles in the farmyard. At the same time, enemy mortars brought down fire on the farmhouse and the enemy counterattacked with the support of a tank. As Griffin and his men withdrew, the flank protection group opened fire on the enemy counterattack force, which was caught in a crossfire. Under pressure from this strong enemy force, B Company was forced to withdraw, having lost eight men killed and 13 wounded. However, the enemy subsequently abandoned the farmhouse and thereafter limited themelves to sniping at the Canadians from the hedgerows.

On the following day, 9 June, a platoon of C Company, commanded by Lieutenant McGowan, was despatched to the village of Bavent to determine the strength of the enemy as well as the number and positions of guns there. The plan was for one section to enter the village and stir things up while three men ran across an open field in full view of the enemy to draw their fire. In the event, having become over-confident and assuming the village to be unoccupied, the platoon came under fire from an enemy machine gun at almost point-blank range. Mercifully no one was hit, and the platoon launched an attack on the village, which they found to be crawling with enemy troops, many of whom brought fire to bear on the Canadians from the upper storeys of buildings. However, the platoon sergeant, Sergeant McPhee, found an enemy 2-inch mortar and brought this into action, raining a shower of bombs down on the village. Meanwhile, the three men designated to draw the enemy's fire, and thus force the latter to reveal the locations of their positions, were sent running across open ground and back. Fortunately, they escaped death and injury.

That night, C Company sent another patrol into Bavent. Twelve men, accompanying a party of 14 sappers from 3rd Parachute Squadron RE, infiltrated into the village. The sappers placed explosive charges on some heavy mortars and in some houses while the C Company men opened fire on the enemy. When the sappers had completed their task the entire force withdrew as the enemy responded with machine guns firing wildly in different directions.

On 10 June the enemy attacked in strength, breaking through Breville and advancing on Ranville, where they were beaten off. However, a wedge had been forced between 3rd Parachute Brigade and 1st Special Service Brigade. Shortly afterwards, a strong enemy force consisting of the 2nd Battalion 857th Grenadier Regiment, a combined body of the 1st and 2nd Battalions 858th Grenadier Regiment and several companies of the 744th Grenadier Regiment, supported by tanks and armoured cars, put in an attack at a point between 1st Canadian and 9th Parachute Battalions, but this was broken up by heavy artillery and machine gun fire. The same fate met two more attacks which were launched to the north of 1st Canadian Parachute Battalion's positions.

Two days later, on 12 June, the whole of 3rd Parachute Brigade's front came under heavy shelling and mortar fire. At 1500 hours that afternoon an enemy battalion attacked 1st Canadian Parachute Battalion while a strong enemy force, supported by six tanks and self-propelled guns, advanced on 9th Parachute Battalion and the 5th Battalion The Black Watch, which lost all of its anti-tank guns and nine of its Bren carriers. The battle raged around the Chateau St Come, The Black Watch doggedly resisting desperate attempts by the enemy to seize it with the support of their armour. Gradually the enemy started to force the Highlanders back towards the Bois de Mont. At the same time the enemy also started to concentrate on 9th Parachute Battalion, and A and B Companies came under fire from tanks and self-propelled guns. The Mortar Platoon kept up a steady rate of fire, dropping bombs 300 yards away into the woods while under constant fire itself. More enemy infantry, supported by two tanks, attacked B Company. One tank received two direct hits from PIAT bombs but remained unscathed and responded by knocking out two machine gun posts. It withdrew only after being hit yet again by a PIAT, followed by the infantry which had managed to advance to within very close range of A and B Companies. At this point Lieutenant Colonel Terence Otway realised that his battalion was so weak that it would not be able to hold out for much longer. When Brigadier James Hill, in his headquarters 400 yards away from 9th Parachute Battalion, received a radio signal from Otway to this effect, he himself immediately led a force of some 40 men from 1st Canadian Parachute Battalion in a counterattack, driving the enemy from 9th Parachute Battalion's area.

Meanwhile, in 5th Parachute Brigade, 7 June had seen 12th Parachute Battalion, which was on the high ground south of Le Bas de Ranville, come under attack from seven tanks supported by approximately a company of infantry. The enemy advanced against A Company and succeeded in knocking out the crew of the single 6-pounder anti-tank gun supporting it. However, the situation was saved by one man, Private Hall, who ran across to the gun and destroyed three tanks in rapid succession, forcing the enemy to withdraw.

In 13th Parachute Battalion's area on the same day, a troop of three self-propelled guns tried to penetrate A Company's positions but were destroyed. On the following day, 8 June, the battalion knocked out six tanks while repelling another attack.

On 10 June, before dawn, a strong force of enemy troops was detected by B Company in the woods south-east of Breville. C Company despatched a reconnaissance patrol which subsequently reported that the enemy were forming up to attack. At 0900 hours the enemy began crossing DZ 'N' and headed for the bridges over the Caen Canal and River Orne. Waiting until the enemy were within 50 yards, 13th Parachute Battalion opened fire with deadly effect. C Company then counterattacked with a bayonet charge, at which point 7th Parachute Battalion brought its Vickers machine guns and 3-inch mortars to bear. The enemy, who by this time had suffered over 400 killed, were routed and withdrew into three areas of woodland at Le Mariquet along the road between Ranville and Le Mesnil. One hundred prisoners were taken after this action had ended.

During that morning, reports had reached Headquarters 6th Airborne Division of heavy fighting in the areas of both parachute brigades and 1st Special Service Brigade, who were all being heavily engaged by enemy units attacking from the direction of Breville. Major General Gale decided that the enemy was to be cleared out of the areas of woodland at Le Mariquet, and had requested armoured support from 1st Corps to assist 5th Parachute Brigade to carry out the task. During the early afternoon, B Squadron 13th/18th Royal Hussars arrived and linked up with 7th Parachute Battalion. Both the squadron leader, Major Anthony Rugge Price, and Lieutenant Colonel Geoffrey Pine Coffin were fully aware that any form of artillery or mortar fire support was impossible because of the risk to 13th Parachute Battalion and to the units of 3rd Parachute Brigade. The task of clearing the enemy from the woods would be carried out by A and B Companies, who would be preceded by a troop of the Hussars' Sherman tanks, which would move over the open ground of the dropping zone to the left of the companies' axis of advance. The tanks would bring fire to bear on the wooded areas for two minutes before signalling the companies to advance by firing smoke rounds. Another troop of Shermans would follow up behind the leading troop while the squadron's reconnaissance troop of Honey light tanks would move along their left flank, covering the Breville ridge.

However, the tanks encountered problems as they moved forward during the attack. One of the reserve troop's tanks was hit and, as the leading troop was laying down fire on the second wood, the reconnaissance troop leader's Honey's tracks became entangled with the rigging lines of parachutes lying on the dropping zone. Immobilised, it was almost immediately knocked out by a self-propelled gun. Meanwhile, the leading troop leader's Sherman had also been hit and set ablaze, the rest of the troop coming under fire from a self-propelled gun. Almost at the same moment, Major Rugge Price's tank was also hit and set on fire. The squadron started to pull back and, as it did so, another Sherman and Honey were hit. A further Sherman was knocked out after it became immobilised, its tracks entangled in rigging lines.

The two companies had been making good progress. B Company had succeeded in clearing the enemy, a battalion of the 857th Grenadier Regiment, out of the first two woods, and the third was being cleared by A Company when the hussars encountered problems. By the end of the afternoon, 20 enemy had been killed and a further 100 prisoners captured. 7th Parachute Battalion had suffered very light casualties, ten men having been wounded, but the hussars had suffered badly, losing one officer and nine other ranks killed as well as one officer and four men wounded. They had also lost three Shermans and two Honeys destroyed.

Two days later, on 12 June, Major General Gale decided that the threat from the enemy forces in Breville had to be removed once and for all. By then his division was sorely depleted after the heavy fighting of the last five days, 3rd Parachute Brigade being exhausted and very low in numbers. He therefore allotted the task of an attack on Breville to his reserve, the understrength 12th Parachute Battalion, which numbered only 300, and D Company of the 12th Battalion The Devonshire Regiment. To support them, he had a squadron of the 13th/18th Royal Hussars and a formidable amount of artillery: four field regiments and one medium regiment. Gale also decided to use the 22nd Independent Parachute Company to deal with any enemy counterattack. The attack was to be mounted at 2200 hours that night, Gale's intention being to catch the enemy off-guard while recovering from the previous fighting that day. It would be mounted from the eastern outskirts of Amfreville, No. 6 Commando having secured the start line beforehand. Lieutenant Colonel Johnny Johnson, the Commanding Officer of 12th Parachute Battalion, thus had little time in which to draw up his plans. He decided that C Company would take and secure the initial crossroads while the Devons' D Company would follow up behind and then deploy to the left on reaching Breville. A Company would move through C Company and push on to secure the south-eastern part of the village, B Company bringing up the rear as the battalion's reserve. The approach to the village consisted of 400 yards of open ground. To provide cover for the battalion as it advanced, a troop of the 13th/18th Royal Hussars would move down the right flank and destroy an enemy strongpoint some 200 yards from the village.

At 2000 hours the battalion prepared for battle while the company commanders attended the Commanding Officer's 'O' Group and carried out a brief reconnaissance. At 2035 hours the battalion moved off for Amfreville, where it assembled in the church. After a while, platoon commanders were called out to receive their orders while the rest of the battalion sat in the pews of the church. Eventually they were called outside, forming up by companies along the roadside. There was no time to give detailed orders, so company commanders could give their men only the briefest of outlines of the planned attack. At 2150 hours the supporting artillery opened fire. As the battalion advanced along the road towards Breville, a constant barrage of shells hurtled overhead. Soon afterwards, however, the battalion came under enemy artillery and mortar fire and was forced to take cover in the ditches on either side of the road or against the walls of nearby buildings. It was some 15 minutes before the fire slackened and the battalion was able to continue its advance to the start line.

On crossing the start line, C Company started to suffer casualties, losing all of its officers and its company sergeant major. Nevertheless, it continued to advance under the command of Sergeant Warcup while still under fire from self-propelled guns. Although enemy mortar and artillery fire continued to rain down, there was no small-arms fire from Breville, which by then was ablaze. Meanwhile, the Sherman tanks of the 13th/18th Royal Hussars were firing tracer from their machine guns to guide the assaulting companies to their objective. By the time C Company reached Breville, however, it was only 15 strong.

As A Company crossed the start line it lost its company commander, Captain Paul Bernhard, who was wounded, and the whole of No. 2 Platoon, under Lieutenant James Campbell, was either killed or wounded. Company Sergeant Major Marwood assumed command of the company, but he was killed as it reached Breville. Captain Paul Bernhard, meanwhile, staggered on after his men, passing C Company's commander, Major 'Steve' Stephens, who was lying wounded by the roadside and urging his men on into the village. On reaching Breville, Bernhard found No. 3 Platoon, which soon afterwards lost its commander, Lieutenant Brewer. Sergeant Nutley took over command of the remaining nine men in the platoon, leading them forward to clear the chateau. Meanwhile, Sergeant Murray and the remaining members of No. 1 Platoon took the chateau garden, which was their objective.

As D Company of the Devons, under second in command Captain John Warwick-Pengelly, was moving past the church in Le Plein on its way to the start line, a number of men were wounded by a shell which burst in the middle of its ranks. Despite this, it continued heading towards Amfreville along a narrow sunken lane. As it did so it met wounded members of 12th Parachute Battalion coming in the opposite direction. Soon afterwards, the Devons met the commander of their battalion's Support Company, Major Eddie Warren, who had been asked by D Company's commander, Major John Bampfylde, to bring the latter's men forward to the start line. As D Company crossed the start line a salvo of shells, later suspected of having been fired by the supporting artillery of 51st Highland Division, fell short and exploded in the middle of a group of officers which included the commanders of 6th Airlanding and 1st Special Service Brigades as well as Lieutenant Colonel Johnny Johnson and Major John Bampfylde. Johnson and Bampfylde were killed, whilst Brigadiers Kindersley and Lovat were badly wounded. Meanwhile, D Company pushed on towards Breville.

B Company brought up the rear, accompanied by Colonel Reggie Parker, the Deputy Commander of 6th Airlanding Brigade. The former Commanding Officer of 12th Parachute Battalion, he had been standing near Lieutenant Colonel Johnson when the latter was killed and, although wounded, had come forward to take over command of his old battalion.

It was now 2245 hours and dusk was falling. The pitifully small remaining element of C Company had secured the crossroads, while the 18 men of A Company had taken up positions on the south-eastern edge of the village. In the north-eastern corner the remaining 20 men of the Devons had taken an orchard which was their objective. At that point Colonel Parker, who was accompanied by a forward observation officer from 53rd Airlanding Light Regiment, RA, called for defensive fire from the supporting artillery to prevent any enemy counterattack. Tragically, there was a misunderstanding at the gun end and Breville itself was subjected to a heavy barrage which caused even further casualties among 12th Parachute Battalion and the Devons. The forward observation officer, Captain Hugh Ward, was killed, and it was his signaller who ordered the guns to cease fire. When the shelling had stopped, it was discovered that Major Paul Rogers, the commander of B Company, had been fatally wounded and that nine men of 12th Parachute Battalion had been hit. A Company's commander, Captain Paul Bernhard, had been wounded again and Captain John Sim of B Company had been hit in the arm.

At 0200 hours the 13th/18th Royal Hussars moved up to the crossroads, where they joined the remnants of C Company. Early on the following morning 22nd Independent Parachute Company, under Major Nigel Stockwell, arrived as reinforcements. Later, the 1st Battalion The Royal Ulster Rifles marched up from Ranville to relieve what remained of 12th Parachute Battalion and the Devons' company.

The battle for Breville had taken a very heavy toll. Casualties in 12th Parachute Battalion and D Company 12th Battalion The Devonshire Regiment totalled nine officers and 153 men killed during the action. Of the 550 officers and men of 12th Parachute Battalion who had been dropped into Normandy on 6th June, only Headquarter Company and 55 men of the rifle companies remained. All of the officers, including the Commanding Officer, and all the warrant officers had been killed or wounded. Enemy casualties during the action at Breville amounted to 77 men killed.

By 14 June all six parachute battalions and 6th Airlanding Brigade were severely weakened as a result of the casualties sustained during the constant fighting which had taken place since 6 June. 6th Airborne Division by then numbered fewer than 6,000 men and consequently was reinforced by 4th Special Service Brigade, commanded by Brigadier B. W. Leicester RM, which comprised Nos. 41, 46, 47 and 48 Commandos Royal Marines. This enabled Major General Gale to withdraw each of his exhausted brigades in rotation for rest and re-equipping. 3rd Parachute Brigade, having suffered particularly heavy casualties, was withdrawn first. 5th Parachute Brigade took over the southern part of the division's sector, while 6th Airlanding Brigade assumed responsibility for the rest of it. 1st and 4th Special Service Brigades were deployed to cover the area from Breville to the coast.

On 14 July Major General Gale received a letter from General Montgomery, the Commander-in-Chief, in which the latter informed him that 55 decorations had been awarded to members of 6th Airborne Division: ten Distinguished Service Orders, 20 Military Crosses, three Distinguished Conduct Medals and 22 Military Medals. On 16 July General Montgomery personally decorated the recipients.

Two days later Operation 'Goodwood' took place. On the morning of 18 July the 7th, 11th and Guards Armoured Divisions advanced behind a barrage of artillery fire down a corridor which had already been bombed continually for three days by the Allied forces. The battle continued for three days as the British armour advanced and Allied bombers attacked targets beyond. It ended two days later when heavy rain turned the ground into a quagmire and heavy German resistance slowed the momentum of the armoured advance. Meanwhile, the bridgehead was expanded with the arrival of 49th Infantry Division, which moved up between 6th Airborne and 51st Highland Divisions. During this period, until 16 August, 6th Airborne Division concentrated on dominating its area of responsibility by patrolling aggressively and hunting down the enemy whenever the opportunity arose.

In 5th Parachute Brigade's area, 7th Parachute Battalion had taken over from 8th Parachute Battalion in the Bois de Bavent where it continued Lieutenant Colonel Alastair Pearson's policy of taking the war to the enemy. In late June, Lieutenant Colonel Geoffrey Pine Coffin tasked B Company, commanded by Major Bob Keene, with carrying out an attack on a farm called 'Bob's Farm'. After making its approach unseen, and having deployed as it approached the start line, the company spotted an enemy company forming up for an attack in the opposite direction. Keene and his men put in an immediate assault, charging through an orchard into the farm. At this point, however, they were subjected to heavy fire, suffering 15 casualties which included two platoon commanders, Lieutenants Poole and Farr, who were wounded. In addition, Company Sergeant Major Durbin had been killed whilst manning a Bren gun. By the time B Company withdrew, however, it had killed 30 enemy, wounded several more, and taken nine prisoners.

Bob's Farm was subsequently raided by 22nd Independent Parachute Company, which was tasked with capturing prisoners. Led by Lieutenant Bob de Latour, a patrol from the company successfully infiltrated the enemy positions and silently took some prisoners. Unfortunately, it was spotted whilst withdrawing and Lieutenant de Latour was killed in the ensuing action. This left only one surviving officer in the company, Lieutenant John Vischer. The original company commander, Major Francis Lennox-Boyd, had been killed during the drop on 6 June, and the second in command, Captain Andrew Tait, had been killed during a raid into Breville soon afterwards. Two other platoon commanders, Lieutenants Bob Midwood and Don Wells, had subsequently been wounded.

On 10 July 7th Parachute Battalion made one final attempt to take Bob's Farm. B Company put in an attack during the afternoon, but this proved to be unsuccessful, the company being forced to withdraw under heavy machine gun and mortar fire, although support was forthcoming from the guns of 53rd Airlanding Light Regiment RA.

THE ADVANCE TO THE SEINE

On 7 August the commander of 1st Corps, Lieutenant General Sir John Crocker, ordered Major General Gale to prepare 6th Airborne Division for follow-up operations, as there were indications of an impending German withdrawal. The overall plan was for 1st Canadian Army to make a breakout from the bridgehead, moving south-east from Caen towards Falaise and subsequently turning eastwards before advancing towards the

River Seine. 1st Corps, which would be under command of 1st Canadian Army, would advance along an axis taking it through Lisieux, which was some 15 miles inland from the coast. 6th Airborne Division's task would be to maintain pressure on the enemy's right flank to reduce resistance on the main axis of advance. To carry out this task the division was allotted the Princess Irene of The Netherlands Brigade, commanded by Lieutenant Colonel A. C. de Ruyter Van Stevenick, and the Belgian Brigade under Colonel Pirron. 6th Airborne Division's final objective was the mouth of the River Seine. There were, however, a number of rivers to be crossed en route. The three main ones were the Dives, the Touques and the Risle, the latter two lying in narrow valleys with water meadows. Of these the Dives was the largest obstacle, lying in a broad and marshy valley with a derelict canal running parallel to it. Between the river and the canal was a large island, while to the east of the valley was a line of hills which dominated it.

Major General Gale had a choice of two routes to the Seine. The first option led from Troarn through Dozule, Pont L'Eveque and Beuzeville to Pont Audemer, the distance by road totalling some 45 miles. The alternative route ran along the coast through Cabourg, Trouville and Honfleur. There was little difference in the terrain on both routes, this consisting of undulating ground with hills covered in scrub and woods, between which was pastureland divided by very thick hedges. Although it meant crossing an 8,000-yard-wide valley of marshes and streams, as well as the major obstacle of the River Dives and the Dives Canal, Gale selected the inland route. His choice was based on the fact that the division was very short of sappers and bridging equipment, which meant that only one route could be maintained. The inland route via Troarn and Pont Audemer would pose fewer bridging problems, being farther from the estuaries where the rivers would be wider, deeper and tidal.

Gale's plan tasked 6th Airlanding Brigade, now commanded by Brigadier Edward Flavell, with the Dutch and Belgian brigades under command, to clear the coastal areas of enemy while the rest of the division advanced along its main axis via Troarn and Pont Audemer. 3rd Parachute Brigade would lead off first, moving to Bures and crossing the River Dives there, then on to the island in the middle of the valley, followed by 5th Parachute Brigade. Meanwhile, 4th Special Service Brigade would remain at Troarn and hold the area to the south, ready, together with 5th Parachute Brigade, to exploit any gains achieved by 3rd Parachute Brigade. Meanwhile, 1st Special Service Brigade would take Bavent and Robehomme, crossing the river at Robehomme if the opportunity presented itself.

On the night of 17 August the enemy started to withdraw. At 0300 hours on the following morning 3rd Parachute Brigade began to advance. By 0700 hours 8th and 9th Parachute Battalions had taken Bures without encountering any resistance, and at 0800 hours 1st Canadian Parachute Battalion started moving through the Bois de Bavent, where its progress was slowed by mines and booby traps. At the same time, 4th Special Service Brigade was advancing towards Troarn and St Pair, whilst 1st Special Service Brigade was heading for Bavent and Robehomme.

3rd Parachute Brigade started crossing the Dives at Bures during the late afternoon of 18 August, having been delayed whilst 3rd Parachute Squadron RE replaced a bridge destroyed on D-day, and by nightfall all of its units were across. By then, 1st Canadian Parachute Battalion had made contact with the enemy at Plain-Lugan, and 8th Parachute Battalion had reached the outskirts of Goustranville. The following morning the brigade advanced on Goustranville, where the enemy put up a stout resistance. At the same time, the brigade came under artillery fire from the heights of Putot, which dominated the area. Because the island was under constant observation, Major General Gale decided that any attack would have to be carried out at night, and that 3rd Parachute Brigade would advance and secure the railway line east of the canal. This would act as the start line for a second-phase attack by 5th Parachute Brigade, which would then push on and attack the heights of Putot.

That night, at 2200 hours, 1st Canadian Parachute Battalion led the way as 3rd Parachute Brigade crossed the start line. By 2235 hours C Company had seized the northernmost railway bridge, which had been blown by the enemy but was passable to infantry. The next two bridges to the south had also been destroyed, but the fourth and southernmost bridge was captured intact by A Company. By 2359 hours the battalion had overrun two fortified positions manned by troops of the 744th Grenadier Regiment and had taken 150 prisoners. 9th Parachute Battalion then moved through the Canadians towards the railway station at Dozule. By 0100 hours on the following morning, 19 August, it had arrived at the outskirts of Dozule, where it was subjected to artillery fire. By 1100 hours the battalion had suffered 54 casualties and its Regimental Aid Post had been hit.

Meanwhile, 5th Parachute Brigade had crossed the canal by the southernmost bridge and had pushed on towards Putot-en-Auge. 7th Parachute Battalion's objective was the spur immediately east of Putot-en-Auge, which it was to secure, after which 12th Parachute Battalion would take the village itself. It would not be an easy task because the enemy were well dug in and showed every sign of putting up a stiff fight.

13th Parachute Battalion, which was to cross the canal and follow up behind 9th Parachute Battalion, attempted to do so via the blown railway bridge. However, by the time it reached the bridge the water level was such that a crossing was out of the question. Lieutenant Colonel Peter Luard then led his battalion to a small footbridge which had been discovered earlier by 1st Canadian Parachute Battalion, and there it waited in reserve.

7th Parachute Battalion, meanwhile, had encountered problems with the thick, impenetrable hedges, which forced it to make detours along its route. Moreover, the enemy had sited sustained-fire machine guns on fixed lines and fired these at frequent intervals while at the same time constantly illuminating the countryside with flares. In addition, the area between the canal and the railway, which was the battalion's start line, had not been completely cleared and several enemy positions and some anti-tank guns were encountered and had to be neutralised. B Company, commanded by

Major B. R. Braithewaite, was in the lead and was pinned down by machine gun fire as it advanced along a hedgerow. At that moment A and C Companies were crossing the start line and there was a danger that the battalion could become bunched in a small area. A section was sent off to locate the machine gun and deal with it. It returned having captured the weapon and its crew.

As the battalion was preparing to continue its advance, troops were spotted approaching in extended line across a field to the left. Initially, in the first glimmer of dawn, it was thought that these were men of 13th Parachute Battalion, but as they drew nearer it was realised that they were enemy troops. The battalion having adopted ambush positions in the hedgerow, Lieutenant Colonel Geoffrey Pine Coffin decided that he would attempt to take the Germans prisoner. A Bren group was despatched to a flank to cover the enemy while the Intelligence Officer, Lieutenant Bertie Mills, having waited until they were only 25 yards away, called out in German and ordered the enemy to lay down their weapons. The Germans were taken totally by surprise, and were so astonished that they stood motionless. Unfortunately, one of their number reacted by dropping to the ground and opening fire on the hedgerow. 7th Parachute Battalion responded by returning the fire and causing devastating casualties. After 15 minutes the remaining enemy surrendered. The battalion then resumed its advance and took its objective, the spur east of Putot-en-Auge, without further problems.

13th Parachute Battalion was by then advancing on its objective, a prominent feature called 'Hill 13' just beyond the village of Putot-en-Auge. Having waited in the open for three hours under constant fire, the battalion was faced with crossing a thousand yards of open terrain. Lieutenant Colonel Peter Luard realised that the only way his battalion had any chance of avoiding heavy casualties was for the whole unit to double across it as one body. His reasoning was that this was the last tactic that the Germans would expect, and would give them the least time to react. In this he was correct. By the time the enemy had realised what was happening, the entire battalion had sprinted over the three-quarters-of-a-mile of open ground and A and B Companies, commanded by Majors John Cramphorn and Reggie Tarrant respectively, were storming up Hill 13 with fixed bayonets. As the two companies reached the top of the hill, however, they were counter-attacked by an enemy battalion which had just arrived to reinforce the positions there. At the same time, a well-sited machine gun opened fire, seriously wounding Major Reggie Tarrant and killing one of his platoon commanders, Lieutenant Bibby, as well as several others. A and B Companies were driven off the hill by the German counterattack which was itself halted by very accurate artillery fire called down just in time. Lieutenant Colonel Luard then despatched C Company, commanded by Major Nobby Clark, to carry out a flanking attack from the right, but this proved unsuccessful as the enemy had the approach well covered. At that point Brigadier Nigel Poett, on learning of the situation, ordered Luard to hold his positions on the ridgeline where the battalion was at that moment deployed.

Although Hill 13 had not been taken, the attack on Putot-en-Auge had otherwise been very successful. Elsewhere the enemy had been driven back and 160 prisoners, two 75mm guns, four mortars and a large number of machine guns had been captured.

The next day, 21 August, saw 3rd Parachute Brigade advancing towards Pont L'Eveque. It soon encountered strong opposition from the enemy, particularly at the village of Annebault, where enemy infantry were supported by armour. 8th Parachute Battalion was given the task of clearing the village, which it took after some very heavy fighting, having initially been held up by an 88mm gun. During that night, 5th Parachute Brigade moved through 3rd Parachute Brigade and pushed on until it reached Pont L'Eveque, on the River Touques, at midday on 22 August. Situated in a valley dominated by wooded hills on either side, Pont L'Eveque is situated on both sides of the Touques, which flows through the town via two channels which are 200 yards apart. Running along an embankment alongside the eastern channel is a railway line. South of the town, which then consisted in the main of wooden houses and buildings, were two fords crossing the river, the southern approach to Pont L'Eveque being dominated by a feature called St Julien.

13th Parachute Battalion was ordered to infiltrate into the town and to establish a bridgehead across both channels of the river. 12th Parachute Battalion, now commanded by Lieutenant Colonel Nigel Stockwell, would meanwhile cross the river via the fords south of the town and secure the railway embankment and St Julien. At 1500 hours A Company, commanded by Captain J. A. S. Baker, led the rest of 12th Parachute Battalion under cover of smoke, laid down by supporting artillery, across the open ground towards the two fords. After it had advanced about 400 yards, however, it came under fire. Once it appeared that A Company had reached the river, B Company started forward. Unfortunately, however, A Company had failed to find the fords, but had been unable to inform Battalion Headquarters because its rear link radio set had been hit and was inoperable. While the rest of his company took cover in ditches on the west bank of the river, Captain Baker took nine men and swam across. On landing on the far side, they succeeded in driving the enemy from the railway embankment but soon found themselves running low on ammunition. By then the smoke laid down by the artillery was thinning out and B Company, commanded by Major E. J. O'B. Croker, had become pinned down in a hedgerow by machine gun and artillery fire from St Julien and from the high ground on the eastern side of the valley. After more smoke had been put down, however, the company managed to advance to some dykes where it became pinned down once more. On the far bank, Captain Baker and his men had run out of ammunition and, as the rest of A Company were unable to join them, they had no option but to withdraw and swim back to the west bank.

With 12th Parachute Battalion's two leading companies pinned down, and with the enemy once more in possession of the railway embankment which dominated all the approaches, Brigadier Nigel Poett realised that there was no chance of achieving success through a daylight attack and ordered the assault to be called off. For the next few hours until dusk fell, A and B Companies were forced to remain in their exposed positions, cut off from the rest of 12th Parachute Battalion. Only after nightfall were they able to withdraw, having suffered one officer and 15 men killed as well as some 50 wounded.

Meanwhile, 13th Parachute Battalion had succeeded in working its way into the town and had crossed the bridge spanning the western channel into the centre of the town. However, it had met stiff opposition and had not managed to clear the main street and thus reach the bridge over the eastern channel. Moreover, the enemy had set fire to several buildings, and this added to the battalion's problems. At this point a troop of Cromwell tanks of 6th Airborne Armoured Reconnaissance Regiment moved up in support, crossing the western channel via a ford rapidly constructed by sappers using an armoured bulldozer. After giving covering fire for a while, however, the tanks were forced to withdraw because of their vulnerability to anti-tank guns and the risk of catching fire from the blazing buildings around them.

On the following morning, 23 August, Brigadier Nigel Poett and Lieutenant Colonel Peter Luard carried out a reconnaissance. By then a patrol from 13th Parachute Battalion, led by Captain F. H. Skeate, had succeeded in crossing the eastern channel via the one remaining intact girder of one of the two bridges which had been blown by the enemy just before the battalion reached them on the previous day. Brigadier Poett considered there was a better chance of establishing a bridgehead on the eastern bank, and ordered Lieutenent Colonel Luard to carry out a crossing a rapidly as possible. Within a short space of time B Company had crossed the river, but soon encountered strong resistance. A Company moved forward to support B Company while C Company remained in reserve and established a firm base at the bridge, at the same time keeping a watchful eye on the battalion's left flank. During the next three hours or so, A and B Companies fought hard against enemy troops in well prepared positions. At 1200 hours the Second in Command, Major Gerald Ford, reported to Lieutenant Colonel Luard that the two companies were held up and that the enemy were attempting to infiltrate their positions. Realising that the bridgehead was too weak and that the attack had little chance of success, Brigadier Poett ordered 13th Parachute Battalion to withdraw to the west bank through a firm base established by 7th Parachute Battalion. A and B Companies withdrew, wading the river with the aid of a rope. One badly wounded man was carried across on a door while Major Nobby Clark gave covering fire with his .45 pistol.

At dawn on 24 August reconnaissance patrols from 7th Parachute Battalion reported that the enemy had withdrawn during the night. Consequently the battalion, on orders from the brigade commander, advanced with all haste across the river and up on to the high ground on the eastern side of the valley, followed shortly afterwards by the other two battalions. The brigade continued to push forward without encountering any resistance until it arrived at a point east of the railway line at Bourg. After meeting some opposition, the high ground at Bourg was taken and secured. At this point Brigadier Poett was told to halt his advance and limit his units to patrolling while 1st Special Service Brigade moved through to take up the van.

The division's front was at this point some ten miles wide. On the left were 6th Airlanding Brigade and the Belgian Brigade, which were advancing on a twin axis towards the towns of Honfleur and Foulbec, while the rest of 6th Airborne Division advanced along the line of the road leading to Pont Audemer. Owing to the lack of resistance, the rate of advance was swift on the southern route until the leading elements of the division arrived on the outskirts of the town of Beuzeville, where strong opposition was encountered once again.

On the morning of 25 August, after 1st Special Service Brigade had been held up outside the town, 3rd Parachute Brigade and 4th Special Service Brigade were ordered to clear the enemy from the town. As they advanced, elements of 3rd Parachute Brigade came under heavy mortar fire. 8th Parachute Battalion, with the support of a troop of Cromwell tanks of 6th Airborne Armoured Reconnaissance Regiment, attacked a farm to the south of the town which was taken and occupied.

During the evening Major General Gale received his orders from Lieutenant General Sir John Crocker for operations for the next day. These specified boundaries for 6th Airborne Division's operations, and these excluded Pont Audemer, which would be on the axis of advance of 49th Infantry Division. However, Gale was convinced that his leading elements were nearer to Pont Audemer than those of 49th Infantry Division, and that they were better placed to reach the town and seize the bridge over the River Risle before the Germans could destroy it. The task of leading the race for the bridge was given to the Princess Irene of The Netherlands Brigade, which was placed under command of 5th Parachute Brigade. On the early morning of 26 August, mounted on the Cromwell tanks of A Squadron 6th Airborne Armoured Reconnaissance Regiment, the Dutchmen raced for Pont Audemer. Unfortunately they were just too late, as the enemy had blown the bridge 20 minutes before they arrived. Soon afterwards, 5th Parachute Brigade reached Pont Audemer after a high-speed march, subsequently occupying the town while the Dutch brigade deployed to positions on the high ground dominating the river.

Meanwhile, 6th Airlanding Brigade and the Belgian Brigade had been advancing rapidly towards the town of Berville sur Mer, which is beyond Honfleur. By 0800 hours on 26 August it was discovered that the enemy had withdrawn and the advances became even more rapid. By the afternoon the town had been occupied. That night found the Belgians in Berville, the 2nd Battalion The Oxfordshire & Buckinghamshire Light

Infantry deployed in Foulbec on the right flank, and the 1st Battalion The Royal Ulster Rifles on the left in the area of a hamlet called La Judee.

On 27 August the division was ordered to concentrate in the area between Honfleur and Pont Audemer. Its task in Normandy was completed, and it was to return to England in early September. Since landing on 6 June it had been in action continually for almost three months and had suffered 4,457 casualties: 821 killed, 2,709 wounded and 927 missing. During the final ten days of action since 17 August it had liberated 400 square miles of enemy occupied territory and taken over 1,000 prisoners.

CHAPTER 5
1st Airborne Division Operations at Arnhem, September 1944

By mid-September 1944 the Allied forces had drawn nearer to Germany's borders and were encountering stiff resistance. The Germans had sent all the troops they could muster to hold the Siegfried Line, which had already been reached by the 1st US Army. Officer cadet schools, training battalions and even convalescent units had been pressed into service. Added to these were six Luftwaffe parachute regiments, with two others formed from men recovering in convalescent depots. Despite the dubious standards of fitness and training of some of them, however, these units succeeded in slowing down the Allied advance, which was also hampered by logistical problems. The leading elements of General Dempsey's 2nd Army in the far north, which had advanced from the River Seine to a line along the River Meuse and the Escaut Canal subsequently found themselves frequently held up by small rearguard units of infantry supported by tanks and self-propelled guns.

A month previously, on 17 August, General Montgomery, the commander of 21st Army Group, had proposed that a major thrust by the 40 divisions of 12th US and 21st British Army Groups be carried out northeastwards. His own 21st Army Group would advance on the western flank to clear the channel coast, the Pas de Calais and West Flanders and take Antwerp and southern Holland, while General Omar Bradley's 12th Army Group would advance on the eastern flank, with the Ardennes on its right, to take Aachen and Cologne. Thereafter, bridgeheads would be established for a subsequent advance into northern Germany via the Ruhr. While he conceded that there was an alternative opportunity for another thrust by General George Patton's 3rd US Army further to the south via Metz and the Saar, Mongomery maintained that the northern one was likely to provide the best and quickest results. He dismissed the idea of two simultaneous advances because such a plan would divide the logistical resources which would be needed to maintain the momentum of a single strong penetration deep into Germany. Montgomery, who was convinced that the Germans were on the edge of collapse, was concerned that any slackening in the momentum of the Allied advance would result in further stiffening of opposition as the enemy gained extra time to prepare their defences against an invasion of Germany. He was well aware of the problems being caused by the lack of ports through which supplies could be landed. This, combined with the speed at which the Allied forces were advancing, had resulted in a shortage of everything including rations, ammunition and fuel. All available transport, including artillery tractors and tank transporters, had been commandeered to transport supplies to the advancing divisions.

Other Allied commanders, such as Patton, also believed that pressure should be maintained on the Germans and that a single strong thrust to Berlin would bring a speedy end to the war. Montgomery initially thought that he convinced General Omar Bradley of his plan, but it transpired that the latter favoured a thrust by his own 12th US Army Group eastwards towards Metz and the Saar. The Supreme Allied Commander, General Eisenhower, had listened to Montgomery's arguments but had been fully aware that adoption of the British general's plan would have meant halting Lieutenant General George Patton's 3rd US Army and diverting logistical resources away from it. This in itself would have caused him major political problems. He had thus decided that a broad-front strategy was to be adopted, and on 23 August directed that 21st Army Group was to take the Ruhr and Antwerp, while 12th US Army Group, whose 1st US Army would support 21st Army Group on its left, was to concentrate its main effort on capturing Metz and the Saar.

Montgomery, who was promoted Field Marshal on 1 September, was still convinced that Eisenhower's approach was wrong, and on 4 September had signalled the Supreme Allied Commander, once again strongly putting the case for a thrust to the north. The two men met on 10 September in Eisenhower's aircraft at an airfield at Brussels. During the meeting Montgomery became somewhat heated in criticising Eisenhower's plans. Nevertheless, the Supreme Allied Commander continued to reject the idea of a single strong thrust and insisted that the port of Antwerp had to be taken and brought into operation before any advance into Germany could begin. At that point Montgomery presented Eisenhower with information concerning German V-2 rocket attacks on England which were being launched from sites in Holland. He stressed that this alone meant that an advance into Holland had to be carried out at the earliest opportunity. This would be carried out by 2nd Army, whose proposed route would take it over several canals and rivers, five of which were major obstacles: the Wilhelmina Canal, the Zuid Willemsvaart Canal, and the Rivers Maas, Rhine and Lower Rhine. These were crossed respectively by bridges at Son, Veghel, Grave, Nijmegen and Arnhem. To facilitate the progress of 2nd Army, he proposed to use elements of the 1st Allied Airborne Army, which had been allocated to him, to seize the bridges and crossing beforehand, providing a corridor along which the divisions of 2nd Army could advance rapidly, eventually crossing over into Germany and subsequently advancing south-eastwards into the Ruhr.

Eisenhower was impressed by Montgomery's plan. Although he appreciated that it would mean the diversion of supplies from 3rd US Army and a delay in the opening up of Antwerp, he also realised that it would inject renewed momentum into the slowing Allied advance and would carry the pursuit of the enemy into Germany itself. However, Eisenhower placed limitations on the operation and emphasised that it was "merely an extension of the northern advance to the Rhine and the Ruhr". Montgomery attempted to argue, but the Supreme Allied Commander was adamant and Montgomery was forced to accept that condition. The plan was codenamed Operation 'Market Garden' — 'Market' was the airborne part of the operation, while 'Garden' covered the advance along the corridor by armoured formations of General Miles Dempsey's 2nd Army. Immediately after his meeting with Eisenhower, Montgomery briefed the commander of 1st Airborne Corps, Lieutenant General 'Boy' Browning, on the proposed airborne operation. In addition to seizing and holding five major bridges and a series of crossings, his airborne forces would also have to hold a 64-mile-long corridor stretching from the Dutch border to Arnhem. Whilst this was the type of operation for which airborne forces had been designed, it was a huge task, and Browning was uneasy that his corps was being overcommitted. Browning returned to England, having been told by Montgomery that planning and preparations for the operation were to be carried out with the utmost speed and that the attack itself was to be mounted within a matter of days. On being pressed for a date by which 1st Airborne Corps could be ready, he had proposed 15 or 16 September.

On his arrival at his headquarters Browning contacted the commander of 1st Allied Airborne Army, Lieutenant General Louis Brereton, and informed him of the planned operation before summoning the commander of 1st Airborne Division, Major General Roy Urquhart, to give him his orders. These were short and to the point. After indicating on an operations map where the 82nd and 101st US Airborne Divisions would be landing in the areas of Eindhoven and Nijmegen respectively, Browning drew a circle around the town of Arnhem. Pointing to the road bridge crossing the Lower Rhine, he told Urquhart that it was to be taken and held. Urquhart had only six days in which to plan his division's part of the operation. Two major problems faced him: the shortage of aircraft and the reported presence of heavy enemy anti-aircraft defences in the area of Arnhem which precluded

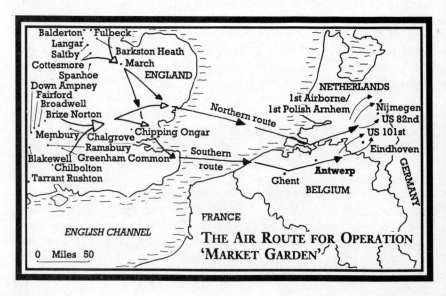

THE AIR ROUTE FOR OPERATION 'MARKET GARDEN'

any landings close to the bridge itself. He and his staff calculated that at least 130 aircraft were required for each of his brigades, but he had been allocated only ten squadrons of Nos. 38 and 46 Groups RAF to tow the gliders which would carry 1st Airlanding Brigade, divisional troops and his headquarters, and the Dakotas of 9th Troop Carrier Command USAAF to transport his two parachute brigades. Urquhart submitted a request for another 40 aircraft, but was told that there were none to spare.

The total aircraft requirement for the 1st Airborne Corps task involving three and a half divisions was 3,790: 2,495 aircraft to carry parachutists and 1,295 to tow gliders. Resources available consisted of 1,175 USAAF Dakotas, 130 RAF Dakotas and 240 RAF bombers, making a total of 1,545 aircraft. This meant that only one third of the corps' forces could be lifted at one time or, alternatively, could be transported in two and a half lifts. The allocation of aircraft was thus made as follows:

101st US Airborne Division — 502 Dakotas (incl. 70 glider tugs)
82nd US Airborne Division — 530 Dakotas (incl. 50 glider tugs)
1st Airborne Division — 463 Dakotas (143 USAAF
                                         para a/c and 320 RAF glider tugs)
Headquarters 1st Airborne Corps — 38 RAF glider tugs

Consequently, Urquhart had no choice but to plan to land his division in three lifts. This obviously entailed major risks: the leading elements would have to take and secure the objectives as well as defending the dropping and landing zones while waiting for the remainder of the division to arrive. Surprise would be lost by that stage, and the enemy would be prepared for further landings. Moreover, any strong enemy counterattack on the leading elements of the division could spell disaster for the operation.

It was suggested by the RAF that the first lift should be flown in just before dawn, the second taking place later on the same day and the third on the following day. This idea was rejected by Lieutenant General Brereton because of the inability of the USAAF crews of 9th US Troop Carrier Command to fly at night. However, the RAF could have performed such a task and could also have carried out a drop on the night of D/D+1.

The suspected presence of heavy enemy anti-aircraft defences, combined with reports from Dutch Army sources on the local terrain, limited Urquhart's options when it came to selecting dropping and landing zones. The RAF insisted that dropping troops near the bridge was out of the question, and maintained that the area of flat land to the south of the river, which otherwise appeared ideal, was unsuitable because it was swampy and was interlaced with deep dykes. This view was supported by reports from the intelligence staff and from the Dutch Resistance, which had provided detailed descriptions of the area. An area of heathland some four miles to the north of the town was considered suitable as a dropping zone, being hard sandy ground, but was too small an area for use as a landing zone by gliders. The RAF did, however, agree to dropping elements of the third lift south of the river near the bridge, as it was assumed that all enemy flak defences would have been neutralized beforehand.

Initially, Urquhart was inclined to reject the RAF's refusal to accept the areas around the bridge and to the south of the river as dropping and landing zones. Attempts were made to persuade the RAF to drop some elements south of the river, but to no avail. Urquhart himself, bearing in mind the experiences of 6th Airborne Division in Normandy, and having been denied the opportunity of dropping or landing his troops near their objectives, accepted the next best alternative, which was to land his forces together and thus enable them to form up as quickly as possible. Eventually he selected five dropping and landing zones to the west of the town: two (LZs 'L' and 'S') to the north of the railway line running between Arnhem and Utrecht; one (DZ 'Y') on Ginkel Heath; and two (DZ and LZ 'X' and LZ 'Z') on Renkum Heath, south of the line. The area chosen was far from ideal, as it was some eight miles from the bridge and there was the danger that the second lift would by then be prevented from linking up with the leading elements of the division holding the objective. Moreover, some of those in the first lift would have to remain on the DZs and LZs to hold them until the remainder of the division had landed, leaving fewer men to take and secure the bridge. However, the nature of the terrain was such that it was suitable for use by parachutists and gliders. In addition to the five main dropping and landing zones, a sixth (DZ 'K') was selected south of the town for use by 1st Polish Independent Parachute Brigade, which would be dropped by USAAF aircraft on the morning of the third day, enemy flak defences supposedly having been neutralised by then. Finally, a supply dropping point (SDP 'V') was located on the north-western outskirts of Arnhem, east of LZ 'L', which would be within the planned perimeter.

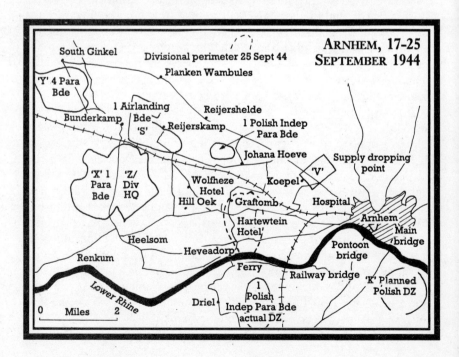

Right: The objective of C Company 2nd Para Bn: the 'Wurzburg' radar site on the French coast at Bruneval. (Imperial War Museum)

Right: 'C' Company 2nd Para Bn arriving at Portsmouth on one of the gunboats which brought it home after the successful raid on Bruneval. Major Johnny Frost is second from the left on the vessel's bridge. (Imperial War Museum)

Right: Flight Sergeant Cox, the RAF radar expert who accompanied C Company 2nd Para Bn on the raid on Bruneval, on his return talks to Group Captain Sir Nigel Norman who was in command of the RAF element of the operation. (Imperial War Museum)

Left: A rigorous programme of physical fitness training was a feature of the selection course for Airborne Forces from the very beginning. Trainees are shown here, at the Airborne Forces Depot at Hardwick Hall, carrying out exercises with logs. (Imperial War Museum)

Below: Trainees were tested for any susceptibility to air sickness by being swung for twenty minutes in a stretcher suspended by ropes. A medical officer is shown here checking a trainee beforehand. (Imperial War Museum)

Right: Flight drills and control of the parachute were learned and practised on a 'trapeze'. In the background of this picture is a group of men standing on a mock-up of a Whitley aperture on which they are being taught exit drills. (Imperial War Museum)

Right: Two sticks of trainees about to make their first exit from a balloon at Tatton Park, the DZ used by No. 1 Parachute Training School at Ringway. (Imperial War Museum)

Left: The interior of a Whitley just before a stick carries out a descent. 'Number One' has just swung his legs into the aperture and is awaiting the command to exit. (Imperial War Museum)

Right: Men of 1st Para Bn setting off on a patrol in the Beja area of Tunisia at the end of December 1942. (Imperial War Museum)

Right: A section commander and Bren gunner of 4th Para Bn in position during an exercise in the Sousse area of Tunisia in July 1943. (Imperial War Museum)

Left: Parachutists and equipment containers being dropped over the DZ at Tatton Park. (Imperial War Museum)

Right: A Vickers medium machine-gun in action in North Africa in 1943. (Imperial War Museum)

Left: A PIAT team covers a likely approach for 'enemy' armour during an exercise in North Africa in 1943. (Imperial War Museum)

Right: Men of 1st Canadian Para Bn being inspected by His Majesty King George VI during a visit to 6th Airborne Div in May 1943. Behind him is Lieutenant General 'Boy' Browning. (Imperial War Museum)

Left: A member of a rifle section of 4th Para Bn throws a No. 36 grenade during training in North Africa in July 1943. (Imperial War Museum)

Right: His Majesty The King and Brigadier James Hill discuss the PIAT while Her Majesty Queen Elizabeth talks to a sniper during the visit by the Royal Family to 6th Airborne Div in May 1943. Standing beside Princess Elizabeth is Lieutenant Colonel Shamus Hickie, AA & QMG 6th Airborne Div. (Imperial War Museum)

Left: A section of 4th Para Bn carries out a final assault under cover of smoke during an exercise in North Africa in July 1943. (Imperial War Museum)

Above: General Montgomery inspects 13th Para Bn during his visit to 6th Airborne Div before D-Day. Behind him is the CO, Lieutenant Colonel Peter Luard. (Imperial War Museum)

Below: Major General Richard Gale addresses men of 6th Airborne Div on the eve of the invasion of Normandy. (Imperial War Museum)

Above: Lieutenant Bob Midwood of 22nd Indep Coy, the divisional pathfinder unit, briefs members of his stick on the tasks they will carry out during the early hours of D-Day. (Imperial War Museum)

Right: Parachutes are drawn and fitted on 5 June 1944, in preparation for the airborne invasion of Normandy the following day. (Imperial War Museum)

Right: A stick of 22nd Independent Coy boards the Albemarle bomber that will drop it over Normandy in the early hours of 6 June 1944. (Imperial War Museum)

Above: The high level of morale in 6th Airborne Div on the eve of battle is reflected in the faces of these parachutists en route to Normandy in a Halifax bomber on the night of 5/6 June 1944. (Imperial War Museum)

Below: These men of 12th Para Bn found themselves dropped behind enemy lines, miles from their dropping zone, in the early hours of 6 June 1944. They engaged in several minor actions with German troops during the following three days before rejoining their unit. (Imperial War Museum)

Above: The northern edge of the village of Breville after the fierce battle that took place there on 12 June 1944. This picture was taken from an enemy anti-tank gun position that overlooked 12th Para Bn's axis of attack. (Imperial War Museum)

Below: Major John Cramphorn, commanding A Coy 13th Para Bn, debriefs three of his men who landed in Troarn which lay to the south east of DZ 'N' on which they should have landed the morning of D-Day. They avoided capture with the help of the French Resistance but were unable to rejoin their unit until after the fall of Caen. Left to right: CSM McParlan, Major Cramphorn, Private Bardsley and Lance Corporal West. (Imperial War Museum)

Above: Elements of 1st Airborne Div landing among gliders on the dropping and landing zone at Wolfheze, north west of Arnhem, on the morning of 17 September 1944. (Imperial War Museum)

Left: A defensive position at one of the brigade headquarters on the day after 1st Airborne Division landed in the area of Arnhem. (Imperial War Museum)

Bottom left: Men of 'C' Troop 1st Abn Recce Sqn covering a crossroads at Wolfheze, near Arnhem. (Imperial War Museum)

Above: A Vickers MMG crew trains its weapon on some houses containing enemy snipers in the area of Arnhem. (Imperial War Museum)

Below: An aerial view of the Arnhem bridge, showing the burnt-out enemy vehicles at the end near 2nd Para Bn's positions. (Imperial War Museum)

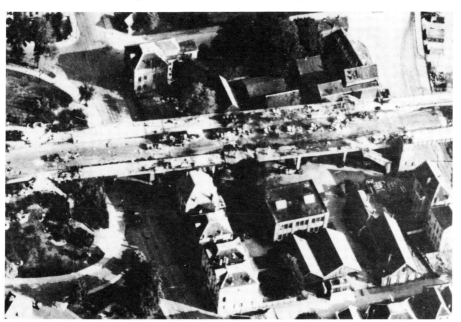

Left: Four men of 1st Para Bn in a position in a shell hole. (Imperial War Museum)

Right: A 6-pounder anti-tank gun in action, in the area of Oosterbeek, against an enemy self-propelled gun at a range of about 80 yards. (Imperial War Museum)

Right: A patrol clears a ruined house in Oosterbeek. (Imperial War Museum)

Left: A Bren gun position in a wood in the area of Oosterbeek. The two men in this picture are Private Jury and Private Malcolm. (Imperial War Museum)

Right: A soldier engages enemy snipers from the ruins of a house in Oosterbeek. (Imperial War Museum)

Above: During the winter fighting in the Ardennes in January 1945, a sniper and patrol commander of 9th Para Bn move forward cautiously to the edge of a wood to observe the terrain in front of them. (Imperial War Museum)

Left: On 24 March 1945, men of 6th Airborne Div don their parachutes while waiting beside the Dakota in which they will shortly embark for Operation 'Varsity', the crossing of the Rhine. (Imperial War Museum)

1st Parachute Brigade and the major part of 1st Airlanding Brigade would land on the first day. 4th Parachute Brigade, together with the remainder of 1st Airlanding Brigade, would be flown on the second day. General Stanislav Sosabowski's 1st Polish Independent Parachute Brigade would complete the division's order of battle on the ground when it arrived on the third day. Meanwhile, Major General Maxwell D. Taylor's 101st US Airborne Division would land and capture the bridges between Eindhoven and Veghel. Its objectives consisted of two canal crossing points and nine road and railway bridges along the 15-mile stretch of road in its sector. Taylor's plan involved the 502nd and 506th Parachute Infantry Regiments landing in the centre between Eindhoven and Veghel, while the 501st would be dropped on two DZs a few hundred yards north and west of Veghel. Its task would be to capture four of the bridges and one of the canal crossings, at Veghel itself, which spanned the River Aa and the Willems Canal.

Brigadier General James Gavin's 82nd US Airborne Division had an equally awesome task. In addition to taking the bridge over the River Maas at Grave, as well as at least one of the railway bridges over the Maas-Waal Canal, it was to seize the bridge which crossed the River Waal at Nijmegen. In addition, it was also to secure and hold the Groesbeek Heights — the high ground between Nijmegen and Groesbeek which dominated the area. The 505th and 508th Parachute Infantry Regiments, accompanied by General Gavin's headquarters, would land in two drops a mile and a half from the Groesbeek Heights and about four miles south west of Nijmegen. The 504th would be dropped on the western side of the heights between the River Maas and the Maas-Waal Canal, a mile from eastern end of the bridge at Grave and two miles from the canal bridges. A company of the 504th would also be dropped a mile from the western end of the Grave bridge, enabling the regiment to attack it from both sides of the river.

Both American commanders were concerned about one factor. While most of their parachute infantry would land on the first day, their artillery, engineers and transport would not arrive until the second and third days of the operation. Nevertheless, they had confidence in their troops and in their ability to carry out the tasks given to them.

The enemy forces along the route to be followed by 30th Corps, the leading formation in 2nd Army, were reported to consist of a small force of six infantry battalions supported by a small amount of artillery and armour. Reports from the Dutch Resistance indicated that a further six battalions, consisting of medically downgraded troops, were stationed in the area of Nijmegen, and that a number of understrength armoured units, which were refitting and reorganising, were based around Arnhem. On 12 September, intelligence reports from 21st Army Group stated that enemy units were understrength, short of equipment and suffering from low morale. Six days later, on 18 September, the day after the start of the operation, further intelligence reports from both 21st Army Group and 2nd Army would still maintain that both the northern and southern areas of Holland were thinly held by enemy forces. Their optimism was such that when the Dutch

Resistance reported the presence of SS troops, including armour, east of the River Ijssel and near Arnhem, the intelligence staffs at both formations refused to regard the report as reliable. However, only two days before the operation was to be launched the Chief of Intelligence at SHAEF, Major General Sir Kenneth Strong, reported the presence of German armour to Lieutenant General Walter Bedell Smith, Chief of Staff to the Supreme Allied Commander. Strong informed Smith that the 9th *Hohenstaufen* and 10th *Frundsberg* SS Panzer Divisions, which had been withdrawn from Normandy before the German retreat, were in the area of Arnhem. This news alarmed General Smith sufficiently for him to bring it to Eisenhower's attention immediately and to advise him that a second airborne division should be landed in the Arnhem area. Eisenhower gave the matter urgent consideration, but was wary of ordering any changes to the operational plan at the risk of incurring the wrath of Field Marshal Mongomery. He decided that any alteration could only be decided by Montgomery, and accordingly despatched his Chief of Staff to Headquarters 21st Army Group at Brussels. However, Smith's fears fell on deaf ears when he advised Montgomery of the presence of the German armour in the Arnhem area; indeed, Montgomery belittled them and the idea of any alteration to the plan.

Thus the general opinion amongst the intelligence staffs at 21st Army Group, 2nd Army and 1st Allied Airborne Army, was that enemy forces around the Arnhem area were at approximately only brigade strength in addition to the heavy anti-aircraft defences thought to be in the area. One individual at Headquarters 1st Airborne Corps, however, did not share this optimism. Major Brian Urquhart, the GSO 2 (Intelligence), was convinced that there was a large concentration of German armour in the Arnhem area. He was in possession of Dutch Resistance reports and aerial reconnaissance photographs which confirmed his belief, and was sufficiently concerned to request a low-level photo-reconnaissance sortie to be carried out over the area by the RAF. The results, in the form of five oblique-angle photographs which clearly showed tanks, confirmed his suspicions, and he brought them to the attention of Lieutenant General Browning without delay. The corps commander, however, made light of the photographs and dismissed Urquhart's fears. Shortly afterwards, Urquhart was removed from his post and sent back to Britain on sick leave on the grounds that he was suffering from nervous exhaustion.

Had Urquhart's warnings had been taken seriously and the operational plan been altered accordingly, it is unlikely that it would have had much effect on the determination of 1st Airborne Division to go to war again. Officers and men had been champing at the bit and had grown impatient with the enforced waiting. One officer was later quoted as saying: "The men were truly and deeply thankful. They'd had to wait far too long." Another commented: "Those responsible for planning were determined that we should see something of the party before it was too late, and were not particular as to how or where we made our entrance." Within the division, as Major General Roy Urquhart himself stated: "There was a dangerous mixture of ennui and cynicism slowly creeping into our lives. We were trained to a fine edge and I knew that if we didn't get into battle soon, we would lose it. We were ready and willing to accept anything, with all the 'ifs'."

While 6th Airborne Division was earning its laurels in Normandy, 1st Airborne Division had been continuing to prepare itself for future action. Since its return to Britain at the end of 1943, the gaps in the ranks of its two parachute brigades caused by the heavy casualties during the Sicily campaign had been filled by trained parachutists, and the period from January until the end of May 1944 had been spent re-equipping all of its units. During the period of operations in Normandy, the division had been warned to be ready to take part in a total of 17 airborne operations. These had all been cancelled because of adverse weather conditions, because enemy opposition in the area was too strong, or because the rapid advance of the Allied armoured formations had dispensed with the need for them. On four occasions the division had been briefed and had moved to the mounting airfields but the operations had been cancelled at the very last moment.

Major General Urquhart gave his orders for the operation to his four brigade commanders on the afternoon of 12 September. In outline, his plan was as follows.

On the morning of 17 September, pathfinders of 21st Independent Parachute Company, commanded by Major B. A. 'Boy' Wilson, would land and mark out the three dropping and landing zones to be used in the first lift. They would be followed by the major part of 1st Airlanding Brigade, commanded by Brigadier Philip 'Pip' Hicks, which would secure and hold the DZs and LZs, and Brigadier Gerald Lathbury's 1st Parachute Brigade, which was to make its way with all speed to Arnhem, where it would capture the railway bridge south of Oosterbeek, the Arnhem bridge itself and a pontoon bridge half a mile to the west. Accompanying the two brigades in the first lift would be 1st Airborne Reconnaissance Squadron, commanded by Major Freddy Gough, which would make a dash in its armed jeeps for the Arnhem bridge, which it would seize and hold until the arrival of 1st Parachute Brigade. In addition to the two brigades and the reconnaissance squadron, the first lift would also include Tactical Head-quarters 1st Airborne Division, 1st Airlanding Light Regiment RA (less one battery), 1st Airlanding Anti-Tank Battery RA, 1st Parachute Squadron RE, 9th Field Company RE, 16th Parachute Field Ambulance and 181st Airlanding Field Ambulance.

2nd Parachute Battalion, under Lieutenant Colonel Johnny Frost, would move into Arnhem via Heelsum and the southern edge of Oosterbeek, making its way along the northern bank of the Lower Rhine. On reaching the bridge, where it would relieve 1st Airborne Reconnais-sance Squadron, the battalion would take up positions on both banks. 3rd Parachute Battalion, commanded by Lieutenant Colonel Tony Fitch would move through Arnhem via Heelsum and Oosterbeek and approach the bridge from the north, taking up positions on its north-eastern approach. Lieutenant Colonel David Dobie's 1st Parachute Battalion initially would be in reserve, but thereafter would move to the high ground immediately north of the town.

On the morning of the second day, 18 September, 4th Parachute Brigade would land together with a battery of 1st Airlanding Light Regiment RA, 4th Parachute Squadron RE, 133rd Parachute Field Ambulance, the rest of 1st Airlanding Brigade, 2nd Airlanding Anti-Tank Battery RA and those divisional troops who had not landed with the first lift on the first day. Its task would be to establish a northern sector, linking up with 1st Parachute Battalion. 1st Airlanding Brigade, meanwhile, would move into the town and establish the western sector of the bridgehead.

On its arrival on the morning of the third day, 1st Polish Independent Parachute Brigade, after landing on DZ 'K' just south of Arnhem bridge, would cross over and deploy into the eastern suburbs of the town. This would result in the complete establishment of the bridgehead on the northern side of the river, awaiting the arrival of 2nd Army from the south.

The morning of Sunday 17 September dawned, any mist having cleared by 0800 hours, when the men of 1st Airborne Division were waiting to emplane. At 0945 hours the first aircraft took off, and soon the massive aerial armada was forming up over south-eastern England before heading for Holland. In the lead was 21st Independent Parachute Company. At approximately 1300 hours Major 'Boy' Wilson and his pathfinders landed. As they did so they came under fire from a small group of Germans who immediately surrendered. Two of their number had been hit, but the pathfinders busied themselves with laying out the coloured cloth drop-zone markers and setting up their Eureka radio beacons to guide in the approaching transport aircraft. At 1330 hours the 145 Horsa gliders carrying 1st Airlanding Brigade, less two companies of the 2nd Battalion The South Staffordshire Regiment, arrived on LZ 'S'. Ten minutes later another 150 gliders, including 18 Hamilcars, carrying Tactical Headquarters 1st Airborne Division, 1st Airborne Reconnaissance Squadron, 1st Airlanding Light Regiment RA (less one battery), two airlanding anti-tank batteries and half of 1st Parachute Brigade's transport, landed safely on LZ 'Z'. These were followed at 1400 hours by 1st Parachute Brigade Group and the advance party of 4th Parachute Brigade, which landed intact.

The landings were unopposed, the enemy in the area of the DZs and LZs consisting of small groups who put up no resistance. Soon after 1500 hours 2nd and 3rd Parachute Battalions, having rallied and joined up with their transport, were on the move towards Arnhem. 1st Parachute Battalion, which was in reserve, moved off at 1530 hours. Although the landings had proceeded almost without mishap, 1st Airborne Reconnaissance Squadron encountered difficulties in unloading some of its gliders. Twenty of its total of 22 Horsas had landed safely on the LZ, but six had made heavy landings. It took some time for the jeeps to be unloaded from them and thus it was not until 1530 hours that the squadron, less its reserve troop, numbering 28 jeeps, moved off towards the level crossing at Wolfheze. Its main task was to move as fast as possible to the Arnhem bridge, which it was to capture in a *coup de main* attack. The squadron reached the level crossing and headed down a track which ran parallel to the railway line towards Arnhem. Having covered about 600 yards C Troop, which was in the lead, came under fire from troops of the 16th SS Panzer Grenadier Depot Battalion, who were in positions on the railway embankment and on a wooded ridge to the north. They had been on exercise in the woods around Wolfheze when the landings had taken place. During the ensuing action the squadron suffered casualties as the enemy engaged it with machine guns, mortars and snipers. Some two hours later the squadron withdrew after being relieved by some glider pilots.

Meanwhile, the three battalions of 1st Parachute Brigade were advancing towards Arnhem along three different routes. 2nd Parachute Battalion moved towards the village of Heelsum, taking the southern route into Arnhem along the river. 3rd Parachute Battalion moved in a south-easterly direction to the Utrechtseweg, the main road to Arnhem, to support 2nd Parachute Battalion at the bridge. 1st Parachute Battalion's route took it towards the main Arnhem–Ede road to the north-east and subsequently into Arnhem itself from the north. 2nd Parachute Battalion pushed on with all speed with A Company, commanded by Major Digby Tatham-Warter, in the lead. On the way the company ambushed a number of enemy vehicles and captured a group of prisoners. As they entered the village the local inhabitants came pouring out of their homes to welcome the battalion with open arms, and it was with difficulty that Frost and his men continued on their way through the throngs of excited men, women and children. On nearing the next village, Heveadorp, A Company came under fire and suffered light casualties. Nevertheless, it pressed on towards Oosterbeek.

On leaving Oosterbeek, Major Victor Dover and C Company headed towards the river and the railway bridge. No sooner had the company reached the bridge and started to cross under cover of smoke and covering fire from some of its Bren guns, than the enemy blew up the bridge, leaving the southernmost span lying half-immersed in the river. Lieutenant Peter Barry, the leading platoon commander, and two of his men were wounded in the blast. As the bridge had been rendered useless, C Company was ordered to move on to its secondary objective, a building reported to house an enemy headquarters.

Meanwhile, A Company had reached a point on the western outskirts of Arnhem near the railway line and had encountered enemy armoured cars which were preventing any further movement along the roads. At the same time, any attempt to cross the railway line itself resulted in heavy machine gun fire and sniping from a feature called Den Brink. Major Douglas Crawley's B Company, which was the battalion's reserve, was despatched by Lieutenant Colonel Frost to deal with the enemy on Den Brink and Major Tatham-Warter called up a 6-pounder anti-tank gun to deal with the armoured cars. At this point Lieutenant Peter Cane, one of the platoon commanders in A Company, was killed. Dusk was falling, and Major

Tatham-Warter led his company through the back gardens of houses and on into Arnhem, where he and his men had another encounter with the enemy. He was followed shortly afterwards by Battalion Headquarters and elements of Headquarter Company, which pushed on quickly through the town to the pontoon bridge, the centre section of which was found to be missing. It was thought at the time that it had been dismantled, but it was later discovered lying alongside the rest of the bridge. Shortly afterwards, Lieutenant Colonel Johnny Frost and his group caught up with A Company, which by 2100 hours had stealthily taken up positions on an embankment near the northern end of the bridge and was watching the traffic crossing to and fro.

While A Company prepared to send a platoon forward to take the southern end of the bridge, Battalion Headquarters commandeered a house overlooking the bridge and Headquarter Company moved into the next building. As they did so, Lieutenant A. J. McDermont and 15 of his men ran up to the embankment and started to cross the bridge to secure the southern end of it. They had not advanced very far before they came under fire from a machine gun in a pillbox. At the same time, an armoured car approached from the southern end of the bridge, opening fire on the battalion's positions. McDermont and his men were forced to withdraw. A second attempt was made shortly afterwards by Lieutenant Jack Grayburn and his platoon, but this was also repulsed. Grayburn himself was wounded in the shoulder, but continued to press forward until forced to withdraw after suffering heavy casualties.

Shortly afterwards, part of Headquarters 1st Parachute Brigade, accompanied by its defence platoon, arrived under Major Tony Hibbert, the Brigade Major. It was followed by the supporting battery commander and his FOOs, a troop of 1st Parachute Squadron RE under Captain Eric Mackay, Major Freddy Gough and the squadron headquarters of 1st Airborne Reconnaissance Squadron, a platoon of divisional RASC troops with a captured enemy truck loaded with ammunition collected from the dropping zone, and a troop of 6-pounder anti-tank guns accompanied by some glider pilots. A platoon of 9th Field Company RE also arrived. During the night further welcome reinforcements arrived in the form of C Company 3rd Parachute Battalion, whose headquarters and one platoon took up positions on the eastern side of the bridge. However, there was no sign of Brigadier Lathbury.

A Company, meanwhile, was still attempting to dislodge the enemy from the bridge. A platoon under Lieutenant Robin Vlasto, accompanied by a small group of sappers equipped with a flamethrower, moved off to carry out an attack from the flank. As they were in the process of doing so, the enemy put in a counterattack supported by mortar fire. This was repulsed and shortly afterwards the pillbox on the bridge was engaged by Vlasto's platoon with PIATs and the flamethrower. This resulted in a number of large explosions and the sound of burning ammunition exploding. A Company was preparing to attempt to cross the bridge again when a convoy of four enemy trucks carrying enemy infantry approached over the bridge from the south. A hail of fire greeted them and they were soon set ablaze, their few surviving occupants surrendering quickly. A major problem faced Lieutenant Colonel Frost, who was out of radio contact with both B and C Companies. The latter company was pinned down by enemy fire near the enemy headquarters building, which was its objective, and was unable to break out to rejoin the battalion. Frost planned to send B Company, which had been detached to take the Den Brink feature, and the brigade headquarters defence platoon across the river using small craft, seen earlier near the pontoons, to attack the southern end of the bridge. C Company would leave its positions at the enemy headquarters and take over B Company's task on Den Brink. A message was taken to B Company, ordering it to move to the area of the pontoon bridge, but it was unable to do so because of heavy enemy activity. A patrol attempted to make its way through to C Company but was unsuccessful. The rest of the battalion spent a quiet night, its signallers continually trying to establish radio contact, but without success.

At dawn on 18 September a number of trucks containing enemy troops drove down the streets dominated by the buildings held by 2nd Parachute Battalion and the other elements of 1st Parachute Brigade, which opened fire at close range, killing most of the occupants. Almost immediately afterwards a column of armoured cars and halftracks of the 9th SS Panzer Division Reconnaissance Company started to cross the bridge, pushing aside the wrecked trucks from the previous action during the night. Somehow avoiding the necklaces of Hawkins grenades laid by the battalion during the night, the first four vehicles drove through at high speed and disappeared into the town. The remaining ten were not so fortunate, and were destroyed by a 6-pounder anti-tank gun and the battalion's PIATs. Shortly afterwards, however, enemy infantry attacked in force and a major battle developed during the next two hours. Heavy fighting took place at close range, buildings being set on fire and destroyed as shells and mortar bombs crashed down into the area. Casualties among the battalion were light, however, and morale was extemely high. The enemy, on the other hand, suffered heavily, losing four more armoured vehicles and a considerable number of men dead or wounded. The guns of 1st Airlanding Light Regiment RA, directed by the battery commander located in an observation post in the attic of a house, provided excellent support for the battalion, their accurate fire helping to break up attacks by enemy infantry. At that point brief radio contact was established with the leading elements of 30th Corps, and shortly afterwards with B Company, who had succeeded in making their way to the area of the pontoon bridge. After fighting their way through the streets, Major Douglas Crawley and the major part of his company arrived to join the battalion. However, there was still no word of C Company. By this time the sounds of fighting could be heard from the west of the town, where 1st and 3rd Parachute Battalions were attempting to break through to the bridge.

3rd Parachute Battalion had set off shortly after 2nd Parachute Battalion, following the middle road to Arnhem. It had rallied with 95 per cent of its strength and just before dusk met up with its gliderborne element with the vehicles and anti-tank guns. At 1600 hours Lieutenant James Cleminson's No. 3 Platoon, which was in the lead, reached a crossroads a mile west of Oosterbeek when an enemy staff car suddenly approached at high speed. This was ambushed from both sides of the road and its occupants killed. Among them was Generalmajor Kussin, the Commandant of Arnhem, who had been paying a visit to the 16th Panzer Grenadier Depot Battalion which was located between Oosterbeek and the nearby village of Wolfheze. The battalion started to push on again, but the enemy brought down mortar fire on the crossroads. As the bombs burst in the trees overhead, the battalion suffered casualties among those who had taken cover in the undergrowth — others who had taken shelter in some old German trenches nearby were more fortunate. Shortly afterwards, Brigadier Lathbury ordered Lieutenant Colonel Tony Fitch to resume his advance. Radio communications were such that Lathbury could not make contact with 1st Parachute Battalion and only occasionally with 2nd Parachute Battalion. As a result, he was becoming increasingly concerned at the lack of information on his brigade's progress. At that point the radio set mounted on the jeep of Major General Urquhart, who had arrived whilst 3rd Parachute Battalion was being mortared, was hit by a mortar bomb and rendered inoperable. Deciding to remain with Lathbury, Urquhart followed 3rd Parachute Battalion as it resumed its cautious advance towards Arnhem.

As dusk was falling B Company, under Major Peter Waddy, came under fire at close range from a self-propelled gun. Having decided how to deal with it, Waddy led a patrol off to the left flank while Lieutenant Cleminson and a group deployed to the right. As both groups were about to engage the gun, a 6-pounder anti-tank detachment appeared on the scene and proceeded to bring its gun into action. It was too slow, however, as the German self-propelled gun quickly put the 6-pounder out of action. Its crew then draped one of the wounded anti-tank gunners across the front of their vehicle, using him as a human shield as it reversed towards the German lines. No sooner had it disappeared and 3rd Parachute Battalion had resumed its march than other self-propelled guns and some armoured cars appeared and prevented any further advance. While the battalion dealt with this problem C Company, commanded by Major Peter Lewis, was despatched in a flanking move to the north. Advancing along a road heading towards the railway, it encountered a number of enemy vehicles near Oosterbeek Station. These were destroyed before the company resumed its advance along the railway line to Arnhem Station. Moving through the town via sidestreets, Lewis and his men succeeded in reaching 2nd Parachute Battalion's positions later that night. This brought the total of Frost's force to 600–700 men.

Meanwhile, the rest of 3rd Parachute Battalion had encountered the 16th Panzer Grenadier Depot Battalion, supported by patrols of the 9th *Hohenstaufen* SS Panzer Division, and was being held up on the outskirts of Oosterbeek, near the Park Hotel at Hartenstein. Dusk was falling, and

Brigadier Lathbury suggested that the battalion should halt for a few hours. While he and Major General Urquhart, together with other members of their group, took shelter in a large house, a patrol from B Company, led by Major Peter Waddy, entered the Park Hotel, where they discovered the remains of a hastily abandoned meal. Waddy then despatched a party to go ahead and find a safe route into Arnhem, but no sooner had it reached the edge of the nearby woods than it came under fire and was forced to withdraw to the hotel.

1st Parachute Battalion had made a perfect drop on the previous day, moving off almost intact from the dropping zone. As it headed towards the high ground north of Arnhem, it too had been met by crowds of jubilant Dutch people waving and cheering. However, as R Company, which was in the lead, approached a crossroads north of the village of Wolfheze at about 1630 hours, it came under fire from armoured patrols of the 9th *Hohenstaufen* SS Panzer Division. Mortar and machine gun fire rained down on the company as it took cover. The failing light and heavy rain compounded the difficulties of engaging the enemy as R Company moved into the woods. Enemy armoured vehicles were moving around in the area of the crossroads, and a company of enemy infantry attacked the unit. The air was filled with the rattle of small arms and the explosions of grenades and mortar bombs as a bitter close-quarters battle was fought. Heavy casualties were suffered on both sides, and by the time R Company managed to extricate itself from the woods and fight its way to the northern outskirts of Arnhem, its strength was reduced by 50 per cent.

Lieutenant Colonel David Dobie had meanwhile decided to bypass the opposition and, leaving R Company heavily engaged, to move eastwards along a track by the edge of the woods before striking north once more to the main road. On reaching it, however, 1st Parachute Battalion encountered tanks and other armour advancing from the south-east and at the same time observed enemy troops digging in in the woods further to the east. At midnight, having waited for a while for R Company to rejoin it, the battalion headed south once more, leaving behind a guide for R Company. At that point, hearing over the radio that 2nd Parachute Battalion was in dire straits at the bridge, Dobie decided that he must go to Frost's aid. His attempts to contact Brigadier Lathbury were unsuccessful and so, taking the responsibility for departing from the plan, Dobie issued orders for the battalion to head for the bridge later that night.

Dawn on Monday 18 September found 3rd Parachute Battalion resuming its advance towards Arnhem after spending most of the night near the Hartenstein Hotel in Oosterbeek. Having moved off through Oosterbeek at 0430 hours, it joined the southernmost road running alongside the river. B Company was again in the lead, followed by Lieutenant Colonel Fitch and his battalion headquarters and some sappers. They were accompanied by Major General Urquhart and Brigadier Lathbury. B Company set a fast pace, passing under the railway bridge at 0530 hours — so much so that, in the dark, A Company, Headquarter Company, the Mortar and Machine Gun Platoons, together with some anti-tank guns, became separated and cut off. On reaching the outskirts of Arnhem, near the St Elizabeth Hospital, the battalion was held up at the junction where the southernmost road joined the central one. There it encountered tanks and self-propelled guns which brought down heavy fire whilst enemy infantry sniped at it and machine-gunned it from the upper storeys of buildings. Before long the battalion was surrounded as more German units closed up around it.

Meanwhile, 1st Parachute Battalion had set off at 0100 hours for the bridge. After crossing the railway at Oosterbeek Station, it turned on to the main road to Arnhem. Shortly afterwards, at 0430 hours, S Company, which was in the lead, came under heavy fire from mortars, sustained-fire machine guns and armoured cars sited on some high ground above a railway bridge to the front. The company responded with a left flanking attack and succeeded in clearing the enemy, but suffered 30 casualties in the process. During this action one of 1st Airlanding Light Regiment's FOOs appeared in a jeep en route to divisional headquarters to report on the situation at the Arnhem bridge. After talking to him, Lieutenant Colonel Dobie decided to continue his move direct to the bridge, and by 0630 hours 1st Parachute Battalion was once again heading for the railway bridge on the southern route along which 3rd Parachute Battalion had, unbeknown to him, passed a few hours earlier. Some 30 minutes later the battalion reached the railway bridge, where it found 3rd Parachute Battalion's Headquarter Company, including some anti-tank guns and detachments of the Machine Gun Platoon, which it added to its own depleted strength.

By now it was dawn, and the enemy brought down mortar fire on the area around the railway bridge. T Company, commanded by Major Chris Perrin-Brown, encountered the enemy in strength in some houses and a factory some 400 yards beyond the bridge, and a number of armoured vehicles were seen on Den Brink. Supported by the guns of 1st Airlanding Light Regiment RA and the battalion's own mortars, together with some of those of 3rd Parachute Battalion, the company put in an attack on some houses on the crossroads nearby, but was held up by an enemy 20mm cannon which opened fire from the factory. At that point, A Company 3rd Parachute Battalion, commanded by Major Mervyn Dennison, arrived. Another attack was mounted, with A Company on the left of the road and T Company on the right, once again supported by mortars, machine guns and the guns of 1st Airlanding Light Regiment RA. The action lasted for about an hour, during which the enemy launched a counterattack on 1st Parachute Battalion's left flank. Nevertheless, the battalion fought its way through to the main road junction ahead, which it reached at about 1500 hours. By that time, however, its strength was down to about 100 men.

The situation by the morning of the second day looked grim. 2nd Parachute Battalion was managing to hold on at the bridge, but had suffered casualties and was running very low on ammunition. 1st and 3rd Parachute Battalions had both been held up in heavy fighting on the outskirts of Arnhem and thus were unable to reinforce Lieutenant Colonel Frost and his men. To make matters worse, Major General Roy Urquhart and Brigadier Gerald Lathbury were both missing from their headquarters, out of contact with their respective formations and their units. The two men had taken cover in a house, together with the battalion headquarters of 3rd Parachute Battalion, watching German tanks and self-propelled guns moving along the street outside. During the morning Captain William Taylor, Lathbury's GSO 3 (Intelligence) who was with them, succeeded in contacting the brigade headquarters at the bridge and learned that it was being held.

During the afternoon the remnants of A Company 3rd Parachute Battalion, numbering only about 40 strong under Lieutenant Burwash, appeared with two Bren carriers loaded with ammunition. At this point Lieutenant Colonel Fitch decided to make a further attempt to reach the bridge by heading north and approaching via the railway. At 1500 hours the battalion moved off but soon found itself hampered by having to clamber over the high fences of gardens and by increasingly heavy machine gun fire from the direction of the railway.

Major General Urquhart and Brigadier Lathbury decided to make their own way to the bridge. Leaving the house where they had been sheltering, they ran across the garden of the house next door under cover of a smoke grenade thrown by Lathbury. At that point they met Lieutenant James Cleminson, together with the remnants of his platoon, who warned them not to go any further. Ignoring his advice, Urquhart and Lathbury, followed by Captain Taylor, ran into the *Alexanderstraat* and headed in the direction of St Elizabeth Hospital. Somewhat alarmed at the idea of the two senior officers moving through the enemy-occupied area unescorted, Cleminson ran after them, calling on his men to follow. As the four officers ran down the street, a machine gun opened fire and Brigadier Lathbury was hit. As the other three dragged him inside the nearest building, a German soldier followed them but was shot by Major General Urquhart through the window with his pistol. Lathbury was paralysed by his wound and unable to walk, so, leaving him in the care of a Dutchman and his wife, Urquhart and the two others continued on their way. However, they were soon forced to take refuge in the attic of a house to avoid capture by a company of panzer grenadiers approaching in the opposite direction. Once again Urquhart was forced to stay where he was and lie low, unable to reach his headquarters.

In Urquhart's absence, the commander of 1st Airlanding Brigade, Brigadier 'Pip' Hicks, had assumed command of the division. Realising 2nd Parachute Battalion's perilous situation, he despatched B and D Companies of the 2nd Battalion The South Staffordshire Regiment (less two companies which would arrive in the second lift), which was one of the three airlanding battalions holding the dropping and landing zones, as reinforcements. Unfortunately, however, they also became held up as they attempted to make their way towards the bridge. The division's only hope therefore lay with 4th Parachute Brigade, which was due to arrive at 1000 hours.

The weather was bright and clear as Major 'Boy' Wilson and the pathfinders of 21st Independent Parachute Company laid out their coloured DZ markers and set up their Eureka beacons. As they did so they were attacked from the air by Messerschmitt Bf 109s. Fortunately, they all managed to take cover in time and thus suffered no casualties. However, there was no sign of the Dakotas carrying 4th Parachute Brigade. Unbeknown to those awaiting their arrival, all the departure airfields were covered in low-lying mist, and it was not until late morning that the weather improved sufficiently for the aircraft to take off. By 1500 hours the leading aircraft were over the landing and dropping zones and the drop and landings started. As on the previous day, the parachutists and gliders were delivered accurately, but on this occasion flak was encountered during the final 20 minutes of the run-in, together with considerable opposition on the DZs and LZs. 10th Parachute Battalion in particular suffered casualties. Nevertheless, all three battalions formed up quickly and headed for their respective rendezvous points. Brigadier John Hackett was himself in fine form, having taken two prisoners soon after landing. Shortly afterwards he was met by Lieutenant Colonel Charles McKenzie, the GSO 1 1st Airborne Division, who briefed him on the situation and on the changed orders which had been issued by Brigadier 'Pip' Hicks.

Two hours after the drop, 4th Parachute Brigade was heading towards Arnhem. Brigadier Hicks' orders specified that 10th and 156th Parachute Battalions were to carry out their previously allocated task of taking and holding the high ground north of Arnhem but, much to Hackett's displeasure, 11th Parachute Battalion was to be detached from the brigade and was to head for the bridge, together with the two companies of the 2nd Battalion The South Staffordshire Regiment, which had just landed. When dusk fell the two South Staffordshire companies were on the march towards Arnhem with Lieutenant Colonel George Lea and his 11th Parachute Battalion following up behind. Soon afterwards, just after nightfall, they met up with Lieutenant Colonel Dobie and the remnants of 1st Parachute Battalion. The three commanding officers between them decided that the advance would be continued at 0400 hours on the following morning, 19 September. 1st Parachute Battalion would head south to the river and then approach 2nd Parachute Battalion's positions along the northern bank, while the South Staffordshire companies and 11th Parachute Battalion moved along the main road.

Brigadier Hackett, meanwhile, had driven to Headquarters 1st Airborne Division, which was by then located at the Park Hotel, Hartenstein, with the intention of trying to sort out what he later referred to as a "grossly untidy situation". Although Urquhart had nominated Lathbury as his deputy in the event of his becoming *hors de combat*, Hicks had taken over command of the division in the latter's absence. However, Hackett was his senior. Having helped Hicks to restore some degree of order, Hackett returned to his brigade after obtaining agreement that 4th Parachute Brigade would move on the following morning to take the area of Koepel, a feature of high ground to the north of Arnhem. From there it would advance into Arnhem north of the railway line. En route, it would collect the 7th Battalion The King's Own Scottish Borderers to replace 11th Parachute Battalion.

By this time, 1st Parachute Battalion was also faring little better. In the early hours of 19 September, after heading for the river, Lieutenant Colonel Dobie and his men encountered enemy infantry and some fierce close-quarter fighting took place near the area of the pontoon bridge. Major John 'Tim' Timothy led his R Company in a bayonet charge, and Major Chris Perrin-Brown did likewise with T Company in attempts to drive the ' nemy back, but achieved only limited success. By 0600 hours the battalion numbered fewer than 40 men, and the arrival of enemy tanks made the situation all the more impossible. As Lieutenant Colonel David Dobie and the other survivors of the battalion attempted to take cover in some houses, enemy troops appeared inside the buildings and opened fire, Dobie himself being wounded by a grenade. Eventually he and six of his men found shelter in a cellar occupied by Dutch civilians. An hour later they were discovered by SS troops, who took them prisoner.

At 0500 hours on 19 September, 156th Parachute Battalion launched its attack through the woods of Johanna Hoeve, heading for the Lichten-beek feature. By 1000 hours, however, it had failed and the battalion had suffered heavy casualties, A Company having lost all of its officers. Lieutenant Colonel Ken Smyth's 10th Parachute Battalion had fared little better, having encountered heavy fire from 88mm anti-aircraft guns being used in the ground target role, as well as from tanks and self-propelled guns on the main Arnhem-Ede road. The battalion had been ordered to establish a firm base 1,000 yards from a small farmstead at Johanna Hoeve. However, Smyth ordered his men to dig in where they were, astride the Arnhem to Utrecht road, planning to attack and seize his objective after nightfall. Throughout the day the battalion was subjected to heavy fire, but stood its ground.

It was not until the morning of 19 September that Major General Urquhart was able to make his way to his headquarters. Having been trapped in the house in which he was sheltering by the presence of a self-propelled gun outside, he was unable to move until 0700 hours, when he heard the gun move off. Shortly afterwards, the owner of the house appeared and told Urquhart that British troops were advancing up the street. These turned out to be the two companies of South Staffordshires and 11th Parachute Battalion attempting to make their way to the bridge to reinforce 2nd Parachute Battalion. Commandeering one of their jeeps, Urquhart sped back towards his headquarters. After assuming command of the division from Brigadier 'Pip' Hicks, Urquhart learned with growing alarm of the chaotic situation reigning in Arnhem. Hicks informed him that 1st and 3rd Parachute Battalions, along with 11th Parachute Battalion and the 2nd Battalion The South Staffordshire Regiment, were advancing independently into Arnhem in an attempt to link up with 2nd Parachute Battalion, which was still hanging on at the bridge. 156th and 10th Parachute Battalions, together with the 7th Battalion The King's Own

Scottish Borderers, were to the north of Arnhem, and it was not known whether they were advancing into the town. The 1st Battalion The Border Regiment was occupying positions on a line running along the western outskirts of Oosterbeek from Westerbouwing to Wolfheze. Another major problem was that of resupply. Because the operation was way behind schedule, Supply Dropping Zone 'V', on the north-western outskirts of Arnhem, had not been secured and the situation was such that it was no longer a feasible resupply point. The same applied to Dropping Zone 'K', south of the town and river, on which 1st Polish Independent Parachute Brigade was due to drop that morning. Messages were transmitted back to England by the divisional headquarters, advising the RAF that new dropping zones would have to be selected. There was no response, and this was to have tragic consequences.

Urquhart was appalled at what he learned from Hicks and his staff, and despatched Colonel Hilaro Barlow, Deputy Commander 1st Airlanding Brigade, into Arnhem in a radio-equipped jeep to co-ordinate the operations of the five battalions operating independently in the town. Unfortunately, Barlow never reached Arnhem. He was never seen again, and it was assumed that he had been ambushed and killed en route. Some time later it was learned that he was killed by mortar fire near the Rhine Pavilion hotel.

Deciding that he must see the situation on the ground for himself, Urquhart drove to Headquarters 4th Parachute Brigade, located near Wolfheze. There he found Hackett and his brigade heavily committed on the northern outskirts of Oosterbeek around the woods of Johanna Hoeve and Lichtenbeek. As he reached the brigade headquarters, Urquhart had a narrow escape when three Messerschmitts suddenly attacked, forcing him to throw himself down a steep bank into the headquarters itself. Urquhart discovered that, despite every effort to push forward to the high ground at Koepel, the brigade had been unable to make any progress. After conferring with Hackett, he decided to withdraw the brigade south to the middle road leading into Arnhem, but ordered Hackett not to implement the withdrawal plan until ordered to do so.

Shortly after Urquhart's departure, however, the 1st Battalion The Border Regiment, which was behind 4th Parachute Brigade on the western outskirts of Oosterbeek, was attacked from the west. Hackett and his brigade were threatened with being cut off, particularly if the enemy took Wolfheze, which possessed the only level crossing over which 4th Parachute Brigade's vehicles could cross the railway line, which otherwise was lined by steep embankments. 10th Parachute Battalion was despatched to take and hold the crossing, and almost immediately afterwards the order to withdraw was received from Headquarters 1st Airborne Division. The withdrawal was carried out in contact with the enemy, who harrassed the brigade as it pulled back. Meanwhile, 10th Parachute Battalion had encountered the enemy on approaching Wolfheze and heavy fighting subsequently took place in the village itself. Captain Lionel Queripel, commanding a composite company of men from two other battalions as well as his own, was wounded in the face as he carried a wounded NCO to shelter. Disregarding his wound, he then led an attack on an enemy strongpoint, killing the crews of two machine guns and a 6-pounder anti-tank gun captured previously by the enemy. At that point enemy infantry counterattacked and Queripel was wounded again in the face and in both arms. Together with some of the men with him, he took cover in a ditch and stood his ground against the enemy, who were by then showering his party with stick grenades. Despite his wounds, Queripel threw several of these back at his attackers. He continued to do so as he ordered his men to withdraw while he covered them. Shortly afterwards the enemy closed in and killed him. His supreme gallantry was subsequently recognised by the posthumous award of the Victoria Cross. By the time 10th Parachute Battalion had withdrawn across the railway line it numbered only some 250 men. 156th Parachute Battalion had also suffered heavily, numbering some 270 of all ranks and having lost virtually all of its transport.

At that point during the withdrawal by 4th Parachute Brigade, some of the gliderborne elements of 1st Polish Independent Parachute Brigade started to land on ground between 10th Parachute Battalion and the enemy. They immediately came under very heavy fire from the Germans on the ground and from Messerschmitt Bf 109 fighters which appeared at the same time. Several gliders caught fire in mid-air, while others exploded on landing. In the confusion and poor visibility caused by smoke, some of the Poles were mistaken for enemy troops by 10th Parachute Battalion, and vice versa, and they opened fire on each other.

In the meantime, the two companies of South Staffordshires had been held up in the main street of Arnhem. After running out of PIAT ammunition, they were overrun by enemy tanks and were forced to withdraw westwards. After reorganising they attacked the Den Brink feature to allow 11th Parachute Battalion to reach the road running north of the feature. No sooner had they taken it than they came under very heavy mortar fire and were driven off by tanks, which then turned their attention on 11th Parachute Battalion, causing heavy casualties. The surviving South Staffordshires, together with those of 11th Parachute Battalion, withdrew to Oosterbeek Station. Together with remnants of 1st and 3rd Parachute Battalions they formed a composite force, later called Lonsdale Force, under the command of Major Dickie Lonsdale, second in command of 11th Parachute Battalion. By then the commanding officers of all four battalions represented in Lonsdale Force had become casualties. Lieutenant Colonel Fitch of 3rd Parachute Battalion had been killed, and Lieutenant Colonels Dobie and Lea of 1st and 11th Parachute Battalions and Lieutenant Colonel McCardie of the South Staffordshires had been wounded and taken prisoner.

During the day, the RAF dropped supplies to the beleaguered division. Unfortunately, the messages from Headquarters 1st Airborne Division to England concerning the necessary changes in dropping zones had not been received, so the Dakotas and Stirlings flew in to meet a heavy barrage of enemy anti-aircraft fire and dropped their containers accurately on to

Supply Dropping Zone 'V', which was by then behind enemy lines. A new dropping zone was marked out near the divisional headquarters and a Eureka beacon was set up nearby, but the coloured marker panels served only to attract the attention of enemy fighters, which strafed the dropping zone. Nevertheless, those on the ground did everything in their power to attract the attention of the aircrew, firing flares, laying out parachutes on the ground and even setting fire to the grass — all to no avail.

As the troops watched, the aircraft flew on through the barrage of flak. One of them was a Dakota of No. 271 Squadron, 46 Group RAF, flown by Flight Lieutenant David Lord. As the aircraft made its run-in over the drop zone it was hit and caught fire. Despite this, the crew proceeded to despatch six panniers of ammunition and Flight Lieutenant Lord turned his aircraft for a second run-in. As the final two panniers were being despatched the flames grew until they enveloped the aircraft, which crashed. One member of the crew, Flying Officer Henry King, survived, and he later revealed that, after the ammunition had been despatched, Lord had ordered his crew to bale out while remaining at the controls and holding the burning aircraft steady. Unfortunately all the despatchers and crew, with the exception of Flying Officer King, had taken off their parachutes while despatching the panniers. As the despatchers were donning their parachutes there was an explosion and the starboard wing broke off. Flying Officer King, who had been standing by the door, was flung clear and somehow managed to pull the ripcord of his parachute. Flight Lieutenant Lord was subsequently awarded a posthumous Victoria Cross for his great heroism.

Other aircraft crash-landed in the area, some landing south of the Rhine. Of the total of 390 tons of supplies dropped, only a tiny proportion fell into the division's hands. During the RAF's resolute and gallant efforts to resupply 1st Airborne Division, its aircraft and aircrews suffered heavy casualties: 13 aircraft were shot down and 97 were damaged.

Chaos reigned in most areas throughout the day. Other than in 2nd Parachute Battalion's area, the only other place where some form of order reigned was in Oosterbeek, where Lieutenant Colonel W. F. K. 'Sheriff' Thompson, the Commanding Officer of 1st Airlanding Light Regiment RA, had established his forward command post with the guns of 3rd Airlanding Light Battery RA. Having already formed a force of glider pilots and anti-tank gunners to protect the battery, Thompson had moved forward to reconnoitre. Whilst doing so he had encountered a number of stragglers from 11th Parachute Battalion and the South Staffordshires withdrawing from Arnhem. Quickly organising them into some form of force, he had placed them under the command of Major Robert Cain of the South Staffordshires and ordered him to deploy them on the high ground west of the Den Brink feature, covering the railway line. Cain and his men were later joined by Lieutenant J. L. Williams, 1st Parachute Battalion's Motor Transport Officer, who had collected some 50 men of Headquarter Company and some 200 from other units. Williams had then attempted to break through to 2nd Parachute Battalion, but had been held up near the St Elizabeth Hospital. By the time dusk fell on 19 September he had decided to withdraw and he and his men, who had been joined by others from 3rd and 11th Parachute Battalions, made their way to the area of the railway south of Den Brink where they met Lieutenant Colonel Thompson's force.

Meanwhile, 2nd Parachute Battalion had been under constant heavy fire from tanks and artillery. By the afternoon of 19 September most of the buildings in which Lieutenant Colonel Frost's men had installed themselves had been set ablaze by phosphorous shells. After each artillery barrage, enemy infantry attacked but were beaten off by the determined defenders, who counterattacked with bayonet charges, some of which were led by Major Digby Tatham-Warter. Morale within the battalion was still high despite the appalling conditions, and the troops carried the war to the enemy whenever they could do so, leaving their positions with PIATs and Gammon bombs to hunt the enemy tanks which crawled through the streets blasting the houses on either side of them. One tank which had proved to be particularly troublesome was destroyed with grenades by Lieutenant Pat Barnett, the commander of the brigade headquarters defence platoon, and three others were knocked out by Captain Tony Frank with a PIAT. However, that evening some Tiger tanks, against which PIATs were useless, appeared and opened fire on the battalion's positions. Major Digby Tatham-Warter, who had taken over as Second in Command after Major David Wallis had been killed, and Father Egan, the battalion's Roman Catholic chaplain, were both wounded.

By the evening of 19 September the remnants of 1st Airborne Division in the area of Oosterbeek were being pushed back on all sides. The majority of them were in an area between Heveadorp and Wolfheze to the west and from Oosterbeek to Johanna Hoeve to the east. Divisional headquarters was roughly in the centre, located in the Hartenstein Hotel. Major General Urquhart decided that his only chance of conserving his remaining forces and hanging on until the arrival of 30th Corps was to withdraw his troops and consolidate them inside a defensive box. This would also form a bridgehead on the northern bank of the river for any subsequent crossings from the south via the ferry at Heveadorp, which had been found to be still in working order. Although it would in effect mean abandoning 2nd Parachute Battalion and the other units at the bridge, Urquhart knew it was the only option open to him. That evening, orders were issued for troops to withdraw into the perimeter around Oosterbeek. As night fell, the sky was brilliantly lit by burning buildings throughout Arnhem.

Dawn on the following day, 20 September, saw the resumption of heavy shelling of 2nd Parachute Battalion. By then, most of the buildings in the battalion's area had been destroyed, and the remnants of Frost's force had been forced to evacuate them and dig in around those sheltering Headquarters 1st Parachute Brigade and Battalion Headquarters. In the cellars of the ruined buildings, wounded men were crammed tightly together and medical officers and orderlies worked under appalling conditions. At about 1000 hours a signaller in Headquarters 1st Parachute Brigade suddenly made contact with the divisional headquarters. On being summoned to the radio, Lieutenant Colonel Frost was told by Major General Urquhart that 30th Corps were expected to arrive within a matter of hours. When told by Frost of the perilous situation which existed at the bridge, Urquhart replied that there was little or no chance of any of the division being able to fight its way through to him. That afternoon, Frost himself was wounded by a mortar bomb whilst talking to Major Douglas Crawley. On being taken to the battalion's Regimental Aid Post, he discovered that he had been wounded in both legs. Major Digby Tatham-Warter, himself also wounded, took over command of the battalion, while Major Freddy Gough, commander of 1st Airborne Reconnaissance Squadron, assumed command of the entire force at the bridge.

During this time Lieutenant Jack Grayburn of A Company once again distinguished himself. His platoon had been holding positions which were a vital keypoint in the battalion's defensive perimeter. Despite several attacks in strength by the enemy, including tanks and self-propelled guns, Grayburn and his men had held out despite suffering severe casualties. Subsequently, despite his wounded shoulder, he had led several fighting patrols which caused such mayhem that the enemy brought up their tanks again. Later, German sappers were spotted placing demolition fuses under the bridge. Grayburn responded by leading out another patrol and beating the enemy back whilst the fuses were removed from the charges. He was wounded again, but refused to leave his men or to desist in carrying the fight to the enemy. During the evening, however, he was killed by fire from a tank at close range while standing up in full view of it and directing the withdrawal of the remnants of his platoon to the battalion's main defensive position. For his great gallantry he was later awarded a posthumous Victoria Cross.

That evening, the single remaining unburnt building which housed the brigade headquarters caught fire several times, but the flames were extinguished. Its cellars were crammed with over 200 wounded, and Captain Jimmy Logan, 2nd Parachute Battalion's Regimental Medical Officer, approached Lieutenant Colonel Frost and told him that the wounded would have to be evacuated and surrendered to the enemy or they would perish. Frost discussed the matter with Major Freddy Gough and told him to be ready to move those troops still able to fight to new positions. Shortly afterwards the building caught fire again and, as the flames began to spread, Frost ordered Gough to move his men out. The wounded remained behind in the cellars, awaiting the arrival of enemy troops. Just after nightfall, under a flag of truce, the wounded were carried up from the cellars by SS troops, who removed them from the area.

Thereafter the battle resumed, with enemy tanks blasting the battalion's positions. By then the northern end of the bridge was no longer held and ammunition was so low that each man possessed only a few rounds. At that point the Brigade Major, Major Tony Hibbert, gave orders that the force was to break up into small groups for the night and then, at first light on the following morning, infiltrate back to the buildings in the area of the bridge. In the event this proved impossible and, as best he could, Hibbert then ordered those whom he could contact to withdraw westwards to the divisional headquarters. However, most of those who tried to do so were killed or wounded and the remainder hunted down and taken prisoner. By dawn on the morning of 21 September there were only 150 men of 2nd Parachute Battalion left as SS panzer grenadiers advanced once again to clear the area. As they did so, the paratroops fought back and conceded ground only when they had been killed or wounded. By 0900 hours the remnants of 2nd Parachute Battalion and the elements of other units of 1st Parachute Brigade in the area of the bridge had been overrun. They had held the bridge for three days and three nights.

Similarly, 4th Parachute Brigade had also been virtually destroyed. At about 0600 hours on 20 September, having been ordered by Major General Urquhart to move to the main divisional area, Brigadier John Hackett and his much depleted battalions made their way towards the divisional perimeter. What remained of 156th Parachute Battalion was in the lead, and it was the 25 men of A Company who came under fire from machine guns and self-propelled guns as they moved through some woods near the Wolfheze Hotel. C Company, commanded by Major Geoffrey Powell, attempted to put in a flanking attack but this failed and the company suffered heavy casualties. Bearing in mind his orders to rejoin the rest of the division, and realising that he must try avoid any major encounter with the enemy, Brigadier Hackett ordered 10th Parachute Battalion to take an alternative route to the east and bypass the enemy, leaving 156th Parachute Battalion to follow as a rearguard while in contact with the enemy. The battalion fought its way through the woods, being harried by machine guns and snipers all the way. On receiving a message from Brigadier Hackett to "pull the plug out" and speed up his advance, Lieutenant Colonel Ken Smyth ordered his men to fix bayonets. Charging through the woods, the remnants of 10th Parachute Battalion fought their way through to the divisional perimeter, which they reached at just after 1300 hours. Besides himself and one of his company commanders, Major Peter Warr, Smyth's battalion numbered only 60 men. Despite the fact that they were exhausted, filthy and covered in blood, Smyth and his men formed up in column and marched to the divisional headquarters, where they were met by Major General Urquhart. They subsequently took up defensive positions in buildings by the main crossroads in Oosterbeek.

Meanwhile, Brigadier Hackett and the remnants of his brigade headquarters and 156th Parachute Battalion were being hard pressed by enemy infantry supported by tanks. Nevertheless, Hackett and his men on several occasions counterattacked and drove the enemy back, but suffered casualties in the process. At one point, several men of 156th Parachute Battalion were killed after being lured out of cover by German troops dressed in parachute smocks. The enemy troops disappeared into a hollow as machine guns opened fire and cut down the unsuspecting paratroops, who had mistaken the Germans for members of the gliderborne element of 1st Polish Independent Parachute Brigade. On an order from Brigadier Hackett, Major Geoffrey Powell and C Company carried out a bayonet charge and drove the enemy out of the hollow, which was then occupied by Hackett and the rest of his force. There they regrouped and beat off more attacks by the enemy. During the afternoon the German armour pulled back for some unknown reason, but the action still continued for most of the time.

Ammunition was now running very low and heavy losses had been suffered. The survivors of 156th Parachute Battalion numbered less than 30, and the rest of Hackett's small force consisted of 12 men from his brigade headquarters, ten from 10th Parachute Battalion, and between 20 and 30 from other units. Among those officers who had been killed during the day's fighting were the Commanding Officer of 156th Parachute Battalion, Lieutenant Colonel Sir Richard des Voeux, the Brigade Major, Major C. W. B. Dawson, the GSO 3 Intelligence, Captain G. L. Blundell, and the commander of the brigade headquarters defence platoon, Captain James.

With some 30 of his men in the hollow now wounded, Brigadier Hackett decided that, rather than stay and be overrun, he and his men would break through the enemy to reach the divisional perimeter, which was about half a mile away. At 1800 hours, charging with fixed bayonets and screaming at the tops of their voices, they swept the Germans aside and ran the few hundred yards to join the other remnants of 1st Airborne Division. The perimeter itself was horseshoe-shaped, with the divisional headquarters located in the centre of the area inside it. After the arrival of the remnants of 4th Parachute Brigade, Major General Urquhart divided the area into eastern and western sectors, commanded by Brigadiers Hackett and Hicks respectively. The northern curved end of the perimeter was manned by men of 21st Independent Parachute Company and the 7th Battalion The King's Own Scottish Borderers. The eastern side was defended by the survivors of 10th and 156th Parachute Battalions, some glider pilots and gunners of 1st Airlanding Light Regiment RA, while on the western side were the 1st Battalion The Border Regiment, glider pilots, sappers, Poles from the gliderborne elements of 1st Polish Independent Parachute Brigade and men from several other different units. The southern end of the area was held by Lonsdale Force, consisting of men of 1st, 3rd and 11th Parachute Battalions, the 1st Battalion The Border Regiment, the 2nd Battalion The South Staffordshire Regiment and divisional troops.

The enemy kept up constant pressure on the perimeter. After 20 September there was a virtually continual bombardment of mortar fire which sometimes reached a crescendo of about 50 bombs a minute. Added to this was the threat of snipers, although many fell victim to the airborne troops. Patrols of two or three men would move out from their positions and clamber to the rooftops of nearby buildings, from where they picked off snipers with unerring accuracy. The men of 21st Independent Parachute Company were particularly adept at this type of tactic, one man killing 18 snipers. Conditions within the divisional area were appalling. All the houses had been badly damaged, and many of them were either demolished or burned down. Those men still capable of holding and using a weapon manned the slit trenches dug in once immaculate gardens and streets, while

Dutch civilians crowded into cellars with the wounded, whom they nursed to the best of their ability. Throughout the area some of the dead lay unburied among the shell craters, burned-out vehicles and general flotsam of war. There was little or no food, and water was scarce. In the dressing stations in the Hotels Schoonoord, Vreewyck and Tafelberg, the medical officers and orderlies worked tirelessly on the endless stream of wounded, who numbered almost 1,200.

The battle raged on. At one point on 21 September the enemy attempted to break through the perimeter, but were driven back by a bayonet charge of men of the 1st Battalion The Border Regiment. Much of the fighting took place at very close quarters, and in the weaker parts of the perimeter enemy tanks and infantry succeeded in infiltrating between individual positions and causing heavy casualties. On the morning of 21 September the first indications that 30th Corps had managed to fight its way to within supporting range of Arnhem came when salvoes of shells crashed down a hundred yards or so in front of the airborne troops. Controlled by Colonel R. C. Loder-Symonds, Commander Royal Artillery 1st Airborne Division, the 5.5 inch guns of 30th Corps' 64th Medium Regiment broke up enemy attacks with unerring accuracy. Meanwhile, the gunners of 1st Airlanding Light Regiment RA continued to serve their own 75mm pack howitzers while under fire, as they had done throughout the battle, in some cases engaging tanks over open sights.

That day also saw the arrival in Arnhem of more enemy units, namely the *Panzerabteilung* 503 equipped with King Tiger tanks, the 171st *Auffrischung* Light Artillery Regiment, a panzer grenadier battalion, several companies of Luftwaffe ground staff reformed as infantry and the Dutch SS *Landsturm Nederland* battalion. By 1600 hours they were all in action against the airborne troops.

On the afternoon of 21 September the western sector of the perimeter was attacked, but the enemy were again driven off by men of the 1st Battalion The Border Regiment. Simultaneously, an assault was made on Lonsdale Force in the south, while at the northern end the 7th Battalion The King's Own Scottish Borderers were driven out of their positions. Fixing their bayonets, the Lowlanders counterattacked and routed the enemy, who were unable to withstand the onslaught. By the end of the action, however, the battalion's strength numbered only 150 of all ranks. At 1900 hours 10th Parachute Battalion, on the east of the perimeter astride the main road through Oosterbeek, was attacked by enemy tanks and self-propelled guns. The houses in which Lieutenant Colonel Ken Smyth and his men were located were set on fire by phosphorous shells and they were forced to withdraw. Smyth himself was fatally wounded, dying a few days later, and the last of his remaining officers was killed.

Urquhart's main hope for resupply and reinforcement had rested on the Heveadorp ferry, a cable-operated craft capable of carrying vehicles and personnel. On 20 September a patrol of sappers had carried out a reconnaissance of the crossing, taking soundings of the river and measuring the current. That night, a patrol of 12 men was despatched to secure the northern end of the ferry, which was to be used to ferry across men of 1st Polish Independent Parachute Brigade on the following day. In the darkness the patrol was unable to find the craft itself, despite searching for quarter of a mile on either side of the landing stage. At dawn on the 21st the patrol returned to the perimeter. It was believed at the time that the ferry had been sunk by artillery fire, but it was eventually discovered by some Dutch civilians, washed up intact on the bank downstream by the Arnhem railway bridge. The loss of the ferry was a bitter blow to Urquhart, as it removed the only effective means of crossing the Lower Rhine.

At 1700 hours on 21 September part of 1st Polish Independent Parachute Brigade dropped on a drop zone east of the village of Driel, just over a mile south of the river. Unfortunately the enemy were well prepared, having received early warning of the columns of Dakotas as they crossed the French coast near Dunkirk. As Major General Stanislaw Sosabowski and his men left their aircraft, which were attacked during the final approach to the dropping zone by two squadrons of Messerschmitt Bf 109s, they jumped into a barrage of anti-aircraft fire which, together with the fighters, shot down a number of the Dakotas. On landing, the Poles suffered further casualties as enemy machine guns, mortars, tanks and artillery were brought to bear on the dropping zone. By the time they had fought their way to cover in nearby dykes and embankments and subsequently regrouped by nightfall, Sosabowski's men numbered only about 750, including the wounded. Only two-thirds of the brigade had been dropped, the aircraft carrying one battalion of 500 men having been forced to return to England because of bad weather. At 2100 hours that night, Captain Zwolanski, the Polish liaison officer attached to Headquarters 1st Airborne Division, arrived at Sosabowski's headquarters after swimming the Rhine. He informed his brigade commander that rafts would be sent across the river later that night to ferry Sosabowski and his brigade across to the northern bank. The Poles moved up to the southern bank and waited for the rafts, but they never came. At 0300 hours on the morning of 22 September, Sosabowski withdrew his men.

Before dawn on the morning of 22 September, Major General Urquhart reduced the size of the northern part of the perimeter, which had become very weak in several areas. 21st Independent Parachute Company, the remnants of 1st Airborne Reconnaissance Squadron, and some sappers were moved to the north-eastern part of the perimeter, while some of the divisional RASC troops were transferred to the south-eastern part. Early that morning, radio contact with 30th Corps was established and its commander, Lieutenant General Sir Brian Horrocks, informed Urquhart that 43rd Infantry Division had been ordered to relieve 1st Airborne Division. However, Horrocks was apparently unaware that the Heveadorp ferry was no longer held by 1st Airborne Division, despite two messages to that effect having been sent to 2nd Army. Urquhart suspected that Horrocks was not fully aware of the situation in Arnhem. Accordingly, that morning, he despatched his GSO 1, Lieutenant Colonel Charles McKenzie, and Lieutenant Colonel Eddie Myers, the Commander Royal Engineers 1st

Airborne Division, to make contact with Horrocks and Browning and brief them accordingly. At the same time, Myers was tasked with organising arrangements for ferrying men and supplies across the river. The two officers crossed the Rhine in an inflatable dinghy and subsequently made their way to the headquarters of 1st Polish Independent Parachute Brigade, which was under attack by enemy troops supported by artillery north of the river. There they discussed with Major General Sosabowski the idea of ferrying some of his men across in small rubber boats. At the same time they sent a signal to Lieutenant General Horrocks, asking for reinforcements and supplies.

To the south, Major General G. I. Thomas's 43rd Infantry Division was attempting to push its way northwards towards Arnhem. Unfortunately, it had been hampered on its way by a traffic jam in Nijmegen, which it had reached on the morning of 21 September, and had subsequently been misrouted over the wrong bridge. Consequently, its leading elements did not reach the village of Oosterhout, some seven miles south of Arnhem, until 0930 hours. By then the enemy had realised what was afoot and made every effort to halt the division's advance. Two attacks were launched by the division, but these failed, and it was not until 1700 hours that afternoon that a third attack, with very heavy artillery support, succeeded in punching a gap in the enemy defences and enabled a column of armour and infantry to thrust towards the Lower Rhine and Arnhem. The 5th Battalion Duke of Cornwall's Light Infantry, supported by a squadron of tanks and bringing with it two amphibious DUKWs loaded with ammunition and supplies, raced for the village of Driel, which was reached at 1730 hours.

Meanwhile, within 1st Airborne Division's area the mortar and shellfire continued and casualties mounted. The pressure was beginning to have serious effects on many of the defenders, some of whom were shell-shocked and were on the verge of breakdown, but despite this the defence was conducted as doggedly as ever by others who fought tenaciously and refused to give an inch against overwhelming odds. In Oosterbeek church Major Dickie Lonsdale roused his exhausted men with a stirring speech delivered from the pulpit while, not far from divisional headquarters, Sergeant 'Cab' Calloway of 3rd Parachute Battalion charged a Tiger tank single-handed with a PIAT and succeeded in immobilising it at the same time as it gunned him down. Major Robert Cain of the South Staffordshires, who was later awarded the Victoria Cross for his gallantry, personally hunted down and knocked out six tanks and a number of self-propelled guns with a PIAT. Throughout the battle, moving among the positions throughout the perimeter, some of which were only yards from those of the enemy, the figures of Major General Urquhart and Brigadiers Hicks and Hackett could be seen constantly braving the shell and mortar fire to visit their men and give encouragement.

At 2100 hours on the night of the 22nd, men of 1st Polish Independent Parachute Brigade moved silently up to the southern bank of the Lower Rhine. Sappers on both sides of the river had set up a hawser on pulleys which would pull four inflatable dinghies and a number of hastily constructed wooden rafts back and forth across the river, ferrying six men and a quantity of supplies at a time. For a while all went well, then suddenly the night sky was illuminated by parachute flares. Almost immediately the crossing point came under heavy mortar fire. Two of the rubber dinghies were destroyed and the Poles on the southern bank took cover. As soon as the flares burned out, the Poles resumed crossing. Throughout the night the desperate attempt to ferry men and supplies across the river continued, despite heavy casualties being suffered by Sosabowski's men. Only 50 men of 1st Polish Independent Parachute Brigade succeeded in reaching the northern bank and 1st Airborne Division. At 0200 hours on the following morning, 23 September, the two DUKWs, brought forward during the night by the 5th Battalion Duke of Cornwall's Light Infantry, moved towards the river. The only approach was via a narrow, ditch-lined road which was immersed in mud caused by heavy rain which had fallen during the previous day. Time after time the cumbersome and heavily loaded vehicles slid off the road and had to be manhandled on to it again. Within a few yards of the river, however, both DUKWs crashed into the ditch, where they remained immovably stuck. At 0300 hours all further attempts to ferry men and supplies across the river ceased.

It was only when Lieutenant Colonel Charles McKenzie eventually reached Headquarters 1st Airborne Corps at Nijmegen on the morning of 23 September that Lieutenant General 'Boy' Browning was able to gain an accurate picture of 1st Airborne Division's appalling predicament. Until then, plagued by the inadequacy of radio communications with 1st Airborne Division, he had possessed only a vague picture of events in Arnhem. There was little that Browning could do, as all troops in the Nijmegen-Arnhem area were under the control of 30th Corps and ultimately of 2nd Army. However, Browning assured McKenzie that every effort would be made that night to ferry reinforcements and supplies to Urquhart and his beleaguered force.

That night, 1st Polish Independent Parachute Brigade once again started to ferry some of its men across the river to join 1st Airborne Division. Again the enemy brought the crossing point under heavy fire, and only 250 men reached the northern bank. Of those, only 200 reached 1st Airborne Division. Meanwhile, 43rd Infantry Division was pushing forward as best it could, but its leading elements, in the shape of 130th Infantry Brigade, did not reach Driel until after the Poles had withdrawn once again from the southern bank of the river.

No account of the battle in Arnhem would be complete without mention of Kate ter Horst. This remarkable woman, a mother of five children, became a source of great comfort and inspiration to those who were brought to her house beside Oosterbeek Church. Not only did she assist Captain Randall Martin, the Medical Officer of 1st Airlanding Light Regiment RA, and his orderlies to nurse the casualties, but she also moved constantly among the wounded and dying men, praying with them and reading to them the 91st Psalm from her prayerbook. Her house, which had suffered appalling damage, was crammed to overflowing from attic to cellar with wounded men, and her garden eventually contained 57 graves. Yet, despite her undoubted fears for herself and her family, she remained outwardly calm and her composure had a marked effect on those around her.

Throughout Saturday 23 September the hell continued. The enemy continued to attack in force at several points along the perimeter, and the mortar and shellfire continued unabated. Still the defenders held on, watching hopelessly as the RAF continued desperately to drop supplies while being shot out of the skies at virtual point-blank range by enemy anti-aircraft guns. All the while, as they fought back against increasingly overwhelming odds, the men of 1st Airborne Division hoped against hope that relief from 2nd Army would be forthcoming.

At 0930 hours on the morning of Sunday 24 September Colonel Graeme Warrack, the Assistant Director Medical Services 1st Airborne Division, told Major General Urquhart that all of the dressing stations were under fire and that he wished to arrange a truce with the Germans for the evacuation of all the wounded. Urquhart agreed, but emphasised that Warrack had to make it clear to the Germans that the approach was being made purely on humanitarian grounds. This was subsequently effected through the senior German medical officer at the Schoonoord Hotel dressing station, which was by then being operated by both German and British medical staff. Warrack, accompanied by an interpreter and a German medical officer, was driven to the headquarters of Obersturmbann-führer Walter Harzer, the commander of the 9th *Hohenstaufen* SS Panzer Division. Shortly afterwards Generalleutenant Willi Bittrich, the commander of 2nd Panzer Corps, arrived and, after discussing the matter with Warrack, agreed to the plan for the evacuation of the wounded. The truce began at 1500 hours that afternoon, and the evacuation of the wounded took place. An unearthly hush settled over the area as the firing stopped. Convoys of vehicles arrived and the wounded were loaded aboard them. During the next two hours the convoys drove out of Oosterbeek towards Arnhem, carrying over 250 men, while more than 200 walking wounded were led out of the area to St Elizabeth's Hospital in Arnhem.

At 1700 hours the battle was resumed in earnest. The enemy had taken advantage of the truce to infiltrate some of their troops into many areas throughout the perimeter, and the situation was such that in certain areas front lines as such no longer existed. German and British troops found themselves in positions only yards apart, these being taken and retaken as the battle raged. Once again the divisional area was subjected to a constant bombardment of mortar and shellfire. The 1st Battalion The Border Regiment, now reduced to little more than an understrength company in size, was attacked by a force of enemy trying to penetrate the perimeter from the west. Members of the Mortar Platoon, whose mortars had all been knocked out, counterattacked and drove the enemy back.

As dusk fell on the evening of the 24th, another attempt to cross the river from the southern bank was under way. The 4th Battalion The Dorsetshire Regiment, supported by the 5th Battalion The Dorsetshire Regiment and the 5th Battalion Duke of Cornwall's Light Infantry, was preparing to cross the river in assault boats. However, some of the trucks bringing the boats never arrived: two took a wrong turning and found themselves in the German lines, and two skidded off the wet roads and ended up in deep ditches. By early on the morning of 25 September only nine boats had reached the Dorsets, who were waiting near the river in the pitch dark. During this time, the south bank of the river was under constant mortar and machine gun fire. As the Dorsets started across the river the enemy machine guns switched to the boats, raking them from stem to stern. Those of the flimsy wood and canvas craft which were hit sank like stones. Others were swept away downstream by the strong current, landing on the north bank outside the perimeter. As they disembarked the Dorsets came under heavy fire and suffered casualties. The battalion was scattered and was unable to regroup, out of 420 officers and men who started across the river, only 239 arrived on the far bank, and many of those were taken prisoner in the area of the ferry, which was by then in German hands. Of those, only a few managed to reach 1st Airborne Division's perimeter.

During that night, after the Dorsets' unsuccessful crossing attempt, Major General Urquhart received a coded message from Major General G. I. Thomas, the commander of 43rd Infantry Division, giving details of Operation 'Berlin' — the plan for the withdrawal of 1st Airborne Division. By then his division numbered only some 2,500 men, and Urquhart knew that, if they were to be saved, the withdrawal had to take place on the following night. Accordingly, at 0808 hours on the morning of 25 September, he sent a radio message to Major General Thomas, informing him that Operation 'Berlin' had to take place that night. Urquhart's plan for the withdrawal depended on being able to deceive the enemy for as long as possible. Groups of men, including those wounded still capable of handling weapons, would keep up a show of force by firing from different positions while the main body of the division withdrew under cover of darkness. Those in the north of the perimeter would withdraw down the eastern and western flanks to the river, across which they would be evacuated in boats manned by British and Canadian sappers. Radio transmissions would be maintained as normal and the guns of 1st Airlanding Light Regiment RA would carry on firing until the last possible moment. Medical officers and orderlies would remain with the wounded. Glider pilots would form a human chain along the escape route which would be marked at intervals with strips of white tape.

At 2145 hours that night, the artillery of 30th Corps opened fire in a massive barrage which rained down on the German positions. This bombardment, combined with the heavy wind and rain which lashed the area, provided cover for the withdrawal, which began at 2145 hours. With their boots muffled and their equipment secured against rattling, the remnants of 1st Airborne Division made their way through the darkness and pouring rain. On the river bank at the southern end of the perimeter the sappers and their assault boats were waiting. To the west of the perimeter, units of 130th Infantry Brigade were carrying out a diversionary attack.

Further to the west, 2nd Army artillery was firing a barrage as part of another diversionary operation by 129th Infantry Brigade.

Eventually, those with the boats spotted the long lines of men making their way slowly towards them through the darkness. Guided by the chain of glider pilots, they reached the boats. Others had not been as fortunate. Some men had lost their way and had been captured, while others had encountered enemy patrols and had been killed. As they reached the boats, the men were loaded into them as fast as possible and the ferrying operation began. At this point the Germans were able to see the boats crossing, and artillery and mortar fire was brought down. Within an hour 50 per cent of the boats had been sunk, but the operation continued. Meanwhile, on the river bank and in the woods and fields leading back to the divisional area, hundreds of men waited for their turn to cross to safety. All the while, machine gun and mortar fire fell on the embarkation point and on the river itself as the boats crossed to and fro. By dawn on 26 September only a few boats still remained, but their crews continued to ferry men across the river. By the time the operation ceased, 2,120 men had been evacuated — this figure including 420 glider pilots. Others had swum across during the night, but 300 men remained on the northern side. By 1200 hours on 26 September the exhausted but still unbowed survivors of 1st Airborne Division had been moved to Nijmegen, where they met the division's administrative 'tail', which had landed by sea and travelled overland. On 30 September, after four days spent reorganising and resting, the remnants of 1st Airborne Division returned to England.

Many bitter lessons were learned from the debacle at Arnhem, and these have since been expounded at length. Suffice it to say that a number of factors mitigated against the success of the operation. The lack of accurate intelligence about the enemy forces in the area led inevitably to incorrect appreciations by the planners. Over-reliance on air photo-reconnaissance and too much emphasis on enemy anti-aircraft defences in the area led to incorrect appreciation of the ground and selection of dropping and landing zones: there was a suitable dropping zone two miles north-east of Arnhem, and another east of the town only two miles from the bridge, while the area south of the river would have been suitable as a dropping or landing zone — contrary to RAF reports. Bearing in mind the lessons learned from 6th Airborne Division's operations in Normandy, dropping parachute troops eight miles from their objective appears little short of lunacy. Air attacks on the enemy flak defences just before the operation would have done much to neutralise that threat. The failure to drop and land 1st Airborne Division in its entirety in one lift was another major error. Although two brigades were initially committed on the first day, one was tied to protecting the dropping and landing zones, thus limiting the offensive capability of the division to one brigade. Moreover, the 24-hour delay until the second lift meant that the vital element of surprise had been long lost by the time of the arrival of the division's third brigade.

Poor radio communications, caused by insufficiently powerful radio sets, also proved disastrous for the operation. With commanders at all levels out of contact with their formations and units, the operation swiftly became uncoordinated. The rear link was non-operational for the first two or three days, and thus there was no communication with 1st Airborne Corps. Moreover, the lack of ground-to-air radios, caused by incorrect crystalling of sets before the operation, meant that air resupply could not be diverted to alternative dropping zones. Another telling factor was the absence, until the last two days of the operation, of close air support. There is no doubt that the availability of 'cab ranks' of Typhoon fighter-bombers on call to the division would have had a major effect in preventing the enemy from mounting any effective threat.

Finally, the failure by 30th Corps to link up with 1st Airborne Division in time was the major factor in sealing the fate of 1st Airborne Division. In later years criticism would be pointed at both the Guards Armoured and 43rd Infantry Divisions for excessive caution during the last phases of the breakthrough to Arnhem. However, much of this was ill-founded, as the terrain was such that vehicles were confined to a single road and traffic conditions became chaotic, movement becoming slow and jams frequent. In Eindhoven the road was almost blocked by the wreckage of a bombed ammunition convoy. Moreover, it was under constant threat from enemy artillery, which shelled any bottlenecks, and from attacks by infantry attempting to cut it. When the Guards Armoured Division pushed on from the Nijmegen bridgehead its leading elements found themselves confronted by anti-tank defences in terrain already divided by a maze of dykes and drainage ditches. Movement off the road was out of the question.

The failure of the Arnhem phase of Operation 'Market Garden' did not detract from the magnificent performance of 1st Airborne Division, which had held on for nine days — having been told that the link-up with 30th Corps would take place within 48 hours. Its casualties numbered 7,578 killed, wounded and missing out of a total of 10,005 men dropped or landed at Arnhem. The division was paid a compliment by Field Marshal Montgomery, the architect of Operation 'Market Garden', when he later wrote to Major General Roy Urquhart:

'So long as we have officers and men who will do as you have done, then we can indeed look forward with complete confidence to the future. In years to come it will be a great thing for a man to be able to say, "I fought at Arnhem".'

CHAPTER 6
North-West Europe, December 1944 to May 1945

THE ARDENNES

Christmas 1944 found 6th Airborne Division in action once again, having been hurriedly deployed to Belgium as a result of a series of powerful German counterattacks against the American forces in the Ardennes. Before dawn on 16 December, 14 German infantry divisions advanced through the Eifel forests. Covering the noise of their advance were salvoes of V-1 rockets launched against the cities of Liege and Antwerp. At 0530 hours 2,000 guns opened fire on American positions between Monschau and Echternach. Behind the heavy creeping barrage advanced infantry supported by five panzer divisions.

The Americans were caught totally unawares. 28th US Infantry Division was attacked by five enemy divisions and was overwhelmed. On the following day, two regiments of the 106th US Infantry Division were outflanked and surrounded by units of 5th Panzer Army, which crossed the River Our to the west. On the American southern flank, 4th US Infantry Division held firm, and to the north 5th US Corps succeeded in halting the advance of 6th Panzer Army. However, the 1st SS Panzer Division succeeded in penetrating some six miles through American positions at the junction between 5th US Corps and 8th US Corps.

German forces in the offensive comprised three armies consisting of 17 infantry, parachute and panzer grenadier divisions advancing behind a spearhead of armoured formations. 6th Panzer Army advanced in the north, its objectives being the capture of Monschau and Butgenbach and the opening-up of the road leading north-west to Eupen and Verviers. 5th Panzer Army was tasked with capturing the key cities of St Vith and Bastogne, and was subsequently to advance westwards to the River Meuse and Namur. In the south, 7th Army was to cross over the river into the Ardennes between Vianden and Echternach, subsequently providing a flank guard north of Luxembourg and Arlon. The Germans' intention was to disrupt the Allied build-up of troops and equipment in preparation for the invasion of Germany, at the same time allowing a breathing space to permit the regrouping and re-equipping of their own forces for the defence of the Fatherland.

On 20 December Field Marshal Montgomery assumed command of all Allied forces north of the German thrust. By that stage 1st US Army was involved in a series of delaying actions, moving forward divisions which were committed to action on arrival. The American reaction at higher command levels had been slow because the scale and strength of the

German offensive had not been fully appreciated, owing to scarce and inaccurate information from the front. Montgomery quickly guessed the enemy's intentions and formulated plans to head the Germans off from their final objectives and force them to advance south-west.

6th Airborne Division, now commanded by Major General Eric Bols, received orders to move to Belgium on 20 December. The main body departed its bases in Wiltshire two days later, and by 26 December the division was concentrated between Dinant and Namur. Three days later it received orders to prepare to advance against the tip of the German salient. 5th Parachute Brigade, on the right of the division, advanced towards Grupont, while 3rd Parachute Brigade occupied the area of Rochefort. Resistance from the enemy was stiff, and Brigadier Nigel Poett decided to mount an attack by 13th Parachute Battalion against the strongly-held village of Bure.

At 1300 hours on 3 January, 1945, the battalion crossed the start line in a wood overlooking Bure. The weather was very cold and there was thick snow on the ground. A Company, commanded by Major Jack Watson, was the left assault company, and Major Bill Grantham's B Company was on the right. As soon as the two companies crossed the start line they came under very heavy fire from machine guns, which pinned them down. During the next quarter of an hour, casualties in A Company amounted to a third of its strength. A Company resumed its advance over the 400 yards to the village, suffering more casualties on the way. B Company, which was attempting to take the high ground above, was also suffering badly after coming under fire from tanks and artillery. Major Bill Grantham had been killed as he crossed the start line, along with one of his platoon commanders, Lieutenant Tim Winser, and Company Sergeant Major Moss. The company second in command and one other platoon commander had been wounded, and thus it was the surviving platoon commander, Lieutenant Alf Largeren, who led the rest of the company forward towards its objective.

On reaching the village, A Company became involved in bitter fighting. As it advanced, clearing each house, it continued to suffer heavy casualties. Fighting took place at close quarters. In some instances German troops were firing from the upper storeys of houses while men of A Company fought downstairs, and vice versa. As the company reached the middle of the village, Tiger tanks appeared and opened fire. The battle raged throughout the day, A Company successfully beating off a series of counterattacks. Support arrived in the form of Sherman tanks of C Squadron Fife & Forfar Yeomanry. However, by the morning of the following day, 4 January, five of the Shermans had been knocked out. C Company 2nd Battalion Oxfordshire & Buckinghamshire Light Infantry, commanded by Major Johnny Granville, also arrived to reinforce A Company, which by then had been reduced to a platoon's strength.

On 5 January both companies were subjected to five more counter-attacks supported by tanks. However, these were broken up with the help of artillery support. The enemy responded with their own guns, subjecting A Company and Major Granville's Light Infantrymen to a series of heavy barrages. Another counterattack, launched by the enemy as Major Granville and his company advanced through A Company's positions, was also beaten off. That afternoon, after some fierce close-quarter and hand-to-hand fighting, the rest of the village was cleared with the help of C Company and was secured by 2100 hours that night. Early on the following morning 13th Parachute Battalion withdrew, having lost seven officers and 182 other ranks. Sixty-eight men had been killed, of whom about half were from A Company.

The wintry conditions made life very difficult for the division, and operations became somewhat hazardous because of the thick snow and sub-zero temperatures. On one occasion a patrol of 22nd Independent Parachute Company, reconnoitring a wood near the town of Marloie, between Namur and Luxembourg, inadvertently entered a minefield. The leading member of the patrol trod on an anti-personnel mine and was wounded. On going to his assistance, the patrol commander also fell victim to a mine. When five medical orderlies arrived to render emergency medical treatment and evacuate the two men, two of them were also wounded. A medical officer arrived and made his way into the minefield, reaching each man in turn and carrying out first aid. Shortly afterwards, Sergeant Lou Carrier and another sergeant from 22nd Independent Parachute Company appeared on the scene with mine detectors and some stretcher bearers. After clearing a path into the minefield, they made their way to the medical officer, who was supporting one of the wounded in a sitting position. On sweeping the area around the two men, the rescuers found a mine where the wounded man's shoulders would have been if he had been lying down, and two more by the medical officer's feet.

By the end of January, 6th Airborne Division had been withdrawn to Holland, where it took up positions near the River Maas in the area of Venlo and Roermond. A vigorous programme of patrolling was conducted by units of all of its three brigades, although such operations were made hazardous by the necessity of having to cross the Maas, which was wide and in full flood. The small assault craft used by patrols were often swept away by the strong current, and landfall at any predetermined spot on the far bank became difficult. Nevertheless, patrol operations continued, although by the middle of February the flood conditions made them even more hazardous. By then, conditions on the front were relatively quiet. After crossing the Maas, 1st Canadian Army had cleared the Reichswald by 13 February and was only a day's march away from the town of Emmerich on the banks of the Rhine.

During the third week of February, 6th Airborne Division, minus its seaborne 'tail', which remained in Belgium, was withdrawn to England to prepare for its role in a major operation which would take place in the latter part of the following month: Operation 'Varsity' — the crossing of the Rhine.

OPERATION 'VARSITY'

The failure of their Ardennes thrust cost the Germans dear. They had lost some 40,000 killed or wounded and over 50,000 captured by the time they withdrew over the Rhine. While the Allies had also suffered heavily, they possessed well supplied forces totalling almost four million men. The invasion of Germany was to be carried out in an operation codenamed 'Plunder', which would involve the 13th, 16th and 19th US Corps of General Simpson's 9th US Army together with the 8th, 12th and 30th British Corps, 2nd Canadian Corps and 18th US Airborne Corps comprising General Sir Miles Demsey's 2nd Army.

Field Marshal Montgomery's plan called for a crossing to be made north of the Ruhr, between the towns of Wesel and Emmerich. It would be carried out on a two-army front, with 9th US Army on the right and 2nd Army on the left. A bridgehead would be established beforehand from which their divisions would fan out and advance into northern Germany. This would extend from Emmerich in the north to Wesel in the south, and would be sufficient in depth to allow divisions to form up before the breakout northeastwards and eastwards into Germany. The bridgehead would be established initially by 18th US Airborne Corps, commanded by Major General Matthew Ridgway, which comprised 17th US Airborne Division, under Major General William 'Bud' Miley, and 6th Airborne Division. Its tasks were to seize and hold a feature called the Diesfordter-wald and the ground north of Wesel up to the line of the River Ijssel, and to defend the bridghead. The codename for the airborne phase of the crossing was 'Varsity'.

Both airborne divisions would be flown in one lift and dropped or landed on their objectives, which were in range of supporting artillery on the west bank of the Rhine. Link-ups with ground troops would take place

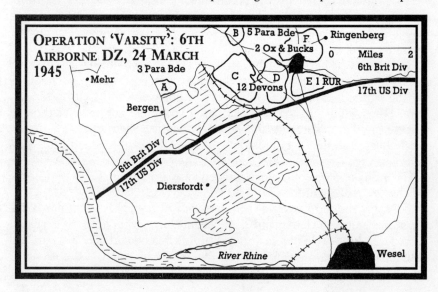

on the first day of the operation. 6th Airborne Division would drop and land on the northern part of the area at 1000 hours on 24 March. Its objectives would be the high ground east of Bergen, the town of Hamminkeln, and certain bridges over the River Ijssel. It was also to protect the northern flank of 18th US Airborne Corps. Subsequently, it was to link up with 17th US Airborne Division on its right and with 12th Corps which, after crossing the river, would move up from the rear on to its left flank. Armoured support would be provided by 6th Guards Tank Brigade as soon as it crossed the river. A squadron of the 3rd Tank Battalion Scots Guards would link up with 6th Airborne Division on the second day, the remainder of the battalion arriving as soon as it had crossed the river. The operation would be supported by a large amount of artillery. Three field regiments and two medium regiments would be in direct support of 6th Airborne Division, with a further two medium regiments being on call. In addition, a battery of American long-range guns would be available for harassing fire tasks.

The enemy forces opposing the Allied crossing consisted of 1st Parachute Army commanded by Generaloberst Schlemm, a veteran of the campaigns in Crete, Russia, Italy and the bitter fighting in the Reichswald. His forces comprised 2nd Parachute Corps, 86th Infantry Corps and 63rd Corps. In reserve was 47th Panzer Corps. 2nd Parachute Corps comprised 6th, 7th and 8th Parachute Divisions, each of which only consisted of between 3,000 and 4,000 men but which were still effective fighting formations. 86th Infantry Corps consisted mainly of 84th Infantry Division, which numbered only 1,500 men, whilst 47th Panzer Corps comprised 116th Panzer and 15th Panzer Grenadier Divisions. Enemy armour consisted of between 100 and 150 vehicles, while artillery was reported as totalling some 50 field or medium guns. However, enemy anti-aircraft artillery was reported as being in strength: 153 light and 103 heavy guns. By the third week of March these figures had increased to 712 light and 114 heavy weapons, indicating that the Germans were anticipating that the Allies would launch some form of airborne operation.

Major General Eric Bols issued his orders to his brigade commanders on 6 March. Commanding officers of units were briefed on 9 March, and by 21 March all officers down to platoon and troop level had received their orders. The plan involved 3rd Parachute Brigade dropping on to Dropping Zone 'A', at the north-west corner of the Diesfordterwald, and seizing the Schneppenberg feature. It would then clear and hold the western side of the forest and the road junction at Bergen, patrolling out to the area of the railway line which ran north-east through the forest — holding it if necessary. 5th Parachute Brigade would drop on Dropping Zone 'B', north-west of Hamminkeln, and would patrol westwards. It was to hold the area east of the railway line and link up with 3rd Parachute Brigade. 6th Airlanding Brigade, now commanded by Brigadier Hugh Bellamy, was given a series of objectives and would land in company groups as close as possible to each of them. Each battalion was allocated its own landing zone, within which there was a carefully planned location for each company. The 12th Battalion The Devonshire Regiment, which was tasked with capturing Hamminkeln, would land south-west of the town on Landing Zone 'R', while the 2nd Battalion The Oxfordshire & Buckinghamshire Light Infantry would land north of the town on Landing Zone 'O' and capture the road and rail bridges over the River Ijssel between Hamminkeln and Ringenberg. The 1st Battalion The Royal Ulster Rifles would land on Landing Zone 'U', south of Hamminkeln, and would capture the bridge over the Ijssel on the main road to Brunen.

On the night of 23 March a massive barrage was brought down on the German positions as 3,500 guns opened fire. For the previous two days the enemy had been subjected to a heavy bombardment by 5,561 bombers, which dropped 15,100 tons of bombs on defensive positions, barracks, roads, railways and airfields. At the same time, Allied fighter-bombers attacked convoys, anti-aircraft batteries and the headquarters of 1st Parachute Army. At 2100 hours on the 23rd, 1st Commando Brigade crossed the Rhine in assault craft while RAF Lancaster bombers attacked Wesel. At 2200 hours 12th Corps started to cross near Xanten, and an hour later 30th Corps crossed the river further north. By 0400 hours on the following morning 9th US Army had started crossing south of Wesel, and by dawn on 24 March a number of bridgeheads had been established on the east bank.

Meanwhile, the weather in England was good as the 'sticks' of parachute and airlanding troops of 6th Airborne Division waited beside their aircraft and gliders to emplane. At 0730 hours the first aircraft took off, and before long a vast armada of aircraft was airborne and heading for Germany and the Rhine. While crossing the Ruhr they met bombers returning from softening up targets on the ground. Over Belgium, the division's aircraft turned north-east and flew alongside the column of Dakotas carrying 17th US Airborne Division. One hour and forty minutes before the time of the parachute and glider landings (P-100) nine field regiments, eleven medium regiments, one heavy regiment, four heavy batteries, one heavy anti-aircraft regiment, one super-heavy battery and three American 155mm battalions opened fire on the areas on which both airborne divisions would land. An hour later, at P-40, they ceased fire. Ten minutes later, at P-30, another massive barrage was brought to bear on the enemy anti-aircraft defences. At P-Hour, as the leading aircraft of Nos. 38 and 46 Groups RAF, along with those of 9th US Troop Carrier Command USAAF, flew over the artillery positions on the west bank, the guns ceased fire to avoid any risk of hitting an aircraft inadvertently.

3rd Parachute Brigade jumped nine minutes late. 8th Parachute Battalion, now commanded by Lieutenant Colonel George Hewetson, was first to land. It was followed by Brigade Headquarters, 1st Canadian and then 9th Parachute Battalions, a troop of 3rd Parachute Squadron RE and 224th Parachute Field Ambulance. As the drop continued, enemy anti-aircraft fire grew stronger as the Germans recovered from the artillery barrages. 8th Parachute Battalion had been allowed only four minutes to secure the dropping zone and clear the enemy from the woods to the south and from two copses which dominated the DZ. As it landed, each company went straight into action. Major Bob Flood and A Company took a small wood in the north-eastern corner of the DZ, whilst C Company, under Major John Shappee, occupied the wood in the south-eastern corner with Battalion Headquarters and the Mortar Platoon. B Company and the Machine Gun Platoon met stiff opposition from two platoons of enemy paratroops when attempting to take their objective, the wood on the southern side of the dropping zone. Unfortunately the company had become disorganised on landing, and found itself under fire on the DZ. The company commander, Major John Kippen, eventually managed to assemble a force of about a platoon with which he assaulted the enemy positions. However, this attack was beaten off and Major Kippen, together with one of his platoon commanders, was killed. Subsequently, another platoon from B Company succeeded in taking the objective under covering fire from the first platoon.

1st Canadian Parachute Battalion came under heavy fire as it jumped from its aircraft, and several men were killed as they dropped or when they landed in some trees. Among these was the Commanding Officer, Lieutenant Colonel Jeff Nicklin, who landed in a tree above a machine gun position. He was killed as he hung in his parachute harness. On his death the Second in Command, Major Fraser Eadie, assumed command of the battalion. C Company was the first to land, coming under heavy machine gun fire as it did so. Misfortune struck when the company commander, Major John Hanson, broke his collarbone on landing, and the aircraft carrying the company second in command, Captain John Clancy, was hit by flak over the dropping zone. Along with two others Clancy managed to jump clear of the stricken aircraft, but landed in an enemy-held area and was captured. One of the other two men was carrying the company headquarters radio set. As he descended, a burst of machine gun fire severed the suspension cord by which his container hung below him. In the absence of both the company commander and second in command, Sergeants Saunders and Murray took over and quickly organised those of their men who had landed nearby. They quickly cleared the enemy on attacking their objective, putting several gun crews out of action.

A Company, commanded by Major Peter Griffin, landed at the eastern end of the dropping zone and put in an immediate attack on the buildings designated for use by Battalion Headquarters. An assault was also carried out on a group of houses which were part of the company's objective, but this met stiff opposition and the attack faltered. On seeing the problem, Company Sergeant Major Green led a group of men to the first house and cleared it after some fierce close-quarter fighting. After that, the remaining houses were successively cleared until the entire objective had been taken.

B Company, under Captain Sam McGowan, attacked a group of farm buildings and an area of woodland from which it was under fire from the enemy. With its own Bren light machine guns, the company assaulted the enemy positions, clearing bunkers and trenches with grenades. In the face of heavy fire, Company Sergeant Major Kemp led an attack on the farmhouse itself. Within 30 minutes the objective had been taken. However, No. 5 Platoon had suffered heavy casualties on the dropping zone, including its platoon commander, Lieutenant Jack Brunnette, who was killed.

The terrain on which 6th Airborne Division dropped was open grassland offering little or no cover. Consequently, casualties suffered on the dropping zones were heavy. In one instance a wounded man was lying in the open and two members of 224th Parachute Field Ambulance attempted to rescue him but were killed in the process. Corporal Topham, a medical orderly in 1st Canadian Parachute Battalion, went forward under heavy fire and rendered first aid to the wounded man. While doing so he was shot through the nose, but in spite of being in severe pain and bleeding profusely, he continued in his task. Having completed first aid, he then carried the man to safety. During the next two hours, Topham continued to bring in and treat wounded men, refusing help with his own wound until all the casualties had been cleared from the dropping zone. Subsequently, while returning to his company, he came across a Bren Gun carrier which had received a direct hit. The area was under heavy fire from enemy mortars and the carrier, which contained mortar bombs, was ablaze. Disregarding the enemy fire and the orders of an officer not to approach the vehicle, Topham went forward and rescued the vehicle's three crew, who were wounded. After carrying them back over open ground he gave them first aid. His great gallantry was subsequently recognised by the award of the Victoria Cross.

The last to drop was 9th Parachute Battalion, commanded by Lieutenant Colonel Napier Crookenden, and 45 minutes after landing it was assembled in its RV area. As the battalion advanced towards the Schneppenberg feature it encountered only light resistance from the enemy, but this was dealt with by A Company under Major Alen Parry. B Company attacked and silenced a battery of 76mm guns sited along the western edge of the woods. By 1300 hours the battalion had secured its objective. A Company was on the Schneppenberg, B Company was deployed astride the main road to the south-east, and C Company was occupying positions in the wood to the south of the road.

5th Parachute Brigade had received a rougher reception when it reached Dropping Zone 'A', because the enemy anti-aircraft gunners had recovered from the anti-flak bombardment by the time the aircraft carrying the brigade arrived over the dropping zone. Jumping with the three battalions were a detachment of 2nd Forward Observation Unit RA, a troop of 591st Parachute Squadron RE, and 225th Parachute Field Ambulance. As the aircraft approached the DZ they encountered heavy anti-aircraft fire and two Dakotas were hit. The DZ itself came under fire as the drop was taking place, and the three battalion RV areas were subjected to mortar and artillery barrages.

7th Parachute Battalion, still commanded by Lieutenant Colonel Geoffrey Pine Coffin, suffered a number of casualties from artillery shells airbursting among its sticks as they descended to the ground. By the time they reached the DZ they were under fire from artillery and mortars. A Company, together with the Mortar and Machine Gun Platoons, suffered particularly heavy casualties from a troop of 88mm guns sited in a small wood about 700 yards away. These were also bringing fire to bear on 12th Parachute Battalion and Brigade Headquarters, and continued to cause considerable damage until silenced. The battalion's initial task was to establish itself on the northern end of the dropping zone and to engage any enemy while 12th and 13th Parachute Battalions took the brigade's objective, which was the ground astride the road leading from the DZ to Hamminkeln, thus preventing any enemy movement through the area. In addition, it had a secondary task, which was to secure and hold an important road and rail junction in an opening in a big wood between 3rd and 5th Parachute Brigades. Lieutenant Colonel Pine Coffin despatched a platoon under Lieutenant Patterson, a Canadian who had joined the battalion in Normandy among a number of reinforcements and who had stayed with it, thereafter qualifying as a parachutist. Patterson and his men reached the area after several near encounters with the enemy. Subsequently, the platoon was subjected to a number of attacks, but these were beaten off in a highly unorthodox but successful fashion. If the attack was a weak one, the platoon would remain in its positions. If it appeared that the enemy were approaching in force, Patterson would withdraw his men to a flank and wait. As the enemy assaulted the empty trenches, the platoon would attack. This tactic was used on a number of occasions and resulted in the enemy suffering heavy casualties.

12th Parachute Battalion moved off rapidly after landing. Lieutenant Colonel Ken Darling had realised that speed was of the essence in this operation, and had therefore organised his battalion so that it could go straight into the attack on landing. During the preceding days the jumping order of each company and platoon had been reorganised so that men jumped in relation to where they were required to be on the dropping zone. In addition, weight of equipment was reduced to the barest minimum, items such as spare clothing, entrenching tools and grenades being discarded. Unfortunately, owing to the poor visibility caused by the pall of smoke and dust covering the area, most of the battalion made its way to the wrong location while seeking its RV. This error was soon discovered, and the Second in Command, Major Frank Bucher, led the battalion to the correct RV. However, as it moved across the dropping zone it came under heavy small-arms fire and was shelled by the troop of 88mm guns which had also caused casualties among 7th Parachute Battalion. Nevertheless, the battalion regrouped and A Company, commanded by Major Gerald Ritchie, proceeded to take its objective. No. 2 Platoon, under Lieutenant C. E. Crook, cleared some enemy from a nearby farm, while Lieutenant Phil Burkinshaw's No. 1 Platoon attacked and silenced the 88mm guns. C Company, under Major Steve Stephens, was meanwhile attacking its objective. A group of buildings were cleared by a group led by Lieutenant

T. Reed and Sergeant Wilson, and the rest of the company followed up and secured the remainder of the area.

Major E. J. O'B. 'Rip' Croker and B Company were having a tough time taking their objective, a group of farm buildings occupied by a large number of enemy who were putting up a stiff fight. Lieutenant Peter Cattell, leading the assault group, was wounded while clearing a building and shortly afterwards Lieutenant Ginger Delaney suffered the same fate. However, Sergeant Dobson and No. 4 Platoon arrived shortly afterwards and took the rest of the objective. The company had suffered several casualties among its officers and senior NCOs. In addition to Lieutenants Cattell and Delaney, Lieutenant M. Mustoe, the commander of No. 6 Platoon, had been captured after dropping some distance from the dropping zone, and Company Sergeant Major Warcup had been wounded.

By the time the aircraft carrying 13th Parachute Battalion arrived over the dropping zone, a thick pall of dust and smoke covered the entire area. Nevertheless, the battalion landed virtually intact and rallied swiftly to the sound of the company commanders' hunting horns. A Company, under Major Jack Watson, went straight into action, one of its platoons capturing an enemy machine gun position. Within a very short time the battalion had secured all of its objectives and had taken a large number of prisoners.

As the day wore on the intensity of the fighting slackened. By 1500 hours 5th Parachute Brigade had taken all of its objectives and 7th Parachute Battalion was ordered to start withdrawing at 1545 hours. This was carried out with some difficulty, as B and C Companies were still in contact with the enemy, but the withdrawal was eventually achieved without loss and the battalion moved into reserve. It had suffered heavy casualties during the day, mainly caused by anti-aircraft fire during the drop and by mortar and artillery fire on its positions. Total casualties numbered 92 out of just over 500 men who had dropped that morning.

Headquarters 5th Parachute Brigade had also suffered losses. Brigadier Nigel Poett had followed his normal custom of jumping with the leading elements of his brigade. He lost his Brigade Major, Major Mike Brennan, his Signals Officer, Lieutenant Crawford, and his DAA & QMG, Major Ted Lough, who was badly wounded while flying in by glider. As a result, Brigadier Poett had to reorganise his headquarters after reaching its RV.

Heavy casualties had been suffered by the gliderborne elements of the two parachute brigades and 6th Airlanding Brigade. As these approached the landing zones the enemy anti-aircraft guns switched their attention to the gliders and their tugs. Several aircraft were hit in mid-air and as they landed, causing heavy losses. Moreover, the poor visibility on the LZs made landing difficult and there were several collisions on the ground. In some instances pilots were unable to find their bearings and landed their gliders in the wrong place. One result of this was that only a small proportion of the vehicles, anti-tank guns, mortars and ammunition reached the parachute battalions. Losses among the glider pilots themselves were high, over 100 being killed, wounded or missing.

Despite the chaos on the LZs, sufficient numbers of all three battalions of 6th Airlanding Brigade were landed in the correct locations and succeeded in taking their objectives. However, only 11 of the 24 pack howitzers of 53rd Airlanding light Regiment RA were in action after landing, the remainder being destroyed or missing. 2nd Airlanding Anti-Tank Regiment RA suffered similarly, only half of its guns being brought into action after landing. Fortunately, the considerable amount of artillery support from the west bank of the Rhine helped compensate for these losses. 6th Airborne Division's own armoured element, 6th Airborne Armoured Reconnaissance Regiment, also suffered badly. Of the eight Locust light tanks flown in by Hamilcar gliders, only four survived the landings and reached the RV. Of those, only two were fit for action.

Major General Eric Bols and his tactical headquarters had landed within 100 yards of the location earmarked for them in a farm. By 1100 hours the main divisional headquarters had been set up, and within ten minutes radio communications had been established with all three brigades. That night, Major General Ridgway, commander of 18th US Airborne Corps, arrived at Headquarters 6th Airborne Division with Major General 'Bud' Miley, commander of 17th US Airborne Division. During their meeting, Major General Ridgway issued Major General Bols with his orders for the advance eastwards, which would begin on the morning of 26 March.

THE ADVANCE TO THE BALTIC

The advance began at 0900 hours, when 6th Airlanding Brigade moved eastwards, supported by a squadron of Churchill tanks of the 3rd Tank Battalion Scots Guards. Two miles after the start line had been crossed, the 12th Battalion The Devonshire Regiment encountered enemy infantry supported by tanks and self-propelled guns. A successful attack was put in with artillery support, and the battalion moved forward to take its main objective, the high ground above the town of Brunen. In the meantime, the 1st Battalion The Royal Ulster Rifles had also met opposition after crossing the River Ijssel and moving up on to the Devons' left flank. As it moved towards the high ground above Brunen, the battalion came under fire and called for support from a 'cab rank' of Typhoon fighter-bombers on call. These hit targets to the rear of the enemy positions as the battalion put in a successful attack. That night, patrols from 6th Airlanding Brigade entered Brunen and found that the enemy had withdrawn.

Meanwhile, 3rd Parachute Brigade had moved forward to the west banks of the Ijssel on being released from corps reserve on the afternoon of 26 March. Patrols were sent out, and it was discovered that enemy positions on the east bank had been abandoned. Brigadier James Hill established a bridgehead on his own initiative and was given permission by Major General Bols to exploit forward towards his objective, the area of the village of Klosterlutherheim and the high ground south-east of Lembeck, on the following day. After crossing the river, the brigade continued its advance during the night of 26 March, with the 3rd Tank Battalion Scots Guards under command.

At 0530 hours on the following morning 1st Canadian Parachute Battalion was advancing on its objective, the village of Burch, when B Company encountered a Tiger tank at close range. After a brief exchange of fire with a PIAT team, the tank withdrew and the battalion pressed on towards its objective, where it began to dig in. As it did so it came under heavy shellfire from some tanks and self-propelled guns in a wood about a quarter of a mile away. B Company was particularly badly affected, suffering a number of casualties. The Commanding Officer, Lieutenant Colonel Fraser Eadie, decided that there was no alternative but to mount an immediate attack on the wood, despite the fact that this would have to be a frontal assault over open ground against concealed armour and without artillery support. Accordingly, the battalion attacked with B Company once more in the van. It was supported by two armed jeeps, equipped with Browning .50 heavy machine guns, which had suddenly appeared as the battalion was preparing for the attack. These laid down a heavy volume of fire as the battalion advanced across the open ground. By the time B Company reached the woods the enemy had withdrawn, so the battalion pushed through into the village beyond the woods, where it established itself.

Meanwhile, 9th Parachute Battalion had attacked Klosterlutherheim, which it captured after a short but fierce engagement in which 12 enemy were killed and 180 taken prisoner.

5th Parachute Brigade was ordered to move through 3rd Parachute Brigade and to take the village of Erle. The advance began at 1100 hours, with 6th Airborne Armoured Reconnaissance Regiment deployed forward as a screen. By 1200 hours the brigade had passed through Brunen, and it was not until the early afternoon that it met an enemy force consisting of an

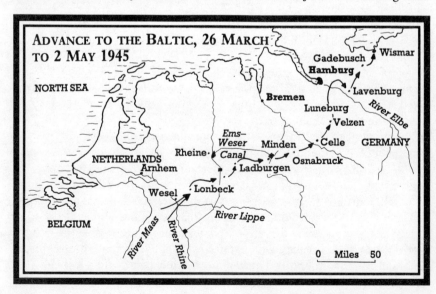

ADVANCE TO THE BALTIC, 26 MARCH TO 2 MAY 1945

infantry company supported by a number of 20mm light anti-aircraft guns and some self-propelled guns. 7th Parachute Battalion was given the task of clearing the enemy positions, which were astride the divisional axis of advance. C Company attacked a crossroads which was held by some self-propelled guns, while the rest of the battalion carried out a flanking move. No. 7 Platoon, under Lieutenant Whitworth, was in the van when it came under fire from some anti-tank guns and 20mm light anti-aircraft guns being used in the ground-target role. After reconnoitring the ground, which was open with fences across the line of advance, Major Bob Keene decided against putting in an attack under cover of smoke. Dusk was now falling, and C Company took up positions on the edge of a wood. At this point the enemy set fire to some haystacks, and the light from the flames illuminated the company's positions, which were on a forward slope. The company was almost immediately pinned down, but was rescued by a fighting patrol from B Company which put in an attack from the north, catching the enemy by surprise. C Company immediately advanced and took the crossroads, capturing 60 prisoners.

By then it was midnight. 13th Parachute Battalion had moved on towards its own objective, the high ground above the village of Erle. Unfortunately, radio communications with the rest of the brigade had been lost, and thus Brigadier Nigel Poett had no way of knowing when and if the battalion had reached its objective.

At 0200 hours the following morning, by which time no news had been received of 13th Parachute Battalion, Brigadier Poett decided that 12th Parachute Battalion would have to start its advance on Erle. However, he changed the plan of attack and the battalion was despatched across country to take up positions at the rear of the village, thereby cutting the enemy's line of supply and communications to the east. The initial five-mile stage of 12th Parachute Battalion's march, which lasted five hours, took it via the high ground on which it met 13th Parachute Battalion. By then there was only another hour and a half before dawn, in which to cover the remaining two miles to the battalion's objective. Leaving Headquarter Company under Major Douglas Freegard, the Second in Command, together with the Mortar and Machine Gun Platoons, Lieutenant Colonel Ken Darling and the three rifle companies set off at speed. Fortunately it was raining heavily, and this helped to reduce visibility and thus increase the chances of surprise being achieved. First light on 28 March found the battalion on the road on the eastern side of Erle and heading for the village. A No. 36 grenade lobbed into the back of a parked truck filled with stick grenades produced startling results, and was the signal for the attack to begin. The enemy responded by firing wildly, but in 15 minutes the battalion had seized its objective. Three self-propelled guns withdrew without firing a shot, and within an hour the village had been secured and 200 enemy taken prisoner. Soon afterwards, enemy artillery brought down a very heavy concentration on A and B Companies and Battalion Headquarters. Fortunately the battalion was well dug in and suffered only light casualties. Brigadier Poett than arrived with some anti-tank guns and ambulances, and Lieutenant Colonel Darling learned that the rest of the brigade would be moving up to the village and that the battalion would be responsible for the defence of the northern approaches.

At midnight on 27/28 March, 6th Airborne Division had passed from under command of 18th US Airborne Corps to that of 8th Corps, commanded by Lieutenant General Sir Evelyn Barker, which was advancing on an axis towards the Baltic. The axis was intersected by two rivers, the Weser and the Elbe, and thus the advance itself was divided into three phases: from the division's locations at that time to the Weser, from the Weser to the Elbe, and from the Elbe to the Baltic. The division's initial objective was the town of Coesfeld, which lay about 35 miles north-east of Erle. With the Inns of Court Regiment under command, it would take the town while 11th Armoured Division advanced on a parallel axis to the north-east, dominating the town from the north.

The advance began at 1200 hours on 28 March. 3rd Parachute Brigade led the way, followed by 6th Airlanding Brigade. The first encounter with the enemy took place 2,000 yards east of Erle, but any resistance was quickly brushed aside as the advance continued. Heavier resistance was met between Rhade and Lembeck, but 8th Parachute Battalion quickly dealt with it before continuing the advance towards Lembeck, which was about 6,000 yards away. As resistance began to grow stiffer, however, 9th Parachute Battalion was despatched on a flanking movement to approach the town from the rear and cut it off. As 8th Parachute Battalion approached the western edges of Lembeck, its leading company became pinned down by fire from some 20mm light anti-aircraft guns. 1st Canadian Parachute Battalion, which was in reserve, moved up along the axis while 8th Parachute Battalion mounted a flanking attack on the town from the south, supported by 6th Airborne Armoured Reconnaissance Regiment. The battle for the town raged throughout the rest of the day and, as dusk fell, Brigadier James Hill ordered 8th Parachute Battalion to take the high ground to the south of the town. The leading company became separated from the rest of the battalion while becoming embroiled in a fierce action with two companies of a panzer grenadier training unit. By midnight, however, the battalion had gained the upper hand. Meanwhile, the detached company fought its way into the western suburbs of the town, where it was subsequently joined by 1st Canadian Parachute Battalion.

While the battle was being waged in Lembeck, 9th Parachute Battalion carried out its flanking move to the east of the town. While moving over the high ground to the north, the battalion came under fire from a battery of four 20mm light anti-aircraft guns. These were engaged by A Company, which pinned down the enemy gunners while a patrol under Lieutenant Harpley attacked from a flank and overran the guns and their crews. The battalion then pushed on and took up positions, cutting off the town from the east.

On the following morning, 29 March, 6th Airlanding Brigade moved through 3rd Parachute Brigade, which remained in its locations until the following day, when it resumed the advance after once again taking over the van. Its objective was the bridge across the River Ems in the town of

Greven, about 35 miles away. 1st Canadian Parachute Battalion led the way in trucks, A Company being mounted on the Churchill tanks of Nos. 1 and 3 Squadrons of the 4th Tank Battalion Grenadier Guards. As the column advanced, pockets of resistance were dealt with by A Company and the Grenadiers, the Canadians dismounting and carrying out sweeps on either side of the road while the tanks opened fire on any likely enemy positions.

By the time dusk fell the battalion had advanced to within three miles of Greven. From here it moved forward on foot while the Grenadiers and their tanks took up covering positions along the river. The bridge was taken within minutes, and shortly afterwards 9th Parachute Battalion arrived to join the Canadians. The Commanding Officer, Lieutenant Colonel Napier Crookenden, and his reconnaissance group moved down the main street, and spotted another bridge as they arrived at the river. As Crookenden went forward to reconnoitre it, the bridge was blown by the enemy. It was only then that 1st Canadian Parachute Battalion discovered that their maps were inaccurate; they showed only one bridge, whereas there were two. The battalion had seized the wrong bridge, which led to an island in the middle of the river. With the main bridge now blown, there was no alternative but to wait for sappers to bring up bridging equipment. 9th Parachute Battalion withdrew and moved southwards along the river where, at 0345 hours, a footbridge was found. At dawn on 31 March two patrols from A Company and one from C Company crossed over. As they did so they came under fire and Lieutenant McGuffie, commanding the C Company patrol, was killed. After a fierce battle lasting an hour the enemy positions were overrun, and by 0730 hours the town had been taken.

That night 1st Canadian Parachute Battalion had been kept busy, its positions along the river bank being constantly under fire. In addition, a troop train, carrying enemy troops returning from leave, had arrived at the town's railway station. Its passengers had suddenly found themselves being taken prisoner and being marched away to a PoW cage. In the early hours of the morning the sky had suddenly been lit up with the noise and flashes of large explosions as the enemy destroyed a large ammunition dump on the far side of the river.

During the morning, sappers constructed a Bailey bridge across the river in the main part of Greven and strengthened another south of the town. After crossing the river, 3rd Parachute Brigade pushed on for another ten miles, with 8th Parachute Battalion in the lead, until it reached the west bank of the Dortmund-Ems Canal during the later afternoon. On its arrival there, however, it was discovered that the main canal bridge and a second smaller one, half a mile to the south, had been destroyed. During the night, 6th Airlanding Brigade moved through 3rd Parachute Brigade to take over the lead. On the following morning, 1 April, sappers of 591st Parachute Squadron RE began bridging the canal. By then, however, two companies of 8th Parachute Battalion had already managed to cross over and had advanced about a mile. Shortly after the sappers arrived, the bridging site came under fire from some self-propelled guns some distance away, and the shelling continued until midday. That night, 6th Airlanding Brigade continued the advance eastwards, men crossing over via the remains of the destroyed canal bridge. At 0300 hours on the following morning, 2 April, vehicles followed over the bridge constructed by 591st Parachute Squadron RE.

The morning of 3 April found 5th Parachute Brigade advancing towards Osnabruck. In the lead was 12th Parachute Battalion, supported by No. 3 Squadron of the 4th Tank Battalion Grenadier Guards. After crossing the Dortmund Ems Canal, the brigade advanced on Lengerich, which it reached at 1400 hours. C Company 12th Parachute Battalion was mounted on the Grenadiers' tanks, and the remainder of the battalion followed on foot after dismounting from its trucks because of the threat from enemy shellfire. After passing through Lengerich the battalion moved up to the forward positions of the 1st Battalion The Royal Ulster Rifles, one of whose supporting tanks had been knocked out by an 88mm gun sited 800 yards away along the road which was the axis of advance. As one of No. 3 Squadron's Churchills advanced to a position from which to engage the gun, it was also knocked out. Under cover of heavy fire from the Grenadiers, who also laid down a thick smokescreen to the right to deceive the enemy as to the direction of attack, A and C Companies carried out a flanking move to the left. No. 8 Platoon, commanded by Sergeant Wilson, attacked the gun and knocked it out. C Company advanced further up the road, while A Company occupied the enemy position as the rest of the battalion followed up.

By then dusk was falling, and the Grenadiers, unable to operate with their tanks at night, withdrew to a harbour area to refuel and replenish ammunition. Meanwhile, 12th Parachute Battalion advanced on foot with Major Gerald Ritchie's A Company in the lead. After about a mile Lieutenant Phil Burkinshaw and No. 1 Platoon, who were in the lead, heard sounds of digging. Shortly afterwards, two enemy sentries were spotted on the edge of the small village of Natrup. These were silently dealt with, and No. 1 Platoon worked its way to within 30 yards of the enemy before opening fire. The rest of A Company then joined the platoon in assaulting the enemy positions, which were rapidly overrun.

At 0230 hours on the following morning, 4 April, 12th Parachute Battalion resumed its advance. An hour later B Company, which was in the lead, encountered an enemy roadblock. At this point Lieutenant Colonel Ken Darling decided to deviate from the axis of advance along the road and carry out a flanking move to the left and round to the rear of the village of Hasbergen. This was situated beyond the high ground in front of the battalion, and at its far end was a road junction from which a road led to the battalion's objective, the town of Osnabruck. Darling planned to carry out a two-phase attack on Hasbergen. The first phase consisted of cutting the village off from the east by positioning A and C Companies, together with himself and his tactical headquarters, astride the road junction, while at the same time securing the high ground which dominated the area. The second phase would be an attack on the village from the rear while Headquarter and B Companies under the Second in Command, Major Frank Bucher, advanced along the main axis.

At that point Brigadier Nigel Poett arrived and directed that the high ground had to be taken by dawn at 0630 hours. By then it was 0430 hours, so the battalion had only two hours to complete the task. A and C Companies moved off at 0520, accompanied by the tactical element of Battalion Headquarters. As they did so, B Company laid down covering fire to provide a diversion and to cover the noise of the two companies during the flanking move. At one point the leading element of A Company came under fire and it was feared that it had been spotted. However, the firing ceased shortly afterwards and there was no further reaction from the enemy. The two companies reached their objective by dawn, and the eastern exits from the village were duly blocked. Shortly afterwards, two platoons were despatched into Hasbergen to clear it, and the village was taken and secured within an hour, over 100 enemy troops being taken prisoner.

Meanwhile, Headquarter and B Companies had advanced, the latter with its three platoons astride the road. Between them and the wooded ridge ahead of them was a row of houses to the right of the road. On the left was open ground, beyond which was a small wood which bordered on the road. Thereafter there was another stretch of open ground to the foot of the ridge. The first three houses were cleared by No. 4 Platoon while a section of No. 6 Platoon cleared the forwardmost building. During this action the company second in command, Captain Kauffmann, was killed. At 0625 hours the Machine Gun Platoon opened fire with its Vickers guns, protecting B Company's right flank as No. 4 Platoon moved forward and took some houses on the forward edge of the ridge. As it did so it came under fire from two 75mm guns and from snipers. Nevertheless, it continued to provide support until ordered to withdraw 35 minutes later. The battalion's mortars were able to fire only three or four rounds before being ordered to cease fire because of the risk of causing casualties among B Company, whose mortar fire controller had lost radio contact with the mortar baseline.

By 0700 hours, when dawn came, Nos. 4 and 6 Platoons had occupied the houses at the foot of the ridge. As radio contact with them had been lost, Major Frank Bucher decided to join them with the rear element of Battalion Headquarters and No. 5 Platoon. While attempting to do so, he and his men came under fire and were pinned down, suffering two casualties. Major Bucher's call for support was answered by a troop of the Grenadiers, whose Churchills advanced to provide covering fire. As Bucher clambered on to the leading tank it was hit by a 75mm gun and he was blown off its turret. A second Churchill attempted to carry out a right flanking attack but shed a track and was immobilised.

At 0730 hours Brigadier Poett came forward to see how the battle was progressing. On seeing the situation, he ordered 13th Parachute Battalion to move up and mount an attack. However, this was forestalled by B Company, which pressed home an assault supported by the third tank in the Grenadier troop. At this point the enemy surrendered. Twenty-seven of them had been killed and five 75mm guns knocked out. 13th Parachute Battalion moved through Hasbergen at 1100 hours with the Grenadiers' tanks in support, taking over the lead from a very tired 12th Parachute Battalion. Lieutenant Colonel Darling and his men had been in operation for 30 hours, had led the division's advance for 25 miles, had fought four major engagements and had killed or captured 300 enemy. Although there had been little or no opportunity to eat and rest, Lieutenant Colonel Darling found his men in great form, with their fighting spirit as keen as ever, when he wandered among them before they resumed the advance to Osnabruck, which was reached at midnight.

Meanwhile, 3rd Parachute Brigade had been advancing on Wissingen, about six miles east of Osnabruck. The entire brigade was travelling in armoured troop carriers and half-tracks or on the backs of tanks. 9th Parachute Battalion was leading the brigade, and took Wissingen after some heavy fighting during the afternoon. On the following morning, 4 April, the brigade advanced on Lubbecke with 1st Canadian Parachute Battalion in the van, its objective being the city of Minden on the River Weser. As the brigade in its vehicles moved swiftly along the road which was the axis of advance, it met large numbers of enemy troops surrendering en masse. Such was the rate of advance that the brigade could do no more than disarm them and send them back towards other formations following behind.

After reaching Lubbecke, 3rd Parachute Brigade pushed on towards Minden and reached the outskirts of the city, where it halted. As dusk fell, 8th Parachute Battalion came under fire and was pinned down. On receiving a report that the enemy force was not large, Brigadier James Hill decided to carry out a night attack. At 2345 hours, with the Grenadier Guards' tanks leading the way, 1st Canadian Parachute Battalion stormed the enemy positions and advanced into the city. The two other battalions were close behind, and throughout the night there was fierce fighting as the enemy were cleared from the streets. By 0230 hours on 5 April Minden had been taken. Its capture by 3rd Parachute Brigade had saved it from a far worse fate — a mass bombing raid before attack by elements of 9th US Army. That afternoon, American units arrived to take over from the brigade, which moved three miles to the north, to the village of Kutenhausen.

That same day 5th Parachute Brigade was concentrated at Friede Walde. It had been intended that 15th (Scottish) Division would take over the lead in the remaining stages of the advance to the Baltic, but it was unable to move up in time. Thus 6th Airborne Division remained the spearhead of 8th Corps. Three days later, on 8 April, the advance resumed with the brigade in the lead. Its tasks were to seize two bridges over the River Leine at Neustadt and Bordenau. Its line of advance would take it over the River Weser at Petershagen, where a bridgehead had been established by 6th Airlanding Brigade, and then on through the towns of Roisenhagen, Bergkirchen and Altenhagen and eventually to some high ground north of Wunstorf, two miles from the Leine. At that point, 12th

Parachute Battalion would take the bridge at Bordenau while 7th Parachute Battalion secured the one at Neustadt, some three miles upstream. 12th Parachute Battalion would once again be leading the brigade. Behind it would be No. 3 Squadron of the 4th Tank Battalion Grenadier Guards, 15th (Scottish) Division Reconnaissance Regiment, a troop of 4th Airlanding Anti-Tank Battery RA, a field battery and a medium battery.

The advance began at 1000 hours, with elements of the reconnaissance regiment deployed forward to reconnoitre the axis and both flanks. C Company 12th Parachute Battalion, mounted on the Grenadiers' tanks, came next, followed by the two artillery batteries which moved in bounds, one being in action and ready to bring down supporting fire whilst the other was moving forward to its next location. The rest of 12th Parachute Battalion, under Major Frank Bucher, followed them in troop carrying vehicles. No enemy were encountered until after the River Weser had been crossed, and these were dealt with as the advance continued. As the column neared Wunstorf, C Company and the Grenadier tank squadron reached the village of Altenhagen. There the enemy were routed by a few rounds fired down the main street by a troop of 4th Airlanding Anti-Tank Battery RA, after which the advance continued.

At this point the River Leine was only five miles away. There were two routes to the objective. The northernmost one ran through a number of small villages and then to some high ground north of an airfield at Wunstorf. The alternative southern route led through more open country. Lieutenant Colonel Ken Darling, travelling with C Company, discussed the situation with the Grenadiers' squadron leader, Major Ivor Crosthwaite, and they decided there was a good chance of taking the bridge if they travelled via the route to the south. After confirming this decision with Major General Eric Bols and Brigadier Nigel Poett, who arrived on the scene at that juncture, Darling led his battalion off on the southern route after ordering C Company and the Grenadiers to cover the distance to the bridge as quickly as possible.

For the first three miles the column made swift progress, and it was not until it had passed through Wunstorf and was approaching the airfield there that any resistance was encountered. However, C Company quickly dealt with it and the column was soon on the move again, bypassing the airfield as it covered the final two miles to the bridge at Bordenau. As the leading Churchill rounded the final bend, the bridge could be seen. However, there was a vehicle and a small group of enemy troops on it. Fearing these to be enemy sappers preparing the bridge for demolition, the column brought every weapon to bear and opened fire as it raced towards them. The enemy fled, swiftly followed by the Grenadiers' tanks, which roared on to the bridge. As they did so, Lieutenant Colonel Darling and C Company leaped off and swiftly disconnected the demolition firing circuits which they found.

Meanwhile, 7th Parachute Battalion was advancing on Neustadt after clearing the airfield at Wunstorf with the help of 13th Parachute Battalion. Having reached the town, it found the bridge intact. B Company, commanded by Major Derick 'Tiger' Reid, was in the lead. As it started to cross the bridge Corporal Taylor, one of the sappers from 591st Parachute Squadron RE attached to the company, spotted that the bridge was prepared for demolition and shouted a warning. Tragically, he was not heard. Seconds later, as the leading platoon was halfway across, the enemy blew the bridge, killing 22 men and wounding several others. However, a bridgehead was established by Captain E. G. Woodman, Lieutenant G. B. Gush and two men who had been the first to cross the bridge and had thus escaped injury.

By the evening of 7 April 5th Parachute Brigade had advanced farther into Germany than any other troops in 21st Army Group. Four days later, on 11 April, 15th (Scottish) Division took over as leading formation in 8th Corps and 6th Airborne Division assumed the task of clearing up the axis of advance. The advance to the Baltic continued, the division passing through the town of Celle and on 16 and 17 April holding several villages east of Uelzen, which was attacked by 15th (Scottish) Division. Enemy resistance in this area was the fiercest that the division had encountered since crossing the Rhine. It was not until 15th (Scottish) Division had taken Uelzen after some fierce street fighting, and 6th Airborne Division had bypassed it and advanced on the town of Rosche to the east, that all opposition was finally overcome.

By 23 April 8th Corps had reached the River Elbe, which was a major obstacle, being 300 yards wide. The far bank, on which enemy positions were sited, consisted of a steep wooded escarpment, while the western bank, from which the crossing had to be launched, was flat marshland offering little or no cover. Six days later, on 29 April, a five-phase operation to cross the river began. 15th (Scottish) Division, with 1st Commando Brigade under command, carried out an assault river crossing, established a bridgehead at Lauenburg and seized the bridges over the Elbe-Trave Canal east of the town. By the end of the first day it had also completed the second phase and extended the bridgehead to the town of Kruzen, two miles north of Lauenburg. On the following day, 30 April, it completed the third phase, which involved extending it a further seven miles. The fourth phase of the operation involved 15th (Scottish) Division handing over the eastern sector of the bridgehead to 6th Airborne Division. 3rd Parachute Brigade, together with 15th Infantry Brigade, crossed the Elbe on the morning of the second day, 30 April, and headed eastwards to an area beyond Boizenberg, where it linked up with American forces. Subsequently, the rest of 6th Airborne Division followed to carry out the fifth and final phase. This involved deploying 15th Infantry Brigade, which was detached from 5th Infantry Division and under command of 6th Airborne Division, to secure the area west of the Elbe-Trave Canal and to seize two bridges over the canal about eight miles north of Lauenburg, the final limits of the bridgehead.

After crossing the canal, 6th Airborne Division was once again under command of 18th US Airborne Corps. On the evening of 30 April, Major General Matthew Ridgway arrived at Headquarters 3rd Parachute Brigade with orders for the division to advance with all speed the following day to the town of Wismar, on the Baltic coast, with the aim of arriving there before the Russians, who were advancing westwards. The division was to prevent them from entering Denmark. On the following morning, 1 May, both parachute brigades set off in a headlong dash for Wismar along separate routes which would take them to a town called Gadebusch, 15 miles south of Wismar. From there it was a single route to Wismar itself. Both brigade commanders were determined to be the first to arrive, but in the event it was 3rd Parachute Brigade which reached Gadebusch first, and ultimately Wismar, on the morning of 2 May. With 1st Canadian Parachute Battalion in the lead, its B Company mounted on the tanks of its supporting squadron of Royal Scots Greys, the brigade had thundered past units of fully armed enemy troops attempting to surrender. Occasional resistance was encountered, but this was quickly countered by fire from the tanks as the column sped onwards. At 0900 hours 1st Canadian Parachute Battalion entered Wismar and encountered an enemy roadblock with enemy troops dug in around it. B Company dismounted and cleared the enemy while the Royal Scots Greys shot their way through the roadblock.

By 1200 hours the rest of the brigade had arrived, and at 1600 hours that afternoon the leading elements of Russian forces were encountered by 1st Canadian Parachute Battalion, which was by then deployed on the eastern side of the town. That afternoon Lieutenant Colonel Napier Crookenden, accompanied by two Russian-speaking sergeants from 1st Canadian Parachute Battalion, made contact with a senior Russian officer. Subsequently, there was a meeting between Major General Bols and a senior Russian commander, who stated that his mission was to capture Lubeck. Major General Bols called the Russian's bluff, indicating that he would use force to stop him if necessary. Needless to say, the Russian backed down. Meetings took place between British and Russian officers at brigade and divisional level, followed by one between Major General Bols and Marshal Rokossovsky. Relations between the two sides were barely cordial, and had deteriorated by 7 May, when Field Marshal Montgomery arrived to meet Rokossovsky, although high-level communications were maintained.

On 8 May 1945 the war in Europe ended and the latter half of the month saw the return of 6th Airborne Division to its bases in Wiltshire. On 31 May it bid a sad farewell to 1st Canadian Parachute Battalion, which began its long journey back to Canada. Having been an integral part of the division almost from its inception, and having proved to be a fighting unit second to none, the battalion had earned itself a special place in the annals of British airborne forces, and it was thereafter much missed by 6th Airborne Division.

CHAPTER 7
2nd Independent Brigade Group in Italy, Southern France and Greece, November 1943 to October 1945

When 1st Airborne Division sailed for England in November 1943, 2nd Parachute Brigade remained in Italy and was redesignated an independent brigade group. In addition to 4th, 5th and 6th Parachute Battalions, it also comprised 2nd Parachute Squadron RE, 127th Parachute Field Ambulance, a REME light aid detachment and a Corps of Military Police provost detachment. Having been placed under command of General Alexander's 15th Army Group, the brigade moved south to Gioia to carry out airborne training in conjunction with aircraft of the USAAF's Troop Carrier Command. It had only just done so when, on the evening of 30 November, it received orders from General Montgomery's 8th Army to move within 48 hours to an area in the British line north of the River Sangro, where it would be deployed in the infantry role.

On the evening of 2 December, by which time it had come under command of 2nd New Zealand Division, commanded by Lieutenant General Sir Bernard Freyberg VC, the brigade was travelling north by road and rail. Eventually, it was advancing in driving rain along a narrow and muddy mountain track to take up its new positions. En route, the brigade met some opposition south of Guardiagrele, but this caused few problems. By 6 December it was holding a 25-mile front north of the Sangro and south of Castelfrentano. The enemy were holding the town of Torricella and the high ground south of Orsogna which overlooked the Sangro. On 8 December, 2nd New Zealand Division mounted an attack, but this failed. A second attack, launched from the east on 13 December, was successful. During this attack a number of patrols from all three battalions operated against the enemy from the south.

The weather during this period was little short of atrocious, and the brigade was ill-equipped to cope with the blizzards which blanketed their positions on New Year's Eve and New Year's Day of 1944. In some areas of the brigade's positions the snow lay six feet deep. Particularly badly affected were those men of 6th Parachute Battalion who had lost their personal equipment and clothing when the minelayer HMS *Abdiel* had been blown up and sunk in Taranto harbour. Some of them were clad only in overalls given to them by the Royal Navy after being rescued. The adverse weather conditions made resupply extremely difficult at times. Roads and tracks became impassable even to jeeps, and ammunition and rations frequently had to be manpacked up to the forward positions, which were on mountain ridges. In some instances these were overlooked by the enemy, making movement during the day difficult.

The brigade was deployed in a series of strongpoints. On identifying any enemy movement within its area it could call for support from the guns of the divisional and corps artillery. The enemy adopted similar tactics, and there was a considerable amount of shelling and mortar fire brought to bear on both sides. In the main, the brigade's operations during this period consisted of patrolling. It was under orders to capture prisoners, as information was urgently required on the order of battle of the German forces commanded by Feldmarschall Kesselring. Much was learned from enemy prisoners. One individual even obliged by assisting a forward observation officer to bring down fire on the positions occupied by his former comrades.

Clad in sheets to provide camouflage in the snow-covered terrain, the patrols ventured forth to raid the enemy positions or lay ambushes. On one occasion, Lieutenant Shepherd, the Intelligence Officer of 5th Parachute Battalion, calmly entered a house occupied by a number of Germans and helped himself to a cooked chicken waiting to be eaten. On another occasion Lieutenant G. L. Mortimer of C Company 4th Parachute Battalion led a patrol into Orsogna and returned with several prisoners.

On 16 January the brigade came under command of 8th Indian Division, which relieved 2nd New Zealand Division. On 16 February it was withdrawn into reserve in the area of Castelfrentano after being relieved by 17th Indian Infantry Brigade. A week later, on 23 February, it returned to the area of Casoli and resumed patrolling and harrassing the enemy at every opportunity. At the end of March the brigade withdrew to Guardia, near Naples, for a rest. By then it had been in action for four months, at the end of which it had suffered a considerable number of casualties. 5th Parachute Battalion, which had been in very exposed positions overlooked by the enemy, had lost a number of men in the Salorola sector facing the enemy's main defensive line along a ridgeline between Orsogna and Guardigrela. Such men could not be replaced easily because no reinforcements were forthcoming from England. The only replacements which could be obtained were volunteers serving in other units in the Mediterranean theatre of operations. These were trained at the Airborne base commanded by the brigade's deputy commander, Colonel T. C. H. Pearson. Co-located with the USAAF Troop Carrier Command, it comprised a staff captain, an officer in charge of parachute training, a number of Army Physical Training Corps instructors who provided instruction in parachute training, and No. 2 Mobile Parachute Servicing Unit RAF. In addition to recruiting and training volunteers, the Airborne base was responsible for the organisation of resupply drops for 15th Army Group. It also operated a convalescent depot for rehabilitation of wounded parachutists which proved successful in reducing the loss of trained men who, if sent elsewhere, might not have been posted back to the brigade. Subsequently, in the autumn of 1944, the base was properly established. Thereafter commanded by Major J. W. Pearson, with a staff of 15 officers and 100 other ranks, it was capable of holding and training up to 50 officers and 750 other ranks. Subsequently, its establishment was increased to include a parachute school.

On 4 April, 2nd Independent Parachute Brigade Group was transferred westwards to the Cassino sector where, with the 10th Battalion The Rifle Brigade under command, it relieved 1st Guards Brigade and some New Zealand units. From its positions, which were overlooked by the famous monastery, the brigade patrolled the line of the River Rapido. Cover during the day was provided to a certain extent by a constant barrage of smoke shells fired by the divisional artillery. At certain points throughout the sector Allied and German positions were within a short distance of each other. When B Company 4th Parachute Battalion occupied the railway station in Cassino itself, it found that enemy troops were established in a hotel across the town square.

Shortly after the brigade's arrival, 6th Parachute Battalion was tasked with carrying out reconnaissances on the far side of the River Garigliano to obtain information on the dispositions of enemy minefields. One such patrol, commanded by Lieutenant J. Pearson, was provided by C Company. Its mission was to find a path through the minefield in front of enemy positions opposing those of the battalion. Accompanied by a party of sappers equipped with mine detectors, Pearson and his men were making their way through the minefield when a mine was set off and four of his men wounded. The patrol started to retrace its path, Pearson leading the way while crawling on his hands and knees. Tragically, he knelt on an anti-personnel mine which blew off both his legs below the knees. Despite his terrible wounds, he ordered his men to evacuate the other wounded first and to leave him behind. This they refused to do and carried the young officer out of the minefield. Eventually, he was evacuated on the back of a mule, the journey taking several hours.

On 16 April the brigade was relieved by 21st Indian Infantry Brigade and withdrew for two days' rest. On 20 April it relieved 6th New Zealand Brigade in another sector north-east of Cassino, once more coming under command of 2nd New Zealand Division. At this point it was joined by 300th Airlanding Anti-Tank Battery RA, deployed in the infantry role. All three battalions patrolled intensively, their tasks being made none the easier by the weather, which deteriorated a week after their arrival. The heavy rain and severe cold, combined with the constant heavy shelling, made life very unpleasant. Nevertheless, the brigade continued to make the enemy constantly aware of its presence. On 21 May, 6th Parachute Battalion was withdrawn, being followed on 27 May by the rest of the brigade less 5th Parachute Battalion, which remained under command of 6th New Zealand Brigade. On the following day the battalion joined the rest of the brigade in reserve at Portecagnano and Filignano, not far from Salerno.

OPERATION 'HASTY'

By this time the Germans were in the process of withdrawing to a line between Pisa and Rimini, closely followed by 5th US Army and 8th Army, the latter now commanded by General Sir Oliver Leese, Bt. As they withdrew, the Germans attempted to delay the Allies by blowing roads, bridges and other key points along the Allied axis of advance. General Leese decided to prevent the Germans from carrying out such measures by harassing them during their withdrawal along the route from Sora to Avezzano. Accordingly, 2nd Independent Parachute Brigade Group was detailed to provide one battalion for this task, which would take place on the night of 1–2 June. However, Brigadier Pritchard was of the opinion that the operation, codenamed 'Hasty', did not justify the commitment of a complete battalion, and it was subsequently agreed that a smaller body would suffice. 6th Parachute Battalion was allotted the task, and a force of 60, including signallers and a detachment of 127th Parachute Field Ambulance, was assembled under the command of Captain L. A. Fitzroy-Smith.

At 1900 hours on 1 June Fitzroy-Smith and his men took off in three aircraft, followed by eight more carrying dummies which would also be dropped to give the impression of a larger force. At 2030 hours the force carried out a successful drop near Torricella, and by 2100 hours had rallied at its RV, having suffered only one casualty, a man with a broken rib. Shortly afterwards, radio contact was established with 2nd New Zealand Division and Fitzroy-Smith requested that a supply drop should proceed as planned. After establishing a base, Fitzroy-Smith divided his force into three groups under himself, Lieutenant Ashby and Lieutenant Evans. For the ensuing week these groups harried the Germans where and whenever they could and with a certain degree of success. In doing so, however, they incurred casualties which included a detachment of signallers who were captured. Moreover, contact with 2nd New Zealand Division was lost when the single remaining radio became inoperable and the force's carrier pigeons failed to reach their home destination.

By 7 June it had been decided to withdraw Fitzroy-Smith and his remaining men, but there was no way of communicating with them. The problem was solved by Brigadier Pritchard, who arranged for leaflets bearing the cryptic message "Proceed Awdry forthwith" to be dropped over the area. While this puzzled the enemy, Fitzroy-Smith and his men were well aware that Captain John Awdry, another officer in 6th Parachute Battalion, was acting as a liaison officer with 2nd New Zealand Division. Accordingly, they made their way back to Allied lines in small groups. Although almost two-thirds of the force had been lost and little physical damage had been caused to the enemy, the operation achieved a certain amount of success in that it caused the Germans, who believed that a much larger number of troops had been dropped, to deploy forces to counter it. The use of the dummies proved highly effective, increasing nervousness among the enemy of possible airborne operations in their rear areas.

OPERATION 'DRAGOON'

For the remainder of June the entire brigade carried out airborne training in the Salerno area. Meanwhile, the Allied invasion of Normandy had begun, and General Eisenhower's plans included a landing in the south of France by 7th US Army, which would land between Frejus and St Raphael and advance to the north up the Rhone valley, subsequently linking up with the American forces as they advanced after breaking out of Normandy. While little opposition to the landings was expected, it was known that the bulk of the enemy forces were being held in reserve inland from the coast. It was essential that these should be prevented from approaching the area of the landings until a beachhead had been well established in strength, so it was decided to deploy an airborne formation, designated 1st Airborne Task Force, for this task. Commanded by Major General Robert Frederick, this comprised five American parachute battalions, an airlanding regiment and 2nd Independent Parachute Brigade Group.

The brigade, which now also included 64th Light Battery RA, was tasked with seizing and holding the area between the villages of Lam Motte and Le Muy, approximately ten miles north-west of St Raphael. Three roads, possible routes for use by advancing enemy formations, traversed the brigade's area, and these were to be denied to the enemy. The brigade was to be transported in Dakotas of the 51st US Troop Carrier Wing USAAF, the gliderborne elements being flown in Horsa and Hadrian gliders. The drop would take place at 0445 hours, pathfinders having dropped approximately an hour beforehand to mark out the dropping and landing zones. The gliders carrying 300th Airlanding Anti-Tank Battery RA and 64th Light Battery RA would land later at 0815 hours. By then, the seaborne forces would have landed at 0700 hours, and it was planned that they should link up with 1st Airborne Task Force 48 hours later. Resupply would be by air, the first drop taking place on the second day of the operation and further drops taking place as requested by the brigade.

On 12 July the brigade moved from Salerno to Rome, where it spent the next four weeks preparing for the operation. In the early hours of 15 August the pathfinders of 1st Independent Parachute Platoon landed without mishap, and by 0323 hours they had marked the dropping zone for the brigade drop, which took place on time. Unfortunately, however, thick cloud caused visibility from the air to deteriorate. Although Eureka beacons had been deployed by the pathfinders, some of them proved to be faulty and 53 of the 126 aircraft dropped their 'sticks' up to 20 miles away. The other 73 aircraft dropped their troops accurately and, once the brigade had rallied on the ground, it was discovered that 4th and 6th Parachute Battalions numbered between 40 and 60 per cent of their full strengths, whilst 5th Parachute Battalion numbered only 25 per cent.

With the exception of Major Bill Corby's B Company, most of 5th Parachute Battalion had been badly scattered in the drop because the pilot of the leading aircraft had been unable to locate the Eureka beacon. Sergeant Tucker of No. 2 Platoon of A Company landed on the roof of a building housing enemy troops. On coming under fire from its occupants, he replied with his Sten gun until forced to surrender by the threat of grenades being thrown on to the roof where he was concealed. On being taken prisoner, he convinced his captors that they were surrounded by two divisions of airborne troops. His story was reinforced by the arrival of the gliders bringing in 64th Light Battery RA, at which point the enemy troops, who numbered over 80, surrendered to him without further ado.

As the battalions moved off to their respective objectives, 2nd Parachute Squadron RE, assisted by the pathfinder platoon, cleared the landing zones of anti-glider defences. At 0920 hours the Hadrians carrying 64th Light Battery landed. However, the Horsas carrying 300th Airlanding Anti-Tank Battery RA had been forced to return to Italy because of the poor visibility. After the tug aircraft had refuelled, they and their respective gliders returned to France, where a successful landing took place shortly after 1630 hours. Meanwhile, the brigade had successfully achieved all of its objectives. Opposition in the area had been very weak, and one of two small enemy garrisons had quickly surrendered to 6th Parachute Battalion. 4th Parachute Battalion had seen some action which resulted in 16 enemy being killed and 29 being taken prisoner. Casualties within the brigade amounted to seven killed and nine wounded.

During the rest of the day missing members of the brigade arrived after making their way back from where they had been dropped. Major Dan Calvert, commanding A Company 4th Parachute Battalion, had been dropped some 20 miles away and had hitched a lift on a bus, concealing himself under a pile of cabbages and being shielded by local people as it passed through enemy roadblocks. Another who was dropped some ten miles from the dropping zone was Lieutenant Colonel Vic Coxen, Commanding Officer of 4th Parachute Battalion. After joining up with a group from one of the American parachute battalions, Coxen and other members of his unit made their way across country and rejoined the battalion in the early hours of the following morning.

On the morning of 16 August the resupply drop took place as planned. On the following day American forces, in the shape of the 142nd Regimental Combat Team, arrived at Le Muy, where they linked up with units of the brigade. The enemy, who by this time had appreciated the strength of the landings, had withdrawn, and thus the brigade was not called upon to block any enemy counter-attempts.

On 26 August, 2nd Independent Parachute Brigade Group returned to Italy and was warned to prepare for deployment to Greece, where, as the Russians advanced through the Balkans, the Germans were preparing to withdraw before the end of September. Greece was a country divided into royalist (EDES) and communist (ELAS) factions which had been warring with one another for some time, even under German occupation. It had become apparent to the British that a German withdrawal would produce a political vaccum, which the Greek communists would seek to fill while requesting support from Russian forces after their entry in Yugoslavia and Bulgaria. Accordingly, it was decided to forestall any such communist intentions by sending in troops to support the pro-Western factions in Greece. 2nd Independent Parachute Brigade, together with 23rd Armoured Brigade, deployed initially as infantry, was given the task of speeding up the Germans' withdrawal by harassing them. Leading elements of the brigade would enter Greece by parachute, the remainder being flown in or landed from the sea after an airfield and a port had been secured. 23rd Armoured Brigade would land from the sea on the following day.

In fact, the Germans did not start to withdraw from Greece until October. By that time 4th Parachute Battalion had been tasked by Brigadier Pritchard with carrying out the initial task of securing the airfield on which elements of the rest of the brigade would land. It had been planned that the brigade would land at an airfield at Kalamaki, on the eastern outskirts of Athens. On the evening of 11 October, however, while briefing his officers on the operation which was to take place on the following day, Lieutenant Colonel Coxen was suddenly informed that his force was to drop on another airfield 40 miles west of Athens, at Megara.

On 12 October at 1200 hours Major James Gourlay's C Company, accompanied by the Commanding Officer, a detachment of 2nd Parachute Squadron RE, the pathfinder platoon, detachments of the Mortar Platoon and some signallers, dropped on Megara airfield. The wind speed was 35 miles per hour, far in excess of the maximum allowed for operational parachuting, and the company suffered several casualties on landing. Lieutenant Donald Marsh and two other men were killed and 40 others injured on landing, men being dragged for considerable distances by their parachutes before they could release themselves from their harnesses. Nevertheless, the airfield was quickly secured, but the weather grew worse and the landing of the rest of the brigade had to be postponed until it improved. Two days later, on 14 October, 6th Parachute Battalion dropped on the airfield. High winds again took their toll and there were several casualties. 5th Parachute Battalion followed a day or two later, rejoining the brigade in Athens.

On leaving Megara, Brigadier Pritchard and the advance elements of the brigade discovered that the road to Athens had been blown by the retreating Germans. Quickly commandeering a fleet of caiques and other fishing craft, they sailed from Megara to Piraeus and made their way in similarly commandeered local transport to Athens. On entering the city, on 15 October, the advance elements of the brigade received a tumultuous welcome from the Greek people and had great difficulty in making its way through the crowded streets. On the following day 23rd Armoured Brigade arrived, and the next few days were spent in restoring law and order throughout the city. B and C Companies of 4th Parachute Battalion departed Athens on the day after their arrival and, with elements of the Special Boat Squadron and the RAF Regiment, formed a composite force for an operation in the north of Greece against a German column withdrawing towards Albania. Codenamed 'Pompforce' and under the command of Lieutenant Colonel The Lord Jellicoe, Commanding Officer of the Special Boat Squadron, this force succeeded in catching up with and harrassing the enemy column.

On 26 October an attack was carried out on the rearguard of the column, which by then was occupying the town of Kozani and the hill overlooking it. The rear of the hill consisted of a sheer rock face, and it was up this that C Company climbed during the night to attack the enemy infantry holding the hill. The company reached the top of the rock face just before dawn. As Major James Gourlay's company headquarters and the leading platoon deployed and began to advance, a trip flare was set off and the battle started. The platoon attacked a bunker from which a heavy volume of fire was being laid down. After a fierce fight, during which it sustained some casualties, the platoon cleared the bunker and took a number of prisoners. Meanwhile, Major Gourlay and Company Headquarters took a building nearby and captured more enemy.

Having reorganised and secured the hill, C Company was attacked by a platoon of enemy, but succeeded in beating it off. Almost immediately afterwards the enemy brought down a heavy concentration of shellfire on the hilltop, causing a number of casualties. At that point a heavy mist settled over the hill and it was decided, in view of the company's heavy losses, to withdraw. Under covering fire from its own Bren light machine guns, C Company withdrew, carrying its wounded. Among them was the company second in command, Captain Rupert Teed, who died after reaching the 'Pompforce' base.

Another attempt was made to attack the enemy column at the Klythe Pass, but this failed because 4th Parachute Battalion had now virtually run out of fuel for its jeeps and had been forced to continue its advance on foot. Only Lieutenant Colonel Vic Coxen succeeded in reaching the pass, being unable to do anything other than watch the German column move through. There was, however, another enemy column known to be approaching through the town of Florissa. When Major Dick Hargreaves and B Company arrived there, a platoon under Lieutenant Nigel Riley was despatched to blow up the railway line between Florissa and Edessa. Having cut the line in two places, Riley and his men derailed part of an enemy train and captured some 400 prisoners.

Meanwhile, 5th Parachute Battalion had sailed in a Royal Navy cruiser for Salonika, together with the brigade headquarters and No. 9 Commando, to deal with increasing trouble caused by the Communist-backed ELAS guerrillas who had been supported and supplied with arms by the Allies during the German occupation of Greece. On their arrival, the troops encountered an unfriendly reception from the ELAS force, which withdrew on the following day to the north. Shortly afterwards, 5th Parachute Battalion, by then under command of 7th Infantry Brigade of 4th Indian Division which had arrived in Greece during November, moved further north to the aptly named town of Drama in eastern Macedonia and Thrace, where it kept an uneasy peace between ELAS forces and those of the EDES royalists. For a while it was successful, but eventually the situation became so explosive that civil war broke out. Shortly afterwards the battalion was withdrawn to Athens, where trouble had also broken out.

6th Parachute Battalion, based in Thebes, had been tasked with maintaining order in central and southern Greece. This task was made none the easier by the presence of 5,000 ELAS guerrillas, who attempted to impose their authority throughout the area but were thwarted by the battalion, which also carried out a great deal of relief work among the towns and villages.

By the end of November the brigade was preparing to return to Italy, where it was required for airborne operations being planned by 8th Army. Brigadier Pritchard and an advance party had already returned to Italy and 5th Parachute Battalion had already embarked on its vessels when the brigade deputy commander, Colonel T. C. H. Pearson, received an urgent summons to corps headquarters, where he received orders to redeploy the brigade in Athens as quickly as possible. It appeared that ELAS forces, several thousand in strength, were advancing on Athens with the aim of seizing control of the city. By the time the ELAS forces arrived, they found themselves facing a force consisting of 2nd Independent Parachute Brigade Group, 23rd Armoured Brigade, the Greek Mountain Brigade and elements of the Greek National Guards. All three parachute battalions soon found themselves heavily committed. The brigade had been ordered to hold the centre of the city, 6th Parachute Battalion holding the area of Omonia Square whilst 4th Parachute Battalion deployed nearby. 5th Parachute Battalion, after moving through Constitution Square, would take up positions in the Acropolis area.

The fighting in the streets was fierce. 5th Parachute Battalion succeeded in pushing forward from Constitution Square towards the Acropolis, but had to storm the headquarters of ELAS before it could secure its objective at dusk, with B Company securing the Acropolis itself which dominated the city. It suffered heavy casualties in the process, Lieutenant Conway being killed and Major W. Hunter severely wounded. By this stage Brigadier Pritchard had returned in haste from Italy, just before the brigade came under heavy attack from ELAS forces and was forced to abandon some areas previously under its control. On 18 December 4th Infantry Division landed and offensive operations against ELAS began. On 22 December 5th Parachute Battalion, supported by two squadrons of tanks and a troop of armoured cars of 23rd Armoured Brigade, attacked the main body of ELAS forces, killing about 50 and taking 400 prisoner. After reaching the Piraeus road the battalion linked up with 6th Parachute Battalion.

On 4 January, 1945, a combined operation with 12th Infantry Brigade was carried out. Some fierce fighting took place during the advance along the Piraeus road and severe casualties were incurred by 5th Parachute Battalion, which lost over 100 men, and 6th Parachute Battalion, in which all the company commanders were wounded or killed. Eventually, after fighting their way forward against stiff resistance, the brigade succeeded in cutting off the ELAS line of withdrawal by seizing a bridge. By that evening, after their ensuing stand, the ELAS forces had suffered 170 killed, 70 wounded and 520 captured. On the following day the remaining ELAS troops withdrew as the brigade continued its advance.

On 16 January the brigade handed over its areas of responsibility to troops of the Greek National Guards, and by the beginning of February had returned to Italy. During the next three months it remained in a constant state of preparedness to carry out airborne operations in support of 8th Army. However, much to its disappointment, it was not called upon to do so. Over 30 operations were planned but subsequently cancelled, on five occasions after the brigade had emplaned and was waiting for take-off.

During May, 2nd Independent Parachute Brigade Group returned to England. Its achievements were best summed up in the words of the Commander-in-Chief, General Alexander, in a letter to Brigadier Pritchard: "You have a wonderful record of successes and in every battle that you have fought you have shown all the true qualities of good soldiers — high morale, dash and fighting efficiency."

CHAPTER 8
5th Parachute Brigade in the Far East, 1945–1946

Shortly after its return from Germany in May 1945, 6th Airborne Division was once again warned to prepare itself for action. With the war in Europe ended, attention was now solely focussed on defeating the Japanese in the war in the Pacific. Allied plans to do so included an airborne operation to be mounted by the division.

Initially, 5th Parachute Brigade was placed under orders for service in South East Asia. Soon after, Major General Eric Bols, accompanied by Brigadier Nigel Poett and two members of the divisional staff, flew to Ceylon. There they were met by Lieutenant General 'Boy' Browning, who was by then Chief of Staff to the Supreme Allied Commander, Admiral Lord Louis Mountbatten. On being briefed by him, Bols and his officers learned that 5th Parachute Brigade was to carry out an airborne operation to seize the causeway linking Singapore with the mainland of Malaya. This would take place after an initial seaborne landing had been carried out and a beachhead established, and would form part of a major operation, codenamed 'Zipper', to recapture the entire Malay Peninsula. It soon became obvious that the operational requirement was for a brigade group, and that there would be no involvement for the rest of 6th Airborne Division. Accordingly, Major General Bols and his two staff officers returned to England, leaving Brigadier Poett, who moved to Bombay to await the arrival of his brigade.

5th Parachute Brigade Group arrived in July and immediately began to prepare for its part in Operation 'Zipper'. In addition to 7th, 12th and 13th Parachute Battalions, it comprised 22nd Independent Parachute Company, 4th Airlanding Anti-Tank Battery RA, a detachment of 2nd Forward Observation Unit RA, 3rd Airborne Squadron RE, 225th Parachute Field Ambulance and other supporting arm minor units.

In early August the atomic bombs were dropped on Hiroshima and Nagasaki and the war in South East Asia came to an abrupt end. Operation 'Zipper' was cancelled, but 5th Parachute Brigade Group was nevertheless despatched by sea on the P & O liner *Chitral* to Malaya, arriving off the west coast on 17 September. 7th and 12th Parachute Battalions landed on the Morib beaches, moving inland a short distance before night fell. That night, however, the brigade received a signal informing it that the capital city, Kuala Lumpur, was already in British hands and ordering it to re-embark on the *Chitral* for Singapore. On arrival, the brigade met an old friend, General Sir Miles Dempsey. Now Commander-in-Chief Allied Land Forces South East Asia, he had known 6th Airborne Division well during operations in Normandy, when he was commanding 2nd Army. The first task given to the brigade was assisting in restoring law and order to Singapore. The city's police force had been virtually destroyed by the Japanese, and the situation bordered on the chaotic. The brigade set to with

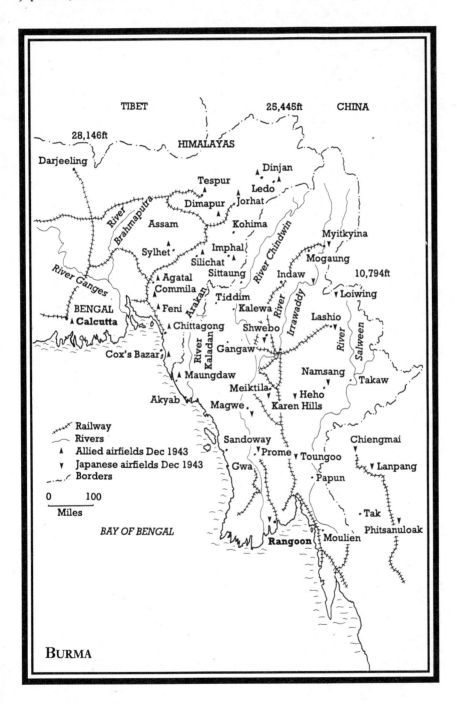

TIBET   25,445ft   CHINA

28,146ft   HIMALAYAS

Darjeeling   Dinjan

                        Tespur   Ledo
                                         Jorhat
                        Dimapur   Jorhat

River Brahmaputra   Assam   Kohima   Myitkyina

                    Sylhet   Imphal   Mogaung
                          Silichat
River Ganges   Agatal   Sittaung   Indaw   10,794ft
                    Commila   Loiwing
                          Tiddim
BENGAL   Feni   Kalewa   Lashio
Calcutta   Chittagong   Shwebo
                              Gangaw
Cox's Bazar   Namsang
                    Maungdaw   Takaw
                          Meiktila
Akyab   Magwe   Heho
                              Karen Hills

Railway
Rivers   Sandoway   Chiengmai
Allied airfields Dec 1943   Prome   Toungoo
Japanese airfields Dec 1943   Gwa   Lanpang
Borders   Papun

0   100
Miles   Tak
                                           Phitsanuloak
BAY OF BENGAL   Rangoon   Moulien

BURMA

a will and restored control, at the same time helping to reconstruct the police force.

In early December 1945, 5th Parachute Brigade Group was moved to Indonesia, where it was deployed in Batavia (now Djakarta), the capital city of Java. Trouble was brewing as a result of agitation by nationalists led by Dr Soekarno, an Indonesian politician who had proclaimed himself President and had declared independence. He was supported by several other Indonesian politicians and a large number of armed extremists. Until 1942 Java had been a Dutch colony, although its administration had not been popular with the Indonesians. Consequently, after the Japanese invasion in 1942, the Indonesians were not unhappy to see their former masters being imprisoned. When the Japanese surrendered in August 1945 they had handed over some of their weapons to the Indonesians and had withdrawn to camps inland to await the arrival of the Allied forces to whom they would surrender. This move was contrary to orders issued by Admiral Mountbatten, who had instructed them to remain in their locations and maintain law and order pending the arrival of Allied troops.

Inevitably, in the vacuum resulting from the withdrawal of the Japanese from the towns throughout the country, there was chaos. Indonesians seized the opportunity to settle old scores while indulging in a wave of crime and terrorism. Only one thing united the various factions: a hatred of the Dutch and a determination that their country would not return to its former status as a Dutch colony. The main initial problem facing the Allies was the thousands of prisoners of war and civilian internees in Java who were at risk from the increasing violence. With the Japanese withdrawn to their barracks and no Dutch troops in the country, law and order had completely broken down, and the situation was worsening as each day passed. The British therefore had to step in and take control.

On its arrival in Batavia 5th Parachute Brigade Group found that the capital had already been occupied by British forces. Elsewhere, serious fighting was taking place on the outskirts of the towns of Semarang and Surabaya. Almost immediately the brigade took part in Operation 'Pounce' — the clearing of Batavia. By day the units of the brigade dispersed riots and carried out searches, and by night they patrolled the sniper-infested streets of the city. Brigadier Poett, unhappy that his brigade was not being used to best effect, approached the commander of 23rd Indian Division, Major General D. C. Hawthorn, under whose command the brigade was operating, and requested that he and his troops be given a role more in keeping with their capabilities. Consequently, as part of the reorganisation and redeployments then being carried out, the brigade was despatched to the town of Semarang on the coast between Batavia and Surabaya. Under command were a number of additional supporting arm units, including A Squadron 11th Cavalry (Prince Albert Victor's Own) and 6th Indian Field Battery Royal Indian Artillery.

Semarang was the most important town and port on the northern coast of Java, handling much of the export traffic from Central Java. The main part of the town was situated on low-lying terrain nearest to the sea, while the residential area was situated on high ground three miles inland. The town itself was well laid out, consisting mainly of modern buildings. It was totally dependent upon supplies of food from further inland, as there was little or no agriculture in the surrounding areas. Electricity and water were supplied from Oengaran, some 15 miles inland. Two miles inland from the residential area was a feature called Gombel Hill, which dominated the town and the surrounding areas for several miles in all directions. Three miles to the west of Semarang lay an airstrip capable of accommodating aircraft up to the size of a Dakota. The town's population consisted of three different ethnic groups: the Indonesians, who numbered some 185,000, about 40,000 Chinese, and approximately 5,000 Dutch, many of whom had held key positions in the administration before the Japanese occupation. While the Dutch were regarded by the Indonesians with distrust, it was the Chinese who fared worst of all. Having suffered badly under the Japanese, they were subsequently treated with hostility by the Indonesians, who accused them of collaborating with the British.

5th Parachute Brigade Group arrived in Semarang on 9 January 1946. As it did so, it found that troops of 49th Indian Infantry Brigade, commanded by Brigadier de Burgh Morris, had completed the final phase of operations to secure the town and had evacuated a large number of Allied prisoners of war and civilian internees to Batavia. During the evacuation fighting had broken out between the troops and Indonesian guerrillas who had been indulging in murder, arson and looting. Despite this, the town was largely intact apart from some buildings in an area called Bodjong, which had been bombed by the RAF two months previously. 49th Indian Infantry Brigade had succeeded in maintaining law and order, the local police force being virtually non-existent and incapable of taking any effective action. Extremists had, however, succeeded in cutting off all supplies of power and water and were refusing to allow any supplies of food into the town.

49th Indian Infantry Brigade had been assisted in maintaining order by a battalion of Japanese troops. Commanded by a Major Kido, this unit had been based at Semarang when the Japanese had surrendered. All had gone well until Sukarno had made his declaration of "independence", which roused the extremists among the Indonesian population and resulted in unrest. At the same time an organisation called RAPWI (Recovered Allied Prisoners of War and Internees), whose role was to provide medical and humanitarian relief to PoWs and internees, had established its headquarters in Semarang. This had caused suspicion and unease amongst the Indonesian extremists, and Major Kido and his troops had thus assumed the task of maintaining order in the town. The situation had worsened when Indonesians established checkpoints in and around the town, halting all traffic and subjecting locals and Europeans alike to interrogation. Major Kido had intervened, explaining the reasons for RAPWI's presence. For a while there was an uneasy peace, but Kido felt it prudent to reinforce the guards on the internment camps, which by then held over 20,000 European internees, and on the airstrip. However, the situation began to deteriorate once again, and eventually the extremists cut the railway line, leaving the airstrip as the only route by which supplies could be brought into the town.

The numbers of extremists in the area of Semarang increased steadily, and once again they entered the town itself and established checkpoints. On 12 October they attacked the Japanese battalion's barracks, demanding that Major Kido and his men lay down their arms. To resolve the situaion, Kido took a delegation of Indonesians to meet his area commander, Major General Nakamura, at the headquarters at Magelang. While the Indonesians were demanding that the Japanese forces hand over all their arms and ammunition, a signal arrived from the commander of all Japanese troops in Java, ordering Japanese forces to retain their arms. Violence exploded in the aftermath of the meeting with Major General Nakamura. Armed Indonesians attacked Europeans, incarcerating British, Dutch and Eurasians alike. All telephone links with the rest of Java were cut, and the RAPWI headquarters and the offices of the Red Cross were attacked. Major Kido's detachment of troops at the airstrip were attacked, overpowered and imprisoned. At the same time, fighting broke out between Indonesian police, who were under orders to arrest all Japanese personnel in Semarang, and 300 Japanese civilians who worked for the Semarang Steel Company.

By 15 October the situation was such that Major Kido had no alternative but to take matters into his own hands and restore order in the town. In the early hours his battalion moved out of its barracks and cleared the area of Djomblang before pushing forward to recapture the internment camps at Bangkong, Sompok and Halmaheira. It then went on to retake key areas and buildings such as the railway station and hospital, which were occupied by extremists. All the time it was under heavy fire from machine guns and snipers. Throughout the following night the Japanese troops fought their way towards the centre of the town. On coming under fire from the Governor's residence they shelled the occupants into submission with an anti-tank gun. On the following day, 16 October, Major Kido and his men stormed the jail at Boeloe, where they found the bodies of 85 Japanese soldiers, airmen and civilians who had been slaughtered. They also discovered a further 50 Japanese and over 300 Europeans due to be executed on the next day.

Fighting continued throughout 17 October, but by then the extremists had begun to withdraw from Semarang, although small groups and some snipers remained behind to harass the Japanese troops. On the night of 18 October Japanese positions on Gombel Hill were subjected to attacks, but these were repulsed after intense fighting, during which the extremists suffered heavy losses. On 19 October extremists were still in possession of the British American Tobacco factory, on the eastern outskirts of the town. The Japanese battalion cleared these, along with others who had infiltrated back into Semarang during the night.

The following day saw the arrival of elements of the 3rd Battalion 10th Princess Mary's Own Gurkha Rifles, commanded by Lieutenant Colonel Dick Edwards. They landed at Semarang docks, but came under fire from a patrol of Japanese troops. Two Japanese soldiers were killed in the ensuing action, after which Major Kido and his men were placed under Edward's command. Shortly afterwards a composite brigade of troops, under the command of 23rd Indian Division's Commander Royal Artillery (CRA), Brigadier Richard Bethell, arrived and began the task of evacuating 11,000 Allied prisoners of war and civilian internees. Despite the fighting which continued in and around Semarang, the evacuation was successfully carried out. By mid-December all PoWs and internees had been moved from camps at Magelang, Ambarawa and Banjobiroe via Semarang to Batavia. Whilst carrying out the evacuation, the CRA's Brigade also restored order to the best of its ability. On 17 December it was relieved by 49th Indian Infantry Brigade, which remained in the town until the arrival of 5th Parachute Brigade Group.

After reviewing the layout of the defensive positions around Semarang, Brigadier Nigel Poett decided to establish a perimeter running along a canal on the eastern side of the town, including the key feature of Gombel Hill, and then along another canal on the western side. The total length of this perimeter was 12 miles, which was far too long for it to be manned throughout, so Poett established platoon and company bases on the main approaches to the town and used patrols to cover the areas in between. A company base was set up at the airfield, and all key points such as the railway station, public buildings and the docks were guarded by detachments of troops. One problem facing Poett was the future deployment of the Japanese battalion. While they had done much to re-establish order before the arrival of the CRA's Brigade, and had since been deployed on guard duties throughout Semarang, their presence was not welcomed by the local people, many of whom had suffered during the Japanese occupation. However, they were a welcome addition to Poett's brigade, whose resources would be stretched in providing the manpower for the defence of the town and restoring essential services. The problem was resolved by deploying Major Kido and his men to Gombel Hill and the south-east sector of the perimeter, where they were out of the town and thus out of sight.

5th Parachute Brigade Group lost little time in settling into Semarang. 13th Parachute Battalion was allocated responsibility for the docks and the centre of the town, while 12th Parachute Battalion assumed the task of defending the western sector of the perimeter and the airfield. 7th Parachute Battalion was held in reserve in the main residential area of the town and provided guards for the RAPWI camps. To prevent extremists infiltrating into the town, a patrol area was established outside the perimeter to a depth of 2,000 yards. Patrols from all three battalions operated frequently throughout this area, visiting local villages or 'kampongs' which were possible concentration points for guerrilla groups consisting of bandits who appeared to recognise the authority of no one but their individual group leaders. They devoted much effort to terrorising the local population while at the same time attacking troops, frequently avowing that their aim was the expulsion of the British and the massacre of the Dutch and Chinese.

The guerrillas were armed with an assortment of weapons which included small arms, a small number of 75mm and 105mm guns, and some mortars. To begin with, guerrilla artillery and mortar fire was extremely inaccurate, but it improved with practice, Gombel Hill being its principal target. To counter this, a number of observation posts were established by 2nd Forward Observation Unit RA from which sound bearings could be taken and reported. Counter-battery fire was provided by 6th Indian Field Battery RIA and the 4.2 inch mortar troop of 4th Airlanding Anti-Tank Battery RA. Brought to bear within minutes of a guerrilla gun or mortar opening fire, these proved to be very effective countermeasures.

Within Semarang itself there were a number of small kampongs comprising a warren of huts positioned haphazardly among trees and undergrowth. The guerrillas frequently used these for concealment, and a number of cordon and search operations were carried out. These were not particularly successful, although some arms and equipment were discovered on occasions. They did, however, cause resentment among the inhabitants of the kampongs, who, because of the damage caused to property, were somewhat naturally dismayed by large numbers of troops descending on them with no warning. Eventually, such operations were abandoned and were replaced by an effective intelligence system operated by the brigade's field security section.

Law and order in the town was reimposed swiftly, as was a curfew between 2230 hours and 0430 hours. Responsibility for this task and for policing the town fell upon Major John Bamford of 2nd Forward Observation Unit RA, assisted by his own officers and men as well as those of 4th Airlanding Anti-Tank Battery RA and 6th Indian Field Battery RIA. The town's police force had to be completely reconstructed by Major Bamford and his gunners. The new force was organised as a headquarters and four divisions, of which two were staffed by Indonesians and one each by Dutch and Chinese personnel. Each division was commanded by a British officer, who was assisted by 20 gunners. Police posts were established throughout the different areas of Semarang, and these were visited each night by troops who patrolled the streets in jeeps. Gradually the confidence of the local population in the police was restored, and this resulted in people bringing their problems and complaints to local posts for investigation. Such was the success of the brigade's law and order operations that one policeman, who had served in the town's pre-war force, stated that there was less crime in Semarang at that particular time than during any comparable period before the war.

3rd Airborne Squadron RE, under Major Peter Moore, lost little time in restoring essential services such as power and water, and soon started repairing the roads, railways and docks damaged by Allied bombing. 225th Parachute Field Ambulance, commanded by Lieutenant Colonel John Watts, organised medical facilities, while the brigade headquarters signal section took over the operation and maintenance of the town's telephone system and two exchanges. The RASC detachment attached to the brigade organised the distribution of food. To assist the brigade in the civil administration of the town, the Allied Military Administration Civil Affairs Bureau (AMACAB) was formed on 15 January, 1946. This was headed by a Dutchman named Dr Angenent, who had previously served in several administrative posts in Java. Major Kenneth Milne of the King's Royal Rifle Corps, who commanded RAPWI Mid-Java, was attached to Dr Angenent as a staff officer and as Brigadier Poett's liaison officer. AMACAB comprised four branches dealing with health, food, engineering and law and order. The head of each branch worked in close co-operation with an officer of 5th Parachute Brigade Group who was responsible for providing technical advice and for obtaining assistance from the appropriate resources within the brigade.

Much of the burden of returning conditions to normal within Semarang fell on the shoulders of the sappers of 3rd Airborne Squadron RE. Assisted by local people who had worked as engineers in the town before the war, they constructed new waterpoints and repaired existing ones. They carried out extensive repairs on the main power station and electricity sub-stations, and installed new generators. They also repaired two drydocks, putting them back into commission, and provided technical assistance in restoring the town's gasworks and refrigeration plant to running order. The squadron constructed a railway culvert, redecked two bridges, and overhauled four locomotives. It also built two sawmills, repaired roads, demolished unsafe buildings and converted a number of warehouses within the docks area into accommodation for 5,000 Japanese internees.

In early February 1946, during a visit to the brigade by General Sir Miles Dempsey, Brigadier Nigel Poett was told that he was to be posted to the War Office as Director of Plans. This was sad news for him, as it meant that he would be leaving the brigade which he had formed and led throughout the operations in Normandy, the Ardennes, the Rhine Crossing and the advance to the Baltic. A few days later, on 16 February, Brigadier Poett handed over command of 5th Parachute Brigade Group to Brigadier Ken Darling, the well-known and much-respected former commanding officer of 12th Parachute Battalion. Poett received a splendid send-off attended by elements of all units of the brigade, Major Kido and some of his battalion, and members of Semarang's Chinese community.

At the end of February Brigadier Darling was informed that the brigade would be relieved by a Dutch formation, namely 'T' Regiment Group of the Royal Netherlands Army. Darling and his staff quickly realised that there could be problems with regard to the reactions of the local people to the return of the Dutch, and that the situation would have to be handled with the utmost delicacy and diplomacy. The first precaution was to ensure that there would no friction between the British and Dutch troops. Consequently all elements of the brigade received strict instructions to this effect. Subsequently, the heads of the different ethnic communities were informed of the impending arrival of Dutch troops, but were assured that they would be under British command until such time as 5th Parachute Brigade Group withdrew. Brigadier Darling emphasised at length to the local leaders that the Dutch would be fully capable of defending the community against extremists. At the same time, he also persuaded them that any form of disturbance would be futile and would only destroy the peaceful conditions prevailing in Semarang. Fortunately, Darling's counsel was heeded by the local people and the arrival of the Dutch troops under Colonel van Langen, at the end of the first and second weeks of March, took place without incident.

During the initial three weeks after their arrival, individual Dutch units were provided with liaison parties consisting of three officers and a small number of NCOs from 5th Parachute Brigade Group. In addition, the brigade provided teams to provide assistance in training signallers, mortarmen and machine gunners, of which there were few in the Dutch ranks. 'T' Regiment Group was also weak in its supporting arm elements, though this was rectified to a certain extent when a Dutch field artillery battery arrived. 5th Parachute Brigade Group also gave logistical assistance, the RASC and RAOC officers of the brigade being kept busy checking and handing over stores of all natures to the Dutch.

On 24 March the first anniversary of the crossing of the Rhine was celebrated. The whole of 5th Parachute Brigade Group, together with all of its supporting arms units, marched or drove through Semarang, the salute being taken by Lieutenant General Sir Montagu Stopford, the Allied Commander Netherlands East Indies. On 15 May 5th Parachute Brigade Group handed over Semarang to Colonel van Langen and his force and left Java. The peaceful state of the town and the harmonious state of co-existence among the different ethnic minorities were a great tribute to the immense effort and great dedication shown by all ranks of the brigade during its time in Semarang. On departing Java the brigade returned to Malaya for a brief period before moving to Singapore. In July it sailed for Palestine, where it arrived on 7 August to rejoin 6th Airborne Division. Shortly afterwards, the 5th Parachute Brigade Group was disbanded and its officers and men absorbed into other units within the division.

CHAPTER 9
Parachute Battalions in India, 1941–1945

October 1941 saw the formation of 50th Indian Parachute Brigade, commanded by Brigadier Bill Gough. Based at Delhi, it comprised 151st Parachute Battalion, a British unit commanded by Lieutenant Colonel Martin Lindsay; 152nd Indian Parachute Battalion commanded by Lieutenant Colonel B. E. 'Abbo' Abbott; 153rd Gurkha Parachute Battalion commanded by Lieutenant Colonel Freddy Loftus-Tottenham; and 411th (Royal Bombay) Parachute Section Indian Engineers under Captain Mike Rolt.

No parachute training facilities existed in India, so the Airlanding School was established at Willington Airport, New Delhi, under the command of Wing Commander J. H. D. Chapple. He was assisted by Flight Lieutenant Bill Brereton, the Chief Instructor, the remainder of his staff consisting of two flight sergeants and five army warrant officers and NCOs. The aircraft attached to the school for parachute training consisted initially of two, and subsequently five, elderly Vickers Valencia biplanes. The main problem facing the RAF instructors was the shortage of parachutes. For some time the only parachutes available were 14 which had accompanied Brereton and the other PJIs when they were posted from No. 1 Parachute Training School RAF to the Airlanding School.

The first parachute descents in India were carried out on 15 October 1941 by Brereton and two officers of 50th Indian Parachute Brigade, Captains Abbott and Hopkinson. Despite the problems caused by the shortage of parachutes and equipment for synthetic training, Wing Commander Chapple and his men set to with enthusiasm to train the officers and men of the parachute brigade. In February 1942 the brigade took part in its first brigade exercise. The airborne part of the exercise consisted of a stick of ten men from 151st Parachute Battalion being dropped, the rest of the brigade being taken to their respective dropping zones by trucks before being deployed.

By the end of March 1942 the situation regarding parachutes and equipment had shown little improvement, only 200 parachutes out of an order for 2,200 having been received from Britain. Attempts were being made to manufacture parachutes in India, but these had so far proved unsuccessful owing to lack of suitable materials and technical expertise. Moreover, as the five Valencias had by then been withdrawn to assist in the evacuation of refugees from Burma, the absence of aircraft for parachute training was also causing major problems. Six Hudson light bombers had been promised, but had not arrived. Eventually the Commander-in-Chief,

General Sir Archibald Wavell, was so frustrated by the delay that he personally sent a signal to the Prime Minister in which he drew the latter's attention to the problem. A reply from the Secretary of State for India revealed that a consignment of parachutes destined for India had somehow been delivered to the Middle East and that two of the Hudsons had crashed. Whilst efforts to resolve these problems were being made behind the scenes, 50th Indian Parachute Brigade continued its rigorous programme of intensive training. A ceaseless round of exercises was maintained to compensate for the lack of airborne training, and in June and July the brigade carried out combined operations exercises at Kharakvasla, near Poona.

At this time, the problem of the shortage of parachutes was remedied by the establishment of a factory at Kanpur by Mr Leslie Irvin, the American parachute manufacturer. By June the supply situation was such that 300 parachutes were being produced each month, the eventual target rate being 1,750 per month.

During this period the organisation and establishment of the brigade and the parachute battalions underwent some changes. The training company within each battalion was withdrawn and incorporated into the Parachute Troops Training Centre at Delhi. In October 1942 151st Parachute Battalion left the brigade and sailed for the Middle East, where it was redesignated 156th Parachute Battalion and joined 4th Parachute Brigade. During the same month, Brigadier Gough handed over command of 50th Indian Parachute Brigade to Brigadier M. R. J. 'Tim' Hope Thomson, who had previously commanded 4th Parachute Battalion in 2nd Parachute Brigade. Shortly afterwards the brigade left Delhi for a new base at Campbellpur in the Punjab, while the Airlanding School moved to Chaklala, near Rawalpindi.

Before its move to its new base, three small airborne operations were mounted by the brigade. The first of these took place in July 1942, when a company of 152nd Indian Parachute Battalion was dropped from Valencias in an operation against the Hurs, a tribe which inhabited Sind province. In May the Hurs had derailed and attacked a mail train. Although troops had been despatched to deal with them, the tribesmen were well armed and punitive expeditions failed to make any impression on them. Despite a successful drop by the company into this bleak and inhospitable territory, the Hurs had been forewarned and avoided contact. The drop was reinforced with a small ground party and the search continued for several days, but to no avail. The officers taking part were Captains Richard Gillett, Mike Webb and L. F. 'Dicky' Richards.

The second operation, codenamed 'Puddle', was an intelligence-gathering mission behind Japanese lines in Burma. The Japanese advance in December 1941 was so unexpected and swift that the Allied forces were forced to withdraw to India. Owing to the difficult terrain of high mountains covered in thick jungle which formed the Assam Divide, separating India and Burma, the gathering of intelligence on Japanese dispositions was very difficult. In this particular instance, information was needed as to whether the enemy were constructing any airfields in the area of Myitkina. It was decided to drop a small group of paratroops into the area to discover whether any airfields were under construction and to ascertain the extent of the enemy's progress northwards along the routes between Fort Hertz and Hukawng Valley. Thereafter the group was to return to Fort Hertz, which possessed an airstrip, from which it would be extracted.

The group of men selected for the mission came from 153rd Gurkha Parachute Battalion. Commanded by Captain Jimmy Roberts, it comprised three Viceroy Commissioned Officers, four other ranks, and three British other ranks who were signallers. Training for the operation was carried out in great secrecy. The group learned to jump from a Lockheed Lodestar, which involved jumping from a door in the fuselage, as opposed to an aperture in the floor as was the case with the Valencia and the Hudson. Parachuting from the door of the Hudson, and also from a slide from the tail gunner's position, had been tried but found to be impractical.

On 24 June Roberts and his men were flown to Dinjan, where they waited to be launched on their mission. At 1615 hours on 3 July they took off, and an hour later were dropped over the flooded paddy fields of the Ningchangyang Valley in the Kachin Hills. After extracting themselves and some of their seven containers from two feet of water, the group spent the night sitting round a fire trying to converse with friendly locals, none of whom spoke either Gurkhali or Hindustani. On the following morning, 4 July, Roberts succeeded in making radio contact with the operational base at Dinjan and reported his group's safe arrival. That afternoon, by which time they had at last established communication with the local people via the village schoolmaster, who spoke a little English, Roberts and his men moved to a local rest-house where they established their base. Soon afterwards, Roberts despatched two patrols, each of two Gurkhas, with Kachin guides to Myitkina and Tiangzup. Before their departure the guides were briefed by Roberts through the schoolmaster, as there was no way in which the Gurkhas could communicate with the Kachins.

The Myitkina patrol returned on 8 July, having been unable to cross the Mali Hka river because the ferry was guarded and controlled by Japanese troops. It was followed on the following day by the other patrol, which had also been unsuccessful. By that time, however, Captain Nimmo of the Burma Levies had appeared at Roberts' base, and proved invaluable as an interpreter. At that point in the operation the batteries of Roberts' radio failed and contact with the base at Dinjan was lost. It had been planned that a Lysander aircraft would be sent to look for the group after the 15th day of the operation if radio contact was lost, but no aircraft arrived and Roberts decided to lead his men to Fort Hertz. This involved a long march of 150 miles along narrow and twisting tracks through very thick jungle. It was the monsoon season, and the heavy downpours made the going very difficult as tracks became slippery and treacherous. Six of Roberts' men had contracted malaria before they started out on the march, and soon the entire group was similarly afflicted. The group reached Kajitu after seven days of marching.

There they were told that a Blenheim bomber had flown over on two successive days looking for them and had dropped messages asking for news of them. Roberts decided to stay at Kajitu for a day to allow his men to rest and perhaps to make contact with the aircraft if it returned.

With no sign of the Blenheim on the following day, Roberts and his men moved on a day later towards Nbyem. That afternoon, however, they saw the aircraft circling over Kajitu. They eventually managed to attract its attention by firing Very flares, and succeeded in communicating with it by laying out messages on the ground. The aircraft's crew replied by dropping a message saying that they would return on the following day with supplies of food. After two days, however, there was no sign of the aircraft, so Roberts and his men resumed their march towards Nbyem. As they did so they encountered the wounded and dead of the Chinese 5th Army, which was retreating into China through the Hukawng Valley.

At Headquarters 50th Indian Parachute Brigade concern was mounting. Eventually Major Paul Hopkinson, the Brigade Major, was dispatched to Assam to make contact with the group. By that time, the monsoon rains had rendered the airstrip at Fort Hertz unusable, so he was only able to overfly the area. Travelling in a Hudson, he arrived over Fort Hertz, where Roberts and his men were spotted. After dropping a message to them, the aircraft returned to Assam and loaded up with supplies which were dropped on Fort Hertz the same day. Meanwhile, preparations were in hand to drop a force on Fort Hertz to repair the airstrip. On 13 August Captain Jack Newland of 153rd Gurkha Parachute Battalion, together with Lieutenant Bob McLune of 411th (Royal Bombay) Parachute Section Indian Engineers, four other ranks from the brigade headquarters, and a Viceroy Commissioned Officer and four other ranks from his own battalion, parachuted into Fort Hertz. The airstrip was repaired and on 20 August a force consisting of a company of infantry, some Burmese Levies, sappers and medical personal were flown in to Fort Hertz. On the same day Captain Jimmy Roberts and his group, all of whom were sick men, were flown out.

In December 1942 a new battalion joined 50th Indian Parachute Brigade to replace 151st Parachute Battalion. This was the 3rd Battalion 7th Gurkha Rifles, which had seen much action during the retreat from Burma, by the end of which it numbered six officers and 300 men out of its established strength of 750. On being converted to the parachute role, for which every man in the battalion volunteered after the vagaries of parachuting had been explained to them, command of the battalion was assumed by Lieutenant Colonel Hugh Parsons of the 2nd King Edward VII's Own Goorkhas. Unfortunately, in February of the following year, Parsons broke a leg whilst on his parachute course and he was succeeded by Lieutenant Colonel George Bond of the 1st King George V's Own Gurkha Rifles. Subsequently, the battalion was redesignated 154th Gurkha Parachute Battalion.

By this time parachute training in India had progressed, and the Airlanding School had been redesignated No. 3 Parachute Training School.

The aircraft attached to the school still consisted of Valencias and a single Hudson until No. 215 Squadron RAF arrived with its Wellington bombers. The parachute course itself lasted 14 days, and trainees were required to complete five descents to qualify for their wings. In February 1943, as a result of a number of accidents in which there were a number of fatalities including the death of an RAF instructor, the Commanding Officer of No. 1 Parachute Training School at Ringway, Wing Commander Maurice Newnham, arrived at Chaklala to investigate and advise on matters. Fatalities had reached the alarming rate of one per cent of trainees, and parachuting had been suspended. It was resumed only after the main faults had been identified and put right. During his three-month visit, Newnham reorganised the training by lengthening the course and increasing the number of qualifying jumps from five to seven. He also investigated parachute maintenance and the facilities for servicing parachutes, subsequently arranging for the posting of Flight Sergeant Campbell from Ringway to Chaklala to take over parachute maintenance. This resulted in a sharp decrease in the number of accidents caused by parachute malfunctions.

In April 1943 improved equipment for synthetic training arrived at No. 3 Parachute Training School, followed by No. 99 Squadron RAF with more Wellingtons. A month later these were replaced by No. 62 Squadron RAF, equipped with Hudsons. However, in June the first Dakota arrived and was in use by the end of July. More followed later in the year, replacing the Wellingtons and Hudsons. The Wellington, with its fabric-covered geodetic fuselage structure and its restricted exit, was the most unpopular and was universally disliked.

At this point 50th Indian Parachute Brigade underwent expansion. Each battalion was allocated a support company comprising a platoon of 3-inch mortars and a platoon of Vickers medium machine guns. In addition, the brigade was also allocated a medium machine gun company, a pathfinder platoon and a brigade headquarters defence platoon. Its engineer element was increased from a section to a squadron, and its medical support was increased to a field ambulance.

In September 1943 Major General 'Boy' Browning, the Major General Airborne Forces, arrived in India. During the first week of October he visited 50th Indian Parachute Brigade, accompanied by the Commander-in-Chief, Field Marshal Sir Claude Auchinleck and Air Chief Marshal Peirse. This visit proved to be very beneficial for the brigade, which impressed both Browning and Auchinleck. As a result, a mobile parachute servicing unit was posted to Chaklala from the Middle East and a number of officers from No. 38 Group RAF were posted to India to assist in forming No. 177 (Airborne Forces) Wing, which comprised a headquarters and four squadrons. The Parachute Troops Training Centre was redesignated as an airborne forces depot and the decision was taken to form an Indian airborne division, which was to be ready for operations in the latter part of 1944. This would be commanded and staffed at senior level by experienced airborne officers from Britain, and would include a British parachute brigade.

During his visit, Major General Browning hinted to Brigadier Hope Thomson and some of his officers that they might find themselves in action in the near future. This was cheering news, as by then all elements of the brigade were keen to put their extensive training to good effect. The operation to which Browning obliquely referred was codenamed 'Bulldozer', and involved the capture of Akyab, a town situated on the coast of Burma 200 miles north of Rangoon, by an amphibious assault carried out by 36th Infantry Division supported by 50th Indian Parachute Brigade.

The brigade began a period of even more intensive training in preparation for 'Bulldozer', the emphasis being on jungle warfare. This was carried out at the Jungle Warfare School at Raiwala, where 153rd Gurkha Parachute Battalion, together with the brigade headquarters and its signals section, arrived for its course by parachute. Transported in 32 Dakotas, they flew 400 miles across the Punjab and performed the largest drop so far carried out by the brigade. By early December 1943 all units had completed their jungle training, and early 1944 found them carrying out the final exercises in preparation for Operation 'Bulldozer'. By this time, the entire brigade was at a high pitch of readiness and excitement over the coming operation, and it was thus with bitter disappointment that it learned that 'Bulldozer' had been cancelled. To provide some compensation, however little, and to allow his troops to acquire some operational experience, Brigadier Hope Thomson succeeded in arranging for the brigade to be moved to Imphal, in the Naga Hills of Assam, which was in a threatened but quiet sector of operations. There it would be able to carry our more jungle training while some of its officers and senior NCOs were attached to units on operations against the Japanese further south.

At the end of February 1944 50th Indian Parachute Brigade, less 154th Gurkha Parachute Battalion, which was still under strength and in the process of carrying out its parachute training, moved 1,500 miles from Campbellpur to Assam by rail and river steamer. The brigade's new location was at Chakabama, ten miles east of Kohima, and its area of patrol responsibility was the Jessami-Ukhrul sector south-east of Kohima. Under command of the brigade were the 1st Battalion Assam Rifles, which was holding Jessami and Kharasom, and two companies of the Shere Regiment (a native state unit) at Phakekedzumi. It was tasked with intensive patrolling over the vast jungle area from Kohima to Ukhrul, down to the River Chindwin, to deter infiltration by small groups of Japanese.

On its arrival the brigade came under command of 23rd Indian Division, commanded by Major General Ouvry Roberts, which together with 17th and 20th Indian Divisions formed 4th Corps, based at Imphal. The corps commander, Lieutenant General Geoffrey Scoones, had deployed two divisions forward: 17th Indian Division in the Chin Hills and 20th Indian Division in the Kabaw Valley, each divisional area being at the end of a road running south of Imphal. In view of its role, the brigade was only lightly equipped and was without defence stores and equipment. It was to use mule transport only, apart from Brigadier Hope Thomson's jeep, which was shared with the GSO 3 (Intelligence), and another jeep for the

Brigade Liaison Officer, Captain 'Dicky' Richards. These vehicles proved invaluable when communications proved impossible in the forward areas.

Imphal itself was a major Japanese objective. In the summer of 1943 the Japanese had decided that its capture was the key to their successful march on Delhi and the defence of Burma against the Allies. Before starting the campaign to achieve their objective, however, they launched an offensive in Arakan with the purpose of diverting Allied reserves away from Imphal. It was at that point that the Allies also began an advance into Arakan up to a line between Foul Point and Rathedaung, of which the cancelled Operation 'Bulldozer' had formed part. The Allied formations met the Japanese offensive head-on and were quickly encircled. It was only through the rapid despatch of reinforcements and resupply from the air that a catastrophe was averted.

Intelligence reports had indicated that the Japanese were preparing for an offensive in Assam. There had been a steady increase in enemy formations and logistical support. The commander of 14th Army, Lieutenant General Sir William Slim, realised that the main threat faced 4th Corps and decided that the best solution lay in fighting a defensive battle in the area of Imphal. Accordingly, 17th and 20th Indian Divisions were ordered to withdraw on 14 March. However, the Japanese moved swiftly and attacked 17th Indian Division in the rear at two locations. Consequently, 23rd Indian Division had rapidly to send forward two of its brigades to cover the withdrawal of 17th Indian Division. One of these was 49th Indian Infantry Brigade, which had been holding the area of Ukhrul and Sangshak. At 1700 hours on 9 March Major General Ouvry Roberts arrived at Milestone 10, near Kohima, and issued orders for 50th Indian Parachute Brigade Group to take over the vast area of mountainous jungle south of Kohima, bounded by the Kohima-Imphal road and River Chindwin to the east, and as far south as the tracks linking Litan, Sangshak, Finch's Corner and Sheldon's Corner. Its task was to patrol the area and to prevent Japanese infiltration via the Somra tracks. A major Japanese attack from this direction was not thought to be possible. The brigade's deployment was to be completed in two phases, coming into effect on 12 and 14 March.

Early on the morning of 10 March, Major General Roberts departed with Brigadier Hope Thomson and the GSO 3 (Intelligence), Captain Lester Allan, to select positions for the brigade group in the area of Kharasom, Ukrul, Sangshak and Sheldon's Corner. Deployment proceeded accordingly, mainly on foot, though some units were ferried down the Manipur road by trucks via Imphal to Litan. On 15 March very heavy rainstorms washed away parts of roads and some of the narrow winding tracks; delays were caused by some transport being put out of action or lost. Nevertheless, by 16 March the deployment phases had neared completion.

On 16 March troops of the Japanese 15th Division crossed the River Chindwin near Thaungdut and advanced on Imphal along an axis through Myothit, Sangshak and Litan. At the same time, the 31st Division crossed the river further to the north, its objectives being the capture of Ukhrul and Kohima.

Five days earlier, on 11 March, 152nd Indian Parachute Battalion had reached the small village of Litan, which lay some 20 miles away from Imphal on the road to Ukhrul. On its arrival the battalion had been ordered to take over positions at Sheldon's Corner, which lay to the east, from a unit of 49th Indian Infantry Brigade. On 14 March it marched 15 miles to Sangshak, passing through Finch's Corner, where the headquarters of 49th Indian Infantry Brigade was located, and on the following day it arrived at Sheldon's Corner, where it relieved the 4th Battalion 5th Mahratta Light Infantry. The battalion position at Sheldon's Corner was intended to block the approaches from a number of tracks which led from the Chindwin river to a narrow road which ran from Imphal to Ukrul. It consisted of a company base at Point 7378, overlooking a track which led from the village of Homalin and divided into two others, leading to Khanggoi and Ukhrul respectively. Over two miles away lay another company base at Gammon Hill. Two miles from Point 7378, on the northern side of Badger Hill, was a hide position manned by the rest of the battalion.

Such was the hostile nature of the terrain that it was not anticipated that the enemy would attempt to channel large numbers of troops through the area. The positions at Sheldon's Corner were therefore designed so that any enemy advance would be blocked by a counterattack from Badger's Hill, the two forward company positions acting as pivots on which any manoeuvre would be based. However, the positions had been designed for a battalion with four rifle companies, whereas all the battalions in 50th Indian Parachute Brigade possessed only three. Thus 152nd Indian Parachute Battalion was unable to man both forward company positions fully and provide a counterattack force whilst also defending the hide position on Badger Hill. During the next two days the battalion improved the positions, strengthening the defences and bringing in stores and equipment. It was, however, hampered by the lack of barbed wire and other defence stores, and by torrential rain.

Meanwhile, a report from 'V' Force, the intelligence organisation which monitored Japanese activity on the Assam and Arakan fronts, indicated that a group of 50 enemy had crossed the river and had dug in. On the morning of 18 March Lieutenant Colonel Paul Hopkinson, Commanding Officer of 152nd Indian Parachute Battalion, despatched a reconnaissance patrol to discover more about the enemy's movements in the area. The patrol returned that evening, having learned that there were no enemy in the area other than the group which had already been reported. Just before nightfall, however, some Naga tribesmen reported that the Japanese had occupied the village of Pushing, which had been a 'V' Force base. C Company, which was holding Point 7378, had deployed an observation post some four miles in front of its main position, on a track leading to Pushing. In the light of this latest information the company commander, Major John Fuller, withdrew the post and decided to send a reconnaissance patrol along the track at dawn on the following day. Later that night a 'V' Force officer arrived at C Company's headquarters and reported that the Japanese had crossed the Chindwin in force. He and his men had been obliged to abandon their base in haste, along with all their equipment at Pushing, such was the sudden and unexpected appearance of the enemy.

At dawn the following day Lieutenant Andrew Faul led C Company's reconnaissance patrol along the track towards Pushing. He and his men had gone only some three miles when they encountered a column of 200 enemy troops approaching in the opposite direction. With great presence of mind, Faul laid some booby traps before withdrawing in haste. On learning of the enemy's approach, Lieutenant Colonel Hopkinson and his tactical headquarters moved to Badger Hill, from where he could control the battle. Having done so, he watched as the 800 men of the 3rd Battalion of the 58th Regimental Group, commanded by Major General Miyazaki, swarmed up the track from Pushing.

Shortly afterwards, C Company's mortars and machine guns engaged the encircling enemy. At 0930 hours the company was attacked from two directions, an outpost of 20 men being overrun in minutes. During the rest of the morning the enemy launched three attacks against C Company, but these were beaten off. At that point Brigadier Hope Thomson arrived at Lieutenant Colonel Hopkinson's command post. After seeing the situation, he decided that a company of Mahrattas would move up to Badger Hill to replace A Company, which would then carry out a counterattack. Meanwhile, another company of Mahrattas would move with all speed to Khanggoi, where it would cut off any enemy heading north to bypass Sheldon's Corner. A Company set off towards C Company's positions at 1630 hours. Meanwhile, the enemy had begun a series of probing attacks on B Company on Gammon Hill while still keeping up the pressure on C Company. During the night radio contact was maintained with C Company, which reported that it had beaten off a number of attacks but urgently required assistance, there having been no sign of A Company. At midnight on 19 March the Japanese attacked C Company again. Once again Major John Fuller's exhausted men repulsed them, inflicting heavy casualties. In the early hours on the following morning the enemy withdrew, suffering further losses from some booby-trapped mortar bombs planted earlier by Lieutenant Andrew Faul.

By just before dawn on 20 March there was still no news of A Company. Lieutenant Colonel Hopkinson despatched a platoon of Mahrattas to work its way as near as possible to C Company and cause a diversion. Having requested a further company of Mahrattas, he planned to launch another counterattack to relieve C Company, which at that point was subjected to a dawn attack whilst calling for help. On hearing Major John Fuller's call for help, Hopkinson immediately despatched the remainder of the Mahratta company at Badger Hill with orders to fight its way through. However, the enemy had already blocked the route to Point 7378 and all attempts to reach C Company were unsuccessful. At 0600 hours a radio message from the surviving men on Point 7378 reported that Fuller and his second in command, Captain John Roseby, had been wounded and that the enemy had overrun the company's forward posts. At 1015 hours Lieutenant Easton, the surviving officer in C Company, reported over the radio that the company was being overrun and that he would attempt to withdraw to Badger Hill with his surviving men. The rest of the Mahratta company was moving up to Badger Hill, and further support had arrived in the form of 582nd Jungle Mortar Battery. Shortly afterwards, radio contact was established with A Company, which was ordered to withdraw to Badger Hill via Khanggoi, where it was to make contact with the Mahratta company there.

Meanwhile, at Brigade Headquarters, which had moved to Milestone 36 on the Litan-Ukhrul road, Brigadier Hope Thomson viewed the situation with extreme gravity. It worried him immensely that his men, far from taking part in a "jungle warfare exercise in long-range patrolling in a quiet area", were about to be plunged into a major conflict with large forces of battle-hardened opponents. The situation had changed dramatically overnight. His men were neither properly equipped nor completely trained for such operations. Moreover, they were still not fully deployed through lack of transport, the battle had begun and time was quickly running out. Hope Thomson thus ordered his Brigade Liaison Officer, Captain 'Dicky' Richards, to take the brigade's Deputy Commander, Colonel 'Abbo' Abbott, some 15 miles forward to Sheldon's Corner and the positions now under attack. After a hazardous two-hour drive, half-expecting to be ambushed at one of the innumerable bends in the tortuously winding mountain track, Richards and Abbott arrived at 1030 hours and climbed the steep slopes on foot. On reaching the headquarters of 152nd Indian Parachute Battalion they discussed plans and air support for further attacks against the advancing Japanese with Lieutenant Colonels Paul Hopkinson and Jack Trim, Commanding Officer of the Mahrattas, as well as with the officers of 582nd Jungle Mortar Battery. At 1830 hours the two officers reported back to the brigade commander. They had also given orders for the 'V' Force dump of 1,500 gallons of fuel and a large quantity of rations to be destroyed; there had been no other way of saving them from falling into enemy hands.

Brigadier Hope Thomson had sent Captain Allan, his GSO 3 (Intelligence), back to Headquarters 23rd Indian Division to report on the situation and to ask where the brigade should establish a point of resistance, should it become necessary to evacuate the Sheldon's Corner area. At 1900 hours he spoke over the radio to the divisional commander, Major General Roberts. On reporting the situation, he obtained 15th Mountain Battery of 9th Mountain Regiment Royal Indian Artillery, located at Litan, to be placed under command of the brigade. Just after midnight on the night of 20/21 March Captain Allan returned from Imphal and reported that the divisional commander wished the whole of 50th Indian Parachute Brigade and its attached units to concentrate at Sangshak, where it was thought there was a good supply of water. At first light on the 21st the brigade headquarters and the medium machine gun company moved off.

That night, Lieutenant Easton and the few exhausted and wounded survivors of C Company 152nd Indian Parachute Battalion reached the battalion hide area. After reporting that the company had been overrun whilst fighting to the bitter end, they were evacuated to Litan for urgent medical treatment. During the night, enemy troops approached Badger Hill, where the positions had been strengthened, but were scared off by booby traps which had been placed on all approaches. They also carried out probing attacks against B Company on Gammon Hill, but were repulsed. Reconnaissance patrols sent out at dawn on 21 March discovered that the number of enemy had increased during the night; a battalion was by then occupying C Company's old positions, while another was between Badger Hill and Point 7378.

By this time it had become clear to Brigadier Hope Thomson that such was the speed of the enemy's advance, and the rapid build-up of his forces, that Sheldon's Corner was rapidly becoming indefensible. 153rd Gurkha Parachute Battalion had arrived on the evening of 20 March, but without its Support Company. At the same time, the brigadier learned from the medium machine gun company, which was evacuating the supply dump at Ukhrul and destroying any stores which could not be carried, that the enemy were approaching Ukhrul itself and thus threatening to outflank the force at Sheldon's Corner.

In the early hours of 21 March orders arrived from Major General Roberts, instructing 50th Indian Parachute Brigade to withdraw westwards to Sangshak. There it was to form a close perimeter 'defensive box' and, in the event of the enemy bypassing it, to harass and cut the enemy lines of communications as part of the operations to defend Imphal. Vital time was required to reinforce Imphal with a major force to prevent the corps and divisional headquarters, airstrips and massive supply dumps from being overrun by this unexpected flanking attack. The withdrawal would have to be carried out at night, and its success depended on the enemy being given no hint of it beforehand. Shortly before dusk a resupply drop took place. This had been ordered before the decision to withdraw, but to strengthen the enemy's belief that the brigade intended to stand its ground it was not cancelled. Accordingly, at 0800 hours, the Brigade Liaison Officer was again sent forward to the battle area by jeep with orders to withdraw to Finch's Corner if the situation did not improve during the day, and to plan to fall back to Sangshak at short notice.

The first unit to withdraw was 582nd Jungle Mortar Battery, whose mules moved off down the narrow track after darkness had fallen. Shortly afterwards, an enemy patrol opened fire on Badger Hill and at 2100 hours another advanced to within a short distance of the positions on the hill and attacked them with grenades. In both instances, the enemy were driven off. At 0200 hours on 22 March the withdrawal began. Burdened with heavy packs and carrying their wounded, the paratroops and the Mahrattas silently made their way through the darkness along the narrow track leading through the jungle. As they did so, they could hear the sounds of battle coming from the direction of Sangshak. By 1000 hours both battalions had reached Kidney Hill, where they met 582nd Jungle Mortar Battery, together with A Company 152nd Indian Parachute Battalion, which had moved there on withdrawing from Khanggoi. At 1230 hours, shortly after their arrival, orders arrived for the entire force to join the rest of the brigade at Sangshak as soon as possible. At the same time a patrol of 153rd Gurkha Parachute Battalion reported that the track leading to Sangshak was still clear but that a large number of enemy were advancing towards Sangshak along the road from Ukhrul.

The rest of the brigade, less Support Company 153rd Gurkha Parachute Battalion and the medium machine gun company, had occupied Sangshak on the evening of 21 March. Under command were 15th Mountain Battery, a detachment of 74th Field Company Indian Engineers, the Kalibahadur Regiment (a Nepalese Army unit) less two companies, and D Company 4th Battalion 5th Mahratta Light Infantry. Sangshak was a Naga village, along the southern side of which ran the road from Finch's Corner to Sheldon's Corner and on to the River Chindwin. From the defensive point of view Sangshak had little to recommend it. Although it was in a commanding position, dominating several important track junctions, the ridgeline on which it was situated was covered in grass and scrub which offered little cover. The slopes approaching it, however, consisted of thick jungle which came up to the brigade's perimeter, affording excellent approaches to the enemy while restricting the defenders' fields of fire. The problems in defending Sangshak were compounded by the fact that no barbed wire, anti-personnel mines or explosives were available to the brigade, making it virtually impossible for the defenders to construct obstacles to channel the enemy into covered approaches or to prevent them from reaching the forward positions. An equally serious problem was discovered when the brigade began to improve the defences on the morning of 22 March. To their dismay, the defenders discovered that they were unable to dig any deeper than three feet because of a thick layer of rock. In many places, outcrops of rock prevented any digging whatsoever. Furthermore, the only water supply was from locations outside the defensive perimeter.

At 1430 hours a column of some 300 enemy troops was sighted approaching along the road from Ukhrul. These were engaged by 15th Mountain Battery which proceeded, with some very accurate shooting, to force the Japanese to abandon the road and take to the jungle. Five hundred yards to the west of the village was a hill on which there was a small number of Naga huts, and it soon became apparent that the enemy were heading for it. The Mahrattas' D Company, commanded by Captain Ray Steele, was ordered to occupy the hill to provide cover for the two battalions from Kidney Hill who were approaching the brigade's positions and arrived there shortly before the enemy. The main track was picquetted by men of 153rd Gurkha Parachute Battalion who had just arrived from Kohima, and the Brigade Liaison Officer, Captain 'Dicky' Richards, was able to maintain constant contact with units of the brigade as they approached Sangshak, keeping the brigade headquarters advised of their progress. At the same time he assisted some of the walking wounded by ferrying their heavy equipment forward to the new positions in his jeep.

152nd Indian Parachute Battalion and the Mahrattas arrived at Sangshak with only an hour and a half of daylight to spare. The former took up positions defending the north-west sector of the perimeter, which included a small wooden church belonging to a Baptist mission, which occupied a commanding position. The Mahrattas, who had the good fortune of being allocated their own defensive positions constructed much earlier when 49th Indian Infantry Brigade had held the Ukhrul-Sangshak sector, assumed responsibility for part of the southern sector with 74th Field Company IE and the brigade headquarters defence platoon. 153rd Gurkha Parachute Battalion defended the western sector and the rest of the southern, while the Kalibahadur Regiment was allocated the eastern sector and part of the northern one. The brigade headquarters was located behind the central ridgeline, and 80th Parachute Field Ambulance was split between two positions — one in the south-eastern corner of the area, behind the Mahrattas and the Kalibahadurs, and the other in the south-western corner to the rear of 153rd Gurkha Parachute Battalion and 74th Field Company IE. The brigade's mortars and the guns of 15th Mountain Battery were located on the plateau in the north-western corner of the area.

At 1900 hours that evening the Mahrattas' D Company was withdrawn from the hill to the west of the village, at which point the enemy brought down a heavy concentration of mortar fire on the hill and occupied it shortly afterwards. At 1920 hours machine guns opened fire on the brigade's positions and caused some casualties. In the absence of slit trenches it was difficult to move without attracting fire.

At 0130 hours on the following morning, 23 March, the enemy launched an attack against the Mahrattas while also carrying out probes to draw fire from the southern and south-western sectors of the perimeter. These then developed into a fierce attack on the area of the church. This assault took a heavy battering from Major John Ball's medium machine gun company and the brigade's 3-inch mortars. The arrival of the enemy assault was heralded by the light of torches and the sound of shouting as the Japanese made their way through the jungle towards their objective, subsequently hurling themselves forward in waves at the paratroopers, who mowed them down the machine guns and mortars. Two Japanese succeeded in infiltrating into the field ambulance headquarters area but were swiftly dealt with. By the time they withdrew at dawn, the enemy had lost 89 men killed. On one of the corpses were found documents and a map giving full details of the enemy's plans for the offensive against Imphal and Kohima. Copies of these were made and taken to Imphal by the GSO 3 (Intelligence) and another member of the brigade headquarters intelligence section.

Throughout 23 March the enemy kept the brigade's positions under fire from machine guns and snipers as well as mortars and artillery, a number of casualties being caused as men moved between trenches. At 0800 hours all the mortars in the brigade were placed under command of 15th Mountain

Battery and all Vickers guns under the medium machine gun company. At the same time Colonel Abbott reorganised the perimeter in the light of the night's activities. A major problem was the lack of water, as the water point, at the north-eastern corner of the perimeter, was under fire. A resupply drop was requested, and this took place during the afternoon, but unfortunately the aircraft flew in at high altitude to avoid enemy fire and the sorely-needed supplies landed outside the perimeter. One aircraft, flown by a crew which had transported units of the brigade during their airborne training, made a low-level approach and dropped its load accurately. During the ensuing days of fighting at Sangshak this same aircrew repeated the performance to ensure that their loads always landed on target. Unfortunately they were the only ones able to do so, and the other aircraft loads continued to fall into enemy hands. As a result the brigade rapidly grew short of essential supplies such as ammunition, rations and medical supplies.

All the while, the enemy kept up the pressure on the brigade. Throughout the night of 23 March the attacks continued and the number of casualties increased. On 24 March Brigadier Hope Thomson decided to attempt to retake the hill to the west of the brigade's positions, but first despatched patrols to discover the enemy's strengths and dispositions. Another air resupply drop of ammunition was requested and took place shortly afterwards, but once again only one aircraft's load landed within the perimeter. Eighty per cent of the drops had fallen into enemy hands and could not be recovered. At about midday a large enemy force of some 400 men with 75mm artillery pieces, using elephants to tow them, was seen approaching along the road leading from Sangshak to Sheldon's Corner. At 1400 hours the brigade headquarters and 152nd Indian Parachute Battalion came under shellfire and shortly afterwards the enemy put in a strong attack which was repulsed only after some fierce fighting at close quarters. Despite the severity of this assault, and others during the afternoon, the battalion held its ground and suffered only four killed and six wounded. Major John Ball, commanding the medium machine gun company, took over a Vickers gun whose crew became casualties, but was himself killed after taking a heavy toll of the enemy. At 1600 hours air support arrived in the form of some Hurricane fighter-bombers which attacked the Japanese, although they were hampered in their pinpointing of targets by the thick jungle, which led to some aircraft firing on the paratroopers' positions.

At 1730 hours the enemy launched another attack on 152nd Indian Parachute Battalion, but supporting fire from 15th Mountain Battery and the brigade's mortars kept them at bay. At 0500 hours on the following morning, 25 March, after further fierce fighting throughout the night, Lieutenant Colonel Paul Hopkinson was forced to withdraw the platoon holding the positions by the church in the north-west corner of the perimeter. Two hours later, however, the positions were reoccupied and a listening post established in the church itself. That evening another strong attack, supported by artillery and mortar fire, was directed against the positions by the church, and the enemy succeeded in taking some of the forward positions before being driven off. A reconnaissance patrol, which had been sent out the day before, returned and reported a heavy build-up of troops and an administrative base being established by the enemy at Milestone 36.

Details of the Japanese build-up were passed to Headquarters 23rd Indian Division while the brigade headquarters staff reviewed the increasingly grim situation. All tracks around Sangshak were cut and held by the Japanese; rapidly mounting casualties could not be evacuated and most were doomed to die. Reinforcements promised by Headquarters 23rd Indian Division had not got through, and now could not do so. Rotting bodies of men and mules lay unburied because of the rocky ground and dysentery had broken out. With the near-total failure of air resupply, it was agreed that only a miracle could save the situation. There was no question of surrender; the battle had to go on.

The rest of the night of 25 March was quiet, but two hours before dawn on 26 March the enemy began to bring mortar fire to bear on the Kalibahadur Regiment. Soon afterwards a very heavy artillery concentration crashed down on A Company 152nd Indian Parachute Battalion, which was then attacked by three companies of enemy infantry. During this action the company commander, Major Richard Gillett, was mortally wounded. By 0530 hours the enemy had established a foothold in the area of the church, less than 200 yards from Brigade Headquarters, and subsequently broke through the perimeter several times but were repulsed. Eventually they took the church which dominated the main brigade position, and from it they then attacked the positions of 15th Mountain Battery and 582nd Jungle Mortar Battery. The two battery commanders, Majors Locke and Smith, were killed while defending their positions. Howitzers were fired over open sights at the Japanese-held trenches within the perimeter, inflicting heavy losses on the enemy.

152nd Indian Parachute Battalion had lost all of its company commanders and its positions were littered with the dead and wounded of both sides. Brigadier Hope Thomson then committed his small reserve, the brigade headquarters defence platoon. Led by their commander, Lieutenant Robin de la Haye, the men of the platoon counterattacked but were cut to pieces by a withering hail of fire from enemy machine guns and mortars. At that point Lieutenant Colonel Hopkinson himself led another counterattack by men of his headquarters and was successful in retaking some of his battalion's positions. However, the enemy attacked again and Hopkinson and his men were driven back, Hopkinson himself being badly wounded in the foot. Brigadier Hope Thomson went forward to encourage the remnants of 152nd Indian Parachute Battalion to hold on at all costs to the church positions. They had taken the worst battering at Sheldon's Corner and had been subjected to continuous heavy attack from the time of their arrival at Sangshak. Nevertheless they had held on, preventing the position from being overrun.

Two more counterattacks by platoons of the Mahrattas on orders from Brigadier Hope Thomson failed to recapture the positions by the church. At 2100 hours the brigade commander ordered 153rd Gurkha Parachute

Battalion to retake the area of the church, and this task was given to A Company, commanded by Major Jimmy Roberts, which had not been involved in the earlier fighting at Sheldon's Corner. The Gurkhas stormed the position, led by Roberts sounding a rallying call on a hunting horn, and the Japanese, unable to face this onslaught, were routed.

Despite the period of relative calm that followed the day's fighting, Brigadier Hope Thomson was well aware that the Japanese would not give up their efforts to take Sangshak, since they were depending on the equipment and stores which they would capture. The scene throughout the perimeter was one of carnage, the dead lying unburied and the majority of the wounded lying in trenches as there was no room for them in the already overcrowded area occupied by the field ambulance. Suffering from lack of sleep and severe thirst, the men of the brigade awaited the next enemy onslaught.

At 1800 hours, however, a British signaller in the brigade signals section, which had struggled against tremendous odds to maintain the rear link, received a verbal message 'in clear' from Major General Roberts, ordering the brigade to fight its way out to the south and subsequently to the west. It was agreed that a properly co-ordinated withdrawal at night in mountainous jungle without communications or ammunition, whilst carrying large numbers of wounded, was quite impossible. This was a heartbreaking moment for Brigadier Hope Thomson and his men, because such an order meant that some of the wounded would have to be left to the mercy of the Japanese, who were renowned for their inhumane and murderous treatment of Allied wounded. Lieutenant Colonel Bobby Davis, the Commanding Officer of 80th Parachute Field Ambulance, volunteered to stay with the wounded, but Brigadier Hope Thomson refused to let him do so, knowing full well what fate would await him. Instead, he ordered each unit to send 50 men to the field ambulance to evacuate as many of the wounded as possible, using makeshift crutches and stretchers fashioned from bamboo.

After darkness had fallen the brigade prepared to disperse into the jungle. Equipment, stores and documents were destroyed, the sounds being masked by diversionary bursts of machine gun fire and the continual heavy shelling by the enemy. At 2230 hours the withdrawal began, the column of small groups of men wending its way in the darkness through the Mahrattas' positions on the southern sector of the perimeter which did not face the Japanese, who had found the steep slopes unassailable after the first attack. Crossing over the road on the southern side of the village, the brigade slowly made its way down the steep slopes into the jungle. As planned, the column soon split up into groups as it laboured its way through the jungle, which at times was so thick that paths had to be cut through it. All members of the brigade had been briefed to head south until 0600 hours, and because the ridgelines ran north-south the going was relatively easy for the first few hours. However, on turning west towards Imphal, which lay some 30 miles away, the groups of exhausted men were confronted with a seemingly endless series of steep ascents and descents over the crests of ridgelines. Although armed, almost all were without ammunition and grenades. Others were far too weak from near-exhaustion or injury to carry their weapons or anything at all. There was water in plenty, but it was polluted and could not be boiled for fear of attracting the enemy. There was little or no food. Caution had to be exercised as each group made its painful way through the jungle because the Japanese had occupied most of the Naga villages and columns of enemy troops were moving along the tracks, heading for Imphal and Sangshak. Some groups of the brigade were ambushed; the Japanese surrounded any area where they had detected movement, set fire to it and shot anyone who came out.

While the journey was arduous for those who had not been wounded in the fighting, it was an appalling ordeal for the wounded. Carrying the mainly improvised stretchers became impossible when moving through thick jungle or climbing over the steep ridgelines, and those who could not walk eventually had to be left in the care of friendly Naga tribesmen. Others of the wounded succumbed before reaching Imphal, many suffering from dreadful wounds which had turned gangrenous. The complete absence of any medical evacuation facilities back to the rear brigade headquarters at Litan added to the great toll, particularly in respect of the exceedingly high casualties suffered by 152nd Indian Parachute Battalion, upon whose position astride the church the Japanese had concentrated their main attacks.

One small group, with only a dozen rounds of ammunition between them, was commanded by the brigade's much respected deputy commander, Colonel Abbott. It included Lieutenant Colonel Paul Hopkinson and was led by Captain 'Dicky' Richards, who carried the only rations, an emergency pack which he had recovered from his jeep, wrecked by enemy gunfire, before leaving. While reconnoitring ahead and about to enter a Naga village, Richards encountered a group of enemy troops who opened fire on his group. Hopkinson, seriously wounded in the foot and unable to walk unaided, managed to escape by rolling downhill into some thick jungle. He was closely followed by the rest of the group, most of whom were in a state of near-collapse. All of them hid in the undergrowth and tall elephant grass while the Japanese searched for them, sometimes passing within a few feet. However, dusk was approaching and the enemy abandoned the search as darkness fell, enabling the three officers and the rest of their group to escape.

That evening, while converging on to the final stage of the escape route, Colonel Abbott and his men met up with other groups, including one led by Major Harry Butchard of 153rd Gurkha Parachute Battalion. At dawn on the next day, after spending the night together, the groups split up once more and continued their journey westwards. On the sixth day after the withdrawal from Sangshak, Abbott and his group met a patrol from the 17th Dogra Regiment which gave them a meal and directions to the road which ran between Imphal and Yaingangpokpi. As they reached the road they met a troop of friendly tanks. Meanwhile, Major Butchard and his group had met Brigadier Hope Thomson, who had been injured in a fall, and his orderly. That evening they encountered two Indian medical officers leading a group of some 30 wounded. Two days later another group joined them as they continued their march, not knowing whether Imphal was still in friendly hands or whether it had been captured by the Japanese. On the morning of the sixth day Butchard and his group of exhausted and near-starving men reached a village where the local people gave them their first proper meal in several days. Later that day they marched into Imphal.

Other feats of survival and endurance came to light once the brigade had regrouped at Imphal. Lieutenant Kynoch Shand of 153rd Gurkha Parachute Battalion appeared after being given up for lost. Having been captured by the Japanese, who had stripped him of most of his clothing and his boots, he had been led by a rope with his hands bound behind his back. During the night, however, he had succeeded in escaping by throwing himself down the side of a ridgeline and rolling several hundred feet to the bottom. He had then wandered barefoot through the jungle, his hands still bound behind his back, until he met a Naga who cut his bonds. Subsequently he made his way to Imphal. Another daring escape was made by Lieutenant Basil Seaton of 152nd Indian Parachute Battalion, who had been wounded in the mouth. He had inadvertently been left behind at Sangshak while lying in a slit trench after being given a dose of morphia. On regaining consciousness after the brigade had withdrawn, he discovered a Japanese soldier sitting nearby and searching through his equipment. Slowly and carefully drawing his fighting knife, he silently killed him before disappearing into the jungle and making his way to Imphal.

After its arrival, 50th Indian Parachute Brigade spent a short period refitting before coming under command of 17th Indian Division on 8th April. During this period it said a sad farewell to Brigadier Tim Hope Thomson, on whom the gallant stand at Sangshak against overwhelming odds and the subsequent trek to Imphal had taken a severe toll. He was admitted to hospital on 31 March and was subsequently invalided back to England. Colonel Abbott assumed command of the brigade.

The defence of Imphal was based on a series of 'boxes' which were sited to provide mutual support as well as covering the airfield. In addition, there was a reserve force tasked with counterattacking any enemy which succeeded in penetrating any 'box'. On coming under command of 17th Indian Division the brigade was split between two 'boxes'. 153rd Gurkha Parachute Battalion was assigned to 'Oyster Box' while the rest of the brigade, reinforced by a company of the West Yorkshire Regiment, assumed responsibility for the defence of the north-eastern sector of 'Catfish Box'. The brigade tactical headquarters, together with a company of 152nd Indian Parachute Battalion and the West Yorkshire company, formed a mobile counterattack force. In addition, Colonel Abbott also formed another mobile reserve consisting of a jeep company, a company of West Yorkshires in Bren carriers, a company of 7th Baluch Regiment and a detachment of 129th Field Battery RA. This force was christened 'Abforce'.

The enemy were by then advancing on Imphal from all directions. Their 15th Division was approaching from the east and the north, the

Yamamoto Force was attacking from the south-east and south, and the 33rd Division was advancing from the west and south-west after coming up the Tiddim road. No sooner had they been blocked at one point than they broke through at another. On 30 March the enemy blew a bridge on the Kohima road 30 miles north of Imphal, cutting 4th Corps off from Kohima and the railhead at Dimapur as well as severing all of 4th Corps' land links with India except for a track leading to Silchar, 57 miles away. Fourteen miles north of Imphal, the ordnance depot at Kanglatongbi was captured by the enemy, who helped themselves to large amounts of stores and equipment which they desperately needed in order to continue their battle into India

The only units in 50th Indian Parachute Brigade which were in reasonable condition after Sangshak were 153rd Gurkha Parachute Battalion and 411th (Royal Bombay) Parachute Squadron IE. 152nd Indian Parachute Battalion had suffered severe losses during the actions at Sheldon's Corner and Sangshak and had to be reorganised into three light companies. Other men from the brigade continued to arrive in groups after trekking through the jungle from Sangshak. Many of these had been captured by the enemy but had subsequently escaped. On 21 April a large party of 25 men from 152nd Indian Parachute Battalion made a very welcome appearance.

On 22 May Brigadier E. G. 'Lakri' Woods assumed command of the brigade. By then the Japanese offensive had begun to peter out with the exception of the 33rd Division, commanded by Lieutenant General Tanaka, which was operating in the Bishenpur sector to the south-west of Imphal. On the night of 20 May Tanaka launched an attack on 17th Indian Division and cut off the divisional headquarters from its forward brigades. No sooner had Brigadier Woods assumed command of 50th Indian Parachute Brigade than he had to move his headquarters and take over responsibility for operations to clear the enemy out of divisional headquarters area. A composite column called 'Woodforce' was formed from units at his disposal, and during the period 27 May to 5 July it cleared the Japanese forces from the area. On 8 July the brigade tactical headquarters returned to Imphal. So stubborn and effective was the resistance from the enemy road blocks, sited high up on the steep ranges, that flame throwers had to be used against them. One strongpoint proved to be particularly stubborn, and was only overcome after a Bofors anti-aircraft gun had been dragged by a group of men, including the brigade commander and his liaison officer, to the top of a peak from where it destroyed the road block.

Meanwhile, the rest of the brigade had been involved in operations to harry the Japanese forces which were withdrawing via Ukhrul, which was a rallying point for the 15th and 31st Divisions. At the beginning of June 152nd Indian Parachute Battalion came under command of 80th Indian Infantry Brigade, a part of 20th Indian Division, which was holding positions astride the road leading from Imphal to Ukhrul. Shortly afterwards B Company, commanded by Major Tom Monaghan, was detached from the battalion and placed under command of 100th Indian

Infantry Brigade. At midnight on the night of 9 June a battalion of the brigade attacked a hill feature called 'Bastion' which dominated the area occupied by the brigade headquarters. Although the attack was supported by tanks, it failed, and B Company was ordered to take the objective. This it proceeded to do with great dash, despite the fact that it came under heavy fire from machine guns and grenade launchers. A bayonet charge resulted in the enemy being cleared from the feature, which was then secured, to the great relief of Brigade Headquarters, which otherwise would certainly have been overrun.

153rd Gurkha Parachute Battalion, also operating under 20th Indian Division, had meanwhile been deployed around Mung Ching. The enemy were fiercely resisting any efforts to dislodge them from the area to the south of Ukhrul, which they were still using as a base, and were particularly active in the area of Tangkhul Hundung, to the east of Imphal. C Company, commanded by Major John Saunders, was tasked with forming a column which would include a detachment of the Assam Rifles and some men of 'V' Force and would be accompanied by the battalion's Medical Officer, Captain Eric Neild. Designated 'Sancol', its task was to monitor Japanese activity in the area, to engage enemy forces and destroy or capture them, and to cut enemy escape routes between Kamjong and Humine. Air support would be available for engagement of large bodies of enemy when sighted. The column was to carry only light equipment, and would have no transport except porters. Wherever possible it was to live off the land, although each man would carry an emergency supply of two days' rations. 'Sancol' departed on its operation on 25 June. Five days later, on 30 June, another larger column was formed. Called 'Tarforce' and commanded by Lieutenant Colonel G. L. Tarver of the Baluch Regiment, it comprised 152nd Indian and 153rd Gurkha Parachute Battalions (less the latter's C Company), a company of the 1st Battalion The Devonshire Regiment, and a company of the 4th Madras Regiment. 'Tarforce' arrived at Tangkhul Hundung on 5 July and 'Sancol' moved on further eastwards to Khongjan.

By now the Japanese had been routed and were in full flight. Their retreat was made none the easier for them by the monsoon rains and the absence of air support. As they streamed back down the tracks towards the River Chindwin they discarded their heavy equipment and their wounded, leaving their dead to lie unburied where they had fallen. 'Tarforce' and 'Sancol' carried out innumerable ambushes against the disorganised Japanese, who were in poor physical condition, suffering from malaria and dysentery as well as jungle sores and wounds. C Company 152nd Indian Parachute Battalion, commanded by Captain 'Dicky' Richards, operating well forward in the Sakok area, ambushed a group of enemy and captured the first Japanese officers in this operation. The enemy's personal equipment and weapons were also in a neglected state, the latter frequently rusted and almost inoperable. Despite their desperate plight, however, the Japanese refused to surrender when cornered and fought hard to the end. When captured they expected to be killed, and were astonished when they were fed and their wounds were treated. There was no doubt, however, about their military skills, their determination and courage.

By 23 July 'Tarforce' had completed its mission. Earlier in the month Brigadier Woods had received a warning order to prepare to withdraw his brigade from the operational area, and on 26 July the two parachute battalions returned to Imphal. Two days later, 50th Indian Parachute Brigade departed for Secunderabad, but before it left the commander of 20th Indian Division, Major General Gracey, arrived at Imphal to bid farewell. On 31 August 1944 the commander of 14th Army, Lieutenant General Sir William Slim, published a Special Order of the Day in which he singled out the brigade from the 26 others which had fought in the battles for Kohima and Imphal. The following is an extract:

"Your parachute brigade bore the first brunt of the enemy's powerful flanking attack, and by their staunchness gave the garrison of Imphal the vital time required to adjust their defences.

To the officers and men of the 50th Parachute Brigade I send my congratulations."

Years later, when writing to the 50th/77th Indian Parachute Brigades Association in England, he would add the following tribute:

"I shall always remember the days you gained for 14th Army at a critical time by the magnificent stand at Sangshak."

On arriving at Secunderabad in early August, the brigade found 154th Gurkha Parachute Battalion waiting for it. Shortly afterwards, it was discovered that the airfields in the area were not capable of accommodating Dakotas, and so by October the brigade moved to the area of Rawalpindi. The brigade headquarters was based near Chaklala, while 152nd Indian and 153rd Gurkha Parachute Battalions were located at Sangjani. 154th Gurkha Parachute Battalion took up residence at Kahuta.

With the return of the brigade from operations, the expansion of Indian airborne forces could be undertaken. The newly formed 9th Indian Airborne Division, commanded by Major General Eric Down, had until then been only a skeleton formation. It had been intended that 44th Indian Armoured Division, which had been formed for operations in the Middle East, should transfer its headquarters and divisional troops to the new airborne formation. However, as a result of the Japanese offensive these had been rapidly transferred to Jorhat, at the foot of the Himalayas, from where they operated the lines of communications for the operations around Kohima.

After the Japanese withdrawal from Assam, the headquarters and divisional troops were withdrawn and 9th Indian Airborne Division was redesignated 44th Indian Airborne Division. A further addition took place when 14th (Long Range Penetration) Brigade, which had operated in an airlanding role during the second operation carried out by the Chindits of Major General Orde Wingate's Special Force, was redesignated 14th Airlanding Brigade. However, owing to the depleted numbers of the British units in Special Force, only one British battalion could be provided with the brigade headquarters, so two Indian battalions had to be transferred to the new formation. Commanded by Brigadier Tom Brodie, it consisted of the 2nd Battalion The Black Watch, the 4th Battalion (Outram's) 6th Rajputana Rifles and the 6th Battalion 16th Punjab Regiment. The divisional troops included 44th Independent Pathfinder Company (formed from the Special Force parachute company); 44th Indian Airborne Division Reconnaissance Squadron (Governor General's Bodyguard), formed from the Viceroy's Bodyguard; 159th Parachute Light Regiment RA; and 23rd Light Anti-Aircraft/Anti-Tank Regiment RA. Sapper elements comprised 40th Indian Airborne Field Park Squadron IE; 33rd Parachute Squadron IE; 411th (Royal Bombay) Parachute Squadron IE; and 12th Parachute Squadron RE. Logistical and transport units of the RIASC consisted of the Parachute Supply Company, 610th Airborne Light (Jeep) Company, and 165th and 604th Airborne GT Companies. A second parachute brigade was still required for the new division. In January 1945, after the disbandment of Special Force, 77th Infantry Brigade was converted to the parachute role and was redesignated 77th Indian Parachute Brigade. Its commander was Brigadier Charles Wilkinson.

A considerable amount of reorganisation took place within the parachute battalions of the division at this time, and it was decided that both parachute brigades would contain a British battalion. Accordingly, two such units were raised by converting two battalions of the disbanded Special Force, the 1st Battalion The King's Regiment and the 1st Battalion The South Staffordshire Regiment, to the parachute role and redesignating them 15th and 16th Parachute Battalions respectively. Both units were initially reduced to cadre strength and their ranks subsequently filled by volunteers in England and from British units in India. They were commanded by Lieutenant Colonels Terence Otway (who had previously commanded 9th Parachute Battalion in Normandy) and A. W. E. 'Danny' Daniell respectively.

On 18 December 1944 authorisation had been given for the formation of The Indian Parachute Regiment, and this was put into effect on 1 March 1945, Lieutenant General 'Boy' Browning being appointed Colonel of The Regiment. The insignia of the regiment was that of The Parachute Regiment of the British Army with the word 'India' inscribed at the base of the parachute. This was worn on the maroon beret which replaced the broad-brimmed Gurkha hat which had been worn until then by all Indian and Gurkha parachute battalions. The divisional sign was the famous Pegasus emblem, as worn by the British airborne formations.

Following the formation of the regiment, the individual parachute battalions underwent changes of designation. 153rd and 154th Gurkha Parachute Battalions respectively became 2nd and 3rd Gurkha Parachute Battalions, while 152nd Indian Parachute Battalion was divided to form two new battalions designated 1st and 4th Indian Parachute Battalions; the 1st Battalion being Hindu and the 4th Muslim. In addition, four in-dependent parachute companies were formed, designated 44th, 14th, 50th and 77th. These were defence units for the divisional and brigade headquarters. 1st Indian, 3rd Gurkha and 16th Parachute Battalions were allocated to 50th Indian Parachute Brigade, whilst 2nd Gurkha, 4th Indian and 15th Parachute Battalions were given to 77th Indian Parachute Brigade. The Indian Airborne Forces Depot had been formed at Rawalpindi in December 1944 from the Parachute Troops Training Centre, and this consisted of a depot company, two Indian and two Gurkha training companies, and a specialist training company comprising medical, signals and engineer elements.

While the expansion and reorganisation of Indian airborne forces had been taking place in early 1945, the campaign in Burma against the Japanese had continued apace. Originally, two airborne operations had been planned as part of 14th Army's operations for the recapture of Burma: one to seize the Yeu-Shwebo plain and the other to capture Rangoon. Consideration had also been given to a third to capture the area of Kalewa and Kalemyo. However, Lieutenant General Slim had been unwilling to divert much-needed transport aircraft from the task of supplying his forward formations, which depended on air resupply. Coupled with the successes and rapid advance of 14th Army, this had led to the abandonment of plans for such operations. 14th Army had advanced south and taken Kalewa and Kalemyo, Slim's intention being to thrust swiftly into Burma and defeat the Japanese forces before they could recover from their defeat at Imphal. The Yeu-Shwebo plain had been taken a month ahead of schedule, but subsequently an unexpected enemy counter-offensive had slowed the advance towards Rangoon, which had to be captured before the arrival of the monsoon rains and the inevitable problems which accompanied them.

An amphibious operation, codenamed 'Dracula', had been planned for the capture of Rangoon, and it was decided at the end of March that it would be carried out in a modified form. The meteorologists had predicted that 2 May was the latest suitable date for the operation, which meant that there was only a month to prepare for it. 'Dracula' consisted of a landing by 26th Indian Division, with naval and air support, on both banks of the Rangoon River south of the city and halfway between Elephant Point and the Bassein Creek. The river itself had been mined by the Japanese, as well as by Allied aircraft, and thus minesweepers would have to precede the vessels and landing craft carrying the division. However, coastal defences were sited on the west bank of the river, and these would have to be neutralised before the minesweepers could enter the river mouth. This would be accomplished by a parachute battalion which would land on 1 May, the day before the amphibious assault.

When details of the operation were passed to 44th Indian Airborne Division, it was in the midst of its reorganisation. Moreover, many of its officers were in England on leave, and the men of the two Gurkha battalions were on leave in Nepal or, in the case of 3rd Gurkha Parachute Battalion, in the process of transferring to 77th Indian Parachute Brigade. As a result, a composite battalion, commanded by Major Jack Newland, was formed from elements of both Gurkha battalions. On moving to Chaklala the battalion was joined by two teams of pathfinders, a section of 411th (Royal Bombay) Parachute Squadron IE, a detachment of 80th

Parachute Field Ambulance, and detachments from the signals and intelligence sections of Headquarters 50th Indian Parachute Brigade. After training at Chaklala the battalion moved to Midnapore on 14 April. Four days later it moved to the mounting airfield at Kalaikunda, where it remained for ten days, assembling its equipment and carrying out a rehearsal of the operation. On 29 April it flew to Akyab on the coast of Burma, 200 miles north of Rangoon. There it was joined by a 200-strong reserve force consisting of men from both Gurkha battalions and the old 152nd Indian Parachute Battalion under Major Maurice Fry.

At 0230 hours on 1 May two Dakotas took off from Akyab. On board were the two pathfinder teams, visual control posts (forward air controllers), some Force 136 agents and a platoon to provide initial defence of the dropping zone. At 0300 hours the main force took off in 38 Dakotas, and at 0545 hours they jumped over Tawhai. It was raining and there was only a slight wind, so casualties were light during the drop. Unfortunately one of them was Captain Merryfield, one of the two medical officers accompanying the battalion. The battalion rallied swiftly in the pouring rain and covered the first two and a half miles towards its objectives well ahead of schedule. At that point it was forced to halt and wait for Liberators of the USAAF to carry out a bombing raid on Elephant Point. Although the battalion was some 3,000 yards from the nearest of the bombers' targets, and despite the fact that officers and men wore yellow recognition panels on their backs and carried orange umbrellas, C Company was bombed and strafed from the air and lost 15 men killed and 30 wounded. As a result, one of the visual control posts called a halt to any further bombing except when ordered. Major Rangaraj, the first Indian officer to join 50th Indian Parachute Brigade in 1942 as Medical Officer to 152nd Indian Parachute Battalion, did sterling work among the wounded, being very adept after his gruelling experiences at Sangshak.

Despite the heavy rain, the battalion pushed on through flooded terrain and at 1600 hours came under fire from an enemy bunker and some small craft on the river. Air support was called in and the craft were neutralised, after which the bunker was attacked by a company supported by flame-throwers. Out of the 37 Japanese inside the bunker only one survived, but the battalion suffered 41 casualties in this action.

The reserve force, accompanied by a field surgical team, dropped on Thaungang at 1530 hours, and 30 minutes later a supply drop was carried out. After joining up with some of the medical personnel who had arrived earlier, the field surgical team moved off after darkness had fallen to link up with the battalion. Unfortunately it was mistaken for an enemy force and was fired upon, losing four of its number, who were wounded. The rain continued unabated and the spring tides that night were so high that the battalion's positions were submerged in three feet of water, men camping wherever they could find a spot of dry ground. On the following morning, as it searched and cleared bunkers in the area, the battalion watched as the convoys of vessels carrying 26th Indian Division headed upriver.

On the following day, 3 May, the battalion moved to Sadainghmut as 36th Indian Infantry Brigade occupied Rangoon without firing a shot. Two days later, leaving a company at Sadainghmut, the battalion marched into Rangoon and occupied the premises of an engineering college, from which it mounted anti-looting patrols and searched for any enemy stragglers. On 6 May General Sir Oliver Leese, the Commander-in-Chief Allied Land Forces South East Asia, visited the battalion and congratulated it on its operation at Elephant Point. On 15 May the battalion, along with the units of 36th Indian Infantry Brigade, took part in a parade in Rangoon and marched past the commander of 26th Indian Division, Major General H. M. Chambers, who took the salute. On the following day it departed by ship for India, and ten days later arrived at Bilaspur to rejoin the rest of 44th Indian Airborne Division. There was naturally considerable pride that The Indian Parachute Regiment had successfully completed its first airborne operation.

In July 1945 the advance headquarters of 1st Airborne Corps, now commanded by Lieutenant General Sir Richard Gale, was established at Gwalior in Central India. The war in Europe had ended, and Allied attention was now focussed on defeating the Japanese. 6th Airborne Division would subsequently form part of the corps and would join it in India in due course. Meanwhile, with the end of the campaign in Burma, Headquarters 14th Army had moved to Secunderabad to prepare for operations to recapture Malaya. Consequently, 44th Indian Airborne Division was moved to Bilaspur to make way for it. Bilaspur had been selected for its proximity to five airfields, its good dropping zones and good facilities and areas for jungle training. Otherwise it had little to recommend it, being an area where malaria, elephantiasis, cholera and other equally deadly diseases were commonplace. The town itself was surrounded by a mixture of thick jungle, paddy fields and open terrain. During the monsoon the entire area was flooded, roads becoming impassable quagmires and living areas within the camps sodden to the point of becoming morasses. After the trauma of operations in Assam and Burma, it was exceedingly difficult to maintain morale. Any enthusiasm for training called for maximum leadership from British officers and Viceroy Commissioned Officers, the latter being Indian and Gurkha. Nevertheless, all units of the division made the best of it, and much effort was put into improving conditions. A high standard of training was achieved, and when Lieutenant General Gale visited the division on 8 August he was pleased with what he saw. He later commented: "I was very much impressed with the high quality of the officers and men of that splendid division. Their professional skill was of the highest, their physique excellent and their discipline all that could be desired."

On 11 August the war with Japan ended. A week later 30 teams from 44th Airborne Division, each consisting of two medical personnel and two escorts, were dropped into Japanese prison camps in Malaya, Java, French Indo-China and Hong Kong. On 30 August another group of six dropped into Singapore. There they found Allied prisoners of war in the most appalling physical condition after years of imprisonment under conditions which beggared description. Many were little more than walking skeletons, and large numbers were dying daily from starvation and disease. Although they carried only limited supplies of medical equipment, the teams from 44th Indian Airborne Division carried out invaluable work in helping to bring relief to the inmates of the camps and in providing treatment for the sick.

On 23 October Headquarters 1st Airborne Corps was disbanded, and a few days later the advance parties of 44th Airborne Division left Bilaspur for its new base near Karachi. At the same time the division was redesignated 2nd Indian Airborne Division, and on 16 November the main divisional headquarters was established under its new name.

The end of the war inevitably meant demobilisation of much of the Indian Army, which had swelled during the war from a peacetime strength of 194,373 to a figure of 2,049,203 by the time hostilities ended. Towards the end of 1945 plans for the reorganisation of Indian airborne forces were announced. All British elements of 2nd Indian Airborne Division would be withdrawn and formed into 6th Independent Parachute Brigade Group under command of the division, and all British staff officers would be replaced by Indian officers. The Indian Parachute Regiment would be disbanded and its officers and men transferred to other parachute battalions, which would be regular units of the Indian Army provided by nominated regiments. All Gurkha troops would be withdrawn from the division and would be transferred to Gurkha regiments. Finally, the division could consist of three parachute brigades, with 14th Airlanding Brigade being converted to the parachute role.

On 8 March 1946 Major General Charles Boucher arrived to take over command of the division from Major General Eric Down. An Indian Army officer who had spent his regimental service with Gurkhas, Boucher had not previously served with airborne forces. Nevertheless, he successfully completed his parachute course at Chaklala and on 31 March assumed command of 2nd Indian Airborne Division from Major General Down, who returned to England a few days later. At 1100 hours on 26 October 1945, on the polo ground at Quetta, The Indian Parachute Regiment was formed up for the last time. It was a sad day for those officers and men who had been with India's parachute battalions from the early days of 1941 and had fought together at Sheldon's Corner, Sangshak, Imphal and Elephant Point, and especially for the men of the Gurkha battalions who would be leaving Airborne Forces. Under the command of Brigadier Paul Hopkinson, The Indian Parachute Regiment marched past Field Marshal Sir Claude Auchinleck, who took the salute. Immediately afterwards there was a low-level flypast by aircraft of the Royal Air Force, which had specifically requested to be allowed to carry it out as a tribute to the Indian parachute battalions with whom they had worked so closely during the previous four years.

Under the reorganisation, the only battalion to remain in the division was the 4th Battalion 6th Rajputana Rifles (Outram's), which converted from being an airlanding battalion to the parachute role. New units joining the division were given the 'Parachute' designation after their battalion numeral and were brigaded as follows.

HEADQUARTERS 2ND INDIAN AIRBORNE DIVISION:
1st Parachute Battalion The Kumaon Regiment
3rd Parachute Battalion 15th Punjab Regiment (Machine Guns)

14TH INDIAN PARACHUTE BRIGADE:
4th Parachute Battalion 6th Rajputana Rifles (Outram's)
1st Parachute Battalion Frontier Force Regiment
3rd Parachute Battalion 16th Punjab Regiment

50TH INDIAN PARACHUTE BRIGADE:
3rd Parachute Battalion 1st Punjab Regiment
3rd Parachute Battalion The Baluch Regiment
2nd Parachute Battalion The Madras Regiment

77TH INDIAN PARACHUTE BRIGADE:
1st Parachute Battalion 2nd Punjab Regiment
3rd Parachute Battalion Mahratta Light Infantry
3rd Parachute Battalion Rajput Regiment (Duke of Cornwall's Own)

In February 1947 it was announced that India would be granted independence in June 1948. Since June of the previous year violence between the Hindu and Muslim populations of India, which had not been uncommon during British rule but was normally isolated in nature, had begun to increase as a result of political agitation between different factions vying for power. With the announcement of independence in the following year, violence broke out anew in the Punjab and North West Frontier Province to such a degree that the civil authorities were unable to maintain law and order. As a result the Army was called in to suppress the disturbances, and units of 2nd Indian Airborne Division were deployed to a number of locations where trouble had broken out, including Rawalpindi, Lahore, Ambala, Jacobabad, Multan, Quetta in Baluchistan and other troublespots in the Punjab.

Because of the violence, the British Government decided to bring forward the date of independence and British withdrawal from India. At the same time the Indian National Congress, the body which had long fought for freedom from British rule, reluctantly accepted that India would have to be partitioned in order to achieve independence. Thus, on 14 August 1947, the state of Pakistan came into being, and at midnight Britain handed over power in India to the Constituent Assembly. Partition meant that 2nd Indian Airborne Division was divided between India and the newly created Pakistan. Officers, Viceroy Commissioned Officers and other ranks were given the choice of staying in India, serving with Pakistan, applying to transfer to the British Army (in the case of British officers) or returning to civilian life. The majority of British officers chose to return to England, while a number transferred to the British Army. Others stayed with the Indian Army, whilst some elected to serve either temporarily or permanently in Pakistan.

50th and 77th Indian Parachute Brigades were allotted to India, while 14th Indian Parachute Brigade went to Pakistan. Of the eleven parachute battalions in the division, six remained in India. The five which went to Pakistan were 3rd Parachute Battalion 15th Punjab Regiment (Machine Gun); 1st Parachute Battalion Frontier Force Regiment; 3rd Parachute Battalion 16th Punjab Regiment; 3rd Parachute Battalion 1st Punjab Regiment; and 3rd Parachute Battalion The Baluch Regiment. Once the division of parachute battalions between India and Pakistan had been agreed, there remained the final step of exchanging Hindus, Muslims and Sikhs between units. With the exception of the Kumaon, Mahratta Light Infantry and Madras Regiment units, the parachute battalions had drawn their men from India and the area now covered by Pakistan. Now it was necessary for those Hindus and Sikhs in battalions allocated to Pakistan to be exchanged for the Punjabi Mussulmans and Pathans in those units remaining with India. In such a situation there was potential for bitterness and disagreement, but such was the mutual regard and high esteem in which the Hindus, Muslims and Sikhs of the parachute battalions held each other that they parted on the friendliest of terms and without incident.

As the Indian and Pakistani parachute battalions marched away to their respective bases, many of their former British officers made their way home to England. As had been the case in all regiments of the Indian Army, it had been a sad moment when the time had come for them to say farewell to the soldiers for whom they felt great affection and respect. For them and for the airborne forces in India, an era had come to a close.

Above: Dakotas of 9th U.S. Troop Carrier Command dropping elements of 3rd Para Bde nine minutes early as the airborne assault across the Rhine commences on the morning of 24 March 1945. As the enemy recovered from the heavy preliminary bombardment, which ceased as the leading aircraft crossed the Rhine, anti-aircraft fire intensified and a number of Dakotas and gliders were shot down. (Imperial War Museum)

Below: Major Gen Eric Bols and Brigadier James Hill in the divisional commander's jeep after the landings across the Rhine on 24 March 1945. Seated behind them are General Bol's ADC and his personal escort. (Imperial War Museum)

Above: Men of 2 PARA enplaning on a Hastings for an exercise; Canal Zone, Egypt, 1952. (Reproduced by courtesy of Bert Goodall)

Below: 'Airborne Assault on El-Gamil airfield, Suez, 1956' by David Shepherd. (Reproduced by courtesy of 3 PARA)

Right: Aden: 'Checkpoint Golf – First Light' by David Shepherd. (Reproduced by courtesy of 1 PARA)

Opposite page, bottom: Borneo, 1965: a 2 PARA patrol moves out of Plaman Mapu. (Reproduced by courtesy of Bert Goodall)

Right: A 3-inch mortar crew of 4th Para Bn in action near Venafro, against enemy mortar positions, in Italy in May 1944. (Imperial War Museum)

Right: Two men of 4th Para Bn guard an approach along one side of a valley that was No Man's Land by day and patrolled by both sides at night during operations north-east of Cassino, Italy, in 1944. This picture shows the mountainous terrain over which the units of 2nd Independent Para Bde operated, much of the time in appalling weather conditions and under constant shellfire. (Imperial War Museum)

Right: Four members of 4th Para Bn enjoying a rare moment of relaxation during operations in Italy in 1944, on this occasion eating their first meal of the day at 1500 hours. Left to right: Lance Corporal Jackson, Privates James, Stringer, Pendrey and Dawson. (Imperial War Museum)

Above: Troops of 6th Airborne Div board transport in the area of Osnabruck during the advance north-eastwards through Germany to the Baltic in April 1945. (Imperial War Museum)

Below: Corporal Moody and men of 9th Para Bn pass through an enemy roadblock at Brelingen on 10 April 1945 during the advance through Germany. 6th Airborne Div's final objective, the town of Wismar on the Baltic coast, was reached on 2 May. (Imperial War Museum)

Opposite page, top: 'Whitleys flying over the Aqueduct at Tragino' by Norman Hughes. (Reproduced by courtesy of the artist and the Airborne Forces Museum)

Left: 'Arnhem Bridge, 5 p.m. the Second Day' by David Shepherd. (Reproduced by courtesy of 2 PARA)

Above: 'Assault Crossing of the Rhine' by John Sellars. (Reproduced by courtesy of the artist)

Above: Men of 2nd Independent Para Bde don their parachutes prior to emplaning for the flight to Greece on 12 October 1944 for Operation 'Manna'. (Imperial War Museum)

Left: Men of the brigade headquarters inside their Dakota en route for Greece and Operation 'Manna' on 12 October 1944. (Imperial War Museum)

Left: 4th Para Bn landing at Megara, in Greece, on 12 October 1944. The wind speed of 35mph caused casualties totalling three men killed and forty injured during the drop. (Imperial War Museum)

Above: Three members of 5th Para Bn take up a position on a street corner during operations against ELAS forces in Athens in December 1944. (Imperial War Museum)

Below: Men of A Coy 6th Para Bn move up behind a Sherman tank of 23rd Armoured Brigade while clearing an Athens street of ELAS snipers in December 1944. On the left, armed with a Thompson machine carbine, is Sergeant Johnson. In front of him is Corporal Baker. (Imperial War Museum)

Below: 'Exercise Casino Royale 1989: 4 PARA FIBUA Training at Hammelburg' by Kelly Ryan (Reproduced by courtesy of the artist and 4 PARA)

Above: An evening drop. (Reproduced by courtesy of Jeremy Flack)

Above: A section of 2 PARA on exercise in England. (Reproduced by courtesy of the Airborne Forces Museum)

Right: On 22 June 1990 all six battalions of The Parachute Regiment and other units of Airborne Forces marched through the City of London on the 50th anniversary of the formation of Airborne Forces Leading the parade was the Regimental Mascot of The Parachute Regiment, Sergeant Pegasus III, seen here with his handler, Corporal D. Soane. Behind him is the Regimental Colonel, Colonel Hamish MacGregor, and the Regimental Adjutant, Major Godfrey McFall. (Reproduced by courtesy of the Airborne Forces Museum)

Above: A Vickers MMG of the Machine Gun Platoon of 5th Para Bn positioned on the roof of the KKE building in Constitution Square, Athens, in December 1944. (Imperial War Museum)

Below: Members of 5th Para Bn in the Acropolis, seen here in action against ELAS snipers in December 1944. (Imperial War Museum)

Above: The CIGS, Field Marshal Lord Alanbrooke, inspects men of 12th Para Bn in Johore, Malaya, during his visit to 5th Para Bde in the Far East on 6 December 1945. (Imperial War Museum)

Below: Privates G. McGreigh and G. Lewis of 12th Para Bn search suspects before passing them on for interrogation during internal security operations in Batavia, Java, in December 1945. (Imperial War Museum)

Above: *Norland* under attack in San Carlos Water; painting by David Cobb. (Reproduced by courtesy of P&O plc)

Below: 'Lieutenant Colonel 'H' Jones preparing to attack Argentinian positions' by Michael Turner. (Reproduced by courtesy of the artist)

Above: 'Sergeant Mackay, VC, attacking Argentinian positions' by Peter Archer. (Reproduced by courtesy of the artist and 3 PARA)

Below: '2nd Battalion The Parachute Regiment, Wireless Ridge, The Falkland Islands, 13/14 June 1982' by David Cobb. (Reproduced by courtesy of the artist and 2 PARA)

Above: Members of 7th Para Bn take cover after coming under fire from snipers during operations in the Kramat quarter of Batavia, Java, in December 1945. (Imperial War Museum)

Left: The CO of 12th Para Bn, Lieutenant Colonel Ken Darling, looks on as a Dutch intelligence officer interrogates an Indonesian suspect during internal security operations in Batavia, Java, in December 1945. (Imperial War Museum)

CHAPTER 10
6th Airborne Division Operations in Palestine, 1945–1948

With the war in Europe and South East Asia over, it was decided that there was no longer a requirement for the British Army to possess two airborne divisions. Although 6th Airborne Division was the junior of the two formations, it was decided to retain it and to disband 1st Airborne Division, which until then had been earmarked for the Middle East as part of the Strategic Reserve.

As a result, 6th Airborne Division became part of the Strategic Reserve, and on 15 September 1945 started moving to Palestine. At the same time there were several changes to its order of battle. 5th Parachute Brigade, by then already deployed to India and subsequently to the Far East, was replaced by 2nd Parachute Brigade. 3rd Parachute Brigade, commanded by Brigadier Gerald Lathbury, and in which 3rd Parachute Battalion had replaced 1st Canadian Parachute Battalion, still formed part of the division, together with 6th Airlanding Brigade. The main body of the division travelled by sea, arriving at the port of Haifa after a ten-day voyage. Continuing its journey by rail, it moved to Nuseirat Hospital Camp near Gaza, where it joined the main divisional headquarters, which had gone ahead. The different elements of the division were accommodated in a number of camps within a short distance of each other, some six miles from Gaza. Living conditions were very spartan, the weather very hot and the terrain sandy and barren.

The division's role was to provide Britain with a strategic reserve in the Middle East. Palestine had been selected because the training facilities and airfields were superior to those available in other locations, such as Egypt or Cyrenaica.

At the time Palestine was plagued by internal dissent and strife between its Arab and Jewish factions. It had been so since 1917, when the British Government had publicly recognised the need for a home state for Jews but had taken no action. Immediately after the First World War the League of Nations had granted Britain a mandate to administer Palestine, which had previously formed part of the Turkish Empire. This mandate, which came into effect in 1923, included in its terms a provision for a Jewish body which would advise the colonial government of Palestine on matters and issues relating to the Jewish national home and the interests of the Jewish community. Until 1929, this role was carried out by the Zionist Organisation, when it was transformed into the Jewish Agency, which included non-Zionist elements and possessed wider terms of reference. While it had no governing function, it exercised a great deal of influence over the Jewish community. The major part of Palestine's population was Arab, but from 1918 to 1939 there was a small but steady flow of Jews into the country. In 1939 the British had placed a limit of 75,000 on Jewish immigration during the following five years. Subsequently, any further immigration would take place only with the consent of the Arabs. By 1945 and the end of the war in Europe, however, large numbers of Jews had been rendered homeless by the Nazi holocaust. Inevitably Palestine, which offered the possibility of a secure home, seemed very attractive to them, and they made increased demands to be allowed to settle there. At the end of 1945 the Jewish Agency, which by then had assumed responsibility for Jewish affairs, tried to force the British Government to lift the restrictions on Jewish immigration. At the same time it attempted to advance the cause of a national home state for Jews.

The reception from the Jewish press, which greeted 6th Airborne Division on its arrival, was hostile. Its troops were referred to as "Gestapo" — a term which the division objected to most strongly, as many of its members had been Jewish and it had seen first-hand evidence of the Nazi atrocities during its operations in Northern Germany earlier in the year. It had suffered many casualties during its 12 months of fighting in Europe, and the Jews' attitude was strongly resented.

Since 1920 the Jews had possessed their own underground defence forces. The Haganah was organized along conventional military lines, being well equipped with weapons which included small-arms and mortars and including many in its ranks who had served with the Allied forces during the war. Within the Haganah was the Palmach, a small elite full-time group which was highly trained. In addition, there were two other guerrilla organisations. The first was the Irgun Zvai Laumi (National Military Organization — IZL), better known simply as the Irgun. This had been formed from a splinter group which broke away from the Haganah in 1937 after disagreeing over armed reprisals against Arab aggression. During the war the IZL had maintained a low profile until February 1944, when it launched a campaign of violence against British rule. The second guerrilla group was the Stern Gang, named after its founder, Abraham Stern, and comprising some 50 members of the IZL who opposed the latter's policy of quiescence during the war. In opposing the British, Stern and his men had actively co-operated with the Axis forces. In 1942 Stern had been killed during an encounter with the police, and his place had been taken by a Pole named Nathan Freedman Yellin. During the following year the gang adopted the name of Lacahamey Heruth Israel (Hebrew Fighters of the Freedom of Israel), but was generally still referred to as the Stern Gang.

The Arabs in Palestine were mostly followers of the exiled Mufti of Jerusalem, Haj Amin al Husseini. Banished by the British, he exercised control from abroad, his rule being maintained by a number of loyal lieutenants. Although they were united in their desire for independence, the Arabs were divided by tribal politics, which caused continual disagreements between the different factions and tended to take prime place in the order of political priorities. In 1936 a body called the Arab Higher Executive

Committee was formed, with the Mufti as its president. It consisted of the heads of the Arab political parties, and its role was to organize and control the Arab revolt which took place in Palestine during that year. Although it was declared illegal by the Palestinian government, no other body replaced it. In November 1945 the Arab Higher Committee was formed, incorporating representatives of all political parties. However, its existence was brief, its downfall being caused by disensions between different factions. The Arab League, which was also formed in 1945 and whose ruling council comprised representatives from all Arab nations, decreed that a new body was to be formed under the leadership of Jamal Husseini, a cousin of the Mufti. This was the Arab Higher Executive, which was given the task of developing and maintaining some form of unity amongst the Palestinian Arabs. The Arab League also exerted influence, not only because of its interest in the affairs of all Arab nations but also due to the lack of any effective Arab political organisation in Palestine.

The British troops in Palestine occupied an uncomfortable position between the two sides. On the one hand were the Jews, with their implacable hostility towards Britain and the Arab population, and on the other were the Arabs, who were constantly in a state of political instability. It was small wonder that the troops found the situation somewhat unpleasant.

6th Airborne Division joined a considerable number of British troops already stationed in Palestine. In addition to 1st Infantry Division and some units tasked with static guard duties, there were some colonial troops as well as units of the Transjordanian Frontier Force and the Arab Legion. Palestine was divided into three military sectors: 15 Area in the north, with its headquarters at Haifa; 21 Area in the south, with its headquarters at Sarafand; and 156 Sub-Area, with its headquarters in Jerusalem. Each area headquarters controlled and administered all the static units and military installations in its area, while the field formations were responsible for conducting internal security operations and were deployed so that maximum contol could be maintained during civil unrest.

By the time of 6th Airborne Division's arrival, the situation in Palestine had deteriorated to the extent that internal security was becoming a matter of growing priority. Even before the division had fully assembled, warning orders were issued with regard to the regrouping and deployment of all forces in Palestine. The division was allocated responsibility for the Southern Sector, consisting of the districts of Lydda, Gaza and Samaria (less the sub-distict of Jenin), in the event of trouble breaking out. As the three brigades and supporting arms arrived they were allotted their respective tasks and immediately set about reconnoitring their areas.

The type of operations facing 6th Airborne Division in Palestine were very different from those it had performed during the war. The very nature of airborne operations demanded a high degree of aggression and elan to compensate for the lack of heavy equipment and firepower. By the end of the war all elements of 6th Airborne Division were very highly trained in all the skills required of them for offensive operations. Internal security operations, however, placed different requirements on units and individuals. While fundamental qualities such as discipline, physical fitness and high standards in military skills remained of great importance, the emphasis was on diplomacy and the use of minimum force when necessary. While carrying out a peacekeeping role between two communities continually at loggerheads, troops were likely to be called upon to act as mediators or to protect one side from the other. Such a role called for a sound knowledge of the historical background and political situation, as well as tact and firm action when required. The troops of the division had to learn the principles of internal security operations, as well as tactics such as cordon and search — the surrounding of a village or settlement with a cordon of men and the techniques of searching for concealed caches of arms or hiding places for personnel. Other tactics included crowd dispersal and riot control, as well as the setting up of roadblocks and checkpoints. Officers and men were also required to learn regulations governing the powers available to them, as well as the rules for opening fire and powers of search and arrest. Troops were also given lectures on the religions and customs of the Jewish and Arab communities, to minimise the risk of any offence being caused during operations which involved the searching of people or property.

As they would be working in close co-operation with the Palestine Police, the troops were briefed on its organisation and role. It was a colonial force composed of constables recruited from the local communities and commanded by British officers and NCOs. Under the control of a Commissioner, it was organised in divisions and districts and possessed specialist branches such as the Criminal Investigation Department. To remind them that they would be operating in support of the civil authorities, all members of the division were required to be fully familiar with the system of government and civil administration in Palestine. Responsibility for government of the country lay with the High Commissioner, who in turn was empowered to delegate powers to the General Officer Commanding in Palestine, who represented the military authorities. Such powers, embodied in the Defence Emergency Regulations of 1945, were considerable and extensive. For civil administrative purposes Palestine was divided into six districts, each of which was under the control of a District Commissioner who was responsible to the Chief Secretary.

On 20 October 6th Airborne Division received orders to deploy to its operational locations, the divisional headquarters moving to 21 Area, where it was co-located with the area headquarters. On the following day 3rd Parachute Brigade moved northwards to the Lydda district, which included Tel Aviv and Jaffa. Meanwhile, 6th Airlanding Brigade prepared for its deployment to the Samaria district. 2nd Parachute Brigade arrived in Palestine on 22 October and was immediately deployed to Gaza, where the threat of unrest was lowest. It was planned that the three brigades should rotate through the different districts within the Southern Sector every six months, with Gaza providing opportunites for refresher training in airborne and tactical skills. The end of the month saw the first serious incidents occur, when, on 31 October, the railway network was attacked in a number of places, including the junction at Lydda and the oil refinery at Haifa. Lines were cut at 240 locations by members of the Palmach, who suffered only one casualty. The security forces suffered four killed and eight wounded.

In the middle of November the British Government made its long-awaited statement on the future of Palestine. In essence, this announced that Palestine itself was unable to solve the problem of Jewish homelessness, and that an Anglo-American committee would be established to examine the political, economic and social conditions in Europe which were relevant to the problems of Jewish immigration and settlement. The committee would also examine the status of Jews in Europe who had been victims of Nazi and Fascist oppression. The statement also indicated that the British Government would conduct consultations with the Arab population in Palestine to ensure that there would be no interruption of the immigration of 1,500 Jews each month. The Jewish Agency and the Jewish community were disappointed by this statement, but were well aware that any resort to violence would be counter-productive. However, the younger and more headstrong elements in the community ignored any such considerations, and on the afternoon of 14 November riots broke out in Jerusalem and Tel Aviv.

The situation was already deteriorating rapidly when 3rd Parachute Brigade moved into Tel Aviv. Attacks were carried out on British property, and troops were stoned. During the evening the District Offices were set ablaze and the police became heavily committed in operations to break up riots in several parts of the city. It was not long before a company of 8th Parachute Battalion moved into Colony Square, shortly afterwards coming under attack from a large mob which proceeded to stone the troops and the police with them. Eventually, after great restraint had been shown, force had to be used and a few rounds were fired. This was successful in dispersing the mob, which then turned its attention on the Post Office and government building, which were looted and set on fire. The remainder of 8th Parachute Battalion arrived during the evening, and a curfew was imposed after order had been restored. During the early morning of 15 November, however, trouble broke out anew when mobs looted buildings and set them on fire. Once again, weapons had to be used to disperse the rioters. Later in the morning the rest of 3rd Parachute Brigade was ordered into Tel Aviv, arriving at 1200 hours with A Squadron of the 3rd The King's Own Hussars under command. After order had been quickly restored, the brigade was reinforced by the 1st Battalion The Royal Ulster Rifles (from 6th Airlanding Brigade), the 6th Airborne Armoured Reconnaissance Regiment and the rest of the 3rd The King's Own Hussars.

The operation in Tel Aviv continued until 20 November, when all troops were withdrawn. This was the division's first taste of internal security operations, and great credit was reflected on the troops, who had shown restraint and steadiness under very difficult circumstances. Casualties numbered 12 wounded and 30 slightly injured, while the Jewish rioters had six killed and 60 wounded. In late November, 6th Airborne Division carried out the first of its cordon and search operations.

During the night of 24 November two groups of the Palmach attacked coastguard stations at Givat Olga and Sidna Ali, which were manned by the police. The stations were located to the north and south of a point at which a schooner had been intercepted two nights previously by the Royal Navy. The craft had been in the process of landing illegal immigrants, and the crew and the immigrants were arrested and interned at the detention camp at Athlit. The Palmach raid was a reprisal. Both coastguard stations were blown up, and 14 policeman were injured. On the following day the police discovered that the saboteurs who had attacked the station at Givat Olga had come from Jewish settlements at Givat Haiyam and Hogla, while those who had attacked Sidna Ali were from Rishpon and Shefayim, which were not far away. Early on 25 November 8th Parachute Battalion moved to the area of Sidna Ali to support the police, who were searching Rishpon and Shefayim. Violent resistance was encountered when the police entered the settlements, and the inhabitants were soon joined by others from nearby. Most of the Jewish reinforcements were prevented from entering the settlements by cordons of troops which had been thrown round them earlier. However, the police made little headway and were eventually forced to withdraw. 8th Parachute Battalion was replaced by 3rd Parachute Battalion and a battalion of 6th Airlanding Brigade, which by then had also been deployed on the operation with 3rd Parachute Brigade.

On the following day the police attempted to search the settlements at Givat Haiyam and Hogla in the north, but once again encountered strong resistance. During the morning troops were called in to quell the rioting, and those in the cordons had to prevent Jews from other settlements from entering the two settlements. At one point attempts were made to break through the cordons and, after warnings had been given, troops were forced to open fire. At Rishpon and Shefayim in the south, meanwhile, 8th Parachute Battalion entered Shefayim and restored order with the use of baton charges and CS gas. Thereafter the inhabitants adopted a policy of non-cooperation, and 900 Jews were arrested. At Rishpon the cordon was attacked by a mob numbering some 1,500 and the troops had no option but to open fire. Later, a large crowd of 3,000 approached a platoon manning part of the cordon. The leader, who was on horseback, ignored warnings and was shot, at which point the crowd dispersed without further ado. The search of the settlement uncovered some explosives and consequently 11 Jews, including the head of the settlement, were arrested. By 1700 hours the operations at all four settlements had been completed and all troops and police withdrawn. 160 Jews were sent to the detention centre at Athlit for interrogation, six had been killed, and 42 were wounded. Casualties among the security forces amounted to no more than a few men slightly injured.

It had rapidly become apparent that the Jews were well organised. The rapid deployment of reinforcements, in answer to calls from the settlements being searched, enabled them rapidly to escalate confrontations with the security forces. A lesson soon learned was that the maximum number of troops had to be deployed on any cordon and search operation, including a strong reserve, and that Jewish reinforcements had to be intercepted as far as possible from the cordons to prevent any interference.

After a lull of about a month, the Jews resumed their operations against the security forces. During the night of 26 December the IZL carried out attacks on police headquarters in Jerusalem and Jaffa, as well as on a military armoury in Tel Aviv and railway installations at Lydda. These resulted in 3rd Parachute Brigade once again being sent into Tel Aviv after intelligence reports indicated that the IZL gang had taken refuge in a large settlement just outside the city. On 29 December the brigade, with 4th Parachute Battalion under command, launched Operation 'Pintail'. A total of 1,500 Jews were interrogated, 59 being arrested and detained. During the following month, January 1946, Operations 'Heron' and 'Pigeon' were carried out, during which the settlement at Rishon-le-Zion and the Shapiro quarter of Tel Aviv were searched. The IZL struck again on 25 February, when it launched a series of attacks on RAF airfields at Lydda, Petah Tiqva and Qastina. These resulted in the withdrawal of aircraft to Egypt and thus the loss of any airborne training for units of 6th Airborne Division. The aircraft eventually returned to Palestine, but responsibility for their security and protection fell on the shoulders of the already heavily committed division.

Early the following month the IZL carried out an operation to secure arms and ammunition. At midday on 6 March nine of its men, dressed in British airborne uniforms, arrived at the camp of the 3rd The King's Own Hussars at Sarafand. After quietly overpowering the guards on the main gate and capturing the guardroom, they proceeded to the hussars' ammunition store, where they held the sentries at gunpoint and loaded cases of ammunition aboard their truck. However, the alarm was soon raised and the Jews withdrew under fire towards the gate. As they did so they placed an explosive charge in the ammunition store which exploded, fortunately without causing any casualties. A small group of hussar officers had run to the main gate with the aim of closing it to cut off the raiders' escape. However, they found it held by the rest of the IZL gang, from whom they came under fire. The Signals Officer, Captain Gerry Barrow, managed to overpower one of the Jews, but came under fire and was forced to take cover. The IZL withdrew with armoured cars of the hussars in hot pursuit. Eventually the Jews succeeded in shaking off their pursuers in the area of Rishon-le-Zion, but subsequently two of the gang, who had been seriously wounded, were captured. Shortly afterwards two vehicles were discovered with nearly all of the stolen ammunition still loaded aboard them. The only casualty suffered by the hussars was Mrs Jean Marjoribanks, one of the YMCA team which ran a canteen service for the troops. She was seriously wounded by IZL gunfire during the raid, but fortunately made a complete recovery. A widow, she subsequently married Lieutenant Colonel Johnny Frost, the Commanding Officer of 2nd Parachute Battalion.

During 1946 a number of changes took place in 6th Airborne Division. Major General James Cassels, who until then had been commanding 51st

Highland Division, took over command from Major General Eric Bols, who departed for the Imperial Defence College. With the disappearance of gliders as a means of airborne delivery, 6th Airlanding Brigade left the division. It was replaced by 1st Parachute Brigade, comprising 1st, 2nd and 17th Parachute Battalions and commanded by Brigadier Hugh Bellamy, the previous commander of the gliderborne formation. 1st Parachute Brigade arrived at Port Said on 1 April. Two days later the brigade headquarters reached Camp 21 at Nathanya, and the remainder of the brigade arriving on 7 April. On the following day it assumed responsibility for the Samaria District.

In early August, 5th Parachute Brigade returned to the division after its operations in South East Asia. Soon afterwards, however, it was disbanded. 7th Parachute Battalion was amalgamated with 17th Parachute Battalion but, as senior battalion, retained its numerical designation. 12th Parachute Battalion was also disbanded, and its officers and men absorbed by other units within the division. 13th Parachute Battalion had already been disbanded before the brigade left Malaya. On 13 September, 21st Independent Parachute Company was also disbanded. Its pathfinder role was assumed by the 3rd The King's Own Hussars, which had taken over as the divisional reconnaissance unit after the disbandment of 6th Airborne Armoured Reconnaissance Regiment earlier in the year. Thus, many members of the company transferred to the hussars, while others joined parachute battalions within the division.

With units committed almost constantly to internal security operations, it was inevitable that airborne and other training would have to take second place. The division was supported by No. 283 Wing RAF, which consisted of Nos. 620 and 644 Squadrons, equipped with Halifaxes. Parachute training was carried out at the Airborne Training School at Aqir, the number of descents during 1946 and 1947 exceeding 20,000. These were mainly carried out during refresher training by trained parachutists in the division, although a number of basic courses were also conducted for those personnel who could not be sent back to No. 1 Parachute Training School in England. The division operated its own battle school, which was initially based at Ein Shemer before being moved to St Jeans, near Acre. It carried out all types of training, except airborne, at the various different levels. Owing to operational commitments, brigade exercises never took place in Palestine, and training at battalion level was rare. One exercise took place in Sudan in May 1946, when 3rd Parachute Battalion, together with a company of 8th Parachute Battalion and detachments of supporting arms, flew from Palestine to Khartoum. Several company exercises took place in Iraq, Transjordan and Cyprus. Plans for training in Libya, Aden and elsewhere in the Middle East were abandoned because of the operational situation in Palestine.

At the beginning of April the IZL attacked the railway network in two places, one north of Haifa and the other in the area of Isdud-Yibna between Lydda and Gaza. The attack north of Haifa was carried out by a gang of 20, who damaged a bridge at Na'amin after overpowering the police detachment guarding it. In the south the attack was carried out by a larger group which cut the line in several places and damaged five bridges, as well as destroying an engine and mining some roads. The IZL also attacked the railway station at Yibna and a police post nearby, but a patrol from 9th Parachute Battalion arrived in the area and encountered some of the terrorists' mines. The patrol followed up and the IZL withdrew, but the pursuit was delayed because of an unfortunate and lengthy exchange of fire in the dark between some Arab railway policemen and the patrol, fortunately without casualties to either side. At this point a patrol from 5th Parachute Battalion arrived, and a company of 6th Parachute Battalion arrived further to the south at about midnight. Dawn the following day found patrols following three trails in hot pursuit. A group of 30 Jews had been reported moving north across the Rishon ranges, while other trails, being followed by police dogs, led to settlements at Kefar Marmorek, Ezra Bitsaron and Isdud. The group heading north was spotted by an observation aircraft, which guided troops from 8th Parachute Battalion to its location. An action subsequently took place which resulted in the capture of 24 Jews and a considerable quantity of weapons.

Towards the end of April the Stern Gang carried out an attack which was notable only for its degree of brutality, and which was remembered long afterwards with considerable bitterness by many members of 6th Airborne Division who served in Palestine. At 2030 hours on 25 April 30 members of the gang opened fire on a detachment from 5th Parachute Battalion guarding a vehicle park in Tel Aviv. Under cover of fire from a commandeered house opposite the entrance to the park, a number of Jews entered the park itself and cold-bloodedly gunned down the unarmed troops taking cover inside tents. The terrorists then withdrew to the Karton quarter of the city. A search of the quarter was carried out on the following morning, and 79 suspects were arrested. Major General Cassels summoned the Mayor of Tel Aviv and made clear his feelings of anger and revulsion at the outrage, at the same time expressing his belief of the involvement of the Jewish community. Some elements within the division, bitterly angry at the outrage, decided to take the law into their own hands on the following night. They vented their fury on the inhabitants of the nearby settlement of Beer Tuvya, beating up several Jews and damaging property. Despite the massive provocation, this breach of discipline could not be permitted and the ringleaders were caught and punished.

During the following month, June, the IZL kidnapped five officers from the British officers' club in Tel Aviv. Its aim was the commutation of the death sentences passed previously on the two Jews captured after the raid on the ammunition store at Sarafand. Two of the hostages were released four days later in Tel Aviv, probably under pressure from moderate Jewish elements who feared drastic repercussions against key Jewish leaders. The other three officers were released on 4 July, by which time the death sentences on the two Jews had been commuted.

Throughout the campaign of terrorism and sabotage waged by the Jews from November 1945 to June 1946, the security forces had suspected that the activities of the underground Jewish organisations had been condoned, if not actively assisted, by the Jewish Agency and leaders of the Jewish community. Consequently, it was decided to carry out a raid on the headquarters of the Jewish Agency, to obtain evidence of its complicity and to arrest those members of Jewish political organisations suspected of involvement in terrorist activities or of supporting them. At the same time, buildings suspected of housing the headquarters of illegal organizations would be searched, and suspected personnel arrested. The operation was to take place throughout Palestine, and would involve the majority of units in the country. 6th Airborne Division was tasked with carrying out all of them, with the exception of the raid on the headquarters of the Jewish Agency. 2nd Parachute Brigade, now commanded by Brigadier J. P. O'Brien Twohig, was based on the Lydda District and had responsibility for Tel Aviv. It was tasked with arresting suspect Jews in its area. 1st Parachute Brigade was to search six settlements in the north, while 3rd Parachute Brigade was allocated the task of searching those at Givat Brenner and No'ar Oved in the south. Security was of paramount importance, and elaborate measures were taken to preserve it. All formations and units involved in the operation maintained normal routines, and knowledge of the operation was restricted to the minimum number of personnel. At the same time, certain deceptive measures were carried out and the briefing of troops was left until the last possible moment.

In the early hours of 29 June the operation was launched. Between 0345 and 0515 hours, telephone exchanges were taken over without warning by detachments of troops and telephone lines to those settlements to be searched were cut. In Tel Aviv, detachments of troops and police raided houses and arrested individuals whose names were on lists which they carried. In the areas of the settlements to the north and south, cordons were positioned quickly and quietly while search parties moved in before the inhabitants were aware of their presence. The operation ended on 1 July, by which time a total of 2,718 people had been arrested. Of these, 571 were released during the following week, and the majority of the remainder over the following months. A total of 636 were despatched to the detention centre at Latrun, of whom 135 were suspected of being members of the Palmach.

Later in the month, the Jews carried out a major attack on the security forces in Jerusalem. During the early afternoon of 22 July a group of 20 disguised as Arab workmen unloaded several milk churns full of explosives and placed them in the basement of the King David Hotel, which housed the Secretariat of the Government of Palestine and Headquarters British Troops in Palestine and Transjordan. As the building also still served as an hotel, the sight of workmen entering its rear entrance did not arouse any suspicion. The explosive charges were placed beneath the section of the hotel accommodating the government secretariat. As the Jews were in the process of positioning them, a British officer became suspicious and was shot as he attempted to investigate. The fuses were lit and the Jews withdrew. The explosion demolished an entire wing of the hotel, killing a large number of people and trapping and injuring many more. Only six survivors were extracted from the wreckage of the building during the rescue operations which took place during the following three days.

On the following day 8th and 9th Parachute Battalions moved into Jerusalem to take part in an operation to track down the perpetrators. Two of them, one wounded and one dead, were discovered, and 37 Jews were arrested and sent to a detention centre. A search was also carried out in Tel Aviv, as intelligence reports indicated that some of those responsible were hiding there. The operation involved four brigades supported by three extra battalions, three regiments of armour and the supporting arms of 6th Airborne Division. It commenced before dawn on 30 July all three parachute brigades and 2nd Infantry Brigade took up their positions. An outer cordon was in position before the alarm could be raised, and inner cordons, dividing the city into four areas, were inserted at dawn. All buildings in the city were searched thoroughly and all inhabitants, with the exception of the elderly and children, were screened. All suspects were sent to the detention centre at Rafah for further screening and interrogation. During the four days of the operation a total of 100,000 people were screened by the battalions of all four brigades, and a further 10,000 were processed by the four brigade headquarters and the police. Those sent to Rafah numbered 787. The troops uncovered five caches of arms, including one in the Great Synagogue, where they also discovered forging equipment and 50,000 worth of counterfeit bearer bonds.

In September 1946 an incident took place which was subsequently to have major repercussions. During a raid on the branches of the Ottoman Bank in Tel Aviv and Jaffa, the IZL lost 13 of its men in an engagement with the police. One of these was a youth named Benjamin Kimchin, who was tried and sentenced to 18 years in prison and 18 strokes of the cane. In retaliation the IZL warned that, if the sentence on Kimchin was carried out, they would capture and flog a British soldier. The authorities disregarded the threat and Kimchin was caned in accordance with his sentence. On 29 December the IZL carried out their threat, kidnapping the Brigade Major of 2nd Parachute Brigade and flogging him. In addition, three British NCOs were also kidnapped and treated in the same manner. The reaction from British troops was such that they were confined to their bases to prevent retaliatory action being taken against Jews. However, men of 1st Parachute Brigade arrested five members of the IZL at a roadblock at Wilhelma, north of Lydda, after a short action in which one of the Jews was fatally wounded. On searching the car in which the terrorists had been travelling, the troops discovered two rawhide whips, together with some weapons. All five were brought to trial and three of them were hanged.

The Stern Gang was also active during this period, carrying out a bomb attack on the South Palestine District Headquarters in early December. The explosive charge was hidden in a vehicle parked inside the headquarters compound and, when detonated, killed two men and injured 28, as well as causing severe damage.

December also saw the return of Major General Eric Bols, who assumed command of the division from Major General James Cassels. Another change in command appointment had been that of Brigadier Gerald Lathbury, who had handed over command of 3rd Parachute Brigade to Brigadier F. D. Rome.

During the final days of 1946 6th Airborne Division took part in three operations. On 30 December 1st Parachute Brigade, with 8th Parachute Battalion and the 3rd The King's Own Hussars under command, carried out a search of the Yemenite quarter of Petah Tiqva for members of the IZL and Stern Gang. 2nd Parachute Brigade, with a squadron of the 12th Lancers under command, searched the south-east quarter of Nathanya. A day later 3rd Parachute Brigade searched the Yemenite quarters of Rishon-le-Zion. Operations continued into the New Year, with further searches being carried out in Tel Aviv, Rehovot, Sht Hat Tiqva and Montefiorre. As a result, 9,000 people were screened and 130 arrested.

On 18 January 6th Airborne Division handed the Southern Sector over to 3rd Infantry Division, which had just arrived from Egypt, and began its move to the Northern Sector, where it was to take over from 1st Infantry Division. Six days later 2nd Parachute Brigade departed Palestine for England, where it was to reorganise before moving to Germany.

The environment in which the 6th Airborne Division found itself was very different to that of the Southern Sector. As opposed to being flat, with fertile areas and orange groves interspersed with stretches of desert, the north of Palestine was hilly and offered spectacular views over the Jordan Valley and Sea of Galilee. Moreover, the relationship between the British troops and the local inhabitants was considerably better than that which they had experienced in the south. Shortly after the division's arrival, however, the IZL kidnapped a district judge and a British civilian in retaliation for the sentencing to death of a Jew named Dov Gruner. 3rd Parachute Brigade, which was based in Haifa, imposed a curfew in the Jewish quarter of the city and roadblocks were established throughout the area. The death sentence was subsequently postponed and the two hostages released.

In addition to maintaining internal security, 6th Airborne Division also had the responsibility of protecting the oil installations belonging to the Iraq Petroleum Company, Shell and other oil companies, as well as the port installations in Haifa itself. Initially, the division was allocated the 2nd Battalion The East Surrey Regiment and a squadron of the Arab Legion under command to assist in fulfilling such a heavy commitment, but these units were withdrawn after a while and it was left to 3rd Parachute Brigade to shoulder the burden.

1st Parachute Brigade was responsible for Galilee, which was a very large area covering the towns of Acre, Safad, Beisan, Tiberias and Nazareth, where the brigade headquarters was based. In addition to maintaining order, the brigade was responsible for conducting anti-smuggling operations and preventing illegal immigration along Palestine's northern and eastern borders with Lebanon, Syria and Transjordan. It was also tasked with protecting the oil pipeline which ran from the refinery at Haifa to the River Jordan. To assist it in this last task, the 3rd Mechanised Regiment of the Arab Legion was placed under command of the brigade. Two of 1st Parachute Brigade's battalions were located on the coast north of Acre and were employed on anti-illegal immigration operations. The third battalion was based at Rosh Pinna, north of Tiberias, and was responsible for maintaining order in Safad, where the threat of unrest was always high. To assist it, the brigade had under command the 1st The King's Dragoon Guards, who were subsequently replaced by the 17th/21st Lancers.

In early February, not long after its arrival in the Northern Sector, 6th Airborne Division took part in the evacuation of British civilians from Palestine. This involved the movement of 1,500 or so people to collection centres, from where they were transported by rail to Egypt before sailing for England. 8th Parachute Battalion was deployed to patrol the railway line which was the first stage of the journey from Haifa to Maadi in Egypt.

February also saw units of the division involved in the most unpleasant of all the tasks it was called upon to carry out during its tour of duty in Palestine: the trans-shipment of illegal immigrants. The immigrants arrived in Europe in vessels on which the conditions were appalling. The ships themselves were old and hardly seaworthy, possessing little or nothing in terms of facilities for their passengers. Accommodation consisted of bunks crammed into every available space on board, one vessel accommodating nine people in six cubic feet. The vessels were shadowed by RAF aircraft which guided Royal Navy warships until interception could be made once the three-mile territorial limit had been crossed. Once boarding parties had taken control of them, the vessels were towed to Haifa, where trans-shipment took place. This was the responsibility of the division's artillery units, under HQRA 6th Airborne Division. Army boarding parties took over from the Royal Navy and any sick immigrants were disembarked and taken to hospital. The remainder were disinfected as a precaution against disease and were searched for arms and explosives before being re-embarked in British vessels which transported them under guard to Cyprus. There the would-be immigrants were put into detention camps to await processing for immigration into Palestine.

On 11 July 4,500 Jews sailed from France in a ship called the *Exodus*, which had been specially fortified to resist boarding by the Royal Navy. Around its decks the ship had been fitted with barricades reinforced with barbed wire and netting, and around the outside ran a steam pipe with jets fitted at 12-inch intervals and powered by the ship's boilers. After being shadowed almost from the start of her voyage from the small port of Setye, near Marseilles, *Exodus* entered Palestinian territorial waters and soon afterwards was boarded by the Royal Navy. After the crew and passengers had surrendered the ship was towed to Haifa, where it arrived on the afternoon of 18 July. Trans-shipment took place as usual and the immigrants were transferred to three British vessels, which sailed on the following morning with a Royal Navy escort. However, once they were at sea the Jews were told that they were not being taken to Cyprus but were being returned to France. This news was greeted with considerable consternation. The voyage to France lasted nine days, during which time all male Jews were confined to their quarters. On arrival at Port de Bouc, near Marseilles, on 28 July the convoy was met by a number of vessels organised by the Haganah, which proceeded to broadcast propaganda and to incite the passengers on the three ships to resist any attempt to disembark them. The immigrants needed little persuading, and consequently only a few sick Jews were disembarked in France. After three weeks of fruitless negotiations between the British, the Jews and the French authorities, the convoy sailed for Germany, reaching Hamburg on 8 September. By this time the Jews were determined to resist any attempt to disembark them, and a violent battle took place before they were eventually ejected from the ships.

News of the *Exodus* operation reached Palestine, and the response of the Jewish population was one of disbelief followed by great anger. The Stern Gang carried out a number of attacks against the security forces, who responded by deploying in force in Haifa on 20 July and imposing a curfew in the Jewish quarter of Hadar hak Carmel. On the following day the Palmach carried out attacks on two radio stations, the second of these being in the area of Headquarters 6th Airborne Division. A group of six saboteurs was spotted by sentries who opened fire, seriously wounding one of the Jews, who fled and left behind some 50lb explosive charges. The IZL also made its presence felt, mining roads and railway lines and attacking oil pipelines and military installations. In Haifa harbour a British vessel, the *Empire Lifeguard*, was sunk by an explosive charge, the Palmach subsequently being suspected of being responsible for this attack.

The latter part of 1947 saw further changes in command appointments and reorganisation within 6th Airborne Division. On 19 August Major General Eric Bols handed over command to Major General Hugh Stockwell, who immediately distinguished himself in the eyes of his new command by undergoing parachute training and successfully qualifying for his wings. A month earlier, Brigadier J. P. O'Brien Twohig had assumed command of 1st Parachute Brigade from Brigadier Hugh Bellamy, who returned to England to take over 2nd Parachute Brigade. There had already been a number of changes in the division's order of battle, mainly as a result of the disbandment of 6th Airlanding Brigade, many of these having taken place among the supporting arms. In October it was proposed that the number of parachute brigades in the division should be reduced to two, and that a number of amalgamations should take place among the battalions. Thus it was decided that 3rd Parachute Brigade should be disbanded and that amalgamations would take place between 2nd and 3rd, 4th and 6th, and 8th and 9th Parachute Battalions. 1st (Guards), 5th (Scottish) and 7th (Light Infantry) Parachute Battalions would retain their separate identities. 1st Parachute Brigade would be composed of 1st (Guards), 2nd/3rd and 8th/9th Parachute Battalions, while 4th/6th, 5th (Scottish) and 7th (Light Infantry) Parachute Battalions would form 2nd Parachute Brigade. These reductions in the number of battalions within the division inevitably resulted in a greatly increased workload for the remainder, although the loss of 3rd Parachute Brigade was slightly offset by the arrival of the 2nd Battalion The Middlesex Regiment, which arrived in December and was based near the prison at Acre, a constant source of trouble.

At the end of November 1947 the United Nations announced its approval of plans for the partition of Palestine between the Arabs and Jews. While the latter were delighted, the Arabs were totally opposed to partition and vowed to oppose it by force if necessary. The immediate result was that the Jewish underground military organisations switched their attentions from the security forces to the Arabs, and violence between the two communities flared up anew. Beginning in Jerusalem and Jaffa on 2 December, the trouble quickly spread to Haifa. On 30 December a major incident occurred when members of the IZL attacked a group of Arab workers outside the oil refinery at Haifa, killing six Arabs and wounding over 40. The Arab reaction was swift and violent, a number of Jews in the refinery being beaten to death. The police arrived soon afterwards, but found themselves outnumbered. Troops from 2nd/3rd Parachute Battalion arrived and quickly restored order, clearing the refinery of all Jews and Arabs, who were subsequently escorted to their respective home areas by the 3rd The King's Own Hussars. Forty-one Jews had been killed and 48 injured during the incident in the refinery. On the following night the Haganah carried out a reprisal attack on the Arab village of Balad es Sheik, killing 14 Arabs and wounding 11. Of those killed, ten were women and children.

Trouble was not confined to the urban areas. Earlier in the month, on 13 December, violence had broken out in Safad, a town in the Frontier Sub-sector, when a Jew had disappeared after entering an Arab market in the town. As the trouble escalated, troops were called in to assist the police, and a company of 8th/9th Parachute Battalion, supported by a troop of armoured cars of the Transjordanian Frontier Force, were despatched.

A few days later, on 18 December, trouble broke out anew in the frontier areas when a number of Jews attacked the Arab village of Khissas, near the border with Syria. Ten Arabs were killed and five wounded during the attack, which was a reprisal for the Jewish casualties suffered during the violence in Safad. 1st Parachute Battalion, together with the 17th/21st Lancers and detachments of divisional troops, was despatched to reinforce the Transjordanian Frontier Force and help it cope with the increasing threat of trouble. A major problem facing the security forces was the defence of Jewish settlements near the frontier, which were dominated by high ground and vulnerable to attacks by snipers. On 9 January, 1948, settlements at Dan and Kafr Szold were attacked by large groups of Arabs. A troop of the 17th/21st Lancers was despatched to each and came under fire as they approached. The lancers replied with their armoured cars' machine guns, but eventually were forced to use their 2-pounder guns, which proved effective in silencing the Arabs' fire. Shortly afterwards, RAF Spitfires carried out mock attacks on the Arab positions, and during the afternoon 1st Parachute Battalion joined the action, using its 3-inch mortars to good effect. Eventually the increasing amount of firepower being brought to bear on them forced the Arabs to withdraw.

The start of 1948 saw the withdrawal of the Transjordanian Frontier Force, which was replaced by the 1st Battalion Irish Guards. On 18 January Headquarters 3rd Parachute Brigade was disbanded and an *ad hoc* formation designated 'Craforce', commanded by Brigadier C. H. Colquhon, who was CRA 6th Airborne Division, was assembled to carry out operations in the frontier areas. This consisted of 1st Parachute Battalion, the 1st Battalion Irish Guards and the 17th/21st Lancers. Meanwhile, 2nd/3rd and 8th/9th Parachute Battalions were maintaining order in Haifa despite the deterioration in the situation after the announcement of partition. The fighting between the Jews and Arabs had escalated from desultory sniping to battles involving the use of small-arms and, eventually, heavy machine guns and mortars, Nevertheless, the security forces retained the initiative and kept a tight grip on the situation. Platoons were deployed in static positions which dominated the city, and patrols remained ready to provide a rapid response to any threat.

At the end of January, 40 Commando Royal Marines arrived at Haifa from Malta and was placed under command of 6th Airborne Division, taking over responsibility for the protection of the port. It had originally been planned that the division would withdraw from Palestine during March and April and return to England before moving to Germany to become part of the British Army of the Rhine. On 18 February, however, it was announced that the division would be disbanded, and that several of its units would remain in Palestine until the end of the British Mandate on 15 May.

In the meantime, law and order had to be maintained. In March it became apparent that the Jews might not wait for the British withdrawal before attempting to defeat the Arabs, who by then had received reinforcements in the form of several hundred Syrian and Iraqi irregular troops, who were reported to be hidden in the Suq in Haifa. Consequently, a mixed troop of tanks and self-propelled guns of the Chestnut Troop of 1st Regiment Royal Horse Artillery was despatched to reinforce the squadron of the 3rd The King's Own Hussars already supporting the two parachute battalions in the city. Thereafter, columns of infantry, armour and artillery patrolled Haifa throughout the day and night, engaging any Arab or Jewish elements which opened fire on the other side. This tactic successfully reduced the levels of confrontation between the two communities.

On 3 April Headquarters 6th Airborne Division closed down and handed over control of the Northern Sector to the divisional commander's tactical headquarters, which was designated Headquarters GOC North Sector. Three days later 1st Parachute Brigade handed over operational control of Haifa to 1st Guards Brigade. On 16 April the brigade headquarters and 2nd/3rd Parachute Battalion sailed for England on the *Empress of Australia*. On 23 April Rear Headquarters 6th Airborne Division and 8th/9th Parachute Battalion followed them on the *Empress of Scotland*, leaving behind them the divisional tactical headquarters, Headquarters 'Craforce', 1st Parachute Battalion and divisional troops. Between 6 and 12 May the division's artillery units also departed for England. On 15 May Major General Hugh Stockwell handed over the Northern Sector to 1st Guards Brigade and boarded an aircraft for England. Three days later his tactical headquarters, Headquarters 'Craforce' and 1st Parachute Battalion embarked on the *Empress of Australia*. The last British unit to leave Palestine was 1st Airborne Squadron RE, which departed on 30 June.

CHAPTER 11
Post-War Reorganisation and Operations in the Middle East, Cyprus and Malaya, 1948–1958

The period after the end of the Second World War inevitably brought reductions and changes in the British Army's order of battle, and its airborne forces were no exception. 1st Airborne Division was disbanded in 1945, after it had been decided that only one airborne division would be retained in the Regular Army. However, on 1 January 1947 another formation was raised in the form of 16th Airborne Division (TA), its numerical designation commemorating the two wartime airborne divisions. Commanded by Major General Roy Urquhart, who had commanded 1st Airborne Division at Arnhem, it consisted of the 4th, 5th and 6th Parachute Brigades (TA), commanded by Brigadiers James Hill, Henry Ricketts and Pat Weston respectively. These three formations comprised nine parachute battalions, designated 10th to 18th respectively. The history of these Territorial battalions of The Parachute Regiment is covered in a later chapter.

In 1948 the decision was taken to disband 6th Airborne Division and to reduce the Regular Army's airborne forces to one brigade. In July of that year 2nd Parachute Brigade was redesignated 16th Parachute Brigade, again to maintain the links with the wartime airborne formations, and 4th/6th, 5th (Scottish) and 7th (Light Infantry) Parachute Battalions were re-formed as the 1st, 2nd and 3rd Battalions The Parachute Regiment (1, 2 and 3 PARA) respectively. 1st (Guards) Parachute Battalion was reduced to company strength and was redesignated 16th (Guards) Independent Company The Parachute Regiment, becoming the pathfinder unit for 16th Independent Parachute Brigade Group. Its designation was later changed to No. 1 (Guards) Independent Company.

In 1947 the Headquarters of the Commander Airborne Establishments, the post then held by Brigadier C. H. V. 'Tag' Pritchard, was located in Aldershot. Early that year Brigadier Pritchard had established Headquarters The Parachute Regiment as a branch of his own headquarters. Its staff included a Deputy Assistant Adjutant General (DAAG), the first incumbent being Major Eddie Warren of the Devonshire Regiment, who had previously served with 6th Airborne Division, and a staff captain, initially Captain David Mayfield. The role of this small regimental headquarters was to liaise with the rest of the infantry with regard to the recruitment of officers and men for secondment to The Parachute Regiment, and to supervise the internal affairs of the regiment itself.

The period from 1947 and 1948 saw reductions in the number of airborne establishments. In November 1947 the Holding Battalion was disbanded, and The Parachute Regiment Training Centre met the same fate on 1 July 1948. A month later, on 1 August, Headquarters Airborne Establishments was also disbanded and the responsibilities of its Commander transferred to the Commandant of the Airborne Forces Depot, the rank of the latter being upgraded to Colonel to reflect the added responsibility. The first officer to hold the new appointment was Colonel Ken Darling, the last commander of 5th Parachute Brigade before its disbandment. At the same time, the DAAG and GSO 2 were also transferred from the disbanded headquarters to the depot as Officer i/c Headquarters The Parachute Regiment (later redesignated as the Regimental Adjutant) and Air Training Officer respectively. The first two officers to hold these posts were Major Peter Hinde and Major John Barrow. While it had established an unsurpassable reputation since its formation in 1942, The Parachute Regiment possessed little or nothing in the way of property or assets as accumulated by other regiments of the infantry during long years of history. It had neither colours nor regimental march, so these and other matters of similar import had to be addressed by Colonel Darling and his small staff at the first available opportunity.

In August 1949 The Parachute Regiment ceased to form part of the Army Air Corps. In a Special Army Order dated 16 August an amendment to the corps warrant was published, in which it was stated: "the Parachute Regiment shall be constituted as a separate Corps of Infantry, entitled The Parachute Regiment". Thus it was established as an infantry regiment of the Line, taking precedent after the Green Jackets Brigade, and was entitled to carry colours. In October that year 16th Independent Parachute Brigade, commanded by Brigadier Walter Kempster, left Germany, where it had been serving with the British Army of the Rhine, and returned to England, where it settled into its new home at Aldershot.

Two years later a momentous event for The Parachute Regiment took place. On 19 July 1950 all three regular battalions formed up on Queen's Parade in Aldershot to be presented with their first colours by His Majesty King George VI. Commanding the parade was Colonel Darling, while the 1st, 2nd and 3rd Battalions The Parachute Regiment were under their commanding officers: Lieutenant Colonels Charles Harington, Bill White, and 'Digger' Tighe-Wood respectively. Also present on that unique occasion were Field Marshal The Viscount Montgomery of Alamein, in his capacity as Colonel Commandant The Parachute Regiment, Lieutenant General 'Boy' Browning (who was by then Comptroller of the Royal Household) and Lieutenant General Sir Richard Gale. The ground was kept on all four sides by the territorial battalions of the regiment, No. 1 (Guards) Independent Company and the Glider Pilot Regiment. The occasion was also enhanced by the presence for the first time of the massed bands and corps of drums of The Parachute Regiment. These had been formed by Bandmasters Penell, Keeling and Rippon, who transferred into the regiment in 1947 and had begun the task of raising the bands for the 1st, 2nd and 3rd Battalions respectively. Bandsmen were recruited from other regiments, which were losing their second battalions as a result of postwar reductions in the size of the Army, and instruments were obtained wherever possible. Meanwhile, corps of drums were also raised in all three battalions. The hard work and dedication of the three bandmasters and others responsible manifested itself in the presence on parade on that great occasion of 110 fully trained bandsmen and drummers.

Much thought had also been given to a regimental march and many tunes including "Lili Marlene", were considered. Eventually the Director of Music of the Royal Military School of Music at Kneller Hall, Colonel Roberts, suggested "The Ride of The Valkyries". After rearrangement by Bandmasters Keeling and Rippon, the march was approved and adopted. Shortly afterwards, "Pomp and Circumstance No. 4" was also adopted as the regimental slow march.

On their arrival, His Majesty King George VI and Queen Elizabeth were greeted by a royal salute. Then followed a service, during which the King's and regimental colours were consecrated, after which they were presented by the King himself to each of the three battalions. His Majesty then addressed the regiment:

"Colonel Darling, officers, warrant officers, non-commissioned officers and men of The Parachute Regiment.

I am very glad to be here today to present you with your first colours, and to inspect The Parachute Regiment for the first time. I have been deeply impressed by what I have seen, and I congratulate you on your fine bearing and drill.

This has been no surprise to me, for I have watched the growth of your regiment from its earliest days, and I recognise in this parade the keenness and spirit which have brought you through the perils of so many difficult operations. Yours has not been a long history. Only a short time separated your first raids on the Tragino Aqueduct and the Bruneval radar station from the fighting in North Africa and Sicily; very soon afterwards, in the 1st and 6th Airborne Divisions, you were adding your weight to those great blows which fell upon the enemy in Normandy, at Arnhem and on the Rhine, and which brought the European War to an end. There were other battles and much varied training, for you had to fight not only as parachutists but often for months at a time as infantrymen. The volunteers who came from all arms of the service to fill your ranks had much to learn; they learned it quickly and they learned it well.

These colours which I have just presented to your three battalions are the traditional symbol of a soldier's loyalty. The qualities which they represent and call forth are those which are common to, and indeed essential, to all good soldiers in all ages: they are qualities which you have shown that you possess alike in war and peace.

I am fully confident that you will maintain the high standard which you have already established, and that these colours will always be safe in your hands."

Following the King's address, all three battalions marched past their Sovereign for the first time to their new regimental march "The Ride of The Valkyries", their new colours flying in the bright sunshine. Watching them on that day were many who had fought with the wartime parachute battalions in the actions and campaigns recorded by the battle honours emblazoned on those colours: Bruneval, Normandy Landings, Pegasus Bridge, Merville Battery, Breville, Dives Crossing, La Touques Crossing, Arnhem 1944, Ourthe, Rhine, Southern France, Northwest Europe 1942, 1944–45, Soudia, Oudna, Djebel Azzag 1943, Djebel Alliliga, El Hadjeba, Tamera, Djebel Dahra, Kef El Debna, North Africa 1942–43, Primosole Bridge, Sicily 1943, Taranto, Orsogna, Italy 1943–44, Athens and Greece 1944–45. For the youngest regiment in the British Army, it was a very proud day.

THE MIDDLE EAST, 1951–54

The year 1951 once again found battalions of the regiment deployed in the Middle East. In May the government of Persia nationalised its oil industry and caused alarm in Britain over future supplies of oil and the safety of British nationals living in Persia. In June, 16th Independent Parachute Brigade Group, commanded by Brigadier Ken Darling, sailed for Cyprus in the aircraft carriers HMS *Triumph* and HMS *Warrior*. However, soon after its arrival there the situation was resolved, and the brigade subsequently moved to Egypt in the autumn.

Towards the end of July of the following year, King Farouk of Egypt was overthrown by a *coup d'etat* led by General Neguib and Colonel Gamal Abd al-Nasser. In the weeks following the coup, political tension between Egypt and Britain mounted as the new regime made plain its anti-British sentiments. In October, Headquarters 16th Independent Parachute Brigade and the three parachute battalions were flown in, being followed by the rest of the brigade and its heavy equipment, which travelled by sea. During the following month civil unrest developed in Egypt when workers in the docks, ordnance depots and other British-controlled establishments went on strike. At that time, British troops stationed in the Suez Canal Zone numbered some 70,000, and many of these now had to be deployed on internal security duties. The three battalions took over responsibility for the docks, while the brigade's artillery unit, 33rd Parachute Light Regiment RA, took over the guarding of the ordnance depot at Geneifa.

Two months later, in January 1952, 16th Independent Parachute Brigade moved into the desert west of Suez, together with other British forces, to counter a threat from Egyptian forces against the Suez Canal itself. 1 PARA was stood by to carry out an airborne operation as part of an attack on Cairo, to be carried out with 3 PARA and a squadron of the 4th Royal Tank Regiment, in the event of the lives of British civilians being threatened. Egyptian forces advanced towards the Canal Zone, halting five miles away. Although there had been no further military threat by February, the political situation continued to deteriorate and anti-British sentiment in

Egypt continued to increase. Terrorist attacks against British military establishments in the Canal Zone increased, and the Egyptian police refused to co-operate in maintaining security. Much of the trouble was centred on the town of Ismailia, where the main British military and civil administration headquarters were based.

On 20 January elements of 2 and 3 PARA moved into Ismailia, carrying out cordon and search operations in the areas of the town suspected of harbouring terrorist elements. The operation met with some resistance. While 2 PARA was clearing a cemetery, an action took place in which four terrorists were killed and 12 captured. Unfortunately the battalion lost one of its officers, who was killed. One of the key points to be taken over was the Egyptian police barracks in the town. The police refused to allow troops of the 1st Battalion The Lancashire Fusiliers to occupy the barracks, and a battle developed. Eventually the police surrendered, but only after a Centurion tank of a supporting armoured squadron was used to shell them into submission. By the end of the action half of the 95 policemen in the barracks had been killed and the remainder wounded. The Lancashire Fusiliers suffered four killed and 11 wounded. On the completion of these operations 16th Independent Parachute Brigade moved into camps in the area of Ismailia and assumed responsibility for the security of the town and surrounding areas. For the next two years it conducted internal security operations which kept it fully committed. Egyptian terrorists continued to attack British troops and installations, which resulted in units of the brigade having to perform patrols, cordon and search operations, guard duties and convoy escorts. Despite its heavy operational commitments, however, the brigade also found time to carry out training, and several exercises were held in Cyprus, Jordan and the desert of Sinai.

In 1952 another important development for The Parachute Regiment occurred when the decision was taken to allow other ranks to enlist direct from civilian life. Previously, volunteers had come from other units, as had been the case during the wartime years. Officers, however, continued to be seconded from other regiments until 1958, when a regular cadre was established. In August of that year 2nd Lieutenant Rudge Penley was commissioned from the Royal Military Academy Sandhurst direct into The Parachute Regiment, the first regular officer to be so commissioned. In July 1954, 16th Independent Parachute Brigade completed its tour of duty in the Middle East and returned to Britain and its home at Aldershot.

MALAYA, 1955–57

The next call to arms for members of The Parachute Regiment came in 1954. By then, elements of the British Army were engaged in operations against Communist terrorists (CTs) in the jungles of Malaya. 22nd Special Air Service Regiment (22 SAS), which had been formed in 1950 from the Malayan Scouts and volunteers from 21st SAS Regiment (Artists') (TA), was engaged in deep penetration patrol operations, seeking out the terrorists' jungle bases while also conducting 'hearts and minds' operations among the local people to win their support. The regiment was reinforced by a squadron of the Rhodesian SAS, which was coming to the end of its tour of operations and would thus need to be replaced by another unit. The Director of Operations in Malaya, General Sir Geoffrey Bourne, suggested that a squadron should be formed from volunteers from The Parachute Regiment to replace the Rhodesians. As a result the Independent Parachute Squadron was formed. Commanded by Major Dudley Coventry, it comprised men from all three battalions.

After flying out to Malaya in the Spring of 1955, the squadron underwent six weeks of training at the Jungle Warfare School at Kota Tinggi before joining 22 SAS at its base at Coronation Park in Kuala Lumpur. The squadron was organised on an SAS squadron establishment: a headquarters troop and four 'sabre' troops, each comprising three patrols of four men. During the latter part of the squadron's tour in Malaya a fifth troop was formed from additional personnel. The troops in the squadron were numbered 11 to 15.

To those of the squadron who had spent their years of soldiering in Europe or Palestine, jungle warfare was a totally different way of fighting. Instead of operating in platoons and companies, they found themselves operating in four-man patrols deep inside the jungle, with only a No. 62 HF radio set as a link with the outside world. In areas of secondary jungle the dense undergrowth restricted visibility and limited fields of fire to only a few yards, so patrols had to be constantly alert to the threat of ambush from terrorists, who sometimes operated in large groups. Movement through the jungle was of necessity slow and cautious, patrols covering as little as a few hundred yards in an hour. Everything had to be carried in packs, with resupply from the air taking place every seven to ten days. Instead of the normal four- to five-day duration, patrols lasted anything up to ten weeks. The constant wetness in the jungle caused clothing and boots to rot and they had to be replaced after only a few days, using aerial resupply. Dropping zones, on to which supplies were parachuted, had to be cut by hand, and if parachutes landed in the jungle canopy there was no way they could be retrieved.

Personal health was of paramount importance, because a sick man created major problems for a patrol. Casualties were evacuated by air if a landing strip could be cut, or were carried out by aboriginal porters on a stretcher, which was a slow and tedious business. The high level of physical exertion in a hostile environment such as the jungle inevitably had a debilitating effect and increased susceptibility to illness or disease. As well as learning to live in the jungle, members of the squadron learned to fight in it. Navigation (using maps on which there was little detail apart from contour lines); patrolling; ambush and anti-ambush drills; contact drills; tracking; close reconnaissance and close-quarter battle marksmanship, which involved engaging moving targets which appeared for a few fleeting seconds, were just a few of the skills that men of the squadron were required to assimilate. Like the other squadrons in 22 SAS, the Independent Parachute Squadron often operated under command of one of the infantry brigades in Malaya. After insertion by helicopter or on foot, patrols would penetrate deep into the areas of jungle where it was suspected that CT bases were located.

The squadron's first operation took place over three months in the Iskander swamp, an area in southern Malaya. The terrain was difficult, consisting of large areas of secondary jungle interlaced with small rivers and streams. To make matters even more difficult, the area was not accurately mapped, making navigation difficult. During the operation the squadron discovered a number of cultivated areas in the jungle and laid ambushes, but without success. At the end of the operation it returned to Kuala Lumpur for rest and further training.

January 1956 found the squadron operating in southern Selangor, in the northern part of the sultanate of Johore. Under the command of an infantry brigade, it was deployed in an area of swamp called Tasek Bera, tasked with collecting information on terrorist activity before taking part in an operation to destroy the CT organisation in the area. The squadron discovered signs of activity in the vicinity of the River Palong, and patrols had several encounters with CTs. During one of them a member of a patrol was wounded and had to be evacuated by helicopter from a hastily cut LZ.

During the following 12 months the squadron was deployed in the area between Ipoh and the Cameron Highlands to its east. It spent much time patrolling the mountainous, jungle-covered terrain but encountered CTs on only a few occasions. One of these was a highly successful ambush by 12 Troop, which resulted in the capture of a CT organiser on the road leading to Tapah. 22 SAS was reinforced at this time by the New Zealand SAS Squadron, and by 1956 the regiment had five squadrons deployed on operations against the Communists, who were estimated as numbering some 2,000. SAS operations proved successful in denying the terrorists safe havens in the jungle, destroying their cultivated areas and forcing them to seek food outside, where other troops were waiting for them. In April 1957 the Independent Parachute Squadron completed its tour of duty in Malaya and sailed for Britain aboard the *SS Nevasa*. After its return to Aldershot in May, the squadron was disbanded.

CYPRUS 1956

Meanwhile, the three battalions of The Parachute Regiment had been in action elsewhere. In January 1956, 1 and 3 PARA were deployed to Cyprus after King Hussein of Jordan had dismissed General John Glubb, the famous 'Glubb Pasha', who had until then been commander of the Jordanian Army. Fearing a threat to British expatriates living in the kingdom, the British government decided to deploy a force capable of intervening rapidly if required. In the event no crisis arose, and the two battalions found themselves deployed on internal security operations in Cyrpus instead.

During 1955 the Greek terrorist organisation EOKA had begun its campaign for *Enosis*, union with Greece. Cyprus had originally formed part of the Ottoman Empire, and had been ruled by Turkey since 1560, when it was handed over to Britain in 1878 as part of a pact between the two countries. In 1914 it was officially annexed by Britain after Turkey had allied itself with Germany at the start of the First World War, and in 1925 it became a British Crown colony. The majority of the population in Cyprus was of Greek descent, outnumbering those of Turkish origin by four to one. From the very beginning, in 1878, Greek Cypriots had made plain their desire for union with Greece. However, *Enosis* was totally unacceptable to their Turkish counterparts and to Turkey itself, whose southern approaches from the sea are dominated by Cyprus.

In 1954, with growing demands for *Enosis* from both the Greek Cypriot community and Greece, the Turkish government threatened to annex the island. A refusal by the Greek government to consider a British suggestion for tripartite government of Cyprus led Greek Cypriot extremists to believe that Greece tacitly supported the idea of *Enosis* and so they launched a campaign of civil unrest and terrorism. Led by a former wartime Greek Army Officer, Colonel George Grivas, the extremists formed the terrorist organisation known as EOKA (National Union of Cypriot Combattants).

After its arrival on the island in January 1956, one of the first tasks given to 3 PARA, by then commanded by Lieutenant Colonel Paul Crook, was the arrest of Archbishop Makarios, who was the Ethnarch — the head of the Greek Orthodox Church in Cyprus, which supported EOKA and its campaign for *Enosis*. Makarios himself had been involved in lengthy negotiations with the British government which, when these proved fruitless, decided to exile him to the Seychelles. 3 PARA cordoned off the archbishop's palace in Nicosia and Makarios was escorted to the airfield at Akrotiri, from where he was flown into exile. Meanwhile, the battalion

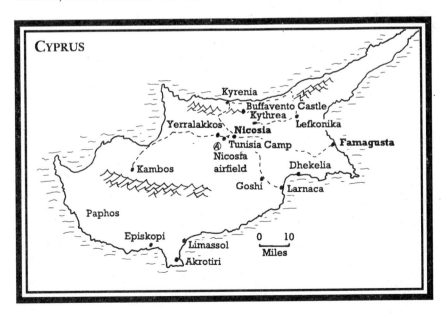

CYPRUS

searched his palace but found nothing other than a bricked-up chamber containing a skeleton some hundreds of years old.

EOKA waged its campaign of terror with ruthless cruelty. The majority of its attacks were directed against Cypriots, to suppress any opposition and to ensure the silence of the people when they were questioned by the security forces. Violence was also directed against the Turkish Cypriot community and the security forces, who were subjected to bomb attacks and ambushes from which EOKA terrorists would rapidly withdraw once the troops and police fought back. Occasionally, attacks were also carried out on off-duty servicemen, and sometimes on their families, whom the EOKA thugs regarded as legitimate targets.

In May both battalions took part in Operation 'Pepperpot' in the forest of Paphos, which concealed the bases of several EOKA cells. Ambushes were laid at night on the narrow tracks which interlaced the forest, and villages were cordoned off before dawn and searched. Persistence paid off and two wanted members of EOKA were captured, a third being taken prisoner two days later. However, the EOKA leader, Grivas, escaped the dragnet. It was known that the Greek Orthodox Church actively supported EOKA, and a search of the monastery at Kykkho confirmed that it was being used as a base by an EOKA cell, although no terrorists were found there.

At the beginning of June, 1 and 3 PARA once again found themselves deployed in Paphos forest, on Operation 'Lucky Alphonse'. It was suspected that Grivas was hiding in a valley within the forest, so the whole area was surrounded by a force consisting of several battalions. The initial task of cordoning the area was difficult and involved approach marches carried out at night, the steep scree-covered slopes making quiet movement very difficult. Navigation in the thick forest was also a problem. Initially luck was with 3 PARA, which uncovered a terrorist hide, but thereafter misfortune seemed to plague it for the rest of the operation. A warrant officer of 1 PARA was ambushed and shot dead after straying over the boundary between the two battalions, and a C Company patrol narrowly missed capturing a group of terrorists, the latter escaping after being alerted by the noise of a patrol member's boot on the scree-covered hillside. A hide was discovered, and a search revealed that the patrol had come close to capturing Grivas himself. Abandoned equipment and documents included the EOKA leader's boots and diary. A few days later misfortune struck 3 PARA again, when a vehicle carrying the second in command of A Company, Captain Mike Walsh, and Captain Michael Beagley became trapped by a forest fire. Together with their driver, Private Hawker, the two officers tried to escape by running downhill through the flames. Walsh survived after falling into a ditch, but Beagley and Hawker both died. Thirty men from other units also perished in the fire.

In early July the two battalions were joined by 2 PARA, commanded by Lieutenant Colonel Bala Bredin, and the rest of 16th Independent Parachute Brigade under its commander, Brigadier 'Tubby' Butler. The reason for the brigade's deployment was the growing threat to the Suez

Canal from President Gamal Abd al-Nasser, who was threatening to nationalise it. America's President Eisenhower and his administration took a neutral stance, but the British and French governments decided that they would respond with military force, if required, to retain the canal under international control. Thus 16th Independent Parachute Brigade was deployed to Cyprus in its entirety, to be able to deploy rapidly if Nasser carried out his threat. Meanwhile, the brigade continued to conduct internal security operations in Nicosia, which was divided into Turkish and Greek areas. Troops patrolled between the two communities, moving in quickly to stamp out any fighting.

In early August 1 and 3 PARA were flown home for parachute training, neither unit having jumped for 11 months. During their ten days in England, the battalions carried out four descents and a battalion exercise, as well as enjoying a brief period of leave. When they returned to Cyprus, both battalions took with them reservists who had been recalled to the colours in view of the impending threat of action in Egypt.

September was spent preparing for a possible airborne operation, but by the end of the month the situation had calmed down and the brigade returned to internal security operations. On 2 October it was deployed on Operation 'Sparrowhawk I' in the mountains of Kyrenia. Three EOKA groups, numbering 20 terrorists in all, were making use of villages in the area for supplies and communications. On the night of 2 October the entire area of the East Kyrenia Range was surrounded by a cordon of troops, while vessels of the Royal Navy sealed off the seaward approach to the area. At dawn on the following day all three battalions and No. 1 (Guards) Independent Company, commanded by Major Kemmis Buckley of the Welsh Guards, moved in and began searching the area. Observation posts were established and patrols were sent out to patrol by day and lay section ambushes by night, the entire area being subject to curfew which was announced by aircraft equipped with loudhailers. Meanwhile, the brigade tactical headquarters was established at Ayios Amvrosios, together with interpreters, cages, screening teams, trackers, dogs and handlers, a platoon of police and intelligence personnel.

2 PARA was deployed with its battalion headquarters at Halevga Forest Station. C Company, commanded by Major Roy Fullick, was based on the Trapeza Plateau, which dominated its area of responsibility. On the early morning of the second day of the operation, a patrol from the company was searching a farmhouse and the surrounding area which lay below the plateau when a soldier, Private Taylor, dislodged a rock and uncovered a hole while searching a nearby hill. His platoon commander's suspicions were aroused, and he ordered his men to search the area thoroughly. Shortly afterwards an NCO, Lance Corporal Staff, uncovered a dugout containing plates of half-eaten food, more food in a basket, blankets and large stocks of tinned food, ammunition and grenades. The dugout was well constructed, and was large enough to accommodate up to three people comfortably. It was obvious that it had been recently occupied and hastily abandoned. A search was then made of the farm buildings, including a byre

occupied by donkeys. Two members of the patrol, Privates Pearce and O'Donnell, removed an old coat hanging from a peg inside the byre and uncovered a hole. On shining his torch through it, O'Donnell saw a face inside. Pearce fired a round through the hole, while O'Donnell dashed round to the far side of the building in time to catch six men scrambling out through a concealed trap door. They surrendered and were taken away for interrogation at Brigade Headquarters. Later that day one of them was escorted back to the farm, where he revealed an arms cache concealed in an oil drum buried in a bank under a large tree. On 7 October another search by C Company produced a further two caches which included a Breda machine gun and some 2-inch mortar bombs. For once, fortune had smiled on the security forces and had presented them with the largest haul of weapons to be discovered since the emergency in Cyprus had begun. Moreover, the interrogation of the six men, four of whom were on lists of wanted terrorists, subsequently led to the arrest of a further 18 suspects and the breaking-up of EOKA groups in the villages of Kartja, Ayios Amvrosios and Kalogrea. It also provided the intelligence staff with information relating to other EOKA groups throughout Kyrenia and as far away as Nicosia.

Elsewhere during the operation, other units in the brigade also had contacts with groups of terrorists. On the morning of 3 October a patrol from 3 PARA was fired upon by a group of men moving north, and during the evening of the following day troops of 9th Parachute Squadron RE ambushed two terrorists. In the early hours of 5 October, men of No. 1 (Guards) Independent Company opened fire on a man seen moving through the area of one of their troop headquarters. Later that morning, at 0500 hours, a cordon and search was carried out at the village of Khardja and some weapons and leaflets were found. Such was the success of Operation 'Sparrowhawk I' that another operation, 'Sparrowhawk II', was mounted in West Kyrenia during 11 to 16 October.

A few weeks later, however, the brigade was not so fortunate. A trap was laid for one particular EOKA group, in the form of a convoy of seemingly harmless trucks engaged on resupply. In the rear of each vehicle, however, were ten soldiers protected by sandbags. Over a period of six weeks the convoy of three vehicles took the same route at the same time of day, the leading truck travelling half a mile ahead of the other two. Nothing happened until one evening, when the terrorists responded to the bait by attacking a vehicle from another unit which had strayed into the area and entered the ambush before the decoy truck.

On 25 October, 16th Independent Parachute Brigade Group was deployed on Operation 'Foxhunter', in the Morphou area, in the Paphos Forest in the Troodos Mountains, when it was suddenly recalled to its camps in Nicosia. The situation in Egypt had deteriorated sharply, and Brigadier Butler was told to prepare for an airborne operation. In fact the brigade had already received a warning of possible operations, and all three battalions had undergone a period of concentrated training in preparation for full-scale war, as opposed to internal security. A series of exercises were conducted during the day and at night down the main road to Dhekelia and Limassol, with battalions carrying out advance to contacts with repeated daylight and night attacks. In the mountainous northern areas of Cyprus, large-scale battalion field firing exercises, including artillery and mortars, were also held.

SUEZ AND OPERATION 'MUSKETEER'

In July President Nasser had carried out his threat to nationalise the Suez Canal, subsequently refusing to withdraw or to permit international use of the waterway. While the British and French continued to make plans to use force to wrest control of the canal from him, Israeli forces attacked the Egyptians and advanced rapidly across the Sinai desert towards the canal. The British and French Governments, who had been well aware of Israeli plans, called on both sides to cease fighting and withdraw or face intervention by an Anglo-French force. The Israelis complied, but the Egyptians disregarded the ultimatum, and Britain and France decided to use force.

The city of Alexandria had been selected as the initial objective of the Anglo-French task force, its capture being followed by an advance on Cairo and subsequently the Suez Canal. However, this was rejected as being politically unacceptable and Port Said, at the northern end of the canal, was chosen instead. This was not popular with the War Office and its planners, which argued that British and French forces, under General Sir Hugh Stockwell, a former commander of 6th Airborne Division, would have a very limited area in which to deploy after landing. The causeway along which they would advance southwards was some 28 miles long and only some 300 yards wide, being bordered to the east by the Suez Canal and to the west by a marsh. The plan, drawn up by the British, involved an initial phase consisting of six days of air attacks by RAF and French aircraft to destroy the Egyptian Air Force on the ground. This would be followed on the seventh day, 6 November, by joint amphibious landings at Port Said, followed immediately afterwards by an airborne assault. Among the many who were not happy with the plan was Brigadier Tubby Butler, who argued that it would be more logical to drop the brigade at Ismailia, halfway down the canal, while French paratroops were dropped at the southern end at Port Tewfik. With the amphibious landings by Royal Marine Commandos and French forces taking place at the same time, the entire area of the canal zone could be secured simultaneously. Unfortunately, the planners disregarded this imaginative and far more logical alternative.

One major factor which placed severe limitations on the British capability to launch an airborne operation was the shortage of transport aircraft. Three types were available: the Beverley, which was capable of dropping vehicles and guns as well as paratroops, the Hastings, and the Valetta. At the time no Beverleys were available for the operation, and the only alternative method of transporting heavy loads for dropping by parachute was to carry them slung underneath a Hastings. Moreover, the

Valetta was manifestly unsuitable for dropping paratroops because the wing spar passed through the cabin, and men heavily burdened with parachutes and equipment containers had to step over it whilst shuffling their way towards the door to make their exit. When one considers the combined capability of the RAF and the British Army to carry out major airborne operations in 1945, the effect of ten years of neglect of airborne forces is immediately apparent.

When Lieutenant Colonel Paul Crook and 3 PARA arrived back at their base on 29 October they noticed a great deal of activity on the nearby airfield, where they observed Noratlas transport aircraft and French troops. It transpired that these were paratroops of the 10th Airborne Division, commanded by General Massu. On the same day, Crook received a warning order from the brigade headquarters to prepare for an airborne operation, although the location was not specified. During the next few days 3 PARA prepared feverishly for the coming operation. Weapons and equipment were prepared and packed, parachutes drawn and fitted, and all members of the battalion underwent synthetic parachute training. On Thursday 2 November Lieutenant Colonel Crook was briefed on the operation by the brigade commander.

The British element of the airborne assault would consist of a battalion group of 3 PARA plus supporting units under command, which would drop at 0715 hours on El Gamil airfield, west of Port Said, and seize it. The battalion would then clear the area between the airfield and Port Said

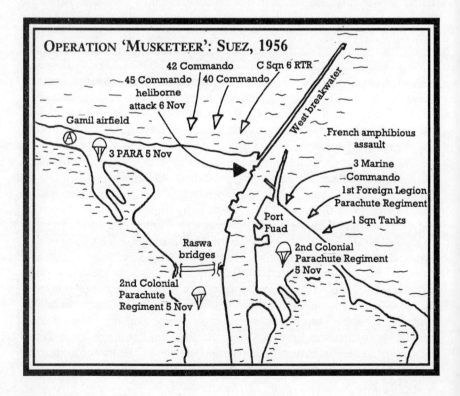

before linking up with 40 and 42 Royal Marine Commandos, who would have already landed north of the town. Amphibious landings would also be carried out north of Port Fuad, which lay immediately to the east of Port Said, by French troops of the 1er Regiment Etranger de Parachutistes (1er REP) and the 2eme Regiment de Chasseurs Parachutistes (2e RCP). Meanwhile, a force of 487 French troops consisting of a commando group of the 11eme Demi-Brigade Parachutiste de Choc (11e Choc) and elements of a battalion of the 2eme Regiment de Parachutistes Coloniale (2e RPC), commanded by Colonel Chateau-Jobert, the Commanding Officer of 2e RPC, would be dropped south of the town at El Raswa. At 1515 hours a battalion of the 1er Regiment de Chasseurs Parachutiste, commanded by Lieutenant Colonel Fossey-Francois, would be dropped immediately south of Port Fuad. Other units of the 10th Airborne Division would be on standby in Cyprus, ready to drop on El Qantara and Ismailia at 0800 and 1500 hours respectively on the second day.

Command of the Anglo-French ground forces was to be exercised by General Gilles from an airborne command post in a Noratlas transport. The aircraft would also provide a communications and command link with the overall commander, General Sir Charles Keightley, who would be on board a headquarters ship with his French deputy, Admiral Barjot, as well as with the operational base in Cyprus.

The French objectives were two bridges over which ran two roads, linking Port Said with the western canal bank, along which British armour, led by 2 PARA, would subsequently head south after landing by sea with Brigadier Butler and a small tactical brigade headquarters. The French force would be accompanied by a stick from No. 1 (Guards) Independent Company, commanded by Captain Murray de Klee of the Scots Guards, and a small party of sappers from No. 3 Troop of 9th Parachute Squadron Royal Engineers under 2nd Lieutenant Graham Owens. De Klee and his men were to reconnoitre the road south for a distance of 8km, accompanied by some of the sappers who would clear any mines or explosive charges, after which they would link up with 2 PARA.

There was very little hard intelligence concerning the Egyptian forces. It was known that there was an armoured division in the desert to the south and a number of units in Port Said itself, including some tanks and a large force from the National Guard. In the area of the airfield there was a battalion group deployed to counter any seaborne or airborne assault. Of one thing Lieutenant Colonel Crook and his men could be sure: the Egyptian troops would not enjoy any air support. Nasser's air force had reportedly been destroyed on the ground within 48 hours by the British and French air attacks which had begun on 31 October. Indeed, the rapid completion of the first phase of the operation, for which six days had been allocated, caused a problem for the planners. The Anglo-French amphibious invasion force was heading for Egypt, but there was no possibility of it landing before the morning of 6 November. The consequent hiatus between the end of the air-attack phase and the landings could afford the Egyptians the opportunity to move reinforcements to the Port Said area. A further complicating factor was that the speed of the Israeli advance had surprised all concerned, and there was the possibility that Israeli forces would seize the canal before the arrival of the Anglo-French force, forcing the Egyptians to surrender. To prevent either of these situations arising, the airborne operation was brought forward 24 hours, to 5 November.

Thirty-two aircraft were allocated to carry the 3 PARA group for the drop: 18 Valettas and seven Hastings transporting the 668 officers and men of the battalion, and seven Hastings carrying the heavy-drop loads of jeeps, trailers and six 106mm recoilless rifles (anti-tank guns), as well as 176 containers. A second drop of 58 men, three jeeps and a trailer, plus 84 more ammunition containers, would be made eight hours later.

Each man in the battalion was loaded on the aircraft in relation to where he was required on landing, each aircraft thus containing men from different platoons and companies. This was a technique previously used by 12th Parachute Battalion for Operation 'Varsity' in 1945, and it had proved extremely effective with regard to the speed of deployment of the battalion from the dropping zone. Men of Major Mike Walsh's A Company, accompanied by sappers of No. 3 Troop of 9th Parachute Squadron RE under Captain Jock Brazier, would be the first to exit from each aircraft, their task being to secure the western end of the dropping zone, which was the airfield itself, and to seize the control tower. They were also to seize a bridge 2,000 yards to the west of the airfield, which the sappers would prepare for demolition. C Company, under Major Ron Norman, would jump after them and would thereafter be the battalion reserve, ready to move wherever it was required. Last to jump would be B Company, under Major Dick Stevens, which would secure the eastern end of the DZ and clear the area of a sewage farm nearby. Battalion Headquarters and the anti-tank gunners, mortar crews and machine gunners of Major Geoff Norton's Support Company would be interspersed among the rifle companies' sticks. D Company, a small *ad hoc* force commanded by Major Noel Hodgson and composed of administrative personnel such as storemen, cooks, clerks and orderlies, would be dropped in the second lift and would provide further reserves and reinforcements. Accompanying the battalion and its attached troop of sappers would be Brigadier Tubby Butler and Major Charles Dunbar, his Brigade Major, detachments of 33rd Parachute Light Regiment RA, the brigade signal squadron and 63 Company RASC, a section of 23rd Parachute Field Ambulance, a field surgical team, 13 Air Contact Team (for control of aircraft giving support) and a party from the brigade RAF detachment.

The original plan was for the airborne assault to be carried out under cover of a naval bombardment which would have begun 30 minutes beforehand, at the time of the amphibious landings. As a result of the drop being advanced 24 hours, the airborne troops would have to carry out their tasks without any such support. Not that this alarmed the officers and men of 3 PARA. All were delighted at the opportunity to carry out an airborne operation and were raring to go.

As dawn was breaking in Cyprus at 0415 hours local time on 5 November, the first aircraft took off. The weather was good and the flight was uneventful, many of the soldiers sleeping during the flight. 'P' Hour was set for 0715 hours GMT. Preceding the airborne force was a Canberra bomber which dropped a flare five miles to the west of the dropping zone, marking the start of the run-in for the Valettas and Hastings. As the aircraft arrived over the dropping zone and disgorged their 'sticks', the Egyptian troops in the area reacted swiftly and brought fire to bear on the DZ. Despite the opposition, however, the 3 PARA group was on the ground in ten minutes. A Company went straight into action on landing, the control tower being swiftly occupied by a group of men led by Sergeant Legg. An enemy machine gun opened fire from a bunker position at the western end of the airfield, but this was attacked and knocked out by a platoon under 2nd Lieutenant Peter Coates, Private Clements scoring a direct hit with his 3.5-inch rocket launcher. Two Egyptians were killed and nine were captured in this action.

Meanwhile, Lieutenant Colonel Paul Crook and his small battalion tactical headquarters had landed without mishap and had set off to find B Company, which had landed virtually on top of some Egyptian positions. Despite encountering some opposition, it was carrying out its tasks. Major Dick Stevens had been wounded in the hand soon after landing, but was given first aid by his second in command, Captain Karl Beale. The company knocked out an enemy machine gun in a bunker and cleared some enemy from positions at the eastern end of the airfield before turning its attention to the sewage farm. No. 5 Platoon under Sergeant Norman pushed forward and cleared half the farm while No. 4 Platoon, commanded by 2nd Lieutenant Chris Hogg, advanced through an area of thick reeds from which it cleared some snipers before occupying some of the farm's buildings. As the platoon continued its advance it came under fire from Egyptians dug in around the cemetery, and was ordered to withdraw. As it did so, it was attacked by two French Mystere fighters and Hogg and his men were forced to take evasive action by diving into some large tanks of sewage nearby. The pilots, who had mistaken Hogg and his men for Egyptians, were called off by the French liaison officer accompanying 13 Air Contact Team.

At this point Lieutenant Colonel Crook called forward one of the Battalion's six anti-tank guns to engage Egyptians using a house as an observation post, and another target which was thought to be a tank dug in on the beach near the cemetery. At the same time, a section of the Machine Gun Platoon came forward to provide B Company with covering fire. As B Company reached the end of the sewage farm it again came under fire from the cemetery. Major Dick Stevens was wounded in the leg and Captain Karl Beale assumed command. Lieutenant Colonel Crook decided to mount a company attack on the cemtery, using C Company.

Just before 'H' Hour at 1030 hours, an airstrike was carried out by Sea Venom and Sea Hawk aircraft of the Fleet Air Arm. Further firepower was brought to bear on the enemy positions by the battalion's mortars and

Vickers medium machine guns before Major Ron Norman and his company advanced to clear the enemy from the cemetery. Unfortunately, over 70 3-inch mortar bombs had been lost during the drop, so the Mortar Platoon, commanded by Captain Norman Morley, could fire only 15 rounds per mortar in support of C Company's attack. The Company advanced towards the cemetery in 'two-up' formation, Nos. 7 and 9 Platoons in the van with Company Headquarters and No. 8 Platoon following behind. Some close-quarter fighting saw the enemy cleared from among the tombs and graves, over 20 Egyptians being killed. At one point an Egyptian soldier who was on the point of shooting Lieutenant Colonel Crook was shot dead by Staff Sergeant Issitt, the battalion's physical training instructor and the CO's bodyguard. A large quantity of weapons and equipment captured during the attack included three Russian SU-100 assault guns, two 3.7-inch anti-aircraft guns, a Bren carrier and a considerable number of small arms.

After capturing the cemetery, C Company called down airstrikes on some apartment blocks which were being used as observation posts by the Egyptians. After these had been successfully attacked by the Fleet Air Arm, Major Norman sent patrols forward to occupy the apartments and a nearby coastguard barracks which dominated the area. While the battle was in progress the field surgical team of 23rd Parachute Field Ambulance, under Major Norman Kirby, had been performing a number of emergency operations on the wounded. The battalion's own medical officer, Captain Sandy Cavenagh, had been wounded in the eye and was removed only after Major Kirby had placed him in charge of some of the most seriously wounded men, who were being evacuated by helicopters from the commando carriers HMS *Bulwark* and HMS *Albion*.

At 1315 hours the second lift arrived in the form of two Valettas and five Hastings, which dropped the men of D Company and more containers of mortar, anti-tank and small-arms ammunition. One member of D Company, Corporal Brackpool of the battalion's pay office, was the leading member of a stick in one of the Valettas. Standing in the door of the aircraft, he was accidentally thrown out when it banked steeply before starting the run-in towards the dropping zone. He landed on the wrong side of the river to the west of the airfield and was unable to cross via the bridge, which had been destroyed earlier by Fleet Air Arm aircraft, so he was forced to strip down to his underwear and swim across. At that point a group of Egyptians appeared, but the timely intervention of a patrol under Sergeant Vokes, the Officers' Mess Sergeant, saved the unfortunate NCO from any harm. On their way to rescue Brackpool, Sergeant Vokes and his men had come under fire from an enemy machine gun in a bunker and had distinguished themselves by knocking it out, killing two enemy and taking the remainder prisoner.

As 3 PARA dropped at El Gamil, Captain Murray de Klee and his stick from No. 1 (Guards) Independent Company jumped from their French Air Force transport over El Raswa. As they did so they encountered heavy anti-aircraft fire, which was answered by the men of 11e Choc and Colonel Chateau-Jobert's 2e RPC firing their sub-machine guns as they hung below their parachutes. When they reached the ground the French troops immediately went into action, clearing the enemy and seizing the two bridges which were their objectives. As de Klee and his men landed, Guardsman Murphy was hit in the stomach as he landed near an Egyptian position. Captain de Klee and Lance Corporal McNab carried him to safety after the Egyptian position had been knocked out by the French. At 0800 hours, after gathering the rest of his patrol, de Klee headed south down the Treaty Road. After covering six kilometres they espied a small hut which was found to contain explosives, and discovered that the road had been prepared for demolition by the Egyptians, who were conspicuous by their absence. By 1230 hours the patrol had covered ten kilometres. After crossing a footbridge it turned and headed northwards up the Canal Road, still seeing no sign of Egyptian troops but again finding that the road had been prepared for demolition at the six-kilometre point. On his return, de Klee reported that the roads leading south were clear.

As dusk fell at 1530 hours, 3 PARA consolidated in the area of the sewage farm. The battalion had advanced beyond its originally stated objectives into the area designated for naval bombardment on the following morning, and thus had to withdraw from the area of the apartment blocks and coastguard barracks. B and C Companies held the right and left hand ends of the sewage farm respectively, while A and D Companies had established themselves in positions at the eastern and western ends of the airfield. Battalion Headquarters and No. 3 Troop of 9th Parachute Squadron RE were located on the airfield itself.

During the night Brigadier Butler and Colonel Chateau-Jobert attempted to negotiate a ceasefire with the commander of the Egyptian forces in Port Said. At one point it seemed as though they would succeed, but a telephone call from the Egyptian president put paid to their efforts. Nasser himself spoke personally to the Egyptian commander, forbidding him to surrender and informing him that Soviet and Egyptian troops were on their way as reinforcements. This outrageous lie was reinforced by the Russian Consul in Port Said, Anatoli Tchikov, who took to the streets and distributed weapons, proclaiming that the Third World War had started and that London and Paris would be attacked by Soviet missiles. Consequently the negotiations failed, and the fighting continued, some of it taking place between the Egyptians themselves as old scores were settled.

Dawn on 6 November was signalled by a surprise low-level attack by an Egyptian MiG fighter, which strafed the airfield but caused no damage. Later in the morning, however, the aircraft returned and carried out a further attack in which one soldier was wounded.

At 0700 hours the amphibious landings began, facilitated by the absence of Egyptian beach defences, which had been cleared by 3 PARA or knocked out by Fleet Air Arm airstrikes on the previous day. The Machine Gun Platoon, under Captain Mike Newall, provided covering fire for 42 and 45 Commandos RM as they landed, while C Company sent a fighting patrol into the area of the cemetery to reoccupy it. A two-platoon attack was mounted on the apartment blocks and coastguard barracks to clear out some snipers, and a patrol was then sent forward to seal off the slum area further to the east. Meanwhile, A Company stood by to advance south down the western side of the canal if required.

A link-up between 3 PARA and the Royal Marines was supposed to take place soon after the landings, but the latter encountered opposition in the town. Accordingly, Lieutenant Colonel Crook decided to push forward to make contact with the commandos. To do so, however, 3 PARA had to move through an area in which there was a hospital, the large slum area and a police barracks. The main road entering Port Said from the east forked, and the hospital lay within the fork itself. To the right of it was the slum area, with the police barracks beyond to the south. A fighting patrol from C Company, under Lieutenant Jack Richardson, the commander of No. 8 Platoon, was sent forward to effect the link-up. It advanced along the left of the main road, moving through some buildings near the beaches until it came under heavy fire from a machine gun at the far end of the hospital and was pinned down. Using fire and movement, Richardson and his men managed to work their way forward and eventually succeeded in entering the hospital itself, where they found terrified patients who had been deserted by the medical staff. At that point the patrol came under very heavy fire from the slum area and the police barracks, Private Penning being wounded in the hand. Richardson and two others, Sergeant Read and Corporal Stead, pushed on and crossed over the road from the hospital into the slum area, taking shelter in the nearest buildings. As the three men moved round the corner of a house they came under fire and Richardson was wounded by a rocket which hit his rifle and severely injured his hand, although it failed to explode. At the same time, Corporal Stead was wounded by a bullet which shattered his elbow.

Fortunately for the patrol Captain Malcolm Elliott, an anaesthetist with the 23rd Parachute Field Ambulance field surgical team, happened to arrive upon the scene in a jeep. Elliott had been en route to the hospital in a search for medical supplies and, after borrowing the jeep belonging to 3 PARA's Adjutant, Captain Gerald Mullins, had driven forward through C Company and had unwittingly proceeded into enemy-held territory. Subsequently, he had come under fire at close range from the Egyptian machine gun sited at the far end of the hospital buildings. Withdrawing at top speed, Elliott and his driver had met some members of No. 8 Platoon sheltering behind a high wall beside the hospital. After returning to C Company's headquarters and briefing Major Ron Norman on the situation regarding Richardson's platoon, Elliott had returned to the hospital, where he learned of the plight of Richardson and his two NCOs. Without hesitation, he drove the jeep across the road and parked under cover before entering the house where the three men were sheltering. After rendering first aid, Elliott loaded the two wounded men aboard his vehicle. He then discovered that he was unable to engage the jeep's reverse gear. The only alternative was to continue driving forwards and turn round as swiftly as possible. Under covering fire from Sergeant Read and his Bren gun, Elliott succeeded in swinging the jeep round and headed at speed for

C Company's headquarters, where he deposited Lieutenant Richardson and Corporal Stead. On returning again to the hospital he was greeted with the news that Sergeant Read had been killed while giving covering fire. He immediately volunteered to recover Read's body, but was told that it would be futile as the sergeant was definitely dead.

Lieutenant Colonel Crook decided to call in an airstrike to suppress the strong opposition coming from the slum area and the police barracks. Unfortunately, his request was denied at higher level to "avoid further damage to civilian property", but he was still permitted to use his own weapons. Accordingly, he ordered one of the battalion's 106mm anti-tank-gun detachments to advance and bring down fire on the slums and police barracks. Five rounds had the required effect. The police barracks was nearly demolished and the slum area set ablaze, causing the Egyptian troops to evacuate them with all haste and flee southwards. C Company resumed its advance into the outskirts of Port Said, while B Company moved forward to the apartment blocks. Battalion Headquarters occupied a large building which was found to be a brothel, its only residents being a large colony of voracious fleas.

It transpired that Sergeant Read had not been killed, although he had been very badly wounded. On regaining consciousness Read discovered that the house in which he was lying was on fire. Unable to walk because one leg was useless, he crawled slowly out of the building and back along the road. Shortly afterwards he lost consciousness again, awaking to find a group of hostile Egyptians bending over him. Continuing his painful crawl, Read then encountered an enemy soldier, who approached him while pointing a rifle at him. With great presence of mind Read went through the motions of throwing a grenade, whereupon the Egyptian fled in haste. By then it was almost dusk. Waving his white handkerchief to avoid being shot at by his friends in C Company, Sergeant Read crawled on. Fortunately he was soon spotted, and a small group led by Major Ron Norman dashed forward to rescue him.

Meanwhile, 2 PARA had been waiting impatiently aboard the landing ship LST *Snowdon Smith*, on which Battalion Main and Tactical Headquarters and other advance elements were embarked, and the troop ship HMT *Empire Parkeston*, which was carrying the rest of the battalion. Late on the night of 3 November the two vessels sailed from Limassol, and at 0600 hours on the following morning they rendezvoused offshore with the convoy carrying the rest of the Anglo-French invasion force. At 1430 hours on the afternoon of 4 November the convoy set sail, and at 0500 hours on the morning of 6 November it anchored 15 miles offshore of Port Said. At 1000 hours news of 3 PARA's success was received by radio, although there was no news of 42 or 45 Commandos.

At 1230 hours 2 PARA's vessels were called forward and the battalion landed soon afterwards. The battalion concentrated by a large block of flats on the waterfront and waited for its transport to be unloaded. Whilst it did so, Major Jim Dunning, the commander of Headquarter Company, went forward to reconnoitre the route of the battalion's advance, as fighting was still in progress along it. At 1600 hours 2 PARA began its advance in the direction of Raswa, accompanied by Brigadier Butler and his tactical headquarters. The leading elements of the battalion were mounted in vehicles, but the main body was on foot. In the van was No. 1 (Guards) Independent Company, followed by B Company, Battalion Tactical Headquarters, A Company and C Company. During the advance No. 1 (Guards) Independent Company was fired on by snipers and a light machine gun. The fire was returned but the Commanding Officer, Lieutenant Colonel Bala Bredin, ordered the battalion to press on. Only one casualty was suffered: Major Roy Dorey, the commander of Support Company, was slightly wounded in the leg.

At approximately 1730 hours 2 PARA arrived at the two bridges at El Raswa held by French paratroops, and concentrated on the Treaty Road to the south. An hour later the battalion continued its advance, and at approximately 2130 hours it linked up with B Squadron 6th Royal Tank Regiment (6 RTR), which had leaguered up for the night. At that point an order came from Brigade Headquarters, stating that a ceasefire would come into effect at 2359 hours and that there was to be no move thereafter. This was due to the great pressure which by then had been brought to bear on the British and French governments by America and the Soviet Union, the latter demanding an immediate cessation of hostilities. The British and French had capitulated to these demands. This meant that there was no time to be lost in pressing on, in order that the battlion should advance to the open ground south of the causeway, where a bridgehead could be established before the ceasefire deadline. Such a bridgehead would be essential for any further operations which might be conducted thereafter. The main body of 2 PARA pushed on from El Raswa at 1900 hours, the battalion's small number of vehicles ferrying men forward, while B Company remained with 6 RTR. It was another three hours, however, before the tanks were ready to move. At 2230 hours they moved off with B Company, commanded by Major John Pine Coffin, riding on their backs. Attached to the company was a section of sappers of 9th Parachute Squadron RE who would deal with any mines that might be encountered. Just before the column moved off, Brigadier Butler came forward to the leading tank and joined B Company. It was not long before the tanks overtook the rest of 2 PARA as it marched south on foot. Soon afterwards, however, a convoy of assorted commandeered vehicles appeared, under the command of a staff officer, and the battalion scrambled aboard.

At 2359 hours the ceasefire came into effect and 2 PARA and its supporting units were forced to halt. However, they found themselves at no particular point on the canal road and the narrow width of the terrain, bordered on the left by the Suez Canal and on the right by the Sweet Water Canal, beyond which lay salt marshes, was such that there was no room for the battalion to deploy into defensive positions. Lieutenant Colonel Bala Bredin had intended that his battalion would reach El Qantara before the ceasefire came into force, but time had run out. However, Brigadier Butler, who was still accompanying the battalion, ordered him to continue the advance to El Cap, the next signal station on the canal, which lay 19 miles south of Port Said. There the ground widened out to a frontage of nearly 600m, which would allow limited deployment. El Cap was reached at 0200 hours on 7 November. The battalion consolidated there, B Company being sited forward 100 yards south of the station with a troop of tanks, while the Anti-Tank, Mortar and Machine Gun Platoons deployed to the rear. Battalion Headquarters established in the El Cap station, while A and C Companies deployed just beyond, in the area of the deserted village where 'A' Echelon was located in a school. A battery of 33rd Parachute Light Regiment RA arrived and took up positions on the forward edge of the village.

At midday a patrol of some 50 enemy, armed but dressed in civilian clothes, appeared through some trees along the bank of the canal across B Company's flank. The company held its fire as the enemy closed to within 50 yards of the forwardmost tank. Without warning, the patrol opened fire on the tank, wounding a 6 RTR sergeant. The second tank in the troop returned the fire, killing two enemy and wounding a third. B Company continued to hold its fire, although the enemy patrol and a 3-ton vehicle were in full view all the time.

On the following day Egyptian troops could be seen in a village to the west of El Cap. In addition, enemy vehicles and troops were also spotted in some woods to the battalion's front about two kilometres away. Major John Pine Coffin despatched a patrol under Lieutenant Douglas McCord to reconnoitre the ridgeline in front of 2 PARA, a distance of some 900 yards or so away, and to discover the whereabouts of the nearest Egyptian positions. As the patrol approached its objective it came under heavy fire from a position occupied by a large number of enemy. McCord and his men withdrew without returning the fire. Radio contact with B Company's head-quarters could not be established, so a runner was despatched to ask for artillery support to be made available, but in the event it was not required.

Two days later, on 10 November, B Company discovered that the Egyptians had advanced during the night and had taken up positions some 800 yards away. Shortly afterwards 2 PARA received an order from the brigade headquarters, forbidding any further patrolling. During the after-noon two war correspondents, one American and one French, drove along the road through the battalion's positions, ignoring all signals to stop. As they drove into the Egyptian positions, firing could be heard and the jeep was seen to plunge into the canal. It was subsequently confirmed that both correspondents had been killed. In the early hours of 11 November the Egyptians opened fire on the battalion's forward positions as it was preparing to hand over to troops of the 1st Battalion The Royal West Kent Regiment (1 RWK). This continued for four hours, during which 2 PARA replied with two belts of ammunition from one of its Vickers medium machine guns. At 0800 hours 1 RWK arrived and relieved 2 PARA, which subsequently concentrated at the hospital in Port Said at 1400 hours. At 1700 hours 2 PARA boarded the MV *New Australia* for the voyage back to Cyprus.

Meanwhile, while 2 PARA had been advancing southwards, 3 PARA had linked up with the Royal Marine Commandos in Port Said at dawn on 7 November. During the day the battalion moved into the town, where it came under command of 3rd Commando Brigade, commanded by Brigadier Rex Maddox RM. There it took over responsibility for a sector of the town, including the area in which it had fought earlier. For the next four days the battalion was employed in collecting weapons discarded by the Egyptian forces and enforcing law and order among the civilian population. On Friday 9 November A Company was despatched southwards to the canal station at El Tina, where it took up positions in support of 2 PARA, which was still deployed at El Cap, dug in over a 600-yard wide front facing Egyptian forces. Apart from the occasional violations of the ceasefire by the Egyptians, the only incident of note which took place was an unexpected visit by Brigadier Butler, who was accompanied by an attractive woman journalist from *Paris Match*. On entering the house occupied by Company Headquarters, the brigade commander and his companion discovered Major Mike Walsh and his second-in-command, Captain Peter Kingston, sharing a large double bed. Needless to say, this caused considerable mirth.

When 1 PARA landed, it moved westwards along the coast, where it took up positions. By then, however, world opinion and political pressure on Britain and France was such that the decision was taken to withdraw from the Canal Zone. On Monday 12 November, 16th Independent Parachute Brigade was embarked on the MV *New Australia* and sailed for Cyprus.

On arrival at Famagusta, a day later, the brigade encountered a strange reception when it was met by a detachment of Royal Military Police who were under orders to search all troops for captured weapons which had been kept as trophies. On seeing the heavy-handed 'Redcaps' starting to body-search his men, Lieutenant Colonel Paul Crook of 3 PARA lost his temper and ordered them to cease doing so. Ignoring the protests of the provost officer, Crook led his battalion back to Tunisia Camp at Nicosia. It later transpired that some of the French airborne troops, after returning to Cyprus, had sold some captured Egyptian weapons to EOKA, and the British military authorities had consequently overreacted.

All three battalions settled back into the routine of conducting internal security operations in Cyprus. In December 1 and 3 PARA returned to England, leaving behind 2 PARA who relieved the 1st Battalion The Gordon Highlanders on operations in the Troodos Mountains. 2 PARA had under command No. 1 (Guards) Independent Company and D Company of the 1st Battalion The Suffolk Regiment (1 SUFFOLK). As a result of the battalion's previous experience, the Commanding Officer had concluded that large-scale counter-terrorist operations were unlikely to succeed. He believed that the emphasis should be on patrols by night and platoon-level operations by day, with further patrols ready to deploy at very short notice, as soon as information was received of terrorists and their whereabouts.

Towards the end of the month it was decided to adopt the tactic of descending without warning on villages known to support EOKA. This would be carried out during the early evening, when terrorists were most likely to appear to replenish their supplies. One area, the mountain of Papoursa, was known to be the hiding place of one particular EOKA gang headed by a much-wanted terrorist named Afxentiou. Intelligence had already indicated that the villages in the area, including those of Alona, Askas, Agros, Zoopiyi, Platanistassa, were involved in supporting the terrorists.

In the following weeks approximately 20 villages were visited each week between 1800 and 2000 hours. The methods used were varied, and former EOKA collaborators were moved in front of the troops to lull the local inhabitants into a false sense of security. These operations resulted in early successes, including the killing of a wanted terrorist at Zoopiyi and the discovery of an arms cache. A further series of operations, combined with night ambushes, led to the discovery of arms and terrorist hides in the area of Ayios Theodoros. As the suspect area on the Papoursa mountain was narrowed down, Operation 'Dragonfly', involving four of 2 PARA's companies, was mounted. Helicopters were used and a contact took place with Afxentiou's gang, which unfortunately escaped.

Further intelligence led 2 PARA to the area of Alona and Askas, this being subsequently narrowed down to the Platanistassa area, where more hides and caches were uncovered, yielding arms, explosives and equipment. At the same time the security forces began to accumulate information about the presence of terrorists and hides in the area of Kannavia and Sarandi. On the night of 18 January a raid on Kannavia resulted in the capture of three armed men who subsequently revealed the whereabouts of a wanted man named Karadimas and three others. On the same night, fortune was again on the side of the security forces when a patrol of D Company 1 SUFFOLK spotted a figure entering its area just after it had taken up its ambush positions. On being challenged the figure, who appeared to be armed, escaped. Later that night another D Company patrol observed a lone figure walking into its ambush and opened fire. The soldiers remained in position for the rest of the night, and it was not until dawn that they went forward to identify the body lying only a few yards away. When they did so, they realised that they had killed Markos Dracos, the EOKA terrorist who, after Grivas himself, was the most wanted man on Cyprus. This was a major blow for the terrorists, and underlined the significant role played by 2 PARA during operations against EOKA.

JORDAN, 1958

In the summer of 1958 16th Independent Parachute Brigade, commanded by Brigadier Tom Pearson, was deployed once again at short notice to Cyprus, in readiness for possible operations in the Middle East after the outbreak of civil war in the Lebanon. The situation appeared to deteriorate further on 14 July, when King Faisal II of Iraq, together with most of his family and his Prime Minister, Nuri al-Sa'id, was murdered during a *coup d'etat* staged by Iraqi army officers led by General Abd al-Karim Qasim. The new military junta in Iraq allied itself with President Gamal Abd al-Nasser of Egypt in an anti-Western alliance, and at the same time announced their support for factions in Jordan which were calling for the overthrow of the government of King Hussein. The situation began to worsen rapidly, and on 16 July King Hussein asked Britain for military assistance.

The advance elements of 16th Independent Parachute Brigade Group, led by Brigadier Pearson and consisting of headquarters and signals personnel, arrived in Jordan on the following day, 17 July. Such was the speed of their move that they arrived before the Jordanian authorities had been appraised of it. Over the next two days the brigade, less 1 PARA, which remained in Cyrpus, arrived and was complete by 20 July. Accompanying it was No. 208 Squadron RAF, a ground-attack unit equipped with Hawker Hunters. It was also supported by the United States Air Force, whose Globemaster transport aircraft carried out a major airlift of men and equipment.

Based at the airfield at Amman, the brigade was given three tasks, namely: the security of Amman airfield, this being the responsibility of 2 PARA; the protection of King Hussein and members of his government; and the safeguarding of British residents in Jordan. The latter two tasks were carried out by a mobile force formed by 3 PARA and No. 1 (Guards) Independent Company under Major Johnny Retallack of the Welsh Guards. On 7 August reinforcements arrived in the form of the 1st Battalion The Cameronians (The Scottish Rifles) who arrived at Aqaba aboard HMS *Bulwark*, a commando carrier. Subsequently, the brigade was further strengthened by the arrival of 17th Field Battery RA, which arrived two weeks later.

During the next few weeks the political situation improved and the threat to King Hussein subsided. This enabled units to carry out training and the brigade to provide assistance to Jordanian hospitals and to the 500,000 refugees living in the country. King Hussein himself paid a formal visit to the brigade, being welcomed on his arrival by a guard of honour from 3 PARA. At the end of September it was announced that British forces would withdraw from Jordan, and the first elements departed on 20 October. 16th Independent Parachute Brigade Group departed by air between 25 and 29 October, returning to Cyprus. Subsequently it flew back to England, leaving behind in Cyprus 1 PARA, which followed it in March of the following year.

CHAPTER 12

Operations in the Middle East, Cyprus, the Far East, British Guiana and Anguilla, 1961–1969

THE PERSIAN GULF 1961–64

n 1961 trouble flared up once again in the Middle East, when Iraq threatened to annexe the tiny oil-rich emirate of Kuwait, which it had long coveted. On 19 June the Emir, Sheikh Abdallah al-Salem al-Sabah, declared independence from Britain. He had, however, taken the precaution of signing a treaty with the British in which the latter would come to Kuwait's aid if it was threatened. In Baghdad the British Ambassador, Sir Humphrey Trevelyan, made it very clear to the Iraqis that any threat to Kuwait would be met by British military intervention. He recommended to his own government that the commando carrier HMS *Bulwark*, which was due to arrive in Kuwait on 4 July, be despatched to the emirate immediately. However, it was soon appreciated in London that Iraqi forces could arrive in Kuwait City after an advance of only a few hours from the border. Shortly afterwards, a formal request for assistance was received from the Emir. It was thus decided to fly in troops as quickly as possible from a number of British outposts, including Aden, Bahrain, Cyprus and Kenya. These units formed an *ad hoc* brigade group under Brigadier Derek Horsford. Among those units flown in from Cyprus was 2 PARA, commanded by Lieutenant Colonel Frank King, which landed at the airport in Kuwait and subsequently deployed to a feature called the Matla Ridge, about 40 miles to the north of Kuwait City. This was about 2,000 yards long and straddled the only good approach which could be used by Iraqi armour.

Within five days of the Emir's request for assistance, 8,000 British troops had deployed to Kuwait. In addition to HMS *Bulwark*, which arrived shortly after the leading troops, a naval task force, which included the aircraft carrier HMS *Victorious*, also took up position in the Gulf. These deployments proved effective as a deterrent against an Iraqi invasion of Kuwait, and by 14 July 2 PARA had moved to Bahrain, where it was based at the airfield at Muharraq. During the next few weeks the battalion carried out training which was interrupted by another tour of duty on the Matla Ridge. In October 3 PARA arrived to relieve 2 PARA, which returned to Cyprus towards the end of the month, and remained in Bahrain until May of the following year, when it handed over to 1 PARA.

These short tours in the Middle East provided valuable opportunities for training in a desert environment. Exercises, several of which included parachute drops, were frequently conducted with the RAF and Royal Navy, as well as with local forces such as the Trucial Oman Scouts and the Sultan of Oman's Armed Forces. Apart from training, there was little else for the parachute battalions, which were carrying out short tours of duty unaccompanied by their families. Bahrain itself did not have much to recommend it, offering little in the way of social life and possessing a climate which was uncomfortably hot for the majority of the year. It was not until early 1964 that appropriate air-conditioned accommodation became available. In April 3 PARA took over again from 2 PARA, bringing some of its families with it. In early 1964 D Company 2 PARA, under Major Jim Burke, was deployed to Aden, in readiness to carry out an airborne operation on the island of Zanzibar, where a Communist-led revolt was in progress. In the event the airborne operation was not required.

1 PARA OPERATIONS IN CYPRUS, 1964

Towards the end of December 1963 the political situation in Cyprus worsened, and violence broke out between the Greek and Turkish elements of the population. The two British battalions stationed on the island were interposed as a peacekeeping force along what became known as the "Green Line", which had been drawn by Major General Peter Young, the General Officer Commanding Cyprus. This divided the city of Nicosia into two halves, with the Turks in the northern half and the Greeks in the south. Initially the British intervention was welcomed, but it was not long before such sentiment was replaced by suspicion and distrust as both Turkish and Greek Cypriots realised that the "Truce Force", as the troops were called, were impartial and would not be aiding either side in its respective aims.

Further battalions arrived from Britain as reinforcements. Among them was 1 PARA which, having been recalled from leave on 1 January 1964, arrived on the island three days later. The battalion, commanded by Lieutenant Colonel Pat Thursby, initially moved to Dhekelia. It spent two weeks there, patrolling into towns such as Paphos and into Nicosia. On 26 February it moved to Nicosia, where it relieved the 1st Battalion The Gloucestershire Regiment and the 1st Battalion The Rifle Brigade. D Company, commanded by Major Joe Starling, had responsibility for the area of Neapolis, while C Company, under Major Mike Heerey, looked after Trakonas. Major Geoffrey Dockerell and Support Company established themselves in a flour mill in the Turkish sector of the city. A Company, under Major Colin Wallace-King, a Coldstream Guards officer on secondment to 1 PARA, was despatched initially to the southern region to carry out any task required of it. Thereafter it was moved to the area of Kokkina Tremetia, a Turkish enclave.

Not long after the battalion arrived in Nicosia, C Company were despatched to evacuate a group of British civilians working in a tin mine at Limni, north of Paphos, who were unable to leave owing to the deteriorating situation in the area. After deploying to the mine, the company called in RAF Whirlwind helicopters, which evacuated the civilians to safety. Four days later C Company withdrew to Nicosia and rejoined the battalion on the Green Line. There it took over the area of

Ayios Nicholaos, establishing itself in houses which had been deserted by their Turkish or Greek Cypriot occupants. On the day C Company arrived, there was a major outbreak of fighting with heavy firing between Turkish and Greek positions. When this died down, a number of Cypriots were found lying in the streets, many of them women. Another major incident occurred in Limassol, when Greek Cypriots used armoured bulldozers to launch an attack on Turkish elements. It so happened that some 130 British families lived in the area where the fighting was taking place, and were trapped in their homes. Support Company was sent in to quell the fighting, which it did by threatening to open fire on both sides. After two days the situation was sufficiently calm to allow the families to be evacuated.

1 PARA had by now developed its own methods of keeping the peace. It discovered that, when its own positions were being sniped at by either side, a few well-placed rounds placed close to a sniper's location was the most effective response. On one occasion the sight of one of the battalion's Mobat 120mm anti-tank guns being brought to bear caused one particular group of snipers to cease fire abruptly.

In March the United Nations assumed responsibility and, along with other British units, 1 PARA was transferred to UN command. A few weeks later the battalion was withdrawn into reserve after handing over its area of responsibility to the Canadian Royal 22nd Regiment. A month later, on 5 May, the battalion flew home to England.

3 PARA OPERATIONS IN THE RADFAN, 1964

In April 1964 3 PARA was deployed to Aden to take part in an operation in the Radfan, the mountainous area which lies some 50 miles to the north of Aden itself. Inhabited by tribes who are almost constantly at war with one another and owe allegiance only to their own chiefs, the Radfan is an extremely inhospitable region through which winds the Dhala Road, an ancient trade route from the Indian Ocean to the Yemen and one of the traditional routes to Mecca. Scattered throughout the mountains are villages of stone houses, each one fortified because of the interminable feuds which have been waged between families and tribes since time immemorial.

The Radfan formed part of what were then the Aden Protectorates, which were under British rule. With the exception of Aden itself, which was a British colony, these were administered by the local rulers under the watchful eyes of political officers in each state. In the early 1960s the protectorates had been brought together to form the Federation of South Arabia. The Aden Protectorate Levies, a local force previously raised by the British, became the Federal Regular Army (FRA), and the local forces maintained by state rulers were incorporated into a new force called the Federal National Guard (FNG). British forces were stationed in Aden, from where they were deployed in the Radfan and other states in support of the FRA and FNG.

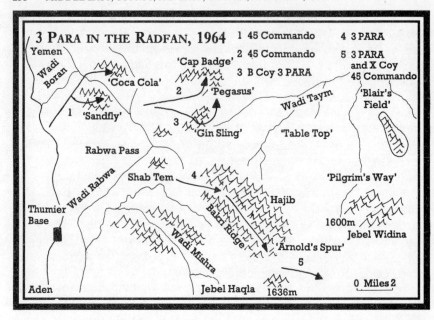

In 1963 trouble had flared up when the principal tribe in the Radfan, the Quteibi, known as the 'Wolves of The Radfan', caused trouble on the Dhala Road by stopping caravans and extorting tolls in defiance of newly introduced laws forbidding such acts. The tribesmen further vented their displeasure by shooting up convoys and mining the road. They were covertly supported in their campaign of insurrection by Egypt which, with the assistance of the Yemen, which had long coveted the Aden Protectorates, was encouraging unrest within the newly formed federation. Egypt's intention was to separate the federation from British dominance and to install a regime sympathetic to its own aims. The Egyptians were encouraged in this by the Russians, as part of their long-term campaign to see the British withdraw east of Suez. The initial response from the British authorities was to send in FRA units. These achieved some success, but were subsequently withdrawn. The tribesmen, who were supplied with arms by the Egyptians and some of whom had received training in the Yemen, grew bolder and the tempo of attacks increased on convoys using the Dhala Road.

It was decided to suppress the insurrection by deploying British troops to the Radfan and quelling the tribesmen. The forces allocated to the task were 45 Commando Royal Marines, B Company 3 PARA, No. 3 Troop of A Squadron 22nd SAS Regiment and elements of the FRA. Christened 'Radforce', it was supported by an RAF ground-attack squadron of Hawker Hunters. Radforce's initial objective was an area of high ground which dominated the Danaba Basin and the Wadi Taym, both of which were tribal strongholds. The two main areas of the objective were codenamed 'Cap Badge' and 'Gin Sling' respectively. The plan called for 45 Commando RM to advance north in transport from a Radforce firm base at Thumier to an assembly area at Milestone 27. From there it would march during the night of 30 April to the high ground north of the Danaba Basin, where it would take two features codenamed 'Rice Bowl' and 'Sand Fly' by first light on 1 May. Meanwhile, a deception force would move up the Wadi Rabwa to give the impression that the main route of advance was via the Rabwa Pass. At 2359 hours on the night of 30 April B Company 3 PARA, commanded by Major Peter Walter, would parachute on to a dropping zone on the Wadi Taym to seize 'Cap Badge' by first light on 1 May. The DZ would have been marked and secured by a patrol of nine men from the SAS troop commanded by Captain Robin Edwards.

The operation ran into difficulties from the start. A convoy of armoured cars carrying the SAS patrol up the Wadi Rabwa came under heavy fire. While the fire was returned, Edwards and his men dismounted and escaped unseen into the darkness. By dawn the following day, having been hampered during the march by their signaller, who had developed symptoms of possible food poisoning, the patrol was concealed in two abandoned sangars (stone redoubts) about 1,000 yards above a small village called Shi'b Taym. Unfortunately, it was spotted during the morning by a tribesman herding goats, and shortly afterwards was pinned down by heavy fire. A battle developed and continued throughout the day, two members of the patrol being wounded and its signaller, Trooper Warburton, being killed. Despite the support of artillery and RAF Hawker Hunters, which attacked the tribesmen's positions, the patrol remained pinned down until just after dusk, when it broke out of its position. Captain Edwards was killed as it did so, but the remainder succeeded in escaping and making their way back to the firm base at Thumier.

As a result of the disaster which befell the SAS patrol, the original plan to drop B Company 3 PARA by parachute was cancelled, and the company travelled to Thumier by road on the evening of 30 April. Two days later, the company was preparing to carry out a fighting patrol at night. Meanwhile, supporting artillery was registering targets, with the guns firing ranging rounds on each. As they did so, a group of dissidents was spotted entering a wadi some two miles from the company's location. Major Peter Walter decided to capture them, and a patrol was dispatched to cut off their line of retreat while Captain Barry Jewkes and some of his platoon laid an ambush. However, the tribesmen foiled Walter's plan by disappearing into a nearby village. The Political Officer for the area refused to allow a search to be carried out, for reasons best known to himself. Captain Jewkes and his patrol proceeded to search and clear three other villages in the area. The third revealed signs of recent inhabitation and a hasty departure, with cooking fires still alight. Above the village, Jewkes and his men discovered fortified caves dug in the hillside. No dissidents were encountered, although a certain amount of sporadic and ineffective sniping was directed at the patrol as it returned to the company base.

On 4 May B Company set out on an operation under command of 45 Commando RM which involved the commandos carrying out a sweep of the area while the company infiltrated by night into the Wadi Taym. Two objectives were to be occupied — the features 'Cap Badge' and 'Gin Sling'. The approach march was long and arduous, with B Company bringing up the rear of 45 Commando. The final stage of the march involved the ascent of some cliffs in the dark, all the troops being heavily burdened with water and ammunition as well as weapons. At the rear of the column Major Peter Walter became irritated by the delays and seemingly incessant halts as the commandos began climbing the cliffs with the aid of ropes. Eventually losing his patience, Walter led his company to a flank and he and his men ascended the cliffs without ropes, overtook the commandos and headed for 'Cap Badge', which was B Company's objective. As the company moved on towards the village of El Naqil, which lay at the southern foot of 'Cap Badge', numbers of shadowy figures carrying lanterns could be seen hurrying through the darkness as tribesmen deployed to their defensive positions. On each occasion the company avoided any contact as it moved silently through the night towards its objective. Even when the tribesmen passed close by, Walter and his men held their fire and let them pass.

As dawn fell the leading platoon, commanded by Lieutenant Tom Walker, began skirmishing forward towards 'Cap Badge', the only cover being provided by bunds, small banks of stones or mud, which separated areas of cultivation. Individual soldiers dashed forward in bounds of a few yards from one bit of cover to the next, covered by others in their section who themselves ran forward as soon as the former had adopted firing positions. It was not long before the company was spotted and came under fire from tribesmen in a number of forts surrounding the village of El Naqil, which lay at the southern foot of 'Cap Badge', and in positions in the hillsides above as well as in the wadi behind it. The company was surrounded, with Lieutenant Tom Walker's platoon pinned down below the dissidents on the hillside and near one of the forts, which was about 300 yards away. In view of the lack of cover, Major Walter realised that the only avenue open to him was to put in an immediate attack on the fort. Led by their company commander, Lieutenant Walker's platoon skirmished forward, one section providing covering fire while the others advanced. On reaching the fort, Walter and his men fired through the apertures in the walls and threw grenades through the single entrance into the building. As they entered the fort they met its single occupant, a shocked and somewhat tattered chicken, making a rapid exit. The dissidents had beaten a hasty retreat.

Meanwhile, a number of tribesmen had left the village and taken up positions on the southern side of the wadi, from where they engaged the company from the rear, wounding two NCOs. At that moment Captain Barry Jewkes and his platoon, who were at the rear, rounded the spur which had until then concealed the scene of action from them. On seeing a group of dissidents working their way into positions to engage the rest of the company, the platoon opened fire and killed four of the tribesmen. The rest took cover behind a stone wall and returned the platoon's fire, but Jewkes and his men put in an immediate assault and killed or wounded most of the remainder as they fled. As the platoon reorganised, it came under fire from enemy mortars located in a village behind them, but there were no casualties. At this point, while engaging the enemy on the hillside above, the platoon called for air support, and shortly afterwards Hawker Hunters of No. 208 Squadron RAF hurtled in at low level to strafe and bomb the forts and village. Unfortunately for Company Headquarters, which had taken up a position inside the captured fort, it was discovered that its set of fluorescent cloth marker panels were with one of the artillery forward observation officers (FOOs), who was some 300 yards away. A member of Lieutenant Walker's platoon volunteered to fetch them and ran across to the opposite side of the wadi to the FOO's position, and back again under fire from the tribesmen. Happily, he survived unscathed and the marker panels were displayed on the fort in time to prevent the RAF from attacking it.

B Company then proceeded to clear the village, killing several dissidents in the process. However, it was still under accurate fire from snipers well concealed in sangars or caves on the hillside. Captain Jewkes arrived at Company Headquarters to make his report, as did Sergeant Baxter from one of the other platoons. As he left to return to his men, Baxter and two soldiers with him were hit by enemy fire. Immediately, Captain Jewkes ran out of the fort and dragged Baxter into cover, pulling in the other two wounded men with the help of two soldiers. Tragically, while administering morphia to Sergeant Baxter, Jewkes inadvertently exposed himself to enemy fire and was hit in the head by a sniper's bullet, which killed him instantly.

In the meantime 45 Commando RM had successfully carried out its night approach march and was ordered to halt after taking 'Sand Fly' and to secure another feature, codenamed 'Coca Cola', which lay a short distance to the east. By 0400 hours on 1 May the commandos had taken both objectives without encountering any opposition. During the afternoon 45 Commando's reserve company was landed on 'Cap Badge' by helicopter. Attacking the tribesmen from the rear, it succeeded in routing them. Subsequently, B Company was able to move out of its positions in El Naqil and join the comandos on its objective. In honour of the company's performance during this operation, El Naqil was christened 'Pegasus Village'.

As a result of the success of this operation, the British forces were subsequently able to dominate the Rabwa Pass and the Wadi Taym, at the same time controlling the Danaba Basin. Active patrolling uncovered caches of arms, ammunition and food, which were destroyed, but few enemy were encountered

On 11 May B Company was withdrawn to Bahrain while the rest of 3 PARA, less D Company, moved to Aden to take part in another operation in the Radfan. The commander of the forces in Aden, General John Cubbon, had decided that further operations with larger forces were required to suppress the troubles in the Radfan. Consequently, Headquarters 39th Infantry Brigade, commanded by Brigadier Cecil 'Monkey' Blacker, was flown out from Britain to command the expanded Radforce. The main objective was the Wadi Dhubsan, known to be one of the main base areas of the dissident tribesmen, who considered it virtually impregnable. Lieutenant Colonel Tony Farrar-Hockley, 3 PARA's Commanding Officer, accompanied two patrols and reconnoitred a route from a deserted village, Shab Tem, which provided a good approach on to the Bakri Ridge, which lay to the north-west of the Wadi Dhubsan. Some ten miles long and reaching 5,000 feet in height at the spur at its south-eastern end, the ridge descended steeply to the wadi below. The eastern side of the ridge consisted of a sheer escarpment.

On the night of 18 May 3 PARA started its advance. Despite the gradual slope of the ridge the going was rough, and the weather was extremely hot. Having been told that no medium-lift helicopter support was available, Lieutenant Colonel Farrar-Hockley decided to use one of his two companies as porters, carrying food, water and ammunition. The average load per man, in addition to personal weapons, was 90lb. By dawn on 19 May the battalion had covered 10,000 yards along the ridge. At this point Major Mike Walsh's A Company, which was 'portering', dumped its loads and returned for more stores. The advance continued during the night of the second day with C Company, commanded by Major Tony Ward-Booth, portering and A Company leading the way. In the van was a fighting patrol of No. 1 Platoon, commanded by Lieutenant Hew Pike, which had been given the task of capturing a feature called Hajib, approximately midway along the eastern escarpment of the ridge. As Pike and his men approached Hajib they came under fire from one of a number of stone towers guarding the feature. As the platoon engaged the tribesmen, fire from the artillery supporting 3 PARA landed uncomfortably close. During the ensuing action in the dark the tribesmen escaped, and Hajib was in the platoon's hands before dawn. On the next night the Anti-Tank Platoon, under CSM Arnold, was ordered to push on and occupy the spur overlooking the Wadi Dhubsan. En route to their objective, Arnold and his men encountered a group of 12 dissidents and succeeded in capturing three of them. The spur, which was subsequently christened 'Arnold's Spur', was occupied without further incident.

Three days later, on 23 May, the rest of 3 PARA continued its advance along the ridgeline until it came under fire from a fortified village, Quedeishi, which lay about a mile to the west of Arnold's Spur. The village was held by a group of tribesmen, some 50 in number, who were armed with automatic weapons. C Company was despatched to attack Quedeishi, supported by artillery and RAF Hunters. The tribesmen put up a stout resistance, withdrawing only after some of their positions had been destroyed from the air and they had been outflanked by A Company. C Company put in an assault on the village and took possession of it, whereupon A Company then advanced to 'Arnold's Spur', where it joined the Anti-Tank Platoon.

Brigadier Blacker decided that an operation would be mounted against the Wadi Dhubsan itself. 3 PARA, with X Company 45 Commando RM under command, would carry out an attack with the task of neutralising any opposition and destroying any supplies of arms and food found there.

Owing to the difficulties of supporting and resupplying it while in the wadi, the battalion was to withdraw within 24 hours. Rather than take the more obvious and easier route via approaches to the south-west, Lieutenant Colonel Farrar-Hockley decided to try and find one descending directly from Arnold's Spur down the escarpment to the wadi 3,000 feet below. Two reconnaissance patrols were sent out to find a usable route, and these discovered a very steep track which ended at the top of a small cliff. From there the route led via a gulley to the rear of a village called Bayn Al Gidr.

As dusk fell on 25 May C Company occupied the Jebel Haqla, which overlooked the Wadi Dhubsan from the west. Under cover of darkness the rest of the battalion descended the track and climbed down the cliff face with the aid of ropes. A Company's task was to clear the wadi up to a point where two stone towers guarded the approach to the main area of the valley. X Company of 45 Commando RM was due to be flown in by helicopter, but weather conditions prevented this and the commandos had to follow 3 PARA's route down the escarpment. A Company secured its objective without incident by 0600 hours on 26 May, and 30 minutes later X Company began its advance into the main wadi. For the first 1,500 yards the commandos encountered no opposition, but, as soon as they were beyond the cover of C Company's picquets on the Jebel Haqla, they came under fire from the area of a feature called La Adhab and the high ground which had not been occupied earlier. The dissidents, who possessed a small number of automatic weapons, numbered over 50, and soon pinned X Company down in the open.

Meanwhile, Lieutenant Colonel Farrar-Hockley and his Intelligence Officer, Lieutenant Ian McLeod, were airborne in a Scout helicopter. Having been given a grid reference of X Company's location by its commander, which indicated that the commandos were a long way out in front, the Commanding Officer was flying forward to see the company's progress for himself. As the aircraft flew low over the hills it came under fire from tribesmen and was hit in the fuel feed line, and fuel began to flow down over the aircraft's canopy. At the same moment, Lieutenant McLeod was hit in the wrist. The pilot of the Scout, Major Jake Jackson of the Army Air Corps, turned his aircraft and flew back until the commandos and elements of 3 PARA were spotted. Although the helicopter was losing power, Jackson succeeded in landing it safely near the leading elements of X Company, who provided covering fire for Lieutenant Colonel Farrar-Hockley and the others as they rapidly disembarked and ran for cover under fire. It transpired that the grid reference given by X Company over the radio was inaccurate by a margin of some 10,000 yards.

A Company moved round to some high ground to the left of X Company as a platoon of C Company did likewise on the opposite side of the wadi. Meanwhile, RAF Hunters were carrying out low level strikes, strafing the dissidents' positions, while the battalion's own mortars and supporting medium artillery also laid down fire. A and X Companies then pushed forward, and by 1400 hours the area had been taken and secured, the tribesmen having withdrawn. Casualties were light, totalling one killed and seven wounded, while enemy losses were estimated at six dead and an unknown number wounded. At first light on the following morning, 27 May, Major Jake Jackson started up his Scout helicopter, which had been repaired during the night by REME fitters flown in at last light on the previous day. To the relief of those watching, and to loud cheers, the aircraft lifted off steadily and flew away without mishap. 3 PARA and X Company then busied themselves with destroying stores of food found in the area and carrying out their various tasks before withdrawing to the Bakri Ridge. From there they were flown out on the following day by Wessex helicopters of No. 815 Naval Air Squadron to the Radforce base at Thumier, thereafter returning to Aden and then Bahrain.

On 8 June D Company 3 PARA was deployed to the Radfan under command of the 1st Battalion The Royal Scots. Between 14 and 18 June the company took part in a reconnaissance in force southwards through an area called the Shaab Lashab, during which light opposition was encountered from small groups of dissidents who contented themselves with sniping at long range. On completion of the operation, D Company returned to Bahrain and rejoined the battalion. It had been an arduous but successful two months for 3 PARA in the Radfan. In an operation which had cost it very light casualties, the battalion had played a major role in suppressing dissident operations and had struck a decisive blow against the dissidents themselves by capturing and destroying their stronghold.

BORNEO CONFRONTATION, 1963–66: NO. 1 (GUARDS) INDEPENDENT COMPANY OPERATIONS, 1964–65

January 1964 found No. 1 (Guards) Independent Company, commanded by Major John Head of the Irish Guards, deployed in Cyprus on internal security operations. Together with the rest of 16th Parachute Brigade, it had been recalled from Christmas leave in England and flown to the Sovereign Base Area at Dhekelia on 4 January. In the middle of December, intercommunal fighting had broken out between the Turkish and Greek elements of the Cypriot population. All telephone lines throughout the island had been cut, and rumours of massacres, arson, pillage and an impending invasion by troops from Turkey had served to heighten fears on either side. Both communities had sealed off their own areas, erecting barricades on all approaches to their villages and cutting all forms of communication.

The company's immediate task was to reopen the whole of the western sector from the other Sovereign Base Area at Episkopi, including the Troodos mountains. Thereafter, its role was to keep the peace between the Turkish and Greek elements of the population in the east of the island, in the area of Episkopi, Paphos and Troodos. It patrolled daily in its Land Rovers and Ferret scout cars, on several occasions intervening between the two factions and preventing violence. The company continued to carry out this task for the next five weeks until early February when, without any warning, it was ordered to return to Britain. Initially, no information was forthcoming to explain this abrupt move, save that the company was to retrain for "special operations in the Far East". A few days later, however, all was revealed, when it transpired that 22nd SAS Regiment (22 SAS) required an additional squadron for its operations in Borneo and that the company had been allotted the task.

For just over a year British forces had been involved in what was known as "Confrontation": a campaign against Indonesian forces on the island of Borneo. President Soekarno of Indonesia had long nurtured the ambition of building his own empire. Called "Maphilindo", it embraced the nations of Malaya, the Philippines and Indonesia. Also included in his ideal were the two British colonies of North Borneo and Sarawak, together with the tiny protectorate of Brunei. Soekarno's plans also included the withdrawal of British forces and military bases in Malaya and Singapore, but his calls for such were strongly opposed by the prime ministers of both countries, Tunku Abdul Rahman and Lee Kwan Yew, who were increasingly concerned by the threat from the rapid spread of communism in the region. Worried by Soekarno's increasingly aggressive posture, Tunku Abdul Rahman conceived the idea of a federation of the Malay states of Malaya, Sarawak, Sabah and Brunei, together with Singapore, under the name of Malaysia. Soekarno, who was under the delusion that the people of Sarawak, Sabah and Brunei would willingly cast off the yoke of colonialism and ally themselves with him, realised that such a federation would thwart his own plans, and thus decided to do his utmost to prevent its creation.

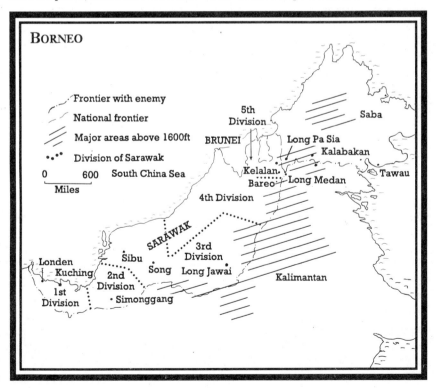

To that end, in December 1962 Soekarno supported a rebellion in Brunei by activists seeking to depose the Sultan. Indonesian forces had been secretly involved in the raising and training of an 8,000-strong force of rebels called the TNKU — the North Kalimantan National Army. However, the revolt had been crushed by British troops of 17th Gurkha Division and 42 Commando Royal Marines rapidly despatched from Singapore and Malaya. The Brunei Revolt was merely a prelude to the campaign which followed. Initially, the British Government underestimated the threat and tended to ignore the warnings sounded by the Director of Operations, Major General Walter Walker, who was under pressure to withdraw his troops to Singapore soon after the revolt had been crushed. Walker, however, was well aware that the leader of the Brunei Revolt, Yassin Affendi, was in the employ of Soekarno, and he was firmly of the opinion that a much greater threat would shortly be posed by the Indonesians themselves. In this he was proved right.

Two principal elements operated against the British and Malay security forces: the Indonesian forces, which initially provided training and commanders for groups of irregulars but subsequently deployed their own units, mainly para-commandos (RPKAD) or marines (KKO), and the Clandestine Communist Organisation (CCO). The latter was a predominantly Chinese organisation whose cells were mainly located in the towns of Sarawak. For some time the CCO had covertly established itself throughout the colony and Soekarno, although not a communist, had recognised in it a potential ally in his campaign against the federating of the Malay states.

It was not until April 1963 that the British Government started to take the situation in Borneo seriously. A group of irregulars, of the type designated by the British forces as Indonesian Border Terrorists (IBTs), crossed the border into Sarawak and attacked a police station. They had been trained by, and were led by, Indonesian regular troops, some of whom had been trained at the British Army's Jungle Warfare School at Johore Bahru in Malaya. In January 1963, the month following the Brunei Revolt, 22 SAS was deployed to Borneo. However, it soon found itself stretched in its task of providing four-man patrols to carry out surveillance along the lengthy border with Indonesia. Initially 'A' Squadron only was deployed, but, after the Indonesian cross-border raid in April 1963, 'D' Squadron was also despatched to Borneo. At that time the regiment consisted of only two squadrons and, bearing in mind its commitments elsewhere, including the Middle East, it soon found itself unable to cope with the demands placed upon it. Consequently, the regiment requested that it be augmented by units which could be converted relatively easily to the SAS role. Accordingly, No. 1 (Guards) Independent Company and the Gurkha Independent Parachute Company were selected for the task. At that time No. 1 (Guards) Independent Company's role in 16th Parachute Brigade was pathfinding, reconnaissance and anti-tank defence. It was organised into four patrols, each consisting of four Ferret scout cars, and an anti-tank troop equipped with 120mm Wombat anti-tank guns mounted on Land Rovers. On leaving Cyprus the company handed over its vehicles to an armoured squadron assigned to replace it, and on returning to Britain was reorganised into four troops, each of which consisted of four four-man patrols. Each man was trained in languages, signals, demolitions and as a medic, as well as in the tactical skills required for the new role. After two months of training at 22 SAS base at Hereford, the company flew out to Malaya, where it underwent a six-week jungle warfare course conducted by 22 SAS instructors. This culminated in a rigorous ten-day test exercise carried out under the critical eye of Lieutenant Colonel John Woodhouse, the SAS Commanding Officer.

Meanwhile, a small advance party under Major John Head was already at the SAS headquarters, at the 'Haunted House' behind the Sultan's palace in Brunei, familiarising itself with SAS operations along the border with Indonesia, gleaning as much information as possible about the area of operations allocated to the company, and laying plans for the deployment of patrols within it. At the same time, the administrative problems of supporting patrols in the jungle had to be considered and arrangements made for the construction of a base camp for the company.

On 8 May, having been passed as fit for its new role, the company moved to Borneo and deployed to Sibu, on the River Rajang, in what was known as the Third Division. There it was met by Lieutenant Colonel Corran Purdon, Commanding Officer of the 1st Battalion The Royal Ulster Rifles, based at Sibu, and his pipe band.

Sarawak was divided into five divisions for civil administration purposes, the First and Second Divisions facing the greatest threat from Indonesia. In the First Division the capital of Sarawak, Kuching, was only some 25 miles from the border. Moreover, half of the territory's population was concentrated in the First Division, including a number of Chinese who provided fertile ground for the CCO. Much of the First Division was under cultivation and accessible by roads which facilitated movement of troops to and from the border areas. Eastwards lay the Second Division, inhabited mainly by Iban tribes, and then the wildernesses of the Third and Fourth Divisions. The small Fifth Division covered the easternmost area of Sarawak around the protectorate of Brunei. Beyond lay the colony of Sabah. The length of the border separating Sarawak and Sabah from Indonesia was approximately 1,000 miles.

The company was responsible for the entire 300-mile stretch of border between the Third Division and Indonesia. Along much of it there was no habitation on the British-held side up to a depth of 80 miles. There were no roads, and tracks — other than those of animals — were few and far between. The main routes for communication and travel lay along the rivers, on the banks of which were scattered the longhouses of the different tribes: Ibans, Kenyas, Kayans, Ukits and Punans, each of which had its own language, as well as a smattering of Malay, and maintained its own traditions and taboos. The border itself followed no logical course, although it was intended to divide the headwaters which ran northwards towards the South China Sea and those that flowed southwards into Indonesian Borneo or Kalimantan. The boken ridge which separated these watersheds rose in places to a height of over 10,000ft, but this was not reflected on maps of the area, which showed no contours and possessed little detail other than the general flow of the main rivers. Nor did they indicate whether different areas were covered by primary or secondary jungle, the latter consisting of almost impenetrable undergrowth through which paths had to be cut. The main town in the Third Division was Sibu, on the River Rajang, which was the base for the British infantry battalion which provided platoons deployed to protect the forwardmost larger villages, or 'kampongs', against any incursions by the Indonesians. Also located there were elements of the Police Field Force and the Special Branch, who were engaged in combatting the internal threat from the CCO. Sibu had a small airport and a paddle-steamer service which operated between the town and the riverside villages and longhouses upstream. It thus offered an ideal site for the company base, and this was constructed on one of two crests of a hill called Bukit Lima, which lay just outside the town.

On 16 May the company deployed 16 patrols by helicopter to carry out surveillance along the mountainous border region in the Third Division. Eleven of these were positioned on the most likely crossing places, while a twelfth was attached to the nomadic Punan Busang tribe which roamed throughout an area of the border known as Ulu Danum. The remaining four patrols were deployed in depth, moving among the kampongs and longhouses and carrying out 'hearts and minds' operations, including the provision of medical aid and the gathering of intelligence. The patrols covering the border remained in the jungle for the entire duration of the company's tour of operations, being extracted only once for a week's rest and recuperation. Initially, the task which faced the patrols over such a vast area seemed overwhelming. However, the Indonesians, although numerically far stronger, were also faced with problems, the major one being the British forces' total air superiority, which denied Soekarno's forces helicopter support. For any incursion to take place, Indonesian forces first had to move up to the border before crossing over and making their way into British-controlled territory towards their target. The choice of routes open to them was limited to navigable waterways on both sides of the border, and naturally these were kept under surveillance both from the air and by patrols on the ground.

Support for the operations of No. 1 (Guards) Independent Company was provided by No. 845 Naval Air Squadron, commanded by Lieutenant Commander 'Tank' Sherman RN, which was also based at Sibu. A forward refuelling point was located at Long Jawi, and a forward supply base at Nangga Gaat, about an hour's flying time from Sibu. All patrols were resupplied by the flight of Wessex helicopters based there. The Fleet Air Arm pilots and their crews soon gained a reputation for never refusing a request for support, earning the company's gratitude and admiration in the process. They flew in even the worst of conditions of weather or failing light, frequently taking their aircraft into the smallest and most awkward of LZs or inching in under the jungle canopy to winch out a casualty. Resupply for the company was the responsibility of CQMS Smurthwaite,

Coldstream Guards. This involved collecting the containers of clothing, equipment, ammunition and lightweight rations which were air-dropped by RAF Argosies or Beverleys based at Kuching, 90 minutes' flying time away in the First Division. These were then broken down and repacked for despatch forward by helicopter to the individual patrol LZs. These deliveries also included other items important for the maintenance of morale, such as mail, one day's fresh rations, and items ordered by individuals from the NAAFI, as well as operationally important items such as new maps and written orders. Resupply took place every ten to fourteen days. Owing to the constant shortage of helicopter hours, any omission of anything other than the most essential of items could not be rectified until the next scheduled resupply mission. Such was CQMS Smurthwaite's meticulous attention to detail, however, that nothing ever went amiss.

Life for the patrols in the jungle was an unremitting round of moving through often difficult terrain for up to eight hours a day, clearing LZs for helicopters, laying ambushes, mapping previously uncharted terrain and coping with the difficulties of communicating by radio over distances of up to 250 miles. Responsibility for maintenance of the company's signals net fell upon Corporal of Horse Kersting of the Royal Horse Guards. He and his radio operators at the company's base worked round the clock, frequently receiving the weakest signals in adverse conditions and reacting to them immediately. Captain Tom Brooke of the Irish Guards commanded the patrol based at a boat station at Ulu Aput. This was considered to be the most likely trouble spot, so Brooke, a tough and irrepressible character, was allocated responsibility for that area. The patrol attached to the Punan Busang was commanded by Captain Algy Cluff, Grenadier Guards, who was renowned for his somewhat unorthodox attitude towards matters military. Other patrols were commanded by Captain Robin Dixon, Grenadier Guards, Captain Charles Fugelsang of the Coldstream Guards, and non-commissioned officers of the company.

In August the Indonesians escalated their campaign, intensifying their incursions and attacks along the Sarawak border and launching sea and airborne attacks on the Malayan mainland. These were unsuccessful, but deprived the Director of Operations of reinforcements which would otherwise have been available to him. By now the Indonesians were deploying units of their regular forces, which were well equipped and highly trained. However, by use of intelligence obtained from the border tribes, the British forces succeeded in remaining one jump ahead of the Indonesians and thus dominated the areas in which they operated. From August to the end of October No. 1 (Guards) Independent Company fulfilled its tasks of watching all the main river routes and crossing points, which by then had been thoroughly reconnoitred and sketched. This had resulted in very detailed maps, containing a wealth of information, being drawn up by CSM Woodfield, Grenadier Guards.

During the latter stages of this, its first tour of duty in Borneo, the company was permitted to take part in Operation 'Claret', the codename for cross-border operations into Indonesia. Until then, only patrols from 22nd

SAS Regiment had been operating on the other side of the border, but such was the company's performance in its new role that it was allocated three 'Claret' missions. One of these, Operation 'Annabel's' (named after the London nightclub frequented by officers of the Household Brigade), involved making contact with members of the Punan Busang tribe who inhabited an area called Long Kihan, which contained an Indonesian base for approximately 600 men. Captain Algy Cluff's patrol, which was living with the Punan Busang, was given the task of linking up with the other half of the tribe at Long Kihan to obtain information on the Indonesian base. However, a problem soon arose. The Sarawak-based Punan, somewhat shy and retiring people who avoided involvement with either side, were somewhat reluctant to lead British troops over the border into Indonesia. The situation was resolved by the company's Second-in-Command and Operations Officer, Captain The Lord Patrick Beresford of the Royal Horse Guards, who persuaded the Punan that the "Great White Queen" would be greatly pleased if they were to render assistance to her soldiers. This statement greatly impressed the tribesmen, who regarded the British Royal Family with great reverence, and they responded by presenting Beresford with a rotan mat as a gift for Her Majesty. This posed another problem, as he would obviously have to provide the Punan with some form of proof that the gift had been delivered. Accordingly, he contacted his mother in England who, at his urgent request, rapidly despatched to him a large photograph of himself shaking hands with Her Majesty The Queen after a polo match. The Punan were extremely impressed by the 'proof', and none of them questioned the fact that it had only taken a few days for their rotan mat to be presented by Beresford to the "Great White Queen" on the other side of the world and for him to rejoin them in the jungle.

Two patrols, commanded by Beresford and Cluff, were subsequently led over the border, and after five days' march into Indonesia reached a track on which lay a broken branch. This was a sign left by the chief of the Sarawak-based half of the tribe, who had gone ahead to warn those at Long Kihan of the troops' arrival, indicating to the patrols' guides that they were expected. Not long afterwards the two patrols met up with the tribesmen. Subsequently the Indonesian base at Long Kihan was reconnoitred, but was found to be unoccupied.

Towards the end of the company's tour of operations another 'Claret' mission was carried out by a patrol commanded by Captain Charles Fugelsang. Crossing the border near the boat station at Balui, the same crossing point used by a large Indonesian force which had attacked a Gurkha and Border Scout post at the village of Long Jawi in the Third Division in September the previous year, Fugelsang and his men reconnoitred the area up to a depth of 3,000 yards from the border. However, the nearest enemy positions were well into Indonesia, and the patrol saw nothing except items of discarded equipment left behind during the enemy's rapid withdrawal after the Long Jawi raid.

On 29 October No. 1 (Guards) Independent Company handed over to the Gurkha Independent Parachute Company and left Borneo, returning via Singapore to England, where it arrived on 9 November. However, it was not long before the SAS once again required the company's services. In March 1965 Major John Head was told that the company was to carry out a second tour in Borneo. This time it would be based at the 'Haunted House' in Brunei and its patrols would be deployed in the more active Fifth Division of Sarawak. It was to leave one troop behind to carry out pathfinding duties with 16th Parachute Brigade, and No. 1 Troop, commanded by Captain Tom Brooke, was allocated this task. Major Head and his advance party flew out to Borneo and began the process of taking over from the Australian SAS squadron which the company was to relieve. On 24 June the main body arrived under Captain John Magnay, Grenadier Guards, who had taken over as Second-in-Command from Captain The Lord Patrick Beresford. Other newcomers to the company included Captain Roger Gabb, Welsh Guards, Captain Mark Carnegie-Brown, Scots Guards, who had taken over as Operations Officer, and Captain Gordon Mitchell, Scots Guards, the company's new Administrative Officer.

During this second tour only 12 patrols were deployed, in most instances for short periods on specific tasks such as 'hearts and minds', intelligence gathering or border surveillance. On a number of occasions patrols were despatched over the border on Operation 'Claret' missions. The company had established a forward operating base at Pensianggan, just under 12 miles north of the border. Patrols were flown in RAF Twin Pioneer or Army Air Corps Beaver aircraft from Brunei to Sepulut, some 16 miles north-east of Pensianggan, and from there were flown by helicopter to the forward operating base. Two of the company's signallers were located at Pensianggan, which was also the base for a company of Gurkhas.

Four of the 'Claret' missions were carried out by Captain Charles Fugelsang's troop. The first, which proved somewhat uneventful, involved carrying out a search for an enemy position which had been established north of the river across the border directly south of Pensianggan. In the event, the patrol was unable to find the site before the rations were exhausted and it was forced to return to Sarawak. After two days at its Brunei base, the patrol was reinserted and successfully located the enemy position. After two days spent observing it, Fugelsang and his men withdrew.

The next 'Claret' mission proved more fruitful. On this occasion Fugelsang led a patrol across the border west of Bareo, which lay near the border some 70 miles to the south-west of Pensianggan. He was accompanied by a section of Gurkhas whose task it was to secure the LZ, on the border, into which the patrol flew by helicopter from Pensianggan. The patrol's mission was to observe an Indonesian airstrip and to bring down fire from a 105mm pack howitzer sited on a ridgeline to shell both the airstrip and some track junctions in the area. On one occasion while the airstrip was under fire, the Indonesians attempted to reinforce the garrison by dropping paratroops from a C-130 transport. Unfortunately the defenders were under the impression that they were being bombed, and opened fire on the aircraft with their 12.5mm anti-aircraft machine guns, hitting it and causing it to crash.

The third mission lasted ten days. Accompanied by a platoon of Gurkhas, Fugelsang's troop crossed the border to lay an ambush on a track to the rear of the Indonesian position which he had located on his first Claret mission of the tour. The Gurkhas would establish a base while Fugelsang and his men moved further into Indonesia to set up their ambush. After three days, not having located any tracks, Fugelsang was convinced that he must be nearing his objective. Taking three Gurkhas, including the platoon commander, and two of his own men, he went forward while the remainder of the force set up a firm base. After about an hour he found a track on a ridgeline which looked promising. Keeping away from the track but deploying the three Gurkhas on either side as stops, he started to consider his next course of action. At that point the Gurkha to his left opened fire and killed two Indonesians moving south down the track. Having been compromised by the sound of the firing, Fugelsang had no choice but to withdraw, as there were obviously other enemy troops in the vicinity. Rejoining the main body as quickly as possible, he led his force back to the border, which was reached two days later after a river crossing made hazardous by two days of heavy rain.

The fourth and final Operation 'Claret' mission carried out by the same troop involved moving through some very difficult terrain which was very badly mapped and in which there was very little 'pattern' to the hills. Consequently, navigation was extremely difficult. The troop's mission was to ambush a track some 9,000 to 10,000 yards over the border, which was believed to be in use by Indonesian units. After ten days or so of searching, however, Fugelsang and his men were unable to find the track and returned to the border LZ into which they had been inserted by helicopter. On the following morning a sentry observing the LZ spotted movement and opened fire on what he believed to be a figure wearing Indonesian camouflage uniform. A platoon of Gurkhas was flown in and the surrounding area searched, but nothing was found.

There were a number of contacts between the company's patrols and the Indonesians, the most serious of which took place on 15 September. A reconnaissance patrol had located a large Indonesian position, estimated to be that of a company, and a company of Gurkhas was tasked with attacking it. Major John Head decided to insert two patrols, under Sergeant McGill, Scots Guards, to the rear of the enemy position to lay an ambush on a river track. They were to destroy any enemy as they withdrew after being attacked by the Gurkhas. The two patrols were inserted four days beforehand. At approximately 0900 hours on the 15th a group of six enemy lead scouts were seen approaching the ambush area. They were moving cautiously, searching the ground carefully, and it was obvious to McGill and his men that the group was the advance element of a large force. About ten minutes later the leading scout encountered the right hand stop group, which consisted of Sergeant Mitchell, Irish Guards, and another member of his patrol. He was shot dead immediately, whereupon the remaining five scouts charged the ambush position. Four were killed at point blank range.

At this point there was a brief lull, during which the enemy main body, which numbered about 50, could be heard and eventually seen moving forward to attack and outflank the ambush position. At the same time, very heavy small-arms and light mortar fire was brought down. Realising the enemy's intentions, McGill withdrew both patrols, using fire and movement, until they reached dead ground and were able to break contact with the enemy. Thereafter the patrols dispersed and headed for their emergency RV, which had been selected beforehand. One man, Guardsman Shepherd of the Coldstream Guards, realised that he was being pursued by some Indonesians and swiftly took up an ambush position. As his pursuers came into view he opened fire and killed two of them before continuing on his way.

On receiving the patrol's contact report, Major John Head had flown forward by helicopter from his headquarters at the 'Haunted House' to the company's forward operating base at Pensianggan. There he waited anxiously for news of the two patrols, whom he knew would be heading for their emergency RV as the first step in withdrawing from the area. The Gurkha company based there had meanwhile deployed patrols forward as a protective screen. To the relief of all concerned, both patrols appeared and moved safely through the Gurkhas' positions on the morning of the following day. Sergeant McGill was subsequently awarded the Military Medal for his exemplary leadership under fire.

At the end of October No. 1 (Guards) Independent Company completed its second tour of operations and left Borneo. Departing on 2 November and again travelling via Singapore, it arrived in England on 6 November. During both tours it had acquitted itself well, and had impressed the SAS with its professionalism to the extent that, when asked by the Director of Operations as to its capabilities, the Commanding Officer of 22 SAS, Lieutenant Colonel Mike Wingate Gray, replied: "They can do anything an SAS squadron can do". This was a very great compliment.

There was a postscript to the company's involvement in Borneo Confrontation. In September 1965 Major General John Nelson, the Major General Commanding The Household Brigade, had visited the company in Borneo. As the Commanding Officer of 1st (Guards) Parachute Battalion, he had been responsible for the formation of the company during the disbandment of his unit, and had taken a keen interest in it ever since. During his visit, Major General Nelson informed Major John Head that the SAS wished to form a Guards squadron from the company. After some deliberation and discussion, Nelson and Head agreed that volunteers should be called for from the company to form the new unit. Consequently, in January 1967, Captain Charles Fugelsang and Sergeant Mitchell, together with a troop of volunteers, departed for 22 SAS's base at Hereford. They formed the nucleus of what subsequently became G Squadron, commanded by Major Murray de Klee, Scots Guards, who had served previously with No. 1 (Guards) Independent Company in the mid-1950s and as a member of it had taken part in Operation 'Musketeer' at Suez in 1956.

GURKHA INDEPENDENT PARACHUTE COMPANY
OPERATIONS IN BORNEO, 1964–65

The Brunei Rebellion in December 1962 had highlighted the requirement for an airborne unit to be based in the Far East. The initial action by British units in the southern part of the tiny protectorate had taken the form of an assault on an airfield at Anduki, a short distance form the town of Seria. The 1st Battalion The Queen's Own Highlanders had landed in an RAF Beverley transport, going straight into the attack as soon as the aircraft came to a halt. The Highlanders were fortunate in that the rebels holding the airfield were taken by surprise. Had they been alert, the consequences could have been disastrous. Landing on an airfield held by the enemy is a questionable tactic to say the least, and such a situation clearly calls for the use of paratroops. It was subsequently decided, therefore, to form a parachute unit for such a role from British Army resources in the Far East, and the task was given to the Brigade of Gurkhas.

The Gurkha Independent Parachute Company was formed on 1 January 1963, and comprised men recruited from all eight infantry battalions and corps units of the Brigade of Gurkhas. Parachute training was carried out in Malaya, a selection course having been established at Johore Bahru under Captain Bruce Niven of the 10th Princess Mary's Own Gurkha Rifles, who had already undergone parachute training at No. 1 Parachute Training School in England. Under the command of Major Peter Quantrill, 6th Queen Elizabeth's Own Gurkha Rifles, the company was initially employed in an infantry role. Shortly afterwards, however, it was redeployed in the First and Second Divisions of Sarawak, where its members were split into groups of two or three tasked with training and commanding sections of the Border Scouts, auxiliary units formed from local tribesmen in the kampongs along the border with Indonesia.

In late 1963 it became apparent that morale in the company was low and that the Gurkhas were not happy working with the Border Scouts. Their task was an unenviable one: trying to carry out surveillance over large areas of the border while attempting to train and lead groups of Ibans of whom they knew little and of whose loyalty they were uncertain. Moreover, the Ibans were unused to military discipline and could at times be somewhat temperamental. The Gurkhas' misgivings about the Border Scouts appeared to be justified to a certain extent when, on 28 September 1963, a strong force of Indonesian irregulars attacked a post at the village of Long Jawi, in the Third Division, which was manned by 21 Border Scouts, a detachment of four Gurkhas and two radio operators of the Police Field Force (PFF). As with all posts, communications were maintained by radio with the Border Scout headquarters at Belaga, some 70 miles to the north-west. However, such links were frequently difficult to maintain and were via high-frequency (HF) radios using Morse on carrier wave (CW) only. Owing to the problems caused by atmospherics, which often resulted in operations being unable to get through, the practice of sounding the alarm when a post failed to make contact was discontinued.

Long Jawi was visited on 25 September by Captain John Burlison of the 1st Battalion 2nd King Edward VII's Own Goorkhas, which was providing the Gurkha detachment. Burlison, who was based at Belaga, brought with him a corporal to relieve the NCO commanding the post and a two-man Bren gun group as reinforcements. On his arrival he was alarmed to find that the post's headquarters and signals centre were established in the village's small school hut beside the main longhouse. He decided to move the post to a small hill a short distance to the east, which would provide a good defensive position. On the night of the 25th Burlison managed to persuade the villagers, who had previously been somewhat unhelpful, to assist in constructing the new defensive positions on the hill. When he departed on the 27th, five trenches had been dug and a new command and signal centre were nearly completed. The Gurkha corporal commanding the post moved his force, less the three signallers, into the new position.

Unbeknown to Burlison or any of those manning the post, however, a reconnaissance patrol from a large Indonesian force had been hiding in the village during his visit. At 0530 hours on the morning of 28 September the alarm was raised by one of the Border Scouts who, against the post commander's orders, had visited his sick wife in the longhouse. Having spotted the enemy force moving into position to attack, he slipped back to the post. As the Indonesians opened fire with automatic weapons and light mortars, the three signallers in the signals hut by the longhouse frantically tried to establish contact with the headquarters at Belaga, but without success. Shortly afterwards a group of enemy attacked the signals hut and opened fire, killing the Gurkha signaller and one of the PFF operators. The second policeman was wounded in the knee, but managed to drag himself under covering fire to the position on the hill.

Shortly afterwards the Border Scouts started to slip away from the position and make their way, in the cover of dead ground, to a stream to the south of the position. However, the Indonesians had established a stop group which captured all of the fleeing scouts except one who, on seeing his comrades' fate, returned to the position. For two hours the defenders, who by then comprised the six Gurkhas and the one Border Scout, put up a stout resistance against a force of 150 Indonesian troops. By 0800 hours, however, one Gurkha had been killed and two others wounded, leaving only three Gurkhas in a fit state to fight. They had already beaten off one assault and were down to only a few rounds per man. At this point the post commander decided to withdraw and, dragging the two wounded men, the three Gurkhas and the Border Scout slowly made their way down from the position into the cover of the jungle. An hour later the enemy attacked the position, but found it abandoned. After looting it and setting the command and signals hut on fire, they brought down heavy fire on the surrounding area for the rest of the day, doubtlessly in the belief that the Gurkhas were still there. After tending the two wounded and concealing them in the jungle, the three Gurkhas and the Border Scout set off for the next Border Scout post at Long Linau. Two days later they reached the village of

Kampong Labuai, where they managed to borrow a longboat. Four days after the action they reached Long Linau and the alarm was raised.

After plundering Long Jawi, the Indonesians returned to the base which they had established five miles upstream of the village. However, one of the captive Border Scouts managed to escape from one of the enemy boats and subsequently provided valuable information which helped pinpoint the enemy base. Lieutenant Colonel Johnny Clements, Commanding Officer of the 1st Battalion 2nd King Edward VII's Own Goorkhas and a seasoned jungle fighter, successfully deduced the escape route which would be taken by the Indonesians and, during the following month, a number of very successful operations were mounted by Clements and his battalion which resulted in some 30 or so enemy being killed before the remainder escaped back into Indonesia. It was later discovered that the Indonesian raiding force had been commanded by a Major Muljono, who had fought against the Japanese during the Second World War and subsequently against the Dutch. He had been trained at several jungle warfare schools, including the British Army's at Kota Tinggi in Johore Bahru, Malaysia.

As a result of the debacle at Long Jawi, the Director of Operations decided to restrict the role of the Border Scouts to one of gathering information, which meant disarming them and removing their uniforms. This difficult task was given to Major John Cross, of the 7th Duke of Edinburgh's Own Gurkha Rifles, who had formed the Border Scouts, and it was due to his skills of diplomacy, exercised as he visited all the kampongs along the 1,000-mile border, that the scouts agreed to their new role and the loyalty of the villagers was retained.

At this time Major L. M. 'Phil' Phillips, 10th Princess Mary's Own Gurkha Rifles, assumed command of the company. The Director of Operations had decided that the company was to be concentrated once more and was to be used in a "Fire Brigade" role, moving wherever it was required at short notice. Phillips spent the first six weeks of his new command walking the length and breadth of the First and Second Divisions, visiting his men and putting new heart into them with news of the impending change in the company's role. In due course the company was concentrated in Kuching, where it was based for the time being. From there it carried out a number of quick reaction tasks in support of 3rd Commando Brigade, which was deployed in the Lundu area.

In early 1964 the company returned to Malaysia, and was based at the Jungle Warfare School at Johore Bahru. There it was joined by Captain David Morgan, 7th Duke of Edinburgh's Own Gurkha Rifles, as its second-in-command and Captain Paddy Verdon, Gurkha Signals, who became the company's Signals Officer. Shortly afterwards, three young officers also joined its ranks: Lieutenant Nigel Walker of the 6th Queen Elizabeth's Own Gurkha Rifles, and Lieutenants Mike Callaghan and Mike Harrison, both of the 10th Princess Mary's Own Gurkha Rifles.

Shortly after the company's return from Borneo, Major Phil Phillips was summoned to attend a meeting with the Director of Operations at the latter's headquarters on the island of Labuan. There he was informed that the company was to operate in the SAS role in Borneo, but he was given little or no information as to how to go about converting his unit to its new role. Fortunately Lieutenant Colonel John Woodhouse, the Commanding Officer of 22 SAS, appeared on the scene, and his assistance thereafter proved invaluable in helping Phillips to plan for the task ahead. Subsequently the company underwent complete reorganisation from three platoons to 16 five-man patrols plus a headquarters and supporting 'tail'. The rationale behind the adoption of the five-man patrol, as opposed to the four-man patrols used by the SAS and No. 1 (Guards) Independent Company, was that the company's primary role was airfield assault, and its strength of 128 all ranks was based on the operational requirement for that role. In addition, there were only sufficient radios available for 16 patrols, the company headquarters, plus a small stock of spare sets. Each patrol consisted of a commander, a medical orderly, two assault pioneers and a signaller.

The company was allowed a short period of time to weed out the weaker members in its ranks and to obtain new recruits before starting to train for its new role, which was to augment the two SAS squadrons and No. 1 (Guards) Independent Company in Borneo. Training was carried out at the Jungle Warfare School, and the company was assisted by two members of 22 SAS. The company's radio operators were provided by the Gurkha Signals, and its patrol medics underwent training at the British Military Hospital in Singapore.

By August 1964 all training had been completed and the company was once again concentrated at the Jungle Warfare School. At this point President Soekarno decided to invade the Malaysian mainland. In the early hours of the morning of 17 August, a force of over 100 Indonesian marines, paratroops and Chinese Communist irregulars crossed the Straits of Malacca in boats and landed on the coast of south-west Johore. This force was intercepted by Malaysian troops, who killed or captured the majority of the Indonesians, hunting the rest as they fled into the jungle.

Two weeks later the Indonesians mounted an airborne assault near Labis, an area in Central Malaysia some 400 miles north of Singapore. Approximately 200 paratroops had embarked in four aircraft at Jakarta, but one was unable to take off. Of the remaining three, one crashed into the sea while flying at low level to avoid detection by radar, and the two surviving aircraft encountered an electric storm over Labis and scattered their parachutists over an area of five miles. Phillips persuaded Lieutenant Colonel 'Bunny' Burnett, the Commanding Officer of the 1st Battalion 10th Princess Mary's Own Gurkha Rifles, which was conducting the operation to hunt down the Indonesians, to let him deploy the company on the north-east flank to cut off the enemy troops. In the event none of the patrols made contact with the enemy, but the operation proved to be a good 'shake-down' for the company.

Towards the end of October 1964 the Gurkha Independent Parachute Company returned to Borneo, where it relieved No. 1 (Guards) Independent Company at Sibu in the Third Division. In addition to deploying patrols in the Third Division, it also had four more attached to a Gurkha battalion in the Fifth Division. One of the patrols on the border in the Third Division, commanded by Lieutenant Mike Callaghan, was based at Long Banai, an area inhabited by the nomadic Punan. After reading a book compiled by a prewar university expedition, Major Phil Phillips became convinced that the patrol's base, which had been taken over from No. 1 (Guards) Independent Company, was nowhere near the border but was in fact a considerable distance from it. Phillips enlisted the aid of the Fleet Air Arm detachment at Nangga Gaat and its commander, Lieutenant 'Tosh' Kennard RN. On the next fortnightly resupply mission to Callaghan and his men, Phillips flew in Kennard's aircraft and, after leaving Long Banai, flew further eastwards until he spotted the escarpment which followed the line of the border. Accordingly, Callaghan's patrol was moved to its new location, followed soon after by the Punan from Long Banai, who missed the tobacco and food frequently dispensed by the patrol. The tribesmen soon proved instrumental in providing Callaghan with information concerning Indonesian activities on the other side of the border.

During the following six months the company patrolled constantly, patrols being rotated to allow them to rest and recuperate at periodic intervals at the company base in Sibu. The longest period spent in the jungle was 12 weeks. There were no contacts with the enemy in either the Third or Fifth Divisions, although some of the company's patrols did make some unauthorised forays across the border into Indonesia. Despite a request from Major Phil Phillips, the Director of Operations refused to authorise the company to take part in cross-border operations.

In April 1965 the company was relieved by C (Independent) Company 2 PARA and returned to Malaysia, where it moved to a new base at Kluang. There Major Phil Phillips handed over command to Major John Cross. The company was given five months to retrain and recruit further members to its ranks, new and stricter selection tests being introduced for potential recruits. The parachute selection course itself had proved to be too easy for Gurkhas, all of whom were superlatively fit. However, while parachuting itself posed no problems to them, navigation and the skills required for the patrol company role frequently did. Tests were therefore introduced which assessed a Gurkha's individuality and his capability to master the necessary skills.

September found the Gurkha Independent Parachute Company in Borneo once more, this time deployed in the Fifth Division. During this second tour the company took part in Operation 'Claret' missions across the border into Indonesia. One such mission was led by the company commander, Major John Cross. Two patrols, one led by Cross, were flown by helicopter to a point a mile from the border. From there they climbed through the jungle until, at 1400 hours, they reached the ridgeline along which, at a height of 4,000ft, ran the unmarked border with Indonesia. Crossing over the border, Cross and his men broke track and took up positions for the night as dusk approached. On the following morning the two patrols headed south to carry out their task of reconnoitring a certain area to check for any Indonesian activity. Subsequently they discovered an enemy position which appeared to have been abandoned only the day before, at about the time that Cross and his men were being dropped off by helicopter.

On another occasion Cross led a force of four patrols from the company on a mission to reconnoitre a track which ran parallel to the border. There was an enemy base in the area, containing a force of between 400 and 500 men, from which the Indonesians had been launching attacks across the border. Cross's mission was to determine whether the track was being used as a route from the enemy base to points on the border from which the incursions were being launched. His four patrols were to spend two days reconnoitring in four different directions, after which they would concentrate at an RV and set up an ambush on the track. The enemy base lay only some three miles to the west, and Cross hoped that sooner or later some Indonesians would approach along the track and encounter his ambush. He had catered for such an eventuality by equipping all four patrols with Claymore mines.

After the patrols had crossed the border, but before they separated to carry out their individual reconnaissance tasks, misfortune struck when a local inhabitant was encountered coming from the direction of the enemy base. After some deliberation Cross decided to let the man continue on his way, but decided that the four patrols would spend only that day reconnoitring. They would concentrate at the RV during the evening, and not on the following day as originally planned. Cross led his patrol to the east, following the local, who had indicated that there were tracks in the area and that there was a longhouse frequented by Indonesians. When the time came to head for the RV, Cross found that he was lost and that there was no sign of the tracks referred to by the local. As the afternoon wore on, he and his three Gurkhas came upon the longhouse. They had passed by at a safe distance and climbed a rise, when Cross saw a tree with the letters 'RPKAD', the initials for the Indonesian para-commando regiment, carved low down on its trunk. Beneath was carved the previous day's date. Although he was unable to find his position on his map, Cross was certain that he and his men were between the enemy base and the ambush location. By then it was getting late in the day and, rather than risk walking into his own ambush, he moved his patrol into a lying-up place under cover of darkness. That evening he sent a message by radio to the other three patrols, instructing them to make their way to his location by 0800 hours the following morning.

Dawn on the next day revealed the patrol's position as being in a clump of trees surrounded by a large expanse of open terrain. By 1000 hours there was no sign of the other patrols, and Cross was becoming anxious. Eventually, at the suggestion of one of his men, he resorted to making cuckoo calls, a method of signalling he had used 18 years previously during the Malay Emergency after learning that there were no cuckoos in Malaya. This ruse worked, and 20 minutes later the three other patrols arrived, having been waiting about half a mile away. They had guessed that Cross would use the cuckoo call and had waited for it. Without further ado, Cross moved his force into the cover of the nearby jungle and decided that he would reconnoitre the longhouse which he and his patrol had passed on the previous day. Approaching it cautiously, he found it inhabited by a small group of elderly locals who made the Gurkhas and their commander welcome.

On the following day the four patrols began the march back to the border and Sarawak. Late that afternoon they camped on a ridgeline above an area which had been the scene of an action between the Indonesians and the 1st Battalion 2nd King Edward VII's Own Goorkhas some months previously, and which featured a large and apparently well maintained LZ. As Cross and his men were eating their evening meal, an Indonesian troop-carrying helicopter, escorted by fighters, suddenly appeared overhead and flew on in the direction of the LZ. From the noise of the engines Cross could tell that the helicopter had landed, and guessed that it was disembarking troops. A few minutes later it reappeared and flew away. Meanwhile, the four patrols had stood to and were ready to engage any enemy who appeared. None did so, and Cross subsequently led his force back across the border without any contact taking place.

In June of the following year it was reported that a force of some 50 Indonesians, led by a Lieutenant Sumbi, was making its way towards the border. Previous reports had indicated that its objective might be the Shell oil installations at Seria, in Brunei, and it was thought that Sumbi planned to cross the border via a remote, jungle-covered ridgeline between the villages of Ba Kelalan and Long Semado in the Fifth Division. The battalion in whose area Sumbi's probable crossing-point lay was the 1st Battalion 7th Duke of Edinburgh's Own Gurkha Rifles. Providing a screen in front of it were patrols of the Gurkha Independent Parachute Company.

On the morning of 29 July two members of a patrol, Corporal Singbahadur Gurung and Rifleman Dharmalal Rai, were carrying out a reconnaissance task when Dharmalal spotted something glinting on the ground. On closer inspection this proved to be a piece of silver foil smelling of coffee. As there were no British troops in the area, and as the Gurkha ration pack does not contain coffee, the two men rapidly concluded that it was possible that the scrap of foil had been dropped by an Indonesian. Further careful inspection of the area revealed tracks made by two or three men heading north from the border into Sarawak. With the other three members of their patrol, the two men continued to track the Indonesians for the next two days and nights. Fearful of alerting the enemy, they did not camp or cook any food. On the third day their patience was rewarded when they discovered three pairs of discarded British-pattern jungle boots and pieces of sacking used by 45 individuals for tying over their feet to prevent any tracks being made on the ground.

The reaction to the patrol's report by radio was initially one of disbelief, and it was ordered to backtrack to make sure that the tracks originated over the border. Corporal Singbahadur and his men did so, and confirmed that the intruders had indeed crossed over from Indonesia. There was no doubt that the raiding force was that of Lieutenant Sumbi. Thereafter the pursuit was taken up by the 1st Battalion 7th Duke of Edinburgh's Own Gurkha Rifles and other units, including five patrols of the Gurkha Independent Parachute Company. A number of contacts were made with Sumbi's force over the next two months, during which some of the enemy were captured while others surrendered or died of starvation. Sumbi himself was captured on 3 September, after 'Confrontation' had officially ended. It transpired that he had attended the British Army's Jungle Warfare School, where his performance had been such that he was awarded a 'B' grading.

Four months previously, in June, the Gurkha Independent Parachute Company had been formally affiliated to The Parachute Regiment, and its members thereafter wore the maroon beret and the badge of the regiment, the latter worn on a backing of rifle green bearing the colours of the Brigade of Gurkhas.

In 1968 the company reverted to the organisation of a conventional rifle company and its role to that of parachute assault on to an airfield and its subsequent seizure. It was based at the Jungle Warfare School at Johore Bahru, where it also performed the duties of demonstration company. In 1971 the Brigade of Gurkhas withdrew from Malaysia to Hong Kong, where no role was envisaged for an airborne unit. Consequently, on 31 October, the Gurkha Independent Parachute Company was disbanded.

2 PARA OPERATIONS IN BORNEO, 1965

In early January 1965 2 PARA, commanded by Lieutenant Colonel Ted Eberhardie, also arrived to take part in operations against Indonesia. On 9 March, after six weeks training at the Jungle Warfare School, it sailed for Sarawak and arrived at Kuching three days later. From there the battalion moved by rail to Balai Ringin, the base location for Battalion Headquarters. The rifle companies were then lifted by helicopter to positions within 2,000 yards of the border, where they relieved men of the 1st Battalion The Argyll & Sutherland Highlanders. A Company, commanded by Major John Daniels, was based at Nibong, while B Company, under Major Jon Fleming, was at Plaman Mapu. D Company, commanded by Major Brian Barnes on secondment from the Irish Guards, moved into a base at Gunan Gajak. C Company, under Major Peter Herring, had been detached from the battalion and reorganised as a patrol company to operate in the SAS role.

Company bases were some 20 miles apart and all resupply was by helicopter. Communications with Battalion Headquarters were via radio, although these were frequently affected by atmospherics and weather conditions which made life for signallers very difficult. Each base was heavily fortified, with defensive positions and living accommodation consisting of bunkers. All trees and undergrowth had been cleared to provide good fields of fire which were floodlit at night, and the defences included barbed wire entanglements, belts of 'punjis' (sharpened bamboo stakes) and remotely-detonated Claymore mines. Each base was roughly circular, being divided into wedge-shaped sectors in each of which there was a position equipped with a tripod-mounted general purpose machine gun (GPMG). Communications within each base consisted of field telephones and radio. Company bases also had their own sections of two 3-inch mortars and, in the case of A and D Companies, a 105mm pack howitzer manned by gunners of a Royal Artillery light regiment. Artillery and mortar defensive fire (DF) tasks were registered around each base, the gunners also registering several on and around B Company at Plaman Mapu.

Lieutenant Colonel Ted Eberhardie had served previously in what was now Indonesia, having been Intelligence Officer of 12th Parachute Battalion during 5th Parachute Brigade's tour of operations in Java in 1945–46. He had very definite ideas as to how operations should be carried out, bearing in mind the huge area to be covered. Unlike the Malay Emergency, where troops acted on intelligence provided by the military/ police Special Branch organisation, information on the movement and locations of Indonesian units, which were usually of company size and were mainly self-supporting, could best be provided by large numbers of small patrols acting as observation and listening posts. Such patrols could make up for their small size and consequent lack of firepower by being able to call upon artillery support and rapid reinforcement by helicopter, with company-sized groups being flown in as required.

Under Eberhardie's tutelage, 2 PARA developed its own techniques for jungle operations. Packs were discarded, everything being carried in pouches on the men's belts, and rations were reduced to the barest minimum on which a man could survive. Tracking was an essential skill for successful operations in the jungle, and much use was made of Iban tribesmen who accompanied patrols. However, there were insufficient Ibans for all units, and it was decided to train members of 2 PARA in the skill. Fortunately the battalion possessed its own resident expert in the unusual form of its Education Officer, Captain Huia Woods of the Royal Army Education Corps. A Maori, he had previously served with the New Zealand SAS in the Malay Emergency, during which he had learned the art, and had subsequently been an instructor at the Jungle Warfare School. As a result of his expertise, each section in 2 PARA possessed a fully trained tracker team of three men which moved in advance of each patrol. Patrols lasted up to ten days, and companies constantly had two platoons deployed on operations and one resting, the third platoon and company headquarters occupying the base.

When 2 PARA took over its area of operations there was a full moon, and it was a period of intense activity on the part of the Indonesians. Approximately ten days after arriving at Plaman Mapu, B Company discovered two enemy observation posts covering its base and signs that enemy patrols had been in the area. D Company also detected activity around its base at Gunan Gajak. During the last week of March and the first week of April, the Indonesians were active in both companies' areas, and on 12 April brought mortar fire to bear on a B Company observation post.

B Company's base, which was approximately 1,000 yards from the border with Indonesia, was not well sited, being on a small hill in a valley. The ridgeline, along which the border ran, dominated the position, and any movement within the base could be clearly seen. Consequently, patrols had to depart and return under cover of darkness. On taking over the position the company had found it to be rat-infested and overgrown, but had quickly taken it in hand, reinforcing the defences with additional punji pits. Further indications of enemy activity came from patrols which reported apparent preparations for an attack in B Company's area. Large numbers of Indonesian troops were observed in kampongs close to the other side of the border, and clearings were being cut for use by mortars. The company could do little more than stay alert and prepare accordingly.

The build-up of enemy activity culminated in a major action which proved to be one of the largest during the Borneo Confrontation. At 0445 hours on the morning of 27 April, in pitch darkness and heavy rain, B Company's base came under heavy fire from artillery, mortars, rocket launchers, rifle grenades and machine guns. At this time the base was held by an understrength platoon of young soldiers who had been sent to join the battalion after completing their basic training at the depot. They were temporarily under the command of Captain Nicky Thompson of Support Company because their own platoon commander, Lieutenant Mike Barton, was absent on a jungle warfare course. The rest of the garrison, which totalled 34, comprised Major Jon Fleming, CSM Williams, CQMS Goodall, an artillery forward observation officer (FOO), two cooks, the two 3-inch mortar crews and the signallers.

As the enemy opened fire and the garrison manned its defences, CSM Williams ran out of the company command post and headed towards the machine-gun position in the sector under attack. As he did so, enemy sappers blew gaps in the barbed wire entanglements with Bangalore torpedoes. The enemy rocket launchers had already proved effective, knocking out the section defending the sector under attack. Advancing through the breached defences, the Indonesians succeeded in capturing one of the 3-inch mortar positions, but were driven out by a counterattack by another section, which lost three or four men wounded. Meanwhile, the enemy bombardment continued.

On realising the situation, CSM Williams returned to the command post and asked the FOO, Captain Webb, to call down artillery supporting fire on the area of the base held by the enemy. He then ran to the position occupied by the platoon commander, Captain Thompson, and told him to follow him with a section to mount a counterattack. As Williams, followed by Thompson and his men, made their way across the position, a mortar bomb exploded in the middle of them. Thompson and half of the section were badly wounded, leaving Williams with only two soldiers, one of whom was a cook corporal, with which to rout the Indonesians, numbering about 30, who now held the captured sector. Williams knew that only heavy fire would dislodge the enemy, and ran across to the sector's GPMG position. As he opened fire, he shouted to Corporal Baughan, the NCO commanding the section to his left, to carry out a counterattack under covering fire of the GPMG. Initially the enemy fell back into a gulley, but shortly afterwards retaliated by launching an attack on Williams' position. Despite the heavy fire, the enemy came storming forward, firing their Kalashnikov assault rifles. One Indonesian nearly succeeded in reaching Williams, falling only two yards from the GPMG. In the darkness visibility was no more than a few yards, the only illumination coming from the flashes from exploding shells and mortar bombs. The rain was still falling heavily and the ground was a quagmire. Eventually the enemy, hampered by the slippery mud as they advanced up the slope of the hill, were driven back to the gulley once more by the fire from Corporal Baughan and his men, who were supported by Private Murtagh and his GPMG.

At that point CSM Williams discovered that the radio beside him had been destroyed and that the GPMG, although still in working order, had been hit four times. He had been wounded and was blind in one eye. Unaware of this, he left the machine gun and, after collecting the wounded and taking them to the company command post, distributed a resupply of ammunition to all the remaining defenders, who by then numbered only about 15. Williams realised that the enemy was preparing to mount a second attack on the same sector. This was heralded by heavy supporting fire and Bangalore torpedoes breaching the defences. One of B Company's mortars had been lost, but Sergeant McDonald was firing the other on almost vertical elevation and dropping bombs 30 yards away on the enemy. At the same time the 105mm pack howitzers at Gunan Gajak were laying down supporting fire. The enemy assault was broken up by fire from Corporal Baughan's section, supported by the two GPMGs.

The enemy made a third attempt, but this petered out. By then it was 0545 hours and dawn was approaching. Williams called for volunteers to make up a patrol and accompany him to clear the enemy from the perimeter of the position. All the remaining defenders volunteered without hesitation, and Williams selected three. As the four of them cleared the perimeter they encountered an Indonesian, who was quickly killed. They had just returned to the position when helicopters arrived, bringing in reinforcements in the form of 2 PARA's quick-reaction force company. Meanwhile, Lieutenant Colonel Eberhardie had despatched three platoons by helicopter to cut off the most likely enemy withdrawal routes. At the same time, two companies of Gurkhas were flown into Plaman Mapu to follow up the fleeing Indonesians. No contact was made with them, however, and it was assumed that the enemy had managed to evade their pursuers.

The sight which met those arriving at Plaman Mapu beggared description. The surviving defenders, clad only in trousers and boots, stood ankle-deep in mud amid the battered bunkers of B Company's base. Only two enemy bodies were found: the man who had fallen only a few feet from CSM Williams' GPMG and the one who had been killed by the patrol clearing the perimeter. There was, however, plenty of evidence pointing to the enemy's route of withdrawal: a trail led towards the border, and along it were copious amounts of blood and discarded equipment. The wounded were evacuated by helicopter, among them CSM Williams, who had been hit in the left side of his face and head by shrapnel from a mortar bomb and had bullet grazes on his skull. He had lost the hearing in his left ear and the sight of his left eye. He was subsequently awarded the Distinguished Conduct Medal for his gallantry and leadership during the action.

It transpired that B Company had been attacked by a battalion of Indonesian RPKAD para-commandos. Two companies had carried out the assault, supported by rocket launchers, 50mm light mortars and machine guns. A firm base for the attack had been established by a third company, while a fourth had been positioned in ambush positions on the Indonesian side of the border to counter any follow-up by British forces. Whereas B Company had suffered only two killed and seven wounded, the casualties among their opponents had been very heavy, numbering some 300. At the time, the absence of bodies caused some mystification. It was only years later that the riddle was solved, when an Indonesian officer who had taken part in the battle attended a course in Britain. He confirmed that his battalion's casualties had been heavy, comprising some 50 per cent of its strength, and explained that the absence of bodies was due to the dead and severely wounded having been thrown into the nearby river which ran towards the border.

The next move against 2 PARA by the Indonesians took place in the centre of the battalion's area of responsibility, when a large body of enemy crossed the border and laid an ambush on a track. A platoon of D Company, based at Gunan Gajak, moved through the area but, as it was moving through the jungle some 20 yards parallel to the track, it missed the ambush. Nevertheless, the Indonesians opened fire on the platoon which, after losing one man killed, pulled back. As the Indonesians withdrew they were pursued by the battalion's helicopter-borne quick reaction force, supported by artillery and 2 PARA's mortars.

Another action resulted from a sighting on 15 May of an enemy reconnaissance patrol near a village called Mongkus. No. 12 Platoon of D Company, under Sergeant Barker, was despatched to follow up. That evening, while lying in ambush, the platoon observed a group of enemy moving across its front. Only one Indonesian actually entered the ambush area, and although he was wounded he managed to escape. The platoon followed up, but the light was fading and by dawn the following day, 16 May, all tracks had been obliterated by heavy rain during the night.

On the following day, 17 May, a strong force of 70 Indonesians appeared in a village called Mujat. News of the appearance of the enemy soon reached 2 PARA, and No. 10 Platoon of D Company, under Lieutenant Gavin Coxen, was sent to the village to investigate. On cautiously approaching the village, Coxen and his platoon succeeded in surprising a small group of Indonesians, who withdrew along a track after an exchange of fire, taking their one casualty with them. Coxen immediately suspected that he was being led into an ambush by the main group of enemy. At that point he and his men were joined by 2 PARA's Reconnaissance Platoon, commanded by Captain John Collinson-Jones, which was accompanied by a tracker team. Following the blood trail left by the wounded Indonesian, the tracker team led the two platoons along the track until it arrived at a junction where the track split into three. The team, led by Sergeant Murray, chose the correct one, because it found itself on the flank of the enemy ambush. The enemy opened fire, but this proved largely ineffective, and the two platoons responded by charging into the Indonesians, who fled. At last light the follow-up was halted until after the moon had risen, when it was resumed. Leading the way was an Iban tracker who tracked with his hand, feeling for marks as he followed the Indonesians' trail. As the gap was closed between the trackers and their quarry, the smell of the enemy became almost overpowering, and it was decided to wait until first light before resuming pursuit. At dawn the following morning it was discovered that the enemy had slipped away. From the tracks left by the Indonesians, the trackers estimated that the enemy had numbered over 200.

A few days later, Indonesian troops were once again reported as being in the area of Mongkus and Mujat. Seven platoons of 2 PARA were inserted by helicopter and, not long afterwards, a section encountered a force of enemy who mistook the paratroops for their own men. Leaving cover, some 40 Indonesians walked forward waving and laughing. Waiting until they were only ten yards away, the section opened fire and cut down 15 of the enemy. The survivors turned and fled back into the jungle where, it transpired, there were more of the enemy. Almost immediately the section came under fire from a light mortar and the enemy started to carry out a flanking attack. However, the section withdrew and broke contact without loss.

During the following month, on 23 June, No. 10 Platoon of D Company, under Lieutenant Gavin Coxen, was flown up to the border just before last light. After leaving the LZ, the platoon moved up as close as possible to the location of an ambush it would lay on the following morning. Codenamed DF11, it was one of 2 PARA's pre-recorded defensive fire tasks for supporting artillery. By dawn on 24 June Coxen and his men, numbering only 15, were ready in their positions. Later that morning a large force of between 50 and 60 Indonesians approached the ambush area. As the enemy lead scout entered it, the platoon radio operator, Private Eltringham, unaware of the Indonesians' approach, continued to transmit a message in Morse. The sound probably alerted the scout, who suddenly opened fire. The ambushers responded likewise, killing some ten of the enemy, who retaliated fiercely. Outnumbered, the platoon carried out a fighting withdrawal with the enemy in hot pursuit. Artillery support was called for, but the platoon was out of radio range. As luck would have it, however, contact was established via a helicopter, which succeeded in relaying details of the Indonesians' position and calling for artillery fire. Shortly afterwards, 105mm shells started landing and the platoon was able to break contact and withdraw. A follow-up was carried out by 2 PARA in the normal way, but by then the enemy had disappeared back into Indonesia.

This was the last major contact for 2 PARA during Borneo Confrontation. It had been a highly successful tour of duty for the battalion, which had inflicted a large number of casualties on the enemy in return for suffering very few of its own. In August, 2 PARA left Borneo and returned to Britain, where it rejoined 16th Parachute Brigade.

C (INDEPENDENT) COMPANY 2 PARA OPERATIONS IN BORNEO, 1965

In September 1964, just after 2 PARA's return from a two-week exercise in Germany, the Commanding Officer, Lieutenant Colonel Neil Gordon-Wilson, was preparing to hand over command to Lieutenant Colonel Ted Eberhardie. As he was doing so, he was informed that the battlion was to provide an independent company to operate in the SAS role. The confrontation with Indonesia in Borneo was continuing and SAS resources of two squadrons were becoming overstretched, despite reinforcements by No. 1 (Guards) Independent Company and the Gurkha Independent Parachute Company.

Time was at a premium, as the company was required to be in the Far East by January 1965, having completed personnel selection and basic patrol skills training. It was decided that it would be based on the existing C Company, commanded by Major Peter Herring, but increased in strength to approximately 120 all ranks. It would include volunteers from throughout the battalion and would be supplemented by signallers and medics from 216 Parachute Signals Squadron and 23 Parachute Field Ambulance respectively. Some 250 hopeful volunteers embarked on the selection course over familiar terrain in Wales. By the end of October the company's provisional order of battle had been agreed, and individuals allocated to specialist roles were ready to begin their skills training in Aldershot and at 22 SAS's base at Hereford. In mid-November an advance party of 12 linguists departed for Singapore to start their training, while others honed their skills in signals, demolitions and field medicine.

Early in January 1965, C (Independent) Company concentrated in Nee Soon, Singapore. Much to its members' annoyance the rest of 2 PARA was also there, en route to Sarawak on a 'Spearhead' deployment. Inevitably, the members of the company took every opportunity to emphasise their independent role.

The company moved to Brunei to carry out the next phase in its preparations — jungle training. Following an initial week's introduction for patrol commanders, all members embarked upon a concentrated month of jungle skills, tactics, navigation and skill at arms. The SAS instructors were all fresh from operations in Sarawak and included Sergeant Geordie Tindale, the brother of Corporal Tindale of D Company who would win a Military Medal later in the campaign. Company Headquarters and the administrative 'tail' were established at the 'Haunted House' in Brunei. Here, Major Peter Herring and his Operations Officer, Captain Derek Jackson, finalised their plans for training operations in Sarawak's Fifth Division, which would follow on from the training phase, and the trial operational deployment to relieve the Gurkha Independent Parachute

Company in the Third Division. The three troop commanders, Lieutenants Simon Hill, Chris Johnson and John Winter, all undertook two-week training operations under the watchful eye of SAS instructors before being declared ready for full-scale operations. Winter later recalled that period, under RSM 'The Gloom' Ross, as being the most testing part of his time in Borneo.

In March the company redeployed to Sibu, where it took over Bukit Lima Camp from the Gurkha Independent Parachute Company and its main administrative base was established under CSM Bing and CQMS Knall. A forward administrative and mounting base, presided over by Colour Sergeant Andrews, was located at Nangga Gaat, a day's journey up the Rajang River. There, too, were the forward elements of No. 845 Naval Air Squadron, which would provide the company with helicopter support. Patrols would deploy forward by air from Nangga Gaat to their operational areas to cover likely Indonesian border crossing routes, gather intelligence, carry out ambush tasks and to live and travel with the local Punan tribesmen. Much effort was expended on mapping. It was not unusual for the map coverage of a patrol's area, the size of a small English county, to consist of a sheet of white paper overlaid with ten-kilometre grid squares. The patrol, equipped only with what it hoped was an accurate grid reference of its start point, a compass and an altimeter, would fill in the rest as it went along.

Initially, operations were to last from four to six weeks. Insertion by helicopter could be a tricky business. With each man carrying 14 days' rations, batteries and ammunition, bergen rucksacks rarely weighed less than 100lb at the start of an operation. The terrain in the border area sometimes reached an altitude of 6,000ft, so it quite often took two elderly Wessex Mk.1 helicopters to deploy a single four-man patrol. Resupply was normally carried out at 14-day intervals. A day's worth of very welcome fresh rations, a mixture of as many different compo rations as could be mustered, mail, a new set of clothing (its life expectancy was slightly less than two weeks), and, above all, radio batteries, were flown in to patrols' LZs from Nangga Gaat. Patrols operated at a range of between 200 and 300 miles from the company headquarters. Their lifelines were their signallers, who operated their sets under frequently adverse atmospheric conditions, more often than not in pouring rain, sending and receiving Morse. Having been well-steeped in HF antenna theory, the signallers frequently found that the best halfwave length dipole was a length of D10 cable thrown over a branch.

Having established its credentials with the SAS, the company was subsequently warned that it would be taking part in Operation 'Claret' cross-border operations. Four patrols, under Lieutenant Simon Hill, were detached to A Squadron 22 SAS based in Kuching, in the First Division, under the command of Major Peter De La Billière. Hill had developed an unconventional tactical style of his own, even when judged by the standards of his mentors. He and his signaller, Lance Corporal Burston, would deploy on a 'Claret' mission, leaving the other two members of their patrol to secure the border crossing-point. The two men would disappear into Indonesia, subsequently re-emerging anything up to ten days later after completing their mission.

A task inherited from No. 1 (Guards) Independent Company and the Gurkha Independent Parachute Company was that of deploying a patrol to live with the Punan who inhabited the border region. The tribesmen existed by hunting and by picking plants and fruit growing wild in the jungle, even the most basic form of agriculture being completely alien to them. The Punan would establish a hutted village under the jungle canopy for a period of weeks or months, hunting in the local areas for wild pig, monkey and sometimes toucan, and moving on when game became scarce. Armed only with blowpipes and parangs, they were a delightful and simple people, but a potentially valuable source of much information. Lieutenant John Winter's patrol became the Punan specialists, at one stage spending 12 weeks with them on one particular operation. Winter, his signaller Lance Corporal Barker and Privates Phelps and Seeney caused much amusement on those rare occasions when they emerged from the jungle. The four of them preferred to keep their own company, and could be found muttering quietly to each other in strange languages in dark corners of various bars in Sibu.

C (Independent) Company's otherwise very successful tour was marred by a tragic accident which occurred in April 1965. Two of No. 845 Naval Air Squadron's helicopters, having extracted Lieutenant Chris Johnson's and Sergeant McNeilly's patrols, were returning to Nangga Gaat one evening when they collided with each other in the gathering gloom, killing all on board. The eight members of the company and the aircrews who perished are commemorated by a memorial erected by the villagers.

No direct contact was made with the enemy during the company's tour in Borneo, but when it completed its tour in July and returned to join the rest of 2 PARA in England, it was confident that it had acquitted itself well in a harsh and unforgiving environment. Moreover, it had laid the foundations for patrol companies to be included in the order of battle of The Parachute Regiment's three regular battalions in the future.

D (PATROL) COMPANY 3 PARA OPERATIONS IN BORNEO, 1966

In July 1965 3 PARA was warned that it was also to provide a patrol company for special operations in Borneo. D Company, commanded by Major Peter Chiswell, was selected for the task, and volunteers were called for from the battalion. Somewhat understandably, competition was fierce. A selection course was held in Wales in August, after which intensive training in the required skills was carried out by those fortunate enough to win places in the company. The company was reorganised into four patrol platoons, each consisting of four four-man patrols, a company headquarters and a base communications section provided by 216 Parachute Signals Squadron Royal Signals. In addition to Major Peter Chiswell, officers in the company included Captain Jeremy Hickman, the Operations Officer, and three subalterns: Lieutenants David Chaundler, Alec Honey and David Hanmer.

Major Chiswell was given four and a half months to train his company to the operational standards demanded by the new role. He was fortunate in that his company sergeant major, CSM Watchus, had just completed a tour of duty with 22 SAS. Basic skills training began in Aldershot. The signallers were introduced to the 125 Set, an HF CW only transmitter/receiver which had been used by agents of the Special Operations Executive during the Second World War. Despite their age the sets were robust, but were difficult to keep dry in damp conditions. The company's medics were trained by 23 Parachute Field Ambulance RAMC to an advanced standard of field medicine and in the communications skills required for consultations with a doctor via radio. By means of a special code, professional medical advice could be obtained for a sick or wounded member of a patrol. Those selected to be linguists flew out to the Far East to learn Malay and subsequently, on their return, carried out a demolitions and explosives course with 9 Parachute Squadron Royal Engineers. Meanwhile, all officers, patrol commanders and NCOs underwent intensive training with 22 SAS, as well as extensive briefings at the Intelligence Centre at Ashford in Kent.

The next phase was platoon and patrol training, which was carried out for prolonged periods in Wales, culminating with a series of arduous exercises in Scotland. After a splendid Christmas party held at the Queen's Hotel in Farnborough, the company went on leave before flying out to Singapore in early January 1966.

At Nee Soon Camp in Singapore, the company, now redesignated D (Patrol) Company, acclimatised and drew up its weapons and equipment. Much time was spent firing on the ranges, and some jungle acclimatisation training was undergone at the Jungle Warfare School at Johore Bahru. The company then flew to the island of Labuan, where the theatre headquarters and that of the SAS were based. From there it travelled by landing craft to Brunei. Before becoming operational, the company had to complete a period of work-up training with the Training Wing of 22 SAS at a jungle base in Brunei. There the tactics, techniques and skills previously learned and practised in England were put into practice under very realistic conditions and under the close supervision of the SAS instructors. In late March, after completing its final training, the company moved to the 'Haunted House', where it relieved the Gurkha Independent Parachute Company. There it became the patrol company of Central Brigade, commanded by Brigadier David House. At the same time the company was given the use of Tutong Camp, some 20 miles to the south, as a base for resting patrols.

The company's principal operational task was to maintain depth surveillance forward of the border ridge, providing patrols to carry out in-depth close reconnaissance tasks on selected targets. It worked extremely closely with Headquarters Central Brigade, and with the SAS headquarters on Labuan Island. Throughout its six-month tour of operations the company successfully completed every one of its missions without loss of life. The number of contacts with the enemy were very few but, nevertheless, a mass of valuable intelligence was obtained. A number of Operation 'Claret' cross-border missions were carried out, the first of these taking place soon after the company became operational. Reports had been received of a large ammunition cache established by the Indonesians on a riverline. A three-man patrol, consisting of Lance Corporal Chivers and Privates Atkinson and Vaughan, was tasked with locating the cache and conducting a close reconnaissance, and this was successfully carried out.

Towards the end of D (Patrol) Company's tour, the confrontation with Indonesia was beginning to cool down. Soekarno's strategic aims had not been achieved, and the joint Commonwealth defence of Eastern Malaysia and Brunei had proved successful. Accordingly, it was decided not to relieve the company with another patrol company of The Parachute Regiment. In late July 1966, D (Patrol) Company returned home to 3 PARA in Aldershot. The Parachute Regiment's involvement in Borneo Confrontation was over.

C (PATROL) COMPANY 2 PARA OPERATIONS IN THE RADFAN, 1966

In September 1965 Major Alex Young took over command of C (Patrol) Company 2 PARA from Major Peter Herring. In January the following year 2 PARA moved to Bahrain, and a few weeks later the company was detached and deployed to Habilayn (formerly Thumier) in the Radfan. As in Borneo, its role was to be one of deep penetration reconnaissance. The company was based in a tented camp near an airstrip, and from there it carried out long-range reconnaissance patrols and strike tasks throughout the Radfan. Observation was carried out on dissident groups, to monitor their movements and to deter attacks on the garrison at Habilayn. The company also established observation posts (OPs), mainly to the north of the base, and also provided a rapid response force which deployed in Army Air Corps Scout helicopters.

The rugged, mountainous terrain made operating conditions very difficult, particularly when OPs were established for any length of time. All water had to be carried in by night at the start of an operation, in addition to ammunition, rations and radios. No movement by day was permissible if an OP was not to be compromised. Patrols were covertly inserted into an area at last light by vehicle or helicopter, and would immediately march for eight hours or so, putting as much distance as possible between themselves and the dropping-off point. Before dawn they would move into lying-up places (LUPs), where they would conceal themselves during the day. The physical strain of operations under such conditions was considerable, and members of patrols were fortunate if they managed four hours sleep in a 24-hour period.

Several brief actions took place when fire was exchanged between patrols and dissidents, and during one contact a member of Lieutenant

John Winter's four-man patrol was seriously wounded. The company suffered only one man killed during its ten months in the Radfan — Bombardier Dane, of 7 Parachute Regiment Royal Horse Artillery, who was attached to the company from 2 PARA's supporting battery in Bahrain. The company was returning from an operation north of Dhala and was moving at night to a rendezvous point from which helicopters would extract it at first light on the following morning. In the darkness Dane became separated from the other members of his patrol and subsequently fell over the edge of a cliff. He was found by some dissidents, who took him over the border into Yemen, where he was murdered. His body was eventually returned. Towards the end of 1966 C (Patrol) Company completed its tour in the Radfan and returned to Bahrain, where it rejoined 2 PARA.

3 PARA IN BRITISH GUIANA, 1965–66

Late 1965 found 3 PARA overseas. In October the battalion was deployed to British Guiana (now Guyana) in South America on internal security duties. The colony was about to receive independence, and there had been considerable inter-racial political trouble among the population, which consisted mainly of Negroes, Indians and a number of Chinese. The different ethnic factions supported different political groups: the Negroes backed the Socialist People's National Congress, and the Indians backed the People's National Congress, which was communist. Both organisations enjoyed the same degree of popular support, so there was a battle for power.

When 3 PARA arrived it relieved the 1st Battalion The Lancashire Fusiliers, which had been maintaining the peace until then. The situation was calm, and remained so, apart from the occasional minor incident. The battalion's area of responsibility was that of Demarara, which forms the eastern part of the country. Companies were thinly spread, their platoons, in some cases, being deployed over 50 miles from their company headquarters, and were rotated through the different locations every four weeks. The reserve company was based at Atkinson Field.

The calm situation enabled the battalion to take advantage of the opportunities for jungle training. A battle camp was established in a disused cattle station five miles from Takama, on the River Berbice. Takama itself consisted of a jetty and a few buildings, one of which was a general store, and was reached from Atkinson Field via a 120-mile unmetalled track. The large areas of uninhabited jungle enabled the battalion to conduct extensive field firing exercises, some of which included support from the Mortar Platoon.

In addition to maintaining the peace, the battalion was also tasked with training the Guyanese Defence Force to enable it to take over responsibility for the country's defence and internal security after independence.

On 4 February of the following year Her Majesty The Queen and His Royal Highness The Duke of Edinburgh arrived in Georgetown, the capital of British Guiana, for the independence celebrations, which lasted three days. On 10 February the leading elements of 3 PARA left the newly independent Guyana for England, the entire battalion being back in Aldershot by the 20th after a successful four-month tour of duty.

2 PARA OPERATIONS IN ADEN, 1966

Two years later, in 1966, 2 PARA provided companies for internal security operations in Aden against terrorists who were indulging in a campaign of sniping and grenade attacks on the security forces there. These initially came under command of the 1st Battalion The Somerset & Cornwall Light Infantry but subsequently operated under command of Headquarters Aden Brigade. During the tours, which lasted for between one and two months at a time, the 2 PARA companies were deployed in a number of roles. These included static tasks such as manning checkpoints, where vehicles were searched and their occupants' identities checked, and provided guards for the detention centre at Al Mansura.

The companies also furnished mobile patrols, mounted in Land Rovers, which covered designated areas and checked possible terrorist targets such as bridges, culverts and pipelines. These patrols also mounted snap vehicle checkpoints, carried out escort duties and enforced curfews at night. Other duties included the provision of stand-by platoons which were employed frequently on area ambushes, cordon and search operations and house searches. Platoons were also deployed to dominate an area known as the 'Salt Pans', which was within mortar range of the RAF airfield at Khormaksar. The platoon carrying out this task was responsible for patrolling during the day and night, by vehicle and on foot, laying ambushes and generally denying the area to the enemy.

In January 1967, B Company, commanded by Major Mike Gray, was dispatched to Habilayn, in the Radfan, under command of the 1st Battalion Irish Guards, which had arrived in Aden during the previous month and was deployed on operations against Communist-supported dissident tribesmen. Located beside an airstrip, Habilayn itself was a heavily fortified base from which machine-guns, mortars and artillery fired defensive fire (DF) tasks at irregular intervals on suspected enemy forming-up points. On occasions, the dissidents replied with Czechoslovakian 'Blindicide' rocket launchers and mortars.

Initially the company was employed in maintaining the security of the base. However, it was soon providing instructors to train the Irish Guards in low-level tactics applicable to the mountainous terrain and its harsh conditions. Subsequently it also provided support for other operations and eventually was deployed on its own, moving into an area and setting up a base from which it dispatched patrols to monitor the activity of the dissidents.

1 PARA INTERNAL SECURITY OPERATIONS IN ADEN, 1967

During the 1960s the political situation in the Federation of South Arabia had been deteriorating gradually. By 1967 two political factions, the Front for the Liberation of Southern Yemen (FLOSY) and the National Liberation Front (NLF) were waging an active guerrilla campaign, seeking to undermine the position of the British and force them to withdraw. At the same time both organisations, who were bitter political opponents, sought to persuade the member states of the federation that they were the only viable contenders for political power after independence. The NLF was formed from a splinter group which broke away from FLOSY in 1966. Egypt, which supported FLOSY and provided troops for training its guerrillas in the Yemen, refused to support the NLF. British troops not only found themselves operating against two guerrilla elements, but also on occasions keeping the peace between them.

Trouble had begun in earnest in December 1963, when an attempt was made to assassinate the British High Commissioner, Sir Kennedy Trevaskis. After the failure of their campaign of insurrection in the Radfan during 1963 and 1964, FLOSY had switched its efforts to a campaign of urban guerrilla warfare within the Crown colony of Aden itself, where the bulk of its support was located. The terrorists of both factions were based largely in the areas of Crater, Tawahi, Ma'alla, Sheikh Othman and Al Mansura, whose warrens of narrow streets and slum areas provided ideal cover and sanctuary after hit-and-run attacks, bombings or sniping at British patrols. In February 1966 the Labour government then in power in Britain

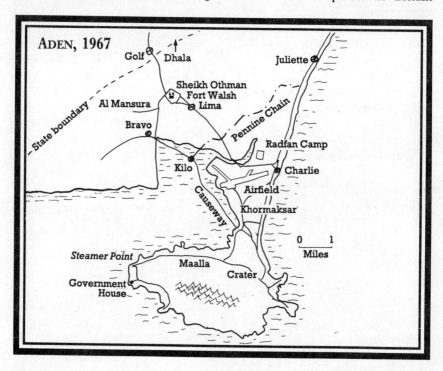

announced that all British troops would be withdrawn from Aden after 1968. This caused those Adenis who had previously backed the British to switch their loyalties, and inevitably led to a sharp drop in intelligence supplied to the security forces while strengthening the hands of the terrorists. The announcement also strengthened the resolve of Egypt's president, Gamal Abd al-Nasser, who had been considering withdrawing his forces from the Yemen, but now declared that his troops would remain there a further five years.

During late 1966 additional British troops were flown into Aden to reinforce the garrison. The 1st Battalion The Royal Northumberland Fusiliers arrived in September, followed by the 1st Battalion Irish Guards in December. Other units subsequently deployed in the colony included the 1st Battalion King's Own Royal Border Regiment, 1st Battalion The Lancashire Regiment, 1st Battalion The Argyll & Sutherland Highlanders, 1st Battalion The South Wales Borderers, 1st The Queen's Dragoon Guards and 45 Commando RM.

In early January 1967 1 PARA, commanded by Lieutenant Colonel Mike Walsh, was despatched to Aden to take part in operations during the final few months of British rule. On the night of 24–25 May the battalion was deployed to the towns of Sheik Othman and Al Mansura under command of Headquarters Aden Brigade. Sheik Othman consisted of a series of parallel streets, on either side of which were stone- or mud-built houses packed tightly together. The two main streets of the town, which formed a cross, were the scenes of most incidents. Situated at the 'cross' was the town's police station, on top of which was sited an OP manned by troops. Inevitably, this became a favourite target for the terrorists. In the centre of the wider of the two main streets was the mosque, from which orders were broadcast to the terrorists over its loudspeaker system. On a number of occasions the minaret was used by snipers, although, they soon discovered that it offered little protection against small-arms fire.

On the day following the deployment into Sheik Othman, Checkpoint Golf, one of the checkpoints manned by the battalion on the northern edge of the town, came under fire from a 60mm mortar. No casualties were suffered because the firing was very inaccurate, the bombs landing some 150 yards away. That same day a position known as the Mansura Picquet, on a crossroads on the eastern edge of Al Mansura, came under fire from an automatic weapon on two occasions during the afternoon. The incidents which took place during the next few days followed a similar pattern, with grenades being thrown at patrols and OPs or checkpoints coming under fire.

A week later a general strike was called by both the NLF and FLOSY to clear the streets of the local inhabitants and enable the terrorists to carry out attacks on the security forces. This was a well-known signal to the British troops to prepare for trouble. Accordingly, at 0200 hours on 1 June D Company, commanded by Major Geoffrey Brierley, and No. 8 Platoon of C Company deployed to eight observation posts (OPs) which commanded the main streets and the area of the mosque which had previously been the scene of several incidents. At approximately 0400 hours trouble began with a grenade attack on a patrol outside the mosque. One of the OPs opened fire and killed three men, while the patrol succeeded in capturing a fourth. Shortly afterwards all the OPs came under heavy fire, some of it at very close range. 1 PARA lost one man killed and one wounded. One of the OPs had to be evacuated during the morning as it had become untenable. The firing lasted for several hours, C Squadron The Queen's Dragoon Guards supporting the battalion with its Saladin armoured cars, which engaged targets with their .30 Browning machine guns. The battle lasted throughout the day, and at one point 1 PARA's ammunition stocks began to run very low. The battalion's Second-in-Command, Major Joe Starling, swiftly arranged for a resupply which was carried out by a group led by the Intelligence Officer, Captain Ted Loden. During the battle broadcasts were made from the loudhailer in the mosque, and it became apparent that these were transmitting orders to the terrorists. As darkness fell, however, the firing slackened, and by 2100 hours the situation had been brought under control and order restored to the town.

For a few days afterwards Sheik Othman was calm, but on 5 June news came of the Israeli invasion of Sinai. It was inevitable that there would be a violent reaction and that trouble would reoccur in Sheik Othman. Lieutenant Colonel Walsh had expected this. In addition to making use of the OPs, he decided to occupy a disused mission hospital which dominated the eastern area of the town and the main road which led to the state boundary. However, the battalion had to fight its way into the hospital, and this was done by C Company, commanded by Major Norman Nicholls, and the Anti-Tank Platoon, which succeeded in doing so against fierce resistance. By dawn the following morning 'Fort Walsh', as the hospital was subsequently christened, had been secured and fortified. It was occupied by Battalion Tactical Headquarters and A Company under Major Graham Farrell.

Two weeks later, on 20 June, trouble once again loomed when, at 0900 hours, fires were lit in Lake Lines, the barracks of the South Arabian Army (SAA), and firing was heard. During the previous week there had been unrest in the SAA after a group of its senior officers were suspended from duty. A number of SAA troops mutinied and attacked both the Officers Mess and the guardroom, setting fire to some buildings within the barracks. Order was eventually restored by SAA officers and NCOs without any British intervention. An hour later firing was heard from within Champion Lines, where the Federal National Guard (FNG), who had heard the firing from Lake Lines, had assumed that British troops were attacking the SAA. The FNG opened fire on a truck carrying men of 60 Squadron Royal Corps of Transport, who were returning from a morning's shooting on the ranges. Seven of the RCT soldiers were killed and five wounded. Shortly afterwards, two British employees of the Public Works Department and two local nationals were killed. The FNG then proceeded to open fire on Radfan Camp, killing 2nd Lieutenant Angus Young of the 1st Battalion The Lancashire Regiment, which was based there with 1 PARA. Subsequently a report was received that British officers seconded to the FNG were being besieged inside the headquarters of Champion Lines. A detachment of C Company 1st Battalion King's Own Border Regiment, which was under command of 1 PARA, was sent in to rescue them, supported by The Queen's Dragoon Guards. That having been accomplished, the remainder of the company was despatched to secure the main armoury in Champion Lines. They did so in the face of strong resistance, suffering one man killed and eight wounded. The Borderers did not return the fire to which they were subjected, and eventually succeeded in restoring order within the barracks.

A week later, acting on information received by the battalion's Intelligence Officer, a force consisting of No. 10 Platoon of D Company 1 PARA and No. 12 Platoon of C Company of the Borderers carried out a cordon and search of a number of houses in Sheik Othman. On entering one building the troops heard shots on the second floor, where they found four local inhabitants bound hand and foot. Two were dead and the others wounded, one seriously. Having been badly beaten, they were in the process of being executed when the troops arrived. Their executioner fled upstairs and attempted to escape over the rooftops, but was shot and wounded by the cordon party, who recovered an AK-47 rifle and ammunition. It transpired that he was a member of the NLF.

One problem facing British troops was the unpredictability and temperamental behaviour of the SAA troops with whom they were frequently required to work. On 29 June an incident occurred which resulted in a confrontation between an SAA detachment and some Borderers who were stationed at Checkpoint Juliet. The Assault Pioneer Platoon of 1 PARA arrived at the rear of the SAA position after completing a task, and the Arab troops immediately suspected that they were being surrounded. The situation grew tense as the SAA troops trained their weapons on the Borderers, and was only defused after an officer from 1 PARA and a SAA staff officer arrived to mediate and restore good relations.

On 13 July the 1st Battalion The Lancashire Regiment took over responsibility for Al Mansura, leaving 1 PARA to devote its attention to Sheik Othman. All was relatively calm until three days later, when a co-ordinated attack was launched against some of D Company's positions. Between 2015 and 2040 hours the terrorists opened fire with blindicides (Czech-made rocket launchers), automatic weapons and a mortar. The command post was hit by three blindicide rockets and one man was wounded. The fire was returned, with the support of two Saladins of the Queen's Dragoon Guards, and three terrorists were killed. The latter part of July saw the daily spate of shooting and grenade incidents, but was otherwise relatively calm. However, on the evening of 28 July the terrorists once again used mortars against 1 PARA positions. Nine 60mm light mortar bombs were fired without causing any casualties, and on the following afternoon Fort Walsh was subjected to two attacks by a 2-inch mortar. Bombs exploded inside the area of the fort, and a trooper of the Queen's

Own Hussars, who had by then relieved the Queen's Dragoon Guards, was wounded in the arm. A mobile reaction force was deployed, but was unable to locate the mortar baseplate position.

Terrorist activity increased in early August, and there was evidence of further strife between NLF and FLOSY. During the first week a number of incidents occurred in which local nationals were gunned down in the streets of Sheik Othman as both organisations strove to increase their influence on the local population. On the evening of 10 August the terrorists once again stepped up their attacks on 1 PARA's positions in Fort Walsh, the police station, and its OPs. These took the form of sporadic but accurate sniping. At midday on 12 August a co-ordinated attack was launched on Fort Walsh and the OPs at Grenade Corner, when heavy fire was brought to bear from automatic weapons firing from several different positions. Twenty minutes later the police station also came under attack. That evening the terrorists tried a different tactic. At 1915 hours an explosive device struck the east inner wall of the police station and exploded. The wall of the station compound was severely damaged, cell doors were blown open, windows smashed and police vehicles damaged. Although there were no casualties among the troops, two policemen were wounded. It transpired that the device had contained some 20lb of explosive and had been rolled through the main gates.

Another variation in terrorist tactics came on 3 September. A Saracen armoured personnel carrier, carrying men of the mobile reaction force from Fort Walsh, was approaching Gunner's Corner in Sheik Othman when an oil drum was spotted in the middle of the road. The vehicle slowly approached it, and the crew saw wires leading from a hole in the drum to a house nearby. As the vehicle reversed rapidly away from it, the drum exploded.

During the first week of September there was increased inter-factional fighting between the NLF and FLOSY, and it was learned that each had kidnapped five of the opposing side. This resulted in a broadcast from the mosque, demanding an end to the killings and kidnappings, and for the hostages to be exchanged. During the afternoon of 9 September fighting broke out between the two organisations, and the civil police called in the Armed Police, a paramilitary force based in the town of Crater, to deal with the problem. A platoon arrived at Sheik Othman that evening and deployed into the area where fighting was taking place. However, the fighting continued through the night and throughout the following day, and the sounds of mortars, blindicides and small arms could be heard.

On 24 September 1 PARA handed over its positions in Sheik Othman to the 3rd Battalion of the South Arabian Army. Thereafter, it withdrew to a position approximately two miles north of Radfan Camp, where it was tasked with establishing a defensive line called the "Pennine Chain". A Company deployed as the left hand company, with D Company on its right. The role of the position was to protect the RAF airfield at Khormaksar, which would be used for the withdrawal of British troops, from attacks from the north, and it was established so that the airfield was out of small-arms and mortar range. During the first week of November the South Arabian Army, which had until then maintained a neutral stance as far as inter-factional strife was concerned, declared its support for the NLF. By then, 29 November had been set as a firm date for the withdrawal of the last British troops. On 27 November 1 PARA handed over its positions to 42 Commando RM, which was covering the withdrawal, and embarked in RAF transports for Bahrain, from where it returned home to England.

ANGUILLA, 1969

In the early part of 1969 trouble broke out on the island of Anguilla when elements of the population stated their objections to federation with other states in the Caribbean. Civil strife led to armed insurrection and, as the island was a British colony, the British Government reacted by sending troops to quell the rebellion. 2 PARA, commanded by Lieutenant Colonel Richard Dawnay, was despatched together with 120 members of London's Metropolitan Police to restore order to the island. While it was expected that the battalion's landing would be opposed, the British Government was keen that it should be as low-key as possible for political reasons. It was thus decided that, instead of an airborne assault, the battalion would carry out a landing from the sea.

The battalion, less B Company, which remained in England, flew to the island of Antigua, where it embarked on two Royal Navy frigates. Just before dawn on 19 March, C (Patrol) and D Companies landed in Gemini assault craft from the two frigates. In the event they encountered no armed opposition, although the islanders proved to be hostile towards the troops. While the landing was taking place, those on board the two frigates, including Lieutenant Colonel Dawnay and the senior naval officer, spotted flashes of light from the darkened coastline. Assuming these to be muzzle flashes from small arms, the observers waited for calls for naval gunfire support from the two companies. Minutes later there was much relief when it was learned that the flashes were not from weapons but from the flashguns of a large contingent of press photographers who were waiting on the beach to record and report on the landing.

Law and order was rapidly restored by the Metropolitan policemen, while 2 PARA directed its efforts towards 'hearts and minds' and winning over the islanders. Six weeks later B Company flew out and the rest of the battalion returned to Britain. The situation on the island by then was calm and the troops' role consisted of providing guards for key points, as well as providing a force to deal with any emergency. At the same time, considerable effort was put into projects such as the building of a school, which was carried out with the support of a sapper squadron which had also been sent out. B Company took part in 'Grass Roots', the codename for a census of the island's population. Patrols visited all parts of the island and recorded all information with regard to the location of each house and the number of occupants. Friendly conversations with local inhabitants led to the gleaning of further information, including opinions on local issues, all of which was recorded carefully on a card index and map at the headquarters of 'Force Anguilla'. This data enabled the island's administration to monitor popular opinion on its policies. One major benefit of 'Grass Roots' was the close contact established between the troops and the islanders. The latter were completely won over by the well disciplined, friendly soldiers, who were always willing to help when asked for assistance or advice.

On 14 September, B Company returned to England. Such was the success of 2 PARA's efforts during its six-month tour of duty on Anguilla that the battalion was awarded the Wilkinson Sword of Peace "for acts of humanity and kindness overseas".

Thus the 1960s drew to a close for The Parachute Regiment. With the British withdrawal from east of Suez, there would be no more campaigns of the type in which battalions and companies of the Regiment had seen action in such far-flung areas as Malaya, Borneo and The Radfan. The coming decade would, however, bring new challenges, not the least of which would be a heavy commitment on internal security operations very much nearer home — in Northern Ireland.

CHAPTER 13
Northern Ireland

n August 1969 the British Army once again found itself keeping the peace between hostile factions, when it was called in to support the civil authorities in Northern Ireland. The causes of the current conflict in Northern Ireland originated some 800 years ago, and it is not within the parameters of this book to examine them. Nor is it possible to cover in any detail all the tours of operations carried out by battalions of The Parachute Regiment during the 23 years of strife in the province since 1969. The story of the part played by The Parachute Regiment is highlighted and summarised in this chapter by accounts of some of the principal events which took place in the early part of the conflict which has plagued Northern Ireland for so long.

The situation in the province began to deteriorate in 1968, when a number of demonstrations and marches, organised by the Northern Ireland Civil Rights Association (NICRA), took place as part of a campaign of massed protest over discrimination against the Catholic community and Protestant domination of virtually every aspect of life in the province, including local government. On 5 October 1968 a major civil rights demonstration took place in Londonderry, during which rioting broke out. The riots lasted two days and spread to other areas of the province, including Belfast. In January 1969 inter-communal strife reared its head when Protestants attacked civil rights demonstrators marching from Belfast to Londonderry and a large number of the marchers were injured. Subsequently a large force of 1,000 Catholics turned the Bogside, the Roman Catholic area of Londonderry, into a defended enclave and refused to allow the Royal Ulster Constabulary (RUC) to enter it. At the same time, trouble occurred at Newry, Armagh and Coalisland. The situation continued to deteriorate further when, on 30 March, an electricity sub-station was attacked by saboteurs. As a result, the 'B' Specials, the Ulster Special Constabulary, were mobilised to provide guards for keypoints and vulnerable installations.

From April to July there was increasing trouble throughout Northern Ireland. On 20 April there was serious rioting in Londonderry which resulted in 209 members of the RUC and 79 demonstrators being injured. At the same time riots took place in Belfast, where a number of post offices were attacked with petrol bombs. On the following day a water pipeline at the Silent Valley reservoir and an electricity pylon at Annabow, Kilmore, were blown up. Three days later saboteurs struck again, attacking another water pipeline near Clady in County Antrim. At this point the Northern

NORTHERN IRELAND

Letterkenny
Londonderry
ULSTER   Antrim
Aldergrove•
•Omagh   Belfast
Dungannon•   'Lisburn
•'Lurgan
Enniskillen   Portadown
•   •Armagh   Ballykinler
Sligo   Newry
0   20   Monaghan   Crossmaglen
Miles   Castleblayney   'Warren Point
Dundalk

Ireland government requested military assistance in the guarding of a number of key installations. This was the first deployment of troops from garrison units within the province.

By this time, rioting and intercommunal strife had become common-place. In Belfast, the Ardoyne area was the scene each night of battles between Catholics and Protestants. In the Catholic area of the Crumlin Road, Protestant homes were attacked and set ablaze. On 2 August serious rioting took place in Belfast during a parade of Junior Orangemen. Protestants and Catholics fought a pitched battle lasting several hours, during which the RUC attempted to keep the two sides apart. However, the violence grew worse, and that night attacks were carried out on the police themselves. The following day shops were looted in the Shankill Road area of Belfast, and the police were again subjected to attacks. On 14 August the 'B' Specials were mobilised to assist in dealing with the riots as the situation in Belfast deteriorated even further. Hundreds of Catholics were forced to flee from their homes, which were set on fire by Protestants. A total of 170 homes were destroyed, together with 16 factories. Ten people died and many hundreds were injured, including 800 policemen.

The British government now despatched more troops to reinforce the garrison units already based in the province, bringing the total to over 6,000 men. Initially, the appearance of the Army was greeted with relief by Protestants and Catholics alike. The situation became calmer in Belfast, although some rioting took place in those areas where Protestant and Catholic communities were in close proximity. This resulted in CS gas being used in the capital for the first time on 7 September. Two days later the 'Peace Line', a barrier dividing the Falls Road and Shankill Road areas, was established to separate the Catholic and Protestant communities and lower the threat of violence from either side. Within a short space of time, however, nationalist sentiments came to the fore and the troops were viewed by the Catholic communities as merely supporting the Protestant-dominated establishment.

1 PARA

On 12 October 1 PARA arrived in the province, the first unit of The Parachute Regiment to carry out an emergency tour in Northern Ireland. Its area of responsibility covered the Falls Road and Shankill Road districts of Belfast. Its arrival coincided with Protestant demonstrations against the disbandment of the 'B' Specials and the announcement of their replacement by the Ulster Defence Regiment (UDR), a part-time military force. During the afternoon a number of demonstrations had taken place in several parts of Belfast, and that evening serious rioting broke out. During the night a large crowd of some 2,000 Protestants, including a number of gunmen of the Ulster Volunteer Force (UVF), assembled on the Shankill Road and advanced towards the area of Unity Flats. On reaching Townsend Street, however, the mob were prevented from going any further by the RUC and troops of the 2nd Battalion The Light Infantry (2 LI), who resorted to the use of CS gas after the demonstrators refused to disperse. At about midnight, members of the 3rd Battalion The Light Infantry (3 LI) came under fire from snipers and were attacked by petrol bombers. At the same time large crowds began to assemble in other areas, including North Queen Street and Limestone Road. The situation grew progressively worse in the early hours of 12 October, when men of 3 LI were attacked by a large crowd of 800 people and came under fire from automatic weapons. By 0300 hours the battalion had suffered 16 casualties. At the same time, men of the 2nd Battalion The Queen's Regiment (2 QUEENS) blocked the advance of a large crowd at the junction of Woodstock Road and Templemore Avenue.

The men of A Company 1 PARA arrived in the province at midnight on the night of 12/13 October, having flown from the Isle of Man, where they had been training, together with a combined force of D (Patrol) Company and Support Company. On their arrival they moved to King Edward's Hall, in Balmoral, the base of 41 Commando RM. All three companies were placed at immediate notice to reinforce 3 LI on the Shankill Road, but in the event they were not required. Battalion Tactical Headquarters and C Company arrived two hours later at 0200 hours on 13 October. At 0300 hours the Commanding Officer, Lieutenant Colonel Michael Gray, was briefed by the commander of 39 Infantry Brigade, Brigadier Peter Hudson, at the latter's tactical headquarters in Belfast. During the afternoon 1 PARA relieved 3 LI in the Shankill Road area. In the aftermath of the rioting of the previous Saturday night and Sunday morning, the atmosphere was very tense and the attitude towards the Army was vicious and outspoken. This feeling was reinforced when a crowd of some 400 assembled at the western end of the Shankill Road during the night. However, 1 PARA remained on standby in the side streets and the situation was defused by the RUC, the crowd dispersing at about 0200 hours on 14 October.

During the battalion's deployment Lieutenant Colonel Gray visited the RUC station in Tennent Street. He quickly discovered that there was no available intelligence on the situation, and that he and his battalion would have to start from scratch. He himself had received orders to reduce the level of tension in the area and to make every effort to return life to normal. In turn, he gave strict orders to all his men to make every effort to establish good relations with the local communities on either side of the Peace Line. At the same time, however, they were to maintain their normal battle disciplines rigidly and ensure that their bearing and turnout was always impeccable. At first the men of 1 PARA found it difficult to break through the wall of animosity which they encountered when talking to the local inhabitants, who were suspicious when they discovered that the soldiers were prepared to be friendly. This was largely due to hundreds of rumours about shooting incidents and alleged brutality by troops. However, within the next two days the atmosphere changed and the battalion established an excellent relationship with the people living in its area of responsibility.

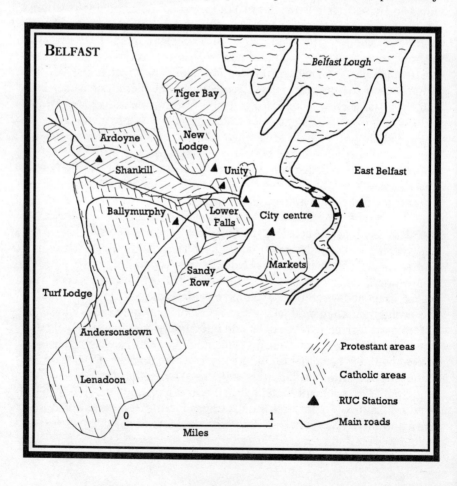

This manifested itself on the morning of Thursday 16 October, when the local inhabitants were woken by the noise of 1 PARA's vehicles and discovered that the battalion was being withdrawn from the Shankill Road. Such was their dismay that they telephoned their local Member of Parliament, who in turn contacted Headquarters Northern Ireland. By the following morning 1 PARA was back in the Shankill Road area.

As part of the 'Community Relations' campaign, the men of 1 PARA found themselves undertaking a wide variety of unfamiliar tasks, from arranging for street lights to be repaired and sewers to be unblocked to organising parties for elderly people and playing football with the local children. At the same time, however, the battalion established its presence with a vigorous programme of patrolling. As it did so, it began to build up a detailed picture of the inhabitants within its area, eventually collecting a mass of information which proved invaluable. It had been mooted to the Commanding Officer that the battalion might be required to carry out cordon and search operations for weapons if reliable information could be obtained. At the time, many commanders were sure that there were large numbers of weapons in the Catholic areas of Unity Flats and the Falls Road, although there were also rumours that there were more weapons and ammunition in the Shankill area than in 1 PARA. However, there was no reliable information to substantiate these reports. The battalion's Intelligence Officer compiled a very detailed dossier on the area, and members of the Intelligence Section accompanied patrols as they went out on the streets each day, acquiring a considerable amount of information. This even extended to details concerning the street lighting system and the local sewers. The Medical Officer spent two days exploring the latter, and discovered that some were sufficiently large for a 4-ton truck to be driven through them.

On a number of occasions 1 PARA found itself confronting mobs in the Shankill Road. In those early days there was none of the specialist equipment subsequently developed for internal security operations in Northern Ireland, and the troops quickly found that the old 'box' formation previously used for riot control in such theatres as Aden and Cyprus was of no use in the streets of Belfast. New tactics therefore had to be devised to cope with rioters throwing petrol bombs and stones.

Shortly after the battalion's arrival, its Training Officer set up a two-day Internal Security course to indoctrinate new drafts of soldiers arriving in the battalion and other Parachute Regiment personnel posted to 1 PARA. With the assistance of the battalion's Second in Command, he also established a deep infiltration exercise to train companies in the art of covertly inserting patrols and OPs. With the assistance of a sniper instructor from 41 Commando RM, cadres were run for the battlion's snipers and instructors were trained in the use of the recently introduced 'Starlight Scope', an American first-generation image intensification night vision device which had just been issued. The battalion was deploying snipers in two of its OPs in the Shankill area, which were manned each night. In addition, positions had been reconnoitred for use by the snipers and members of D (Patrol) Company in the event of trouble. On 5 November 1 PARA took over 41 Commando RM's area in addition to its own, and the entire area of operations, subsequently called the Belfast Central Region, thereafter stretched from the Boyne Bridge in the south of the city to well north of the Shankill Road. It included the majority of the most volatile areas, including the Shankill Road, the area of Divis Flats, a large part of the Catholic 'No Go' land, the Peace Line and the Boyne Bridge/Sandy Row area.

To cope with the tasks allocated by Headquarters 39 Infantry Brigade, 1 PARA was redeployed with Battalion Tactical Headquarters in Hastings Street, opposite the police station; C Company, with the Vigilant ATGW Platoon, Sniper Section, a troop of Saracen armoured personnel carriers and a troop of Saladin armoured cars under command, was based in the Shankill area; A and Support Companies were astride the Peace Line, being responsible for its security and deployed in platoon locations; and D (Patrol) Company was located with A and Support Companies but responsible for all OP tasks. B Company and Rear Echelon were based at Aldergrove. In addition, 1 PARA had a reserve company of 41 Commando RM for use as an immediate reserve and, until the end of the month, a company of 2 QUEENS under command. The Commando company was based at Albert Street Mill, while the Queens company was located in the south of 1 PARA's area and was responsible for the Boyne Bridge.

Lieutenant Colonel Gray soon found that it was difficult to meet his operational commitments and the ever-increasing number of 'Community Relations' projects. The problem was bound to get worse, as the Commander of 39 Infantry Brigade had been ordered to reduce his force level from seven to four battalions by early in the New Year of 1970, assuming that the security situation did not deteriorate before then. To make matters worse, the battalion lost the 2 QUEENS company on 29 November but its tasks remained unchanged. This resulted in a thinning out of the strengths at each of the battalion's locations to create a reserve. In addition to the mobs, 1 PARA, along with all other units in Northern Ireland, found itself coping with the threat from the IRA. Although taken by surprise by the rapid upsurge of trouble in mid-1969, the IRA had soon involved itself in protecting the Catholic community in those area where it was threatened by Protestant attack.

In 1970 the organisation was split in two when a militant splinter group, calling itself the Provisional IRA, broke away from the original body, which thereafter was known as the Official IRA. The 'Provisionals', as they became known, stated their objective as being the withdrawal of the British from Ulster, and proceeded to organise a campaign of terrorism by carrying out indiscriminate bombings against civilian targets, such as shops and business or industrial premises, and attacks on the security forces. As the political situation deteriorated they found increasingly fertile ground among Republican sympathisers within the Catholic community. Within a short period of time their ranks, which until then had been very small in number, had swelled by several hundred. During 1970 the Provisionals established three 'brigades' in Belfast, Londonderry and the rural areas near the border. At that time they were ill-equipped with weapons and were short of funds. However, help appeared in the form of the Northern Aid Association (NORAID), which channelled money from the United States. Within a relatively short period of time the Provisionals had managed to equip themselves sufficiently well to pose a serious threat.

By the time 1 PARA left the province in early February 1970, it had won the locals' confidence and had built up good relations with communities on both sides of the Peace Line. The situation was similar in other parts of Northern Ireland, where other battalions had established a similar rapport with the local people. Unfortunately, however, relieving units found that while they could inherit information and contacts, they had to start from the beginning in establishing their own credibility and winning the trust of the local inhabitants. In this respect the short duration of the four-month emergency tours proved counter-productive.

In September 1970 1 PARA returned to Northern Ireland for a 20-month tour with 39 Infantry Brigade, which comprised six battalions, four of which were deployed in Belfast. The battalion was one of two units which comprised the brigade reserve, and was based at Palace Barracks, Holywood, two miles from the centre at Belfast. Three of its companies were at different degrees of notice to move anywhere in the city, and could reach trouble spots within ten to fifteen minutes of leaving the barracks: one at ten minutes, one at forty and one 'on call', which was about two hours. Each of the four rifle companies was equipped with seven armoured 1-ton Humber 'Pig' armoured personnel carriers and the Reconnaissance Platoon had six Ferret scout cars. Companies frequently came under command of one of the city-based battalions. On the occasions when 1 PARA was deployed for three or four days at a time, it was allocated an area of responsibility and was often given companies from another battalion to augment it. Owing to the experience which it had gained on its previous four-month tour, the battalion possessed a very detailed knowledge of the geography of Belfast and its people.

1 PARA had trained in many different ways of controlling crowd situations in whichever area riots might take place, and its companies became expert at these. The battalion was frequently committed because a situation had gone out of control and the unit in the area could no longer contain the trouble or deal with it. In certain riot situations 1 PARA found that positive action and maintaining momentum into a crowd was a successful tactic. If the companies delayed moving in or deployed short of a crowd, they gave the rioters the initiative and the chance to hurl missiles. Driving directly up to them and deploying fast meant that the range was too short for throwing and the troops could dispense with riot shields and protective equipment. All the men in the companies were trained in arrest techniques, using simple Aikido or Judo holds which enabled a man to make an arrest on his own. Such methods enabled 1 PARA to confront mobs of between 2,000 and 3,000, mainly consisting of youths of between

14 and 20 years old, and to disperse them and make arrests within 30 minutes of being deployed.

By May 1971 the large-scale rioting had died away and the average size of the mobs had diminished to between 300 and 400. However, there was an increase in the number of shooting and bombing incidents. The IRA resorted to ambushing patrols in back streets, as well as bombing shops and public buildings at night.

Owing to the pressure of operational commitments, normal training in the battalion inevitably suffered. However, companies were despatched to the Isle of Man for a series of two-week exercises which began and ended with parachute assaults. These were a welcome change from internal security operations, providing opportunities for recreation and some useful training. The battalion was able to keep its parachuting skills fresh, as the RAF provided two aircraft weekly to enable it to make regular day and night descents. Fortunately there was a Royal Naval airstrip only a few hundred yards from Palace Barracks, and the aircraft would land there to pick up parachutists. Dropping zones were about two hours away and were situated on soft peat bogs on mountainsides.

On 21 July 1971 Lieutenant Colonel Michael Gray handed over command to Lieutenant Colonel Derek Wilford and departed for the Staff College, Camberley, to take up a new post as a GSO 1 on the directing staff.

BLOODY SUNDAY — 30 JANUARY 1972

On 29 January 1972 1 PARA moved from its base at Palace Barracks, Holywood, to Londonderry. Its task was to provide support for the RUC during a Northern Ireland Civil Rights Association march in the areas of the Creggan Estate and Rossville Flats, where trouble was expected in the form of armed opposition from the Provisional IRA. It was placed under command of 8 Infantry Brigade, commanded by Brigadier Pat McLellan, for this operation. Like all such demonstrations in Northern Ireland at the time, the march was illegal and was therefore banned. As a result, the decision had been taken to prevent it from taking place by deploying police and troops. 1 PARA was tasked with carrying out arrests, which would be made within a specified area beyond what was called the 'containment line'.

Early the following morning the battalion moved into Londonderry and took up positions with good access to the routes to be taken by the marchers, who assembled in the Bishop's Field, Creggan, during the early afternoon. At approximately 1445 hours the crowd, some 800 strong, set off through South Creggan, Brandywell, and then via the south then north Bogside until it moved on to its planned route at the intersection of Eastway and Lone Moor Road. It then turned down William Street where it encountered the RUC, who were blocking the route. As the leaders of the march were conferring with the RUC, a number of individuals started to throw stones. The police responded by bringing up a water cannon filled with purple dye, which was used to disperse the crowd. The marchers

Right: A parachute drop being carried out from a Vickers Valencia near New Delhi in 1942. (Airborne Forces Museum)

Below: A stick of 153rd Gurkha Para Bn inside a Dakota. (Airborne Forces Museum)

Left: Gurkha parachutists dropping from a Dakota in India in 1943. (Airborne Forces Museum)

Opposite page, top: Major M. A. Joy, commanding the reinforcements on Operation 'Dracula', organises the moving up of ammunition and supplies with the help of local people. (Airborne Forces Museum)

Below: Operation 'Dracula' – the first lift lands on the DZ at Tawhai, near Elephant Point, on the morning of 1 May 1945. (Airborne Forces Museum)

Above: Field Marshal Sir Claude Auchinleck inspects men of 15th Para Bn in the Bilaspur area of Central India in August 1945. On his left is the CO, Lieutenant Colonel Terence Otway. Behind and in the centre is Major Gen Eric Down, GOC 44th Indian Airborne Div. (Airborne Forces Museum)

Right: Left: Brigadier Paul Hopkinson, Commander 77th Indian Para Bde. Right: Major General Charles Boucher, GOC 2nd Indian Airborne Div. (Airborne Forces Museum)

Left: Vehicles of 6th Airborne Div in front of the Citrus Building, the location of the office of the Town Major, prior to beginning a day of patrolling through the city of Tel Aviv. (Imperial War Museum)

Left: The aftermath of the explosion at the King David Hotel in Jerusalem. Sappers of 9th Para Sqn RE assist in rescue operations. (Imperial War Museum)

Below: Weapons and ammunition found in a cache discovered in a Jewish kibbutz at Dorot in August 1946. (Imperial War Museum)

Above: Airborne training in Palestine was carried out when operational demands so permitted. Here a stick enplanes aboard a Halifax bomber at Aqir during a parachute refresher course. (Imperial War Museum)

Right: Patrolling the Wadi Rushmiya in Haifa. (Imperial War Museum)

Right: 3 PARA march through Aldershot at the start of the move by 16th Independent Para Bde Gp to the Middle East in July 1951. The Escort to the Colours comprised Sergeants Cole, Woodward and McKee with WO2 Cahill in rear. Behind the Escort marches Major Lawrence Scragg, followed by WO2 Chandler. (Airborne Forces Museum)

Left: Troops board a Valletta for a parachute drop into the jungle in Malaya during operations against Communist terrorists in 1955. (Airborne Forces Museum)

Opposite page, top: Operation 'Musketeer' – the first lift of 3 PARA lands on El Gamil airfield just after 0715 hours. (Airborne Forces Museum)

Left: Troops carry out a search for arms in Cyprus during operations against EOKA terrorists in 1956. (Airborne Forces Museum)

Below: Men of 3 PARA wait beside the RAF Vallettas which will drop them over El Gamil airfield at Port Said on the morning of 5 November 1956. (Airborne Forces Museum)

Above: The Commanding
Officer of 3 PARA,
Lieutenant Colonel Paul
Crook, with members of his
Bn Tac HQ near the Egyptian
Coast Guard barracks in Port
Said on 6 November. In the
background is a captured SU-
100 self-propelled gun.
(Airborne Forces Museum)

Right: Troops of 16th Indep
Para Bde Gp on exercise in
Jordan in 1958. (Airborne
Forces Museum)

Above: A patrol of No. 1 (Gds) Independent Coy PARA preparing to deploy into the jungle on an operation during the Borneo Confrontation in 1964. Left to right: Captain Algy Cluff, Guardsman Rowley, a medic from 7 Fd Amb, Guardsmen Gee and Handley and the company commander, Major John Head. (Lord Patrick Beresford)

Below: Captain Tom Brooke's patrol of No. 1 (Gds) Independent Coy PARA at Long Jawi, in the Third Division of Sarawak, after being extracted by helicopter at the end of an operation which lasted two months. Left to right: Lance Corporal Topping, Guardsman Wilson, Captain Brooke and Guardsman Thomas. (Lt Col T. C. P. Brooke)

Above: Members of the Gurkha Independent Para Coy on patrol in the Third Division during operations against Indonesian forces in 1965. Front to rear: Riflemen Kajiman Gurung and Omparsad Pun, Lieutenant Mike Callaghan and Signalman Rudranarayan Limbu. (Maj L. M. Phillips)

Above right: Men of C (Indep) Coy 2 PARA roping down from an RAF Whirlwind helicopter during operations in Borneo in 1965. (Airborne Forces Museum)

Right: Members of B Coy 3 PARA on Cap Badge Ridge, in the Radfan, after the battle against dissident tribesmen at 'Pegasus Village' on 4 May 1964. (Col P. F. Walter)

Right: The Wadi Dhubsan as seen from 'Arnold's Spur'. On the night of 25/26 May 1964, during operations against dissident Radfan tribesmen, 3 PARA and X Coy 45 Commando RM climbed down a steep cliff to, and subsequently advanced along, the wadi bottom. They came under fire in daylight from the hills beyond the second smoke burst from the hill peak. X Coy seized the small house on the pinnacle to the

right of the first shell burst while 3 PARA moved round the hills on both sides to clear the dissidents from their positions. (Airborne Forces Museum)

Left: Members of Support Company 1 PARA round up suspects in the area of Rossville Flats during operations in Londonderry on 29 January 1972. (Imperial War Museum)

Left: Men of 2 PARA embark on HMS *Intrepid* at Portland on 27 July 1972 for a tour of duty in Belfast. (Airborne Forces Museum)

Below: Members of a mobile patrol of B Coy 2 PARA in the autumn of 1972. (Airborne Forces Museum)

Right: A patrol of B Coy 2 PARA takes a break in Duncairn Gardens, Belfast, during operations in the summer of 1972. (Airborne Forces Museum)

Right: The 3 PARA patrol with its haul of weapons after the incident at Belleck in June 1976 when three terrorists were arrested. (Brig Peter Morton)

Below: A 3 PARA patrol in the Bessbrook area making friends of some of the local children. (Brig Peter Morton)

Top: 2 PARA departs from Aldershot at the start of its journey to the Falkland Islands. (Express Newspapers)

Above: Much emphasis was placed on retaining physical fitness during the long voyage south. Tug-of-war competitions, games and runs also helped to break the monotony of shipboard life. (Express Newspapers)

Left: A mattress proved useful as a dummy for bayonet practice. (Express Newspapers)

Opposite page top: All skills, including marksmanship, were practised ceaselessly during the weeks spent on board ship as the Task Force headed south. (Express Newspapers)

Opposite page, centre: 3 PARA landing at San Carlos. (Express Newspapers)

Right: 3 PARA wounded being evacuated by helicopter from the area of Mount Longdon. (Express Newspapers)

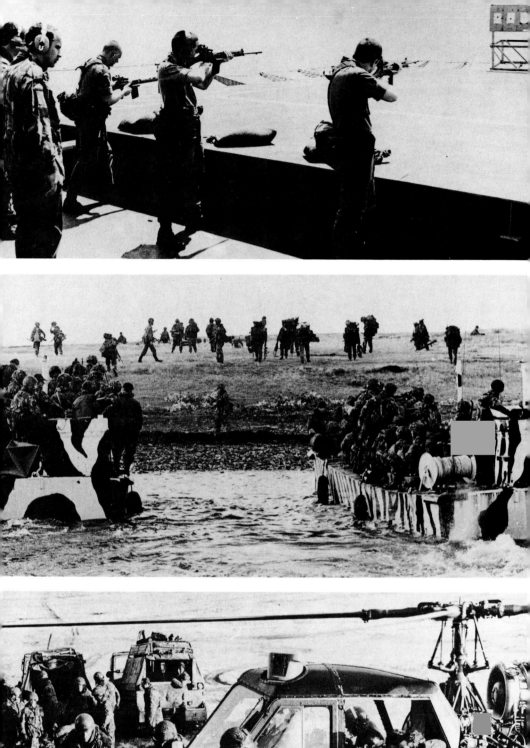

Left: Members of 3 PARA escort prisoner down from Mount Longdon. (Express Newspapers)

Bottom left: Two members of 3 PARA escort the battalion's first prisoner. (Express Newspapers)

Above: Men of 3 PARA tending some of the wounded at the base of Mount Longdon. (Express Newspapers)

Right: Men of 3 PARA enjoy a welcome opportunity to wash and shave in Port Stanley after the cessation of hostilities. (Express Newspapers)

Right: HRH The Prince of Wales, Colonel-in-Chief The Parachute Regiment, welcomes home the two battalions on their arrival back in England. Left to right: General Sir Anthony Farrar-Hockley (Colonel Commandant), HRH The Prince of Wales, Lieutenant Colonel Hew Pike (CO 3 PARA) and Lieutenant Colonel David Chaundler (CO 2 PARA). (Express Newspapers)

Left and below: The Red Devils, the official free-fall parachute display team of The Parachute Regiment and the Army, are world-famous for their displays of skill and precision. (Reproduced by courtesy of the Airborne Forces Museum)

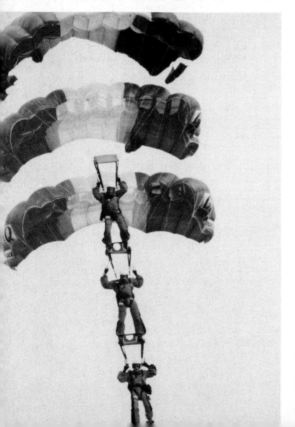

moved 300 yards down Rossville Street to Foxes Corner, where they gathered round a lorry being used as a platform by a number of speakers. A mob of some 150 rioters continued to throw stones and some stolen CS grenades at the RUC and troops.

Meanwhile, Lieutenant Colonel Derek Wilford, accompanied by his company commanders, had reconnoitred the containment line, the road blocks through which they would possibly have to deploy their men, and then William Street and the surrounding area where they might have to carry out arrests. Wilford's plan was to move A Company through Road Block No. 11 to the north-west, C Company through No. 14 up William Street, and Support Company between the two of them through Road Block No. 12. He expected some difficulty in moving a large number of men rapidly through the last of these, and so gave orders that the Machine Gun Platoon was to move forward ahead of the rest of the battalion and occupy a derelict house on the northern side of William Street, some 65 yards from the Presbyterian church nearby.

As the platoon made its way forward it was stoned, and shortly afterwards a single shot was fired at it from a direction of Rossville Flats. As it was occupying the derelict house, at about 1555 hours, a man was seen diagonally across William Street lighting a nail bomb. Two members of the platoon opened fire and the man fell. At 1600 hours Lieutenant Colonel Wilford decided to move in and arrest the rioters, and radioed the brigade headquarters for clearance to do so. Ten minutes passed before permission was granted, and at 1610 hours C Company moved through Road Block No. 14, pushing the rioters down William Street and Chamberlain Street. Two minutes later Support Company passed through Road Block No. 12 in six 1-ton armoured Humber 'Pigs' to move round behind the rioters. Meanwhile, A Company moved further west to the junction of William Street and Creggan Street to take up a flank protection position.

Support Company, led by the Mortar Platoon, moved on to the open ground north-east of Rossville Flats and took up positions cutting off the escape westwards of the rioters who were retreating in front of C Company. As the Mortar Platoon dismounted from its two 'Pigs' and started to make arrests it came under fire from a gunman with a Thompson sub-machine gun on the corner of Rossville House and from another firing from a window in one of the flats. The fire was returned, and both gunmen were shot by one member of the Mortar Platoon. Other gunmen opened fire from some barricades which had been erected at the foot of the flats, and three of these were shot dead. At the same time five rioters were arrested. Meanwhile, bottles filled with acid were being dropped from the top of Rossville Flats, and two soldiers received severe burns. The scene was one of pandemonium. Panic-stricken people were screaming and running in different directions through the troops, who were trying to carry out arrests.

Meanwhile, the Anti-Tank Platoon, supported by a composite platoon of men from Headquarter Company, had dismounted and was moving through some buildings opposite Rossville Flats, but was told to hold fast when the shooting began. Shortly afterwards the platoon came under fire from the area of the Creggan Estate, behind where the civil rights marchers were holding their gathering at Foxes Corner. This fire was returned by some members of the platoon.

Support Company's commander and his company headquarters had established themselves at the foot of Rossville Flats, out of the line of fire from the Creggan Estate, which by then had become heavy. The Mortar Platoon, having placed the bodies of the three dead rioters inside a 'Pig' and despatched them to Battalion Headquarters, was by then deploying round to the left of the flats. Shortly afterwards, Lieutenant Colonel Wilford arrived at Company Headquarters and ordered that fire was not to be returned under any circumstances.

Firing had also come from a barricade which had been erected across Rossville Street and a nail bomb had exploded nearby. Another bomb had been thrown from an alleyway which led into Glenfada Park. Three members of the Anti-Tank Platoon, who were sent into the park to protect the platoon's flank, saw three armed men running. As the three terrorists turned to face the troops, they were engaged. Subsequently, 20 rioters were arrested in Glenfada Park. Meanwhile, C Company had moved through Road Block No. 14 and, after turning south along Chamberlain Street, had linked up with Support Company at Eden Place. The company arrested 22 rioters and handed them over to an arrest team of the Royal Military Police. At 1725 hours Lieutenant Colonel Wilford gave orders for the companies to carry out a phased withdrawal to their original forming-up positions. All of them were clear by 1737 hours.

A total of 13 people had been shot dead during the operation, which was subsequently christened "Bloody Sunday" by the media. The Provisional IRA did not hesitate to use the whole affair for propaganda purposes, accusing 1 PARA of having fired indiscriminately on unarmed people and alleging that the operation had been designed to force a confrontation with the terrorists. However, those who criticised the security forces failed to mention that the organisers of the march had gone ahead with it regardless of the fact that it was illegal and banned. Moreover, the 150 or so rioters had clearly intended to provoke a reaction from the RUC and troops, ultimately using CS gas against them. Once the situation got out of hand, as it was clearly intended to do, the Provisional IRA opened fire on 1 PARA, using the crowd as cover. The charge that the troops opened fire indiscriminately can be refuted by the fact that those killed were all males aged between 18 and 26 years old. Anything other than aimed shots would in all likelihood have resulted in women and children, of whom there were many in the crowd, being among the dead. There were unconfirmed reports that the total of those killed was between 20 and 30, and that the missing bodies had been spirited away across the border, where they were buried. If this was indeed the case, the motive for their concealment can only have been that forensic examination would have revealed that the individuals concerned had been handling and firing weapons.

The subsequent uproar over "Bloody Sunday" resulted in a tribunal being held under Lord Chief Justice Widgery. The summary of the conclusions of his report is as follows:

1 There would have been no deaths in Londonderry on 30 January if those who organised the illegal march had not thereby created a highly dangerous situation in which a clash between demonstrators and the security forces was almost inevitable.

2 The decision to contain the march within the Bogside and Creggan had been opposed by the Chief Superintendent of Police in Londonderry, but was fully justified by events and was successfully carried out.

3 If the Army had persisted in its "low key" attitude and had not launched a large-scale operation to arrest the hooligans, the day might have passed off without serious incident.

4 The intention of the senior Army officers to use 1 PARA as an arrest force and not for other offensive purposes was sincere.

5 An arrest operation carried out in battalion strength, in circumstances in which the troops were likely to come under fire, involved hazard to civilians in the area which Commander 8 Brigade may have under-estimated.

6 The order to launch the arrest operation was given by Commander 8 Brigade. The tactical details were properly left to CO 1 PARA, who did not exceed his orders. In view of the experience of the unit in operations of this kind, it was not necessary for CO 1 PARA to give orders in greater detail than he did.

7 When the vehicles and soldiers of Support Company appeared in Rossville Street, they came under fire. Arrests were made; but in a very short time the arrest operation took second place and the soldiers turned to engage their assailants. There is no reason to suppose that the soldiers would have opened fire if they had not been fired upon first.

8 Soldiers who identified armed gunmen fired upon them in acordance with the standing orders in the Yellow Card.* Each soldier was his own judge of whether he had identified a gunman. Their training made them aggressive and quick in decision, and some showed more restraint in opening fire than others. At one end of the scale some soldiers showed a high degree of responsibility; at the other, notably in Glenfada Park, firing bordered on the reckless. These distinctions reflect differences in the character and temperament of the soldiers concerned.

9 The standing orders contained in the Yellow Card* are satisfactory. Any further restrictions on opening fire would inhibit the soldier from taking proper steps for his own safety and that of his comrades and unduly hamper the engagement of gunmen.

10 None of the deceased or wounded is proved to have been shot whilst handling a firearm or bomb. Some are wholly acquitted of complicity in such action; but there is a strong suspicion that some others had been firing weapons or handling bombs in the course of the afternoon and that yet others had been clearly supporting them.

11 There was no general breakdown in discipline. For the most part, the soldiers acted as they did because they thought their orders required it. No order and no training can ensure that a soldier will always act wisely, as well as bravely and with initiative. The individual soldier ought not to have to bear the burden of deciding whether to open fire in confusion such as prevailed on 30 January. In the conditions prevailing in Northern Ireland, however, this is often inescapable.

Note:
*The Yellow Card is an aide memoire issued to all troops on service in Northern Ireland. It contains the regulations governing the use of firearms by military personnel.

In the aftermath of "Bloody Sunday" the Provisional IRA swore revenge and declared that it had given permission for its members to kill as many troops as possible. Three weeks later it took its revenge on The Parachute Regiment and Airborne Forces as a whole. On 22 February a huge explosion rocked Montgomery Lines, the base of 16 Parachute Brigade, and the town of Aldershot nearby. As a pall of smoke rose into the sky it became clear that the Brigade Headquarters Officers Mess had been demolished by a bomb which had destroyed the front of the building and devastated the interior. There were seven victims of this IRA bomb attack: six civilian mess staff, including some women, and a Roman Catholic padre, Father Gerry Weston.

In May 1972 1 PARA completed its two-year tour as a residential battalion in Northern Ireland and returned to Aldershot and 16 Parachute Brigade. However, it was sent back to the province two months later on an emergency four-month tour. For the first few days the battalion was billeted on board HMS *Maidstone*, a former submarine depot ship which had been converted into a floating barracks and moored at the Harland & Wolf shipyard in Belfast. Five days later it was deployed in the city, divided among the Shankill Road, Woodvale and the Catholic area of Ligoniel. Battalion Tactical Headquarters was located at the police station in Tennent Street, halfway between the Crumlin Road and the Shankill, while the companies were based at the Flax Street Mill, which was shared with the 1st Battalion The Light Infantry (1 LI), and at Ligoniel Mill, where Echelon was also located. One of the companies was attached to 2 PARA in the Ballymurphy area for the duration of the tour. Initially this unit was based in a school, but subsequently was moved to a disused bakery on the Springfield Road.

Two months later 1 PARA was allocated a larger area of responsibility which included New Barnsley, Whiterock and Beechmount. This resulted in relocation of its companies, which were moved to bases in schools in New Barnsley and Beechmount.

Three main incidents marked the battalion's tour. The first occurred when a school bus was hijacked and shots were fired at men of 1 PARA who were guarding the route taken by the bus between children's homes and their schools. The incident escalated, and trouble developed during the next two days after a number of youths were arrested and taken to Tennent Street police station for questioning. A riot developed outside the police station and CS gas grenades were thrown into the station courtyard. Shortly afterwards, a 1 PARA vehicle was attacked and one of its occupants wounded by a small-calibre weapon, the others being injured by stones and bottles which were thrown at them. Another vehicle was stopped by a number of women, one of whom tried to wrest a rifle from one of the soldiers in it. In the ensuing melée a number of the women were injured and, inevitably, the members of the patrol was accused of brutality and of having beaten the women with their rifle butts.

The second incident took place on the following night, when a 1 PARA patrol was ambushed in an area near Berlin Street. Firing took place and two civilians were killed. 1 PARA later alleged that the patrol's assailants were members of the Ulster Defence Association. The third and final incident occurred when an armoured ambulance was ambushed in the area of Woodvale. Once again, a mob gathered and a riot developed.

In November 1 PARA completed its four-month emergency tour and returned to Aldershot, where it once again took its place in 16 Parachute Brigade.

2 PARA

By November 1972 2 PARA, then commanded by Lieutenant Colonel Geoffrey Howlett, had completed four emergency tours totalling 16 months in Northern Ireland. Its first tour started in February 1970 when, accompanied by No. 1 (Guards) Independent Company, it arrived to relieve 1 PARA. During that tour and the following one in 1971, the battalion was based in Londonderry and subsequently Belfast, where it took over from 3 PARA in June 1971. Soon after its arrival the Springfield Road police station, where Battalion Headquarters was located, was attacked by the Provisionals, who threw a bomb over the wall at the side of the station. Shortly afterwards one of 3 PARA's posts overlooking the Springfield Road was attacked by terrorists travelling in a hijacked bus, who opened fire at point-blank range on the two soldiers inside the heavily sandbagged position. Fortunately, only the sandbags were damaged.

One of the battalion's companies was based in the Ballymurphy area, which was considered the most volatile at that time. A Catholic enclave, it is staunchly Republican, and at that time was often the scene of violence and public disorder. During 1970 there were many riots in the housing estates in the area, where the police and Army were regarded with implacable hostility.

OPERATION 'DEMETRIUS' — 9 AUGUST 1971

During 1971 the level of terrorism in Northern Ireland increased to unparalleled levels. On one July night alone, terrorists planted 20 bombs in Belfast and destroyed a number of buildings, including shops, banks, public houses and car showrooms. At the same time there was an escalation of attacks on the Army and police which reached a climax at the end of the first week of August. By that stage mobs were moving through different areas of the city, hijacking buses and setting fire to public buildings, government offices, shops and factories. At that point the decision was taken at the highest level to introduce internment, plans for which had been made some time previously.

In the early hours of Monday 9 August, troops deployed to their respective areas for an operation to arrest individuals who were to be detained and subsequently interned. For this task, 2 PARA had C Company 1 PARA, two troops of the Parachute Squadron Royal Armoured Corps, B Squadron 15th/19th King's Royal Hussars and 54 Battery Royal Artillery under command. These and 2 PARA's companies were allocated areas of houses which were to be searched, and from which nominated detainees were to be extracted, as follows:

A Company — North Suffolk
B Company — Ballymurphy and Turf Lodge
D Company — Clonard and Cavendish
Support Company — Whiterock, Beechmount and St. James
C Company 1 PARA — South Suffolk
B Squadron 15/19H — Malone Road Area
54 Battery RA — Andersonstown

By 0430 hours on 9 August the companies and other sub-units under command of 2 PARA had moved into their areas and within three-quarters of an hour had made all the arrests. Some tasks had proved easier than others, in some instances troops had to make forced entries into houses, and in only two cases had force been necessary to arrest the individuals concerned. Very little trouble was encountered en route to the police stations where those detained were to be held. A crowd of some 40 people attempted to stop the Mortar Platoon at the junction of Donegall Road and the M1 motorway by lying on the road in front of its vehicles. However, they were removed without force and the vehicles went on their way.

The reaction to the introduction of internment was, however, violent. In the Clonard area there were a number of shooting incidents which included sniping at troops in the area of Kashmir Road and Bombay Street D and Support Companies exchanged fire with snipers equipped with automatic weapons. Meanwhile, barricades were erected in the Springfield Road area and riots took place, with petrol bombs and stones being thrown. A mob gathered outside the 2 PARA company base at the Henry Taggart Hall in Ballymurphy, throwing petrol bombs and stones, while terrorists opened fire on the base from the direction of Divismore Park and New

Barnsley. The mob, which numbered some 200, was eventually dispersed with the aid of water cannon. During the evening, fire was exchanged with terrorists near the base.

Such was the level of inter-communal violence that some families had to be evacuated from their homes in Mayo Street and Lanark Street, and the trouble was at its worst in the Springmartin Road area. The evacuation was carried out under Support Company which provided protection. Later that night the company engaged 12 snipers who opened fire in the area of Moyard Flats, hitting five of them. Barricades were erected in several areas, those in Turf Lodge being in place almost immediately after Operation 'Demetrius'. These were allowed to remain until the early hours of 11 August, but in other areas they were removed as soon as possible, often in the face of strong resistance. A Company deployed a platoon to keep the Falls Road clear, and this was attacked with petrol bombs as it removed barricades at the junction with Beechmount Avenue.

By 11 August the situation had calmed down and the level of violence had dropped. By that stage 2 PARA had been further reinforced by companies of 2 and 3 QUEENS and by A and D Companies of 1 PARA. At the end of the month the battalion completed its tour and returned to England.

Four months later, however, at the beginning of February 1972, 2 PARA was back in the province for another four-month emergency tour. Based in north-west Belfast, the battalion was responsible for an area which included the city centre, the volatile area of Unity Flats, Crumlin Road Jail, the western docklands and the northern suburbs of Belfast extending out to Whiteabbey and Rathcoole. A Company had the largest area, stretching from Limestone Road to Whiteabbey. Terrorism was at its height in the province in early 1972. The Provisional IRA directed its campaign of violence at civilian targets, which were subjected to daily bombings. During this tour 2 PARA's companies found themselves carrying out tasks ranging from guarding the Crumlin Road Jail to performing searches for arms, some of which produced large hauls, or patrolling the areas around Unity Flats and New Lodge. Originally, the battalion was due to return to England in mid-June after completing its four-month tour. However, its presence was required for a major operation, and the end of the following month found it still deployed in the province.

OPERATION 'MOTORMAN' — 31 JULY 1972

By the middle of 1972 the political and military situation in Northern Ireland had become intolerable, and the final straw came in the form of "Bloody Friday". In the space of one hour and five minutes on the afternoon of 21 July, the Provisional IRA carried out a total of 19 bomb attacks in Belfast which left nine people dead and 130 seriously injured. At that point it was decided that the Catholic 'No-Go' enclaves in West Belfast and Londonderry would be cleared out and law and order reimposed. The operation to carry out this task was codenamed 'Motorman', and was the largest to be mounted by the British Army since Operation 'Musketeer', the airborne invasion of Suez. It involved a total of 21,000 troops from 27 different units. Supporting the units to be deployed in Londonderry were four Centurion Armoured Vehicle Royal Engineers (AVREs) landed from landing craft which would transport them up the River Foyle.

At 0400 hours on 31 July Operation 'Motorman' began in Belfast. In the west of the city 2 PARA moved into an area which embraced Ballymurphy, Whiterock, New Barnsley, Moyard, and Turf Lodge, while the 1st Battalion Prince of Wales Own Regiment of Yorkshire and the 2nd Battalion Royal Regiment of Fusiliers made their way into Andersonstown. Elsewhere in the city, the 1st Battalion The Light Infantry occupied the area of the Ardoyne and 40 Commando Royal Marines established itself in New Lodge. The 1st Battalion Welsh Guards took over the city centre and moved into Sandy Row, a Protestant area, and the 3rd Battalion Royal Anglian Regiment deployed in the Falls Road area. To the south, the 1st Battalion The King's Regiment did likewise in Beechmount. 19 Field Regiment RA took over another area in the south, while deploying part of one of its batteries to the predominantly Protestant area of Ballynafeigh. The Life Guards occupied Ballymacarrett, a Catholic area.

The operation proved to be a success for the security forces and a disaster for the Officials and Provisionals. The deployment of such a large number of troops forced the terrorists to flee the so-called "No-Go" area and thus lose control of them. After Operation 'Motorman', 2 PARA's area became extremely quiet apart from the occasional incident involving terrorists sniping at patrols. In October the battalion returned to England and Aldershot.

WARREN POINT — 27 AUGUST 1979

In July 1979, 2 PARA, commanded by Lieutenant Colonel Colin Thomson, began a 20-month tour of duty in Northern Ireland. Based at Palace Barracks, Holywood, the battalion undertook the role of reserve for 39 Infantry Brigade.

On the afternoon of 27 August, a convoy consisting of a landrover and two 4-ton vehicles carrying men of A Company was travelling along the coastal road from Ballykinler en route for A Company's base at the border town of Newry. Heading along the northern side of Carlingford Lough, near the village of Warren Point, the convoy approached a lay-by in which was parked a trailer loaded with bales of straw. Across the lough, which is only some 200 yards wide at that point, a group of Provisional IRA terrorists lay in wait, safely within the territory of Eire.

As the convoy passed Narrow Water Castle, a medieval building near the road, and as the rear vehicle drew level with the trailer, the terrorists triggered by remote control a 500lb bomb hidden in the trailer. Six members of A Company died in the blast, which destroyed the 4-ton vehicle in which they were travelling. The other vehicles in the convoy halted and their occupants ran back to help their comrades. As they did so, they came under fire from the terrorists across the lough. As they returned the fire, ammunition in magazines lying in the burning wreckage began to explode.

Meanwhile, a Royal Marine detachment on patrol in Warren Point had heard the explosion and had radioed a contact report to A Company's base in Newry. On hearing the report, two landrover-mounted patrols of 2 PARA's Machine Gun Platoon, which had been patrolling Newry, headed for Warren Point. At the same time, A Company's commander, Major Peter Fursman, accompanied by some of his men, headed for the scene of the incident in another two landrovers. On reaching the area, the two Machine Gun Platoon vehicles set up road blocks to the north and south of the incident location.

Meanwhile, the 1st Battalion The Queen's Own Highlanders, based at Bessbrook in County Armagh, had dispatched its airborne reaction force in RAF Wessex helicopters. On their arrival, the Highlanders circled the area in their aircraft while another Wessex landed on the central reservation in the road and disembarked a medical officer and two medics, who immediately set about treating the casualties. Several members of the A Company convoy had taken up positions near a gatehouse which was located a short distance away. Unfortunately, the terrorists had foreseen that the area of the building offered excellent cover for regrouping troops and had positioned a second bomb accordingly.

Shortly afterwards, a Gazelle helicopter landed in a field to the east of the gatehouse, and the Commanding Officer of the 1st Battalion The Queen's Own Highlanders, Lieutenant Colonel David Blair, disembarked with his signaller. Running down the road, Lieutenant Colonel Blair headed for the gatehouse where he could see Major Peter Fursman's two landrovers parked outside the building. As he did so, the Wessex helicopter on the central reservation, by then loaded with wounded members of A Company, started to take off. At that very moment, the terrorists triggered their second bomb, weighing a massive 1,000lb, which was hidden in the gateway beside the gatehouse. The devastating blast killed twelve more men, including Lieutenant Colonel Blair and Major Fursman, and seriously injured two others. Miraculously, the Wessex helicopter survived, although it suffered some damage.

It transpired later that the terrorists had devoted a great deal of effort and time to planning the attack. As photographs of the location taken a few days earlier later revealed, trailers were often parked in the lay-by, and thus no suspicions had been aroused. The only civilian casualty was a young tourist named Michael Hudson, the son of one of the Queen's coachmen, who was unfortunately caught in the crossfire between the terrorists and the troops and was killed.

3 PARA: SOUTH ARMAGH, 1976

Like 1 and 2 PARA, 3 PARA acquired considerable experience of conducting operations in Belfast. It was during one of the battalion's early tours in 1971 that one of its members received a posthumous award for gallantry. On 25 May, thirty pounds of gelignite, packed in a suitcase, was planted in the police station in the Springfield Road in West Belfast. The station, which was a divisional headquarters, also housed the battalion headquarters of 3 PARA. The battalion was in the process of completing a four-month tour with 39 Infantry Brigade and was handing over to 2 PARA which had previously been in Londonderry as part of 8 Infantry Brigade. Sergeant Willetts of Headquarter Company spotted the bomb and, having sent another NCO to give the alarm and clear the building, shepherded some civilians and several policemen outside. At the same time, he stood in the doorway and shielded them while they escaped. A few seconds later, however, the bomb exploded and killed him. He was subsequently awarded a posthumous George Cross for his great gallantry and self-sacrifice.

On Thursday 15 April 3 PARA, commanded by Lieutenant Colonel Peter Morton, took over from the 1st Battalion The Royal Scots in South Armagh. The battalion was at the start of four-month tour, its role being to provide military support for the RUC in the county. This was the first time that 3 PARA had operated in a rural environment in Northern Ireland. The battalion, which was part of 3 Infantry Brigade at Lurgan, was based principally at Bessbrook Mill. Its companies were deployed a follows:

A Company — Crossmaglen
B Company (less one platoon) — Newtownhamilton
C Company (less one platoon) — Forkhill
D (Patrol) Company — Bessbrook
Support Company — Newry
Battalion reserve (two platoons — one each from B and C Coys)

The first incident occurred only a few hours after 3 PARA had assumed responsibility from the Royal Scots. At 1945 hours an RAF Wessex helicopter landing at A Company's base at Crossmaglen was hit by an RPG-7, a Soviet-made anti-tank rocket launcher, and by small-arms fire from the ground. Fortunately the aircraft suffered only slight damage and was able to land safely without any casualties. A Company, which was prepared to react very swiftly to any threat, responded by opening fire, and during a follow-up operation five men were arrested but subsequently released by the police for lack of evidence of any involvement in the incident. That same night, a patrol on a surveillance task arrested a suspect who was wanted by the security forces. Later, as a helicopter landed to extract the patrol, the suspect attacked the patrol commander, who killed him in self-defence.

These incidents set the pattern for 3 PARA's tour, during which scarcely a day passed without a shooting or bombing incident. Terrorist tactics by this time were very much more sophisticated than in the early days of 1971 and 1972. One of the problems faced by the unit responsible for South Armagh is the border with the Irish Republic. It is 303 miles long, and there are over 290 crossing places. The border is mostly unmarked and meanders invisibly through the middles of fields and farmyards, across roads and tracks. There are no barriers to prevent terrorists crossing it wherever they wish, enabling them to slip back to sanctuary after perpetrating outrages in the North. The British security forces, on the other hand, are not permitted under any circumstances to cross the border, and thus have to exercise great care when operating close to it.

The problems created by the border manifested themselves for 3 PARA in the month following the battalion's arrival. On Saturday 15 May a patrol from C Company discovered seven beer kegs containing a total of 100lb of home-made explosive in a shed in a garage which lay astride the border. Both the RUC and the Gardai Siocchana (the Irish Republic's police force) attended the scene. The latter would not arrest the garage owner, and the RUC, for whatever reason, were unable to call a scenes of crime officer to record fingerprints on the kegs and to collect other forensic evidence. The explosive was subsequently destroyed, but no information was gathered and no arrests resulted from this incident, which was the first of many such frustrating experiences for 3 PARA during this tour.

A week later on one of the border crossings in their area, another C Company patrol discovered a small landmine consisting of two explosive-filled beer kegs. Subsequently, a patrol uncovered a wire leading to a culvert at the location where the main road to Dublin crosses the border. It so happened that a convoy carrying explosives was due to pass that particular point two days later, on 25 May, and it was thought that the wire was intended to activate a mine in an attack on the convoy or its escort. Accordingly, a patrol was inserted covertly that evening to catch the terrorists as they came back to set up their mine and prepare for the attack. In the event, no terrorists appeared.

On 15 June a remotely initiated mine triggered by the Provisional IRA was responsible for a tragedy which occurred immediately after it had been detonated. An eight-man patrol from C Company was manning a vehicle checkpoint (VCP) on the road which runs from Meigh via Drumintee to Forkhill. At 2315 hours a landmine buried in the verge was detonated as the last member of the patrol drew level with it. Although some members of the patrol were hurled to the ground by the blast, there were no casualties, but the troops were shocked and disorientated by the blast. As the patrol commander was checking his men, a Ford Cortina coming from the direction of Meigh stopped nearby. The patrol commander shouted to the driver to switch off his headlights, which were illuminating the scene, and two soldiers were despatched to ensure that he did so. At that point, a second car approached the scene and suddenly accelerated past the stationary vehicle. One of the two soldiers standing by the Ford fired one round and other members of the patrol, who thought that the shot had come from the vehicle, also opened fire and killed the driver, who was a young man from Warren Point. It was subsequently established that he was an innocent civilian who had probably panicked when he saw armed men on the road in the darkness. He was killed by a tragic error made by men who had reacted in a split second while still suffering from the effects of a huge explosion at close range. It was later established that the mine had contained 200lb of explosive and had been initiated from a firing point a few hundred yards away.

A week later, on 22 June, another 3 PARA patrol fell foul of an explosive device. A 12-man patrol, consisting of two sections from A Company, had been deployed in the Cullyhanna area the previous day. During the afternoon it was moving near the border in a quiet and unpopulated area near a crossing point. One section was ordered by the patrol commander to reconnoitre a landing site (LS) for a helicopter which would be flying in to extract the patrol and fly it to Cullaville for another task. Once the LS had been cleared, the rest of the patrol moved in to secure it. As the second section was in the process of making its way through a hedge on top of a bank, there was a massive explosion which injured three men, one seriously. All three were evacuated by helicopter soon afterwards and were taken to Musgrave Park Hospital in Belgrave. The seriously injured man, Private Snowdon, was subsequently transferred to the civilian Royal Victoria Hospital, but died of his wounds. Investigations showed that the device consisted of 40lb of commercial explosive triggered by radio control, probably initiated by a terrorist concealed on the Republican side of the border. The point at which the patrol crossed through the hedge could be clearly seen from the border, which was less than 900 yards away.

Three days later, however, 3 PARA was able to even the score. An eight-man patrol had been carrying out surveillance on the Mountainhouse Inn, halfway between Bessbrook and Newtownhamilton. It had set up an OP, manned by four men, 30 yards from the inn and was photographing those who came and went. The other four members of the patrol were located in a covering position on the northern side of a nearby hill called Drumilly Mountain. At 1735 hours the OP was spotted by a young child, who approached it. Consequently, the patrol commander withdrew the OP and moved on to higher ground before setting off with one of his NCOs to find another location. As he was doing so, he spotted four armed and hooded men getting out of an estate car parked some 450 yards away. Under cover of hedgerows, the four terrorists made their way to a house near the main road, where they met some people in a yard behind the building. Meanwhile, the car was driven off by a fifth man and parked in the garage of a nearby farm.

Leaving the NCO with him to maintain observation on the terrorists, the patrol commander went back to bring up the rest of his OP party. Sending his radio operator back to the covering position to bring up the rest of the patrol, he returned with his light machine gunner to where he had left the NCO. When the two men were 50 yards from the latter's position, they heard him open fire. A fire fight then took place between the patrol and the terrorists, who split up. At that point a Gazelle helicopter carrying the commander of D (Patrol) Company arrived overhead in response to the patrol's contact report over the radio. Two terrorists were seen to run into a nearby bungalow and the Quick Reaction Force (QRF), which at that point arrived in helicopters, was directed to land nearby and engage them. The commander of the QRF, who was a young subaltern in B Company, and three men approached the building. Having failed to persuade the two terrorists to surrender, they fired two shots into the ceiling of one of the bedrooms and two at the front porch, which produced the desired result. Two men, Patrick Joseph Quinn and Raymond Peter McCreesh, surrendered unarmed. An Armalite rifle and an M1 Garand rifle, together with some ammunition, were found inside the bungalow. A search of the surrounding area resulted in the discovery of a Sten gun. During the night, a patrol from B Company remained in the area to watch for any sign of the other three terrorists. This proved to be a wise move, because a thorough search at 0500 hours on the following morning resulted in the discovery of a third man, Daniel McGuinness, asleep in a hiding place with an Armalite rifle in his hands and 32 spent cartridge cases on the ground beside him.

On 17 August 1976 3 PARA handed over responsibility for South Armagh to 40 Commando Royal Marines and departed for England. Although only a few of the incidents which occurred during its tour have been quoted here, it had been a challenging time, and the battalion had worked extremely hard. Like many of the emergency and residential tours carried out before and since by battalions of The Parachute Regiment, it had been unpredictable and interspersed with frustration, disappointment and tragedy, as well as being highlighted with success.

CHAPTER 14
Operation 'Corporate': The Falklands Campaign, 1982

The three regular battalions of The Parachute Regiment were well dispersed on 1 April 1982. 1 PARA was in Edinburgh, having completed a short tour of duty in Northern Ireland, and 2 PARA was in Aldershot, preparing for a six-month tour in Belize. 3 PARA was at its base at Tidworth, where it was the 'Spearhead' battalion. For all three battalions it was a period of routine duties with nothing of any particular import ahead.

However, 8,000 miles away in the South Atlantic, events were taking place which would, within a few weeks, radically alter life for 2 and 3 PARA and result in both battalions taking part in a campaign in which they would be severely tested. At 0430 hours on 2 April 150 men of the *Buzos Tacticos*, an Argentinian special forces unit, landed by helicopter at Mullet Creek, an inlet on the east coast of the Falkland Islands. After moving north the force split into two halves, one heading for Port Stanley and the other advancing on Moody Brook and the barracks housing Naval Party 8901, the small Royal Marine garrison based on the Falkland Islands. Reaching Moody Brook at about 0600 hours, the *Buzos Tacticos* attacked the barracks with automatic weapons and grenades but found them unoccupied, the Royal Marines having deployed to defensive positions four hours earlier.

Meanwhile, the other force of *Buzos Tacticos* had made its way to the residence of the Governor of the Falkland Islands, Rex Hunt, where the commander of Naval Party 8901, Major Mike Norman, had located his small headquarters. At 0615 hours the Argentinians launched their attack on the Governor's residence. Although three of them managed to gain entry to the main building, the attack was repulsed. At 0630 hours Norman received a radio message from one of his OPs which he had deployed on the coast south east of Yorke Point, reporting that Argentinian forces were landing at Yorke Bay. Shortly afterwards the OP reported that a force of some 18 LVTP-7 amphibious armoured personnel carriers (APCs) was advancing towards Port Stanley. After landing at about 0800 hours, the Argentinian APCs headed south-east, passing Stanley Airport and advancing south down the airport road towards the capital. As they did so, they encountered a section of Royal Marines under Lieutenant Bill Trollope which engaged the leading two vehicles, successfully knocking them out. However, the remaining APCs disgorged troops who proceeded to engage Trollope and his men. Naval Party 8901 faced overwhelming odds. After hearing of the attack on Moody Brook and the landing at Yorke Bay, Major Norman had given orders for his entire force, which numbered 80, to withdraw and concentrate at Government House, where a fierce battle was already raging. Some 600 Argentinian troops surrounded the Governor's residence, but the Royal Marines continued to put up fierce resistance.

On receiving news of the continued advance of the Argentinian APCs, and realising that there was no possibility of attempting a breakout, the Governor realised that any further resistance was futile. Moreover, the Argentinians had lost no time in seizing the Falklands Broadcasting Station and the Cable and Wireless office in Port Stanley, thus cutting off any communication with the outside world. At 0925 hours Hunt ordered Major Norman and his force, which had suffered no casualties, to lay down their arms. Shortly afterwards, the Governor and all the Royal Marines were flown out in an Argentinian transport aircraft to Montevideo for eventual repatriation to Britain. The following day a further action took place on the island of South Georgia, 800 miles to the east of the Falkland Islands. Eight days earlier, on 24 March, a small force of Royal Marines, commanded by Lieutenant Keith Mills RM, had landed at the island's port of Grytviken from HMS *Endurance*, the Royal Navy ice patrol ship. Its task was to observe a group of some 40 Argentinian civilians, under a scrap metal merchant named Constantino Davidoff, who had arrived on South Georgia five days earlier for the purpose of carrying out a contract to dismantle an old whaling station at Leith. Permission for them to do so had been granted in early March by the British Embassy in Buenos Aires, which had instructed Davidoff to seek formal authorisation from the commander of the British Antarctic Survey at Grytviken.

Soon after landing, Davidoff and his men had run up the Argentinian flag, an action which had shortly afterwards been reported to the Governor at Port Stanley. While they had complied with the subsequent British request to remove their flag, the Argentinians had refused to seek formal authorisation for their activities from the British Antarctic Survey. The next day, 20 March, HMS *Endurance* had sailed from Port Stanley with 24 marines aboard and had reached South Georgia four days later. Shortly after the ship's arrival, some of the marines had disembarked and had set up their OP to observe the Argentinians, who were busy dismantling the whaling station. On 31 March HMS *Endurance* received a signal which warned of an invasion of the Falkland Islands by Argentinian forces. That night Lieutenant Mills and his small force had disembarked and prepared themselves for a possible landing by the Argentinians, deploying at King Edward Point, the base location of the British Antarctic Survey.

On the morning of 3 April the Argentinian corvette *ARA Guerrico* and the ice patrol ship *ARA Bahia Paraiso* appeared in King Edward Cove. Lieutenant Mills made contact with the vessels and informed them that British troops were on South Georgia and that any landing would be resisted. Shortly afterwards a Puma helicopter landed and disembarked some Argentinian marines, who opened fire on Mills and his men. More helicopters appeared and a second Puma succeeded in landing marines, but was hit by small-arms fire which caused it to land again suddenly. At the same time, two Alouette light helicopters appeared and one of these was also shot down by the Royal Marines. At this point the enemy corvette sailed back into King Edward Cove and opened fire with its 40mm gun. Waiting until it was at close range, Mills and his men responded with their Carl Gustav 84mm medium anti-tank weapon (MAW), and succeeded in punching a hole below the vessel's waterline. A second round hit the corvette's gun and damaged it, while a fusillade of small-arms fire and 66mm LAW rockets scored hits on its hull and superstructure, forcing the vessel to withdraw. The Royal Marines were now surrounded and were under heavy fire. Lieutenant Mills decided that he had fulfilled his brief from the commander of HMS *Endurance*, Captain Nick Barker RN, to put up a token resistance while achieving his own aim of causing the Argentinians as much damage as possible. Accordingly, he ordered his men to surrender. A few days later, Mills and his men were repatriated to Britain via Montevideo.

The invasion of the Falkland Islands and South Georgia by Argentina was the culmination of years of constant dispute between Britain and Argentina over the issue of sovereignty. The military junta in power in Argentina at the time not only wished to force Britain into making concessions during negotiations, but also badly needed a diversion from its political problems at home. It is not within the terms of reference of this book to delve into the history of the dispute between Argentina and Britain over the island. Suffice it to say that General Leopoldo Galtieri greatly misjudged Britain's reaction to the invasion of the islands. He and the other members of the junta were convinced that Britain would concede rather than go to war, particularly if confronted with superior odds. The events of the following weeks would show them how badly they had miscalculated.

The call to arms for 2 and 3 PARA came on Friday 2 April. Lieutenant Colonel 'H' Jones, the Commanding Officer of 2 PARA, and his family were abroad on a skiing trip. As soon as he heard news of the crisis, Jones and his family cut short their holiday and returned to Britain. Although 2 PARA was preparing for its move to Belize, Jones was determined that his battlion would not be excluded in the task force being assembled. On his return to Aldershot he quickly despatched signals to all relevant quarters to this effect. 3 PARA had stood down for the weekend and had to be recalled, telegrams being despatched and notices being posted at railway stations summoning the men of the battalion back to Tidworth. On the morning of Monday 4 April the Commanding Officer, Lieutenant Colonel Hew Pike, attended a briefing in Plymouth by Brigadier Julian Thompson, the Commander of 3 Commando Brigade RM, of which the battalion would form part. There followed five days of frantic activity as equipment and clothing were drawn and preparations made for the coming operation. On 9 April the battalion sailed from Southampton aboard the *SS Canberra*.

Meanwhile, 2 PARA was regrouping at Aldershot, although at that stage no rapid recall had been required. A group of officers and NCOs on jungle training in Belize had been recalled and the Quartermaster, Captain Tom Godwin, and his staff had the problem of exchanging jungle warfare equipment for that required for operations in arctic conditions. Ancient

Larkspur radios were exchanged for the more modern Clansman sets, and an increased number of GPMGs was issued to rifle companies so that each section had two machine guns. As 3 PARA and the rest of the task force headed for the first port of call at Ascension Island, the battalion champed at the bit while the North Sea ferry *MV Norland* was fitted out as a troopship. As the welders and fitters worked night and day, the Quartermaster's advance party began to load tons of stores into the vessel's huge car decks. On 26 April 2 PARA embarked aboard the *Norland* at Portsmouth and set sail for the South Atlantic. The Commanding Officer and his Intelligence Officer, Captain Allan Coulson, had flown ahead to Ascension Island to be briefed on the situation.

During the voyage south, 3 PARA found themselves sharing the *Canberra* with 40 and 42 Commandos RM and Zulu Company of 45 Commando RM. Training had begun soon after the beginning of the voyage. During the day, every available area of deck space was used for training, six laps of the decks being about one mile. Much time was devoted to fitness, which would otherwise have suffered in the cramped conditions aboard the ship. Great emphasis was placed on weapon training, all ranks practising their marksmanship at targets dropped from the stern of the ship and concentrating on their weapon handling skills. Other training included unarmed combat and lectures on first aid.

On 20 April *Canberra* arrived at Ascension Island, where she remained for two weeks. Firing ranges had been constructed on the island, and these were used to good effect by 3 PARA and the three commando units to zero their small arms and to fire their support weapons. 3 PARA also had the chance to practise disembarkation into landing craft, a skill already familiar to its Royal Marine counterparts. On 8 May *Canberra* left Ascension Island and continued south with the rest of the task force.

2 PARA's journey followed much the same pattern as that of 3 PARA and their Royal Marine fellow passengers on the *Canberra*. Shortly after leaving Portsmouth the *Norland* had been joined by the assault ship HMS *Fearless*, and ahead of her was the *Europic Ferry*, which carried the battalion's support weapons, the guns of 4th Field Regiment RA, a large amount of ammunition and the light helicopters of 656 Squadron AAC. Aboard the *Norland* the only source of news was the BBC World Service, relayed over the vessel's Tannoy system. All ranks trained assiduously, honing their skills in shooting, weapon handling, map reading, first aid, aircraft and tank recognition, and signals. Like their comrades in 3 PARA, they concentrated on maintaining their physical fitness. On 6 May the *Norland* reached Ascension Island, where the brief pause in the journey enabled the battalion to rehearse disembarking from the ship by landing craft. Early the following morning Lieutenant Colonel 'H' Jones rejoined his battalion, and at 2200 hours the *Norland* continued its voyage to link up with the rest of the task force.

As the task force was ploughing southwards through the Atlantic, much was happening elsewhere. All diplomatic efforts to produce a peaceful solution to the crisis had failed, the Argentinians refusing to withdraw from the Falkland Islands. On 25 April the island of South Georgia was retaken by a force consisting of the Mountain and Boat Troops of D Squadron 22 SAS, 2 Special Boat Section and M Company of 42 Commando RM. On the night of 30 April, the day Britain declared a 200-mile exclusion zone around the Falkland Islands, the airfield at Port Stanley was attacked by an RAF Vulcan bomber and, in the early hours of 1 May, by Fleet Air Arm Sea Harriers which also bombed an airstrip at Goose Green. On the afternoon of the following day the Royal Navy nuclear attack submarine HMS *Conqueror* torpedoed and sank the Argentinian cruiser *General Belgrano*. On 4 May the Argentinian Air Force attacked and sank the Royal Navy destroyer HMS *Sheffield*. All these events, particularly the loss of the *Sheffield*, served to bring home to the men of the task force the gravity of the situation towards which they were heading.

Since the initial invasion of the islands the Argentinians had reinforced their garrison until it numbered some 12,000 men. Among the units deployed from 12 April onwards were the 3rd, 6th and 7th Infantry Regiments of 10th Motorised Infantry Brigade; the 4th, 5th and 12th Infantry Regiments of 3rd Mechanised Infantry Brigade; 11th Artillery Group, a battery of 1st Marine Anti-Aircraft Regiment, elements of 601st Anti-Aircraft Artillery Group, and 601st Engineer Group. Other units included the 8th and 25th Infantry Regiments, 1st Parachute Regiment, 2nd Airborne Infantry Regiment, 5th Marine Battalion, 602nd Special Forces Group, 302nd and 601st Marine Commando Companies (the *Buzos Tacticos* special forces units which carried out the initial assault on 2 April), elements of the Marine Amphibious Reconnaissance Group (an armoured reconnaissance unit), 9th and 10th Motorised Engineer Companies and a company of the 601st Construction Engineer Battalion. Added to these were logistic support and medical units. Air support for the Argentinian forces was provided by aircraft of the Air Force's 2nd and 3rd Attack and Reconnaissance Squadrons and the 1st and 4th Naval Attack Squadrons, all of which were based on the airfield at Port Stanley. In addition, the Army and Navy had deployed a number of helicopters and STOL light transport aircraft.

The Argentinian commander, Major General Mario Benjamin Menendez, had assumed that the main British objective would be the recapture of Port Stanley. Accordingly, he had deployed 70 per cent of his forces in the area of the town and had also located his headquarters there. To the west he had deployed the 4th and 12th Infantry Regiments on Two Sisters Ridge, Mount Harriet and Mount Kent. The 7th Infantry Regiment, reinforced by one of the *Buzos Tacticos* companies, was positioned on Mount Longdon and Wireless Ridge to the north. The 5th Marine Infantry Battalion and the other *Buzos Tacticos* company were deployed on Tumbledown, Mount William and Sapper Hill, while the low ground between Wireless Ridge and Moody Brook was occupied by a company of the 2nd Airborne Infantry Regiment. The beaches to the south-east of Port Stanley, which had been selected as the most likely locations for landings by British forces, and the airfield itself were held by the 25th Infantry Regiment, supported by the 3rd and 6th Infantry Regiments occupying positions in depth. Supporting batteries of the 11th Artillery Group were sited to the north of Port Stanley, together with a battery of the 3rd Artillery Group, which also had a battery deployed at Moody Brook. The armoured vehicles of the Marine Amphibious Reconnaissance Group were held in reserve in Port Stanley. Goose Green was held by the 2nd Airborne Infantry Regiment, less one company, and a force of over 200 Air Force personnel, together with six Pucara ground-attack aircraft. The rest of East Falkland was covered by posts manned by patrols or sub-units of approximately platoon strength. The Argentinian forces on West Falkland consisted of the 5th and 8th Infantry Regiments, located at Port Howard and Fox Bay respectively, and the 9th Motorised Engineer Company, which was split between the two bases. The rest of the island was covered by patrols.

An Air Force detachment of six Pucaras, a number of Aermacchi MB.339As and 326s, STOL light transport aircraft and two Puma helicopters was based on Pebble Island off the northern end of West Falkland. In addition, the Argentinians had sited a radar there to cover the approaches to San Carlos. Somewhat surprisingly, no Army units were deployed on the island to provide local protection. This proved to be an unwise move, because, on the night of 13 May, an eight-man patrol from the Boat Troop of D Squadron 22 SAS landed on the island and established two OPs from which it carried out surveillance of the settlement, the radar site and the airfield.

On the night of 14 May 45 men of D Squadron, accompanied by Captain Chris Brown, a naval gunfire forward observer from 148 Commando Forward Observation Battery RA, were flown from the task force in Sea King helicopters to an LZ on the island secured by the Boat Troop patrol. Having landed, the men of D Squadron carried out an attack on the airfield. Supported by fire from HMS *Glamorgan*, which was directed by Captain Brown, they destroyed 11 aircraft, the radar, an ammunition dump and an aviation fuel store. On completion of their task the SAS withdrew without loss and, after extraction by helicopter, were flown back to the task force.

LANDINGS AT SAN CARLOS — 21 MAY

On 13 May Brigadier Julian Thompson, Commander of 3 Commando Brigade RM, issued his orders for the forthcoming landings. Codenamed Operation 'Sutton', they would take place at night at San Carlos Water on the north-eastern side of East Falkland, with the purpose of establishing a beachhead before dawn on the following morning. The task force would make its approach to the islands from the north-east, giving the impression that it was heading for Port Stanley. Under cover of bad weather or darkness it would then veer west and sail into Falkland Sound, escorted by HMS *Antrim*, *Plymouth*, *Broadsword* and RFA *Fort Austin*. Falkland Sound itself would be sealed off by the warships to prevent any attack by Argentinian submarines. The plan called for the initial landings to be made by 40 and 45 Commandos RM, which would secure San Carlos Settlement and Ajax Bay, with 2 and 3 PARA landing at first light the following morning and taking Sussex Mountain and the settlement at Port San Carlos respectively. These units would be followed by the guns of 29 Commando Light Regiment RA and the 12 Rapier surface-to-air missile launchers of T Battery (Shah Sujah's Troop) RA. 42 Commando RM would remain at sea as the brigade reserve. Once the beachhead was secure the landing of equipment, stores and ammunition would take place. The intention was that 3rd Commando Brigade would hold the beachhead until the arrival of 5 Infantry Brigade on 1 June. During the landings, supporting fire would be available from the frigate HMS *Plymouth*, directed by naval gunfire forward observers of 148 Forward Commando Observation Battery RA.

Three days later, however, the plan for the landings had to be changed when it became known that the Argentinians had deployed a company-sized force on Fanning Head, which overlooked San Carlos Water. In addition it was reported that a force of airmobile troops, comprising an infantry regiment and a company of special forces supported by some artillery and helicopters, which had previously been thought to be in the area of Fitzroy, was located north of Darwin. Worried that this force could be lifted rapidly to Sussex Mountain in the event of the enemy detecting the landings at San Carlos, Brigadier Thompson decided to alter his plans. 2 PARA would land before first light and move to secure Sussex Mountain as quickly as possible, and 40 Commando would land shortly afterwards and occupy San Carlos Settlement. 3 PARA and 45 Commando would land at dawn to secure the settlement at Port San Carlos and Ajax Bay respectively. Before the landings, at 0100 hours, a diversionary raid would be mounted by 2 Special Boat Section at Fanning Head, to the north of San Carlos Water. Supported by naval gunfire, the SBS would keep the Argentinians occupied while the landings were in progress. Meanwhile, D Squadron 22 SAS, supported by HMS *Ardent*, would carry out an attack on Darwin to divert enemy attention from the landings and to pin down any reserve force there.

On 19 May 40 Commando and 3 PARA were transferred by landing craft from *Canberra* to HMS *Intrepid*, one of the amphibious assault ships. This was part of an operation to pre-position units on certain vessels from which they would land, and to link up supporting arm units or sub-units with the battalions or commandos to which they would be attached on operations ashore. The transfer, or 'cross-decking' as it is called in naval parlance, took place in a heavy swell, but was accomplished without mishap except for a marine of 40 Commando falling into the sea between *Canberra* and a landing craft. He was pulled out wet but uninjured.

As yet, no date for the landings had been announced, although they were believed to be imminent. However, on the afternoon of 20 May HMS *Broadsword* came alongside the *Norland* and a signal was fired on to the troopship's deck. It contained the news that Operation 'Sutton' would start in the early hours of the following morning. The next few hours were spent packing items of equipment, preparing weapons and making final preparations. On board the *Norland* 2 PARA attended a church service held by its Padre, the Reverend David Cooper.

During the night the speed of the task force was reduced as it entered Falkland Sound. On board the *Norland*, which hove to and anchored off Wreck Point outside San Carlos Water, the men of 2 PARA assembled in full equipment before moving down through the ship's car decks to the doors at the stern, through which they would disembark on four landing craft from HMS *Intrepid*. Embarking on the landing craft took longer than expected, the heavily burdened troops having to jump aboard them as they heaved up and down in the swell. Unfortunately, one man in 2 PARA missed his footing and fell between the side of the ship and a landing craft, suffering a crushed pelvis. Once loaded, the craft moved away from the ship and circled as others took their place. Inside them the men of 2 PARA were jammed together in the darkness, waiting for one and a half hours before disembarkation of the battalion from the *Norland* was complete. Their only diversion was the noise of gunfire from one of the frigates as it supported the SBS diversionary raid on Fanning Head. Once the whole of 2 PARA was loaded, the landing craft headed for Bonner Bay in line astern. Ashore, awaiting the battalion's arrival after reconnoitring the area for any enemy presence, would be men of the SBS, who would signal as to whether or not the beach was clear.

As the landing craft neared the shore, no signal could be seen. They moved into line abreast 45 yards apart, and their ramps were lowered for the landing. The craft carrying C Company, which was due to land first, had difficulty in beaching. B Company, whose craft had stopped 15ft from the shore with three feet of water still under it, had no option but to jump into the icy sea and wade on to the beach soaked to the skin. As the leading elements of B Company came ashore they were challenged in English from the darkness. It was rapidly established that it was the SBS who, much to the battalion's relief, confirmed that the area was clear of enemy. In the dark, 2 PARA reorganised and moved off for Sussex Mountain. The march proved difficult for the troops, who were weighed down with heavy packs and weapons, the terrain being covered with tussocks of long grass which caused men to stumble in the dark. C (Patrol) Company went ahead to secure the start line, followed by A, B and D Companies.

Dawn found the battalion beginning to climb Sussex Mountain. The strain of carrying heavy loads over difficult terrain had already proved too much for some, who became casualties and fell by the wayside. These were collected by the battalion's medical section, assisted by the Padre, who administered medicinal tots of whisky once the stragglers had been grouped together and brought into the Battalion RV. Loads were lightened, if only slightly, as each man in the battalion deposited the two 81mm mortar bombs with which he had been issued before leaving the *Norland*. Fortunately the weather was good, and morale rose with the appearance of the sun. Suddenly, a white parachute appeared as from nowhere and floated to earth with the pilot of a Pucara suspended below it. The aircraft had been shot down by a Stinger missile fired by D Squadron 22 SAS, which had been attacked by two Pucaras while withdrawing after its diversionary raid on Darwin. Other aircraft could now be seen, and shortly afterwards an A-4 Skyhawk attacked D Company. The air threat grew as more aircraft could be seen attempting to attack the ships of the task force, which had weighed anchor at dawn and sailed into San Carlos Water. The Blowpipe detachments were not in position on the high ground, and it would be some time before the Rapier battery was ashore and ready for action. As the battalion watched, an aircraft was hit by a missile from HMS *Brilliant*. Shortly afterwards, a Mirage flew over 2 PARA's positions and, after a moment's pause, was engaged by some of the battalion's GPMGs. By that time the Scout helicopters of 656 Squadron AAC were bringing up some of the battalion's equipment from the valley below, and aboard the *Norland* stores were being loaded by B Echelon for despatch to the battalion by helicopter.

2 PARA was deployed with B Company occupying the higher ground to the south, D Company in the centre and A Company on the right. The patrols of C (Patrol) Company, meanwhile, began the long march forward to their OP positions from which they would observe across the terrain towards Goose Green.

Meanwhile, 3 PARA had disembarked from HMS *Intrepid* by landing craft as dawn was breaking. While still some distance from the shore Lieutenant Colonel Hew Pike made radio contact with members of 3 Special Boat Section, who had reconnoitred the area of the beach, and confirmed that it was clear of enemy. Shortly afterwards the larger landing craft (Landing Craft Utility — LCU) found themselves unable to reach the beach because of the shallowness of the water. B Company was being carried in four of a smaller type of craft (Landing Craft Vehicle and Personnel — LCVP), and these were able to reach the shore and disembark the company dryshod before returning to the stranded LCUs to ferry the rest of 3 PARA ashore. First to land after B Company was A Company, followed by the Commanding Officer and his 'R' Group together with some sappers of 9 Parachute Squadron RE. Shortly afterwards, B Company moved off the beach and led the advance towards Port San Carlos. As the leading elements made their way towards the settlement, a Sea King helicopter escorted by two Gazelles, flying towards The Knob, a feature which lay to the east, came under fire from Argentinian troops withdrawing along the northern bank of the San Carlos River. The Sea King, which was carrying a reconnaissance party from the Rapier battery, swerved away unscathed, but both Gazelles were hit. One of them succeeded in remaining airborne and in returning to its parent vessel, but the pilot in the other aircraft was hit and mortally wounded. Nevertheless, still conscious, he succeeded in landing his aircraft on the water. Both he and his crewman managed to extract themselves from the sinking aircraft, but came under fire as they swam towards the shore. Unfortunately, twenty minutes after being pulled ashore by his crewman with the help of some islanders, the pilot died.

As 3 PARA neared the settlement, the Argentinians, comprising a group of 40 and the other half of the company providing the force at Fanning Head, withdrew in haste and fled into the nearby hills. As they did so they shot down another Gazelle as it flew over Cameron's Point towards The Knob. 3 PARA despatched a patrol from A Company to rescue the crew, but they were both found to be dead. By 1300 hours the whole of 3 PARA had landed. C Company moved up the valley and occupied the high ground above Port San Carlos known as Settlement Rocks, while the rest of the battalion took up positions around the settlement itself. Battalion Headquarters established itself in the house belonging to the manager of the settlement, which was inhabited by some 40 islanders.

In the evening, elements of D (Patrol) Company were detached for an operation with the SAS in the Fanning Head area. During the diversionary raid mounted at the time of the landings, the majority of the Argentinian force there had fled just before dawn. Nine prisoners had been captured, but it was suspected that a small number of enemy still remained there, together with a 106mm recoilless rifle and some 81mm mortars. The task of the D (Patrol) Company patrols was to assist in an attack on the enemy position. On the following morning, 22 May, the attack went in on the enemy positions and was successful, the recoilless rifle and mortars being destroyed. During the afternoon an Argentinian soldier waving a white flag surrendered to men of C Company. When he was interrogated by a Spanish speaking member of the company, Private Caraher, it transpired that he had been a member of the force at Fanning Head. After being handed over to members of the brigade headquarters intelligence section, he revealed that he had been involved in the construction of enemy defensive positions at Goose Green.

For the next four days, 2 and 3 PARA remained in the beachhead with the rest of 3 Commando Brigade, and they witnessed the battle for air superiority. The Argentinian Air Force maintained the pressure on the task force, achieving successes despite the air defence umbrella of missiles, guns and Harriers. On the day of the landings the frigates HMS *Antrim* and HMS *Ardent* received direct hits, the latter being sunk with the loss of 20 of her crew killed, while HMS *Argonaut* was seriously damaged. HMS *Brilliant* and HMS *Broadsword* were both hit by bombs which failed to explode. On 23 May HMS *Antelope* was hit by a 500lb bomb which exploded on the following day, sinking her. The air attacks reached a climax on 24 May, when two major raids took place. At 0915 hours the landing ship logistics (LSL) *Sir Galahad* was hit by one bomb and her sister ship *Sir Launcelot* by two bombs, all of which failed to explode. Both vessels were half unloaded at the time, and they were evacuated by their crews until such time as the bombs could be defused and removed. HMS *Fearless*, the amphibious assault ship on which Headquarters 3 Commando Brigade was embarked at the time, was hit by a rocket. On the following day HMS *Broadsword* and HMS *Coventry* were hit, the latter being sunk. In addition, the container ship *Atlantic Conveyor* was hit by an Exocet missile fired from one of the Argentinian Navy's Super Etendard fighters; this was a calamity for the troops ashore, as the vessel was carrying helicopters, including three Chinooks, as well as huge quantities of stores. Despite these successes, losses of Argentinian aircraft were high, totalling 26 during the period 21 to 24 May.

Meanwhile, both battalions patrolled actively. 2 PARA's OPs had reported enemy activity in the area of Canterra House, approximately five miles to the south of Sussex Mountain. As a result, on 23 May No. 12 Platoon of D Company, commanded by Lieutenant Jim Barry, was despatched by Sea King helicopter with the task of clearing the house and the surrounding area. After being dropped off one and a quarter miles from its objective, the platoon located the building with the help of artillery fire and cleared it, finding no sign of any enemy. Barry and his men remained at Canterra House during the night and throughout the following day.

A problem which soon manifested itself was the poor passage of information both within and between units. In some instances this resulted in what were termed 'blue on blue' contacts. Unfortunately, one such incident resulted in several casualties. During the morning of 23 May, A Company 3 PARA reported a strong patrol of between 30 and 50 men moving south in its area. No. 3 Platoon was despatched to find and identify the patrol, but came under fire from elements of C Company, which also brought down artillery fire. The battalion radio net was confused, the lack of a contact report from No. 3 Platoon adding to the belief that C Company was indeed engaging an enemy force. Eventually it was discovered that the 'enemy' was No. 3 Platoon, which had become lost. By the time the firing had ceased, seven members of No. 3 Platoon and an attached sapper from 9 Parachute Squadron RE had been wounded by artillery fire. Unfortunately, such incidents are an inevitable feature of warfare. On the following day a patrol from No. 4 Platoon of B Company 2 PARA narrowly avoided having mortar fire called down on it by C (Patrol) Company, which was unaware of the patrol's presence. Likewise, on the same day, a patrol from D (Patrol) Company 3 PARA reported sighting an enemy OP in the Fanning Head area. Fortunately no action was mounted against the OP as, on investigation, it turned out to be a radio relay station working back to the brigade headquarters, and which had been positioned in the area without 3 PARA being notified.

Both battalions were champing at the bit and wanting to get to grips with the enemy. On 24 May Lieutenant Colonel 'H' Jones was summoned to the brigade headquarters, which had landed two days earlier and established itself at San Carlos Settlement. Immediately after he had come ashore, Brigadier Julian Thompson had visited 2 PARA and had discussed an attack on Darwin and Goose Green, warning the Commanding Officer that the battalion was likely to have to carry out the task. While the Commanding Officer was at the brigade headquarters with his Operations Officer, Major Roger Miller, 2 PARA's Intelligence Officer, Captain Alan Coulson, visited HMS *Intrepid*, where he was able to discuss the enemy forces at Darwin and Goose Green with the commander of the SAS force which had carried out the diversionary raid there on the night of 21 May.

The SAS, who had attacked Burntside House at the northern end of the Darwin isthmus, thought that the Argentinian forces could be overcome without much difficulty. Their estimate of enemy strength was a company, which differed from the assessment given to the battalion before the landings. On his return from the brigade headquarters, Lieutenant Colonel Jones announced that the battalion would move during the night with the aim of reaching Camilla Creek House, some three and a half miles south-east of Canterra House and about eight miles south of Sussex Mountain, by first light the following morning. D Company, which would be joined by No. 12 Platoon from Canterra House, would clear and secure a gun-line for three light guns which would be lifted in after last light by helicopters equipped with passive night vision equipment. In addition, the company would clear Ceritos House, four miles to the east. Meanwhile, A and B Companies would press on to attack Darwin.

Accordingly, D Company set off at last light. After covering more than half the distance to Camilla Creek House, however, it received a radio message telling it to return, as the operation had been aborted because of a problem with the helicopters. Only four were fitted with night vision equipment, and their first task that night had been to fly patrols of D Squadron 22 SAS to Mount Kent to establish OPs to watch the area of Port Stanley. The helicopters had completed this task and were preparing to lift the three light guns to Camilla Creek House when the weather deteriorated to the extent that the aircraft were unable to fly. As the operation could not be accomplished without artillery support, Brigadier Thompson cancelled it. Lieutenant Colonel Jones, frustrated and annoyed, ordered D Company to return to Sussex Mountain and No. 12 Platoon to Canterra House. On the following morning the Commanding Officer decided to move D Company forward by helicopter to Canterra House, from where it would then move on foot to Camilla Creek House. Once again the weather thwarted his plans and the operation had to be cancelled. By that time No. 12 Platoon was running very short of rations and some of the men, like many in the brigade, were suffering from problems with their feet, which had been constantly wet since the landings. The platoon was ordered to return to the battalion, and it arrived at last light, some of its number being completely exhausted.

During the afternoon of 26 May, however, the decision was taken to proceed with the attack on Darwin and Goose Green after all, and Lieutenant Colonel 'H' Jones was summoned to the brigade headquarters. On his return he briefed the commander of D Company, Major Philip Neame, so that the latter could move off as soon as possible with his company to clear Camilla Creek House and secure the gun line for the three guns of 8 Commando Battery RA which would be lifted in by helicopter at first light on the following morning, 27 May. The battalion would be moving in light order, carrying the minimum amount of equipment other than weapons and ammunition. The Commanding Officer initially decided to leave the battalion's 81mm mortars behind because the absence of vehicles meant that only a limited number of bombs could be carried. However, the commander of 8 Commando Battery, Major Tony Rice, persuaded him to take a section of two mortars. Jones also decided that the Machine Gun Platoon should take six of its GPMGs in the light role, and that the Anti-Tank Platoon was to take three Milan firing posts and 17 missiles.

2 PARA ADVANCE TO CAMILLA CREEK

Before last light on 26 May, 2 PARA left Sussex Mountain and set off for Camilla Creek House with A Company, led by 2nd Lieutenant Guy Wallace's No. 3 Platoon. D Company had already departed earlier to clear the route and secure the area of Camilla Creek House and the gun line. Until that afternoon the Reconnaissance and Patrols Platoons of C (Patrol) Company had still been deployed in their OPs and ambush positions. They had now been ordered to move to Camilla Creek House to meet the rest of the battalion on its arrival. The weather was fine and the sun was setting as the battalion headed south towards the track which would lead it to Camilla Creek House. As darkness fell the companies, which had been well spaced out, closed up as they moved over the difficult terrain. Eventually they resorted to using the track, because the tussocks of long grass, the large peat pools and the soft mud, interspersed with steep-sided ravines, were making the going extremely difficult. Although it was risky to use the track, the fact that D Company had cleared it earlier made this acceptable.

Nevertheless, the strain began to tell as 2 PARA filed its way southwards through the darkness. Men became noticeably less alert as fatigue set in. Radio operators and members of the battalion's medical section, who were heavily burdened with packs filled with medical supplies, were particularly badly affected as they struggled to keep up. An RAF forward air controller, Squadron Leader Jock Penman, fell and twisted his ankle. In the darkness he became separated from the battalion, and Captain Peter Ketley of Support Company subsequently spotted him stumbling along parallel to the main body. Two men in A Company also fell, one twisting his ankle and the other lying unconscious. They were left behind with two men to look after them, the Commanding Officer being very concerned that the unconscious man, Private Phillips, was dying. The battalion's medical officer, Captain Steve Hughes, also fell victim to injury when he fell and hurt his ankle. He had been without sleep for two nights while tending injured men on Sussex Mountain, and was exhausted. He continued to carry out his duties while suffering from a badly swollen ankle which he would only allow to be treated when operations ceased three weeks later. It transpired that he had suffered a hairline fracture.

Problems had occured with companies becoming separated. Support Company had fallen behind as a result of having to stop and look after the RAF forward air controller, Squadron Leader Penman, who was left behind with two medics to take care of him. Concerned that there was no sign of the company, the Commanding Officer left some of the members of his 'R' Group to wait for it while he pressed on with A and B Companies.

As 2 PARA continued its march towards Camilla Creek House, artillery air bursts could be seen in the distance to its left. It later transpired that the enemy 105mm guns at Goose Green were shelling a C (Patrol) Company patrol, commanded by Sergeant Higginson, which had been spotted by a helicopter as it made its way to join up with the battalion. Among the battalion the artillery fire caused many to wonder if the enemy was aware of their presence, and whether it was only a matter of time before ranging rounds fell among them. In the event, Fortune smiled on the battalion that night, for it undoubtedly would have presented an easy target for Argentinian artillery had it been observed as it moved along the track in a closely bunched column.

Meanwhile, D Company had neared the area of Camilla Creek House. No. 11 Platoon, commanded by 2nd Lieutenant Chris Waddington, was in the lead. Waddington spotted the house about one and a quarter miles distant, and observed it through a night vision device, seeing no sign of movement among the silhouetted buildings. Nevertheless, Major Philip Neame decided to take no chances and called for artillery fire on the house. Although the target had been registered from an OP the day before, the first salvo of shells fell very wide of the mark. No. 10 Platoon, under Lieutenant Shaun Webster, subsequently put in an assault on the house, which was found to be deserted, although there were signs of very recent occupation — a leg of lamb roasting in an oven and a vest drying on a still warm stove. Having cleared the buildings, No. 10 Platoon vacated them quickly because they were likely to have been registered by the enemy artillery as a defensive fire task (DF). Having ensured that the surrounding area was also clear, Major Neame deployed two of his platoons to cover the most likely enemy approaches and posted men to guide the rest of the battalion in to the RV. Eventually the Commanding Officer and A and B Companies arrived, followed soon afterwards by Support Company, which had made very good time and caught up with the rest of the battalion despite being heavily burdened with the three Milan firing posts and missiles, as well as the two mortars. Despite the risk, Lieutenant Colonel Jones decided to use the house and surrounding buildings. In his mind the benefit to his exhausted men in being warm for the first time in hours, and sleeping under a roof for the first time since landing, outweighed the risk of being shelled. 2 PARA crammed itself into the house, the farm buildings and outhouses. Men slept wherever they could: No. 11 Platoon's headquarters appropriated the lavatory in the house, squatting inside, while one of the rifle sections squeezed into a cupboard. Outside, a screen was established to warn of any enemy approach.

In the meantime, two patrols from C (Patrol) Company, commanded by Lieutenant Colin Connor and Corporal Evans, together with a forward air control party, had pushed on to positions 450 yards apart from where they could observe the Argentinian positions on the Darwin isthmus. At first light the patrols found themselves in somewhat exposed positions on a hillside devoid of any real cover. In front of them, in full view across the water, were the enemy defensive positions. The reports from these two patrols were to prove invaluable. Previous intelligence had indicated an enemy gun line by the bridge over the Ceritos Arroyo, at the north-eastern tip of Camilla Creek, but it was obvious that the guns had been moved. Corporal Evans observed a recoilless rifle being dug in on the eastern side of the track on the northern side of Coronation Point. Further to the south-east he spotted 16 trenches surrounded by men digging-in, while at Burntside House a number of tents were plainly visible. Opposite his own position a company of troops was dug in, and to the south, near Boca House, there was another defensive position consisting of five bunkers. Between Boca House and the company opposite his OP was a platoon in a position overlooking Camilla Creek itself.

Meanwhile, consternation reigned at Camilla Creek House. With the dawn had come a BBC World Service radio broadcast informing the world that a parachute battalion was within five miles of Darwin and Goose Green and was preparing to attack. 2 PARA could hardly believe its ears, and Lieutenant Colonel Jones was thunderstruck. The battalion had succeeded in moving undetected during the night, and had concealed itself under cover, but the whole operation was now jeopardised by a radio broadcast which would undoubtedly alert the enemy of an impending attack. The Commanding Officer and others who listened were naturally infuriated at what appeared to them to have been a monumental breach of security. A few days later, prisoners confirmed that the Argentinians had been alerted by the broadcast but no action was taken to reinforce Goose Green until some seventeen hours after 2 PARA's attack had started. The buildings were immediately evacuated and 2 PARA took up well dispersed positions in the valleys nearby. Battalion Headquarters remained in the house, and Lieutenant Colonel Jones decided that the time had come to start softening up the enemy with some airstrikes. Unfortunately the RAF forward air controller, Squadron Leader Penman, was *hors de combat*. He had suffered an injured ankle and was somewhat dazed from his fall during the night, in which he had lost his weapon and webbing. The Medical Officer had decided that he should be evacuated. Fortunately 2 PARA possessed its own trained forward air controller in Captain Ketley, commander of the Anti-Tank Platoon. He had taken over and had immediately gone forward to make contact with Corporal Evans' patrol in its position observing Camilla Creek. However, those in Battalion Head-quarters were unaware of his departure and, when further information on the enemy's dispositions was received, Ketley was recalled over the radio to collect the information in person. By that time he was with Corporal Evans' patrol and, by the time he reached Battalion Headquarters, air support was on its way in the form of a pair of Harriers.

The Commanding Officer was infuriated at this mix-up, and vented his displeasure on those concerned. In fact, the lack of a forward air controller made little difference to the air strike. The first Harrier made its approach from the north and then banked away after identifying the enemy positions opposite Corporal Evans' position. The second aircraft carried out an attack, but succeeded only in hitting the terrain behind the enemy company. The first aircraft, flown by Squadron Leader Bob Iveson, made a second approach but was hit by enemy anti-aircraft fire and shot down. Iveson ejected safely further to the south over Goose Green, and evaded capture until the battle ended, two days later.

As Captain Ketley and his signaller hurried back southwards along the track towards the OP, they met a civilian Land Rover coming towards them. The vehicle halted as they were spotted and, realising that it contained enemy troops, the two men opened fire. The occupants surrendered rapidly, one of them having been hit in the leg, and were immediately taken to Battalion Headquarters where they were interrogated by the Intelligence Officer, Captain Alan Coulson. He was assisted by a Royal Marine officer, Captain Rod Bell, who had been born in Costa Rica and spoke fluent Spanish. One of the prisoners was an officer, and he revealed that the enemy had been using Camilla Creek House as an OP and that they had been patrolling the area for the previous four days.

At 1530 hours events took a more dramatic turn when both the C (Patrol) Company OPs came under fire from the enemy company opposite Corporal Evans' position. Lieutenant Colin Connor called for artillery support, but this was not available and the battalion's two mortars were not bedded in. The enemy brought down fire from .50 calibre heavy machine guns as Connor and his men crawled 35ft into dead ground. Meanwhile, Corporal Evans had called for air support, and this was forthcoming. As the aircraft attacked, Evans and his men withdrew in pairs, each covering the others' backs. Once they had reached the safety of dead ground they joined the other patrol in withdrawing to Camilla Creek House.

The Commanding Officer had intended to issue orders for the forthcoming operation at 1500 hours, but as a result of the delay in the company commanders arriving at Battalion Headquarters from their dispersed locations, and the news of Captain Ketley's capture of the Argentinian patrol in the Land Rover, he decided to postpone his 'O' Group to 1900 hours. As is normal in briefings for any operations, the 'O' Group began with a detailed description of the ground over which 2 PARA would be fighting. In this instance it was given by Lieutenant John Thurman, a Royal Marine officer who had previously served in the Falkland Islands. He described the terrain in detail, pointing out the features and giving detailed descriptions of the settlements at Darwin and Goose Green. He also suggested possible approaches to objectives. Next to speak was the Intelligence Officer, Captain Coulson, who gave details of the enemy units and their dispositions, including the locations of known minefields. Some of his information had been obtained from a map found on a captured enemy engineer officer. Once Coulson had finished, Lieutenant Colonel Jones revealed the details of his plan and gave his orders. The operation to capture Darwin and Goose Green was to take the form of a six-phase attack which would start before dawn and continue throughout the day until all objectives had been taken. In Phase One, C (Patrol) Company would reconnoitre and clear the route from Camilla Creek House and then secure the start line, which would stretch from Camilla Creek to Burntside, spanning the track between the two points. It would also clear the area of the bridge over the Ceritos Arroyo at the north-eastern tip of Camilla Creek. Phase Two would consist of an attack by A and B Companies on the nearest two enemy positions, A Company attacking the tented area at Burntside House and B Company the company position overlooking Camilla Creek. In Phase Three, A Company would attack the enemy positions on Coronation Point while D Company went for another position on the west coast of the isthmus, to the south of the first one. In Phase Four, B Company would move through D Company and attack the enemy at Boca House. In Phase Five, A Company would exploit forward to Darwin while B and D Companies did likewise to Goose Green. Meanwhile, C (Patrol) Company would clear the airfield. In Phase Six, Darwin and Goose Green would be taken while C (Patrol) Company pushed further south.

Supporting 2 PARA in this operation would be a frigate, HMS *Arrow*, which would be in support until 0830 hours. From first light, Harriers and armed helicopters would be on call, as would helicopters for resupply and casualty evacuation. Artillery support would be provided by the three light guns from 8 Commando Battery RA, which would be in direct support. Air defence would be provided by two Blowpipe detachments, one being located at Camilla Creek to protect the gun line while the other moved with 2 PARA. In addition, each company would be accompanied by a mortar fire controller and A, B and D Companies would each have an artillery forward observation officer. Sapper sections from 59 Independent Commando Squadron RE would also be attached to each company. A fire support base would be set up by Support Company on the western side of Camilla Creek. In addition to the Milan and Machine Gun Platoons, it would also include 2 PARA's snipers and a naval gunfire forward observation officer, Captain Kevin Arnold, who would direct supporting fire from HMS *Arrow* and provide forward air control for any air support. In Phase Four of the operation the fire support team, after having supported the B and C Company attacks, would rejoin the battalion and remain in reserve for Phases Five and Six.

THE BATTLE FOR DARWIN AND GOOSE GREEN

At 2300 hours on 27 May Support Company, led by Major Hugh Jenner, and the other elements of the fire support team moved off from Camilla Creek House and were in position by 0200 hours on the following morning. At 0230 hours HMS *Arrow*, directed by Captain Kevin Arnold, began shelling the Argentinian positions, and in particular an enemy artillery piece firing further to the south. Meanwhile, C (Patrol) Company carried out its initial task of reconnoitring the route and clearing the start line. A and B Companies were led to their start lines by guides from the Reconnaissance and Patrols Platoons respectively. Having met up with its guide, A Company made its way towards its start line through the darkness

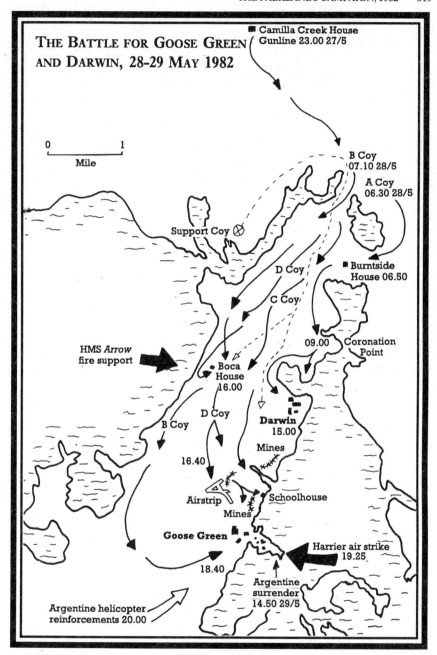

THE BATTLE FOR GOOSE GREEN AND DARWIN, 28–29 MAY 1982

■ Camilla Creek House
Gunline 23.00 27/5

0   1
Mile

B Coy
07.10 28/5

A Coy
06.30 28/5

Support Coy ⊗

D Coy

■ Burntside
House 06.50

C Coy

09.00   Coronation
Point

HMS *Arrow*
fire support

Boca
House
16.00

D Coy

Darwin
15.00

B Coy

Mines

16.40

Airstrip

Schoolhouse

Mines

Goose Green

Harrier air strike
19.25

18.40

Argentine
surrender
14.50 29/5

Argentine helicopter
reinforcements 20.00

and rain. The approach was difficult because the terrain was interspersed with ravines, but the company crossed its start line at 0635 hours in assault formation: No. 3 Platoon, under 2nd Lieutenant Guy Wallace, on the left, 2nd Lieutenant Mark Coe's No. 2 Platoon on the right and No. 1 Platoon, commanded by Sergeant Barrett, following up in reserve. Its officer,

Lieutenant John Shaw, had been injured during the march to Camilla Creek House.

The company's advance on Burntside House was delayed slightly by HMS *Arrow* registering her gun on the objective. However, the flashes from the exploding 4.5-inch shells served to illuminate the house and helped the company locate the building. As No. 3 Platoon moved up to assault the house, 2nd Lieutenant Wallace ordered his 84mm Carl Gustav MAW team to engage the building, but they missed with the first round and then suffered two misfires. The platoon, joined by No. 2 Platoon, resorted to small arms and 66mm LAW rockets, subjecting the building to a heavy volume of fire. As No. 3 Platoon moved in for the final assault, voices could be heard inside, calling out in Spanish. It transpired that these belonged to four civilians who had called out, thinking that the troops outside were Argentinian. They emerged from beneath a heap of mattresses, somewhat shaken but unharmed by their ordeal. A search of the area revealed signs of hasty flight by an enemy platoon, although two dead Argentinians were found later, after the operation was over. Once the area had been cleared No. 1 Platoon moved forward to check an area nearby where one of the C (Patrol) Company OPs had spotted some camouflage nets. In the event, nothing was found.

Meanwhile, B Company had crossed its start line just after 0700 hours. No. 6 Platoon, commanded by Lieutenant Clyde Chapman, was left assault platoon, No. 4 Platoon, under Lieutenant Ernie Hocking, was on the right, and Lieutenant Geoff Weighell and No. 5 Platoon were in reserve. The first contact with the enemy came when Private McKee, in No. 6 Platoon, spotted a figure sitting on the ground. As he shouted a warning, it moved and stood up before walking through the section commanded by Corporal Margerson who, after challenging the figure but receiving no response, opened fire. At that point Margerson spotted some trenches and warned Lieutenant Chapman, who proceeded to lead his men into the attack. Using grenades, machine guns and grenade launchers, the section stormed through the trenches. The majority of the enemy were either unable or unwilling to defend themselves. However, there was some resistance and a total of nine enemy were killed. B Company pushed forward, No. 4 Platoon encountering no resistance on the right, where it expected to find the company position overlooking Camilla Creek. It appeared that the enemy had withdrawn from that area. Six abandoned trenches were found shortly afterwards by No. 5 Platoon which, under company second in command Captain John Young, was moved further to the right as it followed up in reserve.

Major John Crosland then ordered No. 5 Platoon to move through and push forward to the next enemy position, which was to have been D Company's objective in Phase Three. There it found more empty enemy positions, with mortars and rocket launchers lying abandoned. On the left, Corporal Connor's section discovered more trenches. A brief contact took place on the right in which No. 2 Section, under Lance Corporal Dance, took two prisoners. The section next attacked two more trenches, taking another prisoner. Just then, No. 5 Platoon came under fire from more enemy positions in front of it. Parachute illuminating flares were fired, and the firing was pinpointed as coming from two trenches. Sergeant Aird engaged them both with his M-79 40mm grenade launcher, but the enemy continued to direct fire at the platoon. Under covering fire from a member of No. 2 Section, Lieutenant Weighell and Sergeant Aird went forward and cleared the enemy trenches with grenades. During the No. 5 Platoon action, Major John Crosland and his company headquarters were under fire from mortars and artillery. At one point two shells landed between him and his second in command, Captain John Young. Fortunately, they failed to explode.

D Company had followed the Commanding Officer and Battalion Headquarters along the main track leading along the battalion's axis of advance. Although the company was in reserve and behind the other companies, navigation in the dark was difficult and the company took a wrong turning; it had already failed to meet up with its guide from C (Patrol) Company. By the time it reached the Battalion RV the Commanding Officer was becoming extremely anxious about the slow rate of progress. He ordered Major Neame to push forward and sweep both sides of the track to clear a machine-gun position which he thought was on the left and which had been missed by B Company. The Company advanced in 'one up' formation: No. 12 Platoon, commanded by Lieutenant Jim Barry, leading, with No. 10 Platoon, under Lieutenant Shaun Webster, behind and to its left. 2nd Lieutenant Chris Waddington's No. 11 Platoon was behind and to the right. As the company pushed forward it came under fire from the right. Lieutenant Webster spotted six trenches in front of him and, crawling to within throwing range, knocked the nearest one out with a white phosphorous grenade. At that point he and other members of the platoon with him came under fire at close range and two men were wounded. No. 11 Platoon carried out a right flanking movement and put in an assault on the positions, one man being killed, while No. 12 Platoon dealt with some enemy in front of it. Once all opposition had been overcome, D Company went through all the enemy trenches again, ensuring that they had all been cleared.

Support Company now moved forward from its fire support position at 0850 hours. C (Patrol) Company also moved up in reserve, joined by the Assault Pioneer Platoon, which had already brought ammunition forward for resupply and which would now evacuate D Company's casualties of which three, Corporal Cork, Lance Corporal Bingley and Private Fletcher, were dead. Fletcher had been killed while rendering first aid to Corporal Cork, his section commander. By now the enemy artillery was bringing down a considerable volume of fire on the area. Battalion Headquarters, which was located behind D Company, suffered a number of near misses, one of which landed between the Commanding Officer and the Adjutant, Captain David Wood.

A Company now advanced on its Phase Three objective, Coronation Point, which was reached at 0920 hours and found to be clear of enemy. On receiving permission from the Commanding Officer, who joined the company at that point, Major Dair Farrar-Hockley led his company forward to its next objective, Darwin Hill, which dominated the settlement itself. Meanwhile, B Company, was advancing towards the ridge which overlooked Boca House. First light was approaching as A Company advanced, having left No. 3 Platoon to provide fire support from a position overlooking Darwin from the northern side of the inlet. No. 2 Platoon, under 2nd Lieutenant Mark Coe, led the way and, as it moved up a gully, the leading section spotted three men on the high ground to the right of it. These were engaged once it became apparent that they were Argentinians, and shortly afterwards the platoon came under fire from enemy positions on the spur to its right. As Corporal Adams led his section, which was caught in the open, in a charge forward to the other side of the spur where another gully would offer cover, he was hit and wounded in the shoulder. Private Tuffen, the section's machine gunner, was also hit. Only then did Adams realised the size of the enemy position, and withdrew his section to rejoin the rest of the platoon.

By now Company Headquarters and No. 1 Platoon had also come under fire and had been caught in the open. Sergeant Barrett led his platoon up the gully but suffered several casualties. Meanwhile, the artillery forward observation officer attached to A Company, Captain James Watson, and two members of No. 2 Platoon, Corporal Camp and Private Dey, succeeded in knocking out some of the nearest enemy positions with grenades and 66mm LAW rockets. As the platoons fought their way up the gully, Major Farrar-Hockley ordered No. 2 Platoon to carry out a flanking move to the left, but this was thwarted by heavy fire from the right, one member of the platoon being hit. By now the company was scattered in sections in the gully, men seeking what little cover was available as they returned the heavy fire from the enemy, who were superior in numbers and were in well-sited bunkers. As the nearest enemy positions were cleared, Major Farrar-Hockley, who had earlier ordered Sergeant Barrett to concentrate as many of the company's GPMGs as possible into a fire base, now decided to group the guns on a mound at the head of the gully. Six guns were moved up, but it was then discovered that the main enemy positions were further to the right and out of range. No support was available from the battalion's two mortars, as Support Company was still out of range. No. 3 Platoon, which was providing fire support from the northern end of the causeway on the other side of the inlet, had been mortared and had suffered casualties because of the lack of cover. Nevertheless, it continued with its task of providing covering fire.

By then dawn had broken, and the enemy artillery and mortars increased their volume of fire. A Company was calling for artillery support, but the request was refused owing to the confused situation. Moreover, the three light guns of 8 Commando Battery RA, which had been in action virtually constantly since the start of Phase One, were running short of ammunition. They were also receiving counter-battery fire from the enemy artillery, and soon after first light were attacked by two Pucara ground-attack aircraft which were engaged by the Blowpipe detachment defending the gun line. The situation was worsened by the bad weather, which prevented Harriers making air strikes.

While A Company was heavily engaged at Darwin, B Company was attacking the enemy at Boca House. The final approach to the objective was down a slope covered by a line of gorse, and as the company descended towards the buildings the enemy opened fire. Lieutenant Ernie Hocking's No. 4 Platoon was the right assault platoon, and came under fire from a machine gun on the enemy's left flank. Taking cover, the platoon engaged some bunkers and a machine gun position to the south of Boca House. However, it soon found itself too exposed and withdrew into dead ground as the fire from enemy machine guns and snipers increased.

No. 5 Platoon, which was in reserve, had taken cover in a small re-entrant. The platoon commander, Lieutenant Geoff Weighell, decided to withdraw under cover of smoke. As the 2-inch mortarman, Private Street, started to fire the first bombs, he was wounded in the leg. Corporal Standish and Private Brooke ran forward and, despite the heavy machine-gun fire by then raking the slope, succeeded in reaching Street and carrying him back into the cover of dead ground. The platoon suffered further casualties when Private Hall was wounded. Two members of his section, Privates Illingworth and Poole, rendered first aid and dragged Hall into dead ground. Illingworth then went back to retrieve Hall's weapon and webbing, which had been taken off, but was killed. His body was retrieved by Sergeant Aird and the platoon's signaller, Private Williamson. Captain John Young, the company second in command, was seriously wounded shortly afterwards.

No. 6 Platoon, commanded by Lieutenant Clyde Chapman, was the left assault platoon, and had come under fire from two machine guns sited on a hill near the gorse line. Skirmishing forward, Chapman led two of his sections up to an enemy bunker which proved to be abandoned. As he and his men pushed on, they came under fire from a machine gunner who narrowly missed Chapman and then proceeded to make good his escape. At that point the platoon was fired upon from Boca House and took cover in the gorse.

Meanwhile, C (Patrol) Company, was moving up on the left of the axis of advance towards the line of gorse while D Company advanced on the right. Both companies came under artillery and mortar fire which was adjusted as they advanced. Fortunately the soft, boggy ground reduced the effect of the shell bursts, but there were a number of near misses. One mortar bomb landed very close to the commander of the Patrols Platoon, Captain Paul Farrar. On reaching the gorse line, the Company could see A Company below it in the gorse and the enemy positions above which had Major Dair Farrar-Hockley and his men pinned down. Over the radio the company commander, Major Roger Jenner, offered to provide support for an A Company assault with the 12 light machine guns (LMGs) carried by his own men, but this offer was refused by the Commanding Officer. D Company also offered to help, but was ordered to remain where it was.

As both companies watched the A Company action the battalion's mortars attempted to provide support, but this proved to be in vain.

D Company was suffering from the constant attention of enemy artillery, and Major Neame decided to move his men forward into cover. The Commanding Officer mistook this for disregard of his earlier order forbidding any involvement in the A Company's action, and ordered Neame to stay out of the battle. At that point a body of enemy were observed on the western side of the isthmus, heading in the direction of Boca House. They were engaged by members of the Reconnaissance Platoon and by No. 12 Platoon, but to little avail as the range was considerable.

It seemed to make little sense for C and D Companies to remain exposed to enemy shelling, and both therefore pulled back under the lee of a hill. As there was nothing else for it to do at that moment, D Company brewed up in time-honoured British Army fashion. While it was doing so, Major Neame took stock of the shoreline and realised that it offered possibilities for a flanking move to turn the enemy's flank. His suggestion was rejected by the Commanding Officer. Shortly afterwards, Support Company moved up. Major Hugh Jenner's offer of fire support was also rejected by Lieutenant Colonel Jones, who did not want to commit any more of his resources at that moment because of the heavy artillery and mortar fire falling on the spur opposite the enemy positions confronting A Company. Although it offered a good vantage point on to the enemy, casualties would have been high among any troops using it. Moreover, the enemy positions were well sited and the troops in them were putting up stiff resistance.

Indeed, such opposition was causing A Company severe problems. Air support had been requested at 1125 hours, but had to be refused because of bad weather at sea which prevented the aircraft taking off from their carriers. To add insult to injury, three Pucaras flew over en route to carry out an air strike on 2 PARA's 'A' Echelon and 8 Commando Battery's gun line at Camilla Creek House. Ten minutes later they attacked, and one of them was shot down by a Blowpipe; the attack was repeated five minutes later and both aircraft escaped unscathed. A Company was still pinned down, and Lieutenant Colonel Jones made his way forward to the company to see the situation for himself. On his arrival he met Major Dair Farrar-Hockley, who was with the fire team of massed GPMGs on the mound at the head of the gully. The Commanding Officer ordered 2nd Lieutenant Coe to take the Mortar Platoon Commander, Captain Mal Worsley-Tonks, up to the gorse line to a position from which support from the battalion's two mortars could be directed on to the enemy positions. The two officers set off, but were called back after Major Farrar-Hockley had remonstrated with the Commanding Officer and convinced him that such a move was extremely dangerous. Major Farrar-Hockley then ordered Coe to try and take his platoon round to the right of the mound. As the young officer and his men started to move out of the gully they came under heavy fire, and were forced to pull back. Meanwhile, the enemy artillery and mortars kept up an incessant barrage of shelling on the area of open ground in front of the gorse, which was in flames. The seven trenches on the mound had been cleared, and the main weight of enemy fire was coming from positions to the flank of the A Company GPMG fire team. The guns of 8 Commando Battery responded to a call for artillery support, but the high winds affected the accuracy of the shells, some of which landed in the area of B Company's action.

Lieutenant Colonel Jones then ordered Major Farrar-Hockley to attack and take a well-defended position which lay some 55 yards away, above them and to the right. An attempt had been made an hour earlier, but had failed, the company sustaining casualties in the process. Accordingly, Major Farrar-Hockley collected a group of 16 men and led them to the ledge on which the enemy position was located. He was accompanied, among others, by his company second in command, Captain Chris Dent, and unbeknown to him the Adjutant, Captain David Wood, had also joined them. The group did not get far before it came under fire. Captain Dent was killed almost immediately, and two other men were hit. Shortly afterwards Captain Wood and Corporal Hardman were also killed. Under heavy fire, and having suffered such casualties, Farrar-Hockley had no choice but to withdraw into the safety of dead ground.

Only then was it realised that the Commanding Officer had moved off on his own around the spur and into the gully where Corporal Adams and his section of No. 2 Platoon had taken cover in the early part of the action. Just beforehand he had been heard urging A Company on to its feet. At that moment the Mortar Platoon Commander was calling down white phosphorous smoke, and it seemed as though this had achieved some effect, as the enemy fire became more sporadic. As a result the Commanding Officer was apparently under the mistaken impression that only one enemy bunker was still holding out. Already, small groups of Argentinians had attempted to flee from the furthermost positions. At this point Lieutenant Colonel Jones jumped up and ran down to the side of the mound, followed a short distance behind by Sergeants Norman and Blackburn, who called on some of Sergeant Barrett's machine gunners to follow. In the event, only Sergeant Norman and Lance Corporal Beresford managed to keep up with the Commanding Officer as he made his way towards the enemy positions. As Lieutenant Colonel Jones entered the gulley, with Sergeant Norman a short distance behind, he paused in a small re-entrant to check his sub-machine gun before pressing on alone towards an enemy position which he had observed on the left side of the gulley and which had previously remained unnoticed. At that point Sergeant Norman shouted a warning to Jones, who by then was nearing the lone position but was also climbing into view of the other trenches which he had originally intended to attack. Almost immediately a machine gun opened fire and shot Lieutenant Colonel Jones from behind. He fell, mortally wounded. Sergeant Blackburn, the Commanding Officer's signaller, had also arrived on the scene, and he sent the poignant message: "Sunray is down" over the battalion radio net. It was 1330 hours. The news of the loss of the Commanding Officer was immediately flashed from Battalion Headquarters to Headquarters

3 Commando Brigade. Unfortunately, there was an air attack in progress at San Carlos, and thus it was some time before a request for a helicopter to evacuate him could be complied with and an aircraft dispatched to Camilla Creek House where the pilot would be briefed as to where to pick up the wounded man.

Meanwhile, the battle continued, and there was no hope of reaching Lieutenant Colonel Jones, who was unconscious, while the nearer enemy positions were still continuing to put up resistance. Slowly but surely, however, A Company started to win the upper hand. Sections worked their way forward, soldiers skirmishing forward in pairs, each covering the other as they moved. The junior NCOs performed magnificently, keeping firm control of their sections. Just after Corporal Abols had knocked out a trench with a 66mm LAW rocket, a white flag appeared. Major Dair Farrar-Hockley ordered his men not to move until the enemy came forward. Commands to cease fire echoed throughout the company's positions, and calls went out to the enemy troops to surrender. However, the Argentinians were too frightened to move, and firing from the trenches suddenly resumed. A Company responded by firing back, and the white flag reappeared. As the firing died away the enemy troops climbed out of their positions and surrendered.

As they did so, Sergeant Norman ran forward to Lieutenant Colonel Jones, who was still alive but very weak from his wound. Company Sergeant Major Price and Sergeant Blackburn also arrived and rapidly rendered first aid, applying a saline drip. Major Farrar-Hockley then appeared on the scene and gave orders for the Commanding Officer to be moved to the mound at the head of the gully to be evacuated by helicopter. Sadly, Lieutenant Colonel 'H' Jones died 15 minutes later while Major Farrar-Hockley waited beside him. At 1435 hours Battalion Headquarters received a radio message informing it that a helicopter had been despatched to evacuate Lieutenant Colonel Jones. Shortly afterwards the aircraft, flown by Captain Richard Nunn, arrived at Camilla Creek House. After being briefed by 2 PARA's Signals Officer, Captain David Benest, as to the Commanding Officer's location, Nunn took off at 1445 hours and flew southwards towards A Company's location. Unfortunately, his aircraft was intercepted shortly afterwards by two Pucaras, which shot it down. Nunn was killed instantly.

Enemy artillery and mortars continued to shell the area as A Company proceeded to collect prisoners and wounded. It was only then that the strength of the opposition became clear: there were 92 men, of whom 18 had been killed and 39 wounded. Many more had escaped from the furthermost positions. A Company's wounded were tended, as were the casualties amongst the prisoners. Lance Corporal Framingham and Private O'Rourke dressed their wounds, borrowing shell dressings from their comrades to do so. The prisoners were given cups of tea and the wounded were given extra clothing to keep them warm; such treatment was in line with Lieutenant Colonel Jones's insistence that prisoners should be treated correctly. At that point more helicopters appeared, bringing forward, among others, the battalion's Medical Officer, Captain Steve Hughes, who proceeded to treat the most urgent cases. The wounded were then evacuated. As A Company reorganised it was still under constant mortar and artillery fire. It had suffered three killed and 12 wounded. In addition, the Commanding Officer, the Adjutant and Corporal Melia, attached from 9 Parachute Squadron RE, had also been killed.

During A Company's action at Darwin Hill, B Company had remained on the reverse slope of the ridge in front of Boca House. An assault over the open ground to its front was out of the question, so the company had to content itself with engaging the enemy whenever it could. There was little it could do to help A Company, besides trying to knock out the enemy positions on the pyramid-shaped hill which were thought to be giving A Company all the trouble. One of the section commanders in No. 4 Platoon, Corporal Dunbar, had already attacked them at first light with a 66mm LAW but, to make sure that they were out of action, Lieutenant Ernie Hocking and Lance Corporal Barry, covered by Privates Mateland and Walton, prepared to move forward to throw grenades into them. As Hocking moved on to the hill he was ordered to withdraw because an air strike had been called on to Boca House. At the same time he noticed 50–100 enemy troops standing in the open by their trenches, but had no opportunity to engage them because of the imminent air strike. At that moment the flight of Pucaras flew overhead on their way to Camilla Creek House to attack 8 Commando Battery's gun line.

Meanwhile, No. 6 Platoon was still pinned down in the gorse line and being subjected to continuous mortar fire. From a gap in the gorse Lieutenant Clyde Chapman could see two positions about 370 yards apart with a number of tents between them. Corporal Margerson moved his section forward slowly so that it could obtain a better view of the enemy. At that moment a rocket was fired from one of the bunkers and landed among some members of the platoon, but fortunately did not explode. Lieutenant Chapman responded by calling for artillery support, but the shells fell wide of the mark. The platoon remained in this situation for the next 90 minutes, until Major John Crosland decided to withdraw it. Under cover of smoke laid down by the battalion's two mortars and by its own smoke grenades, the platoon pulled back. Corporal Margerson was wounded as he waited for his GPMG group to catch up. As he fell, another bullet hit the stock of his rifle and shattered it. He was dragged to safety by Lance Corporals Bardsley and Barry.

By then the battle at Darwin Hill was over and the battalion's Second in Command, Major Chris Keeble, was coming forward to take over command of 2 PARA. Over the radio he told Major John Crosland to take command of the battle while he was en route. At the same time he ordered C (Patrol) and Support Companies to move forward to the three rifle companies as quickly as possible. An air strike was requested, but had to be refused because of bad weather further to the north. However, an armed helicopter was placed on standby at Camilla Creek House.

Meanwhile, Major Philip Neame of D Company was still contemplating the western shoreline as a route for a flanking attack on Boca House. Although the tide was coming in, the small cliff and a narrow band of rock offered a covered approach which was unlikely to be mined because the beach was hard. Accordingly, Neame set of to reconnoitre the route, accompanied by Lieutenant John Page, Sergeant Bullock and a section. Making their way carefully to the shore, and using the cover of the cliff, Neame and his group moved towards the enemy. Having found a suitable position, he called forward Nos. 11 and 12 Platoons on the radio. On their arrival, he collected all nine of their GPMGs together and positioned them, under command of 2nd Lieutenant Chris Waddington, to provide fire support for an assault. The guns opened fire on the main enemy position, leaving the enemy in no doubt that withdrawal was no longer a possibility. White flags were by this time flying from some of the bunkers. It appeared that a surrender might be in the offing, and Major Phil Neame told his second in command to inform Major Keeble. He and his men could not remain on the beach indefinitely, as the tide was coming in; in any case, a surrender would be the most practical solution. There was a long delay. All was ready for the attack: the machine guns were in position and the artillery was ready and on call to give support if the enemy continued to resist.

Back on the ridgeline, Major John Crosland had asked D Company's second in command, Lieutenant Peter Adams, to request that the Anti-Tank Platoon be sent forward. Major Keeble agreed to this, but ordered D Company not to start its flanking move until B Company had been resupplied with ammunition which he had brought forward with him. Shortly afterwards, the Anti-Tank Platoon, under Captain Peter Ketley, arrived and deployed its Milan firing posts so as to be able to knock out the well prepared bunkers. Two missiles were fired at two positions and a figure appeared and staggered into a nearby bunker, which was also destroyed. At that point the Machine Gun Platoon also arrived and were deployed but ordered not to fire. By then, D Company was beginning its flanking move. The Machine Gun Platoon Commander, Lieutenant Hugo Lister, was then ordered to open fire. Almost immediately a frantic message came over the radio from the platoon commander of No. 10 Platoon, Lieutenant Shaun Webster, telling the company second in command to stop the machine guns as the enemy were indicating that they wished to surrender. To make matters worse, one of the Machine Gun Platoon's GPMGs had jammed, and a further 30 rounds were fired in attempting to clear the stoppage before the gunner received the order to cease fire.

By then No. 12 Platoon was up and moving forward. A member of the platoon shouted to Lieutenant Jim Barry that they were in a minefield but Barry, who had already realised this, told him to keep moving as it was too late to stop. At that moment an anti-tank mine was detonated by Private Spencer walking into a tripwire, the blast knocking him and three others over but not injuring them. Thinking that the platoon was under fire, a GPMG gunner on the ridgeline opened fire, as did one of the Milan firing posts, endangering No. 12 Platoon, which was now out in the open. Had the enemy decided to retaliate, D Company would have suffered heavy casualties. Over the radio, Major Phil Neame ordered all firing to cease.

On the ridgeline, enemy mortar fire was still causing problems. Captain John Young, B Company's second in command, was badly wounded, as were three members of the Anti-Tank Platoon. Behind the ridge, men took cover wherever they could as the medics gave emergency treatment to the wounded, moving them to a makeshift first aid post behind a small wall of peat dug to provide shelter from the wind and rain. The enemy positions around Boca House had now been cleared by D Company. Fifteen prisoners, some of them badly wounded, had been taken and 12 enemy dead had been found. Six more enemy had been seen fleeing over the hill earlier. Without bothering to reorganise, Major Neame pushed on with his company, as he knew that speed was of the essence. He left his company sergeant major and a section to cope with organising the prisoners. The plan was now for D Company to exploit forward to the high ground around the airfield overlooking Goose Green and to attack the enemy position at the schoolhouse. A Company would remain firm on Darwin Hill, less No. 3 Platoon, which would be attached to C (Patrol) Company, which was tasked with clearing all the enemy positions near the gorse line, above the scene of A Company's action on the high ground, before clearing Darwin itself. Meanwhile, B Company would make a flanking move down the western side of the isthmus, looping south to cut off Goose Green from that direction.

The Anti-Tank and Machine Gun Platoons, together with the section of two mortars, adopted positions to support the companies in their respective tasks. One matter causing concern was the problem of providing indirect fire support. The two mortars had done their utmost to provide support but, for much of the time during the actions so far, they had been out of range. The absence of the battalion's other six mortars prevented the leap-frogging of baseplates to ensure continual support. Moreover, the lack of ammunition was also causing problems. The section had run out of bombs at 1300 hours, during A Company's action, and it had become necessary to manpack more ammunition forward from the old baseplate position at the Battalion RV to the new one at Burntside House. This was exhausting work, and there was a limit to the load which could be carried by each man. Despite these problems, the two mortar crews had fired more than 1,000 rounds in two hours during the A Company action. The two mortars had progressively sunk further and further into the soft peat, until eventually only the muzzles of the barrels were visible. The mortars themselves became so hot that the Number Two in each crew had to pour water over them continually. Similarly, the three light guns of 8 Commando Battery RA were confronted by problems. The close proximity of the companies to the enemy positions meant that the risks of bringing down artillery fire were far too great. It was only during the action at Boca House, when B Company was sufficiently far away from the objective, that the guns could be brought to bear, and even then with only dubious accuracy.

While A Company reorganised in the gorse-filled gully where most of its action had taken place, C (Patrol) Company started clearing Darwin, but the plan for the next part of the operation was suddenly changed and Major Roger Jenner was ordered to advance on the airfield at Goose Green. B Company had already begun its long flanking move, and D Company was advancing towards the airfield from Boca House. C (Patrol) Company, followed by the Anti-Tank and Machine Gun Platoons, moved over the crest of the ridgeline above Goose Green and began to descend the slope towards the schoolhouse. In front of it lay the airfield where Argentinian troops stood transfixed, momentarily staring at the sight of the advancing company. When they recovered from their surprise, the anti-aircraft gunners among them manned the three Oerlikon 35mm guns positioned on the airfield and opened fire. Major Roger Jenner immediately called for artillery support, but none was available. At that moment the first salvo from the Oerlikons impacted on the ridgeline and wounded a member of the Machine Gun Platoon, Private Russell. Major Jenner and his signaller, Private Holman-Smith, ran across to the wounded man, who had been badly injured in the neck. Holman-Smith picked up Russell's GPMG but as he did so was killed by a round from another burst of Oerlikon fire, the blast from which also slightly injured Major Jenner and his other signaller, Private Holbrook. Having given Russell first aid and seen him evacuated by a party under Company Sergeant Major Prestfield, Jenner tried to make radio contact with his platoons, whom he could see advancing below, but was unable to establish contact. With heavy fire landing on the slope around him, he made his way back to the gorse line where Major Chris Keeble was observing the action. Despite Jenner's pleas to go on, Keeble told him to withdraw C Company, but all radio contact with his platoons had been lost. The enemy in the area of the schoolhouse had also opened fire and C (Patrol) Company and B Company, which by then was approaching from the west at the end of its flanking move, were both very exposed. No. 3 Platoon, which was still with C (Patrol) Company and in reserve, pulled back and took cover in the gorse line after suffering three casualties, including Sergeant Beattie, the platoon sergeant. The Reconnaissance and Patrols Platoons moved forward and took cover in dead ground, where they were joined shortly afterwards by the company second in command, Lieutenant Peter Kennedy.

Meanwhile, the Anti-Tank and Machine Gun Platoons deployed to the left of C (Patrol) Company, the machine gunners moving forward to positions from which the schoolhouse would be within range of their GPMGs. The battalion's snipers also took up positions in the gorse from which they could bring down harassing fire on the airfield.

D Company, less the section of No. 10 Platoon left behind at Boca House to tend the wounded and guard prisoners, was by then heading rapidly towards the airfield. Lieutenant Jim Barry and No. 12 Platoon were leading the company as it moved in the cover of a re-entrant towards its objective. As Barry and his men caught their first sight of the airfield they saw enemy troops withdrawing on a tractor. Corporal Sullivan's section opened fire and caused casualties. At the same time, more enemy were seen withdrawing into dead ground towards the schoolhouse. The company continued heading south-east, leaving the airfield on its right and keeping under cover from the fire of the Oerlikons by using the river valley which led to the schoolhouse. After advancing a further 900 yards or so, D Company spotted troops crossing a footbridge over the estuary ahead and running towards the schoolhouse. Uncertain whether these were members of C (Patrol) Company or Argentinians, D Company held its fire. At the same time, Major Phil Neame observed what he suspected might be an enemy headquarters in a hollow on the high ground at the western end of the airfield. He decided to despatch No. 10 Platoon to attack and clear it.

Lieutenant Shaun Webster and his remaining two sections advanced on what appeared to be a command post tent and some trenches, but these proved to have been recently abandoned in haste. As they moved further forward, Webster and his men came under fire from the south-west from two snipers. Leaving one section, under Corporal Stodder, to provide covering fire, Webster led the other section and his platoon headquarters in a left flanking attack. Unfortunately he had miscalculated the situation because, as he and his assault group advanced on a second abandoned position beside the airfield runway, they came under very heavy fire from an enemy platoon on the southern side of the airfield. Webster and his men hastily took cover behind the abandoned trenches which were fortunately close at hand. No sooner had their company commander told them to go firm and not move any further, than Webster and his men suddenly found themselves under very heavy and accurate machine-gun fire from behind. Without further ado they leapt into the trenches. It rapidly dawned on them that this was not enemy fire, but that of the Machine Gun Platoon, who had mistaken them for enemy troops. Once the volume of fire had decreased, the platoon hoisted their red berets on sticks and waved them around, while Lieutenant Webster tried to establish radio contact with Company Headquarters. Fortunately the Machine Gun Platoon saw the berets and ceased firing, enabling Webster to regroup his men and rejoin D Company.

The rest of D Company had meanwhile pressed on along the river valley until it neared the estuary. A minefield on the right forced Major Neame and his men to head towards the schoolhouse and the track which led to it. As they watched the building a large number of enemy could be seen regrouping in it, and Neame decided that he would attack this first. At that point the enemy spotted the company and opened fire. Having dropped off No. 12 Platoon to provide fire support from a position on the track, Neame led No. 11 Platoon in an assault from the creek. Lieutenant Jim Barry, the commander of No. 12 Platoon, then spotted white flags flying from the windows of the schoolhouse. He ordered his signaller, Private Knight, to pass this information to Company Headquarters, but in the ensuing confusion of the attack it did not get through. Moreover, despite these indications of surrender, the enemy were still continuing to fire from other positions in the vicinity of the schoolhouse.

As Major Neame and No. 1 Platoon advanced to attack the school-house, the Reconnaissance and Patrols Platoons also came under fire from the same area. From a vantage point higher up on the slope, Captain Paul Farrar watched as enemy troops abandoned three bunkers facing the sea to the east of the schoolhouse and moved into a small building to the south-east, having become aware that the threat was not from the sea but from behind them. The Patrols Platoon had become split, and Company Sergeant Major Greenhalgh had taken half of it forward into dead ground below. Captain Farrar's group now also went forward as an enemy artillery and mortar bombardment came down. He and his group then moved off up the track and shortly afterwards engaged one of the Oerlikon anti-aircraft guns, positioned some 135 yards away, with a grenade launcher before joining forces with Greenhalgh and his men. Farrar divided his platoon into three groups for an assault on the schoolhouse. His own consisted of himself with Corporal McNally, Lance Corporal Sisson and Privates Stokes and Sheap; Company Sergeant Major Greenhalgh took Corporal Graham, Lance Corporals Jackson, McHugh and Walsh, and Privates Myers, Jones, Trick, Wheatley and Yourston. The third group, under Corporal Bishop, com-prised all of the platoon's light machine gunners, Privates Cox, Morgan, Mortimer, Tewson and Warren, who would give covering fire.

Meanwhile, No. 11 Platoon had already attacked the outbuildings to the west of the schoolhouse, firing four 66mm LAWs into one of them. Three of the rockets missed, but the fourth penetrated the building. Under covering fire from the rest of the platoon, Corporals McAuley and Harley charged the building, throwing grenades into it and setting it ablaze. No enemy appeared. The platoon then turned its attention to the next, smaller building, which was already burning. At that moment heavy artillery fire started to fall on the area of the edge of the creek, and the company aid post was prevented from coming forward to tend the wounded. Private Dixon was hit by shrapnel and, despite first aid from the platoon medic, Private Sharp, he later died. The Platoon then began to engage the enemy in the schoolhouse itself. The commander, 2nd Lieutenant Chris Waddington, moved forward along the side of the inlet, taking with him two GPMGs and five men, while the rest of the platoon covered them. At the bottom of the inlet he met Captain Paul Farrar and his group of the Patrols Platoon.

The area of the schoolhouse was under fire from enemy positions at Goose Green Point to the south-east, where a heavy anti-aircraft gun and some Oerlikons were sited, and artillery and mortar rounds were falling on the northern bank of the inlet. From his position, Captain Farrar observed several enemy in the upper story of the main school building and more in the smaller building towards the shoreline. He could not see any white flags. Company Sergeant Major Greenhalgh's group took up positions in an extended line on the edge of the crest north of the school and began to fire 66mm LAWs and M-79 40mm grenades into the building. Meanwhile, Captain Farrar and his group moved round on a small track to the east side of the building. At this point Corporal Bishop's group of the Patrols Platoon joined No. 11 Platoon's fire support group to increase its firepower. A joint assault on the schoolhouse then took place, as elements of the Patrols Platoon and No. 11 Platoon charged the school building. On the right was 2nd Lieutenant Chris Waddington's group, in the centre Company Sergeant Major Greenhalgh's, and on the left Captain Paul Farrar's. As the attack went in, heavy supporting fire came from Corporal Bishop's and Corporal Harley's groups.

Company Sergeant Major Greenhalgh's group attacked the main building, throwing grenades into the ground floor, while the fire support groups concentrated their fire on the upper storey windows. As the grenades exploded, the building began to catch fire. Meanwhile, Captain Farrar and his men were crawling towards the area of the smaller building to the east of the schoolhouse. There they cleared the bunkers with grenades, two of which failed to explode. Because the area was under heavy fire from the enemy on Goose Green Point, Farrar and his men did not move up to the building itself. Suddenly, a heavy anti-aircraft gun opened fire on the schoolhouse, blowing large holes in the roof. At the same time, enemy artillery and mortar fire intensified, much of it landing in the inlet, although several bombs bounced off the crest line between the school and the inlet, ricochetting on to the beach or into the water. Captain Farrar decided to pull his men back and take cover against the shoreline.

Second Lieutenant Chris Waddington and his group had been caught in the open by the fire from the heavy anti-aircraft gun. Forced to take cover behind a tractor, Waddington spotted the bunkers cleared earlier by Captain Farrar's group. Unaware that they had been cleared, he and one of his men moved forward, but once again heavy fire came down around them and Waddington was forced to take evasive action by diving into a nearby pool of water, where he was pinned down for the next 15 minutes. Eventually he was able to move and join his men in clearing the bunkers before withdrawing them into the inlet and back along the track.

During the battle for the schoolhouse, No. 12 Platoon's task had been to provide supporting fire. Looking up the hill, Lieutenant Jim Barry spotted what he thought to be a white flag and, having informed his platoon sergeant that he was going to take a surrender, made his way up the hill accompanied by his runner, Private Godfrey. Sergeant Meredith sent the platoon's signaller after him and told Corporal Sullivan to follow behind. On hearing of this over the radio, Major Phil Neame replied that Lieutenant Barry was not to make any such move, but unfortunately this order never reached Barry. Accounts differ as to what happened next. As Barry and his signaller moved forward, with Private Godfrey behind, five Argentinians appeared with their weapons held above their heads and stood on the other side of a fence. Godfrey stopped, as he sensed that all was not well, while Corporal Sullivan, who could see more enemy in bunkers further to the right, ordered his GPMG group to deploy forward to cover the platoon commander. Face to face with Barry, one of the Argentinians climbed over the fence in between and, levelling his weapon, gestured to the young officer to surrender. Barry refused, gesticulating with his own weapon that the soldier should put his down. At that point a burst of machine gun fire, possibly from the action taking place at the schoolhouse, went overhead and the five enemy, and those in the bunkers, responded by firing at Barry, who was killed instantly.

A slightly different account was later given by Sergeant Meredith, who observed events from his position by a building by the side of the track. According to him, two Argentinians approached Lieutenant Barry unarmed and waving a white handkerchief. Another six were behind them, sitting down under cover. The two men pointed at the action still taking place around the schoolhouse, ducking as rounds whistled over their heads. Barry told his signaller to contact Company Headquarters and ask them to stop the firing. According to Meredith, Barry then appeared to lean his weapon against the fence, but at that moment a long burst of fire, later thought to be from the Machine Gun Platoon, went overhead, and the enemy retaliated by opening fire and killing Barry. Whichever version is true, the area subsequently came under heavy fire from the bunkers. Private Godfrey withdrew and took cover as two of the enemy skirmished towards him, the others taking refuge in a bunker. Both were killed by Private Knight, who then reported the events to Company Headquarters on his radio. Sergeant Meredith opened fire but, finding that rifle fire was ineffective against the enemy in the bunkers, brought forward Private Bresling and his GPMG to bring heavier fire to bear on the bunkers and on a group of enemy hiding behind a pile of ammunition. Meredith then moved up the track with Corporal Kinchen's section, covered by Corporal Barton's section and Bresling's GPMG. There he found the body of Lieutenant Jim Barry.

Meanwhile, Lieutenant Peter Kennedy, the second in command of C (Patrol) Company, had found himself under fire on the forward slope. Together with Corporal Cole he had taken cover in a shellhole and had then crawled down the side of the track, where he met Corporals Raynor and Pearson. Passing the Reconnaissance Platoon by the bridge, Kennedy made his way up the track to the flagpole. With Lieutenant Barry dead, he took over command of the troops in the immediate area and, taking two GPMG groups with him, continued along the track. As he approached the two bunkers where the enemy had earlier attempted to surrender, it became evident that all of the enemy in the area had either fled or had been killed. At that point Corporal Kinchen, who was with one of the GPMG groups, was ordered to return to his platoon, and Kennedy told him to inform A Company's commander that the high ground was clear and provided a good position for putting down covering fire to the front and on to the airfield. Kennedy pressed on with his other GPMG group, Private Sheepwash and Private Slough, and eventually the three of them took up a position in a gap in a hedgerow. From there they could see the enemy artillery firing 370 yards away behind a barn in Goose Green itself. To their right they could hear the noise of fighting, and saw men running into the settlement. Unfortunately, because he had no radio, Kennedy was unable to pass on the information about the location of the enemy guns. Had he been able to do so, the guns could have been put out of action.

The Machine Gun Platoon was now running low on ammunition. Having fired over 6,000 rounds, the sections were forced to link up belts from abandoned enemy ammunition. As the platoon came under heavier and more accurate mortar fire, Lieutenant Hugo Lister decided to move his men forward under cover of smoke. However, as they moved forward they came under fire from Goose Green Point, and were forced back into the abandoned enemy positions in which they had been sheltering. One man, Private Coxall, had been wounded in the leg and was evacuated by being dragged up the hill on a makeshift stretcher fashioned from abandoned enemy ponchos. Lieutenant Lister had a narrow escape when a shell landed very close in front of him but failed to explode.

The Anti-Tank Platoon had also been busy, engaging the anti-aircraft guns on the airfield and a bunker with its Milan missiles. Unfortunately, two of the missiles went out of control and missed. The platoon also attempted to engage the enemy anti-aircraft guns and positions at Goose Green Point, but they were just outside the maximum range of the missiles. Captain Peter Ketley sent forward Corporal Bolt's section, which fired another missile, but it landed 12ft short of the target. Nevertheless, the sight of the missiles homing in undoubtedly had a psychological effect on the enemy gunners and those in the bunkers. The Milan teams were aided by the battalion's snipers who, equipped with laser rangefinders, indicated targets to them. Subsequently, the snipers proved their worth while engaging enemy troops inside Goose Green itself, creating panic with their accurate harassing fire.

During the action around the airfield and the schoolhouse, B Company had carried out its long flanking move via dead ground en route to the south-west side of Goose Green itself. The march had not been without incident, the company moving through a minefield, where it found stocks of anti-personnel mines. As they approached the airfield No. 6 Platoon put down covering fire while Nos. 4 and 5 Platoons pressed onwards. As the company reached the edge of the airfield No. 5 Platoon began to move forward into the attack and No. 4 Platoon was ordered to occupy two large bunkers on the south-east corner. All the other bunkers along the perimeter were abandoned, and a large number of enemy could be seen milling around on the airfield itself in apparent confusion. The platoon spotted 16 enemy to the south who, when approached, were only too willing to surrender and be disarmed. Others further away indicated that they also wished to lay down their arms. Meanwhile, D Company's action on the airfield was taking place, and there was a risk that the two companies would become entangled. B Company's platoons were thus told to hold their fire. At that point, enemy mortars started to bring down fire on No. 5 Platoon.

The operation was now approaching its closing stages. 2 PARA was offered reinforcements by Brigade Headquarters, but these were turned down. At 1809 hours, with less than 30 minutes of daylight left, the battalion requested an airstrike on the enemy positions on Goose Green Point, because the heavy volume of fire being put down by the anti-aircraft weapons sited there was causing problems. However, the first aircraft to appear were two Argentinian A-4 Skyhawks, followed shortly afterwards by a Pucara, which proceeded to strafe B and D Companies as they were regrouping, the latter having moved up the valley away from the schoolhouse. The first aircraft sprayed the track with cannon fire, using the footbridge over the estuary as a target, but caused no casualties. At that point No. 10 Platoon received news over the radio of a flight of three Harriers approaching from the south, and seconds later the second Skyhawk exploded in mid-air, destroyed by a Sidewinder missile from one of the Harriers. Meanwhile, the Royal Marine Blowpipe detachment, now located in the gorse line, engaged the Pucara and shot it down. The aircraft crashed in B Company's positions, fortunately causing no casualties. The three Harriers hurtled over the battalion and attacked Goose Green Point. All available information had been passed to the pilots by Captain Kevin Arnold, the naval gunfire forward observer, and by Major Hugh Jenner, but the target was a difficult one with only one line of approach. Any attempt to attack by passing over Goose Green itself would have put at risk the lives of the settlement inhabitants, who were being held prisoner by the Argentinians inside buildings in the settlement. The first Harrier attacked from the north-west, but its cluster bombs fell harmlessly in the water. The second aircraft, approaching from the same direction, also missed. The third attacked from the north-east and hit the target. After the aircraft had departed, however, the Oerlikon guns continued to fire. It later transpired that the one successful strike had caused several casualties. Moreover, the airstrike as a whole had a psychological effect on the Argentinians in the settlement; the islanders later told of the enemy troops panicking and screaming in abject terror.

D Company was ordered to go firm by Major Keeble, and the company moved to a reverse slope position north-west of the flagpole, which was located by the track between the airfield and the schoolhouse. Just before last light another Pucara appeared and attacked D Company. B and D Companies retaliated by turning their weapons skywards and pouring fire into the aircraft, which plunged earthwards. The pilot ejected and was later captured by Corporal Kinchen and Private Spencer of No. 12 Platoon.

B Company had regrouped on the outskirts of Goose Green and was in the process of producing a much needed 'brew' when Lieutenant Geoff Weighell heard the sound of helicopters. To his dismay, he observed an enemy Chinook followed by six UH-1 'Hueys' in close formation, which shortly afterwards landed to the south and disembarked troops. Reacting rapidly, Weighell and Sergeant Aird worked out the position of the helicopters and called down artillery fire. The guns were accurate but by the time a 15-round fire mission impacted in the area of the LZ, the aircraft were taking off and an enemy company of some 100 men was making its way towards the settlement which it reached without loss. During this time B Company came under fire from Argentinians in the settlement, and Major John Crosland was concerned that this might be a prelude to a counterattack. Accordingly, he pulled his men back to the edge of the airfield, where they took up positions by an abandoned Oerlikon anti-aircraft gun. The ground was littered with Argentinian 7.62mm ammunition, so the company was able to refill its magazines and link up belts for its GPMGs. All digging tools had been left with the battalion's packs at Camilla Creek House, so the men had to dig shell scrapes as best they could with bayonets, knives and mess tins. The weather was cold, it was raining, and rations and drinking water were scarce.

Near the gorse-filled gully, C (Patrol) Company was regrouping. Gradually the platoons came in, having received no orders following the battle for the schoolhouse. Major Roger Jenner was suffering from wounds, and Major Chris Keeble ordered him to be evacuated, but he could not be found. He was discovered on the following morning and evacuated by helicopter to the Main Dressing Station at Ajax Bay for treatment. The company second in command, Lieutenant Peter Kennedy, remained unaccounted for and was presumed missing. In fact, he and his D Company GPMG group had remained forward by the flagpole. At last light Kennedy had decided to seek out the enemy artillery pieces which he had observed earlier, and which were still firing, and attack their positions. Accompanied by Private Slough, and covered by Private Sheepwash with the GPMG, Kennedy set off towards the area of the barns where he had previously observed the enemy guns firing. As darkness fell it became increasingly difficult to locate the guns, which by then had ceased firing. Approaching the barns, Kennedy and Slough searched for them without success. Eventually they withdrew, pausing only to remove an Argentinian flag still flying on the flagpole. Seeing or hearing no sign of the rest of the battalion, Kennedy and his two men moved back to the footbridge near the schoolhouse. As they reached it they saw some campfires but, having already decided that the battalion had either withdrawn or had been wiped out, assumed that these belonged to the enemy and that they had been cut off. They moved on and approached the gorse line, whistling the regimental march 'The Ride of The Valkyries' in the hope that this would reduce the chances of being shot by their own side. Detecting no sign of the battalion, they took up positions in the gorse line for the night.

It was bitterly cold during the night, and men huddled together for warmth as there were no sleeping bags or dry clothing. Battalion Headquarters, A and C (Patrol) Companies were fortunate in that, after last light, they received a resupply of water, ammunition and rations. However, there was no hope of finding B and D Companies in the darkness so, unfortunately, they went hungry. In addition, 30 sleeping bags also arrived for use by the wounded. Far too late in the day, but still sorely needed, the battalion's other six mortars also arrived from Sussex Mountain by helicopter. The Mortar Platoon was busy during the night, resiting the base plate position in the gorse-filled gully where Battalion Headquarters was also located. The matter of 2 PARA's casualties was causing great concern, the only method of evacuation being by helicopter. The Regimental Aid Post (RAP) was operating in two groups: one under Captain Rory Wagan at Boca House and the other under Captain Steve Hughes in the gorse-filled gully. They were hampered by the continual rain and the problem of evacuating the more seriously wounded grew steadily worse. In particular, evacuation of the wounded from Boca House was not going well. Captain Wagan contacted Battalion Headquarters by radio, and shortly afterwards a Gazelle helicopter arrived to pick up the sitting wounded. However, several stretcher cases remained and Captain John Young, B Company's second in command, was suffering from the effects of his wounds and the cold.

Inevitably, unaware of other pressing operational commitments, to the men at Goose Green the brigade headquarters' attitude to the problems in organising the evacuation seemed somewhat unhelpful. Six casualties needed urgent evacuation and two of them, Captain Young and a young Argentinian prisoner, were priority cases. At 2240 hours the brigade headquarters eventually agreed to collect them. A Sea King helicopter later appeared briefly, but flew away again. Just before midnight the brigade headquarters located the aircraft but then informed 2 PARA that it could not return. Battalion Headquarters remonstrated with them, and eventually one casualty evacuation flight was granted. This was a Scout helicopter flown by Captain John Greenhalgh, who had volunteered for the task. The casualties were now in dire need of further medical attention, having lain in the darkness for five hours. Captain Greenhalgh's aircraft arrived, guided in to the LZ by a green light. Captain Young, who had been wounded 14 hours earlier, was evacuated. All that Captain Rory Wagan and his medics could do was to sleep as close to their remaining patients as possible in an attempt to keep them warm. They could not be evacuated until first light the following day, some 20 hours after being wounded.

It was a similar story with the RAP's other group, in the gorse-filled gully. Captain Steve Hughes' first priority had been the wounded from the A Company action. Most of these had been quickly evacuated by helicopter early in the day, despite the increase in artillery fire which occurred every time the helicopters made their appearance. Captain Mike Ford had been busy organising stretcher parties to go forward during the C Company action. They had heard of one man, Private Grey, who had suffered wounds to his leg, which had almost been severed. Captain Ford and a medic, Lance Corporal Bentley, went forward under fire and, with minimal instruments, Lance Corporal Bentley saved Private Grey's life by amputating his leg below the knee. The two men then brought Grey back and he was evacuated soon afterwards, by which time he had lost consciousness. After last light Lance Corporal Bentley again went forward to help Captain Greenhalgh evacuate the remaining C (Patrol) Company casualties as they withdrew back up the hill. By then, Corporal Evans and two other men, Privates Smith and Boland, had lain in a despression on the forward slope for over four hours with mortar fire landing around them continually. They were eventually found by Corporal Owen's section, which literally stumbled on them in the dark. As his section and the three wounded men moved off, Corporal Owen fired a green Very flare to make contact with other members of the company; seconds later a shell landed on the exact spot where they had been. When the helicopter arrived, there was insufficient room for all three caualties. Corporal Evans was evacuated in the dark on a stretcher back to the gorse line by Captain Ford and Lance Corporal Allen, a member of the MT Platoon, while Privates Smith and Boland went in the helicopter.

Throughout the night, Captain Hughes's group continued to work as the dead were brought to the bottom of the mound in the gully and were laid out. Meanwhile, the wounded were kept as warm as possible to await evacuation in the morning. Those who could do so, slept. Many suffered hallucinations in their sleep, hearing once again the din of machine guns, mortars and artillery.

The main problem facing Major Keeble was how to persuade the Argentinians to surrender. His initial plan was simply to flatten the Goose Green settlement with artillery and mortars and then attack it. However, the news of the presence of civilians forced him to dismiss the idea. It then occurred to him to try and make contact with the Argentinian commander by sending two prisoners into the settlement with an ultimatum: surrender or face the consequences, including responsibility for the fate of the civilians. Having obtained the brigade commander's permission over the radio, Keeble formulated his plan. His aim was to extend the period of surrender negotiations as long as possible to enable him to bring up reinforcements, in the form of J Company 42 Commando RM, and replenish ammunition and supplies. At the back of his mind, however, was the nagging question of what action could he take if the Argentinians refused to negotiate and kept the civilians as hostages. During the night Major Keeble, Captain Alan Coulson, and Captain Rod Bell worked on the text of the ultimatum, which Bell translated into Spanish. At 1000 hours on the following morning, 29 May, two prisoners, who had been well briefed, were sent into Goose Green with the instruction that, if they were not back within the hour, it would be assumed that the Argentinians wished to continue the battle and 2 PARA would attack. The two men were back within the space of a few minutes, and arrangements were made for a meeting at a hut on the western side of the airfield. A and D Companies deployed standing patrols nearby.

Major Keeble, accompanied by Major Hector Gullan (a Parachute Regiment officer on the staff of 3 Commando Brigade and attached to 2 PARA as a liaison officer), Major Tony Rice (the commander of 8 Commando Battery), Captain Rod Bell as interpreter, and Robert Fox of the BBC and David Norris of the *Daily Mail*, moved to the hut, above which flew a white flag. Shortly afterwards a group of Argentinian officers arrived. These included the commander of the Goose Green garrison, Air Vice-Commodore Wilson Dosio Pedroza, and the commander of Argentinian Army troops there, Lieutenant Colonel Italo Pioggi. The Argentinians agreed to the removal of the civilians. The garrison commander seemed willing to come to terms immediately, but Colonel Pioggi stated that he wished to consult General Menendez in Port Stanley by radio. Major Gullan interjected, emphasising that there was no time for any prevarication and that General Menendez should know that his men had fought well but were now in a very dangerous situation. Captain Rod Bell reinforced this remark by stressing the consequences if there was no surrender. Both groups then left the hut, having arranged that, if there was a surrender, it would take place on an area of flat ground above the settlement.

At 1310 hours Major Keeble and his party arrived at the designated area. There was an atmosphere of tension and uncertainty, although Argentinian troops could be seen packing their equipment in the settlement below. Suddenly, a column of troops marched out of the settlement to where Keeble and his group were standing. After forming a hollow square, and having been addressed by Air Vice-Commodore Pedroza, they sang the Argentinian national anthem and then lay down their arms. Pedroza marched over to Keeble's group, saluted, and handed over his pistol. Keeble realised that the men were all Air Force personnel, and asked Pedroza what had happened to the remainder of the garrison. The latter pointed towards the settlement, where hundreds of men could be seen pouring out and heading towards them. They assembled with the Air Force men, their numbers growing until they totalled some 1,000 in strength. Having been disarmed under the watchful eye of Regimental Sergeant Major Simpson, they were placed under guard of D Company. Their senior officers were removed from the scene without further ado and despatched to Brigade Headquarters by helicopter. Soon afterwards Major Chris Keeble, accompanied by Major Tony Rice and Robert Fox, walked down to the settlement. As they did so, the local inhabitants began to pour out of the buildings, overwhelmed to be free, happy to be alive and full of gratitude to the men of 2 PARA, for whom the battle of Goose Green was finally over.

2 PARA had suffered 15 killed and 30 wounded during the actions at Darwin and Goose Green. Enemy casualties totalled 55 killed and between 80 and 100 wounded, with over 1,000 men taken prisoner. Equipment captured by 2 PARA amounted to six 120mm mortars, four 105mm pack howitzers, six 20mm and two 35mm anti-aircraft guns, two Pucara ground-attack aircraft and large quantities of ammunition and stores. On the morning of 31 May Major Chris Keeble, accompanied by all six company commanders, the Regimental Sergeant Major and the Padre, flew back to Ajax Bay for the burial of 2 PARA's dead in a large grave dug by Royal Engineers on the hillside above San Carlos Water. Witnessed by troops from other units, the burial, conducted by the Reverend David Cooper, was very simple, lacking the normal ceremony of a military funeral. Those watching saluted as the Regimental Sergeant Major scattered a handful of earth over the shrouded bodies.

3 PARA — THE ADVANCE EASTWARDS

On 27 May, while 2 PARA was lying up at Camilla Creek House before its advance on Darwin, 3 PARA was also moving out of the beachhead. At 1315 hours the battalion, minus D (Patrol) Company, which remained at Port San Carlos with Battalion Main Headquarters and Echelon, began a move from Port San Carlos to a settlement at Teal Inlet, on the east coast of East Falkland, halfway to Port Stanley. Originally it had been intended that it should follow 45 Commando to Douglas Settlement and then move through to Teal Inlet. However, after consulting an islander who knew the route well, Lieutenant Colonel Hew Pike had decided that a more direct route would be preferable, and had obtained agreement from Brigadier Thompson that the battalion should move concurrently with 45 Commando to the settlement.

During the next 24 hours 3 PARA carried out a gruelling march which ended at 1100 hours on the following morning, 28 May, at a lying-up position in the valley of the Arroyo Pedro River, some five and half miles short of Teal Inlet. Led by A Company, which was accompanied by the Commanding Officer and his 'R' Group, the battalion had moved at a punishing pace in appalling weather, halting only for brief breaks. Unlike their comrades in 45 Commando, however, the men of 3 PARA were travelling light. Hearing that the terrain was difficult, Lieutenant Colonel Pike had persuaded some local farmers at Port San Carlos to help by loading the battalion's packs, heavier weapons and equipment, including the mortars, on to trailers and towing them with tractors behind the battalion as it made its way over the hills. Nevertheless, during the night 3 PARA suffered several cases of exhaustion and exposure, and these had to be evacuated by helicopter the following morning. The battalion lay up during the remaining hours of daylight on 28 May. There it was joined by the tractors and trailers carrying its equipment, and by the Mortar Platoon which had travelled with them. After last light the battalion resumed its advance on Teal Inlet. B Company, under Major Mike Argue, carried out a flanking move and took up positions to the south east of the settlement to cut off any attempt at escape by the enemy. That afternoon, in fact, the battalion had received an SBS report that Teal was clear of enemy, but at 2300 hours a civilian reported that there could be up to 11 wounded Argentinians in the settlement. At 0230 hours on the following morning, 29 May, A Company, together with Lieutenant Colonel Pike and his 'R' Group, made its way slowly into Teal. By 0300 hours the area of the settlement had been cleared and secured, only one enemy soldier having been taken prisoner, although there were reports of stragglers in the area.

In the morning the rest of 3 PARA, which had remained behind at Port San Carlos, began flying out to join the battalion at Teal. Part of D (Patrol) Company was the last to be lifted forward. Unbeknown to the rest of 3 PARA, four patrols of the company, under its Operations Officer, Captain Matt Selfridge, and Company Sergeant Major Quinn, had been withdrawn earlier to the brigade headquarters for an operation. As the battalion was preparing to depart from San Carlos, the patrols were despatched by Sea King helicopter to be inserted by parachute on to Great Island, which lies at the southern end of Falkland Sound, for a surveillance task. However, bad weather forced the operation to be cancelled and the aircraft returned to San Carlos. Subsequently, the patrols were embarked on a frigate and were landed on the island by boat. After setting up two OPs, they observed Fox

Bay, on the east coast of West Falkland, for movements of enemy shipping and aircraft, and gave early warning of air strikes and movement of enemy troops by helicopter between East and West Falkland. Eight days later the patrols were withdrawn and returned to 3 PARA. The battalion was also joined at Teal by 4 Troop of the Blues & Royals under Lieutenant Mark Coreth. The troop had originally been due to move with the battalion from Port San Carlos, but had been delayed because of a shortage of fuel. On the following morning Lieutenant Coreth had appropriated some fuel for his Scorpions and Scimitars and had set off in hot pursuit after 3 PARA. Following up behind, 4 Troop had picked up casualties along the battalion's line of march before eventually arriving at Teal. During 29 May 3 PARA dug in around Teal, but that evening the battalion received a warning order to continue its advance at first light on the following morning.

The battalion's objective, along with that of 45 Commando, was Estancia House, some 15 miles to the south-east of Teal Inlet. 3 PARA would arrive first, after which 45 Commando would move through and take Long Island Mount. Brigadier Thompson's plan was that, once Mount Estancia, Mount Kent, Mount Challenger and Long Island Mount had been secured, he would hold the ground dominating Port Stanley from the west and north-west and would be able to use the inlets of Port Salvador.

At first light on 30 May 3 PARA set off, led by D (Patrol) Company under Major Pat Butler, and by the evening had reached and crossed the bridge north of Lower Malo House. Marching almost non-stop through the night, the battalion advanced until it was close to its objective. During the following day it lay up, overlooked by enemy positions on Smoko Mountain to the south but remaining undetected. After last light on 31 May the battalion pressed on and, after a close reconnaissance had been carried out by D (Patrol) Company, cleared and secured the settlement at Estancia House. A Company, commanded by Major David Collett, then moved on to Mount Estancia, the high ground above the settlement, and was joined there on the following morning, 1 June, by Battalion Tactical Headquarters. Major Mike Argue and B Company occupied the southern shoulders of Mount Vernet, covering the valley across to Mount Kent, while C Company, under Major Martin Osborne, took up positions on Mount Vernet itself. On 1 June Major Pat Butler despatched nine four-man patrols and two sections of sappers of 9 Parachute Squadron RE to carry out 48-hour close reconnaissance tasks on Mount Longdon. The following day one of the sapper patrols found an abandoned enemy position consisting of six sangars, around which were seven tents containing sleeping bags, personal equipment, some 2-inch mortar bombs and a 3.5-inch rocket launcher. That night another of the patrols was engaged by enemy mortar fire which, although close, caused no casualties.

As the battalion established itself around Estancia, it was assisted in the movement of its support weapons, equipment and stores by local farmers, who volunteered the use of their Land Rovers or tractors and trailers. A screen of patrols was deployed forward and found evidence of a company-sized enemy force which had withdrawn before 3 PARA's arrival. These included signs of casualties. Subsequently, small groups of Argentinians returned to the area and surrendered. By this time the weather had deteriorated even further, and this caused problems in the move eastwards of 3 Commando Brigade. Driving rain, heavy mist and snow made flying impossible, and it was not until two days later, on 3 June, that 79 Commando Battery RA could be lifted forward by helicopter to Mount Estancia. Two days earlier 7 Commando Battery RA had been flown on to Mount Kent along with L Company, and some of Support Company, of 42 Commando and a troop of sappers of 59 Independent Commando Squadron RE. The rest of 42 Commando joined them on the following two nights. The forces being assembled on Mount Kent, Mount Challenger and Mount Estancia were, however, within range of Argentinian artillery, and in particular of three 155mm guns. Any visible movement on skylines or crests immediately attracted shellfire which added to the problems caused by night bombing raids carried out by Argentinian Air Force Canberra bombers, which became increasingly accurate. Problems of helicopter resupply, owing to priority for aircraft being given to 5 Infantry Brigade, which had just landed at San Carlos, were such that the two Commando batteries were limited to 100 rounds of 105mm ammunition per battery each day. This meant that any counter-battery fire was very tightly controlled, and on many occasions targets could not be engaged.

At 1100 hours on 3 June Lieutenant Colonel Hew Pike held an 'O' Group on the top of Mount Estancia. The battalion would move out during the afternoon for Mount Longdon. It would be supported by a fire base consisting of the Mortar Platoon, the Anti-Tank Platoon, the Machine Gun Platoon and the Scorpions and Scimitars of 4 Troop of the Blues & Royals. In the first phase of the operation, A Company would attack the north-eastern area of the objective. In the second phase, C Company would take the western end and B Company the eastern end. While the Commanding Officer's 'O' Group was in progress, Captain Matt Selfridge and the reconnaissance patrols returned to Estancia House. Having worked their way to within 50 yards of the enemy positions on Mount Longdon, they were able to report that it was held by approximately two companies of infantry and an independent platoon located to the north-east of the main feature. These were supported by two 81mm mortars and two 120mm mortars. The patrols had also located the positions of three machine guns and an administrative area at the base of the eastern end of Mount Longdon.

At 1600 hours 3 PARA began its advance to contact eastwards. At 1824 hours that evening, however, the brigade commander ordered the battalion to halt, as he was concerned that it was moving on too fast and that it would find itself in a position from which it could not extricate itself. Accordingly, 3 PARA consolidated and established new positions with A Company deployed forward some two and a half miles west of the Murrell Bridge, just north of the track leading from Estancia to Port Stanley. B Company was situated in a reverse slope position 2,000 yards west of A Company, where it discovered a recently occupied Argentinian position and some equipment which was put to good use. Meanwhile, C Company remained on Mount Estancia while Echelon was established at Teal Inlet and Estancia House. D (Patrol) Company established a patrol base 430 yards north of the Murrell Bridge, from which it mounted reconnaissance patrols on Mount Longdon. Protected by No. 4 Platoon of B Company, the base reduced the distance which patrols had to cover to reach Mount Longdon and return each night, allowing them more time on the objective. However, by the afternoon of 4 June the base had started to attract the attention of enemy artillery and was withdrawn. Thereafter, patrols were mounted from A Company's positions, in some instances staying out for two to three nights at a time because of the increased distance to be covered. At the same time, the rifle companies carried out a large number of fighting patrols, many of which ventured very close to enemy positions on Mount Longdon. The Mortar Platoon also played its part, engaging the enemy positions with harassing fire.

On the afternoon of the following day, 4 June, Lieutenant Colonel Hew Pike issued orders confirming changes to plans for future operations on Mount Longdon. A Company would now attack the northern half of the objective on the western side; B Company's task remained the same, but it was to move along the northern edge of the western end of Mount Longdon and then attack the eastern end of the feature. Phases One and Two would now be carried out simultaneously. Unfortunately, the battalion would no longer have the support of the Blues & Royals troop, as it had departed earlier that afternoon after being reallocated to 2 PARA.

Meanwhile, 3 PARA continued to harass the enemy. In the early hours of 5 June two of the battalion's snipers, Corporal Phillips and Private Absolon, were engaging opportunity targets on the western end of Mount Longdon. At 0200 hours Corporal Phillips shot an Argentinian officer as he left a command bunker on the side of the hill. Private Absolon then proceeded to destroy the bunker with a direct hit from a 66mm LAW. Both soldiers, who were only 100 yards from the enemy positions, then withdrew under fire. During the afternoon, one of D (Patrol) Company's reconnaissance patrols successfully engaged an enemy mortar position and some OPs with artillery fire. That night, another reconnaissance patrol pinpointed two heavy machine guns, a section of 81mm mortars and another position with at least one 120mm mortar. It also discovered a minefield with a frontage of about 550 yards. One of the mines was lifted, and was discovered to be of Spanish manufacture.

On the following morning, 6 June, two patrols under Corporals Brown and Haddon rendezvoused 200 yards north of the Murrell Bridge to compare notes before returning to Estancia House. It was nearly first light, and the sentry in the patrol base reported nine men crossing the skyline on the eastern side of the river. They were seen to approach the bridge, two men crossing it and apparently checking it with regard to demolition. The two patrols waited as the rest of the enemy joined the two men on the bridge, then opened fire, killing five of the enemy. The remainder fled while the patrols came under immediate mortar and artillery fire from a fire base on the side of Mount Tumbledown. They were forced to evacuate their position rapidly, leaving behind their packs and radio, but succeeded in withdrawing without suffering any casualties. The location was checked on the evening of 8 June by another patrol, but there was no sign of the packs or radio, which meant that the battalion's radio net could have been compromised.

On the evening of 8 June three large fighting patrols, each consisting of a half-platoon and accompanied by a D (Patrol) Company guide and two civilian guides, Terry Peck and Vernon Steen, left B Company's area and headed for Mount Longdon. Their mission was to find suitable approaches to the objective and to test enemy reactions. Unfortunately, bright moonlight made all three patrols feel somewhat conspicuous and prevented them from penetrating the enemy positions. They saw only six enemy, a command post and an artillery piece which was engaged by one of the Commando batteries. The patrols then withdrew and returned to their own companies by first light the following morning.

On 10 June Brigadier Julian Thompson held an 'O' Group at which he issued orders for the next phase of operations, which would be a brigade night attack. 3 PARA was to take Mount Longdon and exploit forward to Wireless Ridge if possible, while 45 Commando would attack Two Sisters and aim to exploit forward to Mount Tumbledown. 42 Commando would capture Mount Harriet and be ready to move behind 45 Commando over Mount Tumbledown on to Mount William. 2 PARA would be in reserve, moving in the centre behind 3 PARA and 45 Commando. It was possible that the battalion would be tasked with taking Wireless Ridge via a flanking move to the north of Mount Longdon. The 1st Battalion Welsh Guards, which had landed with 5 Infantry Brigade, would secure 42 Commando's start line for the attack on Mount Harriet and thereafter be ready to provide support if required.

2 PARA — THE MOVE TO FITZROY

While 3 PARA was taking up positions on Mount Estancia and preparing for operations on Mount Longdon, 2 PARA was enjoying a much-needed respite. Until then the Quartermaster, Captain Tom Godwin, and 'B' Echelon had remained aboard the MV *Norland* where they had assisted in the embarkation of part of 5 Infantry Brigade which had boarded the vessel at South Georgia on 29 May. During the night of 1 May, however, Captain Godwin and his men had followed the 1st Battalion 7th Duke of Edinburgh's Own Gurkha Rifles ashore at Ajax Bay. Fortunately for 2 PARA, 'B' Echelon was subsequently co-located with one of the helicopter squadrons and the Quartermaster soon established a good rapport with the pilots, bartering extra flights in exchange for items such as paraffin heaters. Thereafter, conditions improved markedly for 2 PARA as its long-awaited resupply took place.

On 2 June the relative calm was shattered by a huge explosion among the huge piles of ammunition being cleared by Argentinian prisoners. They were doing so of their own volition because of the proximity of the ammunition to the large shed in which they were being accommodated at the time. Three prisoners were killed and nine others badly injured; one of the latter was seen lying burning in the flames and, despite efforts by the battalion's Medical Sergeant, could not be rescued. As the prisoner was thought to be still alive, three or four shots were fired at him to spare him further suffering. The casualties were given immediate treatment in the RAP and were then evacuated to the Main Dressing Station at Ajax Bay, where they underwent emergency surgery. Unfortunately one man, who had lost both legs in the explosion, died, but the others recovered from their injuries.

During a chance conversation between Major Dair Farrar-Hockley and the manager of the Darwin settlement, Mr Brooke Hardcastle, the question arose as to where the battalion would be moving next. The latter suggested that the quickest way to discover the situation further to the east would be to telephone his counterparts at Fitzroy and Bluff Cove. On hearing of this suggestion, Major Chris Keeble gave his approval and a patrol was despatched to Burntside House, but the telephone lines were found to be down. Another settlement was located further to the east at Swan Inlet, and B Company was ordered to send a platoon to discover whether there was a working telephone there. Lieutenant Clyde Chapman's No. 6 Platoon had already received a warning order to carry out a raid on an enemy OP on Mount Usborne, but was tasked instead with providing a group to go to Swan Inlet. On 2 June Lieutenant Chapman and nine of his men, accompanied by 2 PARA's Intelligence Section NCO, Colour Sergeant Morris, and Major John Crosland, took off in three Scout helicopters. Accompanying them were another two Scouts armed with SS-11 missiles. Crosland's plan was to approach at low level from the south of Swan Inlet. The armed helicopters would then fire their missiles while the other three landed the small assault force. The three groups, commanded by Major Crosland, Lieutenant Chapman and Corporal Bradford, would then clear the buildings.

The operation went as planned, except that two of the missiles missed their targets. The third SS-11 destroyed two of the buildings. Major Crosland and Colour Sergeant Morris found a telephone and succeeded in making contact with the settlement manager at Fitzroy, Mr Ron Binney, who informed them that there were no enemy forces there. This information was relayed back to 2 PARA by radio, after which Major Crosland and his force flew back to Goose Green. On receiving this information Brigadier Wilson cancelled his plans for a march to Fitzroy and decided to lift 2 PARA there by helicopter that evening. The main problem was the lack of helicopters; only one Chinook was available, three others having been lost with the sinking of the *Atlantic Conveyor* on 25 May. The only other aircraft were 656 Squadron's Scouts, which could lift only four men at a time. Nevertheless, planning for the move went ahead and, after a hurried 'O' Group in the settlement's community hall, the Chinook took off with the first lift, comprising two platoons of A Company, B Company headquarters with one platoon and detachments of the Mortar and Anti-Tank Platoons. Meanwhile, Scout helicopters had already deployed two patrols from C (Patrol) Company into Bluff Cove and two others into Fitzroy to check for any sign of the enemy and to mark the LZs for the battalion. 3 Commando Brigade were unaware of 2 PARA's move, and troops on Mount Kent who observed the landings initially assumed the helicopters to be enemy aircraft. One artillery forward observation officer was about to call down artillery fire on the LZs when he realised from the markings on the aircraft that the troops being landed were British.

That day, 2 PARA had been joined by its new Commanding Officer, Lieutenant Colonel David Chaundler. He joined one of C (Patrol) Company's patrols being lifted into Fitzroy, leaving Major Chris Keeble in command of the battalion during the move. When Lieutenant Colin Connor and his patrol were dropped off at Fitzroy, they were unaware that the pilot of their Scout had delivered them to the wrong location. Accordingly, they switched on the strobe signal which would guide in the aircraft bringing in Major Keeble, his 'R' Group and the B Company group. On his arrival, Keeble and his party accompanied Connor on to higher ground to estalish communications with the A Company group, which he assumed had landed safely at Bluff Cove. In the darkness, however, contact was lost with the B Company group below, and Keeble decided to press on to Fitzroy. It was only then that he and the others with him realised that they were two and a half miles from where they should have been delivered. Leaving the B Company group on the ridge, Keeble and his group, led by the two Reconnaissance Platoon patrols, set off for Fitzroy, which was reached without further mishap. There they met Ron Binney, the settlement manager, who confirmed that there were no enemy in Fitzroy but that they had tried to destroy the bridge on the track to Bluff Cove. This was confirmed by Lieutenant Connor and his men, who were sent to inspect it. They found some of the bridge, which was only slightly damaged, still prepared for demolition and some mines laid on the far side. The bridge itself, however, could easily be repaired by sappers.

On the following morning Lieutenant Colonel Chaundler assumed command of 2 PARA, and during the day the rest of the battalion arrived at Fitzroy and Bluff Cove. Brigadier Wilson arrived by helicopter and informed the Commanding Officer that his brigade headquarters and logistic support elements would be moving to Fitzroy. Meanwhile, sappers of 9 Parachute Squadron RE had begun lifting the mines by the bridge and 29 Field Battery RA was being flown in to provide artillery support. There was some confusion during the deployment of the companies. B Company's planned location was on the high ground which overlooked Fitzroy, while A Company's was on that dominating the settlement at Bluff Cove. C (Patrol) Company's area would be to the north-east, while D Company was to be tasked with holding the high ground to the east of Bluff Cove on the far side of the inlet. Battalion Tactical Headquarters would be located in a farm at Bluff Cove. Unfortunately, the deployment itself did not go smoothly. C (Patrol) Company's headquarters was landed at Bluff Cove instead of Fitzroy, and the pilot of the aircraft carrying D Company spent some time searching for a suitable LZ, eventually landing the company on the eastern side of their location, where it was in full view of enemy positions on Mount Harriet. This resulted in the company coming under fire from enemy heavy artillery almost immediately. Despite these problems, 2 PARA busied itself with establishing its new positions. The battalion had moved in light order, and it was not until 24 hours later that it received its packs and a ration resupply.

The rest of 5 Infantry Brigade followed during the next few days. The 1st Battalion Welsh Guards initially set off on foot to march from San Carlos, but the going was such that after 12 hours it was recalled. It was decided instead to send the battalion, together with the 2nd Battalion Scots Guards, by sea to Fitzroy. Accordingly, on the evening of 5 June, the Scots Guards embarked on HMS *Intrepid* and sailed from San Carlos to Lively Island. There the battalion transferred to landing craft which took it to Bluff Cove, where it landed on the morning of 6 June. The weather and sea conditions were bad, and the battalion had a very rough voyage to the settlement, arriving soaked to the skin. It had originally been intended that it would move off immediately to positions further up the coast, but it was decided instead that the battalion should relieve 2 PARA at Bluff Cove, enabling the latter to concentrate at Fitzroy. It was also decided that 2 PARA would move immediately to Fitzroy, but the appalling weather ruled out the use of helicopters. The only alternative was to use landing craft, but these could not be contacted by radio and their location could not be verified. Major Chris Keeble was despatched by helicopter to find them and ask them to sail to Bluff Cove to pick up the battalion. This he did, and by the late afternoon the landing craft had arrived at the inlet to the east of Bluff Cove and 2 PARA embarked. The voyage to Fitzroy proved to be a somewhat fraught affair. Land was sighted after three hours, but turned out to be Bluff Cove once more, the landing craft having sailed in a large circle. By then the sea state was even worse, with water coming over the sides and making the already soaked battalion even more miserable. Eventually, however, the battalion arrived at Fitzroy after first light on the following morning, 7 June.

Meanwhile, the 1st Battalion Welsh Guards had embarked on HMS *Fearless* and sailed to Lively Island. However, the deteriorating weather and a shortage of landing craft resulted in only two companies completing the rest of the journey to Bluff Cove, where they landed on the night of 6 June, the rest of the battalion sailing to Goose Green. There the Prince of Wales' Company, No. 3 Company, the Mortar Platoon and the battalion's Echelon, along with 16 Field Ambulance, was re-embarked on the landing ship *Sir Galahad*, which then sailed for Bluff Cove. On arrival there it was discovered that the vessel could not use the channel up to the disembarkation beach, so she moved to Fitzroy, arriving there before dawn on 8 June. Also anchored there was another landing ship, *Sir Tristram*, which had arrived the day before and had brought 2 PARA's 'B' Echelon together with some brigade troops. The Welsh Guards were under orders to join the rest of their battalion at Bluff Cove. When it was suggested that they would have to disembark at Fitzroy and march 12½ miles around the coast to Bluff Cove, the senior officer on board refused and requested that landing craft be made available to take him and his men to their destination.

Major Ewen Southby-Tailyour, the Royal Marine officer in command of the landing craft, was horrified at the sight of the LSLs moored in the bay in broad daylight. He sailed out to *Sir Galahad* in a landing craft already half-loaded with ammunition, and urged the Welsh Guards to disembark as quickly as possible, emphasising the danger from the air threat and pointing out that both the vessel and the men aboard were at great risk, and that the ship should be allowed to sail as soon as possible. After a sometimes heated argument, Major Southby-Tailyour returned to the shore and made his way to Headquarters 5 Infantry Brigade, where he sought the assistance of the relevant staff, who initially would not believe that there were troops aboard the LSL. Subsequently, the brigade headquarters ordered the landing craft to go alongside *Sir Galahad* and take off the Welsh Guards. However, the Commanding Officer of 16 Field Ambulance, which was also aboard, had discussed the situation with the Welsh Guards senior officer, who had agreed that the field ambulance could disembark first, as it had been given a priority task of setting up a field hospital at Fitzroy. The field ambulance was disembarked but, when it came to the turn of the Welsh Guards, it was discovered that the bow ramp of the landing craft on to which the men and their equipment were to be transferred was jammed upright. Unloading would therefore have to be carried out over *Sir Galahad's* side, rather than via her bow ramp.

By then it was too late. At 1310 hours an air raid warning was sounded, and shortly afterwards four enemy aircraft, two Skyhawks and two Mirages, hurtled low over Fitzroy and attacked *Sir Galahad* and *Sir Tristram*. Both vessels received direct hits and within minutes were ablaze. The attack caught everyone at Fitzroy completely by surprise. At the time, 2 PARA was making use of a makeshift range to zero weapons. As the aircraft flew past they were engaged by a Blowpipe detachment, but the missiles failed to find their mark. All available helicopters were directed to the scene, and despite the hazards of exploding ammunition and fuel on the two vessels, succeeded in evacuating casualties to 2 PARA's RAP. Both ships managed to launch their lifeboats and liferafts, and as these reached the shore they were met by men from 2 PARA and other units who assisted them ashore. After emergency treatment, the casualties were flown to the Main Dressing Station at Ajax Bay. An hour after the attack on *Sir Galahad* and *Sir Tristram*, enemy aircraft returned to attack Fitzroy. This time the troops were alert, and put up a concentrated barrage of machine-gun fire, shooting down the leading aircraft. The others turned and flew away. Later in the day there was another raid which caused no damage, although a landing craft en route to Goose Green was sunk by a Skyhawk as it flew on from Fitzroy. The air attacks on the two landing ships and the settlement served to emphasise the vulnerability of those elements of 2 PARA, the brigade headquarters and logistics troops who were concentrated in buildings in Fitzroy itself. As a result, Battalion Headquarters moved from its location in a large bunkhouse to the settlement manager's house, which was situated away from the main part of Fitzroy and, being surrounded by trees, was well covered from the air.

That night, Lieutenant Colonel Chaundler was informed by Brigadier Wilson that 2 PARA was once again to come under command of 3 Commando Brigade. During the next two days, 9 and 10 June, the battalion worked hard on digging in and improving its defences, and was left undisturbed except for a warning of an attack on Fitzroy which turned out to be a false alarm. On 10 June Lieutenant Colonel David Chaundler flew to Headquarters 3 Commando Brigade to be briefed on 2 PARA's role in the coming operation — the assault on Port Stanley. The battalion would be in reserve, advancing on a northern axis and ready to support either 3 PARA, which would be attacking Mount Longdon, or 45 Commando, whose objective would be Twin Sisters. On the following day 2 PARA would be moved by helicopter from Fitzroy to an area a short distance to the west of Mount Kent. It would have in support a troop of the Blues & Royals, the reconnaissance troop of 59 Independent Squadron RE, and a troop of 9 Parachute Squadron RE.

On the morning of 11 June the Commanding Officer and the company commanders flew to Mount Kent. From an OP there they studied the ground over which the battalion would have to move during the next phase of operations. Later that day 2 PARA was ferried in Sea King helicopters from Fitzroy to a lying-up position to the west of Mount Kent and in the rear of 3 Commando Brigade. The redeployment of the battalion was completed by last light, the perfect weather having facilitated the move. During the evening the Commanding Officer and the company commanders returned from Mount Kent. Later, as last light approached, Lieutenant Colonel David Chaundler gave his orders for the following day.

3 PARA — THE BATTLE OF MOUNT LONGDON

At 1930 hours on 10 June Lieutenant Colonel Hew Pike held an 'O' Group at which he gave his orders for an attack which would be part of a three-phase operation by 3 Commando Brigade on Mount Longdon, Two Sisters and Mount Harriet. The latter two objectives would be taken by 45 and 42 Commandos respectively. Mount Longdon was a long narrow feature running from east to west with two summits, and covered with rocks. There was only sufficient area for one company to advance along it. Running north-east from the western summit was a spur. To the west of Mount Longdon was a stream running north, and to the east lay Wireless Ridge, which continued eastwards towards Moody Brook. To the south was Mount Tumbledown. Enemy forces holding Mount Longdon were reported to consist of the 7th Infantry Regiment reinforced by special forces troops of 601st Company. The estimated total strength of the enemy was some 800 men, and they were supported by three 105mm guns sited at Moody Brook

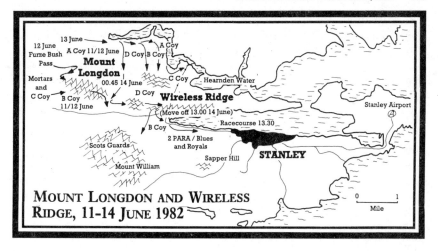

MOUNT LONGDON AND WIRELESS
RIDGE, 11-14 JUNE 1982

and a 155mm gun on Sapper Hill near Port Stanley. Enemy defences consisted of sangars and bunkers which were well sited and dug in and were protected by a number of minefields. Support weapons consisted of 81mm and 120mm mortars, 105mm recoilless rifles and a large number of machine guns.

In direct support of 3 PARA would be a frigate and 79 Commando Battery RA, as well as its own support weapons. In addition, 2 Troop of 9 Parachute Squadron RE, under Captain Robbie Burns, would provide engineer support. The battalion would attack from the west, because minefields from the south precluded any approach from that direction and enemy positions on Wireless Ridge covered the eastern side of Mount Longdon. In the initial stage of the operation the three rifle companies and Battalion Tactical Headquarters, led by guides from D (Patrol) Company, would move independently during the night through an assembly area to the start line, which was the stream west of the objective. Like the other key features of ground to be covered in the attack, this had been given a nickname: in this case 'Free Kick'. A Company, on the left, would take 'Wing Forward', which was the spur running north-east of the western summit, while B Company on the right would attack along the ridgeline, taking the two summits nicknamed 'Fly Half' and 'Full Back' respectively. C Company would be in reserve. The Mortar Platoon would establish its baseline behind the start line and the sections of the Machine Gun and Anti-Tank Platoons would remain there until called forward.

At 2035 hours, just after last light, 3 PARA moved out of its positions. A Company led the way, followed by the Commanding Officer and his 'R' Group, who were in turn followed by B and C Companies. Each company was led by men of D (Patrol) Company who acted as guides. Eventually the battalion came to the Murrell River, which was crossed by a bridge constructed earlier from ladders by sappers of 2 Troop 9 Parachute Squadron RE. The crossing was slow, each man gingerly making his way over the bridge, and the Commanding Officer urged A Company to speed up. A further delay was caused by elements of Support Company cutting across and disrupting the rifle company columns, with the result that No. 5 and 6 Platoons of B Company were separated from the rest of the company for about 30 minutes. As a result, Major Mike Argue, the commander of B Company, changed the direction of his advance to approach the objective direct from the west, thus moving well south of the intended route and well to the right of A Company. Eventually the whole battalion was across with dry feet and arrived at the start line, having bypassed the assembly area on Lieutenant Colonel Pike's orders. It was crossed by A and B Company at 0015 hours, only 15 minutes late. A mist was rising to the east of Mount Longdon, and in the moonlight the jagged features of the objective, as well as the degree to which it dominated the area, could be clearly seen. This latter fact, and the ground visibility, made Major Mike Argue change his plans slightly and order his platoons to move closer to the rocks to seek cover for the subsequent fighting through on the objective. No. 6 Platoon, under Lieutenant Jonathan Shaw, had been tasked with clearing the southern slopes of the objective, where an enemy command post was known to be located. Company Headquarters and Nos. 4 and 5 Platoons, commanded by Lieutenant Andrew Bickerdike and Lieutenant Mark Cox respectively, would clear the northern slopes, where there was a company and a medium machine gun.

After crossing the start line, No. 6 Platoon moved forward to the south-west corner of 'Fly Half', while Nos. 4 and 5 Platoons shook out into close extended line, No. 4 on the left and No. 5 on the right. Company Headquarters was behind them but in visual contact. Once the start of the rocky feature had been reached, No. 5 Platoon began to file out and upwards into slightly better cover. No. 4 Platoon was still on low ground which was not quite 'dead' to any enemy on the feature.

At that point Corporal Milne, commander of the forward left section of No. 4 Platoon, stepped on an anti-personnel mine and this alerted the enemy, who immediately opened fire on No. 5 Platoon, who were protected by the rocks. At that moment No. 6 Platoon also reported contact, and heavy automatic fire could be heard from the southern part of the objective. Lieutenant Mark Cox, the commander of No. 5 Platoon, deployed one of his GPMG groups higher up the rock face, and this engaged the enemy position holding up the platoon's advance. At the same time, one of the forward sections knocked out an enemy machine gun with a 66mm LAW and fire from the platoon's 84mm Carl Gustav MAW. No sooner had this been done than the enemy brought more automatic fire to bear from a heavy machine gun further east along the ridge. Some of No. 5 Platoon were on the ridge, and were straying into No. 6 Platoon's area. They were ordered to make contact with No. 6 Platoon to confirm their locations. Meanwhile, the machine gun position was attacked by Privates Gough and Grey with grenades, under covering fire from Lance Corporal Carver and other members of their section, after attempting to knock it out with a 66mm LAW which misfired twice. At this point enemy snipers opened fire from the platoon's rear, but these were not dealt with because of the proximity of No. 6 Platoon.

No. 6 Platoon, commanded by Lieutenant Jonathan Shaw, advanced for some distance without making contact. In fact, it later transpired that it had bypassed an enemy position high up on 'Fly Half' that subsequently fired on its rear. The platoon moved through an unoccupied enemy sangar and then came under accurate sniper fire which fatally wounded four soldiers in quick succession. As the platoon attempted to deal with the source of fire, the platoon came under fire from the rear and eight more soldiers were wounded before the enemy positions were cleared. The platoon's situation was even more precarious as it had inadvertently moved into No. 5 Platoon's field of fire. Lieutenant Shaw was by then very concerned that any further attempt to advance would result in further casualties among his men; most of those already suffered lay among rocks covered by snipers. Over the radio he contacted Major Argue and asked that he be allowed to go firm to reorganise, recover his casualties and give them first aid. Argue agreed to his request, but informed him of the serious situation building up ahead of the platoon and warned him that he might be called upon to provide assistance for Nos. 4 and 5 Platoons in dealing with their problems.

Meanwhile, on the northern side of 'Fly Half', No. 4 Platoon was pushing forward on the left of No. 5 Platoon, and its right forward section became intermingled with the latter's forward left section, which was in partly dead ground to the enemy. Both platoons had arrived at an area forward of the summit of 'Fly Half' where the rock ridges started to break up and the ground began to slope away eastwards. 'Full Back', the eastern summit of Mount Longdon, could be seen in the distance. At that point both platoons came under fire from what transpired to be the western end of a company defensive position. Their immediate problem was how to deal with the nearest platoon, which was well-sited and supported by a recoilless rifle, a heavy machine gun and at least two GPMGs. In addition, the position also contained a number of snipers whose weapons were obviously equipped with image intensifiers. The commander of No. 4 Platoon, Lieutenant Andrew Bickerdike, decided to carry out a quick reconnaissance. Accompanied by Sergeant McKay, his platoon sergeant, he moved forward cautiously but was spotted. The enemy fire was very accurate and Lieutenant Bickerdike and his signaller were both hit. Private Burt was killed and Privates Gross, Parry, Logan and Kempster were wounded. Sergeant McKay assumed command of No. 4 Platoon, and decided to attack the heavy machine gun, which was located at the base of a sangar and protected by some riflemen, with three men from Corporal Bailey's section. As they went forward, however, Corporal Bailey and one other man were seriously wounded. Sergeant McKay continued forward on his own but was killed as he was clearing the enemy position with grenades. His body was later found in one of the sangars.

On hearing that Lieutenant Bickerdike had been wounded, Major Argue went forward to see the situation for himself. On observing the volume of fire confronting his two forward platoons, he ordered Sergeant Fuller to go forward to take command of No. 4 Platoon and to report on the situation as quickly as possible. Sergeant Fuller found some of the platoon uncommitted. Having regrouped them, and having acquired a section of No. 5 Platoon, he began to advance up to and behind the machine-gun position. Unfortunately the enemy spotted Fuller and his men, and caused severe casualties among them with grenades. However, a small group under Corporal McLaughlin succeeded in reaching the top of the ridge. They crawled to within grenade throwing distance of the enemy machine gun but, despite several attempts to knock it out with 66mm LAW and grenades, were eventually forced to withdraw under heavy fire. It seemed to Major Argue that little more could be done to deal with the enemy position. There were at least two GPMGs and a heavy machine gun still firing, and several enemy were still putting up stiff opposition further to the east. His own position was also under fairly heavy fire, although it was afforded good cover by rocks. Having discussed the situation with the platoon sergeants of Nos. 4 and 5 Platoons, who had returned to brief him, Argue decided to withdraw both platoons to a safe distance and to call for artillery support.

When B Company had started its advance, the artillery forward observation officer accompanying Company Headquarters, Captain Willie McCracken of 148 Commando Forward Observation Battery RA, had laid the guns of 79 Commando Battery RA on 'Full Back', the eastern summit, and recorded the target. When Corporal Milne had stepped on the anti-personnel mine, Major Argue had given the order for the target to be fired on, and since then artillery fire had been coming down at a steady rate, hitting areas where the enemy were believed to be located. At the moment when Argue decided to withdraw the two platoons, the shells were falling only 50 yards in front of them, owing to the excellent observation and direction carried out by Captain McCracken. Major Argue despatched Company Sergeant Major Weekes to supervise the withdrawal, with particular concern to the large numbers of casualties which were lying forward. He found Lieutenant Bickerdike and his wounded signaller still firing from the positions where they had fallen, and some of No. 5 Platoon still active on the ridge under Corporal McLaughlin. Under covering fire, Nos. 4 and 5 Platoons, withdrew, but another man was killed and others wounded in the process. At that point, Lieutenant Colonel Hew Pike and his 'R' Group arrived on the scene and Major Argue briefed him on the situation. Shortly afterwards, Company Sergeant Major Weekes reported that both platoons had pulled back to a safe distance and that all the wounded had been recovered. The dead, however, had to be left where they had fallen. Meanwhile, on the southern slope of the objective, the wounded from No. 6 Platoon were being evacuated while the rest remained under cover of the rocks.

Subsequently, heavy fire was brought down on the enemy positions in front of B Company. 79 Commando Battery RA continued to bombard the heavy machine gun position and other positions further to the east. In addition, the supporting frigate fired 300 rounds with her 4.5-inch gun and the Machine Gun Platoon also engaged the enemy with GPMG (SF) fire.

Nos. 4 and 5 Platoons were amalgamated into a composite force under Lieutenant Mark Cox to carry out a left-flanking attack on the enemy machine gun. Accompanied by Major Argue and his 'R' Group, it moved off the ridge to the north and then headed for the enemy position before pausing for the supporting fire from 79 Commando Battery, the battalion's mortars and the Machine Gun Platoon. As Captain McCracken lifted the artillery fire and adjusted it to the east, the platoon continued its advance. Suddenly, at a range of only 33 yards, the enemy opened fire, killing Private Crow and wounding Lance Corporal Carver. Much of the fire passed over and along the line of march, so more casualties were fortunately avoided. On orders from Major Argue, Captain McCracken fired a 66mm LAW from the rear of the platoon to indicate the enemy position. Despite this, however, Lieutenant Cox was uncertain of the location of the enemy position and ordered his rear section to throw grenades so that he could extricate himself and his signaller. He also threw his own grenades and withdrew to a position from which he could observe the enemy, from whom all firing had ceased. He and Private Cox then fired two 66mm LAWs before charging the position to clear it. Three enemy were found dead, and it was assumed that they had moved off the ridge to seek shelter from the bombardment.

The advance continued and, after breaking cover close to where No. 4 Platoon had come under fire previously, the platoon came under automatic fire from two flanks. Major Argue decided to move back up on to the ridge and move round behind the enemy. As the platoon was attempting to do so, the enemy opened fire once again and wounded three men. Very shortly afterwards, Major Argue and his men were subjected to a heavy bombardment by enemy artillery, suffering one man killed and four others wounded.

It was now 0725 hours on 12 June, and B Company had suffered heavy losses. Lieutenant Colonel Pike therefore decided to move A Company, commanded by Major David Collett, through to take 'Full Back' by first light. Having sent a situation report to this effect back to the battalion command post, the Commanding Officer was informed that there would be reinforcements at first light, in the form of 2 PARA, who would reinforce the northern flank. A patrol from D (Patrol) Company was despatched to rendezvous with 2 PARA and guide them up and through C Company.

After crossing the start line, A Company pushed on as the battle on the hill started. On coming out of dead ground and breaking the top of the ridge, however, it came under fire from the eastern end of Mount Longdon. The company moved forward to a series of peat banks but, as it did so, the fire grew heavier and heavier. Once it was under cover it was realised that Corporal Hope, the Company Headquarters signaller, was missing, and shortly afterwards it was discovered that he had been wounded in the head. The two company medics, Corporal Lovett and Private Wright, had stayed behind to treat him. No. 1 Platoon, commanded by 2nd Lieutenant Ian Moore, was in a good covered position along a peat bank, and soon identified some enemy snipers, which were engaged by Private Evans of No. 2 Section and the GPMG gunner of No. 3 Section, Private Dennis. No. 2 Platoon, under 2nd Lieutenant Mark Kearton, was not so fortunate because it had less cover, consisting of one small peat bank. During the first few minutes Private Jenkins was shot in the head and killed. The platoon identified some enemy positions and engaged them with its GPMGs, but had to cease fire eventually as it was endangering B Company.

A Company was coming under increasingly heavy and accurate fire. Initially, the enemy artillery had concentrated on its pre-recorded defensive fire (DF) tasks, but then began to adjust its fire on to A and C Companies, the latter being in reserve. Private Brebner of No. 1 Section of No. 3 Platoon was hit in the leg by shrapnel during the shelling, and was evacuated to the rear after being given first aid. Unable to advance any further over the open ground without incurring heavy casualties from the sustained machine-gun and sniper fire from the high ground above, the company was pulled back and ordered to move round the western end of Mount Longdon to come up behind B Company to move through and take 'Full Back'. No. 2 Platoon moved up into the rocks while No. 1 Platoon went firm at the base. No. 3 Platoon and the Company Headquarters Support Group, under Captain Adrian Freer, the company second in command, came under fire and were forced to take cover before they reached the main feature. At this point three members of the support group went to assist in the evacuation of Corporal Milne of B Company, who had earlier stepped on an anti-personnel mine. As they were helping to load him aboard a BV 202 'Bandwagon' tracked vehicle which had come forward to collect him, another NCO, Lance Corporal Bassey, stepped on a mine and was wounded. Two of the men from the support group, Corporal Black and Private Darke, were slightly injured. Meanwhile, Major Collett, accompanied by his signaller, Private Kipling, and Sergeant French, had gone forward to B Company's position for a briefing and to carry out a quick reconnaissance. Soon afterwards, A Company was moved forward by platoons and took up positions under cover among rocks on the northern slope, ready to resume the advance.

It was by then obvious that any further attempt to outflank the northern side of the feature would only incur further losses, so the Company Headquarters Support Group moved forward under Captain Freer and sited its GPMGs to provide covering fire for the advance eastwards along the ridge. The artillery forward observation officer attached to A Company, Lieutenant John Lee, also moved up and began bringing down fire on the enemy positions. As soon as the supporting fire from the guns and the GPMGs had begun, Corporal Sturge led No. 2 Section of No. 1 Platoon over the ridge and it began working its way forward. The lack of cover restricted all movement to crawling. Moreover, B Company's earlier experience had shown the importance of systematic clearing of enemy positions to minimise the threat of enemy sniping from the rear. Behind No. 2 Section came the platoon commander, 2nd Lieutenant Ian Moore, who was followed by Corporal Bland and No. 1 Section. Progress was slow, as the enemy fire directed at No. 2 Platoon and the Company Headquarters Support Group was very accurate and heavy. In spite of the covering fire from the group's two GPMGs, the artillery and the Machine Gun Platoon's SF guns, the leading section was forced to use all of its grenades and 66mm LAWs, and the following section's LAWs, to clear the positions as they moved forward. As the last men of No. 3 Section crossed the ridge, some enemy were seen beginning to withdraw. Supporting fire had to be lifted as No. 1 Platoon followed No. 2 Platoon over the crest, as it would otherwise have posed a hazard to them. The two platoons then proceeded to clear numerous positions with fixed bayonets, No. 1 Platoon taking the southern slopes and No. 2 Platoon the northern. As they advanced, more enemy were engaged as they withdrew towards positions to the east. Once 'Full Back' had been secured, No. 3 Platoon moved forward to take over and hold the extreme eastern end of Mount Longdon, which consisted of a long, narrow forward slope running towards Wireless Ridge.

As first light arrived, A Company reorganised. Fortunately, a heavy mist shrouded the company's positions from enemy-held features. Meanwhile, soldiers moved among the enemy positions, checking the dead. It was not long before the enemy artillery once again brought fire down, but it was sporadic because of the mist. No. 3 Platoon, in its forward slope positions, came under fire from snipers on Mount Tumbledown to the south. Two men were pinned down for four hours, and were subsequently able to move only under cover of smoke laid down by artillery and GPMG covering fire. The fire support provided by the Support Company fire base played a key part in the operation. Commanded by Major Peter Dennison, it consisted of two elements: a manpack group and a vehicle-borne group. The former, under Major Dennison, consisted of the six GPMG (SF) detachments of the Machine Gun Platoon with 18 ammunition bearers, each carrying 600 rounds of linked ball ammunition, five firing Milan posts of the Anti-Tank Platoon with 15 missiles, and the primary group of the RAP. Accompanying this group were two journalists: Les Dowd of Reuters and Tom Smith of the *Daily Express*. The vehicle-borne group, under Major Roger Patton, 3 PARA's Second in Command, consisted of the mortars, a resupply of Milan missiles and GPMG ammunition, the secondary group of the RAP, a Blowpipe section and 2 Troop of 9 Parachute Squadron RE, less its reconnaissance sections, which were attached to the rifle companies. While the manpack group accompanied the battalion, the vehicle-borne group remained in a location north of Mount Kent, as it would only advance once Two Sisters had been taken by 45 Commando.

Shortly before midnight Sergeant Colbeck reported over the radio to Major Dennison that he was in his allocated position due west of the objective, with his two GPMGs and a Milan firing post. By 0015 hours the rest of the fire base teams, under Major Dennison, Captain Tony Mason and Colour Sergeant Knights, were also in position. As A and B Companies closed swiftly on their objectives without encountering any significant opposition, the Commanding Officer ordered Captain Mason's group to regroup with A Company on 'Wing Forward'. B Company then started suffering casualties and called for medics, to be told by Major Dennison that the forward RAP and some stretcher bearers were already moving to the western end of Mount Longdon with Colour Sergeant Knights' fire team. Major Dennison's group, accompanied by Sergeant Colbeck's, followed soon afterwards with the remainder of the stretcher bearers. Colour Sergeant Knights and his team joined No. 6 Platoon on the ridge dominating the western end of the objective and engaged some snipers firing from the centre of the ridge. Major Dennison's team advanced up the hill underneath the enemy tracer. Captain Mason's team supported A Company's assault by firing two Milan missiles at enemy positions. Meanwhile, the GPMG groups in Sergeant Colbeck's team were assisting No. 6 Platoon to engage snipers on the forward slopes. Colour Sergeant Knights' team engaged some other snipers with 66mm LAW, Carl Gustav 84mm MAW, GPMG (SF) and ultimately with Milan.

By then it was about 0400 hours, and Lieutenant Colonel Pike ordered Major Dennison to re-form the fire base. Meanwhile, Major Roger Patton's vehicle-borne group, which had begun its move at 0200 hours, was crossing the Murrell Bridge and moving through 45 Commando's start line. At about 0400 hours the mortars were bedded in on their base line at 'Free Kick', 3 PARA's start line, and subsequently provided support for A and B Companies. Meanwhile the fire base itself, which comprised six GPMGs, one light machine gun and three Milan firing posts, was sited on the objective. Fire support was given for A Company's attack, during which an enemy recoilless rifle fired a round along the ridge, killing Private Heddicker and wounding Corporal McCarthy, Lance Corporal Cripps, and Privates West and Sinclair. Corporal McCarthy and Private West subsequently died before they could be evacuated. During this last stage of the battle the enemy artillery once again started to bring down fire on the eastern end of Mount Longdon while A Company was reorganising. Throughout this bombardment the already exhausted stretcher bearers continued to recover the wounded and evacuate them.

By the time the battle for Mount Longdon ended, at approximately 1100 hours on the morning of 12 June, 3 PARA had suffered 19 killed and some 47 wounded. Between then and the afternoon of 14 June, when it headed north for Port Stanley, further casualties included six more men of the battalion killed and several more wounded. Enemy casualties amounted to over 50 killed, ten wounded and 40 taken prisoner. In addition, two 120mm mortars, 50 FN rifles, several GPMGs and heavy machine guns, several rocket launchers, one recoilless rifle and a Soviet-made SA-7 'Grail' shoulder-fired surface-to-air missile were among the weapons and equipment captured by 3 PARA.

Lieutenant Colonel Hew Pike vividly described the scene on Mount Longdon at the end of the battle when he later wrote:

'The misty scene as dawn broke will perhaps be the most haunting memory of this long, cold fight. The debris of battles was scattered along the length of the mountain, encountered round every turn in the rocks, in every gully. Weapons, clothing, rations, blankets, boots, tents, ammunition, sleeping bags, blood-soaked medical dressings, web equipment, packs — all abandoned, along with the 105mm recoilless rifles, 120mm mortars and .50 Brownings that had given us so much trouble during darkness. The enemy dead lay everywhere, victims of shell, bullet and bayonet. The sour odour of death lingered in the nostrils long after many of these corpses had been buried, for this was a slow job, which eventually had to be abandoned when their artillery and mortars started again. The enemy bunkers provided an Aladdin's Cave of Camel cigarettes, bottles of brandy, huge cakes of solid cheese and, of course, bully beef! Standing amongst the shell holes and shambles of battle watching the determined, triumphant but shocked, saddened faces of those who had lost their friends on this mountain, the Iron Duke's comment was never more apt "There is nothing half so melancholy as a battle won. . . unless it be a battle lost".

And then — more artillery — and once again the urgent cry from down a re-entrant, "Medic!" . . . Yes, we had all lost friends, and the battalion some of its finest, most devoted soldiers.'

3 PARA's performance on Mount Longdon was later summed up by an Argentinian prisoner: 'It was terrible! You threw company after company against us and we couldn't stop them. They kept coming even through the mortar fire, it was incredible! You have the bravest and most professional troops in the world.'

2 PARA — THE BATTLE OF WIRELESS RIDGE

'At midnight on the night of 11 June 2 PARA, having left its packs with 'A' Echelon, moved off on a march to an assembly area north of Mount Kent. There it would wait while 3 PARA and 45 Commando attacked Mount Longdon and Two Sisters and 42 Commando took Mount Harriet. Led by patrols from C (Patrol) Company, the battalion pressed on through the darkness. Ahead could be seen the flashes of light and noise of battle coming from 3 PARA's and 45 Commando's objectives. Shells whistled overhead as the supporting artillery batteries laid down supporting fire on Mount Longdon and Twin Sisters. On reaching the assembly area below the feature between Mount Kent and Mount Estancia, the companies moved to their allocated areas and settled down to wait. Men soon began to feel the bitter cold which seeped through the quilted clothing and waterproofs that they carried in bundles on their webbing.

At last, after a long wait, the battalion received orders to move. As it pushed forward it became apparent that 3 PARA was still in action on Mount Longdon, and it was assumed that the battalion was moving up in support. As first light was approaching, 2 PARA neared the Murrell Bridge, where it was due to rendezvous with 3 PARA, when the brigade commander appeared and confirmed that the battalion should continue its advance. However, it was forced to change direction northwards, following the line of the valley along the western side of Mount Longdon, because a minefield had been discovered on its line of route; this took the battalion through an area known to be an enemy DF task. Meanwhile, enemy heavy artillery fire continued to be brought down, but fortunately caused no casualties in the sometimes closely bunched column. As dawn broke, the battalion swung east and pushed on along the Murrell River. At that point Major John Crosland went forward and reconnoitred Furze Bush Pass, a large gully above which a rocky escarpment afforded excellent protection against artillery fire. There he met a group of 3 PARA's D (Patrol) Company under their company commander, Major Pat Butler, who briefed him on the night's action on Mount Longdon. Without further ado 2 PARA moved into Furze Bush Pass and dug in. The rest of the day passed without incident except for the arrival of 3 Troop of the Blues and Royals under Lieutenant The Lord Robin Innes-Ker. The Commanding Officer had also acquired his own adviser on the use of armour, Captain Roger Field of the Blues & Royals, who until then had been employed as a watchkeeper in the brigade headquarters. Having originally been sent with the task force to advise on the use of the Scorpions and Scimitars, and anxious that they should be used properly and their potential maximised, Field had volunteered to accompany 2 PARA.

At 1800 hours that evening Major Hector Gullan, the Brigade Liaison Officer, arrived in a helicopter with orders for 2 PARA to carry out an attack on Wireless Ridge that night. Somewhat naturally, the Commanding Officer was unhappy at the lack of time to prepare for a battalion night attack. Having summoned his company commanders, he held a hurried 'O' Group. Shortly afterwards, however, a message arrived from Brigade Headquarters which informed 2 PARA that the attack was cancelled because 5 Infantry Brigade, which had been due to attack Mount Tumbledown that night, was not ready and its commander, Brigadier Tony Wilson, had asked Major General Jeremy Moore, the commander of the land forces, for an extra 24 hours. Mount Tumbledown, which was to be attacked by the 2nd Battalion Scots Guards with the 1st Battalion 7th Duke of Edinburgh's Own Gurkha Rifles in support, dominated Wireless Ridge and had to be taken before the latter feature could be attacked. The Commanding Officer subsequently flew to the brigade headquarters, where he learned from Brigadier Julian Thompson that the operation was not cancelled but postponed for 24 hours. This gave him more time to prepare a proper plan and orders, as well as for the battalion to prepare for battle.

At 1200 hours on the following day, 13 June, Lieutenant Colonel David Chaundler held his 'O' Group, at which he gave his orders for an attack on Wireless Ridge. Together with the 2nd Battalion Scots Guards' operation on Mount Tumbledown, this would be the prelude to a four-phase attack on Port Stanley by 3 Commando Brigade, starting at midnight on 14 June. Wireless Ridge was a feature to the east of Mount Longdon, running eastwards towards Moody Brook. At its western end was a 300ft-high feature from which a spur ran northwards; as it ran eastwards, the ridgeline narrowed. To the eastern end of the ridge was a line of telegraph poles which crossed it and ran due south to the barracks occupied by the Royal Marine garrison before the Argentinian invasion on 2 April. A track from the north also crossed the ridge to the west of the telegraph poles and led southwards to the road leading from below Two Sisters to Port Stanley. Enemy forces on Wireless Ridge consisted of elements of the 7th Infantry Regiment and 1st Parachute Regiment. Additional troops were thought to be located in the area of the barracks at Moody Brook, including elements of a squadron of armoured cars of the Marine Amphibious Reconnaissance Group. Further east, some anti-aircraft guns were sited on Stanley racecourse.

In support of 2 PARA would be two batteries of artillery, HMS *Ambuscade* (a Type 21 frigate armed with a 4.5-inch gun) and 3 Troop of the Blues & Royals. In addition to the battalion's own mortars, those of 3 PARA would also be providing support. Two squadrons, D and G, of 22 SAS would be deployed on Wireless Ridge to the east of the line of telegraph poles, and they would carry out a diversionary attack. 2 PARA's mission was to attack and capture Wireless Ridge west of the telegraph poles. This would be carried out by a two-phase noisy night attack from the north for which C (Patrol) Company would secure a start line. Phase 1 would consist of A Company capturing the northern spur. B and D Companies would then move through and attack the main part of Wireless Ridge, B Company taking the western end of the feature while D Company took the ridgeline east of the track. The Mortar Platoon, on moving forward from its position near Brigade Headquarters to the rear of Mount Kent, would establish its baseline south of Drunken Rock Pass near Battalion Main Headquarters.

After the 'O' Group, the Commanding Officer and the Battery Commander, Major Tony Rice, flew by helicopter to Mount Longdon, where they met Lieutenant Colonel Hew Pike and his artillery forward observation officer, Captain Willie McCracken, who controlled the artillery OP. They were briefed on the enemy forces on Wireless Ridge, which were stronger than had previously been thought, and had pointed out to them a hitherto unknown enemy position to the north-east, on a feature on a small headland at the mouth of the Murrell River. The two Commanding Officers agreed arrangements for 3 PARA's Mortar, Machine Gun and Anti-Tank Platoons to provide support for 2 PARA during the attack, and these were co-ordinated. In addition, it was agreed that 3 PARA's C Company, commanded by Major Martin Osborne, would be available as a reserve for 2 PARA.

Nine Skyhawks were then observed to the north, flying very low and heading westwards for Mount Kent. Shortly afterwards they carried out an air strike on the area where 2 PARA's Mortar and Machine Gun Platoons were located, close to Headquarters 3 Commando Brigade. Fortunately no casualties were caused, but all helicopter flights were halted and thus there were subsequent delays in the movement of personnel and equipment throughout the brigade. Eventually, however, Lieutenant

Colonel Chaundler was able to proceed on to Brigade Headquarters and the 2 PARA company commanders were flown up to Mount Longdon to observe the ground over which they would be moving that night. While they were studying the terrain they noticed that a position previously thought to belong to 3 PARA was in fact occupied by an enemy company. Situated west of the northern spur of Wireless Ridge, it lay on the flank of 2 PARA's intended axis of advance. Moreover, it soon became apparent that Wireless Ridge itself was heavily defended; the absence of any artillery fire on their positions had brought the enemy troops out to stand in the open in full view of those on Mount Longdon. The company commanders were also able to see that the enemy frontage extended further east than had been thought, beyond the line of telegraph poles.

During the evening Lieutenant Colonel Chaundler returned from the 'O' Group at the brigade headquarters and was given the new information. Accordingly, he changed his plan to that of a four-phase noisy night attack. Phase One would consist of an attack by D Company on the enemy position west of the northern spur of Wireless Ridge, nicknamed 'Rough Diamond'. In Phase Two, A and B Companies would take the northern spur, nicknamed 'Apple Pie', and in Phase Three C (Patrol) Company would capture the feature on the headland by the Murrell River. In Phase Four, D Company would advance down Wireless Ridge itself, nicknamed 'Blueberry Pie', from the west to east as far as the telegraph poles, taking out enemy positions from their flank. In support would be the two artillery batteries, the frigate and the mortars of both battalions. The Anti-Tank Platoon would move with the battalion, and in addition there would be 3 Troop of the Blues and Royals with its Scimitars armed with 30mm Rarden cannon and Scorpions with 76mm guns. Fire support would be allocated to companies for their particular phases.

Before last light the Mortar Platoon, the Blues and Royals and the Reconnaissance Platoon, whose task was to secure the start line, moved off from the LUP. The weather was deteriorating, with snow and sleet making visibility bad. At 0015 hours on 14 June the two artillery batteries and both mortar platoons opened fire and brought a massive concentration of fire on the enemy positions. A and B Companies, led by guides from C (Patrol) Company, moved up to the start line. At 0045 hours D Company crossed its own start line further to the west and advanced, under supporting fire from the Blues & Royals and the Machine Gun Platoon, towards the enemy positions on 'Rough Diamond'. The fire from the Scimitars and Scorpions, which were equipped with second-generation night vision systems, was particularly effective. The crews used their main armament to shell the bunkers and, as the occupants came out and tried to escape, they were engaged by the vehicles' co-axial machine guns.

As D Company approached its objective, enemy troops could be seen running away and, on taking the position, it found it abandoned apart from some dead. As the company reorganised, however, it came under fire from 155mm heavy artillery firing airbursts overhead. Major Phil Neame immediately pushed forward another 300 yards to get clear of the enemy

DF. D Company went firm as A and B Companies began their advance southwards towards 'Apple Pie', one on either side of the track. As they did so, the first casualties were suffered when Colour Sergeant Findlay, moving in the rear of A Company, was killed by shellfire and some men of Headquarter and Support Companies were wounded. Again, as with D Company's objective, the enemy were seen abandoning their positions and withdrawing in haste. Unbeknown to both companies, B Company was walking through an enemy minefield. Only Major John Crosland was privy to this fact, having been informed by the Commanding Officer just before moving off. It was too late for another change of plan, so nothing was said and Crosland did not tell his men until afterwards, when none had fallen prey to a mine. The two companies found a position equipped with communications facilities, which indicated that it was a command post. While they were reorganising they came under fire from some of the trenches on the feature. These positions were quickly cleared, and it became apparent that only some 20 enemy had remained in their positions, the rest having fled. Shortly afterwards both companies came under increasingly heavy artillery fire and they began to dig in. Once A and B Companies were firm on their objective, C (Patrol) Company moved off for the feature on the headland to the east. Here again, the enemy had fled and the company found abandoned tents and equipment. Before moving off to join A and B Companies, however, Major Roger Jenner enjoyed the luxury of sitting in a deserted officers' mess.

The attack was proceeding very smoothly, and the first three objectives had been taken with great speed and very few casualties despite the heavy enemy artillery fire. D Company moved up to its start line for Phase Four while the Blues and Royals and the Machine Gun Platoon joined A and B Companies, ready to provide D Company with supporting fire. As they did so they came under fire from artillery and from anti-tank weapons on Wireless Ridge further to the south. D Company began moving down the ridge with No. 12 Platoon, commanded by Lieutenant John Page since Lieutenant Jim Barry's death, in the lead, followed by Major Phil Neame and his 'R' Group. On the left was 2nd Lieutenant Chris Waddington's No. 11 Platoon, and bringing up the rear was Lieutenant Shaun Webster and No. 10 Platoon.

At this stage the enemy, who were still being subjected to very heavy fire from artillery, mortars, the Scimitars and Scorpions, the Machine Gun Platoon and A and B Companies, were unaware of the company's presence. As D Company reached the feature on the western end of Wireless Ridge, No. 11 Platoon cleared the bunkers and trenches which it found on the reverse slope, but these had been abandoned. The company pushed on, the supporting fire being switched to the rest of the objective. Unfortunately an error occurred in the adjustment of the artillery and five rounds fell very near to No. 11 Platoon. No. 3 Section took the brunt, Private Parr being killed and Corporal McAuley being blown into some rocks. There was a lengthy delay while the problem with the supporting batteries was sorted out, during which D Company was under constant fire from enemy machine guns in well-sited bunkers.

As the company continued its advance No. 12 Platoon came to a gap in the ridgeline. As it moved through, past some ponds, it came under heavy fire from a machine gun to its front. At that point the leading section, commanded by Corporal Barton, spotted a line of string and stopped, fearing it marked a minefield. Nevertheless, the platoon pressed on. No. 11 Platoon had also encountered a suspected minefield. One of its section commanders, Corporal Harley, tripped on what looked like a tripwire and gingerly freed himself, fearing that it might be connected to a mine. The platoon continued to press forward, however, until it encountered barbed wire obstacles. Sappers came forward, but shortly afterwards paths were found between the obstacles and these proved to be safe.

Meanwhile, No. 12 Platoon continued to advance, with No. 10 Platoon now deployed on the left, whilst No. 11 Platoon made its way through the minefield. Suddenly, a heavy burst of fire caused the company to falter in its advance and a brief but fierce fire fight took place. However, No. 12 Platoon continued to press forward and eventually could see the lights of Moody Brook below. No. 10 Platoon also moved up, and the two platoons kept up the pressure on the enemy, who withdrew eastwards along the ridgeline under fire from the Blues and Royals, whose fire was being directed by Major Phil Neame. Eventually D Company reached the limit of its advance: the telegraph wires. 12 Platoon reorganised and went firm there while Nos. 10 and 11 Platoons did likewise further back. Enemy artillery fire grew heavier, and snipers also began to open fire from positions further to the east. For the next two hours D Company was under constant bombardment and small-arms fire as it sheltered in the abandoned enemy positions. Lieutenant John Page suffered a very narrow escape when a bullet passed between two grenades fastened to his webbing and hit a magazine in a pouch. Although knocked over by the force of the round, he was miraculously unharmed; even more so because, as he lay on the ground, a 7.62mm round exploded in the magazine without setting off his grenades.

Meanwhile, the Commanding Officer was attempting to contact Major Neame on the radio to obtain a report on the company's situation. However, Neame was elsewhere and Lieutenant Shaun Webster, the commander of No. 10 Platoon, was the only officer in the vicinity of Company Headquarters. As the latter was briefing Lieutenant Colonel Chaundler, Argentinians were heard talking below. The platoon opened fire and a group of enemy, estimated to be ten to fifteen strong, responded with automatic weapons. No. 11 Platoon moved up in support and joined the fire fight. At that point Major Neame reappeared and told the Commanding Officer that he suspected that an enemy counter-attack was imminent. At the same time the company started to come under fire from enemy troops on Mount Tumbledown, which had not at that moment been cleared by the 2nd Battalion Scots Guards. Neame reorganised his company, leaving a standing patrol forward while Nos. 10 and 11 Platoons moved on to the reverse slope, where they made use of some enemy positions. No. 12 Platoon remained by the telegraph poles. A and B Companies were still in their positions on 'Apple Pie', where they had been joined by the Mortar Platoon, which had established a new baseline on the side of the feature. Its main problem, encountered by all mortar and artillery gun crews during the campaign, was the ground, which was either soft peat or hard rock. During the action at Wireless Ridge the mortars were firing on supercharge for extra range, and the platoon had been forced to improvise to stop the baseplates from sinking down in the peat. Another problem was that the tubes would occasionally jump out of the baseplates on recoil. To prevent this happening, members of the crews took it in turn to stand on the baseplates, but the shock was so great that four of them had suffered broken ankles by the end of the battle. Nevertheless, the mortars continued to put down effective supporting fire, as did those of 3 PARA.

Throughout the battle men of 'A' Echelon did sterling work bringing forward ammunition and evacuating wounded. They were assisted by the men of the Assault Pioneer Platoon, under WO2 Grace, who ensured a steady supply of ammunition for the Machine Gun Platoon, whose six GPMGs were constantly in action. The command element of the battalion also came in for its share of attention from the enemy. A Canberra bomber flew low and dropped a stick of bombs in the vicinity of Battalion Headquarters, wounding Private Steele, a member of the Defence Platoon. A signaller in the Commanding Officer's 'R' Group, Private McLoughlin, was hit by a bullet which pierced his helmet but did not harm him.

At first light a small group of enemy carried out a counterattack on the section of No. 10 Platoon, under Corporal Owen, which had been deployed forward by D Company as a standing patrol. The section opened fire, Corporal Owen engaging the enemy with his M-79 grenade launcher, as did the rest of the platoon, which came forward to support Owen and his men. One member of the section, Private Lambert, heard an Argentinian shouting close to his position and threw a grenade in the direction of the voice, which abruptly ceased as the grenade exploded. No. 11 Platoon spotted another small group which ignored a challenge from 2nd Lieutenant Waddington. The platoon opened fire and the enemy withdrew in haste. Artillery fire was then brought down to discourage any further attempts to mount a counterattack on D Company. Enemy artillery responded by bringing down very accurate fire on No. 11 Platoon. Major Neame, concerned that the muzzle flashes of the company's weapons were enabling the enemy to pinpoint his positions, ordered his men to cease fire. He then noticed a large force of enemy moving up towards Sapper Hill to the south-east and called for an artillery fire mission, but the two supporting batteries were fully engaged on other tasks. Twenty minutes later, however, by which time the enemy had gained the top of the feature, support became available and the guns opened fire.

Shortly afterwards the Commanding Officer arrived on D Company's position and ordered it to engage the enemy, who were by now in full flight towards Port Stanley. To the south-west other enemy troops could be seen fleeing in large numbers down Mount Tumbledown as they were routed from the feature by the 2nd Battalion Scots Guards. As D Company opened fire with its machine guns, three armed Scout helicopters of 656 Squadron AAC, under Captain John Greenhalgh, appeared and engaged an enemy artillery battery with their SS-11 missiles. The enemy rapidly responded with anti-aircraft fire and the helicopters were forced to take evasive action and quickly withdraw.

Meanwhile, the Commanding Officer ordered A and B Companies, supported by the Blues and Royals, to move forward on to Wireless Ridge with all speed. He appreciated the importance of reaching Port Stanley before the enemy had a chance to reorganise. At that point Brigadier Julian Thompson arrived in a helicopter and walked forward to see the situation for himself. After discussing the next move with the Commanding Officer, the brigade commander told him to move 2 PARA forward to a building known as the 'Esro Building', situated on the edge of Port Stanley. There the battalion was to go firm while the rest of 3 Commando Brigade moved up.

By then B Company had reached the ridgeline and was told to move down to Moody Brook. No. 5 Platoon led the way, and shortly afterwards cleared the ruined barracks before pushing on and clearing the area of the bridge over the Murrell River. The platoon was moving somewhat cautiously, watching for any mines or booby traps, and was continually exhorted to keep moving by Major John Crosland. B Company then moved south on to high ground on the other side of the valley, covering A Company as it moved down the road towards Port Stanley with C (Patrol) and D Companies following up behind. Meanwhile, the Blues & Royals moved eastwards along Wireless Ridge to provide covering fire if necessary. At that point news of a ceasefire was announced over the battalion radio net.

At 1330 hours on 14 June A Company, led by No. 2 Platoon under 2nd Lieutenant Mark Coe, entered Port Stanley — the first British troops to do so. Shortly afterwards, the rest of the battalion arrived. During the battle at Wireless Ridge 2 PARA suffered very light casualties of three killed and 11 wounded. The enemy, later estimated at 500 in total, lost some 100 killed and an unknown number wounded, as many had fled. Seventeen prisoners were taken.

On 25 June representatives of 2 and 3 PARA flew from Port Stanley to Darwin Hill where a black cross, erected by the inhabitants of Darwin and Goose Green, already stood on top of the hill beyond the gorse line in memory of those who had fallen during the bitter fighting. Islanders from both communities joined the semi-circle of officers and men as 2 PARA's Padre, the Reverend David Cooper, held a service and wreaths were laid at the base of the cross.

THE RETURN HOME

On the evening of 25 June 2 and 3 PARA embarked on MV *Norland* and sailed for Ascension Island. On their arrival they were met by the Chief of the General Staff, Field Marshal Sir Edwin Bramall, who had flown out from England to greet them and to pay them his respects. From there the two battalions flew home in VC10 aircraft to RAF Brize Norton, where they were met by their Colonel-in-Chief, His Royal Highness The Prince of Wales, their Colonel Commandant, General Sir Anthony Farrar-Hockley, and their families.

Forty members of The Parachute Regiment were killed and 82 wounded during the Falklands campaign. On 1 October a memorial service in memory of them, and of the four sappers of 9 Parachute Squadron Royal Engineers who died with them, was held at Aldershot. It was attended by His Royal Highness The Prince of Wales and a very large number of people, including the relatives of those who had fallen.

On 8 October 1982 the awards for gallantry and conspicuous service to members of the task force were announced. Foremost among those awarded to the 2nd and 3rd Battalions The Parachute Regiment were two posthumous Victoria Crosses, awarded to Lieutenant Colonel 'H' Jones of 2 PARA and Sergeant Ian Mackay of 3 PARA. Other awards included two Distinguished Service Orders, five Military Crosses, five Distinguished Conduct Medals (one posthumous), 12 Military Medals (two posthumous), 34 Mentions in Despatches (four posthumous) and one Member of the British Empire. Awards to members of The Parachute Regiment serving with other units comprised one Military Cross and six Mentions in Despatches. Four days later, on 12 October, the nation was able to salute the men of the task force during a parade through the City of London. Along with their comrades of 40, 42 and 45 Commandos Royal Marines, the Blues and Royals, 2nd Battalion Scots Guards, 1st Battalion Welsh Guards, and 1st Battalion 7th Duke of Edinburgh's Own Gurkha Rifles, the 2nd and 3rd Battalions The Parachute Regiment marched behind their regimental bands to a tumultuous reception from the enormous crowds which lined the streets.

On 25 October 1982 four of those killed during the seven-week campaign were reburied at Blue Beach Military Cemetery at San Carlos Settlement. Among them was Lieutenant Colonel 'H' Jones VC OBE. The bodies of 36 officers and men of the 2nd and 3rd Battalions The Parachute Regiment and 9 Parachute Squadron Royal Engineers were brought home to Britain for burial. On 26 November 16 members of both battalions were reburied in a private funeral attended by their families, friends and comrades. Among them was Sergeant Ian Mackay VC. Subsequently, two more were also buried there. The remaining 18 were buried at private funerals which were attended by representatives of The Parachute Regiment.

CHAPTER 15
The Parachute Regiment and Airborne Forces Today

REORGANISATION OF AIRBORNE FORCES, 1977

Operations in Northern Ireland apart, the first four years of the 1970s were relatively uneventful for The Parachute Regiment and the rest of Airborne Forces. 3 PARA completed a six-month tour of duty with the United Nations forces in Cyprus from May to October 1972, followed by 1 PARA, which carried out an eight-month tour from May to December 1973. In 1974 an occasion of major importance took place, with the presentation of new colours to the three regular battalions of the regiment and 4 PARA (V) by Her Majesty The Queen at Aldershot on 15 July. Those presented to 1, 2 and 3 PARA replaced those presented by His Majesty King George VI, 24 years previously.

In the following year, however, Airborne Forces suffered a major blow when the government in power at that time announced in its Defence Review the decision to disband 16 Parachute Brigade and its Territorial Army counterpart, 44 Parachute Brigade (Volunteers). On 31 March 1977 16 Parachute Brigade ceased to exist. In its place was 6 Field Force, commanded by Brigadier Michael Gray, who until then had commanded 16 Parachute Brigade. It was his unenviable task to conduct the drastic reduction in the British Army's airborne forces to one parachute battalion group. Those units which were disbanded included No. 1 (Guards) Independent Company, 1 Parachute Logistics Regiment, 216 Parachute Signals Squadron, and 16 Heavy Drop Company RAOC. Others, such as 7 Parachute Regiment RHA and 23 Parachute Field Ambulance RAMC, were retained by their parent regiment or corps as non-airborne units. The airborne role for the regular battalions of The Parachute Regiment was reduced to one in-role battalion with limited support which comprised 9 Parachute Squadron RE, which had survived the cuts, and 29 (Corunna) Field Battery of 4th Field Regiment RA, which was to possess a limited airborne capability. This group was designated the Parachute Contingency Force (PCF). A second battalion of The Parachute Regiment was designated as next-for-role, and as such had a reduced parachute training requirement. The third battalion was deployed as an infantry battalion in a non-airborne role. The sadness and anger within Airborne Forces at the policy of reductions and disbandments in 1977 was alleviated somewhat by the appointment in June of His Royal Highness The Prince of Wales as Colonel-in-Chief The Parachute Regiment. In April the following year he successfully qualified as a parachutist at No. 1 Parachute Training School at RAF Brize Norton.

1 PARA was the first to serve as the PCF battalion, remaining with 6 Field Force for three years until March 1981. Meanwhile, 2 PARA was posted to Berlin for a two-year tour from April 1977 to June 1979. 3 PARA served in BAOR at Osnabruck from January 1977 to April 1980, when it returned to England and 8 Field Force at Tidworth. In 1980 a second battalion, 3 PARA, was returned to in-role parachute status and was allocated the Priority Two role. At the same time the third battalion was thereafter required to be kept in date with its parachute training. At the beginning of 1982 the British Army dispensed with 'field forces' and reverted to 'brigades'. 8 Field Force moved from Tidworth to Aldershot, swapping with 6 Field Force, and was redesignated 5 Infantry Brigade. Its airborne elements comprised two parachute battalions tasked with the PCF and Priority Two roles, 9 Parachute Squadron RE and parachute trained elements of 7 Regiment RHA, which had replaced 4 Field Regiment RA.

5 AIRBORNE BRIGADE

On 14 November 1983, 5 Infantry Brigade was redesignated 5 Airborne Brigade, and once again the British Army included an airborne formation in its order of battle. Today, 5 Airborne Brigade forms part of 3rd (UK) Division, one of two British divisions forming part of the Allied Command Europe Rapid Reaction Corps, and has a secondary role of conducting Out of Area operations. In addition to its two parachute battalions, the brigade's airborne elements comprise 7 Parachute Regiment RHA, 9 Parachute Squadron RE, 23 Parachute Field Ambulance RAMC, 216 Parachute Signals Squadron, and 5 Airborne Brigade Logistics Battalion. Other units within the brigade include two infantry battalions (one of them Gurkha) and an armoured reconnaissance regiment provided by the Household Cavalry, elements of which are parachute trained. On operational deployments these units would be inserted via tactical airlanding operations (TALO) from RAF C-130 transports.

Pathfinding and reconnaissance for the brigade is carried out by its Pathfinder Platoon. Commanded by a captain, with a lieutenant as second-in-command, this numbers approximately 30 of all ranks. All members of the platoon, who are recruited not only from The Parachute Regiment but also from volunteers from other regiments and corps, are required to undergo a selection process. Thereafter they are trained in pathfinding skills as well as High Altitude Low Opening (HALO) tactical free-fall parachuting techniques. In the reconnaissance role, the platoon operates in four-man patrols. Members of the platoon are also trained in requisite skills such as tactics, signals, and demolitions, and as medics.

THE REGULAR ARMY PARACHUTE BATTALIONS

Each of the three regular battalions of The Parachute Regiment has an established strength of 603 all ranks. The order of battle of each battalion differs slightly from the others, but in essence there are three rifle companies, a patrol company, a fire support company and a headquarter company. Each rifle company comprises a company headquarters and three platoons, each of the latter consisting of a platoon headquarters and three sections of eight men. With the introduction of the L85A1 Individual and Light Support Weapons, which entered service in 1986 to replace the L1A1 Self-Loading Rifle, the Sterling sub-machine gun and GPMG, the organisation of the section was changed to two fire teams, each of four men. Other weapons used by the rifle companies include the 51mm light mortar, which has a maximum range of 800 metres, the L2A2 HE hand grenade and the No. 80 WP (white phosphorous) grenade. For short-range anti-tank defence the rifle companies are equipped with the LAW 80 94mm HEAT rocket, which has a maximum range of 540 yards and has replaced the L1A1 66mm LAW.

Within the battalion, a total of up to 16 men are trained as snipers in addition to their role as members of rifle companies. These form eight pairs, each pair being equipped with the L96A1 sniper rifle, which replaced the L42A1 in 1986. This 7.62mm NATO bolt-action weapon, designed by Olympic gold medallist Malcolm Cooper, enables a sniper to kill with his first round at 650 yards and to lay down harassing fire at 1,100 yards.

The patrol company within each battalion comprises the Signals Platoon, Patrols Platoon, Assault Pioneer Platoon, Intelligence Section and Training Wing (in the case of 2 PARA, the Training Wing is combined with the Air Training Cell under the Air Adjutant). The Signals Platoon is responsible for the provision of radios and other signals equipment at battalion level, and for the supply of signallers to each company headquarters. The battalion's rear link with the brigade or higher formation headquarters is operated by a rear link detachment from 216 Parachute Signals Squadron.

The Patrols Platoon comprises from six to eight four-man patrols, the exact number differing in each battalion. Mounted in stripped-down armed Land Rovers or moving on foot, the platoon provides the battalion with its own reconnaissance element. Commanded by a warrant officer, the Assault Pioneer Platoon is responsible for providing assistance in basic defence tasks such as wiring, mining, demolitions and construction of defensive obstacles within the battalion. In 2 PARA the platoon is provided by the Corps of Drums, while in 3 PARA it forms part of Headquarter Company and also provides the Provost Section.

The fire support company consists of the Mortar Platoon, the Anti-Tank Platoon and the Machine Gun Platoon, the latter usually being formed from the Corps of Drums. Within the Mortar Platoon there are four sections, each of two mortars and a mortar fire controller (MFC) party which would be attached to one of the rifle companies during exercises and operations. The 81mm mortar, which is standard issue throughout the infantry, has a maximum range of 6,160 yards and a maximum rate of fire of 12 bombs per minute. In addition to high explosive, it can fire smoke and illuminating rounds.

The Anti-Tank Platoon is equipped with the Milan anti-tank guided missile and currently is organised into a platoon headquarters and two sections, each comprising three firing posts. With a maximum range of 2,125 yards, the Milan provides the battalion with medium-range anti-tank defence. All three regular battalions are also equipped with the Wombat 120mm recoilless anti-tank gun, being the only units in the Army which still retain this weapon. With a maximum effective range of 1,100 yards, the Wombat provides a short range anti-tank capability.

The role of the Machine Gun Platoon, which is organised into six detachments of three men each, is to provide supporting firepower with its General Purpose Machine Guns (GPMG) in the sustained fire (SF) role. Mounted on a tripod and fitted with the same dial sight as the 81mm mortar, the GPMG (SF) has a maximum range of 1,200 yards (1,960 yards if strike is observed), and a rate of fire of up to 1,000 rounds per minute. These weapons can thus bring very heavy fire to bear in support of the rifle companies in both attack and defence. In addition the platoon is also equipped with four Browning .50in calibre heavy machine guns which provide an air defence and direct fire capability.

Headquarter Company provides the administrative and logistical support for the battalion. It comprises the Battalion Headquarters Platoon, which incorporates the Provost and Medical Sections, as well as the Orderly Room, Quartermaster Platoon, Catering Platoon, Motor Transport Platoon, and Pay Section.

THE TERRITORIAL ARMY PARACHUTE BATTALIONS

During the post-war reorganisation of Airborne Forces, a Territorial Army airborne division was formed on 1 January 1947. Designated 16th Airborne Division (TA), to perpetuate numerals of the two wartime airborne formations, it was commanded by Major General Roy Urquhart, who had commanded 1st Airborne Division at Arnhem three years earlier. The new division consisted of the 4th, 5th and 6th Parachute Brigades (TA) commanded respectively by three famous Airborne officers: Brigadiers James Hill DSO MC, Henry Ricketts DSO, and Pat Weston DSO OBE. In turn, these three formations comprised nine battalions designated 10th to 18th respectively. Of these, the 11th, 14th and 17th were formed from the 8th Battalion The Middlesex Regiment (Duke of Cornwall's Own) (TA), the 5th Battalion The Royal Hampshire Regiment (TA) and the 9th Battalion The Durham Light Infantry (TA) respectively.

In 1956 the three brigades were redesignated the 44th, 45th and 46th Parachute Brigades (TA). In the same year, however, major reductions in the Territorial Army took place, and 16th Airborne Division was reduced to one brigade, the 44th Independent Parachute Brigade Group (TA). This initially comprised five battalions: 10th (City of London), 12th (Yorkshire), 13th (Lancashire), 15th (Scottish) and 17th (Durham Light Infantry) Battalions The Parachute Regiment (TA). These were subsequently reduced to four in October 1956, when the 12th and 13th Battalions were amalgamated to form the 12th/13th (Yorkshire & Lancashire) Battalion. In 1967 a further reduction took place when the 12th/13th and 17th Battalions were amalgamated to form the 4th (Volunteer) Battalion. Thereafter, the Territorial Army's one parachute formation, by then designated 44 (Volunteer) Parachute Brigade , comprised three battalions of The Parachute Regiment: 4th (Volunteer) Battalion, with its headquarters at Pudsey, near Bradford, and its companies at Liverpool, Oldham, Gateshead and Stockton-on-Tees; 10th (Volunteer) Battalion, based in the London area with companies at Chelsea, White City, Croydon and Finchley; and 15th (Scottish Volunteer) Battalion with its headquarters in Glasgow and companies at Troon and Aberdeen, and a platoon at St Andrews. The brigade's pathfinder unit was 16th (Volunteer) Independent Company, which was located at Lincoln.

As part of the reductions of Airborne Forces in 1977, 44 Parachute Brigade was disbanded. The three battalions retained their airborne capability and were given wartime roles within BAOR. 16th (Lincoln) Independent Company was initially absorbed into the 15th (Scottish Volunteer) Battalion as a fourth rifle company. Subsequently, in July 1984, it was transferred to the 4th (Volunteer) Battalion.

In 1991 the government announced sweeping cuts within the British Army as part of *Options for Change*, its programme of major reductions within the armed forces. Included in these was the amalgamation of the 4th (Volunteer) Battalion with the 15th (Scottish Volunteer) Battalion. The latter was reduced to company strength, with its headquarters and one platoon based in Glasgow and detachments located at Edinburgh, Irvine, Aberdeen and Glenrothes.

THE PARACHUTE REGIMENT GROUP

In January 1989 an *ad hoc* Territorial Army parachute formation was formed on trial as The Parachute Regiment Group (PRG). Commanded by the Regimental Colonel, its headquarters was drawn from Regimental Headquarters and additional personnel drafted in from elsewhere. Its role was to provide a brigade headquarters-type function for the three Territorial parachute battalions. It possessed no organic supporting arm elements apart from 266 Observation Post Battery (V) RA and Royal Signals rear link detachments.

THE DEPOT THE PARACHUTE REGIMENT & AIRBORNE FORCES

At the time of writing, it was announced that, along with all other regimental and corps depots, the Depot The Parachute Regiment & Airborne Forces (Depot PARA) would be disbanded. As part of the programme of reductions within the Army under *Options For Change*, all depots would be replaced by five training regiments based at Pirbright, Winchester, Lichfield, Bassingbourn and Glencorse. Recruits for all arms would undergo Common Military Syllabus Phase One (Recruits) training at one of these regiments, those of The Parachute Regiment being sent to Lichfield, in Staffordshire. Phase Two special-to-arm training would be carried out at advanced training establishments. In the case of The Parachute Regiment, it was initially announced that this would take place at an infantry training centre at Crickhowell, in Wales, which would also train recruits of the Guards Division. However, at the time of writing, that arrangement was being reconsidered on the grounds of cost.

Depot PARA is currently located at Browning Barracks, Aldershot, where it has been based since February 1968 when it moved, together with Regimental Headquarters, from Maida Barracks in Aldershot, which had been its home for the previous 22 years. The depot's organisation consists of a headquarters, Recruit Company comprising five platoons and a remedial training platoon, 'P' Company and Headquarter Company — the latter being responsible for providing all administrative and logistical support.

Until 1983 the depot also incorporated the Junior Parachute Company, formed in 1961, which trained junior soldiers and junior bandsmen for the regiment. Based at Malta Barracks in Aldershot, the company was at one point over 400 boys in strength and produced almost 100 adult soldiers annually. Boys of 15 years of age (subsequently 16 when the school leaving age was raised) underwent two years training of six 15-week terms, during which they carried out training in military skills, education, sports and adventure training. Thereafter they joined Recruit Company platoons, who at that point had reached their third week of training. In 1983 the company moved to the Guards Depot at Pirbright, where it remained until 1991, when it was reduced to a platoon and was incorporated into Waterloo Company, the Guards Depot's recruit training company.

Also based at the depot are the Red Devils free-fall parachute display team and the Regimental Training Team. The latter conducts pre-course training for all NCOs of The Parachute Regiment who are due to attend the Platoon Sergeants and Section Commanders Courses at the NCOs Tactics Wing of the School of Infantry. In addition, the Regimental Training Team also conducts Potential Lance Corporal Courses for those soldiers being considered for promotion.

The Parachute Regiment is the only regiment in the British Army for which recruits are required to undergo a pre-selection course. Aspiring paratroopers spend two days at Browning Barracks, during which their suitability is assessed. At the same time they are able to look at Army life before making the final decision to enlist. Parachute Regiment recruits undergo 26 weeks of training at the depot. The emphasis at the beginning, reflecting a more thoughtful approach than was previously the case, is on retaining recruits' interest and encouraging their aspirations. Much of the previously meaningless aspects of training, such as the making of 'bed-blocks' every morning, has been discontinued. Training is divided into five phases. The first, lasting ten weeks, is devoted to the Common Military Syllabus which is completed by every recruit enlisting in the British Army, regardless of regiment or corps. During this phase, recruits undergo training in individual military skills such as skill at arms with the Individual Weapon, drill, fieldcraft, map reading, nuclear biological chemical defence, and first aid. At the end of the ten weeks recruits fire their Annual Personal Weapon Test. The second phase starts with External Leadership. This consists of a week's adventure training in Wales, during which recruits carry out such activities as canoeing, abseiling and rock climbing. This is followed by a further five weeks training devoted to infantry team skills, including section battle drills, and skill at arms training in other weapons such as the Light Support Weapon, the 51mm mortar and the LAW 80.

By this time the recruits have completed 16 weeks' training, and they now undergo their parachute selection course. During their four months at the depot they will have undergone a systematic programme of physical fitness training designed to ensure that they are of the standard required. On completion of the course, providing they have passed it successfully, they are awarded their red beret. Immediately afterwards they proceed to Wales, where they carry out three and a half weeks of advanced battle training, known as "Advanced Wales", which incorporates all aspects of tactical training up to platoon level and includes live firing of all platoon weapons.

In the early 1980s it was recognised that remedial training would do much to reduce wastage. As a result, the 'Falklands Platoon' was formed. If recruits are failing to reach the standards required of them at the various stages in their training, they are transferred to the Falklands Platoon, where instructors provide concentrated training to rectify weaknesses. This has brought about a large reduction in the number of recruits failing to complete their training, and during the last two years remedial training at the depot has been enhanced by greater assets and resources.

On completion of "Advanced Wales" the recruits proceed to No. 1 Parachute Training School at RAF Brize Norton, where they carry out their parachute training. Having successfully passed the course and qualified for their 'wings', they return to the depot for Exercise 'Last Fence'. Carried out on Salisbury Plain, this provides the recruits with transitional training, during which they use their parachuting skills under tactical conditions. The final, 26th week is devoted to drill and rehearsing for the passing-out parade, which is the culmination of the recruits' training. Attended by their families, it is always a proud occasion for the young men who march off the parade ground at Browning Barracks as newly qualified paratroopers.

'P' COMPANY AND THE PRE-PARACHUTE SELECTION COURSE

The Pre-Parachute Selection Company, or 'P' Company as it is better known, has its roots in the wartime Training Company of the Depot School Airborne Forces, which was established in 1941 at Hardwick Hall in Derbyshire. Commanded by a major, 'P' Company is a small organisation, comprising a company sergeant major and four instructors: four NCOs from The Parachute Regiment and one from 7 Parachute Regiment RHA. It is responsible for carrying out pre-parachute selection courses which must be completed by anyone volunteering for service with The Parachute Regiment and Airborne Forces. Records show that, since 1955, 19,361 officers, NCOs and soldiers have passed through 'P' Company. Three different courses are conducted by 'P' Company: All Arms, Recruits and Territorial Army.

All Arms Course. The All Arms course must be completed by volunteers from other arms and Regular officers commissioned into The Parachute Regiment. It takes three weeks and consists of two parts: Build-up Phase and Test Phase. The first phase lasts until the Wednesday of the second week. On each day trainees carry out a run and a session in the gymnasium to build up their strength and stamina. During the afternoon they carry out a march while carrying a rucksack and rifle. Test Phase starts on the Thursday of the second week. The first test is the Steeplechase: trainees complete a two-mile course which incorporates obstacles including water jumps and which requires them to jump into water at certain points. This is carried out against the clock, and individuals are marked on their timings. Other tests during Test Phase include the Log Race: eight men carrying a 160 lb log and trainees being assessed on their individual efforts; the Ten Mile Bash: a ten-mile march to be completed in 1 hour 45 minutes; the Assault Course: three laps to be completed against the clock; the Confidence Course: a test of trainees' heads for heights, carried out on the trainasium; and finally Milling: pairs of trainees face each other in the boxing ring for one minute — they must stand firm and upright, no flinching, dodging, weaving or turning the back is permitted. The aim of this test is to test the trainees for courage and controlled aggression.

The first part of the Test Phase is completed on the Wednesday of the third week, when the course moves to Wales for its final phase. This consists of three tests. The first, called "Endurance 1" and carried out over tracks and paths, is an 18-mile march of which the various sections are timed. This is completed in squads, each under its own instructor. On the morning of the second day trainees carry out "Endurance 2", an eleven-mile march over Pen-y-Fan, the highest peak in the Brecon Beacons, and then south to the equally well known Fan-Fawr before ending at the Storey Arms, a building on the roadside below Pen-y-Fan. After a 30-minute rest, trainees carry out a ten-mile speed march which ends at Cwm Gwdi Camp in a valley below the northern face of Pen-y-Fan. On the following day comes the third and final test: the Stretcher Race. Teams of 12 trainees, wearing skeleton webbing and carrying rifles, carry a 200lb steel stretcher over a course of approximately seven miles under the supervision of their instructors, who assess them on their individual efforts.

On completion of the Test Phase trainees are then told whether they have passed or failed the course. The average pass rate on the All Arms course is 45 per cent. Since 1984 the assessment of those undergoing the course has been more objective than was the case earlier. Previously, character was taken into account and trainees were graded. Under the current system, points are awarded strictly on their performance during individual tests. Officers are also assessed on their powers of leadership, man management and motivation.

Recruits Course. As has already been mentioned, recruits carry out their pre-parachute selection course at the end of their 16th week of training at the depot. They undergo Test Phase, identical to that of the All Arms course, which lasts until the third day of the 17th week. On completing it successfully, recruits then proceed to Dering Lines, Brecon, where they carry out "Advanced Wales".

Territorial Army Course. All recruits of the three Territorial battalions of The Parachute Regiment are required to undergo two weeks basic training at the depot, the culmination of which is a two-day pre-parachute selection course conducted during the final weekend. During the two weeks, recruits carry out the assault course, steeplechase and milling. On the final test weekend they complete the ten-mile march, confidence course, log race and the stretcher race. If they fail the ten-mile march, which is the initial test, they fail the course.

THE PARACHUTE COURSE ADMINISTRATIVE UNIT

The Parachute Course Administrative Unit is a detached unit of the depot based at No. 1 Parachute Training School at RAF Brize Norton. Numbering 14 strong and commanded by a major, it is responsible for administering all trainees, not only those from Airborne Forces but also those from the SAS, RAF Regiment, commando forces and other units who are required to be parachute trained. On average, it administers some 2,000 trainees each year.

THE PARACHUTE REGIMENT BATTLE SCHOOL

In 1960 Depot PARA established a wing at Dering Lines in Brecon, to conduct advanced infantry training for its recruits. In 1962 the wing was expanded with further personnel from the depot to run tactics courses for junior NCOs and assumed the title of The Parachute Regiment Battle School. Three years later, in 1965, the school was further enlarged to conduct tactics courses for senior NCOs. In addition, it also ran courses for NCOs of the Territorial battalions of The Parachute Regiment.

In 1967 the school was separated from the depot and became an independent command under the aegis of Regimental Headquarters. Early the following year it became a lieutenant colonel's command, the first Commanding Officer being Lieutenant Colonel Joe Starling MBE MC. In the same year the school also began senior NCOs tactics courses for the School of Infantry, its staff being augmented by personnel from other infantry regiments. In 1969 it was redesignated The Parachute Regiment Battle School/NCOs Tactics Wing School of Infantry. At this point Lieutenant Colonel Peter Walter MBE MC assumed command. Subsequently, in the mid-1970s, the school was further expanded to run tactics courses for junior NCOs from all infantry regiments. In 1976 the school was transferred to the School of Infantry and the title of The Parachute Regiment Battle School was relinquished.

THE RED DEVILS

The Parachute Regiment Free-Fall Team, or the Red Devils as they are better known, was formed in January 1964 with the principal role of promoting public relations and recruiting for the regiment in particular, as well as for the Army in general. The name "The Red Devils" was officially adopted in October of that year. Fifteen years later, in 1979, the Red Devils were designated the official British Army free-fall display team. During the early years of the team's existence, the Red Devils played an active part in the development of military free-fall parachuting techniques and in their tactical applications as a means of delivery. The early types of parachute and harness were similar to those of conventional military static line parachutes still in use today, consisting of a main pack worn on the back of the parachutist and a reserve on the front, with an altimeter attached to indicate the height above ground. In the late 1960s new types of parachutes were introduced. These were of different shapes and included one which was configured like a wing, allowing the parachutist greater control of how and where he could land. Currently, the Red Devils use the latest type of parachutes, which are rectangular high-performance ram-air canopies. Owing to the advances in design over the years, both the main and reserve parachutes are now contained in a compact pack worn on the parachutist's back.

The team always jumped from its own aircraft. Shortly after its formation the team acquired a de Havilland Rapide, which was followed during the ensuing years by other types. The current aircraft, which was purchased in 1985, is a Britten-Norman Islander which carries the civil registration G-ORED.

The Red Devils' displays take several forms, and the team constantly strives to improve them. They take many hours of planning, briefing, rehearsing and debriefing until the various formats are perfected. In essence, the displays include Relative Work, which consists of free-fall manoeuvres carried out as members of the team plummet earthwards at speeds of up to 120 mph, and Canopy Relative Work, which requires a number of parachutists 'docking' together with their canopies to create larger and technically more difficult display formats.

The team can frequently be seen training on the Queen's Parade dropping zone in Aldershot, where it also conducts basic training for members of the public, who subsequently have the opportunity to carry out a static-line descent. A relatively recent innovation, introduced five years ago, is the tandem descent. An individual is linked by a harness to one of the Red Devil 'Tandem Masters', who is a skilled and qualified instructor. Pupil and instructor make their exit from the aircraft at a height of 12,000ft and free-fall to 5,000ft, at which point the instructor deploys the parachute.

During the rest of the descent the pupil is given the opportunity of steering the parachute towards the dropping zone.

The Red Devils play a very active part in media related events. These have included parachuting into the River Thames to mark the launching of the Airborne Forces Golden Jubilee Appeal, and playing the part of wartime German paratroopers for the London Weekend Television production "Wish Me Luck" by jumping from a Junkers-Ju 52 transport aircraft. On one occasion the team responded to a challenge from the London Weekend Television programme "You Bet". Two parachutists were required to jump from a hot-air balloon, deploy their parachutes and endeavour to re-enter the balloon, which had descended rapidly to enable both of them to climb back into the basket before it landed. Unfortunately they failed. Other spectacular events in which the Red Devils have been involved include the establishing in August 1980 of the record for the fastest non-powered crossing of the English Channel. Sergeant Mark Sheridan was one of a group of parachutists who jumped from 25,000ft over Dover Castle and flew for 26 minutes before landing successfully at Sangatte in France.

During their 18 years of existence the Red Devils have become renowned in many parts of the world for their skill in free-fall parachuting. They have travelled throughout Europe and many other countries, including the United States, Mexico, Kenya, Malaysia, Hong Kong and Cyprus, taking part in international competitions and giving displays for which they are much in demand. Wherever they perform, they make their mark as ambassadors for The Parachute Regiment and for the British Army.

NO. 1 PARACHUTE TRAINING SCHOOL RAF AND THE BASIC PARACHUTE COURSE

In 1946 No. 1 Parachute Training School (No. 1 PTS) moved from its wartime location at Ringway to RAF Upper Heyford in Oxfordshire, trainees being accommodated in a nearby camp at Middleton Stoney. Four years later the school moved again to RAF Abingdon, where it remained for 26 years until, in 1976, it moved to its current location at RAF Brize Norton. By then it had trained approximately 112,000 parachutists, who had carried out some 1,115,000 training descents. The one millionth descent was carried out in 1969 by Private Norman Blunn, a recruit at the Depot The Parachute Regiment and Airborne Forces, during Regular Basic Course No. 701 at RAF Abingdon.

Commanded by a wing commander, the school comprises four squadrons. The Static Line Training Squadron conducts basic parachute courses for regular and reserve forces personnel of all three services, as well as training RAF parachute jumping instructors (PJIs). In addition, the squadron conducts courses in the use of steerable static line parachutes for specialist personnel required to use them. The Free-Fall Training Squadron provides training in tactical free-fall techniques for special forces personnel of the Special Air Service and the Royal Marines' Special Boat Service, as well for 5 Airborne Brigade's Pathfinder Platoon and RAF PJIs. The

Support Squadron provides support in the form of training co-ordination, programming, logistical support, parachute packing and servicing of ground training equipment. Finally, the PTS Ops Squadron is responsible for the co-ordination of aircraft required for parachute training, the balloons required for the basic courses, ambulances for stationing on dropping zones and transport for movement of trainees.

In addition to its four squadrons, No. 1 PTS also has four detachments deployed elsewhere. One detachment provides support for the Regular and Territorial SAS regiments and for the Royal Marines, while another performs a similar role for the three Territorial battalions of The Parachute Regiment. A third detachment is based at Depot PARA, where it provides support for the parachute training carried out under tactical conditions by recruits after they have undergone their basic course and before they pass out from the depot. This detachment is also responsible for supervising the annual parachute training which the depot's staff must carry out to remain qualified as parachutists. The fourth and largest detachment is based at RAF Pitts Road, Aldershot, where it is responsible for providing synthetic training facilities and support for 5 Airborne Brigade.

The Basic Parachute Course is of four weeks' duration for regular troops. During that time trainees are instructed in exit, flight and landing techniques. They are required to complete eight descents, one at night, to qualify for their 'wings'. Exit training is carried out from full-size mockups of C-130 Hercules fuselages. In groups of eight, each with its own RAF parachute jumping instructor (PJI), trainees are taught the techniques of jumping individually and in 'sticks', both with and without equipment. Trainees are taught flight drills while suspended in parachute harnesses hung from the hangar roof on cables. They learn to control their parachutes while descending, and to carry out emergency measures such as untwisting their rigging lines, taking the necessary action on colliding with another parachutist, and landing in water. The techniques of landing safely are taught on rubber mats. As trainees become more proficient, the height from which they jump is increased by the use of steps and eventually ramps up which they run and jump off. Forward, side and backwards landings are practised by use of a six-sided trapeze from which trainees hang by their hands while being swung in the air. On the command from their PJI, trainees let go and drop to the ground, carrying out the appropriate roll.

The next stage involves the fan trainer. Wearing a harness connected to a cable wound round a drum fitted with fan blades, trainees jump from a platform located near the roof of the hangar; as they fall, their rate of descent is controlled to simulate that with a parachute. More advanced training comes with the exit trainer, designed to simulate the effect of the slipstream as the parachutist makes his exit from the aircraft. The trainer consists of a wooden cabin, mounted on a structure of girders, equipped with doors representing those on the port and starboard side of a Hercules. On either side cables run from above the trainer to a point near the ground some 55 yards away. Wearing harnesses suspended from them, trainees jump from the trainer and travel the length of the cables in a gradual descent towards the ground, where their progress is arrested by an instructor.

The next stage of the course consists of a parachute descent from a balloon at the dropping zone at Weston-on-the-Green. This is carried out from a height of 800ft in what is known as "clean fatigue" — without equipment. Subsequently, trainees carry out their first descent from a C-130 Hercules in single 'sticks' of six without equipment from one door of the aircraft. Their second descent is again in 'clean fatigue', in single 'sticks' of eight or ten. Trainees then make their third descent, jumping in simultaneous 'sticks' of six from both sides of a Hercules. This is followed by a night descent without equipment. Thereafter, descents are made with equipment, initially in a single 'stick' of six, subsequently in simultaneous 'sticks' of eight or ten and finally in the maximum size of 'stick' possible, depending upon the number of personnel on the course. On successful completion of their eight descents, trainees are presented with their 'wings' by the Officer Commanding No. 1 Parachute Training School, and return to their respective units as qualified parachutists.

The course for members of Territorial Army units and Royal Marines Reserve lasts only two weeks, and trainees are required to complete only seven descents without one at night. Before taking the course, however, they will have undergone a considerable amount of synthetic training to enable them to be of a sufficient standard to carry out their balloon descent and their first aircraft descent by the end of the first week at Brize Norton. The rest of their descents are carried out during the second week of the course.

THE FUTURE FOR THE PARACHUTE REGIMENT AND AIRBORNE FORCES

The momentous changes in Eastern Europe and the dissolution of the Soviet Union during 1991 have had far-reaching effects, and these have been reflected in *Options for Change*. One of the main results has been the formation of the Allied Command Europe Rapid Reaction Corps (ARRC), under British command and comprising four divisions. Two of these will be British formations: 1st (UK) Armoured Division and 3rd (UK) Division, the latter being based in Britain and comprising 1 and 19 Mechanised Brigades and 5 Airborne Brigade. 3rd (UK) Division will also provide Britain with a strategic reserve which will provide a capability to conduct Out of Area operations with airborne or mechanised forces. If amphibious operations appear likely, the United Kingdom/Netherlands Amphibious Force (comprising 3 Commando Brigade RM and 1 Battalion Royal Netherlands Marine Corps) could be placed under command of the division. Similarly, if airmobile operations are envisaged, 24 Airmobile Brigade, which will be based in Britain but will be a component of a multi-national airmobile division forming part of the ARRC, could be added to 3rd (UK) Division's order of battle.

There is no doubt that the stereotyped battalion group drop from aircraft flying in a stream to a dropping zone is now considered too conventional and outmoded, and that the concept of parachute assault will have to change dramatically. It has already been perceived by some in Airborne Forces that, for the majority of future operations in which troops are delivered by parachute against a sophisticated enemy, entry would have to be at low level, below radar cover, at heights of approximately 300ft or even less. In such instances, bearing in mind the capabilities of current types of air defence systems, troops would in all probability have to be delivered on to multiple dropping zones as near as possible to objectives. Such changes in operational methods may well require changes in the organisational structure of units, deployment of aircraft, pathfinding techniques and other aspects. Thought would also have to be given to assessment of types of aircraft and parachute equipment for the future.

Today's officers and men of The Parachute Regiment are well aware that versatility is all-important. In addition to being dropped by parachute, they are well versed in the techniques of Tactical Air Landing Operations (TALO), a method of delivery practised often by all units in 5 Airborne Brigade, and in the use of helicopters. Such versatility will be a key factor in ensuring the survival of The Parachute Regiment and Airborne Forces in future years. With the disappearance of the threat from the now-dissolved Soviet Union, Britain's forces must be able to respond to a wider range of threats, both in the defence of Europe and in Out of Area operations. Such roles call for flexibility and a high degree of mobility, qualities long possessed by British airborne forces and the battalions of The Parachute Regiment.

BIBLIOGRAPHY

Allen, Charles. *The Savage Wars of Peace*. Michael Joseph, 1990.

Arthur, Max. *Men of the Red Beret*. Hutchinson, 1990.

Barzilay, David. *The British Army in Ulster*, Vols I, II and III. Century Books, 1973–8.

Benest, Major D. *2 PARA Operations During the Falklands Campaign*.

Cavenagh, Sandy. *Airborne to Suez*. William Kimber, 1965.

Crook, Brigadier Paul. *Come the Dawn*. Spellmount, 1989.

Crookenden, Napier. *Drop Zone Normandy*. Purnell Book Services, 1976.

— *Airborne At War*. Ian Allan, 1978.

— *9th Bn The Parachute Regt – Normandy 1944, The First Six days*.

Cross, Colonel J. P. *In Gurkha Company*. Arms & Armour Press, 1985.

— *Jungle Warfare*. Arms & Armour Press, 1989.

Darling, Lieutenant-Colonel K. T. *The 12th Yorkshire Parachute Battalion in Germany, 24th March-16th May 1945*.

Dickens, Peter. *SAS – Secret War in South East Asia*. Greenhill Books, 1991.

Frost, Major-General John. *A Drop Too Many*. Cassell, 1980.

— *2 PARA Falklands – The Battalion At War*. Buchan & Enright, 1983.

Gale, Richard. *With the 6th Airborne Division In Normandy*. Sampson Low, 1948.

Harclerode, Peter. *'Go To It!' — The Illustrated History of the 6th Airborne Division*. Bloomsbury Publishing, 1990.

Harold, James, and Denis Sheil-Small. *The Undeclared War*. Leo Cooper, 1971.

— *A Pride of Gurkhas — 2nd King Edward VII's Own Goorkhas (The Sirmoor Rifles) 1948–1971*. Leo Cooper, 1975.

Hastings, Max, and Simon Jenkins. *The Battle for the Falklands*. Michael Joseph, 1983.

Hibbert, Christopher. *The Battle of Arnhem*. Batsford, 1962.

James, Julian. *A Fierce Quality*. Leo Cooper, 1989.

McKee, Alexander. *The Race For The Rhine*. Souvenir Press, 1971.

McManners, Hugh. *Falklands Commando*. William Kimber, 1984.

Montgomery, Field Marshal The Viscount. *The Memoirs of Field Marshal Montgomery*. Collins, 1958.

Morton, Brigadier Peter. *Emergency Tour — 3 PARA in South Armagh*. William Kimber, 1989.

Norton, G. G. *The Red Devils*. Leo Cooper, 1971.

Otway, Lieutenant-Colonel T. B. H. *Official Account of Airborne Forces 1939–1945*. The War Office, 1951.

Pimlott, John. *Guerilla Warfare*. Hamlyn, 1985.

Pocock, Tom. *Fighting General*. Collins, 1973.

Praval, K. C. *India's Paratroopers*. Leo Cooper, 1975.

Saunders, Hilary St. George. *The Red Beret*. Michael Joseph, 1950.

Sim, Major J. A. N. *With The 12th Battalion The Parachute Regiment in Normandy*.

Thompson, Julian. *No Picnic – 3 Commando Brigade in the South Atlantic 1982*. Leo Cooper, 1985.

— *Ready For Anything*. Wiedenfield & Nicholson, 1989.

Widgery, Lord Justice. *The Widgery Report*. Her Majesty's Stationery Office, 1972.

Wilmot, Chester. *The Struggle For Europe*. Collins, 1952.

Wilson, Major-General R. Dare. *Cordon and Search with the 6th Airborne Division in Palestine*. The Battery Press, 1949.

6th Airborne Division — Report on Operations in Normandy 6th June — 27th August 1944.

By Air to Battle — The Official Account of The British 1st & 6th Airborne Divisions. Her Majesty's Stationery Office, 1945.

Directing Staff Edition BAOR Battlefield Tour 'Operation Varsity'.

Falklands Campaign — 3 PARA War Dairy.

APPENDIX 1
Colonels Commandant The Parachute Regiment, 1942–1992

1942–4   Field Marshal Sir John Dill, GCB, CMG, DSO, LLD

1944–56   Field Marshal The Viscount Montgomery of Alamein, KG, GCB, DSO, DL

1956–61   General Sir Richard Gale, GCB, KBE, DSO, MC

1961–5   General Sir Gerald Lathbury, GCB, DSO, MBE

1965–7   Lieutenant General Sir Kenneth Darling, KCB, CBE, DSO

1967–72   General Sir Mervyn Butler, KCB, CBE, DSO, MC

1972–7   General Sir Roland Gibbs, GCB, CBE, DSO, MC, ADC, GEN

1977–83   General Sir Anthony Farrar-Hockley, GBE, KCB, DSO, MC, ADC, GEN

1984–90   General Sir Geoffrey Howlett, KBE, MC

1990–   Lieutenant-General Sir Michael Gray, KCB, OBE

APPENDIX 2
Regimental Colonels and Regimental Adjutants of The Parachute Regiment

Regimental Colonels 1948–92

1948–50 Colonel K. T. Darling, DSO, OBE

1951–2 Colonel A. W. E. Daniell

1952–5 Colonel R. G. Pine-Coffin, DSO, MC

1955–7 Colonel H. B. Coxen, DSO, MC

1957–60 Colonel G. Hewetson, DSO, OBE, TD

1960–3 Colonel G. C. A. Gilbert, MC

1963–5 Colonel G. R. Flood, MC

1965–8 Colonel P. D. F. Thursby, OBE

1968–9 Colonel J. D. C. Graham, OBE

1969–72 Colonel K. G. Came, OBE

1972–5 Colonel J. G. Starling, MBE, MC

1975–8 Colonel G. O. Mullins

1978–81 Colonel J. U. H. Burke

1981–4 Colonel G. D. Farrell, MBE

1984–8 Colonel E. A. J. Gardener

1988–91 Colonel J. A. MacGregor, MC

1991–2 Colonel D. C. Parker

Regimental Adjutants 1947–92

1947–9 Major E. J. Warren, DSO

1949–51 Major J. Awdry

1951–64 Major D. M. Mayfield, MBE, TD

1964–6 Major W. R. Corbould

1966–9 Major J. E. N. Giles

1969 Major P. S. Field, MC

1969–71 Major S. G. Lorimer

1971–3 Major R. G. Southerst

1973–4 Major J. P. Epplestone

1974–7 Major J. A. Orr

1977–80 Major N. J. Nichols

1980–2 Major J. D. A. Baker

1982–4 Major B. K. Martin

1984–5 Major A. H. Clark

1985–7 Major J. J. P. Poraj-Wilczynski

1987–9 Major C. F. Hicks

1989–90 Major G. J. J. McFall

1991–2 Major D. G. Benest, MBE

APPENDIX 3

Honorary Colonels of Territorial Army Battalions and Independent Companies of The Parachute Regiment, 1947–1992

4th (Volunteer) Battalion The Parachute Regiment*†
*Formed from amalgamation of 12/13 PARA (TA) and 17 PARA (TA) in 1966
1967–77 Colonel B. H. Parker, OBE, DCM, TD, JP, DL
1977–86 Brigadier C. F. O. Breese, CBE
1986– Colonel B. C. F. Arkle, MBE, TD
†To amalgamate with 15 PARA(SV) in 1993; to retain title of 4 PARA(V)

10th (Volunteer) Battalion The Parachute Regiment
1947–52 Brigadier The Hon H. Kindersley, CBE, MC
1952–60 General Sir Kenneth Crawford, KBE, MC
1960–5 General Sir Geoffrey Bourne, GCB, KBE, SMG, ADC
1965–73 General Sir John Hackett, GCB, CBE, DSO, MC, BLett, MA, LLD
1973–8 General Sir John Mogg, GCB, CBE, DSO
1978–84 Brigadier P. D. F. Thursby, OBE
1984–9 Lieutenant General Sir Michael Gray, KCB, OBE
1989– Colonel J. Holland

11th (8th Middlesex (DCO)) Battalion The Parachute Regiment (TA)
1947–56 Brigadier E. E. F. Baker, CB, CBE, DSO, MC, TD, JP

12th Battalion The Parachute Regiment (TA)*
1947–56 Brigadier J. B. Gawthorpe, CBE, TD
*Amalgamated with 13 PARA (TA) in Oct 1956 to form 12/13 PARA (TA)

13th Battalion The Parachute Regiment (TA)*
1947–56 Brigadier D. Mills-Roberts, CBE, DSO, MC, JP

*Amalgamated with 12 PARA (TA) in Oct 1956 to form 12/13 PARA (TA).

12th/13th Battalion The Parachute Regiment (TA)*
1956–66 Colonel R. G. Parker, DSO
*Amalgamated with 17 PARA (TA) in 1966 to form 4 PARA (V)

14th Battalion The Parachute Regiment (TA)
1947–52 Brigadier S. J. L. Hill, DSO, MC
1952–6 Lieutenant Colonel J. M. Pearson

15th (Scottish Volunteer) Battalion The Parachute Regiment
1947–51 Colonel Sir William Scott, CBE, DSO, MC, TD, DL
1951–8 Colonel Sir Jackson Millar, CBE, DL
1958–63 Colonel H. Waddell, CB, TD
1963–77 Brigadier A. S. Pearson, CB, DSO, OBE, MC, KStJ, TD
1977–83 Colonel L. Robertson, OBE, TD, MA, DL
1983–9 Brigadier A. S. Pearson, CB, DSO, OBE, MC, KStJ, TD
1989– Colonel A. G. Rutherford
To amalgamate with 4 PARA(V) in 1993.

16th Battalion The Parachute Regiment (TA)
1947–56 Colonel Sir G. Llewellyn, CB, CBE, MC, TD, DL, JP

17th (Durham Light Infantry) Battalion The Parachute Regiment (TA)*
1947–55 Colonel Sir T. Bradford, Bt, DSO, DCL, DL
1955–8 Lieutenant Colonel R. C. Kelly, TD, DL
1958–63 Colonel H. L. Swinburn, TD, DL, JP

1963–6   Colonel His Honour Judge
         C. Cohen, MC, TD, DL
*Amalgamated with 12/13 PARA (TA) in 1966 to form 4 PARA (V).

18th Battalion The Parachute Regiment (TA)
1947–56   Colonel Sir H. Chance, DL

16th (Volunteer) Independent Company The Parachute Regiment*
1952–74   Colonel C. F. H. Gough, MC, TD
1974–85   Brigadier P. E. Crook, CBE, DSO, MA
1985–6   Colonel B. C. F. Arkle, MBE, TD
*Lost independent title and role in 1977 on absorption into 15 PARA (SV), but retained honorary colonel until 1986.

APPENDIX 4

Commanding Officers of the Regular and Territorial Army Battalions and Independent Companies of The Parachute Regiment, The Depot The Parachute Regiment & Airborne Forces, and The Parachute Regiment Battle School, 1940–1992

No. 2 Commando/11th Special Air Service Battalion*

1940	Lieutenant Colonel C. I. A. Jackson
1941	Lieutenant Colonel E. E. Down

*Redesignated 1st Para Bn in Sept 1941

1st Parachute Battalion

1941–2	Lieutenant Colonel E. E. Down
1942	Lieutenant Colonel S. J. L. Hill, MC
1942–3	Lieutenant Colonel A. S. Pearson, DSO, MC
1943–4	Lieutenant Colonel P. Cleasby-Thompson, MBE, MC
1944	Lieutenant Colonel K. T. Darling, DSO
1944–5	Lieutenant Colonel D. T. Dobie, DSO
1945	Lieutenant Colonel T. C. H. Pearson, DSO

1st (Guards) Parachute Battalion*

1946–8	Lieutenant Colonel E. J. B. Nelson, DSO, OBE, MC

*Reduced to company strength and initially redesignated 16 (Gds) Indep Coy PARA in May-Jun 1948. Subsequently redesignated No. 1 (Gds) Indep Coy PARA

1st Battalion The Parachute Regiment*

*1 PARA formed in Jul 1948 from 4th/6th Para Bn

1948–50	Lieutenant Colonel J. H. Cubbon, OBE
1950–1	Lieutenant Colonel C. H. P. Harrington, DSO, MC
1951–2	Lieutenant Colonel D. W. Jackson
1952–4	Lieutenant Colonel H. L. E. C. Leask, DSO, MC
1954–6	Lieutenant Colonel J. S. S. Gratton
1957–9	Lieutenant Colonel G. G. Reinhold, MC
1959–61	Lieutenant Colonel J. Awdry
1961–2	Lieutenant Colonel T. J. Pine-Coffin, DSO
1962–4	Lieutenant Colonel P. D. F. Thursby, OBE
1964–6	Lieutenant Colonel J. D. C. Graham, OBE
1966–9	Lieutenant Colonel M. J. H. Walsh, DSO
1969–71	Lieutenant Colonel M. S. Gray, OBE
1971–3	Lieutenant Colonel D. Wilford, OBE
1973–6	Lieutenant Colonel P. S. Field, MC
1976–9	Lieutenant Colonel J. B. Brierley, OBE
1979–81	Lieutenant Colonel D. M. G. Charles
1981–4	Lieutenant Colonel I. McLeod, OBE, MC
1984–6	Lieutenant Colonel M. D. Jackson, MBE
1986–8	Lieutenant Colonel J. G. Reith, OBE
1988–90	Lieutenant Colonel R. W. Trigger, MBE
1990–	Lieutenant Colonel A. W. J. Kennett

2nd Parachute Battalion*

1941–2	Lieutenant Colonel E. W. C. Flavell, MC
1942	Lieutenant Colonel G. P. Gofton-Salmond, OBE

1942–6   Lieutenant Colonel J. D.
            Frost, DSO, MC
1946–7   Lieutenant Colonel D. R. W.
            Webber
*Amalgamated with 3rd Para Bn in Dec
1947 to form 2nd/3rd Para Bn

2nd/3rd Parachute Battalion*

1947–8   Lieutenant Colonel T. H.
            Birkbeck, DSO
*Disbanded Jul 1948

2nd Battalion The Parachute Regiment*

*Formed in Jul 1948 from 5th (Scottish)
Para Bn
1948   Lieutenant Colonel P. S.
            Sandilands, DSO
1948–52   Lieutenant Colonel G. W.
            White, MBE
1952–5   Lieutenant Colonel H. B.
            Coxen, DSO, MC
1955   Lieutenant Colonel R. C. C.
            Langrishe
1956–8   Lieutenant Colonel H. E. N.
            Bredin, DSO, MC
1958–60   Lieutenant Colonel D. A.
            Beckett, DSO, OBE
1960–2   Lieutenant Colonel F. D.
            King, MBE
1962–4   Lieutenant Colonel N. F.
            Gordon-Wilson, MBE
1964–6   Lieutenant Colonel C. E.
            Eberhardie, MBE, MC
1966–8   Lieutenant Colonel J. M. H.
            Roberts, OBE
1968–71   Lieutenant Colonel R. W.
            Dawnay, OBE
1971–3   Lieutenant Colonel G. H. W.
            Howlett, OBE, MC
1973–5   Lieutenant Colonel C. J.
            Bowden, MBE
1975–8   Lieutenant Colonel D. W. F.
            Taylor
1978–81   Lieutenant Colonel O. G.
            Thomson, OBE
1981–2   Lieutenant Colonel H. Jones,
            VC, OBE
1982–4   Lieutenant Colonel D. R.
            Chaundler, OBE
1984–7   Lieutenant Colonel D. Parker

1987–9   Lieutenant Colonel P. E.
            Dennison, MBE
1989–92   Lieutenant Colonel C. F.
            Hicks, OBE
1992–   Lieutenant Colonel A. R.
            Freer

3rd Parachute Battalion*

1941–2   Lieutenant Colonel G. W.
            Lathbury, DSO, MBE
1942–3   Lieutenant Colonel R. G.
            Pine-Coffin, DSO, MC
1943–4   Lieutenant Colonel E. C.
            Yeldham
1944   Lieutenant Colonel J. A. C.
            Fitch
1944–5   Lieutenant Colonel R. T. H.
            Lonsdale, DSO
1945–6   LieutenantColonel W. P. D.
            Brandish
1946–7   Lieutenant Colonel G. P.
            Rickord, DSO
*Amalgamated with 2 Para Bn in Dec
1947 to become 2nd/3rd Para Bn

2nd/3rd Parachute Battalion*

1947–8   Lieutenant Colonel T. H.
            Birkbeck, DSO
*Disbanded in Jun 1948

3rd Battalion The Parachute Regiment*

*Formed in Jul 1948 from 7th (Light
Infantry) Para Bn
1948–50   Lieutenant Colonel P. D.
            Maud, MBE
1950–3   Lieutenant Colonel W. D.
            Tighe-Wood, MC
1953–4   Lieutenant Colonel V. W.
            Street, DSO, OBE, MC
1954–7   Lieutenant Colonel P. E.
            Crook, DSO, OBE
1957–60   Lieutenant Colonel M.
            Forrester, DSO, OBE, MC
1960–2   Lieutenant Colonel R. C.
            Gibbs, DSO, MC
1962–5   Lieutenant Colonel A. H.
            Farrar-Hockley, DSO, MBE, MC
1965–7   Lieutenant Colonel F. H.
            Scobie, OBE
1967–9   Lieutenant Colonel F. A.
            Ward-Booth

1969–71 Lieutenant Colonel P. I. Chiswell, MBE

1971–3 Lieutenant Colonel S. G. Lorimer

1973–5 Lieutenant Colonel K. Spacie, OBE

1975–8 Lieutenant Colonel P. S. Morton, OBE

1978–80 Lieutenant Colonel K. Coates, MBE

1980–2 Lieutenant Colonel H. W. R. Pike, DSO, MBE

1982–5 Lieutenant Colonel R. A. Smith, OBE, QGM

1985–7 Lieutenant Colonel C. D. Farrar-Hockley, MC

1987–8 Lieutenant Colonel R. D. Llewellin

1988–91 Lieutenant Colonel H. M. Fletcher, OBE

1991– Lieutenant Colonel T. W. Burls, MC

4th Parachute Battalion*

1942 Lieutenant Colonel M. R. Hope Thomson

1942–3 Lieutenant Colonel J. A. Dene

1943–4 Lieutenant Colonel H. B. Coxen, DSO

1944–5 Lieutenant Colonel De V. Martin

1945–6 Lieutenant Colonel G. P. Rickord, DSO

1946 Lieutenant Colonel P. H. C. Hayward

1946–7 Lieutenant Colonel H. B. Coxen, DSO

*Amalgamated with 6th Para Bn in Dec 1947 to become 4th/6th Para Bn

4th/6th Parachute Battalion*

1947–8 Lieutenant Colonel H. B. Coxen, DSO

1948 Lieutenant Colonel J. H. Cubbon, DSO

*Redesignated 1 PARA in 1948

4th (Volunteer) Battalion The Parachute Regiment*†

*Formed in Apr 1967 from 12/13 PARA (TA) and 17 PARA (TA)

1967–8 Lieutenant Colonel K. C. Came, OBE

1968–70 Lieutenant Colonel D. W. Callaghan

1970–3 Lieutenant Colonel L. P. Weeks

1973–5 Lieutenant Colonel J. A. Rymer-Jones

1975–7 Lieutenant Colonel L. J. H. Kent

1977–80 Lieutenant Colonel P. M. Beaumont, MBE

1980–2 Lieutenant Colonel E. C. Loden, MC

1982–5 Lieutenant Colonel J. A. MacGregor, MC

1985–7 Lieutenant Colonel A. H. Clark

1987–90 Lieutenant Colonel B. K. Martin, OBE

1990–2 Lieutenant Colonel A. W. Snook

1992– Lieutenant Colonel J. C. Gallagher

†To amalgamate with 15 PARA(SV) in April 1993; to retain title of 4 PARA(V)

5th (Scottish) Parachute Battalion*†

*Formed from 7th Bn The Cameron Highlanders in May 1942

1942 Lieutenant Colonel A. Dunlop

1942–3 Lieutenant Colonel C. B. Mackenzie, DSO, OBE

1943–5 Lieutenant Colonel D. R. Hunter, MC

1945–7 Lieutenant Colonel J. N. H. Christie

1947 Lieutenant Colonel A. G. F. Munro

1947–8 Lieutenant Colonel P. S. Sandilands, DSO

†Redesignated 2 PARA in Jul 1948.

6th (Royal Welch) Parachute Battalion*†

*Formed from 10th Bn The Royal Welch Fusiliers in Aug 1942

1942–3 Lieutenant Colonel C. H. V. Pritchard

1943– Lieutenant Colonel J. R. Goodwin

1943–5 Lieutenant Colonel V. W. Barlow

1945–6   Lieutenant Colonel A. Tilly
1946–7   Lieutenant Colonel J. H.
Cubbon, DSO
†Amalgamated with 4th Para Bn in Dec
1947 to form 4th/6th Para Bn

7th (Light Infantry) Parachute Battalion*†‡
*Formed from 10th Bn The Somerset
Light Infantry in Nov 1942
1944–7   Lieutenant Colonel R. G.
Pine-Coffin, DSO, MC
†Amalgamated with 17th Para Bn in July
1946, but remained as 7th Para Bn
1947   Lieutenant Colonel T. C. H.
Pearson, DSO
1947–8   Lieutenant Colonel P. D.
Maud
‡Redesignated 3 PARA in Jul 1948.

8th (Midland) Parachute Battalion*†
*Formed from 13th Bn The Royal
Warwickshire Regiment in Nov 1942
1943   Lieutenant Colonel Hildersly
1943–4   Lieutenant Colonel A. S.
Pearson, DSO, MC
1944–7   Lieutenant Colonel G.
Hewetson, DSO
1946–8   Lieutenant Colonel J. H. M.
Hackett, DSO
†Amalgamated with 9th Para Bn in Jan
1948 to form 8th/9th Para Bn

9th (Eastern & Home Counties) Parachute Battalion*†
*Formed from 10th Bn The Essex
Regiment in Dec 1942
1943–4   Lieutenant Colonel M.
Lindsay
1944   Lieutenant Colonel T. C. H.
Otway DSO
1944–6   Lieutenant Colonel N.
Crookenden, DSO
1946–7   Lieutenant Colonel M. A. H.
Butler, DSO, MC
1947–8   Lieutenant Colonel P. C.
Hinde, DSO
†Amalgamated with 8th Para Bn in Jan
1948 to form 8th/9th Para Bn

8th/9th Parachute Battalion*
1948   Lieutenant Colonel J. H. M.
Hackett, DSO

*Disbanded June 1948

10th Parachute Battalion*
1943–4   Lieutenant Colonel K. B. I.
Smyth, OBE
*Disbanded Nov 1945. Re-formed in
1947 as 10th (City of London) Para Bn
(TA)

10th (City of London) Parachute Battalion (TA)*
1947   Lieutenant Colonel D. M. L.
Gordon Watson, OBE, MC
1947   Lieutenant Colonel R. G.
Lewthwaite, MC
*Redesignated 10 PARA (TA) in 1948

10th (City of London) Battalion The Parachute Regiment (TA)*
1948–50   Lieutenant Colonel R. G.
Lewthwaite, MC
1950–1   Lieutenant Colonel H. J.
Mogg, DSO
1951–3   Lieutenant Colonel P. H. M.
May, DSO, MC
1953–6   Lieutenant Colonel P. D.
Maud, MBE
1956–9   Lieutenant Colonel E. L.
Richards, MBE, MC
1959–62   Lieutenant Colonel G. C. A.
Gilbert, MC
1962–4   Lieutenant Colonel E. G. Lee,
OBE, TD
1964–7   Lieutenant Colonel W. J.
Lloyd, MC
*Redesignated 10 PARA (V) in 1967

10th (Volunteer) Battalion The Parachute Regiment
1967–9   Lieutenant Colonel P. M. R.
Stewart-Richardson, MBE
1969–72   Lieutenant Colonel G. O.
Mullins
1972   Lieutenant Colonel J.
Christian, TD
1972–5   Lieutenant Colonel R. J.
Jenkins, MBE
1975–7   Lieutenant Colonel P. M.
Kingston, MC
1977–80   Lieutenant Colonel J. A. Orr
1980–2   Lieutenant Colonel F. E. W.
Martin

1982–5 Lieutenant Colonel J. Q. Winter, MVO

1985–7 Lieutenant Colonel R. C. Patton

1987–90 Lieutenant Colonel M. A. Davidson, MBE

1990–2 Lieutenant Colonel P. Neame

1992– Lieutenant Colonel R. J. Kershaw

11th Parachute Battalion*

1943–4 Lieutenant Colonel R. M. C. Thomas

1944 Lieutenant Colonel G. Lea, DSO

*Amalgamated with 3rd Para Bn in Nov 1944. Disbanded in Nov 1945

11th (8th Middlesex (DCO)) Parachute Battalion (TA)*†

*Formed from 8th Bn Middlesex Regt (TA) in 1947

1947–8 Lieutenant Colonel C. F. H. Gough, MC

†Redesignated 11 PARA (TA) in 1948

11th (8th Middlesex (DCO)) Battalion The Parachute Regiment (TA)*

1948–53 Lieutenant Colonel S. Terrell, OBE

1953–6 Lieutenant Colonel R. A. Corby, OBE, TD, DL

*Reverted to 8th Bn Middlesex Regt (TA) in Aug 1956

12th (Yorkshire) Parachute Battalion*†

*Formed from 10th (E. Riding Yeo) Bn The Green Howards in May 1943

1943–4 Lieutenant Colonel R. G. Parker

1944 Lieutenant Colonel A. P. Johnson

1944 Colonel R. G. Parker

1944 Lieutenant Colonel W. A. B. Harris, MC

1944 Lieutenant Colonel N. C. Stockwell

1944–6 Lieutenant Colonel K. T. Darling, DSO

1946 Major D. R. W. Webber

†Disbanded in Jul 1946. Re-formed as 12th Para Bn (TA) in 1947

12th Parachute Battalion (TA)*

1947 Lieutenant Colonel G. N. Lea

*Redesignated 12 PARA (TA) in 1948

12th Battalion The Parachute Regiment (TA)*

1948–9 Lieutenant Colonel G. N. Lea

1949–51 Lieutenant Colonel O. G. Brooke, DSO, MBE

1951–4 Lieutenant Colonel R. B. Marshall

1954–6 Lieutenant Colonel J. W. B. Marshall

*Amalgamated with 13 PARA (TA) in Oct 1956 to form 12/13 PARA (TA)

13th (Lancashire) Parachute Battalion*†

*Formed from 2nd/4th Bn The South Lancashire Regiment in May 1943

1943 Lieutenant Colonel Russell

1943–6 Lieutenant Colonel P. J. Luard, DSO, OBE

1946 Lieutenant Colonel R. Leyland

†Disbanded and absorbed into 3rd Para Bn in 1946. Re-formed in 1947 as 13th (Lancashire) Para Bn (TA)

13th (Lancashire) Parachute Battalion (TA)*

1947 Lieutenant Colonel D. R. Hunter, MC

*Redesignated 13 PARA (TA) in 1948

13th (Lancashire) Battalion The Parachute Regiment (TA)

1948–52 Lieutenant Colonel D. R. Hunter, MC

1952–4 Lieutenant Colonel P. Cleasby-Thompson, MBE, MC

1954–6 Lieutenant Colonel R. Crawshaw, OBE

*Amalgamated with 12 PARA in Oct 1956 to form 12/13 PARA (TA)

12th/13th (Yorkshire & Lancashire) Battalion The Parachute Regiment (TA)*

1956 Lieutenant Colonel J. W. B. Marshall

1956–7 Lieutenant Colonel R. Crawshaw, OBE

1957–61   Lieutenant Colonel G.
          Pollard, OBE, MC, MM, TD
1961–4   Lieutenant Colonel G. W.
          Hawkes, MC
1964–6   Lieutenant Colonel P. J.
          O'Kane
*Amalgamated with 17 PARA (TA) in
1967 to form 4 PARA (V)

14th Parachute Battalion (TA)*†
*Formed from 5th Bn Royal Hampshire
Regiment (TA) in May 1947
1947–8   Lieutenant Colonel F. M.
          Butcher, DSO
1948–9   Lieutenant Colonel A. G. F.
          Munro
1949–51   Lieutenant Colonel R. G. F.
          Frisby, DSO, MC
1951–4   Lieutenant Colonel H. D.
          Nelson-Smith, MC
1954–6   Lieutenant Colonel H. W.
          Le Patourel, VC
†Reverted in Apr 1956 to 5th Bn Royal
Hampshire Regt (TA)

15th (British) Parachute Battalion*†
*Formed from 1st Bn The King's
Regiment in 1945
1945   Lieutenant Colonel G. Astell
1945   Lieutenant Colonel T. C. H.
          Otway, DSO
1945–6   Lieutenant Colonel P. G. F.
          Young
1946   Lieutenant Colonel G. Lea,
          DSO
          †Disbanded Dec 1946. Re-
formed in 1947 as 15th (Scottish) Para
Bn (TA)

15th (Scottish) Parachute Battalion (TA)*
1947   Lieutenant Colonel A. S.
          Pearson, DSO, MC
*Redesignated 15 (Scottish) PARA (TA)
in 1948

15th (Scottish) Battalion The Parachute Regiment (TA)*
1948–3   Lieutenant Colonel A. S.
          Pearson, DSO, MC
1953–6   Lieutenant Colonel P. S.
          Sandilands, DSO

1956–9   Lieutenant Colonel J. S.
          Cousland, TD
1959–62   Lieutenant Colonel J. H.
          Graham, MBE, TD
1962–5   Lieutenant Colonel R. C. V.
          Stewart, TD
1965–7   Lieutenant Colonel L.
          Robertson, TD
*Redesignated 15 PARA (SV) in 1967.

15th (Scottish Volunteer) Battalion The Parachute Regiment*
1967–9   Lieutenant Colonel L.
          Robertson, TD
1969-71   Lieutenant Colonel J. G.
          Starling, MBE, MC
1971–3   Lieutenant Colonel J. E. N.
          Giles, MBE
1973–6   Lieutenant Colonel J. U. H.
          Burke
1976–8   Lieutenant Colonel H. M.
          Pollock
1978–81   Lieutenant Colonel P. E.
          Wood, MBE
1981–4   Lieutenant Colonel E. A. J.
          Gardener
1984–6   Lieutenant Colonel C. P. B.
          Keeble, DSO
1986–9   Lieutenant Colonel W. P.
          Conn
1989–91   Lieutenant Colonel M. H.
          Argue, MBE, MC
1991–   Lieutenant Colonel S. D.
          Cave, TD
To amalgamate with 4 PARA(V) in April
1993.

16th (British) Parachute Battalion*†
*Formed from 1st Bn The South
Staffordshire Regiment in Jan 1945
1945   Lieutenant Colonel P. G. F.
          Young
1945–6   Lieutenant Colonel A. W. E.
          Daniell
†Disbanded in 1946. Re-formed in 1947
as 16th (Welsh) Para Bn (TA)

16th (Welsh) Parachute Battalion (TA)*
1947   Lieutenant Colonel J. T.
          Bannantyne, DSO, MC
*Redesignated 16 (Welsh) PARA (TA) in
1948

16th (Welsh) Battalion The Parachute Regiment (TA)*

1948   Lieutenant Colonel J. T. Bannantyne, DSO, MC

1948–51   Lieutenant Colonel B. C. Bradford, DSO, MC

1951–2   Lieutenant Colonel F. F. Powell

1952–3   Major D. F. Cunliffe, MC

1953–6   Lieutenant Colonel P. C. Hinde, DSO

1956   Lieutenant Colonel W. R. Crawshaw

*Disbanded in Oct 1956

17th Parachute Battalion*

1945   Lieutenant Colonel McCardie

*Amalgamated with 7th Para Bn in Aug 1946

17th (Durham Light Infantry) Parachute Battalion (TA)*†

*Formed from 9th Bn Durham Light Infantry (TA) in 1947

1947   Lieutenant Colonel J. C. Slight, DSO

†Redesignated 17th (DLI) PARA (TA) in 1948

17th (Durham Light Infantry) Battalion The Parachute Regiment (TA)*

1948   Lieutenant Colonel J. C. Slight, DSO

1948–50   Lieutenant Colonel T. H. Birkbeck, DSO

1950–3   Lieutenant Colonel R. B. Humphreys

1953–6   Lieutenant Colonel J. R. P. Montgomery, MC

1956–8   Lieutenant Colonel C. F. O. Breese

1958–60   Lieutenant Colonel W. G. S. Mills

1960–2   Lieutenant Colonel R. E. Morton

1962–5   Lieutenant Colonel H. L. Carey, TD

1965–6   Lieutenant Colonel K. C. Came, OBE

*Amalgamated with 12/13 PARA (TA) in 1967 to form 4 PARA (V)

18th Parachute Battalion (TA)*

1947–8   Lieutenant Colonel W. P. Scott, DSO

*Redesignated 18 PARA (TA) in 1948

18th Battalion The Parachute Regiment (TA)*

1948–9   Lieutenant Colonel J. H. M. Hackett, DSO

1949–52   Lieutenant Colonel S. L. A. Carter, MC

1952–4   Lieutenant Colonel E. J. O'B. Croker, OBE, MC

1954–6   Lieutenant Colonel A. J. C. Prickett

*Disbanded Oct 1956

151st Parachute Battalion*

1941   Lieutenant Colonel M. A. Lindsay

1942   Major Thomas

1942   Lieutenant Colonel M. C. R. Hose, DSO

*Redesignated 156th Para Bn in Nov 1942

152nd Indian Parachute Battalion*

1941–3   Lieutenant Colonel B. E. Abbott

1943–4   Lieutenant Colonel P. Hopkinson

1944–5   Lieutenant Colonel J. Martin

*Divided into two battalions in Mar 1945 and redesignated 1st & 4th Bns Indian Para Regt

1st Battalion The Indian Parachute Regiment*

1945–6   Lieutenant Colonel J. Martin

*Disbanded in Oct 1946

4th Battalion The Indian Parachute Regiment*

1945–6   Lieutenant Colonel G. E. A. Beale

*Disbanded in Oct 1946

153rd Gurkha Parachute Battalion*

1941–2   Lieutenant Colonel F. J. Loftus-Tottenham

1942–5   Lieutenant Colonel H. R. E. Willis

*Redesignated 2nd Bn Indian Para Regt in Mar 1945

2nd Battalion The Indian Parachute Regiment*

1945–6   Lieutenant Colonel H. R. E. Willis

*Disbanded in Oct 1946

154th Gurkha Parachute Battalion*†

*Formed from 3rd Bn 7th Gurkha Rifles in Aug 1943

1943   Lieutenant Colonel H. Parsons

1943–4   Lieutenant Colonel G. H. W. Bond

1944–5   Lieutenant Colonel J. White

†Redesignated 3rd Bn Indian Para Regt in Mar 1945

3rd Battalion The Indian Parachute Regiment*

1945–6   Lieutenant Colonel J. White

*Disbanded in Oct 1946

156th Parachute Battalion*

1942   Lieutenant Colonel M. C. R. Hose, DSO

1943–4   Lieutenant Colonel R. de B. Voeux

*Disbanded Sept 1944

21st Independent Company The Parachute Regiment*

1942–3   Major J. Lander, TD

1943–5   Major B. A. Wilson, DSO, MC

1945–6   Major R. E. Spivey

*Disbanded in Sept 1946

No. 1 (Guards) Independent Company The Parachute Regiment*

1948–9	Major R. Steele	Coldstream Guards
1949–51	Major J. Agnew	Coldstream Guards
1951–3	Major E. I. L. Mostyn MC	Scots Guards
1953–5	Major G. P. Burnett	Scots Guards
1955–7	Major W. K. Buckley	Welsh Guards
1957–8	Major P. N. R. Stewart-Richardson	Coldstream Guards
1958–9	Major J. D. N. Retallack	Welsh Guards
1959–61	Major J. N. P. Watson	Royal Horse Guards
1961–3	Major E. C. Whiteley	Irish Guards
1963–5	Major J. G. F. Head, MBE	Irish Guards
1965–8	Major Sir N. K. L. Nuttall	Royal Horse Guards
1968–70	Major D. V. Fanshawe	Grenadier Guards
1970–2	Major The Hon. W. D. Coleridge	Coldstream Guards
1972–4	Major M. M. Carnegie-Brown	Scots Guards
1974–5	Major R. J. S. Corbett	Irish Guards

*Disbanded in Oct 1975

22nd Independent Company The Parachute Regiment*

1943–4   Major F. Lennox-Boyd

1944   Major N. Stockwell

1944   Captain J. de T. Vischer

1944–5   Major M. G. Dolden

1945–6   Major J. H. S. Lane

1946   Major D. D. Campbell, MC

*Disbanded in Jul 1946

44th (British) Independent Pathfinder Company*

1945   Major F. E. Templer, BEM

*Redesignated 2nd Independent Pathfinder Company in Nov 1945

2nd (British) Independent Pathfinder Company*

1945–6   Major F. E. Templer, BEM

*Disbanded in Oct 1946

16th Airborne Divisional (Lincoln) Independent Company The Parachute Regiment*

1950–2   Major G. H. Seal

1952–3   Captain J. H. Smith

1953–6   Major A. J. Bennett, MBE

*Redesignated 16 (Lincoln) Indep Coy PARA in 1956

16th (Lincoln) Independent Company The Parachute Regiment*

1956–60 Major A. J. Bennett, MBE

1960–1   Major D. J. M. Sheddon

1961   Major W. R. A. Oddie

1961–4 Major D. M. Fletcher, MC
1964–5 Major K. Spacie
1965 Captain J. C. H. Harvey
1965–8 Major R. J. Jenkins
1968 Major P. E. Wood
*Redesignated 16 Indep Coy PARA (V) in 1968

16th (Volunteer) Independent Company The Parachute Regiment*
1968–70 Major P. E. Wood
1970–1 Major D. W. F. Taylor
1971–2 Major C. G. Thomson
1972–4 Major H. W. R. Pike
1974–5 Major A. H. Clark
1975–7 Major J. H. Insley
*Absorbed into 15 PARA (SV) in Mar 1977. Transferred to 4 PARA (V) in Jul 1984

Airborne Forces Depot*
Commandants
1942 Lieutenant Colonel L. W. Giles, MC
1942–6 Lieutenant Colonel R. J. F. Campbell
1946–7 Lieutenant Colonel T. J. Firbank, MC
1947–8 Lieutenant Colonel T. G. D. Rowley
*Redesignated Depot PARA & Airborne Forces in 1948

Depot The Parachute Regiment & Airborne Forces
1948–50 Colonel K. T. Darling, DSO, OBE
1951–2 Colonel A. W. E. Daniell
1952–5 Colonel R. G. Pine-Coffin, DSO, MC
1955–7 Colonel H. B. Coxen, DSO, MC
1957–60 Colonel G. Hewetson, DSO, OBE, TD

Commanding Officers
1959–60 Lieutenant Colonel G. R. Flood, MC
1960–2 Lieutenant Colonel J. L. Waddy, OBE

1962–5 Lieutenant Colonel S. C. A. N. Bishop, OBE
1965–8 Lieutenant Colonel M. A. J. Tugwell
1968–70 Lieutenant Colonel M. H. Jones, MBE
1970–2 Lieutenant Colonel P. L. F. Baillon
1972–4 Lieutenant Colonel P. F. Walter, MBE, MC
1974–7 Lieutenant Colonel R. G. Southerst
1977–9 Lieutenant Colonel G. D. Farrell, MBE
1979–81 Lieutenant Colonel M. A. Benjamin
1981–4 Lieutenant Colonel S. D. R. W. Brewis, MBE
1984–7 Lieutenant Colonel D. L. Roberts, MBE
1987–9 Lieutenant Colonel T. A. Marsh
1989–91 Lieutenant Colonel D. J. Campbell
1991– Lieutenant Colonel J. J. P. Poraj-Wilczynski

The Parachute Regiment Battle School*†‡○
*Initially formed as Battle Camp from permanent staff of Depot PARA
1960–2 Captain J. Taylor
1962–4 Captain L. J. H. Kent
1964–7 Major A. M. L. Watson
†Formed as PARA Battle School in 1967
1967–9 Major J. J. L. Thorpe
‡Upgraded to a lieutenant colonel's command in 1968
1968–9 Lieutenant Colonel J. G. Starling, MBE, MC
1969–71 Lieutenant Colonel P. F. Walter, MBE, MC
1972–4 Lieutenant Colonel J. J. L. Thorpe, MBE
1974–6 Lieutenant Colonel J. P. Epplestone
○Transferred to the School of Infantry and redesignated NCOs Tactics Wing in 1976

APPENDIX 5
Battle Honours of The Parachute Regiment

Bruneval
Normandy Landings
Pegasus Bridge
Merville Battery
Breville
Dives Crossing
La Touques Crossing
Arnhem 1944
Ourthe
Rhine
Southern France
Northwest Europe 1942, 1944–45
Soudia
Oudna
Falkland Islands 1982
Mount Longdon

Djebel Azzag 1943
Djebel Alliliga
El Hadjeba
Tamera
Djebel Dahra
Kef El Debna
North Africa 1942–43
Primosole Bridge
Sicily 1943
Taranto
Orsogna
Italy 1943–44
Athens
Greece 1944–45
Goose Green
Wireless Ridge

INDEX

Aa, River, 97
Aachen, 92
Abols, Cpl, 2 PARA, 326
Abbott, Capt, 50th Indian Para Bde, 165
Abbott, Lt Col B. E. 'Abbo', 152nd Indian Para Bn. Later Col, Deputy Comd 50th Indian Para Bde, 165, 174, 178, 181, 182
Absolon, Pte, 3 PARA, 344
Acre, 200, 204
Acropolis, The, 154
Adams, Lt Peter, 2 PARA, 328
Adams, Cpl, 2 PARA, 322, 325
Aden, 200, 235, 236, 237, 241, 244
Aden Protectorates, 237, 238
Aden Protectorate Levies, 237
Aermacchi MB339A, 307
Aermacchi MB326, 307
Afxentiou, 233
Agros, 233
Aird, Sgt, 2 PARA, 321, 323, 336
Air Ministry, 18
Ajax Bay, 308, 337, 340, 345, 346, 349
Akrotiri, 217
Akyab, 170, 188
Albania, 20, 23, 152
Albemarle bomber, 27, 28, 66
Aldershot, 211, 214, 216, 271, 273, 292, 296, 302
Alexander, Gen Sir Harold, Comd 15th Army Group, 146, 155
Alexandria, 221
Algeria, 32
Algiers, 30, 32, 36, 43
Allan, Capt Lester, GS03 Int HQ 50th Indian Para Bde, 171, 174
Allen, L/Cpl, 2 PARA, 339
Allfrey, Lt Gen Sir Charles, Comd 5th Corps, 48
Allied Command Europe Rapid Reaction Corps (ARRC), 369
Allied Military Administration Civil Affairs Bureau, 163
Al Mansura, 273, 274, 275
Alona, 233
Alouette light helicopter, 303
Alpini, 45
Al-Sabah, Abdallah al-Salem, Emir of Kuwait, 235
Altenhagen, 142, 143
Ambala, 191
Ambarawa, 161
America, United States of, 230
Amesbury Abbey, 58
Amfreville, 73, 76, 81
Amman, 234
Anderson, Gen Sir Kenneth, Comd 1st Br Army, 30, 32, 42
Andrews, C/Sgt, C (Independent) Company 2 PARA, 268
Anduki, 254
Angenent, Dr, head of AMACAB in Semarang, 163
Anguilla, 279

Annebault, 88
Anti-aircraft guns: 20mm, 137, 138, 340; 35mm, 330, 340; 88mm, 88, 133, 140; 3.7 inch, 226
Anti-aircraft machine-gun, 12.5mm, 251
Antigua, 279
Anti-tank gun, 6-pdr, 53, 79, 103, 104, 111
Antwerp, 92, 125
Apple Pie, 2 PARA objective on Wireless Ridge, 362, 363, 365
Apulia, 21
Aqaba, 234
Aqir, 200
Arab Higher Committee, 195
Arab Higher Executivee, 195
Arab Higher Executive Committee, 194
Arab League, 195
Arab Legion, 195, 204
Arab Legion: 3rd Mech Regt, 205
Arakan, 171, 172
Ardennes, 125
Argentina, 304

Argentinian Units and Formations (Falklands Campaign):
Argentinian Air Force:
2nd Attack & Recce Sqn, 306
3rd Attack & Recce Sqn, 306
Argentinian Army:
3rd Mech Inf Bde, 306
10th Motorised Inf Bde, 306
1st Para Regt, 306, 361
2nd Abn Inf Regt, 306, 307
3rd Inf Regt, 306
4th Inf Reg, 306
5th Inf Regt, 306, 307
6th Inf Regt, 306, 307
7th Inf Regt, 306, 350, 361
8th Inf Regt, 306, 307
12th Inf Regt, 306
25th Inf Regt, 306
3rd Arty Gp, 307
11th Arty Gp, 306, 307
601st AA Arty Gp, 306
9th Armoured Engr Coy, 306, 307
10th Motorised Engr Coy, 306
601st Construction Engr Bn, 306
601st Engr Gp, 306
602nd Special Forces Gp, 306
Argentinian Marines: 303
1st Marine AA Regt, 306
5th Marine Bn, 306
302nd Marine Cdo Coy, 302, 306
601st Marine Cdo Coy, 302, 306, 350
Marine Amphibious Recce Gp, 306, 307, 361
Argentinian Navy: 311
1st Naval Attack Sqn, 306
4th Naval Attack Sqn, 306
ARA *Bahia Paraiso* 303
ARA *Guerrico* 303

General Belgrano, 306
Argosy transport aircraft, 249
Argue, Maj Mike, 3 PARA, 341, 342, 352, 353, 354, 355
Arlon, 125
Armalite rifle, 301
Armed Police, Aden, 278
Army training regiments, 372
Arnhem, 93–124
Arnold, Capt Kevin, 148 Cdo Fwd Obsn Bty RA, 318
Arnold, CSM, 3 PARA, 242
Arnold's Spur, 242, 243
Arroyo Pedro, River, 341
Artillery pieces: 75mm guns, 72, 88, 141, 142, 178; 75mm pack howitzers, 117, 135; 105mm guns, 350; 105mm pack howitzers, 251, 262, 264, 340; 155mm guns, 343, 351; 5.5in gun, 117
Ascension Island, 305, 367
Ashby, Lt, 6th Para Bn, 149
Ashford, Maj Dick, 2nd Para Bn, 38, 45
Askas, 233
Assam, 168, 171, 172, 185, 189
Assam Divide, The, 166
Assault gun, SU-100, 226
Athens, 152, 153, 154
Athlit, 198
Atkinson, Pte, D (Patrol) Company 3 PARA, 271
Atkinson Field, 272
Atlantic Conveyor, 311, 346
Auchinleck, Field Marshal Sir Claude, C-in-C India, 169, 190
Augusta, 52
Australian Special Air Service, 251
Austrian troops, 45
Avezzano, 149
Awdry, Capt John, 6th Para Bn, 149
Ayios Amvrosios, 219, 220
Ayios Nicholaos, 237
Ayios Theodoros, 233

Badger Hill, 172, 173, 174, 175
Baghdad, 235
Bahrain, 235, 236, 241, 244, 271, 272, 279
Bailey, Cpl, 3 PARA, 353
Bailey bridge, 139
Ba Kelalan, 260
Baker, Capt J. A. S., 12th Para Bn, 88
Bakri Ridge, 242, 244
Balad es Sheik, 207
Balai Ringin, 261
Ball, Maj John, 50th Indian Para Bde MMG Coy, 177, 178
Balloon, parachute training, 27
Baltic, the, 138, 142
Baluchistan, 191
Baluch Regiment, 184
Balui, 250
Bamford, Maj John, 2nd Fwd Obsn Unit RA, 162

Bampfylde, Maj John, 12th Bn Devonshire Regt, 82
Bangalore torpedo, 68
Bangkong, 160
Banjobiroe, 161
Bardsley, L/Cpl, 2 PARA, 327
Bareo, 251
Bari, 20
Barjot, 223
Barker, Lt Gen Sir Evelyn, Comd 8th Br Corps, 138
Barker, Sgt, 2 PARA, 265
Barker, L/Cpl, C (Indep) Coy 2 PARA, 269
Barker, Capt Nick RN, Captain of HMS *Endurance*, 304
Barlow, Col Hilaro, Dep Comd 1st AL Bde, 110
Barnes, Maj Brian, 2 PARA, 261
Barnett, Lt Pat, HQ 1st Para Bde Def Pl, 113
Barrett, Sgt, 2 PARA, 319, 322
Barrow, Capt Gerry, 3rd The King's Own Hussars, 199
Barrow, Maj John, Air Trg Offr HQ The Para Regt, 211
Barry, Lt Jim, 2 PARA, 312, 321, 328, 330, 331, 333, 334, 363
Barry, Lt Peter, 2nd Para Bn, 101
Barry, L/Cpl, 2 PARA, 326
Barton, Lt Mike, 2 PARA, 263
Barton, Cpl, 2 PARA, 364
Basic Parachute Course, 379, 380
Bassein, Creek, 187
Bassey, L/Cpl, 3 PARA, 356
Bastion, hill feature, 184
Bastogne, 125
Batavia, 158, 159
Battle School, 26
Battle training, 28
Baughan, Cpl, 2 PARA, 263, 264
Bavent, 68, 78, 85
Baxter, Sgt, 3 PARA, 241
Bayn Al Gidr, 243
BBC World Service, 316
Beagley, Capt Michael, 3 PARA, 218
Beale, Capt Karl, 3 PARA, 224
Beattie, Sgt, 2 PARA, 330
Beaver aircraft, 251
Bedell Smith, Gen Walter, Chief of Staff to Supreme Allied Commander, 98
Beer Tuyva, 201
Beisan, 204
Beja, 32, 33, 35, 46
Belaga, 255
Belgian Brigade, 85, 90
Belize, 302
Bell, Capt Rod RM, 317, 339, 340
Bellamy, Brig Hugh, Comd 6th AL Bde. Later Comd 1st and 2nd Para Bdes, 129, 200, 206
Bellerophon, 25
Benest, Capt David, 2 PARA, 326
Benouville, 63
Bentley, L/Cpl, 2 PARA, 338
Berbice, River, 272
Beresford, Capt The Lord Patrick, No. 1 (Guards) Indep Coy, 250, 251
Beresford, L/Cpl 2 PARA, 325
Beret, maroon: adoption by Abn Forces, 25; adoption by Gurkha Indep Para Coy on affiliation to The Para Regt, 26; adoption by The Indian Para Regt, 186
Bergen, 129
Bergkirchen, 142
Berlin, 369
Bernhard, Capt Paul, 12th Para Bn, 82, 83

Bersaglieri, 50
Berville-sur-Mer, 90
Bethell, Brig Richard, CRA 23rd Ind Div, 161
Beuzeville, 85, 90
Beverley transport aircraft, 221, 248
Bibby, Lt, 13th Para Bn, 87
Bickerdike, Lt Andrew, 3 PARA, 352, 353, 354
Bilaspur, 189, 190
Bing, CSM, C (Indep) Coy 2 PARA, 268
Bingley, L/Cpl 2 PARA, 321
Binney, Ron, manager of Fitzroy settlement, 346, 347
Bishenpur sector, 183
Bishop, Cpl, 2 PARA, 332, 333
Bittrich, Generalleutnant Willi, Comd 2nd Panzer Corps, 121
Bizerta, 30, 34
Black, Cpl, 3 PARA, 356
Blackburn, Sgt, 2 PARA, 325, 326
Blacker, Brig Cecil, Comd 39 Inf Bde, 241, 242
Blair, Lt Col David, 1st Bn Queen's Own Highlanders, 297
Bland, Cpl, 3 PARA, 356
Blenheim bomber, 168
Blindicide rockets, 277, 278
Bloody Friday, 295
Bloody Sunday, 288–292
Blowpipe surface-to-air missile, 310, 318, 323, 324, 336, 349, 357
Blue Beach Military Cemetery, 367
Blueberry Pie, 2 PARA objective on Wireless Ridge, 362
Bluff Cove, 346, 347, 348, 349
Blundell, Capt G. L., GS03 Int HQ 4th Para Bde, 116
Blunn, Pte Norman, carried out 1,000,000th descent at No. 1 PTS at RAF Abingdon, 378
Bob's Farm, 7th Para Bn objective, 84
Boca House, 316, 318, 322, 323, 324, 327, 329, 330, 337, 338
Bodjong, 159
Boeloe, 160
Bofors anti-aircraft gun, 183
Bois de Bavent, 73, 77, 85
Bois de Mont, 74, 79
Boizenberg, 144
Boland, Pte, 2 PARA, 338, 339
Bols, Maj Gen Eric, GOC 6th Abn Div, 126, 129, 135, 143, 145, 200, 204, 206
Bolt, Cpl, 2 PARA, 335
Bombay, 156
Bond, Lt Col George, 154th Gurkha Para Bn, 168
Bone, 31, 32
Bonner Bay, 309
Bordenau, 142, 143
Border Scouts, 254, 255, 256
Borneo, 245–253, 256–258, 267, 269, 280
Borneo Confrontation, 245, 253, 261, 263, 266, 271
Bou Arada, 43, 46
Boucher, Maj Gen Charles, Comd 2nd Indian Abn Div, 190
Boufarik, 51
Bourg, 90
Bourne, Gen Sir Geoffrey, Dir of Ops during Malay Emergency, 215
Bowler Hat, 2nd Para Bn objective, North Africa, 48
Brackpool, Cpl, 3 PARA, 226
Bradbrooke, Lt Col George, 1st Cdn Para Bn, 59, 71
Bradford, Cpl, 2 PARA, 346

Bradley, Gen Omar, Comd 12th US Army Group, 92, 93
Braithewaite, Maj B. R., 7th Para Bn, 87
Bramall, Field Marshal Sir Edwin, Chief of the General Staff, 367
Brazier, Capt Jock, 9 Para Sqn RE, 224
Brebner, Pte, 3 PARA, 356
Breda machine-gun, 220
Bredin, Lt Col H. E. N. 'Bala', 2 PARA, 218, 230
Bren carrier, 79, 132, 182, 226
Bren light machine-gun, 34, 75, 87, 101, 255
Brennan, Maj Mike, Bde Maj 5th Para Bde, 134
Brereton, Flt Sgt Bill, later Wg Cdr, 94, 95
Brereton, Lt Gen Louis, Comd 1st Allied Airborne Army, 94, 95
Bresling, Pte, 2 PARA, 334
Breville, 75, 76, 80, 81, 84
Brewer, Lt, 12th Para Bn, 82
Brierley, Maj Geoffrey, 1 PARA, 275
Brindisi, 20
Britain, 193, 213, 214, 217, 221, 232, 235, 241, 265, 267, 279, 304
British Antarctic Survey, 303

British Army:
Bde of Gurkhas, 254
British Army of The Rhine (BAOR), 208, 211, 369, 372
HQ British Troops in Palestine & Transjordan, 202
HQ GOC North Sector Palestine, 208
HQ South Palestine District, 203
1st Army, 30, 32, 37, 38, 40, 42
1st Allied Abn Army, 93, 98
2nd Army, 61, 92, 93, 97, 98, 118, 120, 123
8th Army, 52, 148, 154, 155
14th Army 185, 189
15th Army Gp, 146, 147
21st Army Gp, 92, 93, 97, 98, 144
1st Abn Corps, 94, 95, 98, 124, 189, 190
1st Corps, 61, 76, 80, 84, 85
5th Corps, 42, 43, 48, 51
8th Corps, 128, 138, 142, 144
12th Corps, 128, 129, 130
13th Corps, 52
30th Corps, 61, 97, 103, 113, 118, 120, 122, 124, 128, 129, 130
1st Abn Div, 13, 14, 24, 25, 30, 51, 52, 56, 57, 64, 93–124, 146, 210, 211
1st Inf Div, 195, 204
1st (UK) Armd Div, 380
3rd Inf Div, 61, 204
3rd (UK) Div, 369, 380
4th Inf Div, 154
5th Inf Div, 144
6th Abn Div, 58–91, 96, 99, 125–145, 156, 164, 189, 193–209, 210, 211
6th Armd Div, 43, 46, 164
7th Armd Div, 83
11th Armed Div, 83, 138
15th Scottish Div, 142, 144
16th Abn Div (TA), 210, 371
17th Gurkha Div, 246
36th Inf Div, 170
43rd Inf Div, 118, 119, 120, 122, 124
46th Inf Div, 46, 49
49th Inf Div, 84, 90
51st Highland Div, 76, 82, 84, 200
78th Inf Div, 43
Guards Armd Div, 83, 124
1st Para Bde, 23–26, 30–37, 42–57,

97–124, 200–208
1st Airlanding Bde, 24, 52, 57, 94–124
1st Cdo Bde, 130, 144
1st Guards Bde, 148, 208, 209
1st Special Service Bde, 60, 63, 66, 72, 73, 78, 80–85, 90
1 Mech Bde, 380
2nd Para Bde, 25, 30, 52, 56, 57, 146–155, 166, 193, 196, 202–206, 210
2nd Indep Para Bde Gp, 57, 146–155
3rd Para Bde, 51, 52, 58, 61–67, 73, 79–86, 88–91, 126, 129, 130, 133, 135, 136, 138, 139, 142, 144, 145, 193, 196–199, 202, 204, 206, 207, 208
3rd Inf Bde, 298
4th Para Bde, 51, 52, 56, 57, 97, 100–124, 166
4th Para Bde (TA), 210, 371
4th Armed Bde, 54, 55
4th Special Service Bde, 83, 85, 90
5th Para Bde, 58, 63–65, 73, 79, 80, 83, 84–91, 126, 129, 132–136, 140, 142, 144, 156–164, 193, 200, 211, 262
5th Para Bde (TA), 210, 371
5 Inf Bde, 308, 343, 345, 349, 360
5 Abn Bde, 369, 379, 380, 381
6th Indep Para Bde, 190
6th Para Bde (TA), 210, 371
6th Airlanding Bde, 58, 63, 73, 85, 90, 129, 134, 135, 138, 139, 142, 193, 196–198, 200, 206
6th Guards Tk Bde, 128
6 Fd Force, 368, 369
8 Fd Force, 369
8 Inf Bde, 288, 291, 298
12th Inf Bde, 154
15th Inf Bde, 144
16th Indep Para Bde, 210, 211, 213, 214, 218, 219, 220, 232, 233, 234
16 Para Bde, 244, 246, 251, 292, 293, 368
19 Mech Bde, 380
23rd Armd Bde, 151, 152, 154
24 Airmob Bde, 380
26th Armd Brigade, 45
31st Indep Inf Bde, 24
36th Inf Bde, 43, 49
39 Inf Bde, 241, 283, 286, 287, 296
44th Para Bde (TA), 371
44th Indep Para Bde Gp (TA), 371
45th Para Bde (TA), 371
46th Para Bde (TA), 371
44 (V) Para Bde, 368
129th Inf Bde, 123
130th Inf Bde, 120, 122
138th Inf Bde, 49
139th Inf Bde, 45, 47, 48
153rd Inf Bde, 76
Aden Bde, 273
Central Bde – Borneo Confrontation, 270
Craforce, 208, 209
Pompforce, 152, 153
Radforce, 238, 241, 244
Airborne Forces: 292, 368, 372, 375, 381
Abn Forces Battle School, 26, 27
Abn Forces Depot, 25, 26, 58, 210
Abn Forces Development Centre, 58
Abn Forces Golden Jubilee Appeal, 378
Abn Trg Sch, Aqir, 200
Army Air Corps, 24, 26, 211
Commander Abn Establishments, 58, 210
Depot Sch Abn Forces, 374

Glider Pilot Regt, 24, 26, 211
HQ Abn Establishments, 211
Parachute Contingency Force (PCF), 368
Parachute Course Admin Unit (PCAU), 368, 376
P Company, 374–376
1st Airlanding Lt Regt RA, 54, 99, 100, 103, 106, 112, 116, 120, 122
2nd Airlanding A/Tk Bty RA, 100
2nd Airlanding A/Tk Regt RA, 135
2nd Fwd Obsn Unit RA, 132, 156, 162
3rd Airlanding Lt Bty RA, 112
4th Airlanding A/Tk Bty RA, 66, 143, 156, 162
53rd (Worcestershire Yeomanry) Airlanding Lt Regt RA, 67, 82, 84, 135
33rd Para Lt Regt RA, 213, 224
7 PARA Regt RHA, 368, 369, 374
159th Para Lt Regt RA, 186
300th Airlanding A/Tk Bty RA, 146, 151
Abn Lt Tk Sqn, 52
6th Abn Armd Recce Regt, 63, 89, 90, 135, 136, 138, 197, 200
1st Abn Recce Sqn, 99, 100, 102, 114, 118
Para Sqn RAC, 294
No. 1 Air Tp RE, 23
1st Para Sqn RE, 13, 32, 35, 37, 40, 46, 53, 99, 102
1st Abn Sqn RE, 209
2nd Para Sqn RE, 146, 152
3rd Para Sqn RE, 51, 69, 78, 86, 130
3rd Abn Sqn RE, 156, 162, 163
4th Para Sqn RE, 51, 100
9 Para Sqn RE, 220, 223, 224, 227, 230, 310, 312, 327, 342, 347, 350, 351, 357, 367
9th Fd Coy RE, 99, 102
12th Para Sqn RE, 186
591st Para Sqn RE, 64, 65, 132, 139, 140, 144
216 Para Sigs Sqn, 369, 370
16th Para Fd Amb, 32, 36, 37, 39, 42, 99
23 Para Fd Amb, 224, 226, 228, 368, 369
127th Para Fd Amb, 146, 149
133rd Para Fd Amb, 51, 100
181st Airlanding Fd Amb, 99
224th Para Fd Amb, 51, 67, 71, 130, 132
225th Para Fd Amb, 132, 156, 162
1st Para Log Regt, 368
16 Hvy Drop Coy RAOC, 368
5 Abn Bde Log Bn, 369

The Parachute Regiment:
Para Regt, The, 18, 26, 186, 210, 211, 214, 215, 216, 271, 281, 283, 292, 302, 339, 369, 374, 375, 376, 379, 381
HQ The Para Regt, 210, 211
Para Regt Trg Centre, 211
Holding Bn, 210
Regimental Colonel, 372
RHQ The Para Regt, 372, 373, 376
Regt Trg Team, 373
Depot The Para Regt & Abn Forces, 372, 373, 374, 376, 378, 379
Para Regt Battle School, 376, 377
Para Regt Group (PRG), 372
Junior Para Coy, 373
Red Devils, The, 373, 377, 378
No. 2 Cdo, 19
11th SAS Bn, 20–23

X Troop 11th SAS Bn, 21, 22
1st Para Bn, 23, 25, 31–35, 43–48, 50–55, 100–124, 200, 216, 218
1st (Guards) Para Bn, 206–210
1st Bn The Para Regt (1 PARA), 210, 211, 213, 219, 232, 234–237, 283–295, 302, 368, 369
2nd Para Bn, 13, 14, 23, 24, 31, 36–39, 42, 45–57, 99–124, 199, 200, 206
2nd Bn The Para Regt (2 PARA), 18, 210, 211, 214, 218, 219, 223, 229, 230, 233, 234, 235, 236, 261–267, 273, 292–298, 302, 304, 305, 308–312, 314–340, 344, 345–350, 355, 359–366, 367–370
3rd Para Bn, 31, 32, 46–55, 99–124, 198, 200, 206
3rd Bn The Para Regt (3 PARA), 210–220, 222–228, 232, 234–244, 272, 293, 297–302, 304, 305, 308, 310–312, 340–345, 350–359, 360–362, 365–370
2nd/3rd Bn The Para Regt, 206, 207, 208
4th Para Bn, 24, 25, 56, 146–154, 166, 199, 206
4th (Volunteer) Bn The Para Regt (4 PARA (V)), 368, 372
5th (Scottish) Para Bn, 25, 56, 146–154, 201, 206, 210
6th (Royal Welch) Para Bn, 25, 56, 146–154, 201, 206
4th/6th Para Bn, 206, 210
7th (Light Infantry) Para Bn, 51, 58, 64–66, 73, 80, 84–86, 132–134, 137, 143, 156
8th (Midlands) Para Bn, 51, 58, 64, 66, 69, 73, 77, 84–86, 130, 138, 139, 142, 197, 198, 200, 200–206
9th (Eastern & Home Counties) Para Bn, 51, 58, 64, 66, 68, 70, 73–76, 79, 85, 86, 130, 132, 138, 139, 142, 186, 201, 203, 206
8th/9th Para Bn, 206–208
10th Para Bn, 51, 56, 108–124
10th (City of London) Bn The Para Regt (TA), 371
10th (Volunteer) Bn The Para Regt (10 PARA (V)), 372
11th Para Bn, 51, 57, 108–124
11th Bn The Para Regt (TA), 371
12th (Yorkshire) Para Bn, 59, 65, 66, 73, 79, 81–83, 86, 88, 133, 137, 140, 142, 143, 156, 161, 163, 200, 224, 262
12th (Yorkshire) Bn The Para Regt (TA), 371
13th (Lancashire) Para Bn, 59, 64, 65, 73, 79, 80, 86–89, 126, 127, 133, 134, 137, 141
13th (Lancashire) Bn The Para Regt (TA), 371
12th/13th (Yorks & Lancs) Bn The Para Regt (TA), 371
14th Bn The Para Regt (TA), 371
15th Para Bn, 186, 187
15th (Scottish) Bn The Para Regt (TA), 371
15th (Scottish Volunteer) Bn The Para Regt (15 PARA (V)), 372
16th Para Bn, 186
17th Para Bn, 200, 371
17th (DLI) Bn The Para Regt (TA), 371
18th Bn The Para Regt (TA), 371
151st Para Bn, 51, 165, 166
156th Para Bn, 51, 56, 109–124, 166
21st Indep Para Coy, 59, 99, 100, 108, 116, 118, 200

22nd Indep Para Coy, 59, 64, 81, 83, 84, 127, 156
1st Indep Para P1, 150
16th (Guards) Indep Coy PARA, 210
No. 1 (Guards) Indep Coy PARA, 210, 211, 219, 220, 223, 226, 230, 232, 234, 244, 246, 248, 249, 250
16th (Volunteer) Indep Coy PARA, 372
5 Abn Bde Pathfinder P1, 369, 378
Indep Para Sqn, 215, 216
Gurkha Indep Para Coy, 246, 250, 254–261
C (Indep) Coy 2 PARA, 267, 269
C (Patrol) Coy 2 PARA, 271, 272
D (Patrol) Coy 3 PARA, 269, 270, 271
Wartime airlanding battalions:
1st Bn The Border Regt, 110, 116, 117, 121
1st Bn The Royal Ulster Rifles, 59, 83, 91, 130, 135, 140, 197
2nd Bn The Black Watch, 186
2nd Bn The Oxfordshire & Buckinghamshire Light Infantry, 59, 61–65, 90, 126, 130
2nd Bn The South Staffordshire Regt, 52, 100–119
7th Bn The King's Own Scottish Borderers, 109, 116, 117
12th Bn The Devonshire Regt, 59, 73, 81–83, 130, 135
Infantry battalions converted to wartime parachute role:
1st Bn The King's Regt, 186
1st Bn The South Staffordshire Regt, 186
2nd/4th Bn The South Lancashire Regt, 59
5th Bn The Royal Hampshire Regt (TA), 371
7th Bn The Queen's Own Cameron Highlanders, 25
8th Bn The Middlesex Regt (DCO) (TA), 371
9th Bn The Durham Light Infantry (TA), 371
10th Bn The Essex Regt, 51
10th Bn The Somerset Light Infantry, 51
10th Bn The Green Howards, 59
10th Bn The Royal Welch Fusiliers, 25
13th Bn The Royal Warwickshire Regt, 51
Commando Units:
No. 1 Cdo, 42, 48
No. 3 Cdo, 68
No. 6 Cdo, 32, 69, 81
No. 9 Cdo, 153
29 Cdo Lt Regt RA, 308
8 (Alma) Cdo Bty RA, 313, 314, 318, 322, 324, 327, 329, 339
7 (Sphinx) Cdo Bty RA, 343
79 (Kirkee) Cdo Bty RA, 343, 351, 354, 355
148 (Meiktila) Cdo Fwd Obsn Bty RA, 307, 308, 354
59 Indep Cdo Sqn RE, 318, 343, 350
Special Forces:
Malayan Scouts, 214
Special Air Service (SAS), 57
21 SAS Regt (Artists') (TA), 214
22 SAS Regt, 214–216, 238, 239, 245, 247, 250, 251, 253, 257, 267, 268, 306–308, 310–313, 361
G Sqn 22 SAS Regt, 253
Special Boat Squadron, 57, 152
Infantry:
1st Bn The Royal Ulster Rifles, 247
1st Bn The Devonshire Regt, 184

1st Bn Irish Guards, 208, 273
1st Bn Welsh Guards, 296, 345, 348, 367
1st Bn The Gloucestershire Regt, 236
1st Bn The Rifle Brigade, 236
1st Bn Somerset & Cornwall Light Infantry, 273
1st Bn South Wales Borderers, 275
1st Bn Royal Northumberland Fusiliers, 275
1st Bn The Lancashire Fusiliers, 214, 272
1st Bn The Lancashire Regt, 275, 276
1st Bn The King's Own Royal Border Regt, 275
1st Bn The Cameronians (The Scottish Rifles), 234
1st Bn The Gordon Highlanders, 232
1st Bn The Argyll & Sutherland Highlanders, 261, 275
1st Bn The Queen's Own Highlanders, 254, 297
1st Bn The Royal Scots, 244, 298
1st Bn Prince of Wales' Own Regt of Yorkshire, 296
1st Bn The King's Regt, 296
1st Bn The Royal West Kent Regt, 231
1st Bn The Suffolk Regt, 232, 233
1st Bn The Light Infantry, 292, 296
2nd Bn Scots Guards, 348, 360, 364, 366, 367
2nd Bn The Queen's Regt, 283, 286, 295
2nd Bn The Light Infantry, 283
2nd Bn The East Surrey Regt, 204
2nd Bn The Middlesex Regt, 206
2nd Bn Royal Regiment of Fusiliers, 296
2nd/5th Bn The Leicestershire Regt, 48
3rd Bn The Queen's Regt, 295
3rd Bn Royal Anglian Regt, 296
3rd Bn The Light Infantry, 283
3rd Bn Grenadier Guards, 44
4th Bn The Buffs, 43
4th Bn The Dorsetshire Regt, 121, 122
5th Bn The Black Watch, 76, 79
5th Bn The Dorsetshire Regt, 121, 122
5th Bn The Duke of Cornwall's Light Infantry, 119, 120, 121
5th Bn The Sherwood Foresters, 47
9th Bn The Durham Light Infantry, 55
10th Bn The Rifle Brigade, 148
Green Jackets Brigade, 211
King's Royal Rifle Corps, 163
Royal West Kent Regt, 43
West Yorkshire Regt, 182
2nd King Edward VII's Own Goorkhas, 255, 256
6th Queen Elizabeth's Own Gurkha Rifles, 254, 256
7th Duke of Edinburgh's Own Gurkha Rifles, 256, 260, 261, 345, 360, 367
10th Princess Mary's Own Gurkha Rifles, 254, 256
13 Air Contact Team, 224, 225
Guards Division, 377
Guards Depot, 373
Gurkha battalion – element of 5 Abn Bde, 369
Gurkha Signals, 256, 257
Jungle Warfare School, 215, 246,

256, 257, 261, 270
School of Infantry – NCOs Tactics Division, 373, 376, 377
Armour & Reconnaissance:
15th (Scottish) Div Recce Regt, 143
56th Recce Regt, 37
Blues & Royals, The, 342, 343, 344, 350, 360, 361–364, 366, 367
Household Cavalry – element of 5 Abn Bde, 369
Life Guards, The, 296
1st The King's Dragoon Guards, 205
1st The Queen's Dragoon Guards, 275
3rd The King's Own Hussars, 197, 199, 200, 204, 207, 208
3rd Tank Bn Scots Guards, 128, 135, 136
4th Tank Bn Grenadier Guards, 139, 140, 143
4th Royal Tank Regt, 213
6th Royal Tank Regt, 230, 231
12th Lancers, 204
13th/18th Royal Hussars, 80–83
15th/19th King's Royal Hussars, 294
17th/21st Lancers, 205, 207, 208
Royal Scots Greys, 145
Queen's Own Hussars, 278
Fife & Forfar Yeomanry, 126
Inns of Court Regt, 138
Artillery:
1st Regt RHA, Chestnut Troop, 208
4th Fd Regt RA, 305, 369
17th Fd Regt RA, 43, 44
17th Fd Bty RA, 234
19th Fd Regt RA, 296
23rd Lt AA / A/Tk Regt RA, 186
29 (Corunna) Fd Bty RA, 347, 368
266 OP Bty (V) RA, 372
54th Bty RA, 294
64th Med Regt RA, 117
64th Lt Bty RA, 151
129th Fd Bty RA, 182
T Bty (Shah Sujah's Troop) RA, 308
Army Air Corps, 243, 251
656 Sqn AAC, 305, 310, 346, 366
Army Physical Training Corps, 19, 26, 147
Border Scouts, 250, 254, 255, 256
Corps of Military Police, 146
Intelligence Centre, 270
Royal Army Medical Corps, 16 Fd Amb, 348, 349.
Royal Army Service Corps, 19, 60, 118, 162
63 Coy RASC, 224
Royal Artillery, 262
Royal Corps of Signals, 372
Royal Corps of Transport, 60 Sqn RCT, 276
Royal Electrical & Mechanical Engineers, 146, 244
Royal Engineers, 340
Royal Military Academy Sandhurst, 214
Royal Military Police, 232, 290
Royal Military School of Music, 212
Territorial Army, 371–372, 379, 380
Ulster Defence Regiment, 283

British Government, 193, 194, 197, 246, 279, 282
British Guiana, 272
British Mandate in Palestine, 193, 208
British Military Hospital, Singapore, 257
Britten-Norman Islander G-ORED, Red Devils aircraft, 377

Brodie, Brig Tom, Comd 14th AL Bde, 186
Bromley-Martin, Maj P. E., Bde Maj 1st Para Bde, 23
Brooke, Gen Sir Alan, Chief of General Staff, 25
Brooke, Capt Tom, No. 1 (Guards) Indep Coy, 249, 251
Brooke, Pte, 2 PARA, 323
Brown, Lt, 8th Para Bn, 70
Brown, Cpl, 3 PARA, 344
Brown, Capt Chris, 148 Cdo Fwd Obsn Bty RA, 307
Browning, Maj Gen F. A. M. 'Boy', GOC 1st Abn Div. Later Maj Gen Abn Tps. Subsequently Lt Gen, Comd 1st Abn Corps, Chief of Staff to Supreme Allied Commander S. E. Asia. Col of The Indian Para Regt. Comptroller of Royal Household post-war, 13, 14, 24, 25, 43, 51, 61, 94, 98, 118, 120, 169, 170, 186, 211
Browning Barracks, 373
Browning .50 cal heavy machine-gun, 136, 359
Browning .30 machine-gun, 276
Brunei, 245, 246, 251, 260, 267, 271
Brunei Rebellion, 246, 254
Brunen, 130, 135, 136
Bruneval, raid on, 13–18
Brunnette, Lt Jack, 1st Cdn Para Bn, 132
Buchanan, Lt, 2nd Para Bn, 37
Bucher, Maj Frank, 12th Para Bn, 133, 141, 143
Buckley, Maj Kemmis, No. 1 (Guards) Indep Coy, 219
Buenos Aires, 303
Bukit Lima Camp, 248, 268
Bullock, Sgt, 2 PARA, 328
Burch, 136
Bure, 126
Bures, 63, 85, 86
Burke, Maj Jim, 2 PARA, 236
Burkinshaw, Lt Phil, 12th Para Bn, 133, 140
Burlison, Maj John, 1st Bn 2nd KEO Goorkhas, 255
Burma, 165, 166, 171, 187, 188, 189
Burnett, Lt Col 'Bunny', 1st Bn 10th PMO Gurkha Rifles, 257
Burns, Lt Robbie, 9 Para Sqn RE, 351
Burntside House, 313, 316, 318, 320, 329, 346
Burston, L/Cpl, C (Indep) Coy 2 PARA, 268
Burt, Pte, 3 PARA, 353
Burwash, Lt, 3rd Para Bn, 107
Butchard, Maj Harry, 153rd Gurkha Para Bn, 181, 182
Butgenbach, 125
Butler, Brig Mervyn 'Tubby', Comd 16 Indep Para Bde. Later Gen Sir Mervyn , Col Comdt The Para Regt, 218, 220, 221, 223, 224, 227, 230, 232
Butler, Maj Pat, 3 PARA, 342
BV 202 'Bandwagon' tracked vehicle, 356

Cable & Wireless, Port Stanley, 303
Cabourg, 67, 85
Caen, 62, 84
Caen Canal, 61, 64, 79
Cain, Maj Robert, 2nd Bn South Staffs Regt, 112, 119
Cairo, 213, 221
Callaghan, Lt Mike, Gurkha Indep Para Coy, 256, 258
Calloway, Sgt, 3rd Para Bn, 119

Calvert, Maj Dan, 4th Para Bn, 151
Cameron Highlands, 216
Cameron's Point, 311
Camilla Creek, 316, 318, 320
Camilla Creek House, 313–317, 320, 324, 326, 327, 337, 340
Camp, Cpl, 2 PARA, 322
Campania, 21
Campbell, Lt James, 12th Para Bn, 82
Campbell, F/Sgt RAF, No. 1 Para Trg Sch. Later Airldg Sch., 169
Campbellpur, 166, 170
Canadian Army:
  1st Canadian Army, 85, 127
  2nd Canadian Corps, 128
  1st Canadian Para Bn, 59, 64, 66, 70, 71, 73, 77, 85, 86, 130, 131, 132, 136, 138, 139, 142, 145, 193
  Royal 22nd Regt, 237
Canberra, SS, 304, 305, 308
Canberra bomber, 225, 343, 365
Cane, Lt Peter, 2nd Para Bn, 101
Canterra House, 312, 313
Cap Badge, Radforce objective, 238–241
Caraher, Pte, 3 PARA, 311
Carl Gustav 84mm Medium Anti-Tank Weapon, 304, 320, 352, 358
Carnegie-Brown, Capt Mark, No. 1 (Guards) Indep Coy, 251
Carrier, Sgt, 22nd Indep Para Coy, 127
Carver, L/Cpl, 3 PARA, 352, 355
Casoli, 147
Cassels, Maj Gen James, GOC 6th Abn Div, 199, 201, 203
Cassino, 148
Castelfrentano, 146, 147
Catfish Box, def posn at Kohima, 182
Cattell, Lt Peter, 12th Para Bn, 134
Cavenagh, Capt Sandy, RMO 3 PARA, 226
Cecil, Lt The Hon Henry, 2nd Para Bn, 39
Celle, 144
Centurion tank, 214
Ceritos Arroyo, 316, 318
Ceritos House, 313
Chakabama, 170
Chaklala, 166, 169, 187, 188, 190
Chambers, Maj Gen H. M., GOC 26th Ind Div, 189
Champion Lines, Aden, 276, 277
Chapman, Lt Clyde, 2 PARA, 320, 327, 346
Chapple, Wg Cdr J. H. D., Airldg Sch, 165
Charlton, Maj Eddie, 9th Para Bn, 75
Charteris, Lt Euen, 2nd Para Bn, 14, 16, 40
Château d'Amfreville, 69, 74
Château de Benouville, 65
Château de Heaume, 73
Château de Varaville, 71
Château St Come, 74, 76
Château-Jobert, Col, 2e RPC, 223, 226, 227
Chaundler, Lt David, D (Patrol) Coy 3 PARA. Later Lt Col, 2 PARA. Subsequently Brig, Comd 5 Abn Bde, 270, 347, 350, 360, 362, 364
Checkpoint Gold, Aden, 275
Checkpoint Juliet, 277
Cherbourg Peninsula, 61
Chesterfield, 26
Cheylus, 37
Chin Hills, 170
Chindwin, River, 170, 171, 172, 176, 184

Chinese 5th Army, 168
Chinook helicopter, 312, 336, 346
Chiswell, Maj Peter, D (Patrol) Coy 3 PARA, 269, 270
Chitral, SS, 156
Chivers, L/Cpl, D (Patrol) Coy 3 PARA, 270, 271
Churchill, Winston, 19
Churchill tank, 135, 139, 140, 141, 143
Clancy, Capt John, 1st Cdn Para Bn, 131
Clandestine Communist Organisation (CCO), Borneo, 246, 248
Clansman radios, 305
Clark, Maj Nobby, 13th Para Bn, 87, 89
Claymore mine, 259, 261
Cleasby-Thompson, Maj Peter, 1st Para Bn, 34
Cleaver, Maj Frank, 2nd Para Bn, 39
Clements, Lt Col Johnny, 1st Bn 2nd KEO Goorkhas, 256
Clements, Pte, 3 PARA, 224
Cleminson, Lt James, 3rd Para Bn, 104, 107
Cluff, Capt Algy, No. 1 (Guards) Indep Coy, 249, 250
Coates, Lt Peter, 3 PARA, 224
Coca Cola, Radforce objective, 241
Coe, 2/Lt Mark, 319, 322, 324, 366
Coesfield, 138
Colbeck, Sgt, 3 PARA, 358
Cole, Cpl, 2 PARA, 334
Collett, Maj David, 3 PARA, 342, 355, 356
Collingwood, Maj Bill, Bde Maj 3rd Para Bde, 66
Collinson-Jones, Capt John, 2 PARA, 265
Cologne, 92
Colquhon, Brig C. H., CRA 6th Abn Div, 208
Commando Hill, 43
Communist Terrorists (CTs), Malaya, 214, 216
Connor, Lt Colin, 2 PARA, 315, 317, 347
Connor, Cpl, 2 PARA, 320
Conron, Maj, 1st Para Bn, 35
Constitution Square, Athens, 154
Conway, Lt, 5th Para Bn, 154
Cooper, Capt The Revd David, Padre 2 PARA, 309, 340, 366
Corby, Maj Bill, 5th Para Bn, 150
Coreth, Lt Mark, Blues & Royals, 342
Cork, Cpl, 2 PARA, 321
Cork Wood, 50
Coronation Point, 316, 318, 321
Cos, Island of, 57
Coulson, Capt Alan, 2 PARA, 305, 312, 317, 317, 339
Coventry, Maj Dudley, Indep Para Sqn, 215
Cox, Flt Sgt RAF, Bruneval raid, 15, 16
Cox, Pte, 2 PARA, 332
Cox, Pte, 3 PARA, 355
Cox, Lt Mark, 3 PARA, 352, 355
Coxall, Pte, 2 PARA, 335
Coxen, Capt Gavin, 2 PARA, 265, 266
Coxen, Capt H. B. 'Vic', 1st Para Bn. Later Lt Col 4th Para Bn. Subsequently Col and Regtl Col, 44, 151, 153
Cramphorn, Maj John, 13th Para Bn, 65, 87
Crater, 274

Crawford, Lt, 5th Para Bde Sigs Sect, 134
Crawley, Lt, later Maj, Douglas, 2nd Para Bn, 40, 99, 101, 103, 114
Cripps, L/Cpl, 3 PARA, 358
Crocker, Lt Gen Sir John, Comd 1st Br Corps, 61, 76, 84, 90
Croker, Maj E. J. O'B. 'Rip', 12th Para Bn, 88, 134
Cromwell tank, 89, 90
Crook, Lt C. E., 12th Para Bn, 133
Crook, Lt Col Paul, 3 PARA, 217, 222, 223, 225, 226, 228, 229, 232
Crookenden, Lt Col Napier, 9th Para Bn, 132, 139, 145
Crosland, Maj John, 2 PARA, 320, 321, 327, 328, 336, 346, 360, 362, 366
Cross, Maj John, Border Scouts. Later Gurkha Indep Para Coy, 256, 258, 259, 260
Crosthwaite, Maj Ivor, 4th Tank Bn Gren Gds, 143
Crow, Pte, 3 PARA, 355
CS gas, 282, 289, 290
Cubbon, Maj Gen John, Comd British forces in Aden, 241
Cunningham, RSM, 9th Para Bn, 74
Cyprus, 200, 205, 213, 214, 216, 217, 219, 221, 223, 231, 232, 233, 234, 235, 236, 244
Cyrenaica, 193

Daily Express, 357
Daily Mail, 339
Dakota, C-47 transport aircraft, 30, 31, 54, 95, 111, 112, 118, 130, 169, 170, 188
Daly, Capt G. F. K. RE, att 11th SAS Bn, 21, 22, 23
Dan, 207
Dance, L/Cpl, 2 PARA, 320
Dane, Bdr, 7th Para Regt RHA, 272
Daniell, Lt Col A. W. E., 16th Para Bn. Later Col, Regtl Col, 186
Daniels, Maj John, 2 PARA, 261
Darke, Pte, 3 PARA, 356
Darling, Lt Col Ken, 12th Para Bn. Later Brig, Comd 5th Para Bde. Comdt Abn Forces Depot and Regt. Subsequently Regt Col The Para Regt. Later Brig, Comd 16th Indep Para Bde. Subsequently Lt Gen Sir Kenneth, Col Comdt The Para Regt, 133, 137, 140, 142, 143, 211, 213
Darwin, 308, 310, 312, 313, 315, 316, 317, 318, 323, 327, 330, 340, 366
Darwin Hill, 322, 366
Davidoff, Constantino, Argentinian scrap merchant, 303
Davies, Sgt, 1st Cdn Para Bn, 72
Davis, Lt Col Bobby, 80th Para Fd Amb, 180
Dawnay, Lt Col Richard, 2 PARA, 279
Dawson, Maj C. W. B., Bde Maj 4th Para Bde, 116
Deane Drummond, Lt, 11th SAS Bn. Later Maj. 1st Abn Div Sigs, 21
De Burgh Morris, Brig, Comd 49th Ind Inf Bde, 159
De Klee, Capt Murray, No. 1 (Guards) Indep Coy. Later Maj, G Sqn 22 SAS, 223, 226, 227, 253
De la Billière, Maj Peter, 22 SAS, 268
De la Haye, Lt Robin, 50th Ind Para Bde, 179
Delaney, Lt Ginger, 12th Para Bn, 134
De Latour, Lt Bob, 22nd Indep Para Coy, 84
Delhi, 166, 171
Demarara, 272
Dempsey Gen Sir Miles, Comd 2nd Br Army. Later C-in-C Allied Land Forces S. E. Asia, 92, 128
Den Brink, 103, 106, 112
Dennis, Pte, 3 PARA, 356
Dennison, Maj Peter, 3 PARA, 357, 358
Dennison, Maj Mervyn, 3rd Para Bn, 106
Dent, Capt Chris, 2 PARA, 325
Depienne, 37
Dering Lines, Brecon, 376
Derwent Valley, 85
De Ruyter Van Stevenick, Lt Col A. C., Comd Princess Irene of The Netherlands Bde, 85
Des Voeux, Maj Sir Richard, LO att 1st Para Bn. Later Lt Col. 156th Para Bn, 33, 116
Devonshire, Duke of, 26
Dey, Pte, 2 PARA, 322
Dhala, 272
Dhala Road, 237, 238
Dhanaba Basin, 238, 239, 241
Dhekelia, Sovereign, Base Area, 221, 236, 244
Diesfordterwald, 128, 129
Dimapur, 183
Dinant, 126
Dinjan, 167
Dives, River, 63, 67, 71, 85, 86
Dives Canal, 85
Divette, River, 71
Dixon, Capt Robin, No. 1 (Guards) Indep Coy, 249
Dixon, Pte, 2 PARA, 332
Djakarta, 158
Djebel Abiad, 48
Djebel Alliliga, 44
Djebel Bel, 47
Djebel el Mengoub, 41
Djebel Mansour, 44
Djebel Salah, 45
Djebel Sidi Bou Hadjeba, 39, 41
Djomblang, 160
Dobie, Maj, later Lt Col, David. 1st Para Bn, 50, 100, 105, 106, 108, 109, 111
Dobson, Sgt, 12th Para Bn, 134
Dockerell, Maj Geoffrey, 1 PARA, 236
Dorey, Maj Roy, 2 PARA, 230
Dortmund-Ems Canal, 139, 140
Douglas Settlement, 341
Dover, Capt, later Maj, Victor. 2nd Para Bn, 49, 53, 56
Dowd, Les, Reuters correspondent, 357
Down, Lt Col Eric, 1st Para Bn. Subsequently Brig, Comd 2nd Para Bde. Later Maj Gen, GOC 44th Ind Abn Div (later 2nd Ind Abn Div), 47, 56, 185, 190
Dozule, 67, 85, 86
Dracos, Markos, EOKA terrorist, 233
Drake Group, C Coy 2nd Para Bn, Bruneval raid, 14, 15, 16
Drama, 153
Driel, 119, 120
Drunken Rock Pass, 361
Drury, Sgt RE, att 11th SAS Bn, 22
Dublin, 299
DUKWs, 119, 120
Du Maurier, Daphne, 25
Dunbar, Maj Charles, Bde Maj 16th Indep Para Bde, 224
Dunbar, Cpl, 2 PARA, 327
Dunlop, Lt Col A., 5th Para Bn, 25
Dunning, Maj Jim, 2 PARA, 227
Durbin, CSM, 7th Para Bn, 84
Dutch Resistance, 95, 98
Dyer, Maj Ian, 9th Para Bn, 76

Eadie, Maj, later Lt Col, Fraser. 1st Cdn Para Bn, 131, 136
East Falkland, 341
Easton, Lt, 152nd Ind Para Bn, 174, 175
Eberhardie, Lt Col Ted, 2 PARA, 261, 264, 267
E-boat, 18
Echternach, 125
EDES, Greek royalist faction, 151, 153
Edessa, 153
Edinburgh, 302
Edwards, Lt Col Dick, 3rd Bn 10th PMO Gurkha Rifles, 160
Edwards, Capt Robin, 22 SAS, 239
Egan, Father, Padre 2nd Para Bn, 113
Egypt, 193, 204, 205, 213, 214, 219, 220, 223, 234, 238, 274
Egyptian Air Force, 221
Eifel, 125
Eindhoven, 94, 97, 124
Ein Shemer, 200
Eire, Irish Republic, 298
Eisenhower, Gen Dwight, Supreme Allied Comd Later President of the United States, 30, 93, 98, 149, 219
El Aouina airfield, 32
El Aroussa, 43
ELAS, Greek Communist faction, 151, 154
Elbe, River, 138, 144
Elbe-Trave Canal, 144
El Cap, 231, 232
Elephant Point, 187–189
El Gamil airfield, 222, 226
Elliott, Capt Malcolm, 23 Para Fd Amb, 228
El Naqil, 240, 241
El Qantara, 223, 230
El Raswa, 223, 226, 230
El Tina, 232
Eltringham, Pte, 2 PARA, 266
Emmerich, 127, 128
Empire Lifeguard, troopship, 206
Empress of Australia, troopship, 208, 209
Empress of Scotland, troopship, 208
Ems, River, 138
Enfidaville, 36
England, 208, 209, 219, 232, 234, 237, 253, 273, 279, 280, 296, 301
Enosis, 216, 217
EOKA, Cypriot terrorist organisation, 216–220, 233
Episkopi, Sovereign Base Area, 244
Erle, 136, 137
Escaut Canal, 92
Escoville, 77
Esro Building, Port Stanley, 366
Estancia, 342, 343
Estancia House, 343, 344
Eupen, 125
Eureka, pathfinding radio beacon, 59, 66, 100, 112, 150
Europic Ferry, 305
Evans, Dvr, No. 2 Cdo, 19
Evans, Lt, 6th Para Bn, 149
Evans, Cpl, 2 PARA, 315, 316, 339
Evans, Pte, 3 PARA, 356
Ewing, Piper, 2nd Para Bn, 151
Exocet missile, 311
Exodus, Jewish refugee ship, 205, 206
Ezra Bitsaron, 201

Faisal, King of Iraq, 233
Falaise, 84
Fallschirmjaeger, 32
Falklands Broadcasting Station, 303
Falkland Islands, 18, 302, 303, 304, 306, 317
Falkland Sound, 307, 309, 341
Famagusta, 232
Fanning Head, 309, 311, 312
Fan trainer, 27
Farouk, King of Egypt, 213
Farr, Lt, 7th Para Bn, 84
Farrar, Capt Paul, 2 PARA, 323, 332, 333
Farrar-Hockley, Maj Dair, 2 PARA, 322–326, 346
Farrar-Hockley, Lt Col Tony, 3 PARA. Later Brig, Comd 16 Para Bde Subsequently Gen Sir Anthony and Col Comdt The Parachute Regiment, 242, 243, 367
Farrell, Maj Graham, 1 PARA. Later Col, Regt Col, 276
Faul, Lt Andrew, 152nd Ind Para Bn, 173
Federal National Guard, South Arabia, 237, 276
Federal Regular Army, South Arabia, 237, 238
Fenwick, Maj Ian, 26
Ferret scout car, 244, 246, 287
Field, Capt Roger, Blues & Royals, 360
Figheldean, 24
Filignano, 148
Finch's Corner, 171, 172, 175, 176
Findlay, C/Sgt, 2 PARA, 363
Fitch, Lt Col Tony; 3rd Para Bn, 104, 105, 107, 111
Fitzroy, 308, 346–350
Fitzroy-Smith – Lt L. A., 6th Para Bn, 149
Flamethrower, 102, 183, 188
Flavell, Lt Col Edward, 2nd Para Bn. Later Brig, Comd 1st Para Bde Subsequently Comd Abn Estbs and later Comd 6th Airlanding Bde, 51, 58, 85
Fleming, Maj Jon, 2 PARA, 261, 263
Fletcher, Pte, 2 PARA, 321
Flood, Maj Bob, 8th Para Bn., 131
Florissa, 153
Fly Half, 3 PARA objective on Mount Longdon, 351–353
FN rifle, 358
Foggia, 21, 23
Force 136, 188
Force Anguilla, 280
Ford, Maj Gerald, 13th Para Bn, 89
Ford, Capt Mike, 2 PARA, 328, 339
Fort Hertz, 167, 168
Fort Walsh, 276–278
Forward Observer Bombardment (FOB), 75
Fossey-François, Lt Col, 1er REP, 223
Foulbec, 90, 91
Foul Point, 171
Fox, Robert, BBC correspondent, 339, 340
Fox Bay, 307, 341
Framingham, L/Cpl, 2 PARA, 326
France, 205, 206, 221, 232
Franceville Plage, 63
Frank, Capt Tony, 2nd Para Bn, 113
Frederick, Maj Gen Robert, Comd 1st Abn Task Force, 150
Freegard, Maj Douglas, 12th Para Bn, 137
Free Kick, 3 PARA objective on Mount Longdon, 351, 358

Freer, Capt Adrian, 3 PARA, 356
Frejus, 149
French, Sgt, 3 PARA, 356
French Army:
  19th French Corps, 43
  4th Chasseurs d'Afrique, 43, 45
  4th Régt Tirailleurs Tunisiens, 43
  4th Spahis, 43
  2nd Bn 9th Régt Tirailleurs Algeriennes, 42
  43rd Régt Infanterie Coloniale, 43
  10th Abn Div, 222, 223
  11th Demi-Bde Parachutiste de Choc, 223, 226
  1st Régt de Chasseurs Parachutistes, 223
  1st Régt Etranger de Parachutistes, 223
  2nd Régt de Chasseurs Parachutistes, 223
  2nd Régt de Parachutistes Coloniales, 223, 226
  Foreign Legion, 43, 44
  Goums, 49
French Indo-China, 189
Freya, German radar, 13
Freyberg, Lt Gen Sir Bernard, Comd 2nd NZ Div, 146
Friede Walde, 142
Front for the Liberation of Southern Yemen (FLOSY), 274, 275, 278
Frost, Maj, later Lt Col, Johnny. 2nd Para Bn, 13–18, 36–38, 40, 45, 49, 53, 54, 56, 102, 103, 105, 106, 113, 114, 199
Fry, Maj Maurice, 152nd Ind Para Bn, 188
Fugelsang, Capt Charles, No. 1 (Guards) Indep Coy. Later G Sqn 22 SAS, 249–253
Full Back, 3 PARA objective on Mount Longdon, 351, 353–356
Fuller, Maj Clayton, 1st Cdn Para Bn, 71
Fuller, Maj John, 152nd Ind Para Bn, 172, 173
Fuller, Sgt, 3 PARA, 354
Fullick, Maj Roy, 2 PARA, 219
Furna, 40
Fursman, Maj Peter, 2 PARA, 297
Furze Bush Pass, 360

Gabes, 43
Gabb, Capt Michael, No. 1 (Guards) Indep Coy, 251
Gadebusch, 145
Gale, Brig Richard, Comd 1st Para Bde. Later Maj Gen, GOC 6th Abn Div. Subsequently Lt Gen Sir Richard, Comd 1st Abn Corps. Col Comdt The Parachute Regiment, 58, 60, 61, 63, 65, 73, 80, 81, 83, 84, 85, 90, 189, 211
Galilee, 204
Galtieri, Gen Leopoldo, leader of Argentinian junta, 304
Gammon bomb, 34, 35, 66, 71, 113
Gammon Hill, 172, 173, 175
Garand rifle, M1, 301
Gardai Siochana, 299
Garigliano, River, 148
Gavin, Brig Gen James, Comd 82nd US Abn Div, 97
Gaza, 193, 195, 196, 200
Gazelle helicopter, 297, 300, 310, 311
Geary – Capt, 1st Para Sqn RE, 35
Gebirgsjager – German mountain troops, 45
Gemini assault craft, 279
Geneifa, 213

General Purpose Machine-Gun (GPMG), 262, 263, 264, 305, 310, 314, 322, 324, 325, 328, 330, 334, 337, 352–358, 365
Georgetown, 272
Germany, 204, 206, 217, 267
German Army & Air Force:
  1st Parachute Army, 57
  5th Panzer Army, 92, 129, 130
  6th Panzer Army, 125
  7th Army, 125
  2nd Panzer Corps, 121
  2nd Parachute Corps, 129
  47th Panzer Corps, 129
  63rd Corps, 129
  86th Infantry Corps, 129
  1st Fallschirmjaeger Div, 56
  1st SS Panzer Div, 125
  9th Hohenstaufen SS Panzer Div, 98, 104, 105, 121
  10th Frundsberg SS Panzer Div, 98
  12th SS (Hitler Jugend) Panzer Div, 63
  6th Para Div, 129
  7th Para Div, 129
  8th Para Div, 129
  15th Panzer Grenadier Div, 129
  21st Panzer Div, 63, 70
  84th Infantry Div, 129
  116th Panzer Div, 129
  352nd Infantry Div, 63
  4th Fallschirmjaeger Regt, 54
  10th Panzer Grenadier Regt, 47
  16th SS Panzer Grenadier Depot Bn, 101, 104
  125th Panzer Grenadier Regt, 66
  171st Auffrischung Lt Arty Regt, 117
  744th Grenadier Regt, 78, 86
  857th Grenadier Regt, 74, 76, 77, 78, 80
  858th Grenadier Regt, 77, 78
  Barenthin Regt, 47
  Tunisian Regt, 47, 50
  Witzig's Regt, para engrs, 47, 49, 50
  Dutch SS Landsturm Nederland Bn 117
  Panzerabteilung 503, 117
  9th SS Panzer Div Recce Coy, 103
Gibraltar, 31
Gilles, Gen, Comd of Anglo-French land forces at Suez during Operation Musketeer, 223
Gillett, Capt Richard, 152nd Ind Para Bn, 166, 179
Ginestra, River, 22
Ginkel Heath, 96
Gin Sling, Radforce objective, 238, 240
Gioia, 146
Givat Brenner, 202
Givat Haiyam, 198
Givat Olga, 198
Glider pilots, 122, 123
Globemaster, transport aircraft, 234
Glubb, Gen Sir John, Comd of Jordanian Army, 216
Godfrey, Pte, 2 PARA, 333, 334
Godwin, Capt Tom, 2 PARA, 304, 345
Goften Salmond, Maj, 2nd Para Bn, 24
Goia del Colle, 56
Gombel Hill, 160–162
Goodall, C/Sgt, 2 PARA, 263
Goodwin, Lt Col, 6th Para Bn, 56
Goose Green, 18, 307, 310–313, 315–318, 329, 330, 334, 335, 336, 338, 340, 348, 349, 366
Goose Green Point, 306, 332, 333, 335, 336

Gordon-Brown, Capt Robert, 9th
   Para Bn, 68, 75
Gordon-Wilson, Lt Col Neil, 2
   PARA, 267
Gough, Brig Bill, Comd 50th Ind
   Para Bde, 165, 166
Gough, Maj Freddy, 1st Abn Recce
   Sqn, 99, 102, 114
Gough, Pte, 3 PARA, 352
Gourlay, Maj James, 4th Para Bn,
   152, 153
Goustranville, 86
Government House, Stanley, 303
Grace, W02, 2 PARA, 365
Gracey, Maj Gen, Comd 20th Ind
   Div, 185
Graham, Cpl, 2 PARA, 332
Grantham, Maj Bill, 13th Para Bn,
   126
Granville, Maj Johnny, 2nd Ox &
   Bucks LI, 126, 127
Grave, 93, 97
Gray, Maj Michael, 2 PARA. Later Lt
   Col, 1 PARA. Subsequently Brig,
   Comd 16 Para Bde and 6 Fd Force
   Later Lt Gen Sir Michael and Col
   Comdt The Para Regt, 273, 283, 284,
   286, 288
Grayburn – Lt Jack, 2nd Para Bn,
   102, 114
Great Synagogue, The, 203
Greece, 151–154, 216, 217
Greek Mountain Bde, 154
Greek National Guards, 154
Greek Orthodox Church – in Cyprus,
   217
Green, CSM, 1st Cdn Para Bn, 131
Greenhalgh, Capt John, 656 Sqn
   AAC, 338
Greenhalgh, CSM, 2 PARA, 332, 333
Green Hill, 43
Green Line, 236
Greenway, Capt The Hon Paul, 9th
   Para Bn, 68, 76
Grenade Corner, 278
Grenade launcher, M-79, 321, 332,
   365
Grenade No. 36 Mills, high explosive,
   137
Grenade No. 80, white phosphorous,
   370
Greven, 139
Grey, Pte, 2 PARA, 338
Grey, Pte, 3 PARA, 352
Griffin, Capt, later Maj, Peter. 1st
   Cdn Para Bn, 77, 78, 131
Grivas, Col George, leader of EOKA,
   217, 218, 233
Groesbeek, 97
Groesbeek heights, 97
Gross, Pte, 3 PARA, 353
Gruner, Dov, 204
Grupont, 126
Grytviken, 303
Guardia, 147
Guardigrele, 146, 147
Gue, 35
Gullan, Maj Hector, 3 Cdo Bde LO
   att 2 PARA, 339, 360
Gun, 2 pdr, armoured car main
   armament, 207
Gun, 76mm, Scorpion CVR (T) main
   armament, 362
Gun, naval, 4.5 inch, 355, 361
Gunan Gajak, 261, 262, 264, 265
Gurung, Cpl Singbahadur, Gurkha
   Indep Para Coy, 260
Gush, Lt G. B., 7th Para Bn, 144
Guyana, 273
Guyanese Defence Force, 272

Gwalior, 189

Habilayn, 271, 273
Hackett, Brig John, Comd 4th Para
   Bde, 51, 108, 110, 115, 116, 119
Hadar hak Carmel, 206
Haddon, Cpl, 3 PARA, 344
Hadrian glider, 150, 151
Haganah, 194, 206
Haifa, 197, 200, 204, 205, 206, 207,
   208
Hajib, 242
Halevga Forest Station, 219
Halifax bomber, 27, 28, 200
Hall, Pte, 12th Para Bn, 79
Hall, Pte, 2 PARA, 323
Halliburton, Lt, 9th Para Bn, 69
Halmaheira, 160
Hamburg, 206
Hamilcar glider, 73, 100, 134
Hamminkeln, 129, 130, 133
Hanmer, Lt David, D (Patrol) Coy 3
   PARA, 270
Hanson, Capt, later Maj, John. 1st
   Cdn Para Bn, 70, 72, 131
Happy Valley, 45
Hardman, Cpl, 2 PARA, 325
Hardcastle, Mr Brooke, manager of
   Darwin settlement, 346
Hardwick Hall, 23, 26
Hardy Group, C Coy 2nd Para Bn,
   Bruneval raid, 14, 15, 16
Hargreaves, Maj Dick, 4th Para Bn,
   153
Harington, Lt Col Charles, 1 PARA,
   211
Harley, Cpl, 2 PARA, 332, 333, 364
Harold, CSM, 9th Para Bn, 67
Harpley, Lt, 9th Para Bn, 138
Harrier, GR1, 316, 323, 336
Harrison, Lt Mike, Gurkha Indep
   Para Coy, 256
Hartenstein Hotel, 105, 113
Hartigan, Cpl, 1st Cdn Para Bn, 72
Harvey, Gp Capt L. G., Stn Comd
   Central Landing Establishment, 20
Harzer, Obersturmbannfuhrer
   Walter, Comd 9th SS Panzer
   Division, 121
Hasbergen, 140, 141
Hastings transport aircraft, 221, 224,
   225, 226
Hauger, 68, 73, 74
Haunted House, The, 247, 251, 253,
   267
Hawker, Pte, 3 PARA, 218
Hawker Hunter fighter bomber, 234,
   238, 239, 241–243
Hawkins anti-tank grenade, 34, 35,
   36, 103
Hawthorn, Maj Gen D. C., GOC 23rd
   Ind Div, 158
Head, Maj John, No. 1 (Guards)
   Indep Coy, 244, 247, 251–253
Heddicker, Pte, 3 PARA, 358
Heelsum, 99, 104
Heerey, Maj Mike, 1 PARA, 236
Hennessy, Sgt, 9th Para Bn, 74
Hercules C-130 transport aircraft,
   251, 369
Hereford, 22 SAS base, 247, 253, 267
Her Majesty Queen Elizabeth, 212
Her Majesty Queen Elizabeth II, 272
Herring, Maj Peter, C (Indep) Coy 2
   PARA, 261, 267, 271
Hervey, H. E. Sqn Ldr, OC Glider Trg
   Sch at Central Landing
   Establishment, 20
Heveadorp, 101, 113
Heaveadorp ferry, 17, 118

Hewetson, Lt Col, 8th Para Bn. Later
   Col and Regtl Col, 130
Hibbert, Maj Tony, Bde Maj 1st Para
   Bde, 102, 114
Hickman, Capt Jeremy, D (Patrol)
   Coy 3 PARA, 269
Hicks, Brig Philip 'Pip', Comd 1st
   Airlanding Bde, 52, 99, 107–110,
   116, 119
Higginson – Sgt, 2 PARA, 315
Hill, Lt Col James, 1st Para Bn. Later
   Brig, Comd 3rd Para Bde.
   Subsequently Comd 4th Para Bde
   (TA), 32–36, 58, 61, 67, 72, 73, 76,
   79, 135, 138, 142, 210
Hill, Lt Simon, C (Indep) Coy 2
   PARA, 268
Hill 13, 13th Para Bn objective, 87, 88
Hinde, Maj Peter, first Regt Adjt The
   Para Regt, 211
Hiroshima, 156
His Majesty King George VI, 211, 212
His Royal Highness The Duke of
   Edinburgh, 272
His Royal Highness The Prince of
   Wales, Col in Chief The Para Regt,
   368
Hocking, Lt Ernie, 2 PARA, 320, 323,
   327
Hodge, Capt Vere, 1st Airlanding
   Regt RA, 54
Hodgson, Maj Noel, 3 PARA, 224
Hogg 2/Lt Chris, 3 PARA, 225
Hogla, 198
Holbrook, Pte, 2 PARA, 330
Holman-Smith, Pte, 2 PARA, 330
Holophane lamps, 59
Homalin, 172
Honey, Lt Alec, D (Patrol) Coy 3
   PARA, 270
Honey light tank, 80
Honfleur, 85, 90, 91
Hong Kong, 189, 261
Hope, Cpl, 3 PARA, 355
Hope Thompson, Lt Col M. R. J.
   'Tim', 4th Para Bn. Later Brig, Comd
   50th Ind Para Bde, 24, 166, 170, 171,
   173, 175, 178–182
Hopkinson, Brig G. F., Comd 1st
   Airlanding Bde. Later Maj Gen,
   GOC 1st Abn Div, 24
Hopkinson, Capt, 50th Ind Para Bde,
   165
Hopkinson, Maj, later Lt Col, Paul,
   152nd Ind Para Bn Later Brig,
   Comd 50th Ind Para Bde, 172–174,
   178, 179, 181, 190
Horsa glider, 73, 100, 150, 151
Horsford, Brig Derek, Comd of ad
   hoc brigade during 1961
   deployment of British forces to
   Kuwait, 235
Horrocks, Lt Gen Sir Brian, Comd
   30th Corps, 118, 119
Hotel Schoonord, 117, 121
Hotel Vreewyck, 121
Hotel Tafelberg, 121
House, Brig David, Comd Central
   Brigade in Borneo, 270
Howard, Maj John, 2nd Ox & Bucks
   LI, 64
Howlett, Lt Col Geoffrey, 2 PARA.
   Later Brig, Comd 16 Para Bde.
   Subsequently Lt Gen Sir Geoffrey,
   Col Comdt The Para Regt, 293
Howlett, Brig 'Swifty', Comd 139th
   Inf Bde, 45
Hudson, Brig Peter, Comd 39 Inf
   Bde, 283
Hudson light bomber, 165, 166–169

Hughes, Capt Steve, RMO 2 PARA, 314, 327, 337–339
Hukawng Valley, 167, 168
Humber 'Pig' armoured personnel carrier, 287, 289
Humine, 184
Hunt, Governor Rex, 302, 303
Hunter, Maj David, Bde Maj 1st Para Bde, 54
Hunter, Maj W., 5th Para Bn, 154
Hurricane fighter, 57, 178
Hurn airfield, 31
Hurs, 166
Hussein, King of Jordan, 216, 234
Husseini, Haj Amin al, Mufti of Jerusalem, 194
Husseini, Jamal, cousin of Mufti, 195

Iban tribesmen, 247, 262
Iban trackers, 266
Ijssel, River, 98, 129, 135
Illingworth, Pte, 2 PARA, 323
Imperial Defence College, 200
Imphal, 170, 171, 172, 175, 180, 181, 182, 185
India, 166, 191–193

Indian Army:
14th Army, 185, 189
4th Indian Corps, 170, 171, 183
2nd Indian Abn Div, 190
4th Indian Div, 147
8th Indian Div, 147
17th Indian Div, 170, 171, 182
20th Indian Div, 170, 171, 183–185
23rd Indian Div, 158, 161, 170, 171, 174, 179
26th Indian Div,'187–189
44th Indian Abn Div, 185, 187, 189, 190
44th Indian Armd Div, 185
7th Indian Inf Bde, 153
14th Airlanding Bde, 185, 190
14th Indian Para Bde, 192
14th (LRP) Bde, 185
17th Indian Inf Bde, 147
21st Indian Inf Bde, 148
36th Indian Inf Bde, 170, 189
49th Indian Inf Bde, 158, 161, 171, 172, 177
50th Indian Para Bde, 165–171, 174, 175, 182–188, 192
77th Indian Inf Bde, 186
77th Indian Para Bde, 186, 187, 192
80th Indian Inf Bde, 183
100th Indian Inf Bde, 183
CRA's Bde – Java, 161
Special Force (Chindits), 185, 186
Jungle Warfare School, Raiwala, 170
V Force, 172, 173
Abforce, 182
Sancol, 184
Tarforce, 184, 185
Woodforce, 183
Indian Abn Forces Depot, 187
Indian Para Regt, The, 186, 189, 190
Para Tps Trg Centre, 166, 169, 187
1st Indian Para Bn, 186
2nd Gurkha Para Bn, 186, 187
3rd Gurkha Para Bn, 186, 187
4th Indian Para Bn, 186, 187
152nd Indian Para Bn, 165, 166, 172–178, 182–185, 188
153rd Gurkha Para Bn, 165, 167, 168, 170, 175–179, 181–185
154th Gurkha Para Bn, 168, 170, 185
1st Para Bn 2nd Punjab Regt, 191
1st Para Bn Frontier Force Regt, 191
1st Para Bn The Kumaon Regt, 191

2nd Para Bn The Madras Regt, 191
3rd Para Bn 15th Punjab Regt (Machine-Guns), 191
3rd Para Bn 1st Punjab Regt, 191
3rd Para Bn 16th Punjab Regt, 191
3rd Para Bn Mahratta Light Infantry, 191
3rd Para Bn Rajput Regt (DCO), 191
3rd Para Bn The Baluch Regt, 191
4th Para Bn 6th Rajputana Rifles (Outram's), 191
44th Indep Pathfinder Coy, 186
44th Indian Abn Recce Sqn, 186
44th Indep Para Coy, 186
45th Indep Para Coy, 186
50th Indep Para Coy, 186
77th Indep Para Coy, 186
1st King George V's Own Gurkha Rifles, 168
2nd King Edward VII's Own Goorkhas, 168
3rd Bn 7th Gurkha Rifles, 168
3rd Bn 10th Princess Mary's Own Gurkha Rifles, 160
4th Madras Regt, 184
4th Bn 6th Rejputana Rifles (Outram's), 186, 190
4th Bn 5th Mahratta Light Infantry, 172, 175, 176, 177, 179
6th Bn 16th Punjab Regt, 186
7th Baluch Regt, 182
17th Dogra Regt, 181
1st Bn Assam Rifles, 170, 184
Burma Levies, 167
Shere Regt, 170
11th Cavalry (Prince Albert Victor's Own), 158
6th Indian Fd Bt RIA, 158, 162
9th Mountain Regt RIA, 174
15th Mountain Bty RIA, 174, 176, 178, 179
582nd Jungle.Mortar Bty RIA, 174–176, 179
33rd Para Sqn IE, 186
40th Indian Abn Fd Pk Sqn IE, 186
411th (Royal Bombay) Para Sect IE, 165, 168
411th (Royal Bombay) Para Sqn IE, 183, 186, 187
74th Fd Coy IE, 176, 177
80th Para Fd Amb, 180, 188
Royal Indian Army Service Corps (RIASC), 186
165th Abn GT Coy RIASC, 186
604th ABn GT Coy RIASC, 186
610th Abn Lt (Jeep) Coy RIASC, 186
Para Supply Coy RIASC, 186

Indian National Congress, 191
Indonesia, 245, 247, 249, 250, 252, 254, 256, 258, 261, 263, 269
Indonesian Border Terrorists (IBTs), 246
Innes-Ker, Lt The Lord Robin, Blues & Royals, 360
Internment, Northern Ireland, 294
Ipoh, 216
Iraq, 200
Iraq Petroleum Company, 204
Irgun Zvai Leumi (IZL), 194, 199, 200, 201, 203, 206, 207
Irish Republican Army (IRA), Officials, 286, 296; Provisionals, 286–288, 290, 295, 296, 299
Irvin, Leslie, American parachute manufacturer, 166
Isdud, 201
Isdud-Yibna, 200
Iskander Swamp, Malaysia, 216

Isle of Man, 283, 288
Ismailia, 214, 223
Ismay, Gen Sir Hastings, head of Military Wing of War Secretariat, 19
Issitt, S/Sgt APTC att 3 PARA, 226
Italy, 56, 57, 146–149, 151
Iveson, Sqn Ldr Bob, 317

Jackson, Lt Col C. I. A., No. 2 Cdo, 19
Jackson, Capt Derek, C (Indep) Coy 2 PARA, 267
Jackson, Maj Jake, Army Air Corps, 243, 244
Jackson, L/Cpl, 2 PARA, 332
Jacobabad, 191
Jaffa, 196, 199, 203, 207
James, Capt, HQ 4th Para Bde, 116
Japanese Imperial Army:
15th Div, 171, 182, 183
31st Div, 171, 183
33rd Div, 183
3rd Bn 58th Regt Gp, 173
Yamamoto Force, 183
Java, 189, 262
Jebel Alliliga, 43
Jebel Haqla, 243
Jebel Mansour, 43
Jellicoe, Lt Col The Lord, Special Boat Squadron, 152
Jellicoe Group, C Coy 2nd Para Bn, Bruneval raid, 14, 15, 16
Jenin, 195
Jenkins, Pte, 3 PARA, 356
Jenner, Maj Hugh, 2 PARA, 318, 324
Jenner, Maj Roger, 2 PARA, 323, 330, 337, 363
Jerusalem, 197, 199, 202, 203, 207
Jessami, 170
Jewish Agency, 193, 194, 197, 202
Jewkes, Capt Barry, 3 PARA, 239, 240, 241
Johanna Hoeve, 110, 113
Johnny I, II & III, 2nd Para Bn objectives in Sicily, 53–55
Johnson, Lt Chris, C (Indep) Coy 2 PARA, 268, 269
Johnson, Lt Col Johnny, 12th Para Bn, 65, 81, 82
Johore, 216, 257
Johore Bahru, 246, 254, 256, 261
Jones, Lt Col 'H', 2 PARA, 18, 304, 305, 312, 313, 315, 316, 317, 324, 325, 326, 367
Jones, Pte, 2 PARA, 332
Jordan, 214, 216, 234
Jordan, River, 205
Jordan Valley, 204
Jorhat, 185
Jowett, 2/Lt G., 11th SAS Bn, 22

Kabaw Valley, 170
Kachin Hills, 167
Kachins, 167
Kafr Szold, 207
Kahuta, 185
Kairouan, 52
Kajitu, 167, 168
Kalaikunda, 188
Kalamaki, 152
Kalashnikov AK-47 rifle, 264, 277
Kalemyo, 187
Kalewa, 187
Kalogrea, 220
Kalibahadur Regt, 176, 179
Kalimantan, Indonesian Borneo, 247
Kamjong, 184
Kampong Labuai, 256
Kanglatongbi, 183
Kannavia, 233
Kanpur, 166

Karachi, 190
Karadimas, 233
Kartja, 220
Karton quarter, 201
Kauffmann, Capt, 12th Para Bn, 141
Kayans, 247
Kearton, 2/Lt Mark, 3 PARA, 356
Keeble, Maj Chris, 2 PARA, 327, 328, 330, 336, 337, 339, 340, 347, 348
Keeling, Bandmaster, 2 PARA, 211, 212
Keene, Maj Bob, 7th Para Bn, 84, 137
Kefar Marmorek, 201
Keightley, Gen Sir Charles, overall comd of Operation 'Musketeer', 223
Kellas, Lt Arthur, 1st Para Bn, 34, 35
Kemp, CSM, 1st Cdn Para Bn, 132
Kempster, Brig Walter, Comd 16th Indep Para Bde, 211
Kempster, Pte, 3 PARA, 353
Kennard, Lt 'Tosh', Comd of Fleet Air Arm det at Nangga Gaat, 258
Kennedy, Lt Peter, 2 PARA, 330, 334, 337
Kenya, 235
Kenyas, 247
Kersting, Cpl of Horse, No. 1 (Guards) Indep Coy, 249
Kesselring, Feldmarschall, Comd German forces in Italy, 147
Ketley, Capt Peter, 2 PARA, 314, 316, 317, 328, 335
Khanggoi, 172, 173, 174, 176
Kharakvasla, 166
Kharasom, 170, 171
Khardja, 220
Khartoum, 200
Khissas, 207
Khongjan, 184
Khormaksar, 273, 278
Kidney Hill, 176
Kido, Maj, Comd of Japanese unit in Semarang, 159, 160, 161, 163
Kilkenny, Flt Lt, later Wg Cdr, J. C., 20
Kimchin, Benjamin, 203
Kinchen, Cpl, 2 PARA, 334, 336
Kindersley, Brig Hugh, Comd 6th Airlanding Bde, 59, 82
King, Lt Col Frank, 2 PARA, 235
King, F/Offr Henry, No. 271 Sqn RAF, 112
King David Hotel, 202
King Edward Cove, 303, 304
King Edward Point, 303
King Tiger tank, 117
Kingston, Capt Peter, 3 PARA, 232
Kipling, Pte, 3 PARA, 356
Kippen, Maj John, 8th Para Bn, 131
Kirby, Maj Norman, 23rd Para Fd Amb, 226
KKO, Indonesian marines, 246
Klosterlutherheim, 135, 136
Kluang, 258
Klythe Pass, 153
Knall, CQMS, C (Indep) Coy 2 PARA, 268
Knight, Pte, 2 PARA, 331, 334
Knight, Sgt, 9th Para Bn, 68
Knights, C/Sgt, 3 PARA, 357, 358
Knob, The, 310, 311
Knutsford, 19
Koepel, 108, 110
Kohima, 170, 171, 176, 177, 183
Kokkina Tremetia, 236
Kota Tinggi, 215
Kozani, 152
Kruzen, 144
Kuala Lumpur, 215, 216
Kuching, 247, 248, 256, 261, 268

Kussin, Generalmajor, Commandant of Arnhem, 104
Kutenhausen, 142
Kuwait, 235
Kuwait City, 235
Kykko, 218
Kyrenia, 219, 220

L1A1 66mm Light Anti-Tank Weapon (LAW), 304, 320, 322, 326, 327, 332, 344, 352, 354, 355, 357, 358
L1A1 7.62mm Self-Loading Rifle, 370
L2A2 HE Hand Grenade, 370
L42A1 Sniper Rifle, 370
L85A1 Individual & Light Support Weapons, 370
L96A1 Sniper Rifle, 370
LAW 80 94mm HE Anti-Tank Rocket, 370
La Adhab, 243
Labis, 257
Labuan Island, 257, 270
Lacoste, Maj Gerry, GS02 (Int) HQ 6th Abn Div, 73
Lahore, 191
La Judee, 91
Lake Lines, Aden, 276
Lambert, Pte, 2 PARA, 365
Lam Motte, 150
Lancaster bomber, 67, 71, 130
Landing Craft Utility (LCU), 310
Landing Craft Vehicle & Personnel (LCVP), 310
Lane – Maj Johnny, 2nd Para Bn, 47, 53
Langford, RSM, 6th Para Bn, 56
Largeren, Lt Alí, 13th Para Bn, 126
Larkspur radios, 305
Lathbury, Lt Col Gerald, 3rd Para Bn. Later Brig, Comd 1st Para Bde. Subsequently Comd 3rd Bde. Later Gen Sir Gerald, Col Comdt The Para Regt, 51, 53–56, 99, 102, 104, 105, 107, 193, 204
Latrun, 202
Lauenberg, 144
Lea, Capt C. G., 11th SAS Bn, 22
Lea, Lt Col George, 11th Para Bn, 108, 111
League of Nations, 193
Lebanon, 204, 233
Le Bas de Ranville, 63, 65, 73, 79
Lee, Lt John, FOO att 3 PARA, 356
Lee Kwan Yew, Prime Minister of Singapore, 245
Leese, Gen Sir Oliver, Comd 8th Army. Later C-in-C Allied Land Forces S. E. Asia, 148, 149, 189
Legg, Sgt, 3 PARA, 225
Le Havre, 13
Leicester, Brig B. W., Comd 4th Special Service Bde, 83
Leine, River, 142, 143
Leith, 303
Le Mariquet, 80
Lembeck, 135, 138
Le Mesnil, 69, 71, 72, 73, 77, 80
Le Muy, 150, 151
Le Plein, 68, 73, 82
Le Presbytère, 15, 16
Lengerich, 140
Lennox-Boyd, Maj Francis, 22nd Indep Para Coy, 84
Lewis, Maj Peter, 3rd Para Bn, 104
Liberator bomber, 188
Libya, 200
Lichtenbeek feature, 110
Liège, 125
Limmasol, 221, 229, 237

Limni, 236
Lindsay, Lt Col Martin, 151st Para Bn, 165
Lisieux, 85
Lister, Lt Hugo, 2 PARA, 328, 335
Litan, 171, 172, 181
Litan-Ukhrul road, 174
Lively Island, 348
Lloyd-Jones, Maj Taffy, 1st Para Bn, 47
Locke, Maj, 15th Mountain Bty RIA, 179
Locust light tank, 134
Loden, Capt Ted, 1 PARA, 276
Loder-Symonds, Col R. C., CRA 1st Abn Div, 117
Lodestar, Lockhead, 167
Loftus-Tottenham, Lt Col Freddy, 153rd Gurkha Para Bn, 165
Logan, Capt Jimmy, RMO 2nd Para Bn, 114
Logan, Pte, 3 PARA, 353
London, City of, 367
Long Banai, 258
Long Island Mount, 342
Long Jawi, 250, 255, 256
Long Linau, 255, 256
Long Kihan, 250
Long Semado, 260
Lonsdale, Maj Dickie, 11th Para Bn, 53, 111, 119
Lonsdale Force, 111, 116, 117
Lord, F/Lt David, No. 271 Sqn RAF, 112
Lough, Maj Ted, DAA & QMG 5th Para Bde, 134
Lovat, Brig The Lord, Comd 1st Special Service Bde, 61, 82
Lovett, Cpl, 3 PARA, 355
Lower Malo House, 342
Lower Rhine, 93, 94, 118, 119
Luard, Lt Col Peter, 13th Para Bn, 59, 86, 87, 89
Lubbecke, 142
Lübeck, 145
Lucky, Sqn Ldr, att 11th SAS Bn, 21
Lundu, 256
Luxembourg, 125, 127
LVTP-7 amphibious armoured personnel carrier, 302
Lydda, 195, 196, 197, 199, 200, 202, 203
Lysander aircraft, 167

Maadi, 205
Ma'alla, 274
Maas, River, 93, 97
Maas-Waal Canal, 97
Macdonald, Padre, 2nd Para Bn, 39, 42
Macedonia, 153
Mackay, Capt Eric, 1st Para Sqn RE, 102
Maddox, Brig Rex, Comd 3rd Cdo Bde, 232
Magelang, 160
Magnay, Capt John, No. 1 (Guards) Indep Coy, 251
Maida Barracks, Aldershot, 337
Main Dressing Station, Ajax Bay, 346, 349
Maison Blanche, 32, 33, 36, 37
Makarios, Archbishop, 217
Malacca, Straits of, 257
Malaya, 189, 214–216, 245, 246, 247, 254, 259, 280
Malay Emergency, 259, 262
Malaysia, 245, 257, 258, 261
Mali Hka, River, 167
Malta, 21, 23, 208

Mansfield, 26
Mansie, RSM, PJI No. 1 PTS Ringway, 19
Mansura Picquet, 275
Maphilindo, 245
Margerson, Cpl, 2 PARA, 320
Marjoribanks, Mrs Jean, 199
Marloie, 127
Marseilles, 205, 206
Marsh, Lt Donald, 4th Para Bn, 152
Martin, Capt Randall, RMO 1st Airlanding Lt Regt RA, 120
Marwood, CSM, 12th Para Bn, 82
Mascara, 52
Mason, Capt Tony, 3 PARA, 357, 358
Massicault, 39
Massu, Gen, Comd French 10th Abn Div, 222
Mateland, Pte, 2 PARA, 327
Mateur, 36, 43
Mathinet, Gen, Comd 19th French Corps, 43
Matla Ridge, 235
Mayfield, Capt Richard, Staff Capt HQ The Para Regt, 210
McAuley, Cpl, 2 PARA, 332, 363
McCardie, Lt Col, 2nd Bn South Staffs Regt, 111
McCarthy, Cpl, 3 PARA, 358
McCord, Lt Douglas, 2 PARA, 231
McConney, Cpl, 2nd Para Bn, 41
McCracken, Capt Willie, 148 Cdo Fwd Obsn Bty RA, 354, 355, 361
McCreesh, Raymond Peter, 301
McDermont, Lt A. J., 2nd Para Bn, 102
McDonald, Sgt, 2 PARA, 264
McGavin, Lt Jock, 16th Para Fd Amb, 39, 42
McGeever, Sgt, 9th Para Bn, 74
McGill, Sgt, No. 1 (Guards) Indep Coy, 252, 253
McGowan, Lt, later Capt Sam. 1st Cdn Para Bn, 78, 131
McGuffie, Lt, 9th Para Bn, 139
McGuinness, Daniel, 301
McHugh, L/Cpl, 2 PARA, 332
McIntyre, Pte, 2nd Para Bn, 16
McKay, Capt Eric, 1st Para Sqn RE, 102
McKay, Sgt, 3 PARA, 353, 367
McKee, Pte, 2 PARA, 320
McKenzie, Lt Col Charles, GS01 HQ 1st Abn Div, 108, 118, 120
McLaughlin, Cpl, 3 PARA, 354
McLoughlin, Pte, 2 PARA, 365
McLellan, Brig Pat, Comd 8 Inf Bde, 288
McLeod, Lt Ian, 3 PARA, 243
McLeod, Maj Murray, 1st Cdn Para Bn, 71, 72
McLune, Lt Bob, 411th (Royal Bombay) Para Sect IE, 168
McNab, L/Cpl, No. 1 (Guards) Indep Coy, 227
McNally, Cpl, 2 PARA, 332
McNeilly, Sgt, C (Indep) Coy 2 PARA, 269
McPhee, Sgt, 1st Cdn Para Bn, 78
Mecca, 237
Medjerda, River, 39
Medjez El Bab, 35, 41
Megara, 152
Melia, Cpl, 9 Para Sqn RE, 327
Mellor, Lt Philip, 1st Para Bn, 34
Meredith, Sgt, 2 PARA, 334
Menendez, Maj Gen Mario Benjamin, Comd of Argentinian forces on the Falkland Islands, 306, 339

Merryfield, Capt, RMO att composite Indian para battalion for Operation Dracula, 188
Merville Battery, 63, 67, 71
Messerschmitt 109 fighter, 38, 108, 110, 111, 118
Metropolitan Police, 279
Metz, 92
Meuse, River, 92, 125
MG-42 machine-gun, 75
Midnapore, 188
Midwood, Lt Bob, 22nd Indep Para Coy, 84
Milan anti-tank guided missile, 315, 328, 335, 357, 358
Mildenhall, 21
Miley, Maj Gen William 'Bud', Comd 17th US Abn Div, 128, 135
Miller, Maj Roger, 2 PARA, 312
Miller, CSM, 9th Para Bn, 67
Mills, Lt Bertie, 7th Para Bn, 87
Mills, Lt Keith RM, 303, 304
Milne, Maj Kenneth KRRC, RAPWI staff officer, 163
Milne, Cpl, 3 PARA, 352, 354, 356
Minden, 142
Mirage fighter, 310, 349
Mitchell, Sgt, No. 1 (Guards) Indep Coy, 252
Mitchell, Capt Gordon, No. 1 (Guards) Indep Coy, 251
Miyazaki, Maj Gen, Comd Japanese 58th Regt Gp, 173
Mobat 120mm anti-tank gun, 237
Mobile parachute servicing unit, 169
Monaghan, Maj Tom, 152nd Indian Para Bn, 183
Mongkus, 265, 266
Monschau, 125
Montefiorre, 204
Montevideo, 303, 304
Montgomery, Gen Sir Bernard, Comd 8th Army. Later Comd 21st Army Group. Subsequently Field Marshal Viscount of Alamein, Col Comdt The Para Regt, 52, 83, 92, 93, 98, 124, 125, 126, 128, 145, 146, 211
Montgomery Lines, Aldershot, 292
Moody Brook, 302, 306, 307, 350, 360, 364, 366
Moore, Maj 'Dinty', 2nd Para Bn, 45
Moore, Maj Peter, 3rd Abn Sqn RE, 162
Moore, 2/Lt Ian, 3 PARA, 355, 356
Moore, Maj Gen Jeremy, Comd of British land forces during Falklands Campaign, 360
Morgan, Capt David, Gurkha Indep Para Coy, 256
Morgan, Pte, 2 PARA, 332
Morib beaches, 156
Morley, Capt Norman, 3 PARA, 226
Morphou, 220
Morris, C/Sgt, 2 PARA, 346
Mortar, light 2in, 72, 78, 200, 277, 323, 342; 20mm, 88; 50mm, 265; 51mm, 370; 60mm, 275; medium 3in, 34, 35, 37, 38, 46, 53, 74, 75, 80, 169, 177, 207, 226, 262; 81mm, 309, 311, 313, 343, 344, 351; heavy 120mm, 340, 343, 344, 351, 358, 359
Mortimer, Lt G. L., 4th Para Bn, 147
Mortimer, Pte, 2 PARA, 332
Morton, Lt Col Peter, 3 PARA, 298
Moss, CSM, 13th Para Bn, 126
Mountbatten, Admiral Lord Louis, Chief of Combined Operations. Later Supreme Allied Commander S. E. Asia, 14, 156
Mount Challenger, 342, 343

Mount Estancia, 342–345, 359
Mount Harriet, 306, 345, 348, 350, 359
Mount Kent, 306, 342, 343, 350, 357, 359, 361
Mount Longdon, 306, 342–345, 350, 351, 353, 355–362
Mount Tumbledown, 306, 345, 350, 357, 360, 364, 366
Mount Usborne, 346
Mount Vernet, 342
Mount William, 306, 345
Muharraq, 235
Mujat, 265, 266
Muljono, Maj, comd of Indonesian raiding force in Borneo Confrontation, 256
Mullet Creek, 302
Mullins, Capt Gerald, 3 PARA, 228
Multan, 191
Mung Ching, 184
Murphy, Gdsm, No. 1 (Guards) Indep Coy, 227
Murray, Sgt, 12th Para Bn, 82
Murray, Sgt, 1st Cdn Para Bn, 131
Murray, Sgt, 2 PARA, 266
Murrell Bridge, 343, 358, 359
Murrell, River, 351, 360, 361, 362, 366
Murtagh, Pte, 2 PARA, 264
Mustoe, Lt M., 1st Cdn Para Bn, 134
Myers, Lt Col Eddie, CRE 1st Abn Div, 118
Myers, Pte, 2 PARA, 332
Myitkina, 167
Myothit, 171
Mystère fighter, 224

Na'amin, 200
Naga Hills, 170
Naga tribesmen, 172, 181, 182
Nagasaki, 156
Nakamura, Maj Gen, Japanese area comd in Java, 160
Namur, 125, 126, 127
Nangga Gaat, 248, 258, 268, 269
Naples, 23, 147
Nasser, Col Gamal Abd al, President of Egypt, 213, 219, 221, 223, 227, 234, 275
Nastri, Rfm, Rifle Bde, att X Tp 11th SAS Bn, 21
Nathanya, 200
National Guard, Egyptian, 223
National Liberation Front (NLF), Aden, 274, 275, 277, 278, 279
Natrup, 140
Nazareth, 204
Nbyem, 168
Neame, Maj Philip, 2 PARA, 313, 315, 321, 324, 329, 331–333, 362, 363–365
Neapolis, 236
Nee Soon, 267, 270
Neguib, Gen, co-leader of coup against King Farouk of Egypt, 213
Neild, Capt Eric, RMO 153rd Gurkha Para Bn, 184
Nelson, Maj Gen John, Maj Gen Comd Household Bde, 253
Nelson Group, C Coy 2nd Para Bn, Bruneval raid, 14, 15, 16
Neustadt, 142
Nevasa, SS, 216
Newall, Capt Mike, 3 PARA, 227
New Australia, MV, 231, 232
Newland, Capt, later Maj, Jack. 153rd Gurkha Para Bn, 168, 187
Newnham, Wg Cdr Maurice, CO No. 1 PTS RAF, 20, 169

Netherlands Army:
1 Bn Netherlands Marine Corps, 380
Princess Irene of The Netherlands Bde, 85, 90
T Regt Gp, 163, 164
New Zealand Army:
2nd NZ Div, 146–149
6th NZ Bde, 148
NZ SAS Sqn, 216, 262
Nibong, 261
Nicholls – Maj Norman, 1 PARA, 276
Nicklin – Maj, later Col, Jeff. 1st Cdn Para Bn, 71, 131
Nicosia, 217, 219, 220, 232, 236
Nijmegen, 93, 94, 97, 119, 120, 123, 124
Nimmo – Capt, Burma Levies, 167
Ningchangyang Valley, 167
Niven – Capt Bruce, 10th PMO Gurkha Rifles, 254
No'ar Oved, 202
Noratlas transport aircraft, 222
Norland, MV, 305, 308, 309, 310, 345, 367
Norman, Wg Cdr, later Gp Capt, Sir Nigel. Comdt Central Landing Establishment, 20, 21
Norman, Maj Ron, 3 PARA, 224, 226, 228, 229
Norman, Sgt, 3 PARA, 224
Norman, Maj Mike, comd of Naval Party 8901, 302, 303
Norman, Sgt, 2 PARA, 325, 326
Normandy, 61, 64, 96, 99, 123, 149, 150
Norris, David, *Daily Mail* correspondent, 339
North Africa, 20, 23, 30
North Borneo, 245
Northern Aid Association (NORAID), 287
Northern Ireland 280–301, 302
Albert Street Mill, 286
Aldergrove, 286
Andersonstown, 294, 296
Annabow, Kilmore, 281
Ardoyne, 282, 296
Armagh, 281
Ballykinler, 296
Ballymacarrett, 296
Ballymurphy, 292, 293, 294, 296
Ballynafeigh, 296
Beechmount, 292, 296
Beechmount Avenue, 295
Belfast, 281, 282, 283, 285, 287, 293, 294, 295, 297
Belfast Central Region, 286
Berlin Street, 293
Bessbrook, 298, 300
Bessbrook Mill, 298
Bishop's Field, Creggan, 288
Bogside, 281, 288, 290
Bombay Street, 294
Boyne Bridge, 286
Brandywell, 288
Carlingford Lough, 296
Cavendish, 294
Chamberlain Street, 289, 290
Clady, County Antrim, 281
Clonard, 294
Coalisland, 281
County Armagh, 297
Creggan Estate, 288, 290
Creggan Street, 289
Crossmaglen, 298
Crumlin Road, 282, 292
Crumlin Road Jail, 295
Cullaville, 300
Cullyhanna, 300

Divis Flats, 286
Divismore Park, 294
Donegall Road, 294
Drumilly Mountain, 300
Drumintree, 299
Eastway, 288
Eden Place, 290
Falls Road, 282, 283, 285, 295, 296
Flax Street Mill, 292
Forkhill, 298, 299
Foxes Corner, 288, 289, 290
Foyle, River, 296
Glenfada Park, 291
Harland & Wolf shipyard, 292
Hastings Street, 286
Henry Taggart Hall, 294
Kashmir Road, 294
King Edward's Hall, Balmoral, 283
Lanark Street, 295
Ligoniel, 292
Ligoniel Mill, 292
Limestone Road, 283, 295
Londonderry, 281, 287, 288, 291, 293, 295, 298
Lone Moor Road, 288
Lurgan, 298
Malone Road, 294
Mayo Street, 295
Meigh, 299
Moyard, 296
Moyard Flats, 295
Musgrave Park Hospital, 300
Narrow Water Castle, 296
New Barnsley, 292, 295, 296
New Lodge, 295, 296
Newry, 281, 296, 298
Newtownhamilton, 298, 300
North Queen Street, 283
North Suffolk, 283
Palace Barracks, Holywood, 287, 288, 296
Peace Line, The, 282, 284, 286, 287
Queen Street, 283
Rathcoole, 295
Rossville Flats, 288, 289, 290
Rossville Street, 288, 289, 290, 291
Royal Victoria Hospital, 300
Sandy Row, 286, 296
Shankill Road, 282, 283, 285, 286, 292
Silent Valley reservoir, 281
South Armagh, 298, 300
South Creggan, 288
South Suffolk, 294
Springfield Road, 292, 298
Springfield Road Police Station, 298
Springmartin Road, 295
St James, 294
Templemore Avenue, 283
Tennent Street, 282, 292, 293
Townsend Street, 283
Turf Lodge, 294, 296
Unity Flats, 285, 295
Warren Point, 296, 297, 299
West Belfast, 295, 298
Whiteabbey, 295
Whiterock, 292, 294, 296
William Street, 288, 289
Woodstock Road, 283
Woodvale, Belfast, 292
Northern Ireland Civil Rights Association (NICRA), 281, 288
North West Frontier Province, 191
Norton, Maj Geoff, 3 PARA, 224
Nottingham, 26, 27
Nunn, Capt Richard RM, 326
Nuri al-Said, Prime Minister of Iraq, 233
Nuseirat Hospital Camp, 193
Nutley, Sgt, 12th Para Bn, 82

O'Brien Twohig, Brig J. P., Comd 2nd Para Bde. Later Comd 1st Para Bde, 201, 206
O'Donnell, Pte, 2 PARA, 220
Oengaran, 159
Oerlikon anti-aircraft guns, Goose Green, 330, 331, 332, 336, 337
Officers' Mess, HQ 16 Para Bde, bombing by IRRA, 292
Omonia Square, Athens, 154
Oosterbeek, 99, 104, 106, 111, 113, 117, 120, 121
Oosterbeek church, 119, 120
Oosterhout, 119
Operations:
'Annabel's', 250
'Berlin', 122
'Bulldozer', 170, 171
'Claret', 249, 250, 251, 252, 268, 271
'Colossus', 20–23
'Corporate', 303–367
'Demetrius', 294, 295
'Dracula', 187
'Dragonfly', 233
'Dragoon', 149
'Foxhunter', 220
'Goodwood', 83
'Grass Roots', 279, 280
'Hasty', 148, 149
'Heron', 199
'Lucky Alphonse', 218
'Market Garden', 94, 124
'Motorman', 295, 296
'Musketeer', 221, 253, 296
'Overlord', 61, 64
'Pepperpot', 218
'Pigeon', 199
'Pintail', 199
'Plunder', 128
'Pounce', 158
'Puddle', 166
'Sparrowhawk I', 220
'Sparrowhawk II', 220
'Sutton', 307, 308
'Varsity', 127, 128, 224
'Zipper', 156
Options for Change, 372
Oran, 52
O'Rourke, Pte, 2 PARA, 326
Orne, River, 61, 64, 70, 79
Orsogna, 146, 147
Osborne, Maj Martin, 3 PARA, 342, 361
Osnabruck, 140, 142
Ottoman Empire, 217
Otway, Lt Col Terence, 9th and 15th Para Bns, 58, 64, 67, 68, 69, 74, 75, 79, 186
Oudna, 37, 38
Oued el Medene, River, 48, 50
Our, River, 125
Ousseltia Valley, 45
Out of Area Operations, 369, 381
Owen, Cpl, 2 PARA, 338, 365
Owens, Lt Graham, 9 Para Sqn RE, 223
Oyster Box, defensive position at Imphal, 182

Page, Lt John, 2 PARA, 328, 363, 364
Pakistan, 191, 192
Palestine, 193–209
Palestine Police, 195
Palmach, 194, 198, 202
Palong, River, 216
Paphos, 236, 244
Paphos Forest, 220
Papoursa, 233
Parachute, X Type, 30
Parachute course, 27

Parachute jumping instructors (PJIs), 19, 20, 27, 378
Parachute packing section – No. 38 Wing RAF, 33
Parfitt, Lt John, 9th Para Bn, 75
Paris Match, 232
Park Hotel, Hartenstein, 104
Parker, Lt Col Reggie, 12th Para Bn. Later Col, Dep Comd 6th Airlanding Bde. 59, 82
Parr, Pte, 2 PARA, 363
Parry, Maj Allen, 9th Para Bn, 67, 132
Parry, Pte, 3 PARA, 353
Parsons, Lt Col Hugh, 3rd Bn 7th Gurkha Rifles, 168
Pas de Calais, 92
Paterson, 2/Lt A. RE, att 11th SAS Bn, 22
Patterson, Lt, 7th Para Bn, 133
Patton, Gen George, Comd 3rd US Army, 92, 93
Patton, Maj Roger, 3 PARA, 357, 358
Pearce, Pte, 2 PARA, 220
Pearson, Maj Alastair, 1st Para Bn. Later Lt Col, 1st and 8th Para Bns, 35, 36, 43, 46, 47, 48, 50, 53, 55, 58, 69, 73, 77, 84
Pearson, Lt J., 6th Para Bn, 148
Pearson, Maj J. W., Comd 2nd Ind Indep Para Bde base, Italy, 147
Pearson, Colonel T. C. H., Deputy Comd, 2nd Indep Para bde, 147, 154
Pearson, Brig Tom, Comd 16th Indep Para Bde, 233, 234
Pearson, Cpl, 2 PARA, 334
Pebble Island, 307
Peck, Terry, civilian guide to 3 PARA during Falklands Campaign, 345
Pedroza, Air Vice Commodore Wilson Dosio, Comd of Goose Green garrison, 339, 340
Pegasus emblem, 25, 186
Peirse, Air Chief Marshal, 169
Penley, 2/Lt Rudge, first officer direct commissioned into The Para Regt, 214
Penman, Sqn Ldr Jock, RAF FAC att 2 PARA, 314, 316
Pennell, Bandmaster, 1 PARA, 211
Pennine Chain, The, 278
Penning, Pte, 3 PARA, 228
Pensianggan, 251, 253
Peoples National Congress, British Guiana, 272
Perrin-Brown, Maj Chris, 1st Para Bn, 106, 109
Persia, 213
Petah Tiqva, 199, 204
Peters, Lt, 9th Para Bn, 72
Petershagen, 142
Phakekedzumi, 170
Phelps, Pte, C (Indep) Coy 2 PARA, 269
Philippines, 245
Phillips, Maj L. M. 'Phil', Gurkha Indep Para Coy, 256, 258
Phillips, Pte, 2 PARA, 314
Phillips, Cpl, 3 PARA, 344
Picchi, Fortunato, civilian att X Tp 11th SAS Bn, 21, 22, 23
Pickard, Wg Cdr Charles, No. 51 Squadron RAF, 13, 16
Pike, Lt, later Lt Col, Hew. 3 PARA, 242, 304, 310, 341, 343, 344, 352, 354, 355, 358, 361
Pimples, The, 2nd Para Bn objective in North Africa, 48
Pine Coffin, Lt Col Geoffrey, 3rd and 7th Para Bns. Later Col and Regtl Col, 31, 32, 48, 59, 64, 65, 80, 84, 87,

132, 133
Pine Coffin, Maj John, 2 PARA, 230, 231
Pioggi, Lt Col Italo, Comd of Argentinian Army troops at Goose Green, 339
Piraeus, 152, 154
Pirron, Col, Comd Belgian Brigade, 85
Pisa, 148
Plain-Lugan, 86
Plaman Mapu, 261, 262, 264
Platanistassa, 233
Playford, Lt Pat, 2nd Para Bn, 39
Poett, Brig Nigel, Comd 5th Para Bde, 59, 64, 73, 87, 89, 90, 126, 134, 137, 141, 143
Point 7378, 172, 174, 175
Policed Field Force (PFF), Malaya, 248, 254, 255
'Pomp and Circumstance' No. 4, regimental slow march of The Para Regt, 212
Pond, Lt Hugh, 9th Para Bn, 68
Pont Audemer, 85, 90, 91
Pont L'Eveque, 85, 88
Pont du Fah, 37
Ponte Grande, 52
Poole, Lt, 7th Para Bn, 84
Poole, Sgt, 3rd Para Sqn RE, 71
Poole, Pte, 2 PARA, 323
Poona, 166
Pope, Maj Alec, DAA & QMG 3rd Para Bde, 73
Port de Bouc, 206
Portecagnano, 148
Port Fuad, 223
Port Howard, 307
Port Said, 200, 221, 222, 223, 228, 229, 231, 232
Port Salvador, 342
Port San Carlos, 310, 311, 340, 341, 342
Portsmouth, 18, 305
Port Stanley, 306, 307, 313, 341, 342, 343, 350, 351, 358, 360, 361, 365, 366
Port Tewfik, 221
Powell, Maj Geoffrey, 156th Para Bn, 15
Prestfield, CSM, 2 PARA, 330
Price, CSM, 2 PARA, 326
Primosole Bridge, 52–55
Prise del'Eau, 38, 39
Pritchard, Lt Col C. H. V., 6th Para Bn. Later Brig, Comd 2nd Indep Para Bde. Subsequently Comd Abn Establishments, 56, 149, 152, 154, 155, 210
Pritchard, Maj T. A. G., 11th SAS Bn, 21, 22
Polish Army:
1st Polish Independent Parachute Brigade, 64, 96, 97, 100–124
Pucara ground attack aircraft, 307, 309, 310, 322, 326, 327, 336, 340
Puma helicopter, 303, 307
Punan Busang, 248, 249, 250
Punan tribesmen, 247, 258, 269
Punjab, The, 166, 170, 191
Punjis, 261
Purdon, Lt Col Corran, 1st Bn Royal Ulster Rifles, 247
Pushing, 172
Putot, 86
Putot-en-Auge, 86–88

Qasim, Gen Abd al Karim, leader of coup against King Faisal of Iraq in 1958, 233
Qastina, 199
Quantrill, Maj Peter, Gurkha Indep Para Coy, 254
Quedeishi, 242
Queripel, Capt Lionel, 10th Para Bn, 110, 111
Quetta, 191
Quinn, Patrick Joseph, 301
Quinn, CSM, 3 PARA, 341
Quiteibi, 'Wolves of The Radfan', 238

Rabwa Pass, 239, 241
Radcliffe, Capt Willoughby, 2nd Para Bn, 47
Radfan, The, 237, 238, 241, 244, 271, 272, 273, 278, 280
Radfan Camp, Aden, 276
Radio Set No. 22, 54
Radio Set No. 62, 215
Radio Set No. 125, 270
Rafah, 203
Rai, Rfm Dharmalal, Gurkha Indep Para Coy, 260
Raiwala, 170
Rajang, River, 247, 248, 268
Ramat David, 57
Rangaraj, Maj, RMO att 152nd Ind Para Bn, 188
Rangoon, 170, 186, 188, 189
Rangoon, River, 186
Rann, Capt, 1st Para Bn, 53
Ranville, 63, 66, 76, 80
Rapido, River, 148
Rapier surface-to-air missile, 310
Rarden Cannon, 30mm, Scimitar CVR(T) main armament, 362
Rathedaung, 171
Rawalpindi, 166, 187, 191
Raynor, Cpl, 2 PARA, 334
Read, Sgt, 3 PARA, 228, 229
Rebecca, aircraft-mounted receiver for Eureka pathfinding beacon, 59
Recovered Allied Prisoners of War & Internees (RAPWI), 159
Recoilless rifles: 105mm, 351, 359; 106mm, 224, 225, 229, 311; 120mm, 371
Reed, Lt, 12th Para Bn, 134
Rehovot, 204
Reichswald, 127
Reid, Major Derick, Para Battle Sch and 7th Para Bn, 27, 144
Renkum Heath, 96
Retallack, Maj Johnny, No. 1 (Guards) Indep Coy, 234
Reuters, 357
Rhade, 138
Rhine, River, 93, 112, 127–130, 144
Rhine Pavilion Hotel, 110
Rhodesian SAS Squadron, 215
Rhone Valley, 150
Rice, Maj Tony, Comd 8 (Alma) Cdo Bty RA, 314, 340, 361
Rice Bowl, Radforce objective, 239
Richards, Capt L. F. 'Dicky', 152nd Ind Para Bn. Later LO 50th Ind Para Bde, 166, 171, 174, 176, 181, 184
Richardson, Lt Jack, 3 PARA, 228, 229
Ricketts, Brig Henry, Comd 5th Para Bde (TA), 210
'Ride of The Valkyries', regimental quick march, 212, 213, 337
Ridgway, Gen Matthew, Comd 18th US Abn Corps, 128, 135, 144
Riley, Lt Nigel, 4th Para Bn, 153
Rimini, 148

Ringenberg, 130
Ringway, 19, 27, 28
Rippon, Bandmaster, 3 PARA, 211, 212
Rishon-le-Zion, 199, 204
Rishon ranges, 201
Rishpon, 198
Risle, River, 85
Ritchie, Maj Gerald, 12th Para Bn, 65, 133, 140
Robehomme, 63, 64, 70, 85
Roberts, Capt, later Maj, Jimmy. 153rd Gurkha Para Bn, 167, 168, 180
Roberts, Maj Gen Ouvry, GOC 23rd Ind Div, 170, 171, 174, 175, 180
Roberts, Col, Dir of Music Royal Mil Sch of Music, 212
Rochefort, 126
Rock, Maj John RE, later Lt Col, Central Landing School, 19, 20, 21
Rocket launcher 3.5 inch, 225, 342
Rodney Group, C Coy 2nd Para Bn, Bruneval raid, 14, 15, 16
Roermond, 127
Rogers, Maj Paul, 12th Para Bn, 83
Roisenhagen, 142
Rokossovsky, Marshal, 145
Rolt, Capt, later Maj, Mike. 411th (Royal Bombay) Para Sqn IE, 165
Rome, 42, 150
Rome, Brig F. D., Comd 3rd Para Bde, 204
Rosche, 144
Roseby, Capt John, 152nd Ind Para Bn, 174
Roseveare, Maj Tim, 3rd Para Sqn RE, 69
Rosh Pinna, 205
Ross, RSM, 22 SAS, 268
Ross, Capt, later Maj, John. 2nd Para Bn, 38, 40, 49, 50
Rotheray, Maj Geoff, 2nd Para Bn, 47
Rough Diamond – 2 PARA objective, Wireless Ridge, 362
Royal Air Force:
  Royal Air Force, 13, 15, 21, 27, 30, 57, 96, 98, 110, 111, 112, 121, 123, 130, 190, 199, 205, 207, 221, 222, 224, 235, 236, 239, 242, 243, 249, 251, 288, 298, 306, 314
  No. 38 Group, 61, 63, 95, 168
  No. 46 Group, 61, 63, 95, 112
  No. 38 Wing, 33
  No. 177 (Abn Forces) Wing, 168
  No. 283 Wing, 200
  No. 51 Squadron, 13, 14
  No. 62 Squadron, 169
  No. 91 Squadron, 21
  No. 99 Squadron, 169
  No. 208 Squadron, 234, 241
  No. 215 Squadron, 169
  No. 271 Squadron, 112
  No. 620 Squadron, 200
  No. 845 Squadron, 200
  Air Landing School, 156, 166, 168
  Airborne Training School, Aqir, 200
  Central Landing Establishment, 20
  Central Landing School, 19
  No. 1 Parachute Training School, 58, 165, 169, 200, 368, 374, 378–380
  No. 3 Parachute Training School, 168
  No. 2 Mobile Parachute Servicing Unit, 147
  RAF Abingdon, 378
  RAF Brize Norton, 367, 378
  RAF Henlow, 20
  RAF Pitts Road, Aldershot, 379

RAF Upper Heyford, 378
RAF Regiment, 152
Royal Fleet Auxiliary:
  LSL *Sir Galahad*, 311, 348, 349
  LSL *Sir Launcelot*, 311
  LSL *Sir Tristram*, 348, 349
  RFA *Fort Austin*, 307
Royal Marines:
  Royal Marines, 221, 228, 297, 302, 303, 304, 317, 336, 361, 379, 380
  Royal Marines Reserve, 380
  3 Commando Brigade, 232, 256, 304, 307, 308, 311, 326, 339, 343, 347, 350, 360, 361, 366, 380
  40 Commando RM, 208, 223, 296, 301, 305, 308, 367
  41 Commando RM, 83, 283, 285, 286
  42 Commando RM, 223, 227, 229, 246, 305, 306, 308, 339, 345, 350, 367
  45 Commando RM, 227, 229, 238, 239, 240, 241, 242, 243, 305, 308, 342, 345, 350, 357, 358, 359, 367
  46 Commando RM, 83
  47 Commando RM, 83
  48 Commando RM, 83
  Naval Party 8901, 302
  Special Boat Service, 308, 309, 341, 378
  2 Special Boat Section RM, 306, 308
  3 Special Boat Section RM, 310
Royal Navy:
  Royal Navy, 14, 56, 146, 205, 219, 235, 288
  1st Cruiser Squadron, 56
  Fleet Air Arm, 225, 226, 227, 306
  Abdiel 56, 146
  Albion, 226
  Ambuscade, 361
  Antelope, 311
  Antrim, 307, 311
  Ardent, 308, 311
  Arethusa, 75
  Argonaut, 311
  Arrow, 318, 320
  Brilliant, 310, 311
  Broadsword, 307, 308, 311
  Bulwark, 226, 234, 235
  Conqueror, 306
  Coventry, 311
  Endurance, 303, 304
  Fearless, 311, 348
  Glamorgan, 307
  Intrepid, 308, 309, 310, 312, 348
  Maidstone, 292
  Plymouth, 307, 308
  Sheffield, 306
  Triumph, 21, 23, 213
  Victorious, 235
  Warrior, 213
  Empire Parkeston, 229
  Snowdon Smith, 229
  No. 815 Naval Air Squadron, 244
  No. 845 Naval Air Squadron, 248
  Royal Ulster Constabulary, 281–284, 288, 289, 290, 298, 299
  RPG-7 anti-tank rocket launcher, 298
  RPKAD, Indonesian para-commando regiment, 246, 259, 265
  Rugge Price, Maj Anthony, 13th/18th Royal Hussars, 80
  Ruhr, the, 93, 128, 130
  Russell, Pte, 2 PARA, 330

SA-7 Grail surface-to-air missile, 358
Saar, River, 92
Sabah, 245, 247
Sadainghmut, 189
Safad, 204, 205

Sakok, 184
Saladin armoured car, 276, 286
Salerno, 148, 150
Sallanelles, 63
Salonika, 153
Salorola sector, 147
Salverno, 21
Samaria, 195, 196, 200
San Carlos, 307, 326, 341, 343, 348
San Carlos, River, 310
San Carlos Settlement, 308, 312
San Carlos Water, 307, 308, 309, 310, 340
Sand Fly, Radforce objective, 239, 241
Sangjani, 185
Sangro, River, 146
Sangshak, 171–183, 188
Sapper Hill, 306, 351, 365
Saracen armoured personnel carrier, 278, 286
Sarafand, 199, 201
Sarandi, 233
Sarawak, First, Second, Third, Fourth and Fifth Divisions, 245–251, 254, 256, 257, 260, 261, 267, 268
Saunders, Sgt, 1st Cdn Para Bn, 131
Saunders, Maj John, 153rd Gurkha Para Bn, 184
Schlemm, Generaloberst, Comd 1st Para Army, 129
Schneppenberg feature, 129, 132
Scimitar CVR(T), 342, 343, 360, 362, 363
Scoones, Lt Gen Sir Geoffrey, Comd 4th Ind Corps, 170
Scorpion CVR(T), 342, 343, 360, 362, 363
Scout helicopter, 243, 244, 271, 310, 338, 346, 347, 366
Seago, Maj Edward, designer of Pegasus emblem, 25
Sea Harrier FRS1, 306
Sea Hawk fighter, 224
Sea King helicopter, 307, 310, 312, 338, 341, 350
Sea of Galilee, 204
Seaton, Lt Basil, 152nd Ind Para Bn, 182
Sea Venom, 225
Secunderabad, 185, 189
Sedjenane, 43, 46
Seeney, Pte, C (Indep) Coy 2 PARA, 269
Seine, River, 85, 92
Selangor, 216
Sele, River, 21, 23
Selection course, 26
Self-propelled guns, 66, 136, 137, 139
Selfridge, Capt Matt, 3 PARA, 341, 343
Semarang, 158–164
Sepulut, 251
Seria, 254, 260
Settlement Rocks, 311
Setye, 205
Seychelles, 217
Sfax, 43
Shaab Lashab, 244
Shab Tem, 242
Shand, Lt Kynoch, 153rd Gurkha Para Bn, 182
Shapiro quarter, Tel Aviv, 199
Shappee, Maj John, 8th Para Bn, 131
Sharp, Pte, 2 PARA, 332
Shaw, Lt John, 2 PARA, 320
Shaw, Lt Jonathan, 3 PARA, 352, 353
Sheap, Pte, 2 PARA, 332
Sheepwash, Pte, 2 PARA, 334, 337
Shefayim, 198

Sheikh Othman, 274–278
Sheldon's Corner, 171–180, 183
Shell Oil Company, 204
Shepherd, Lt, 5th Para Bn, 147
Shepherd, Gdsm, No. 1 (Guards) Indep Coy, 253
Sheridan, Sgt, Red Devils, 378
Sherman, Lt Cdr 'Tank', Comd No. 845 Naval Air Sqn FAA, 248
Sherman tank, 80, 82, 126
Shi'b Taym, 239
Short, Capt Jock, 2nd Para Bn, 40
Sht Hat Tiqva, 204
Sibu, 247, 248, 257, 258, 268
Sicily, 52
Sidewinder air-to-air missile, 336
Sidi N'Sir, 34, 35
Sidna Ali, 198
Siegfried line, 92
Silchar, 183
Sim, Capt, later Maj, John. 12th Para Bn, 83
Simeto, River, 52
Simpson, Gen, Comd 9th US Army, 49
Simpson, Capt RE, att 2nd Para Bn, 49
Simpson, Lt John, 1st Cdn Para Bn, 71
Simpson, RSM, 2 PARA, 340
Sinai, 214, 221, 276
Sinclair, Pte, 3 PARA, 358
Sind Province, 166
Singapore, 189, 245, 246, 253, 257, 267, 270
Sisson, L/Cpl, 2 PARA, 332
Skeate, Capt F. H., 13th Para Bn, 89
Skyhawk, A-4, 310, 336, 349, 361
Slade, Lt Dennis, 9th Para Bn, 74
Slim, Lt Gen Sir William, Comd 14th Army, 171, 185, 187
Slough, Pte, 2 PARA, 334, 337
Smith, Maj. 582nd Jungle Mortar Bty RIA, 179
Smith, Maj George, 9th Para Bn, 67, 68, 69
Smith, Pte, 2 PARA, 338, 339
Smith, Tom, Daily Express correspondent, 357
Smoko Mountain, 342
Smurthwaite, CQMS, No. 1 (Guards) Indep Coy, 248
Smyth, Lt Col Ken, 10th Para Bn, 109, 115, 117
Smyth, Capt Hugh, 9th Para Bn, 76
Snowdon, Pte, 3 PARA, 300
Socialist Peoples National Congress, British Guiana, 272
Soekarno, Dr, Indonesian politician. Later President of Indonesia, 158, 245, 246, 248, 257
Sompok, 160
Somra, 171
Son, 93
Sora, 149
Sosabowski, Maj Gen Stanislav, Comd 1st Polish Indep Para Bde, 97, 118, 119, 120
Souk El Arba, 32, 33
Souk El Khamis-Souk El Arba plain, 33, 41, 42, 43
Sousse, 36, 52, 55
Southampton, 304
South Arabia, Federation of, 237, 274
South Arabian Army, 276–279
Southby-Tailyour, Maj Ewen RM, Comd of landing craft during Falklands Campaign, 349
South China Sea, 247
South Georgia, 303, 304, 306, 345

Soviet Union, 230
Special Branch, Malaya, 248
Spencer, Pte, 2 PARA, 328, 336
Spender, Capt Dicky, 2nd Para Bn, 49
Spion Kop, 46
Spitfire fighter, 32, 207
Squirrell, Capt J. G., Staff Capt 1st Para Bde. Later Lt Col, Comdt Abn Dev Centre, 23, 58
SS-11 guided missile, 366
St Charles, 32, 43
St Cyprien, 37
St Elizabeth Hospital, 106, 107, 112, 121
St Julien, 88
St Jeans, 200
St Pair, 85
St Raphael, 149, 150
St Vith, 125
Staff, L/Cpl, 2 PARA, 219
Standish, Cpl, 2 PARA, 323
Stanley Airport, 302
Stark, Capt Ronnie, 2nd Para Bn, 39, 46
Starlight scope, first generation image intensifier, 285
Starling, Maj Joe, 1 PARA. Later Lt Col, Para Battle School and 15 PARA (V) Subsequently Col and Regt Col, 236, 276
Stead, Cpl, 3 PARA, 228, 229
Steadman, CSM, 2nd Para Bn, 35
Steele, Capt Ray, 4th Bn 5th Mahratta Light Infantry, 176
Steele, Pte, 2 PARA, 365
Steen, Vernon, civilian guide to 3 PARA during Falklands Campaign, 345
Sten gun, 32, 33, 71, 150, 301
Stephens, Maj 'Steve', 12th Para Bn, 82, 133
Sterling submachine-gun, 370
Stern, Abraham, founder of Stern Gang, 194
Stern Gang (Lecahamey Heruth Israel), 194, 201, 203, 206
Stevens, Maj Dick, 3 PARA, 224, 225
Stevenson, L/Cpl, 8th Para Bn, 69
Stinger surface-to-air missile, 310
Stirling bomber, 27, 28
Stockwell, Maj Gen Hugh, GOC 6th Abn Div. Later Gen Sir Hugh, Comd Br forces during Operation Musketeer, 206, 209, 221
Stockwell, Maj Nigel, 22nd Indep Para Coy. Later Lt Col 12th Para Bn, 83, 88
Stodder, Cpl, 2 PARA, 331
Stokes, Pte, 2 PARA, 332
Stopford, Lt Gen Sir Montagu, Allied Comd Netherland East Indies, 164
Strachan, CSM, later RSM, 2nd Para Bn, 16
Straits of Malacca, 257
Strange, Sqn Ldr Louis, CO Central Landing School, 19, 20
Strategic Reserve, 193
Street, Lt, 2nd Para Bn, 30
Street, Pte, 2 PARA, 323
Strong, Maj Gen Kenneth, Chief of Intelligence SHAEF, 98
Stuka dive-bomber, 32, 38, 47
Sturge, Cpl, 3 PARA, 356
Sudan, 200
Suez, 238, 280
Suez Canal, 218, 221, 230
Suez Canal Zone, 213, 214, 232
Sullivan, Cpl, 2 PARA, 330, 333
Sultan of Brunei, 246

Sultan of Oman's Armed Forces, 235
Sumbi, Lt, comd of Indonesian raiding force, 260, 261
Super Etendard, 311
Surabaya, 158
Sussex Mountain, 308, 309, 312, 313, 314, 337
Swan Inlet, 346
Sweet Water Canal, Suez, 230
Syracuse, 52, 55
Syrencote House, 24, 58
Syria, 204, 207

Tactical Air Landing Operations (TALO), 369, 381
Takama, 272
Tamera, 46
Tanaka, Maj Gen, Comd Japanese 33rd Div, 183
Tangkhul Hundung, 184
Taranto, 20, 57, 146
Tait, Capt Andrew, 22nd Indep Para Coy, 84
Tapah, 216
Tarrant, Maj Reggie, 13th Para Bn, 87
Tarver, Lt Col G. L., Baluch Regt, 184
Tasek Bera, 216
Tate, Wg Cdr, J. B., 21
Tatham-Warter, Maj Digby, 2nd Para Bn, 101, 102, 113, 114
Tawahi, 274
Tawhai, 188
Taylor, Gen Maxwell D., Comd 101st US Abn Div, 97
Taylor, Capt William, GSO3 Int HQ 1st Para Bde, 107
Taylor, Cpl, 591st Para Sqn RE, 144
Taylor, Pte, 2 PARA, 219
Tchikov, Anatoli, Russian Consul in Port Said, 227
Teal, 342
Teal Inlet, 341, 342, 344
Teed, Capt Rupert, 4th Para Bn, 153
Teichman, Maj Philip, 2nd Para Bn, 40
Tel Aviv, 196, 197, 199, 201, 202, 203, 204
Telecommunications Research Establishment, 13
Ter Horst, Mevrouw Kate, 120
Terrell, Maj Steven, 3rd Para Bn, 31, 43, 50
Tewson, Pte, 2 PARA, 332
Thaungdut, 171
Thaungang, 188
Thebes, 153
Thomas, Maj Gen G. I., GOC 43rd Inf Div, 119, 122
Thomas, Lt Col R. M. C., 11th Para Bn, 57
Thompson, Brig Julian, Comd 3 Cdo Bde, 304, 307, 308, 312, 313, 341, 345, 360, 366
Thompson, Capt Nicky, 2 PARA, 263
Thompson, Lt, 8th Para Bn, 69
Thompson, Lt Col W. F. K. 'Sheriff', 1st Airlanding Lt Regt RA, 112, 113
Thompson submachine-gun, 289
Thomson, Lt Col Colin, 2 PARA, 296
Thrace, 153
Thruxton, 13, 15
Thumier, 238, 239, 244
Thurman, Lt John RM, 317
Thursby, Lt Col Pat, 1 PARA. Later Col and Regt Col, 236
Tiangzup, 167
Tiberias, 204
Tiddim Road, 183
Tidworth, 302

Tiger tank, 113, 119, 126, 136
Tighe-Wood, Lt Col 'Digger', 3
  PARA, 211
Tilshead, 14
Timothy, Lt, later Maj, John 'Tim'.
  2nd Para Bn, 15, 16, 57, 109
Tindale, Sgt, 22 SAS, 267
Tindale, Cpl, 2 PARA, 267
TNKU, North Kalimantan National
  Army, 246
Topham, Cpl, 1st Cdn Para Bn, 132
Torricella, 146, 149
Toseland, Lt Norman, 1st Cdn Para
  Bn, 70, 71, 78
Touffreville, 69
Touques, River, 85, 88
Tragino, 21, 22
Trakonas, 236
Transjordan, 200, 204
Transjordanian Frontier Force, 195,
  208
Trapeza Plateau, 219
Trevaskis, Sir Kennedy, British High
  Commissioner in Aden, 274
Trevelyan, Sir Humphrey, British
  Ambassador to Iraq, 235
Trick, Pte, 2 PARA, 332
Trim, Lt Col Jack, 4th Bn 5th
  Mahratta LI, 174
Tripolitania, 43
Troarn, 63, 69, 70, 77, 85
Trollope, Lt Bill RM, Naval Party
  8901, 302
Troodos, 244
Troodos Mountains, 220, 232, 244
Trouville, 85
Truce Force, 236
Trucial Oman Scouts, 235
Tucker, Sgt, 5th Para Bn, 150
Tuffen, Pte, 2 PARA, 322
Tunis, 30, 32, 34, 36, 37, 38
Tunisia, 30, 32
Tunisia Camp, 232
Tunku Abdul Rahman, Prime
  Minister of Malaya (later Malaysia),
  245
Turkey, 217, 244
Turkish Empire, 193
Turnbull, Capt John, 12th Para Bn, 65
Tutong Camp, 270
Twin Pioneer aircraft, 251
Two Sisters, 345, 350, 359, 361
Two Sisters Ridge, 306
Typhoon fighter-bombers, 124, 135

Uelzen, 144
UH-1 'Huey' helicopter, 336
Ukhrul, 170, 172, 175, 176, 183, 184
Ukhrul-Sangshak sector, 177
Ukits, 247
Ulster Defence Association, 293
Ulster Special Constabulary, B
  Specials, 281–283
Ulster Volunteer Force, 283
Ulu Aput, 249
Ulu Danum, 248
United Kingdom/Netherlands
  Amphibious Force, 380
United Nations, 207, 237
Urquhart, Maj Gen Roy, GOC 1st
  Abn Div. Later GOC 16th Abn Div
  (TA), 94, 96, 98, 99, 104, 106, 107,
  109, 110, 113–119, 121, 122, 124,
  210
Urquhart – Maj Brian, GSO2 Int HQ
  1st Abn Corps, 98
US Air Force, 234
US Army:
  12th US Army Gp, 92, 93
  1st US Army, 92, 93, 125

3rd US Army, 92, 93
5th US Army, 148
7th US Army, 149
9th US Army, 128, 130
2nd US Corps, 43
5th US Corps, 125
8th US Corps, 125
13th US Corps, 128
16th US Corps, 128
18th US Abn Corps, 128, 129, 135,
  138, 144
19th US Corps, 128
4th US Inf Div, 125
9th US Inf Div, 51
17th US Abn Div, 128, 129, 130, 135
28th US Inf Div, 125
82nd US Abn Div, 94, 95, 97
101st US Abn Div, 94, 95, 97
106th US Inf Div, 125
501st Para Inf Regt, 97
502nd Para Inf Regt, 97
2nd Bn 503rd Para Inf Regt, 30
504th Para Inf Regt, 97
505th Para Inf Regt, 97
506th Para Inf Regt, 97
508th Para Inf Regt, 97
39th Regt Combat Team, 50
142nd Regt Combat Team, 151
1st Abn Task Force, 150
US Army Air Force (USAAF), 30,
  31, 60, 95, 96, 147, 188
9th Troop Carrier Command
  USAAF, 95, 130
51st Troop Carrier Wing USAAF,
  33, 150
No. 60 Group USAAF, 30
No. 62 Group USAAF, 37
No. 64 Group USAAF, 33, 37
Utrecht, 96, 109
Utrechtseweg, 101

V-1 rocket, 125
V-2 rocket, 93
Valencia, Vickers, 165, 167, 169
Valetta transport aircraft, 221, 224,
  225, 226
Van Langen, Col, Dutch T Regt Gp,
  164
Varaville, 63, 64, 70, 71, 72
Vaughn, Pte, D (Patrol) Coy 3 PARA,
  271
Veghel, 93, 97
Venlo, 127
Verdon, Lt Paddy, Gurkha Indep
  Para Coy, 256
Vernon, Capt Dennis, 1st Para Sqn
  RE, 15, 16
Verviers, 125
Vianden, 125
Vickers medium machine-gun, 69,
  74, 75, 80, 141, 169, 178, 226, 231
Villers-sur-Mer, 70
Vischer, Lt John, 22nd Indep Para
  Coy, 84
Vlasto, Lt Robin, 2nd Para Bn, 102
Vokes, Sgt, 3 PARA, 226
Vulcan bomber, 306

Waal, River, 97
Waddington, 2/Lt Chris, 2 PARA,
  315, 321, 328, 332, 333, 363, 365
Waddy, Maj Peter, 3rd Para Bn, 104,
  105
Wadi Dhubsan, 241, 242, 243
Wadi Rabwa, 239
Wadi Taym, 238, 239, 241
Wagan, Capt Rory, RMO 2 PARA,
  337, 338
Walker, Lt 'Chug', 1st Cdn Para Bn,
  72

Walker, Lt Nigel, Gurkha Indep Para
  Coy, 256
Walker, Lt Tom, 3 PARA, 240, 241
Walker, Maj Gen Walter, Dir of Ops
  Borneo Confrontation, 246
Wallace, 2/Lt Guy, 2 PARA, 314, 319,
  320
Wallace-King, Maj Colin, 1 PARA,
  236
Wallis, Maj David, 2nd Para Bn, 113
Walsh, Capt, later Maj, Mike, 3
  PARA., Later Lt Col, 1 PARA, 218,
  224, 232, 242, 275, 276
Walsh, Cpl, 2 PARA, 332
Walter, Maj Peter, 3 PARA. Later Lt
  Col, Para Battle Sch, 239, 240
Walton, Pte, 2 PARA, 327
Warburton, Tpr, 22 SAS, 239
Warcup, Sgt, later CSM, 12th Para
  Bn, 81, 134
Ward, Capt Hugh, 53rd Airlanding Lt
  Regt RA, 83
Ward-Booth, Maj Tony, 3 PARA.
  Later Brig, Comd 16 Para Bde, 242
Wardle, Maj Mickey, 2nd Para Bn, 49
War Office, 21, 24, 25, 221
Warr, Maj Peter, 10th Para Bn, 115
Warrack, Col Graeme, ADMS 1st
  Abn Div, 121
Warren, Maj Eddie, 12th Bn
  Devonshire Regt. Later DAAG HQ
  The Para Regt, 82, 210
Warren, Pte, 2 PARA, 332
Warwick-Pengelly, Capt John, 12th
  Bn Devonshire Regt, 82
Watchus, CSM, D (Patrol) Coy 3
  PARA, 270
Water cannon, 288
Watson, Maj Jack, 13th Para Bn, 126,
  134
Watson, Capt James, FOO att 2
  PARA, 322
Watts, Lt Col John, 225th Para Fd
  Amb, 162
Wavell, Gen Sir Archibald, C-in-C
  India, 165
Weathersbee, Lt R., 1st Cdn Para Bn,
  71
Webb, Capt Mike, 152nd Ind Para
  Bn, 166
Webb, Lt Col R., 3rd Para Bn, 25
Webb, Capt, FOO att 2 PARA, 263
Webster, Lt Shaun, 2 PARA, 315,
  321, 363, 364
Weekes, CSM, 3 PARA, 354
Weighell, Lt Geoff, 2 PARA, 320, 321,
  323, 336
Wellington bomber, 169
Wells, Lt Don, 22nd Indep Para Coy,
  84
Wesel, 128, 130
Weser, River, 138, 142, 143
Wessex helicopter, 244, 248, 268,
  297, 298
West, Pte, 3 PARA, 358
Westerbouwing, 110
West Falkland, 342
West Flanders, 92
Weston, Father Gerry, Roman
  Catholic Padre 16 Para Bde., 292
Weston, Brig Pat, Comd 6th Para Bde
  (TA), 210
Wheatley, Pte, 2 PARA, 332
Whirlwind helicopter, 236
White, Lt Col Bill, 2 PARA, 211
Whitelock, Capt Miles, 1st Para Bn,
  36
Whitley bomber, 13, 15, 19, 21, 22,
  23, 27, 28
Whitworth, Lt, 7th Para Bn, 137

Widgery report, summary of
    conclusions, 291
Wilford, Lt Col Derek, 1 PARA, 288,
    289, 290
Wilhelma, 203
Wilhelmina Canal, 93
Wilkinson, Brig Charles, Comd 77th
    Ind Para Bde, 186
Wilkinson Sword of Peace, 280
Willems Canal, 97
Willetts, Sgt, 3 PARA, 298
Williams, Lt J. L., 1st Para Bn, 112
Williams, CSM, 2 PARA, 263, 264,
    265
Williamson, Pte, 2 PARA, 323
Willingdon airport, New Delhi, 165
Wilson, Maj B. A. 'Boy', 21st Indep
    Para Coy, 99, 100, 108
Wilson, Sgt, 12th Para Bn, 134, 140
Wilson, Brig Tony, Comd 5 Inf Bde,
    346, 347, 350
Wingate, Maj Gen Orde, Comd
    Special Force (Chindits), 185
Wingate Gray, Lt Col Mike, 22 SAS,
    253
Wing Forward, 3 PARA objective on
    Mount Longdon, 351, 357
Winser, Lt Tim, 13th Para Bn, 126
Winter, Lt John, C (Indep) Coy 2
    PARA. Later Lt Col 10 PARA (V),

268, 269, 272
Wireless Ridge, 306, 351, 357, 360,
    361–366
Wismar, 145
Wissingen, 142
Wolfheze, 101, 104, 105, 110, 113
Wolfheze Hotel, 115
Wombat 120mm anti-tank gun, 246
Wood, Capt David, 2 PARA, 18, 321,
    325
Woodfield, CSM, No. 1 (Guards)
    Indep Coy, 249
Woodhouse, Lt Col John, 22 SAS,
    247, 257
Woodman, Capt E. G., 7th Para Bn,
    144
Woods, Brig E. G. 'Lakri', Comd 50th
    Ind Para Bde, 183, 185
Woods, Capt Huia, Edn Offr 2 PARA,
    262
Worsley-Tonks, Capt Mal, 2 PARA,
    324
Wreck Point, 309
Wright, Pte, 3 PARA, 355
Wunstorf, 142, 143
Wurzburg radar, Bruneval, 13

Xanten, 130

Yaingangpokpi, 181

Yassin Affendi, leader of Bruni
    Rebellion, 246
Yellin, Nathan Freedman, successor
    to Abraham Stern as leader of Stern
    Gang, 194
Yellow Card, regulations governing
    use of weapons by British military
    personnel in Northern Ireland, 291,
    292
Yemen, 237, 238
Yeu-Shwebo plain, 187
Yibna, 200
Yorke Bay, 302
Yorke Point, 302
Young, Maj Alex, C (Patrol) Coy 2
    PARA, 271
Young, 2/Lt Angus, 1st Bn The
    Lancashire Regt, 276
Young, Capt John, 2 PARA, 320, 321,
    323, 329, 338
Young, Maj Gen Peter, GOC Cyprus,
    236
Yourston, Pte, 2 PARA, 332

Zanzibar, 236
Zionist Organisation, 193
Zoopiyi, 233
Zuid Willemsvaart Canal, 93
Zwolanski, Capt, Polish LO att HQ
    1st Abn Div, 118